# THE AGE OF CHARISMA

# THE AGE OF CHARISMA

Arthur Schweitzer

Nelson-Hall nh Chicago

LIBRARY OF CONGRESS CATALOGING AND PUBLICATION DATA

Schweitzer, Arthur.
  The age of charisma.

  Bibliography: p.
  Includes index.
  1. Leadership. 2. Politics, Practical. 3. Despotism.
4. Democracy. 5. Personality. I. Title.
HM141.S417    1984    303.3'4    83-17268
ISBN 0-8304-1015-5

Manufactured in the United States of America

10 9 8 7 6 5 4 3 2 1

The paper in this book is pH neutral (acid free).

# CONTENTS

Preface                                                    ix

## PART ONE
### Past Perspectives

CHAPTER ONE   Varieties of Charisma                        3

*Charismatic Giants*                                       4
*Charismatic Luminaries*                                   6
*Charismatic Failures*                                     8
*Charismatic Aspirants*                                    11
*Comparative Charisma*                                     12
*Theoretical Approaches to Charisma*                       18
*Synergistic Charisma*                                     25

CHAPTER TWO   Weber's Theory of Charisma                   31

*Origin and Validity of Charisma*                          32
*Natural Charisma*                                         34
*Instability of Personal Charisma*                         37
*Value Charisma*                                           39
*Faith Charisma*                                           42
*Charisma and Democracy*                                   45
*Revolutionary Charisma*                                   51
*Dictatorial Charisma*                                     56

## PART TWO
### Dictatorial Charisma

CHAPTER THREE   Hitler's Dictatorial Charisma              65

*Personal Magnetism*                                       66
*Supernatural Charisma*                                    68
*Religious Limits to Charisma*                             71

Providential Charisma   77
Personality Cult   79
Plebiscitary Charisma   85
Gigantic Charisma in Dictatorship   87

CHAPTER FOUR   Charisma and Ideology   95

Charismatic Ideology   97
Ideological Charisma   103
Internal Counterrevolution and Charisma   108
Ideological Schism and Charisma   113
External Counterrevolution and Charisma   118
Racial Counterrevolution and Charisma   123

CHAPTER FIVE   Charisma and Organization   129

Dictatorial Party   131
Ideocratic Organizations   137
Interlocking Organizations   139
Political Monopoly   141
Charismatic Groups   147
Charismatic and Ideocratic Apparatus   152
Control of State Bureaucracy   159

CHAPTER SIX   Charisma and Despotism   163

Different Crises   165
Superhuman Qualities   166
Charismatic Appeal   167
Dictatorial Ideology and Charisma   168
Legal and Charismatic Authority   171
Charisma and Organization   173
Charisma and Discipline   175
Charismatic Succession   179
Legendary Charisma   182
Manufactured Charisma   187

# PART THREE
## Democratic Charisma

CHAPTER SEVEN   Conscience and Charisma   199

Ideal Democracy and Leadership   205
Charisma, Caste, and Class   210
Black Charisma   212
Achievements of Black Charisma   215
Crisis of Value Charisma   217
White Resistance and Charisma   221

Ideologies of Segregated Democracy 223
Charismatic Achievements and Failures 227
Dual Charismatic Leadership 230

CHAPTER EIGHT   Crisis and Charisma 237

Political Parties and Charisma 238
Superimposition of Charismatic Leadership 242
Charisma and Political Talent 246
Charismatization of the Crisis 250
Ethical Mission 253
Interests and Charismatic Achievements 257
Charisma and the Supreme Court 265
Limits of Democratic Charisma 269

CHAPTER NINE   War and Charisma 273

Military Bureaucrats and Charismatic Rivals 274
Democratic and Dictatorial Bureaucracies 278
Nefarious and Absolute Bureaucracies 283
Military Dictatorship 285
Military Crisis and Charismatic Leadership 288
Ideological Split and Charisma 296
Peace Goals and Empowered Charisma 300
War Goals and Preponderant Charisma 303
Achievements and Failures 306

CHAPTER TEN   Charismatic Rulership 309

Theory of Synergistic Charisma 312
Transitional Charisma 320
Pure Type of Weberian Theory 326
Stymied Charisma 332
Reformist Charisma 338
Conservative Charisma 341

Notes 343
Glossary 391
Selected Bibliography 399
Index 407

# PREFACE

ONE YEAR AFTER HIS retirement from the University of Chicago, Frank H. Knight came to Indiana University to deliver a lecture. Since he had been my advisor as a Rockefeller Fellow in 1939, and a fatherly friend during my tenure as Research Associate at Chicago in 1945 and 1946, I felt justified in asking him privately an unusual question: "If you had to do it over again, what would you do differently?" The answer was clear and unhesitating: "There has been the work of one man whom I have greatly admired. If I were to start out again, I would build upon his ideas. I am referring, of course, to Max Weber." This was a revelation to me, because Knight's theories had appeared to me far removed from Weber's ideas. Finding myself in an intellectual crisis, nine chapters on hand but no integrated book in sight, I accepted Knight's remark as personal advice, started a systematic study of Weber, taught for eight years a course on the Theory of Social Economics, and wrote two books and published a series of articles based upon Weber's ideas.

There was especially one part of Weber's work that puzzled and eventually fascinated me. As a young man I was a strict believer in scientism in most of its aspects. So his theory of charismatic leadership seemed to me utter speculation, of not finding any place in the social sciences. But this negative attitude disappeared under the influence of two research projects. As a Rockefeller Fellow, I planned to write a book on the New Deal for a European audience. This assignment was never completed, mainly because I could not adequately interpret Roosevelt's personal contribution to that impressive experiment. A similar experience was repeated two decades later in a study of the Nazi economy. In the first period of that regime, Hitler made no significant economic decisions, so that his ideas did not significantly influence the course of economic events. In the second period, however, Hitler clearly determined the economics and politics of the regime. For the second time I ran into the leading personality whose power in a crisis created a barrier for my studies.

Reluctantly, I arrived at the conclusion that this personalistic influence was an important component in the attempts to overcome the respective crises in their countries. Yet each leader directed a quite different system. Roosevelt's leadership helped significantly in revitalizing democracy, whereas Hitler was the leading builder of a Fascist dictatorship. This suggested fundamental questions: How can the same type of extraordinary personality attract a huge mass following, but each one personifying so diametrically opposed political systems? Could a theory be found that would permit us to explain the similarities and differences of the mass-supported leaders and regimes?

In turning to Weber's theory of charisma, I had to face two quite different hurdles. Weber had given such great emphasis to pure charisma, but barely touched upon the relationship between such leaders and the respective political regimes. At least, his theory seemed to be in need of a significant extension. But such an effort was declared useless by some very articulate critics. Several counterarguments were advanced that assertedly undermined the validity of the theory. Instead of receiving useful assistance in applying the theory to new charismatic personalities, everyone was assured by the critics that the original thesis was either fatally defective or without foundation.

Yet there emerged a curious divergence between the negative assessments and the rise of new charismatic leaders. By coincidence, the more the theory was condemned, the greater was the number of new charismatic claimants. Since the need for an explanation was undiminished, it became essential to examine the validity of the critical arguments which included the following:

1. The basic charismatic act is only a self-serving belief that is not observable and exists "only in the eyes of the beholder."
2. The theory is presented primarily in a "pure" form, it is not placed in any historical setting, and has little or no explanatory capacity.
3. If charisma really exists, then its internal structure is oversimplified because there is a need to distinguish hysterical from spiritual leaders.
4. The concept of charisma, emanating from religion, is meaningful only for the prophets, and is completely irrelevant for the politicians.
5. Charismatic leadership is so alien to democracy that if it should occur would certainly undermine democracy by means of demagogy and misused plebiscites.
6. Charismatic leadership is inherently dictatorial because the leader alone determines the policies, tells the masses what they have to believe and do, and imposes a stifling obedience.

The opponents thus arrived at two conclusions. Either the whole concept and theory has to be discarded, or only dictators can (and will) claim superior abilities which they use to justify their power.

A careful comparison between Weber's theory and the counterarguments suggested that the critics were not able to prove their negative judgments, but they certainly raised important issues that demanded further investigations. One deals with the peculiar method of Weber; the other with the transformation from the pure to the historical leaders. Preliminary studies were thus required before the Weberian theory could be applied to the historically identifiable leaders.

An examination of Weber's ideal-typical method reveals that it contained two similar but still different ways of typifying ideas and events. One was to formulate a construct, whether rational or heuristic, the characteristics of which would then be compared with particular historical events. If the "ideal" and actual components match, then the construct becomes a tenable theory. The other version of the method formulates a prototype, in which the selected features are not taken from a construct, but from the most exemplary example available to the researcher. The exemplary case permits a prototypical analysis that arrives at the formulation of a cause and effect relationship.[1] There is a clear statement that Weber was not adverse to the prototypical method in the study of charisma, for he underlined that "historical reality constitutes combinations, mixtures, adaptations, and modifications of the pure type" of charisma. This dictum entails the injunction that there arises the synergistic charisma in which the charismatic and noncharismatic features are so combined that they differ significantly from pure charisma. The major purpose of this book, thus, is to investigate the synergistic kind of charismatic leadership.

In concentrating upon the combinations, instead of Weber's transformation, we had to discover how Weber linked charismatic leadership with the political systems of democracy and dictatorship. A preliminary study, published first in 1974 and then revised as chapter 2 below, revealed that Weber had a theory of democratic and revolutionary, but not of dictatorial charisma. The main reason for this omission was one of experience. He and his contemporaries knew only of the military dictatorship which was perceived by him as being primarily a bureaucratic phenomenon. The monumental charismatic leadership in totalitarian regimes looms so large that a detailed investigation seems imperative.

These preliminary studies clearly suggested that Weber's theory could function as an effective guide for a factual study of charismatic leadership in our generation. Not only was the typological method to be modified, but the bulk of the book had to be divided between democratic and dictatorial charismata. Weber's theory of four different types of democracy made it possible to link each with a particular subtype of charismatic leadership. Since Weber was unable to write his planned study of revolutionary charisma, it became our task to show how charismatic leadership operated in revolutionary and counterrevolutionary dictatorship, and how in each it culminated into despotism.

During the years of reflection on these problems, there evolved a new view on the types of leadership and their relations to particular situations. Crises are not continuous over time; they come and go in a repeated but irregular fashion. Hardly any field of human endeavor is completely and permanently immune to some kind of crisis. While not only differing from each other, the crises are unlikely to be eliminated in the foreseeable future. Repeatable crises mean that every relevant theory of the social sciences is in need of being divided in two parts. One seeks to typify and explain the facts of regular evolution; the other tries to understand the courses and meanings of irregular situations. This duality of evolution applies to any of the contemporary political systems, for democratic as well as dictatorial regimes.

The sequence of regular and irregular situations calls for different kinds of political leadership. A type of pragmatic leadership tends to arise in regular situations, whereas passionate leadership has greater opportunities and is more readily accepted by the electorate in irregular situations. For, in a crisis, not only are we faced with objective but deteriorating conditions, but we must focus on the threats to our accustomed patterns of beliefs and actions. The emotions of the millions of participants demand politics that mitigate and eventually overcome the particular crisis. A theory of irregularity of leadership as well as of situations is either implicit in Weber's work or is required for fully appreciating the relevance of his ideas on leadership for our time.

Given the irregularity and the diversity of the crises, one can formulate the thesis that there has to be more than one singular and isolated type of charismatic leadership. Minor crises attract fickle emotions of the followers and an insecure calling of the leader. In major crises, however, definite charismatic assignments await the leader, and many voting groups are ready for policies aiming at significant political changes. The leader must demand more of himself, must possess extraordinary capacities to fulfill his assignments. The followers not only tolerate but insist upon quick action that tends to counteract the destructive influences of the particular crisis. This thesis means that our study has to begin with the variety of charismatic leadership in our time, seeking to arrive at an empirically verifiable typology of the subtypes of charismatic leadership. We then have to examine Weber's theory of charisma and compare his theoretical typology with our descriptive typology. Such a comparison will permit a choice of the most relevant subtype of charismatic leadership for detailed study. As a side effect, comparison and selection dispose of the notion that charismatic leadership is a historical accident that we can only endure but never understand or analyze adequately.

In the light of this perspective on the history and theory of charismatic leadership, we then place it into the political setting of dictatorships and democracies in the expectation that the political systems will simultaneously provide quite different opportunities for the originally similar kind of leadership, while at the same time being so strongly differentiated that we can adequately describe and contrast the democratic from the dictatorial types of leaders and find for each its proper place in the age of charisma.

Anyone interested in examining how exceptional leadership seeks to overcome particular crises in two diametrically opposed political systems, creating or modifying them,[2] should find in this comprehensive study of modern political charisma an illuminating guide and we hope also a persuasive interpretation.

# PART ONE
# PAST PERSPECTIVES

# CHAPTER ONE

# VARIETIES OF CHARISMA

THE AGE OF CHARISMA is one of the features of the twentieth century. The previous century could not muster such a galaxy of charismatic leaders. In reviewing the few examples of charismatic leadership in previous periods, Max Weber concluded in 1918 that "a political genius . . . [can] be expected only once every few centuries."[1] (p.1405).

Instead of witnessing a dying species, we have been blessed, or cursed, with a long sequence of charismatic leaders on practically all continents. While frequency has been accompanied by variety, continuity from one leader to the next has been almost completely absent. New external opportunities and new favorably disposed followers had to appear before another charismatic leader could arise in the same or in a different country. In spite of variety and discontinuity there has been a remarkably similarity in the kinds of emotions felt, and beliefs held, by the various charismatic leaders. In comparison with other kinds of leadership, this similarity has been so pronounced that one is justified to speak of the age of charisma.

A similar core and various forms of actions call for a typification of these leaders according to their degree of success and the political system in which they worked and struggled. If we presuppose that each one possessed a distinct charismatic quality and was acknowledged by a significant number of followers,[2] then those who succeeded in getting control of old or new political parties and headed a government in one of the world powers will be called *charismatic giants*. Others who had a similar degree of success in building up a movement and/or party, taking over the government, but were limited to a small country overshadowed by superpowers, shall be known as *charismatic luminaries*. Those who tried their best but failed in succeeding to national leadership, for whatever reason, will be named *frustrated* or *charismatic failures*. Finally, those who have put up a claim and are in the process of trying but have not yet been successful will be regarded as *charismatic aspirants*. In presenting this typology of charismatic leadership, we can merely give a bare outline so as to place our problem in a proper perspective and indicate the scope of our analysis.

3

## Charismatic Giants

In this country, the two Roosevelts were the outstanding charismatic leaders. Theodore Roosevelt was so much convinced of his personal destiny that after two terms as president he ran as the candidate of a third party and thereby assured the defeat of the Republican candidate for the presidency in 1912. Franklin D. Roosevelt, after running an ordinary campaign in 1932, rose to the challenge of his time by initiating the New Deal as a means of fighting the great depression and by gradually uniting the country for joining the war to destroy the Nazi regime.

Contrary to the prediction of Karl Marx that proletarian revolution would arise in West Europe, communism was victorious in the backward countries of Czarist Russia and agrarian China. Its two leaders were more than ideologists. Lenin was so convinced of his vanguard mission and indispensability as a leader that he seized power by violence and behaved as a charismatic leader during the bitter years of the civil war. Mao in war-torn China followed Lenin's example of violence and civil war but went beyond by jumping from backward to Communist agriculture. While Marx remained their ideological leader, the emotional appeal and missionary zeal of these Communist leaders were so strong that they succeeded in incorporating personal charismatic leadership into their rule of a single party dictatorship.

The most flamboyant and supremely confident form of charismatic leaders carried the banner of fascism. While the March of Rome was more a symbolic than a violent act, once in office Mussolini gained the admiration of millions and never ceased to praise the virtues of superior leadership until he was overthrown by his own generals prior to military defeat. While his revolt of 1923 failed, Hitler rose to power as the head of a large Fascist mass movement, supported by the benevolent neutrality of the army. In a relatively short period he utilized his charismatic qualities to head government, state, and armed forces, and in all three offices became the most emotional and glamorous or hated charismatic leader of the last generation. As in communism, charisma was reconciled and integrated with the most ruthless form of the single party dictatorship of fascism.

Charisma entered the British and French democracies during times of war. Lloyd George became the war hero of civilians and soldiers during World War I. Even more pronounced were the exceptional leadership qualities of Churchill who came out of his political isolation of the 1930s as the man most capable of mobilizing the resources required for war. Soon after Hitler started World War II, Churchill became the prime minister and leader of the Conservative party. As head of the government he personified the British will of resistance and endurance during the most trying period in British history.[3] While being only a symbol of French resistance during World War II, General de Gaulle presented himself as the liberator of the nation for a short time in office after World War II. But he was recalled as the unifier of the nation in the Algerian war and secured a peace without civil war in France. He resigned the presidency in dismay, if not in disgust, when the majority of the voters did not accept enthusiastically his plan for administrative reform, but he left to France the legacy of a plebiscitary democracy.[4]

On the Asian continent, Mahatma Gandhi became the most inventive and celebrated charismatic leader of India. Being a humble person, he shunned any display and bravado, never accepted any state office, but succeeded in becoming the generally recognized leader of the Congress party and national liberation from British colonial rule. Gandhi not only possessed the typical charismatic secret of "hearing what the masses were willing to listen to," but he was also willing to accept personal sacrifices so that his actions would not inflict any physical harm upon others.[5] While not accepting Gandhi's nonviolence, his follower Nehru grew into a charismatic leader in his own right and established the largest democracy in a poor and overpopulated land. Nehru was the only immediate and blessed successor of a great leader in the age of charisma.

This succession has been further handed over by Nehru to his daughter, Indira Gandhi, who has become a charismatic leader, in spite of her setback once during an election. Unless her leadership is interrupted by unforeseen circumstances, she may well qualify to be a charismatic giant, as she shows signs of being a successful charismatic leader, the leader of her own Congress party and also the leader of the world's largest democracy. A close look at the leadership of this Asian democracy shows that there has been a tendency to nominate a member of the family as a charismatic successor. Unfortunately due to accidental death of Indira Gandhi's son, Sanjay Gandhi, she has lost her immediate charismatic successor, but is grooming her older son for the top position. It remains to be investigated how charismatic leaders have been able to nominate their relatives as their successors in this underdeveloped democracy, and what measures have been taken by them to achieve these goals. Another question which needs to be investigated is how the fierce and cutthroat competition from other charismatic aspirants has been systematically and ruthlessly suppressed. However, such an inquiry is beyond the scope of the present investigation.

These thirteen leaders comprise the group of charismatic giants if we include Clemenceau in our record.[6] Giantism means two things in this context. Each of them was extremely successful as charismatic leader, party leader, and leader of his or her respective nation. They also had the good fortune of becoming the leaders of actual or potential world powers that offered them sufficient resources and opportunities for playing the role of a world leader.

It should be underlined that these leaders were only "great" in the sense of having achieved many of their own goals. Only a few of them were great personalities in terms of generally accepted moral values. Whoever equates charisma with moral greatness will create for himself an unsolvable dilemma. This was the predicament of Thomas Mann who spoke of "brother Hitler" as the embodiment of botched-up greatness and of an inferior genius.[7] Unfortunately, this moral judgment was not shared by the millions of Hitler's admirers. For a scientific analysis, however, we have to accept the stricture of Max Weber that it is entirely indifferent how the charismatic qualities and achievements "would be ultimately judged from any ethical, aesthetic or other such point of view. . . . What is alone important is how the individual is actually regarded by those subject to charismatic authority, by his 'followers' or 'disciples' " (p.242).

## CHARISMATIC LUMINARIES

If compared with the giants, charismatic luminaries suffered from one of three defects. For one, their charismatic quality was not sufficiently developed, so they failed to be recognized by the majority of the voters. The outstanding example of this was John F. Kennedy whose charismatic gift did not become visible before the primaries of 1960. In the presidential election his charismatic appeal was responded to primarily by ordinary voters of the Democratic party. It required a shift of some Catholic voters who for religious reasons edged him into the presidency by the smallest of margins. Had Kennedy lived, he most likely would have grown into a charismatic giant. The bullets of the assassin kept him in the category of charismatic luminary.

A quite different defect arose in early democracies of less-developed countries. The new leaders like Sukarno in Indonesia, Nkrumah in Ghana, Nyerere in Tanganyika, and Ben Bella in Algeria mustered an effective charismatic appeal whose exceptional quality gave them control over a political party and headship of the government. In order to sustain their authority, most of these leaders were tempted to establish or succeeded in establishing a single party. But this prop was not sufficient. In three of these countries, the new military establishment became increasingly powerful and at the appropriate moment overthrew the regime of the charismatic leader. The major defect was that the charismatic leaders could not retain their control over party and armed forces. For Ghana, specialists limit the period of personal charisma to the years 1949–55, which was followed or complemented by the institutional charisma of the single party, until both were overthrown by military force.[8] In the African cases the charismatic personal quality was partly short-lived and diluted gradually from within, but was also terminated by military leaders from without. In Indonesia the military deposed Sukarno in self-defense, while the overthrow of Mujibur Rahman in Bangladesh culminated in an awful bloodbath of himself, his family, and of the most important ministers of his government.

In claiming charismatic qualities successfully, military officers enjoyed a greater chance of retaining their charismatic leadership. Usually the military coup preceded the visibility of the charismatic quality. Ataturk of Turkey, Nasser of Egypt, Amin of Uganda, and Quaddafi of Libya began their careers as military usurpers. It was as the victor of the war against Greece that Kemal Ataturk became the founder of the Turkish Republic. His was primarily a heroic charisma. Nasser was only one of the members of the Free Officers Movement that formed the Revolutionary Command Council. The military branch of this movement was under the command of Nasser and the civilian branch was directed by Sadat. Once in power, the council dissolved the political parties and established a military dictatorship. Ministers became responsible to the council, and the Liberation rally became the single party with Nasser as its secretary-general and the council comprised the executive committee of the party. As spokesman for the council and the rally, Nasser formed his own government. It was this joint military and political springboard that enabled Nasser to reveal his extraordinary qualities and to remain the charismatic dictator until his death.[9]

While Kemal Ataturk prepared the country for democratically elected parties,[10] Nasser retained his charismatic appeal as well as his control over the interlinked military and political organizations. Perón in Argentina failed in this because he gained power by means of a plebiscite, emphasized more the single party, and was eventually overthrown by the regular army. But he bequeathed to his country a legendary charisma that ended only with his recall, his death, and the breakup of his movement.[11] The two more recent military dictators with charismatic abilities, Amin of Uganda and Quaddafi of Libya, follow closely the pattern of Nasser. As he sought to play a role in world politics, Amin presented himself as the unifier of Angola and the spokesman of Pan Africa, while Quaddafi used his oil fortune to finance terrorist groups in various parts of the world. Chances are that the world ambitions of the latter will be as effectively curbed as was Nasser's goal of becoming the unifier of all Arabian states.

A military element also played a significant role in the rise of four communists into the role of charismatic luminaries. Kim of North Korea, Ho Chi Minh of Indochina, Tito of Yugoslavia, and Castro of Cuba gained political leadership through their actions as guerrilla fighters. In coordinating political and military campaigns, they were able to show their charismatic qualities and attain the personal attachment of their followers, strengthened by often ruthless discipline. Victory in the partisan war gave the leaders the opportunity to keep control over the reorganized armed forces and also gain a mass basis for their Communist party and government. Another accomplishment of these luminaries was to combine Communist as well as nationalist ideologies and infuse both with their charismatic leadership. Intertwined charisma and nationalism helped significantly to unite the various political and economic groups behind the charismatic hero.

Coming to power without the direct assistance of Russia's Red army, except for Kim, it was the misfortune of the four luminaries that they had to live within the shadow of first one and then two Communist superpowers. Tito had to accept isolation within the Communist world as the price for resisting Stalin's orders. Each of the various Soviet agents failed in undermining Tito's charismatic leadership. Kim's foreign policy was and is controlled by Communist China, and Castro's by Communist Russia, after the abortive attempt to place Soviet missiles at the American doorstep. Ho Chi Minh was the only one of these luminaries who was able to pursue an independent policy of nationalist expansion by playing the two Communist superpowers against each other and getting substantial assistance from both when sending his troops into South Indochina. While internally autonomous, except for Cuba, international standing of these regimes of national communism was largely an unintended consequence of the furious conflict between the two superpowers. The manifold imposed reforms in these small lands were as much a result of the enthusiasm aroused by charismatic leadership as of the oppressive rule of single party and secret police. Charismatic luminaries, magnified by propagandistic manipulation, were not deposed but they became the typical form of leadership for national communism.[12]

In spite of these defects of a not fully developed charismatic qualification, of an incapacity to control simultaneously a party and military, or of being limited to a small country by superpowers, charismatic luminaries succeeded in combining control over a party and a government for a significant period. It is this achievement in leadership during a crucial test of their abilities marching at the heads of their respective movements and regimes that stamped them as moderately successful charismatic leaders.

## CHARISMATIC FAILURES

The age of charisma includes not only the successful but also the frustrated leaders. The causes for the frustration have been diverse. We shall speak of charismatic failures whether their initial attempts have failed because of injury to their body or because of having their chances for success eliminated. Pretenders may be shot by assassins, castrated by party leaders, deposed by superior holders of power, or deprived of their opportunities by political opponents. The effect of the intervention is always the same. An initial success is undercut so that the jump from the charismatic community to the subsequent mass movement, headship of a party, and taking over of the government, are effectively prevented by opposing forces. In a few cases, failure has also been the result of either an insufficient charismatic quality or its inadequate use in a specific situation. Frustrated charisma has been almost as frequent as consummated charisma.

In the Fascist orbit, the early Hitler was the first charismatic pretender. The economic crisis of hyperinflation, and the political conflict between the Bavarian and the Reich governments, created a situation of collective excitement. While the charismatic appeal found increasing support in the middle class, Hitler's coup failed because the upper class withdrew its support at the crucial moment, and the riot police shot at and dispersed the Nazi demonstration. Hitler learned the lesson of his failure and decided to come to power by parliamentary means. Hitler's charismatic abilities were visible at that early time. "Hitler united in his physically insignificant person the talents and characteristics of Demosthenes, Ferdinand of Aragon, and Robert de Bruce; and he added to them the ambition . . . of Alexander and Napoleon."[13]

In presenting a program for creating employment, Sir Oswald Mosley sought to implement his ideas through a Fascist party. "He understood crowds as he never understood individuals. . . . When he added to his usual incisiveness the moral fervor of the prophet preaching in a great cause, he became one of the great orators of England, and convinced himself that political power lay in the response of a large audience to a stirring speech."[14] But the voters did not recognize him as a man of destiny whose charismatic appeal was rejected by the overwhelming majority of the electorate.

A similar fate befell the Belgian Fascist leader Degrelle. "An extraordinary dynamism . . . seemed the keynote of his personality, but he combined this with an unusual sense of the dramatic. . . . In his public speeches he seized his audience by the throat and left them panting. His self-confidence was unlimited, and so were his ambitions."[15] When in 1936, Degrelle challenged the democratic parties in a by-election in Brussels, he was soundly defeated, and his splinter party was destined to collaborate with the Nazis.

The Romanian charismatic community of the Legion of the Archangel Michael praised its leader Codreano in the following terms: "Him we love, to him we listen. We are at his orders. He is our hope and the hope of Romania tomorrow. We get strong through him. We are feared through him. We shall win through him."[16] Codreano's charismatic appeal was peculiar because he was playing down his oratorial inability by relying upon individual terror and hooded riders by night, not supported by any kind of proper organization for the masses. Sentenced by a court to ten years of hard labor on a treason charge, Codreano was strangled to death by the police on his way to prison.[17] Hitler was in a position to intervene in his behalf, but he was more interested in steady oil delivery and in a military assistance pact with the Romanian rulers. The aggressive policy of the Fascist giants undercut unintentionally the charismatic chances of the Fascist leaders in Belgium and England, while the same policy led to Hitler's deliberate disinterest in the chances of Fascist charisma in Romania.

In the Communist orbit, there has developed recently an outright hostility to those charismatic leaders who do not stay within the orthodox ideology of communism. The anti-Soviet revolts of Hungary in 1956 and of Czechoslovakia in 1968 led to military suppression by the Soviet Union, while the similar revolts in Poland in 1956 and 1980 brought forth some Soviet concessions. Gomulka as a noncharismatic leader was recognized, while Imra Nagy was killed after being deposed, and Dubcek banned into a little town, although both responded more to a charismatic disposition of the masses than they created new followers by a powerful charismatic appeal.[18] In fully subdued satellites, Communist hegemony tends to eliminate leaders with even the smallest self-image of a charismatic mission.

Early democracies are often afflicted with individual terrorism. In the young Weimar Republic, one socialist and two democrats were killed shortly after the revolution of 1918. The charismatic leader Kurt Eisner was one among them, who was shot to death by a terrorist in Munich a few months after he had become minister-president of Bavaria. The same happened to Patrice Lumumba of the Belgian Congo soon after he was installed as the first native minister-president of this African country. But only Fascist leaders drew from the murder of Eisner the correct conclusion that a charismatic leader must be carefully protected by a special praetorian guard.

In advanced democracies, charismatic pretenders have faced two quite different hurdles that condemned them to failure. One was castration; the other assassination. Both methods of attack indicate clearly that charismatic leaders arouse not only great enthusiasm in their followers but also intense hatred in their enemies. Under certain conditions, antagonism can and does cause the eventual impotence or elimination of charismatic leaders.

Castration of charismatic leadership could be observed in West Germany, Great Britain, and the United States in the aftermath of World War II. The decisive personality of Kurt Schumacher was easily able to make him the unquestioned leader of the Social Democratic party. But he was stalled in forming the new Federal government by Konrad Adenauer who became chancellor by one vote—his own. Sickness and bitterness incurred in the long years of concentration camp tempered the effectiveness of Schumacher's charismatic appeal with the electorate whose majority yearned for a capitalist restoration. A social-psychological study which recognizes his charisma sees the personal defect mainly as the inability to sense the feelings or appreciate the values of others and to turn this knowledge to his advantage.[19] The "brilliant personality" of Aneurin Bevan effectively expressed the bitterness of many British workers, but he remained the petrel of the Labor party in the 1950s and was effectively prevented from becoming the party leader by the heads of the trade unions.[20]

In 1950 Senator Joseph McCarthy started the charismatic appeal that enabled him to bring half the voting population behind him at the climax of his career.[21] This success was soon dissipated through his greater emphasis on hatred than enthusiasm, his ill-advised attack on some military leaders, and his threat to well-established leaders of the Republican party. Simultaneous dilution of the charismatic quality and censure by the senate jointly terminated the leadership and movement of McCarthyism.

Assassinations disrupted three charismatic drives prior to any sign of dilution. Robert F. Kennedy had proved the effectiveness of his charismatic appeal in the senatorial election of New York, in spite of Governor Rockefeller's intervention.[22] Enthusiasm was overflowing for the candidate of the Democratic nomination in 1968, especially among the students, although Kennedy openly opposed their deferment from military service. The bullets of the assassin prevented us from knowing whether the majority of the voters would have accepted him as a charismatic leader.

Martin Luther King, Jr. was well on his way to becoming the charismatic leader of the articulate and growing black middle class. But it is uncertain whether he would have overcome the challenge of the black power group of students, and especially if he would have possessed the stamina and fortitude of adding long-term fasting to nonviolence, thereby qualifying as a true follower of Gandhi.[23] His despicable murder not only deprived the blacks of a nationally respected leader who was not followed by any successor, but also destroyed any opportunity for transplanting successfully the Gandhian type of charisma to the United States.

A thoroughly indigenous kind of charisma was presented by Governor George Wallace, who not only wanted to retain segregation but also to restore the days of intimacy and smallness, whether in business, government, or labor. Another gunman shot him down in 1972 and crippled him for life. Individual terrorism has been one powerful force turning promising futures into charismatic failures.

## CHARISMATIC ASPIRANTS

In the aftermath of Watergate, American charismatic aspirants faced four distinctly different moods in the electorate. One was a severe disappointment, if not disgust, with government and a condemnation of politicians in general. There was a conservative swing that insisted upon financial soundness, streamlining of government, personal honesty and openness in public affairs as well as a fight against crime and permissiveness. A third sentiment was provoked by all forms of bribery, corruption, and underhandedness in high places of government and big business, as well as by wire tapping, electronic surveillance, police brutality, and a call for measuring all present and future leaders by high moral standards. Last but not least was the economic discontent, and the suffering from unemployment and inflation that was turning into anger against all incumbents. An eagerness developed to "throw the rascals out." These four popular sentiments created an extraordinary situation of mass restlessness. These moods did not turn into a charismatic disposition to acclaim a new leader because of the disgust with a dishonest president, and the increasing emphasis upon moral qualities and honesty as the predominant requirements of the new president.

Among the many candidates for public office in 1976, there were not more than two potential charismatic leaders. Governor Reagan possessed great photogenic glamour over television and polish on the platform. Twice he was able to turn these abilities into electoral victories in California. His ample financial support permitted him to employ all modern means of mass manipulation. Personifying the conservative mood among Republicans helped him in the primaries. When his attractiveness became known, one Republican county chairman interpreted it as a sign that Republican voters were "looking for a political messiah."[24] While the charismatic appeal won increasing acclaim, Reagan failed to get the nomination because of Gerald Ford's incumbency and the negative impact of a too conservative ideology.

Elected four times in his home state, Governor Wallace drowned all opponents and inveigled substantial majorities not only for himself but once also for his wife. Personifying traditional values and inveighing against red tape, federal tyranny, heavy tax burdens, and waste in government became his powerful emotional appeal. Wallace showed a strutting disrespect for all the powerful and eggheads. His identification with the "little man" increased his following from 1968 to 1972. His open racism was disguised but turned it into a powerful political issue of attacking the busing of children for racial reasons. But this emotionally saturated slogan could no longer be monopolized by Wallace, as it was by Nixon in 1972, when most of the other rivals in the Democratic primaries of 1976 pointed to the failure of mass busing as an educational policy. But the greatest handicap of Wallace was his physical disability in 1972. Personal vigor turned out to be an indispensable condition for a successful charismatic appeal. Partial paralysis and insufficient moral righteousness together produced a charismatic failure.

In the primaries after Watergate, intense moral indignation and aversion to any kind of paramount leadership precluded any charismatic opportunities for Senator Edward Kennedy and Governor Jerry Brown. Jimmy Carter was the leading man of the campaign because he combined charismalike self-confidence and endurance with personal honesty, devotion to high moral principles, and compassion for the unemployed and poor of any color. Coming from the South, attracting some of Wallace's voters, and condemning the corruption of Washington enabled Carter to reunite the old Roosevelt coalition and thereby gain the presidency. Charismatic leadership was still effective in the Californian campaign of 1978, when Governor Brown garnered a decisive majority of the votes in spite of his switch in support of Proposition 13. The career of charismatics is full of surprises, and no aspirant has any assurance of eventual victory.

## COMPARATIVE CHARISMA

Our summary of the historical record presents overwhelming evidence for the relative frequency and variety of charismatic leadership. In all we found the minimum of fifty-three leaders of which thirteen were charismatic giants, twenty luminaries, seventeen failures, and three aspirants. By any standard this is a conservative estimate. The names of such men as Bourguiba, Kenyatta, Munoz, and Houphouet-Boigny have been suggested, and some readers may want to include others. If so, our list would be incomplete, but each of the included names seems to be empirically verifiable. There is no doubt, however, that much historical work will have to be done to give us an adequate profile of each of these or other charismatics. For the sake of convenience, we shall bring together the record of leaders in a list and place each of them under the political system in which he operated (table 1.1).

In addition to frequency and variety, most striking is the differential effect of these leaders. Some achieved an outstanding success on a world scale, others only within their particular country, a significant number of them tried their best but failed, and many aspirants still have to meet the test of their capacity. If we take these differential results as the objective criterion, and operation in their political system as the place of action, then our record would lead to the suggestion "that an objective typology of charismatic leadership is necessary."[25] What can we learn from a comparison of these kinds of charisma?

The most obvious suggestion is that charisma is a kind of leadership, but not by itself a political system. These leaders did not exist in a political vacuum. One important condition for their success was that they associated themselves with a particular political system. If they remained apolitical, then their range of activities was limited to charismatic communities. All of the fifty-five leaders developed an affinity for one specific political system. Affinity was either positive or negative to the prevailing system. Either they rose within such a system, personified its major characteristics, and modified its institutions to suit their particular purposes, or they fought against the existing system, developed a force of opposition, and if successful created a new system for their own country. While the leaders were modifiers of old systems or creators of new ones, there is not sufficient evidence for the contention that they single-handedly created the political systems of their own choice. Instead of saying "National Socialism became Hitlerism,"[26] it seems more appropriate to say that the leader personified and led the system but he was not a substitute for it. There is thus a reciprocal, not a direct causal, relationship between charismatic leader and associated political system.

A comparison reveals nothing definite about the origin of charisma because our record proceeds in terms of effects. But the irregularity of occurrence and the absence of successors, except for Nehru following Gandhi, suggest an accidental origin of the charismatic personality. Irregularity has two significant reasons. The charismatic quality may lie dormant for a significant period of time. As Weber has emphasized, "charismatic powers can be developed only in people or objects in which the germ already existed but would have remained dormant unless evoked by some ascetic or other regimen" (p.400). The timing of the awakening may be strictly personal so that an aspirant may become conscious of his qualities at a time when no followers are awaiting him. Conversely, discontent, estrangement, and alienation may give rise to a charismatic readiness at a time when no charismatic leader appears on the horizon. The frantic demonstrations in Portugal during 1975 revealed quite clearly a charismatic disposition of followers who searched but did not find a charismatic aspirant able to transform the emotional uproar into the enthusiasm for his genius, thereby opening the road for a mass movement and a charismatically led government.

Extraordinary situations thus establish only the presumption that a charismatic aspirant will appear at the appropriate time. Instead of a causal nexus between exceptional situations and the right kind of charismatic leader, there is only a happy coincidence for situation and personality to appear at the right moment in time. But as the long list of failures indicates, pretenders arise more frequently than situations, so that they have to struggle for lengthy periods, in which they may gain a partial success, but then fail in the end.

Arousing emotions and kindling enthusiasm in disposed masses is the first and crucial task of aspirants. There is always the danger that the exceptional ability is too small or transitional, or the response too insignificant, for a particular aspirant. Ephemeral charisma is not a part of our historical record. Once the initial success is achieved, there is a continuous struggle to keep the exceptional quality undiluted, to renew and enlarge the enthusiasm. The latter can be greatly facilitated through access to modern mass media, from the microphone to the television. But the use of

TABLE 1.1. CHARISMATIC LEADERS IN THE TWENTIETH CENTURY.

| Political Systems | Giants | Luminaries | Failures* | Aspirants |
|---|---|---|---|---|
| *Early Democracies:* | Gandhi<br>Nehru<br>I. Gandhi | Magsaysay<br>Sukarno<br>Nkrumah<br>Nyerere<br>Ben Bella<br>Mujibur Rahman<br>Carol A. Pérez | Eisner<br>Lumumba | |
| *Advanced Democracies:* | T. Roosevelt<br>F. D. Roosevelt | J. F. Kennedy<br>Ben Gurian<br>Reagan | W. Willkie<br>Bevan<br>Schumacher<br>R. F. Kennedy<br>M. L. King<br>Joe McCarthy<br>George Wallace | G. Wallace<br>E. Kennedy<br>J. Brown |
| *Military Regimes:* | Lloyd George<br>Clemenceau<br>Churchill<br>de Gaulle | Ataturk<br>Nasser<br>Perón<br>Amin<br>Quaddafi<br>Juan Velasco | Z. A. Bhutto | |

14

TABLE 1.1. *Continued*

| Political Systems | Giants | Luminaries | Failures* | Aspirants |
|---|---|---|---|---|
| *Communist Regimes:* | Lenin<br>Mao | Tito<br>Kim<br>Ho Chi Minh<br>Castro<br>Ceausescu | Trotsky<br>Dubcek<br>I. Nagy<br>L. Walesa | |
| *Fascist Regimes:* | Mussolini<br>Hitler | | Hitler<br>Mosley<br>Degrelle<br>Codreano | |
| Total: | 13 | 21 | 18 | 3 |

55

*Hitler and Wallace are counted twice because of their repeated attempts.
For a typology according to the relationship between charisma and office, see Ann Ruth Willner, *Charismatic Political Leadership: A Theory* (Princeton: Center of International Studies, 1968), p. 32.

such instruments has created opportunities as well as dangers for leaders. On the one hand, rivalry among charismatic claimants is decided not only by rhetoric but also by photogenic abilities. Whoever has no access to or cannot "sell" himself over the television screen is likely to be a charismatic failure. On the other hand, perfecting the technique of modern mass media has greatly reduced the distance between charismatic ability and the cosmetic talent of a mere performer. A relatively small charismatic ability may be magnified through an extensive television campaign. Mass manipulation calls for a huge campaign fund, so the son of a millionaire has substantially greater chances than a mere college graduate with a calling but no funds. Financial ability creates more aspirants, while financial poverty constitutes a new cause for turning an exceptional rhetoric ability into a failure. Once in power, a charismatic leader has many opportunities of manipulating public opinion, even in a democracy.

There is no equal opportunity for charismatic stability for the four types of leaders. All claimants take a considerable degree of risk for the safety of their person. Individual terror may destroy some, whereas others luckily escape the bullets or bombs of assassins.[27] Charisma generates not only enthusiasm in the followers, but also a tremendous hatred in some of the leader's opponents. Hatred provides the motivation and charismatic visibility presents the ready target for the physical attack by murderers. Single assassins without any accompanying conspiracy tend to be an unanticipated by-product of charismatic leadership.[28] An inspection of our list shows that a relatively high percentage of the failures were victims of antagonistic assailants. Devising some form of personal protection compatible with mass appeal taxes the ingenuity of charismatic leaders.

Another danger to stability is the always present fear of the leader that his exceptional power may be diluted. He is thus often overly eager to test anew his ability to generate mass enthusiasm. If John F. Kennedy had followed Johnson's advice not to visit Texas in 1963, he could not have been murdered in Dallas. Uncertainty about the strength of the charismatic attraction makes leaders receptive not only to manipulation, but also to various forms of personality cult. The extent of such cults depends upon the degree of control over the means of information, over the media, and effective secrecy in general. The greater the dictatorial power of the leader, the greater is the temptation and opportunity for personality cult. Also, extraordinary deeds, performed repeatedly and successfully, can rekindle the enthusiasm of the masses and strengthen the leader's belief in his extraordinary abilities. Instead of an inevitable process of dilution, some leaders have thus the opportunity to counteract this tendency and develop into charismatic giants, whereas others fall by the wayside.

Durability of followership is also influenced by the nature of the extraordinary situation. If the leader was accepted for mastering an emergency, then his very success limits the time of his leadership. Both British prime ministers during the two world wars were deserted by the majority of the voters soon after military victory. De Gaulle's claim as a liberator faded soon after Nazi occupation ended. His subsequent indispensability in the conflict with Algeria diminished some years after the fear of a civil war had vanished. Mass anxiety and devotion can thus be limited to periods of emergencies. But the theory of charisma as a function of emergencies[29] is true only for strictly military debacles. Combating economic depressions, winning civil wars, or beating back actual invasions (Turkey) do not by themselves terminate followership. It is essential that the charismatic leader devises policies appropriate for new situations, and hopefully succeeds in infusing in additional masses the same kind of enthusiasm for him.

The very fact that charismatic leadership prevailed in leading specimens of five different types of political systems proves that charisma was linked effectively with particular ideologies. Instead of being immune to any or all sets of ideals, new or old, charismatic leaders became the personification and the first articulators of their particular ideologies. This was especially true for the giant leaders of Communist and Fascist regimes, who sponsored quite different ideologies and infused them with mass enthusiasm for their own person. In democracy, charismatic leaders were not the originators of a new ideology, but they usually became the implementors of prevailing ideals in a new situation, whether in promoting a new recovery or founding a new state. Finding and implementing the right kind of ideals, adequate for the situation and acceptable to particular followers, explains why the giants build their power upon different masses.[30]

Some of the pretenders failed because they did not originate or implement the appropriate ideology for removing the ills of the particular situation. The anticommunism of Joseph McCarthy, whose violent attacks were directed primarily against actual or alleged fellow travelers, is a case in point. He failed to develop even a rudimentary theory directed against communism itself. His inept ideology and misdirected policy proposals were important reasons why he turned into a charismatic failure. Other pretenders also proposed ideologies that were insufficiently acceptable to potential followers. Schumacher was kept in the position of minority leader on the national scene. The Social Democrats were able to move forward only after they dropped their opposition to the Schumann Plan. Bevan ran into the determined resistance of some trade unions and became a member of the Shadow Cabinet of Labor only after he stopped toying with some aspects of revolution. In adopting a Fascist ideology, Mosley drove his former associates of Labor from his new party and deprived himself of any chance of success.[31] One can thus generalize that an appropriate ideology contributed significantly to the success of the giants and luminaries while an inept ideology produced a stultifying effect for the failures.

Another contradictory relationship existed between charisma, party, and state bureaucracy. Each of the giant leaders found it compelling either to build up or to take over the leadership of a political party. Churchill alone reversed the sequence and became party leader only after he already had become prime minister.[32] It was a difficult but manageable task to combine party leadership with charismatic authority. These giants also succeeded in using and subduing the state bureaucracy, and even the generals, for their particular purposes. This was less true for some democracies than for single party dictatorships.

Comparison of charismatic leadership establishes the facts of two differences and two similarities. One is the variety but irregular occurrence of such leaders. Another is the distinction among four types of charismatics, whether one compares the degrees of success or the periods of operation. Very striking is the fact that almost all the giants and luminaries adopted certain ideologies and developed their own political or even paramilitary apparatus during the process of coming to power. Finally, each of these successful leaders showed a definite preference for one political system, whether he sought to reform an existing one or tried to build a new one.

These four findings of variety in kind and degree of success, or the linkages between charismatic and ideological elements, or between charismatic and organizational elements, or the preference for a specific political system constitute the factual basis for our typology of four kinds of charismatic leadership. This typology provides one great advantage. It calls for a differentiation of leaders, identifies them as different historical figures, and permits each kind of leadership to be studied by different scholars. In seeing them active in different historical settings, we obtain the opportunity for comparative analysis. In bringing in a differential time sequence, however, the analysis becomes complex and our typology is rendered incomplete. The distinguishing characteristics utilized are exclusively of an external nature. In seeking to link comparison with theory it becomes necessary to examine also the internal features. Are they essentially identical or are they so different that they call for a reassessment of Max Weber's theory of charisma?

## THEORETICAL APPROACHES TO CHARISMA

In concentrating mainly upon the similarities, Weber regarded the extraordinary quality of the leader and the intense devotion of the followers as the central features of charismatic leadership. The internal characteristics of the innate capacity of one man and the worship by the many constitute the core of his theory. Coexistence and interaction created a charismatic community. Clear factual evidence for such an interaction, he insisted, can be found only in the very beginning of their existence. "Faith of the leader himself and of his disciples in his charisma . . . is undiminished, consistent and effective only in *statu nascendi*" (p.1121). These reciprocal beliefs constitute together the essentials of the inner structure of such a community, which provide the basis for the charismatic authority and legitimacy.

But "this entirely pure charismatic authority . . . is rare." For Weber, "pure types . . . are considered merely border cases which are of special and indispensable analytical value, and bracket historical reality which almost always appear in mixed forms" (p.1002). This statement was applied to all forms of authority. "The forms of domination (*Herrschaft*) occurring in historical reality constitute combinations, mixtures, adaptations, or modifications of these 'pure' types" (p.954). The theory of charisma is thus divided into two parts. The "pure" part presents the internal structure of charisma, whereas the "impure" part deals with the realization of charismatic leadership in historical reality. In principle, this division provides the opportunity for incorporating and explaining the four external types of charisma in the second part of Weberian theory.

Unfortunately, Weber himself did not build his theory upon a typology. He proposed that all kinds of pure leadership, apart from strictly ephemeral charisma, become uniformly subject to a process of transformation. "When the tide that lifted a charismatically led group out of everyday life flows back into the channels of workaday routine, at least the 'pure' form of charismatic domination will wane and turn into an 'institution'; it is then either mechanized . . . or imperceptibly displaced by other structures, or fused with them in the most diverse forms, so that it becomes a mere component of a concrete historical structure" (p.1121). In including "fusion" in his impure type, Weber left an opening for the study of gigantic and luminary charismata. But his routinization is a process of gradual deterioration of charismatic quality and authority. He expected that routinization would transform leadership in one of two directions. Charisma would eventually be institutionalized and then smothered by a bureaucracy or it would become incorporated and then suffocated in a traditional regime. Ultimately, "it is the fate of charisma to recede with the development of permanent institutional structures of either bureaucracy or tradition" (p.1133)."

While possible in principle, there is considerable doubt whether gigantic and luminary charismata can be adequately explained by the theory of routinization. The reasons for this doubt lie in the different time dimensions, in the *growth* of charismatic authority, and in the more extensive view of political systems than is presented by Weber's bureaucratic and traditional regimes.

Instead of the pure and routinized phases, charismatic giants live through three phases as soon as they enter the political arena. In actively opposing the existing power holders, the leader and followers go through a period of challengership. With the ascent to governmental power, the leader and paladins significantly increase their power relative to other power groups. The leader is able to place his charismatic authority above the legal authority vested in him as head of the government. His personal apparatus increasingly occupies the leading positions and eventually controls the regular state bureaucracy. Finally, the leader and authority go through a terminal phase that only occasionally resembles routinization. The leader either changes into a despot, or is recalled by the electorate. His charisma may terminate with his natural death or his charismatic influence is perpetuated by a legendary charisma.

There is no doubt that the charismatic leader has to combine charismatic and noncharismatic features for gaining political power. In question is the thesis that acquiring such power must, sooner than later, dilute the exceptional quality, change the paladins into a bureaucratic or patrimonial staff, and eventually produce a bureaucratic regime. As we shall see, gigantic leaders adopt one of several ideologies, originate and control a charismatic apparatus, formulate a political program of their own, and seek either a reform or a shift in political systems. Simultaneously, the non-charismatic political, military, or economic allies of the leader gradually lose much of their power or disintegrate as a going concern. Instead of experiencing deterioration of his charisma, the leader and followers grow into a political regime of their own and by doing so become agents of either significant reforms or elevate themselves to the builders of a new political regime. Rather than acting as temporary intruders, gigantic leaders and followers utilize the mobilized masses to change the course of history.

It is a deplorable fact that Weber could not complete his sociology of the state. His major contribution was the theory of the three kinds of traditional, legal, and charismatic authorities and legitimacies. While this theory differentiates between authorized and unauthorized power, contrasts interest constellations with socio-political orders, there is in this theory a separation of types of political systems only for traditional regimes. The distinction between patriarchism, patrimonialism, and sultanism has illuminated some political systems in traditional regimes.[34] While there is certainly a theory of democracy, there is nothing similar for military dictatorships and single party regimes.[35] But each modern political system has to operate with a bureaucratic administration. The missing theory of the state makes it extremely difficult to answer the two pertinent questions. Why did charismatic leadership act effectively in both democratic and dictatorial systems? Did charismatic leadership superimpose itself upon the prevailing system, or did gigantic charisma succeed in establishing new political systems that possessed the chance of durability?

Whether Weber's theory of the phasing, combining, and ruling of charismatic leadership can readily be applied to gigantic leaders depends especially upon his theory of transformation. We shall thus first summarize and assess his theory of routinization, and subsequently examine four new theories of contemporary sociologists who have presented new interpretations of the interactions of charismatic and non-charismatic elements in charismatic authority. The central issue is whether the theory of routinization furnished an adequate explanation of such combinations of divergent components or whether an improvement or revision of the theory is required.

In Weber's theory of transformation, one finds different causes as well as different effects for routinization. One cause generates from the inside, the other from the outside, of the charismatic structure. The major external cause is the disappearance of the extraordinary situation. The imposing pressures of everyday events are so strong that leader and followers must enter into some form of accommodation, even if the reciprocal relationship among the charismatics remains intact. The internal cause originates primarily from the desires of leader, paladins, and followers "to transform charisma and charismatic blessing from a unique transitory gift of grace of extraordinary times and persons into a permanent possession for everyday life. . . .

Inevitably, this changes the nature of charismatic structure" (p.1121). Each cause routinizes charismatic leadership.

The two major consequences of routinization arise in the political and economic fields. The controllers of party machines resist the charismatic challengers and in the end "succeed in this castration of charisma" (p.1132). A similar outcome may result from an election by free and independent voters seeking the best spokesmen for their concerns. When the representative principle is radically applied, "the elected person is formally the agent and hence the servant of the voters. . . . This means that structurally the charismatic basis has been completely abandoned" (p.1128). In the struggle between a charismatically led movement and an ideological party, the latter will be hit but the outcome is unpredictable because "the internal dynamics of party organization and the social and economic conditions are too intimately interwoven in any given situation" (p.1133). In election campaigns, the "charismatic of the rhetoric" enjoys a demagogic advantage and the great role played by emotions may force the bureaucrats of the party "into the service of charismatic hero worship" (p.1130). The outcome of the political struggle between leadership and parties is thus not uniform. In the first two cases, charismatic leadership was defeated, whereas in the two subsequent cases the charismatic leader could or actually did win his prize.

In the economic and administrative fields, however, the process of routinization is said to be unavoidable. What the economy wants and what means the movement needs require an impure charisma. On the one hand, "the more highly developed the interdependence of different economic units in a monetary economy, the greater the pressure of the everyday needs of the followers becomes." On the other hand, the size of a mass provisioning of goods has its effect on the attitudes of the paladins and followers." As soon as control over large masses of people exists, [charisma] gives way to the forces of everyday routine" (p.252). Indeed, "the process of routinization of charisma is in very important respects identical with adaptation to the conditions of the economy, since this is the principal continually operating force in everyday life" (p.254).

Bureaucracy asserts an almost similarly detrimental impact upon charisma. There is an "objective necessity of adapting the order of the staff organization to the normal, everyday needs and conditions of carrying on administration" (p.252). This bureaucratic pressure is reenforced by the desire for security of the charismatic assistants which lies not only in the continued advantages of charismatic leadership, but calls for a bureaucratic status of their own. The paladins set up norms for recruitment, tests for training are required, tenure and promotion are granted, all of which turn the recipients of such advantages from believers into bureaucrats.

There is thus a certain finality with which the noncharismatic elements dilute the charismatic qualities and beliefs as well as deteriorate the corresponding authority and legitimacy. The study of the relationships of economy and administration with charisma turns into one grand generalization: "Every charisma is on the road from a turbulently emotional life that knows no economic rationality to a slow death of suffocation under the weight of material interests; every hour of its existence brings it nearer to its end" (p.1120).

This generalization leaves little choice for students in the Weberian tradition.[36] The growth in authority and power of gigantic and luminary leaders may be interpreted in terms of pure charisma, but then they cannot be associated with political parties and ideologies. Or the giants may be placed in the framework of routinization, but then the continued effect of the noncharismatic components will deteriorate charismatic leadership and authority. Must one thus conclude that Weber's theory of charisma needs a definite improvement before there can be an adequate explanation of growing charismatic movements and regimes led effectively by the same charismatic leader?

It so happens that sociological scholars have recently tried to overcome this impasse and presented their own solutions. In his lucid integration of Weber's ideas, Reinhard Bendix introduced two modifications. Rather than seeing a uniformly negative impact of political parties upon charismatic leaders, it is emphasized that there occurs a "regularization of the leadership function." Charismatic war lords and civilian Caesars successfully resist, while representative agents and charismatic figureheads succumb, to the pressure of party bureaucracies. There also is a differentiation of routinization which "produces both institutional permanence and decline of charisma."[37] The decline arises when charisma is withdrawn by a higher power or is no longer believed in by the followers. Permanency is achieved "when the charismatic message becomes variously dogma, theory, legal regulation, or the content of an oral or written tradition."[38] The two lines of development do not necessarily interact at each step but they may run parallel, or dogma and theory may substitute for the declining mission so that a routinized charisma can acquire relative permanence.[39]

The new organizational theory of charisma by Amitai Etzoni gives a narrower definition of the charismatic act. It consists in "the ability of the actor to exercise diffuse and intense influences over the normative orientation of other actors . . . for charisma is a form of normative power."[40] Men of such abilities are aspirants for an office, are appointed to an office, operate within and fulfill the requirements of specific organizations. Their main task is to formulate the ends of the organizations and obtain the compliance of others by noncoercive means. There is a mutual affinity between the charismatic aspirants and the needs of the organizations. "People who have the psychological syndromes of generalists are more likely to be charismatics than segmentalists or specialists." In the organization, the charismatics link norms to controls. "The more normative power is relied upon . . . the greater is the need for charisma."[41] Loose control by the superior of the subordinates requires less and more control calls for more charismatic abilities in the controllers.

While all voluntary organizations require charismatic talents, the particular use made of them depends upon the type of organization. In utilitarian organizations, concentration of charisma in the top position is functional, but expert charisma is dysfunctional. The opposite prevails in professional organizations, in which a top charismatic administrator is dysfunctional, whereas the charismatic professional is functional. Normative organizations distribute charismatic talents in two different ways. At the top level, charismatic generalists are functional, but the expertise of specialist is hindered by charismatic qualities. Hierarchically, however, different "amounts of charisma are required."[42] The higher the rank, the greater the necessary charisma and vice versa so that an association develops between personality and role in normative organizations.

Behind this ingenious linkage between charisma and internal structure, there is a novel theory of the organization. Since organizations are rational social units, their transactions are determined by two quite different kinds of decisions. Decisions about the means require rational calculations about cost and benefits. Decisions on ends consist of or involve values that can be appropriately selected only by those who appreciate norms, can translate them into moral obligations for others, and obtain their voluntary compliance. Since these men of norms also enjoy the power of their superior offices, persuasion by the charismatics tends to become "the controls of the elites over their subordinates."[43]

What does this organizational theory contribute to the Weberian problem of charisma as a historical reality? Obviously, the existence and requirements of the organizations occupy a primary position. Without such organizations, there would be few normative tasks, and men of charismatic abilities would wither on the vine. Yet the organizations constitute only the situation and provide the opportunity for charismatics. Organizations hire people with charismatic qualities; they do not possess the charismatic qualification themselves, even when defined in normative terms. The organizations are continuously a "component of everyday life," but they do neither depersonalize charisma nor do they change their character on account of their status as employees. Nor is there an inherently alien relationship between charisma and organization, so that the process of deterioration is missing. Since "personal . . . charisma may be originally achieved in organizational offices,"[44] the charismatic appeal is neither addressed to followers, nor is there a devotion to a leader because of his strictly personal qualities. The requested compliance is expected of subordinates so that noncharismatic power of the office penetrates into the relationship. Moral persuasion by the charismatics and obligation of the compliers do satisfy the "needs" of the organization. The result is a constriction of both groups to their specified organizational tasks so that constriction—without deterioration—becomes the substitute for routinization with its diminishing charismatic qualities.

Quite different results ensue from the contact theory of Edward Shils which seeks to explain charismatic leadership in less developed countries. Central to his efforts are the enlargement of the charismatic act, the professionalization of the leadership function, and reversing of the personal with institutional charisma.

The charismatic quality is redefined as a vital force. Anyone coming in contact with it is a bearer of charisma. Instead of a strictly personal calling, charisma is an "inspiration, embodiment, or perception, with the vital force, which underlies man's existence, his coming-to-be and passing away." This vital force permits the distinction between centrality and periphery. "Centrality is constituted by its formative power initiating, creating, transforming or destroying what is vital in man's life."[45] The charismatic quality, although including every form of creation and innovation, can appear in a distinctly concentrated form, leading to a highly visible kind of leadership. On the periphery, however, the crucial quality becomes merely a "charismatic sensitivity" which permits a "responsiveness to sacredness," and opens the road to followership. When the emphasis is on sacredness, charisma can readily become an element of either traditional or legal authority.[46]

In its concentrated form, charisma finds its bearers primarily in the professions of publicists, politicians, and especially lawyers. "Politicians and civil servants are convinced that they must arouse the work force . . . to a readiness to accept goals beyond those they have been accustomed to achieve." These leaders "counsel abstention from consumption" and urge "an ethic of austerity." A particular economic, not religious, ethic becomes a part of the charismatic mission.

Most significant is the shift to an institutional charisma. "The nation becomes the charismatic object and it is only through their connection with it that charisma flows into persons." Recipients become rulers because they have "experienced the revelation of nationality." A circle of charisma arises comprising especially members of the receptive professions. "The rulers of a country are the most charismatic persons of that country, because they are the closest to the source from which charisma radiates."[47] While the source of charisma becomes impersonal, not endowment but a process of radiation selects the members of the circle of charisma.

But there is one innovating group that falls outside of this circle. Innovation is (or will) arise in the economy. "The economizing attitude is a creative attitude. It gives expression to the genius, i.e., the individuality of its bearer. It expresses a charismatic quality." This charisma resides in the successful business enterprisers. There is a dispersal of such creativity, since economizers operate independently of others. For self-development to emerge, there must be a dispersion of charisma "from the sphere of political authority onto . . . the economic sphere."[48] Dispersal is resisted by the national circle of charisma. Against their claim of a "monopoly of virtue and charisma" there arises a "countercharisma" of those "imbued by the spirit of economizing innovation." But the economic innovator cannot be deliberately created, he must be a self-confident man who carries within him a "spark of divinity."[49]

A conflict arises between the universality of the charismatic authority with its single political center and the countercharisma of the economizing men whose spirits and actions are occupationally and emotionally dispersed. The theory of charisma becomes linked with the one of social conflict. Living in a less developed country, two charismatic opponents suggest two different roads to modernity. In a sense, Shils faced the same issue as did Weber in his search for the capitalist spirit. Weber found the spark of divinity in one branch of Pietism "which glorifies the worker who did not seek acquisition, but lived according to the apostolic model, and was thus endowed with the charisma of the disciples."[50] Whether we look at the charisma of disciples or at countercharisma, divinity of each refers to a religious belief of single individuals inspired by a higher being. There is no reciprocal relationship of two or more persons so that it falls outside of our main concern, namely charismatic leadership in politics.

What is the contribution of the contact theory to the transformation of charisma? In its concentrated form, charisma becomes intermingled with power. "Corporate bodies—secular, economic, governmental, and political—come to possess charismatic qualities simply by virtue of the tremendous power concentrated in them." The noncharismatic power thus creates a magnification of institutional charisma. In its dispersed form, "every legitimation of effective large-scale power contains a charismatic quality."[51] This personal charisma does neither diminish nor become routinized because every powerful authority evokes charismatic responses and retains this capacity because of its ability to create consensus and establish a moral order.

Whereas the contact theory emphasized institutional charisma, S. N. Eisenstadt investigates the sequential development from personal to institutional charisma so as to discover why charisma is one of the most important modes of building institutions. The charismatic act is even more broadly defined, including creativity, freedom, and responsibility. "It is in the charismatic act that the potential creativity is . . . manifest. . . . Such actions are either constructive or destructive but the former are stronger because of the "necessity of the charismatic leader or group . . . to assure the continuity of its organization."[52] Seeking to close the gap between the charismatic act as an extraordinary quality and as a constituent element of any orderly social life, Eisenstadt develops two themes. The charismatic propensity arises whenever people "experience some shattering of the existing social and cultural order." In relying upon the concepts of centrality and order of Shils, it is inferred "that the process of routinization of charisma and the charismatic qualities may differ greatly among different institutional spheres." The reason is seen in the "difference in the organizational needs and problems" in each institutional sphere and in different types of societies." But the problems of "how the ordinary and the charismatic are continuously interwoven in the process of institution building,"[53] what patterns of interaction do occur, or how the two components remain steadily compatible, remain unresolved.

## Synergistic Charisma

This lively theoretical activity in the Weberian tradition suggests some important conclusions. On the one hand, there is agreement that the new kinds of charisma call for some modification of Weber's theory, who did not anticipate the various historical types of charisma. Empirical studies have not been able to identify constricted charisma among leaders of German and American businessmen.[54] On the other hand, there is no agreement on the definition of the new problems or on the nature of the modifications required. The first two theories discussed accepted Weber's theory of pure charisma, but then distinguished different modes of its transformation. The proposed additions in the form of relative permanency and organizational constriction appear as a valid extension of Weber's theory.

The other two theories propose a revision of Weber's theory along the line of an expanding influence of charisma, especially in politics. The concept of charisma now includes everything that is vital and sacred as well as any creative actions. Designation of creation as a charismatic act was opposed by Weber with the following argument. In charisma as well as creation there is a psychological similarity because creators are experiencing the same emotional seizure (*Ergriffenheit*) just as much as a charismatic leader. But creators are absorbed by and limited to their "work," the product they seek to create. "The broad masses of the led merely accept or adapt themselves to the external, technical results which are of practical significance for their interests . . . whereas the substance of the creator's ideas remains irrelevant for them" (p.1117). Incorporating creation, especially the "economizing attitude," in the charismatic act suggested the distinction between concentrated and dispersed charisma. At best, the latter is a certain kind of religious charisma and does not seem a contribution to political charisma.

Fundamental for the contact theory is the thesis that in our time charisma resides in institutions. But it is not the Weberian office or kingship charisma that is of special interest. Charismatic quality is said to attach to the ideal of nationality, to national independence of the newly liberated countries. Charismatizing the nation requires a linkage of the sacred with charisma; this sacred quality radiates out to the believers. The charismatic circle becomes the beneficiary of such sacredness. But is it theoretically appropriate and historically accurate to regard an ideal as an institution? The more common practice seems more acceptable that identifies nationalism as an ideology to which the adherents are committed, and to its realization they devote their energy. Such ideologically directed goals may be effective without any relationship to the charismatic quality. But there is also ample evidence for the mutual interpenetration of charisma and ideologies. We shall try to discover how and why ideologies become fused with charisma.

A similar reservation applies to the claim of the contact theory "that charismatic responses are evoked by the manifestations of powerful authority as such, without regard to the concentration in individual personalities, or possession by divinity."[55] Here, too, we find a definite position in Weber. "It should be kept clearly in mind that the basis of every authority, and correspondingly of every kind of willingness to obey, is a *belief*, a belief by virtue of which persons exercising authority are lent prestige" (p.263). Decisive is the "composition of this belief," the underlying motives of which permit a separation of different kinds of authority. There is no inherent reason for identifying each kind of authority with charisma, and defining both in such a way as to exclude personal charisma. It seems more appropriate to follow Weber's suggestion and investigate when and why in historical reality legal authority and legitimacy supplement charismatic authority and legitimacy.

The contact theory seeks to establish a novel relationship between charisma and power. On the one hand, power creates authority and order. "Great power announced itself by its power over order; it covers order, creates order, maintains it and destroys it. Power is indeed the central, order related event." This seems to imply that power is the core of the charismatic institution which then creates order. On the other hand, power or authority seems to have the capacity to command charismatic responses from the ruled. Implicitly, this raises the question about the nature of the relationship between charisma and politics. "Today, almost all rulers of state-bound societies claim legitimation from the charismatically endowed citizens who form the electorate—although they do so with different degree of reluctance."[56] Does this mean that charisma is limited to democracies? Or do certain leaders of personal charisma develop a definite preference for being leaders in dictatorships? The relationship between charismatic leadership and political systems will be a major concern of this study.

Finally, there is the relationship between charisma, bureaucracy, and vested interests. Here too we find two not quite compatible positions in the contact theory. Bureaucrats and private interest groups may oppose the claims and authority of institutional charisma so that there will arise some disobedience impelled by interests. But other corporate bodies in economic, political, and military spheres "come to possess charismatic qualities simply by virtue of the *tremendous power* concentrated in them." A subsequent power struggle among the various charismatic institutions is avoided only by "creating a social order consonant with a transcendent moral standard."[57] Important in this discussion is that in political charisma some accommodation has to be found with bureaucratic and economic interests. We will have to examine the Weberian thesis that either these noncharismatic powers will subdue and deteriorate charisma or a charismatic institution will turn out to be stronger because of its reliance upon a moral standard.

There is no intention of criticizing the theory of institutional charisma for its own sake. Eventually, definite institutions may be identified, the theoretical defects may be removed, and the historical relevance established by our successors. The sole reason for examining the contact theory critically was to discover the particular causes that were said to be responsible for the required revision of the Weberian theory. Briefly, political charisma has to come to grips with supplementing legal authorities and legitimacies, incorporating certain ideologies, opting either for democracy or dictatorship, and finding an accommodation with bureaucratic and economic interest groups.[58]

It so happened that the leaders of gigantic charisma faced and overcame these difficulties in their rise and exercise of power. But these were all personal leaders so that we are compelled to stay within personal charisma. There is one implicit finding in the contact theory that is also relevant for gigantic charisma. Rather than seeing their charismatic quality deteriorate when interacting with the noncharismatic features, the giants experienced a flowering of their quality and a magnification of their authority. We will have to discover whether this growth of charismatic leadership will replace the process of routinization or whether some giants still suffered from deterioration. In other words, the contact theory unintentionally prepared the ground for the study of gigantic charisma. The four reasons speaking for its revision are almost the same as those faced by gigantic charisma. There also is the helpful, but still implicit, thesis that the charismatic quality and authority increase—not diminish in relative significance—as the charismatic and noncharismatic features interact and gigantic leadership becomes the outstanding feature of political systems.

As a first step towards an improvement of Weber's theory we have to replace his inadequate concept of "impure" charisma with a substantive definition. We shall speak of synergistic charisma when the charismatic and noncharismatic features interact in such a way as to either maintain or strengthen the charismatic component in the interaction. Synergistic charisma prevails when (1) the charismatic quality is combined with political talents; (2) scope and strength of the charismatic appeal is multiplied by the use of mass media; (3) the charismatic group transforms itself into a mass following; and (4) charismatic authority and legitimacy are linked with noncharismatic authority. Each of these combinations modifies but also maintains the internal structure of charisma. A synergistic charisma also exists when (5) one or several ideologies furnish the political content for the charismatic mission; (6) the leader builds up his own apparatus for the control of the indispensable bureaucracy; (7) the leader placates private interest groups with alliances and profitable projects in the future; and (8) the leader and paladins become partisans either by fighting for a reform of a prevailing system or building up a new one. These last four fusions or coordinations permit the leader and his movement to a sphere of extraordinariness within an ordinary society, thereby avoiding or neutralizing the pressures making for the routinization of charisma.[59]

In studying the patterns of interaction typical for gigantic charisma, our work shall be guided by four hypotheses. The *change* thesis recognizes the time dimension. The growth of gigantic charisma exhibits the three phases of challengership, rulership, and standpatship. For the rulership to flourish the leader creates for himself a new "lead role" to be operative in his political party and government. It is the leader who determines the role, not the other way round.[60] The *culmination* thesis postulates that a leader's influence becomes gigantic because he is able to cumulate more and more subtypes of charisma in his person and thereby charismatizes various situations and proposes appropriate charismatic policies. The *partisan* thesis stipulates that a gigantic leader is hardly ever neutral or indifferent to political systems and sets out to either reform an old or build a new political system. Partisanship gives rise to either democratic or dictatorial charisma. Finally, there is the *exit* thesis of an abrupt ending of gigantic leadership. The giant either dies a natural death, is recalled by the electorate, is assassinated by opponents, or turns into a despot because he faces exceptionally difficult problems which he cannot handle by charismatic policies.

Definition and hypotheses of synergistic charisma define the task and set the limits for this book. It stays within the sphere of personal charisma, concentrates upon our experience with gigantic charismatic leadership, and seeks to explain the causes and consequences of its success.[61]

# CHAPTER TWO

# WEBER'S THEORY OF CHARISMA

OF THE MANY CONTRIBUTIONS of Max Weber to the social sciences, his theory of charisma has received the greatest attention. It has been applied to Hitler and the Nazi party,[1] to Lenin and the Bolshevik party,[2] to presidents in democracy,[3] and to rulers of dictatorial parties in newly formed nations.[4] In addition, the scope of charisma has been widened considerably. Charisma should not be limited to supernatural powers but include any kind of human genius and creative activity.[5] Nor need personal and institutional charismata always follow each other but can run concurrently during the reign of the charismatic leader.[6]

Increasing acceptance has been accompanied by some significant criticism. Not only is Weber accused of an incoherent or inconsistent presentation of his arguments but the concept itself is regarded as being either overextended or useless for empirical research. The lack of a clear statement of what are the charismatic qualities, it is said, deprives us of the specific factual referents for discovering whether and when voters see charismatic abilities in a particular leader.[7] One critic denies the charismatic act itself because the so-called leader behaves like any other concerned politician who selects only those issues and grievances that are of passionate concern to his prospective voters.[8] If the gift of grace is accepted, it is said to be transferable only to those who possess sincere religious beliefs. The political sphere is declared to be beyond any form of charisma and political leaders are assertedly free of charismatic qualities.[9] Finally, an old methodological criticism has been restated. Weber's theories of religion and charisma allegedly concentrate upon typical characteristics. The resultant "trait atomism" falls short of a consistent theory and permits only *ad hoc* solutions.[10]

It is the aim of this chapter to realize three goals. We shall present Weber's ideas in the form of a consistent theory of charisma, making use of all parts of his writings on this theme. In doing this we shall also examine the theoretical criticisms advanced and, if possible, incorporate the acceptable arguments into our interpretation. If Weber's typologies can be translated into falsifiable hypotheses, then the methodological criticism seems to be of little merit. Finally, we hope to indicate which hypotheses of the theory can be regarded as being in accord with experience and which ones are in need of a major revision.

## ORIGIN AND VALIDITY OF CHARISMA

As is well known, Weber defined charisma "as a certain quality of an individual personality by virtue of which he is considered extraordinary and treated as endowed with supernatural, superhuman, or exceptional powers or qualities."[11] In religion the charismatic power is believed to be of divine origin, while in other fields the distinct quality springs from extraordinary human sources. Such human qualities include the magic power of the sorcerer, the legal wisdom of the gifted judge, and the extraordinary courage of the leaders of the hunt or of war. Each of these endowed persons gives rise to a particular type of charisma, the characteristics of which can be schematically presented in an oversimplified fashion (table 2.1).

In his extensive writings on these three types Weber supplies us with the relevant evidence for these characteristics. While lying outside of our study, these three types furnish us with a convenient reference for analyzing political charisma. Weber not only gave greatest attention to religious charisma but often treated prophets as the prototypes for the other kinds of charismata. We shall follow this comparative procedure whenever the features of political charisma are incomplete or derived from religious charisma.

TABLE 2.1. TYPES OF PURE PERSONAL CHARISMA.

| Situation: | Military | Magic | Religious |
|---|---|---|---|
| Personality: | War Lord | Sorcerer | Prophet |
| Quality: | Great Courage | Ecstasy | Ascetic |
| Attitude of followers: | Hero Worship | Awe, Fear | Reverence |
| Achievement: | Conquest | Oracle | Revelation |
| Group Formation: | Daring Soldiers | Sacrificial Community | Community of Disciples |
| Organization: | Armed Forces | Secret Societies | Sects |

The original meaning of charisma was religious in nature. As Rudolf Sohm has emphasized before Weber: "The charisma is from God . . . and the service to which the charisma calls is a service imposed by God, and an office in the service of the church, and not of any local community."[12] In accepting the original meaning of charisma as a divine gift, Weber added also the "free gifts of grace," attainable without ordination, and acceptable outside the established church. His theory of the religious prophet rests largely upon these free gifts of grace. This extension from the church to the religious community of the prophet is accepted by the critic. It is the shift from the sacred to the secular sphere that is rejected because charisma "implies a transcendental faith in God," and depends for its validity "on the conception of the deity with which it is associated" and who alone can dispense such favor or grace.[13] Since divinity is not typically bestowed upon politicians, it is inferred that there can be no political charisma.

Indeed, there is not only a distinction but a substantive difference between the two positions. Friedrich sees the central charismatic act in the divine favor granted to a particular person by a supernatural being. In Weber's view, however, the central point lies in the endowment of the selected person and in his belief to be called upon to perform a great and life long task. There is certainly an intricate relationship between endowment and bestowal or endowment and calling. In religious prophecy, endowment and bestowal coexist, precondition and interact with each other. If they are not coequal, bestowal usually has greater significance. In political charisma, however, the belief in a calling can take the place of a bestowal whenever the calling is not of divine origin but attributed to an unspecified destiny or fate.

At any rate, Weber places greatest emphasis upon the belief of a calling whatever its particular origin: "Devotion to the charisma of the prophet, or the leader in war, or to the great demagogue in the *ecclesia* or in parliament, means that the leader is personally recognized as the innerly called leader of men. Men do not obey him by virtue of tradition or statute, but because they believe in him. If he is more than a narrow and vain upstart of the moment, the leader lives for his cause and strives for his work. The devotion of his disciples, his followers, his personal party friends is oriented to his person and to its qualities."[14] In making the sense of a calling the common denominator of all types of charisma, Weber's theory gains three advantages. In playing down the source or justifier of the calling, whether divine or fateful, he gets away from the unknowable "supernatural force" which cannot possibly be a secure foundation for any science. The inner calling becomes an objective criterion as soon as it generates a rising confidence and self-assurance of the incipient or actual leader. The "extraordinary quality of the person" becomes so clearly identifiable that the followers can sense whether he acts out of conceit or an inner obligation. The actual linkage of self-confidence with duty constitutes for the followers the genuine charismatic quality of the leader. It is this quality to which they become devoted and because of which they accept his claim to leadership.

Evolution of confidence in the inner self is usually an arduous and hazardous process. The incipient leader has to prepare himself for his assigned task. He has to engage himself in a series of actions that indicate a growing strength of will, of courage, and of exceptional abilities. At the same time he has to refrain from certain worldly pleasures of the multitude and thus show his single-minded commitment to his task.

As Edward M. Kennedy's vicissitudes indicate, abilities and self-restraint may not grow together harmoniously. Or the abilities may be limited to a certain occasion and not be transferable to other situations, as was illustrated by the partial victory of Senator Eugene McCarthy in the primaries of 1968. Inadequacies of various kinds can thus lead to sporadic or temporary charismatic leadership or the charismatic ambition may falter completely when tested by risky events.

Evolution of the devotion by the followers faces similar difficulties. The required psychological predispositions in potential followers are not available everywhere or at any time. Certain cultural experiences, such as admiration for autocratic government, may generate the emotional readiness for a leader. Or certain extreme crises may create widespread fear for the future of a group or country so that the extreme difficulties seem to be controllable only by a gifted leader. It is only when such latent predispositions exist that the claim of the self-confident leader can be accepted by the masses and translated into a devotion of the followers.

The validity of charisma requires that the self-confidence of the leader and the devotion of the followers interact and reenforce each other. In fact, Weber emphasizes the role of recognition and deeds as the two indispensable criteria for the validity of charisma. "If those to whom he feels sent do not recognize him, his claim collapses; if they recognize him, he is their master as long as he 'proves' himself" (p.1113). There is thus a twofold authentication of charisma. Self-confidence and calling have to be supplemented by extraordinary deeds before the claim of the leader is accepted by the followers. The genuineness of charisma depends thus upon all three criteria simultaneously. While calling and self-confidence initiate the claim, recognition accepts the quality of one person, and exceptional deeds attest to the continued effectiveness of the extraordinary power. As soon as the devotion of the followers turns into a sense of duty, leadership becomes charismatic authority. Devotion creates the inner urge to obey the leader's wishes, even when this should not be in the interest of the followers themselves.

These ideas can be condensed into a hypothesis on the validity of charisma. The personal charisma—sense of calling and self-confidence—becomes valid because of the leader's capacity to perform exceptional deeds and because a sense of duty moves the followers to accept his claim and follow his leadership. Expressed negatively, if the exceptional capacity or the dutiful devotion are missing, an inner sense of calling cannot flower into charismatic leadership.

## NATURAL CHARISMA

In addition to the sense of calling, linked with the belief in a supernatural force, there was also another kind of charisma that sprang from natural forces. In his sociology of religion, Weber said: "Charisma may be either of two types. Where this appellation is fully merited, charisma is a gift that inheres in an object or person simply by virtue of natural endowment" (p.400). This natural capacity becomes especially personified in the magician. He worked primarily through extraordinary emotions so that natural became emotional charisma. It is in this emotional form that this type of charisma is also relevant in the political sphere. In this section we shall look at the specific nature of these emotions in order to see how far they are a part of the charismatic personality.

It has been asserted that Weber failed to distinguish among the exceptional emotions that are associated with his various types of charisma. "Even psychologically, this lumping together of demagogues, leaders of totalitarian movements and founders of religions is misleading."[15] It can be shown, however, that if one compares all the relevant passages one finds a careful distinction among ecstasy, euphoria, and political passions, which are considered as "the distinctive subjective conditions" of particular types of charismata.

There is first the ecstasy creating ability of the magician and mystic prophet. Ecstasy may be created by the potential magician by means of alcohol or other intoxications. Legend has it that the accomplished magician moves into an ecstatic state because the "soul" in him takes possession of his person. The magician personifies the soul when he produces his miracles. Eventually, "magic is transformed from a direct manipulation of forces into a symbolic act" (p.405). Even after this shift from natural to symbolic charisma, ecstatic feelings remain a part of the magician's emotional experience. It either retains some form of orgiastic ecstasy or becomes sublimated into intellectual ecstasy. "Professional magicians and warriors need permanent charisma as well as acute ecstasies" (p.536). Charisma and ecstasy are thus not identical but such a feeling becomes fused with and greatly strengthens the charismatic quality of the magician and warrior.

Whether ecstasy appears as a personified soul, as an intellectual sublimation, or as a form of orgiastic intoxication, it is also a part of the mystic salvation prophet. Especially the older Israelite prophets engaged in emotional cults and represented an "emotional prophecy based upon 'speaking with tongues'; and highly valued intoxicating ecstasy interrupted the unfolding of theological rationalism" (p.441). This kind of prophet not only had to develop his own "ecstatic abilities" but also had to help his followers break down their own "organic inhibitions" to ecstasies. This could be done by orgies and also "by the provocation of hysterical or epileptoid seizures among those with predispositions toward such paroxysms" (p.535). As a rule, however, the initiative lay with the mystic prophet who by his own ecstasy engendered the emotional seizure of his followers. Implicitly, Weber developed a distinction between followers and adherents to a prophet. Minor emotional involvement would make a man merely an adherent but a definite emotional predisposition would transform a person into a true follower of a mystic prophet.

The emotional situation is quite different for the ethical prophet. He not only is able to break the power of the demons by the force of his spirit and redeem his followers from demoniac control, but he also effectively creates a "realm of blessedness upon this earth, purged of all hate, anxiety, and need" (p.527). A magician with some ethical orientation feels a "dream revelation" that gives him a healing or counseling ability. The truly ethical or exemplary prophet assures himself of a much more enduring possession of the charismatic capacity if he relies upon "those milder forms of euphoria which may be experienced as either a dreamlike mystical illumination or a more active and ethical conversion." The ethical prophet does not need orgiastic intoxication, since any ecstasy "actually stands in the way of their ethical pattern of life" (p.536). His knowledge of a divine mission or his assurance of grace gives him the ability to engage in exceptional deeds.

This leads us to the role of emotions in political charisma. In economics as well as in politics, there can be a coupling of interest with rationality which together create a sphere of affective neutrality. Policies are selected and applied free of emotions. Beyond this usually small sphere, Weber distinguishes between ordinary and extraordinary emotions that become politically relevant. Feelings of passion and hatred can become associated with political charisma. The particular role of these emotions depends upon the type of political charisma. An emotionally gifted but responsible party or Caesarian leader is able to place his passions at the service of his "cause." This ability to be activated by his passions but not unpredictably torn by his hatreds can create in his followers admiration for his personality and an emotional commitment to his policies (p.1389). Controlled passions are thus as important as exceptional deeds for engendering the indispensable confidence of the followers in the political leader.

A charismatic demagogue, however, may either not possess a cause or lack the sense of responsibility for the consequences of his actions. He is constantly in danger of becoming an actor by playing upon the emotions of his listeners. In possessing the power to arouse ecstasies, he generates the enthusiasm of the masses and derives power from their emotional attachment to him. The enthusiasm for a charismatic figure may thus be misplaced if the leader himself feels no commitment either for the cause or for the well-being of his followers. Conversely, the center of attention may be more the enemy than the leader. Hatred may be deliberately generated by the leader in attacking the enemy, in defaming his honor, and in holding him responsible for various misfortunes. Or the leader has to satisfy the "hatred and the craving for revenge . . . [and] the opponent must be slaughtered and accused of heresy."[16] The followers can thus demand emotional compensation for their devotion to the leader.

At the point of emotional culmination, there frequently occurs an emotional surrender of the followers to the leader and an emotional seizure of the leader. Together these phenomena create a gripping emotional union of leader and followers. An "emotional form of a communal relationship" arises that can lead to a mutual commitment of master and disciple to a "charismatic community," of all those feeling the inner bond of a union. A sense of psychological compulsion penetrates into the charismatic quality and becomes attached to the followers' devotion. These powerful emotions turn the inner calling into a "natural endowment" and transform enthusiasm into a dutiful obligation to fulfill the leader's wishes. Rather than containing only attitudes towards the supernatural, charisma becomes simultaneously a supernatural as well as a natural force for the participants that invariably governs their destiny.

While the emotional bond has been called the core of charisma[17] the felt linkage between the natural and supernatural has been widely overlooked. In Talcott Parsons' interpretation of Weber's prophetic charisma, for instance, the personal quality acts like a breakthrough to a higher cultural order. Charisma is a "process of rationalization" from magic to the enlightened "program for life as a whole," thereby squeezing out all emotional forces.[18]

Even more surprising is the recent assertion that Weber's theory contained no psychological components and thus needs to be supplemented by Freud's theory of repression. Charisma is redefined as "an unconscious force" which is released from repression by a man of creative ability.[19] Actually, Weber already considered and rejected this "supplement" when he spoke of "the dubiousness of applying the conceptual scheme of 'repression' almost universally" (p.499). Instead of deriving ecstasy, euphoria, and political passions globally from unconscious forces, he could discover "an unconscious desire for vengeance" only in the theodicy of the disprivileged whose resentment attributed the unequal distribution of goods to the sinfulness and the illegality of the privileged.

In rejecting repression as an explication, Weber did not create a gap in his theory of charisma because he traced the three extraordinary emotions to one common denominator. Each of them constitutes an "emotional seizure" (*Ergriffenheit*, p.1116) in which the conscious and unconscious feelings are in full accord and together generate definite attitudes by and towards the leader, other followers, adherents, and enemies. While they usually originate in the unconscious sphere, these attitudes do not change when they become conscious. The emotional seizures intermingle with the awe felt by the leader for his calling, by the creator for his work, and by the follower for the exemplary personality of his leader. Seizure and awe merge in the moment of joyous elation when the followers are able to touch their leader, as it happened to Robert Kennedy during the primary of 1968.

In all, Weber's three extraordinary emotions can be condensed into a hypothesis of natural charisma. The emotional appeal of the leader, driven by his own inner calling, causes an effectively internalized response because he can generate ecstasy, euphoria, and politically relevant passions in his followers who feel united with him by an emotional bond.

## INSTABILITY OF PERSONAL CHARISMA

Coexistence of natural and supernatural charismata leads to a strengthening of the leader's power as soon as both interpenetrate and reinforce each other. Emotional seizure and awe together create a much stronger confidence in the leader than each one could accomplish alone. The great trust in his personality grants the leader a significant degree of freedom in selecting his own policies. It is within his power either to neglect or to overrule the particular interests of his followers and, under certain conditions, those of his supporters. The opposition of Robert Kennedy to the draft deferment of students did not appreciably dilute their elation for him. This relative freedom from particular interests has been overlooked by some critics. The charismatic leader, we are told, "gets his support very largely from the issues he is associated with" and his strength depends on how effectively he is "making these issues and grievances the passionate concern of those whom he thinks will be his followers."[20] Actually, the motive to please his followers by adopting any kind of possible issue fits the political manipulator; the intent to propagandize a cause and gain believers as well as supporters is typical of the political ideologist. The leader of the interacting charisma—natural and supernatural—has to recognize primarily two limits in the choice of his policies: he must select, attack, and defame the "correct" enemy; he must stay within the very broad limit of maintaining the trust of most of his followers. Trust and duty, not issues, interests, and grievances, are the hallmarks of the interacting charisma.

The difficulties in gaining and maintaining this trust reside primarily in the emotional sphere. In magic and religious charisma, "acute ecstasies are transitory in their nature and apt to leave but few positive traces in everyday behavior" (p.535). In political charisma, moreover, the emotions of the demonstrators in the street may be fickle and peter out after the meeting has ended. Or the enthusiasm tends to disappear if the demagogue worships mainly his vanity or is engaged in self-glorification for its own sake. The result of these emotional fluctuations is a temporary charisma.

The stability of the charisma may also be endangered by the nature of the crisis situation. "The charisma of the hero or the magician is immediately activated whenever an extraordinary event occurs: a major hunting expedition, or drought or some other danger precipitated by the wrath of the demons, and especially a military threat" (p.1134). Special occasions or crises thus create, but also limit, the opportunities for leaders to exemplify their emotional capacities and inner calling.

Other situations may bring forth several contenders who claim "specific gifts of body and mind," leading to a differential distribution of the charismatic quality. Conflicting claims may be settled either by "epileptoid seizure as a means of falling into a trance" (p.242), or by exceptional deeds in the form of a miracle or victory. The trust of the followers may thus be delayed until the proof for exceptional ability is forthcoming. The dispute among contenders may also be settled by assigning a specialized function to each leader. These difficulties thus give rise to either sporadic or specialized charisma.[21] A durable charisma becomes possible only if and when the crisis or its danger is regarded as permanent. "The warlord becomes a permanent charismatic figure when there is a chronic state of war" (p.1142).

These emotional and situational limits can be supplemented by a third one that springs from the nature of the mission itself. "As a rule, charisma is a highly individual quality." This implies that the mission and the power of its bearer is qualitatively delimited from within, not by an external order. "Normally, the mission is directed to a local, ethnic, social, political, vocational or some other group, and that means that it also finds its limits at the edges of these groups" (p.1113). While history indicates a long list of groups capable of providing charismatic leaders and the corresponding disposition of devotion, Weber especially emphasizes that traditional and bureaucratic groups do not fall for a charismatic appeal. While many a converted group has sent out swarms of missionaries, outside resistance has often limited the spatial spread of charisma. Even successful acceptance and authority can thus not overcome the limit of charismatic leadership to certain regions or periods.

There is on hand sufficient material for us to formulate a hypothesis on the limits of charisma. Leadership is of short duration because the ecstatic feelings of the leader and followers are not continuous over time, the various crisis situations occur irregularly, and various groups lack the receptiveness for a charismatic mission. Nevertheless, this delineation of a nondurable and not easily repeatable regime raises the question as to the stability of personal charisma wherever it did exist. As one critic has correctly emphasized,[22] Weber failed to specify the conditions for a relative stability of charismatic authority prior to succession. The strengthening effect of the interacting emotional seizures and feelings of awe is not sufficiently appreciated. The possibility of recurrent renewal of the extraordinary emotions, especially of political passions, able to sustain charismatic leadership for a significant time, is not fully investigated. It is most surprising that Weber's extensive historical material does not turn up any evidence for the attempts of leaders to declare themselves infallible. A belief in infallibility, if accepted, could counteract the impact of fickle emotions or delayed deeds by the leader. But could there have been some other reasons for charismatic instability?

## VALUE CHARISMA

In turning to the role of the mission in personal charisma, we shall have to distinguish between value and faith charisma. While the personal call distinguishes the prophet from the priest, the religious prophet either proclaims a religious doctrine or a divine commandment. The ethical prophet believes in the value of his doctrine and thus personifies value charisma. The exemplary prophet lives according to the faith implicit in the divine commandment and thus exemplifies faith charisma. In addition to bringing out the similarities and differences between these two kinds of charisma, we shall also have to inquire into the critic's contention that because of their religious nature neither values nor faith can give rise to political charisma.

Whether a religious prophet is predominantly of the ethical or exemplary variety, "prophetic revelation involves for both the prophet himself and for his followers . . . a unified view of the world derived from a consciously integrated and meaningful attitude towards life" (p.450). This view constitutes a religious postulate that "produces the strongest tensions in man's inner life as well as in his external relationship to the world" (p.451). What is the significance of this conflict for the religious sphere and does such tension also prevail in the political sphere?

The ethical prophet was primarily concerned with indicating the proper roads to religious salvation. In mystic charisma, specified rituals seek the redemption of guilt and thus influence the distribution of sacramental grace. Since salvation by sacrament could be obtained only by those who have become ethically purified in the sight of God, it became the function of the prophet to evolve an ethic that systematized the requirements for gaining salvation. Whether the conditions for salvation called for good works, self-perfection, or sanctification, the behavioral result was to create "a pattern of life integrally and methodically oriented to the values of religion" (p.534).

In ascetic charisma, however, the world is viewed as sinful but still created by God. In seeking to reform the world, the prophet's unique religious charisma can prove itself by means of rational, ethical conduct. The ascetic life calls for abstaining from any excess of emotional feeling, avoiding passion or revenge, but also insists upon repressing or punishing sin. The believer has to participate soberly in the various rational and purposive institutions of the world, and especially acquire a vocation for devoting this time and energy to rational economic activity. The ascetic's assurance of grace is achieved when "he has succeeded in becoming a tool of his God, through rationalized ethical actions completely oriented to God" (p.546).

In these value charismata, the prophet performs two functions of worldly significance. He formulates an ethic of a religiously oriented life, the values of which convey a clear message to the believers as to what kinds of actions are permissible or forbidden. In seeking to implement these values, the prophet is engaged in a systematic regulation of life and is subordinating himself to the religious values, whether for the sake of a charismatic rebirth or for spreading the values to the masses of potential believers.

It is because of those empirical aspects of the ethical doctrine that a value charisma can also arise in the ideological field. This is exemplified by the teachings of religious sects or revolutionary intelligentsia. Some of the sects translated the ascetic ideals into natural rights and thereby became reformers or revolutionaries. "Examples of this were seen in the 'Parliament of the Saints' under Cromwell, in the Quaker state of Pennsylvania, and in the conventicle communism of radical Pietism" (p.542). Certain plebeian intellectuals turned against religion and developed an eschatology looking towards new worldly institutions of the future. This new involvement gave rise either to a "veneration of science" or to a worship of violence. The former knew its "prophet of social revolution, in the sense of a salvation from the class struggle" (p.515). The latter tried to establish new societies by revolutionary action. But "the only remaining variant of socialism in western Europe equivalent to a religious faith, namely syndicalism, can easily turn into a romantic game played by circles without direct economic interests" (p.515).

There are thus two specific reasons for the rise of value charisma in the ideological and political fields. One was the development of an ideological belief that became the equivalent of a religious doctrine. The other was the veneration of science by means of which the scientist turned into a prophet of social revolution or—one has to add—

of social evolution. There was thus in Weber's thinking an easy transition from a religious to an ideological doctrine and from an awe of the supernatural gift to the veneration of that science which predicted the coming utopia. The ideological doctrine became suffused with this veneration by means of an outstanding personality who personified the ideological values and enunciated the appropriate slogans. The veneration confessed for Marx and Lenin in Communist regimes clearly shows how suffusion can remain politically relevant even after the scientist-revolutionary has passed away and his science retains at best only a modicum of predictive capacity.

Weber's analysis permits us to assess the merit of the suggestion that charismatic leadership ought to be limited to the religious field. We are told that such an extension to politics forces us to identify the ideological with the religious values. But the charge that in Weber's theory "Hitler and Jesus, Mussolini and Moses are being identified as essentially engaged in the same kind of work"[23] cannot be substantiated. In the thesis of religious equivalents, religious and ideological values remain clearly distinct. Neither the prophet nor the ideologist will accept each other's values. In each case, the different values occupy the same guiding position. Equivalence is primarily concentrated on the emotional process of suffusion: each distinctly different set of values will become illuminated by the glow of the leader's charisma. Theoretical doctrines turn into religious or ideological beliefs only if the values enter into the charismatic message that guides the leader and the led simultaneously. Conflict between these values can lead to a polarity between religion and politics, as it happened in the religious sects opposing either the power of, or the military service for, the state. But such a clash between religious and ideological values does not eliminate the similarity of charismatic leadership as long as the emotional bond and the common awe for the calling unite each leader with his followers.

Although Weber was primarily interested in ethical prophecy, his application of charisma to ideological beliefs enables us to arrive at a hypothesis on value charisma. Religious, ideological and political values turn into a value charisma if a leader—who personifies these values—follows his inner calling and if the glow of his personality enables his followers and adherents to accept his values and be guided by them.

It is true that Weber did not use the term value charisma explicitly. This omission affects mostly his terminology, not the substance of his theory, because the values are a part of the ethical religion. But he finds it difficult to assess adequately the role of the charismatic message. "Even though the apostle admonishes the followers to maintain the purity of the spirit, the charismatic message inevitably becomes dogma, doctrine, theory, reglement, law or petrified tradition" (p.1122). While the message is derived from the doctrine and both play an effective role in the pure value charisma, one gets the impression from this passage that doctrine is important only in the phase of routinized charisma. This uncertain place of doctrine and its fuzzy link to the message is another reason why Weber could not specify the time period required for the process of dogmatization[24] and failed to state the stability conditions for value charisma.

## FAITH CHARISMA

A quite different situation arises in faith charisma which is usually free from any particular set of values in regard to worldly affairs. Religious faith not only takes on the quality of inwardness but becomes the source for "the specific charisma of an extraordinary and purely personal reliance upon God's providence, such as the shepherds of souls and the heroes of faith must possess. By virtue of this charismatic confidence in God's support, the spiritual representative and leader of the congregation, as a virtuoso of faith, may act differently from the layman in practical situations and bring about different results, far surpassing normal human capacity" (p.567). This unlimited trust of the prophet in his God often springs from a personal involvement that may call for a "sacrifice of the intellect" and then leads to an antirational attitude to religion. There thus arises the "difficulty of establishing an unequivocal relationship between ethical demands and a religion . . . based upon faith, i.e., a genuine salvation religion based upon an attitude of utter trust" (p.569).

Such a religious charisma of faith, free of a specific ethical content, generates a primarily emotional relationship to the divine, and calls for an emotional communication of the exemplary prophet with his God. The prophet claims to know the will of God because of the gift of grace. This gift enables him to strengthen his own will and lead an exemplary life so that others can follow his example. "The preaching of the exemplary prophet says nothing about a divine mission or an ethical duty of obedience, but rather directs itself to the self-interest of those who crave salvation, recommending to them the same path as he himself traverses" (p.447). Thus the asserted identification of the will of the prophet with God's will is crucial. Since the latter cannot possibly be known, the exemplary prophet has to rely upon his intuition and perhaps clairvoyance to discover which religious symbols and policies can and should be employed to please God.

Several different methods were utilized to gain the sense of an "unconditional reliance on God's providence" (p.567) via a charismatic personality. The traditionally transmitted sacred lore became the sacred knowledge that was passed on orally among the prophets within the twice born, as in India. This resulted in the formation of aristocratic religious groups which could not be joined by the masses of believers. Charisma became aristocratic in nature. A controversy raged in early Christianity whether sacred knowledge or simple faith is the higher religious quality. "Every prophetic religion has based religious faith upon something other than real understanding of theology" (p.565). If the emphasis is upon simple faith, the prophet becomes persuaded of his own powers, and the believers can rely upon God's providence by having confidence in these powers of the prophet. Religious faith thus led to providential charisma.[25]

Emotional worship of providential charisma creates serious problems either for the prophet or for his followers. The lack of any ethical doctrine or of orally transmitted knowledge has to be compensated for by an exceptionally strong will of the leader. If successful, the strong will permits the leader a greater discretion in selecting his policies and symbols. His preaching tends to stir in an authoritarian direction. A shift in emphasis from the trust in God to the asserted identity of wills is usually called for to justify the dictatorial elements in such a discretional interpretation of charisma.

The same lack of doctrinal guidance and absence of a definite message, however, can also create periods of spiritual uncertainty. Doubts about the charismatic authenticity can be overcome by emotions derived from natural charisma. In seeking to gain the appropriate emotional capacities, the leader hibernates before making his great decisions. In addition to his ecstatic abilities, the leader develops his intuitive powers, seeks an insight into the emotional needs of his followers, divines the urges of the masses, exposes the hidden intentions of his enemies so as to arrive at the correct decisions, and imposes his will upon others. Providential charisma thus adds intuition to the feelings of natural charisma and both interpenetrate in the experience of the exemplary prophet. The new emotional abilities intermingle with his trust in God and the "primarily emotional relationship to the divine" gives him the inner assurance of possessing God's grace.

Similar problems of authenticity and uncertainty arise for the followers. In discretional charisma, most followers do not participate in the leader's emotional tribulations of arriving at the great decisions. In placing their confidence in the will of the leader, the followers' trust in God becomes effective only through the medium of the prophet. In experiencing an intermingling of confidence and trust, followers can make a spiritual connection with God and thereby become eligible for providential blessing.[26] In emotional charisma, however, confidence in the leader springs from the ecstatic experience which is linked by the exemplary prophet with trust in God. Another process of suffusion takes place, whether by connection or involvement, of trust in the divine with confidence in the leader. In consequence of this suffusion, giving one's confidence becomes the religious duty of the followers who obey the prophet as much as they believe in God.

The different demands and involvements of followers call for a modification of Weber's thesis on the limits of charisma, as stated above. It is only in the providential charisma, whether discretional or acclamatory, that the authentic charismatic qualification has to be proven by exceptional deeds. In value and natural charisma, however, ethical doctrines and the emotional bond can sustain the belief of the followers in the leader through his whole life. Indeed, legendary and institutional charisma occurring after his death need the ethical beliefs and emotional bonds to survive the leader himself.[27]

Faith charisma can be accompanied by diverse attitudes towards politics. "A purely personal religion of faith frequently generated political indifference" as in the case of the "mystical apoliticism" (p.595). Autonomous religious laws could turn indifference into opposition to politics. Wherever congregational religion requires that its members avoid violence, "the conflict between religion and politics has led either to martyrdom or to passive antipolitical sufferance of the coercive regime" (p.594). The most extreme opposition to the state was presented by religious anarchism but its weak intensity of faith made it only an "ephemeral charisma."

Certain aspects of religious faith, however, can lead to a call for reform or revolution. "A distinctive concern with social reform is characteristic of Israelite prophets" (p.443). Such programs were introduced only to mitigate God's wrath toward his chosen people. Also, the social admonitions of the prophets were expressed under the influence of agrarian social movements whose energies were directed against urban land magnates and financial nabobs. Such genuine social concerns, however, were already influenced by an ethical religion.

Eschatological expectations did give rise to political charisma. Springing from messianic religions, desires for salvation turned into beliefs of worldly utopia. The impetus came from proletarian or parish intellectuals who either resented the long and fruitless waiting for the return of the messiah or objected to their low social status. In seeking release from suffering, these intellectuals formed groups who turned their religious emotions into an eschatological faith in socialism. Some of these groups were led by charismatic revolutionaries who engaged themselves in a struggle against capitalism and called for a chiliastic socialism. A similar development may change the direction of the charismatic mystic whose feeling of brotherly love can induce him to build communities among men. "The transformation of a mysticism remote from the world into one characterized by chiliastic and revolutionary tendencies took place frequently, most impressively in the revolutionary mysticism of the sixteenth century Baptists" (p.550).

In faith charisma, too, Weber identified certain religious equivalents that could become associated with political charisma. Fear of God's wrath engenders social reform while resentment over the missing messiah or feeling of brotherly love turned charismatic leaders towards chiliastic socialism. However, the transition from faith to political charisma was not accomplished through suffusion or illumination but through a process of diverted dedication. The faith in salvation was diverted into a semireligious faith in political reform or revolution. It is because of this emotional linkage that we can formulate a hypothesis on faith charisma. A religious, ideological, or political faith turns into faith charisma if the leader's inner calling and the devotion of the followers induce both to dedicate their lives to the fight for salvation or for some political or social utopia on earth.

Just as Weber emphasized the fickleness of certain emotions in natural charisma so he was concerned about the caprice of confidence in the leader (or of trust in God) in faith charisma, or about the infrequency of semireligious equivalents in political charisma. Adverse events or changes of moods can diminish or terminate each of these emotions, thereby creating instability for the respective leader and giving rise to additional limits of charisma. Strangely enough, Weber did not investigate the various devices for deliberately maintaining or strengthening the emotions underlying each charisma. His extensive material did not turn up any evidence of leaders seeking to generate a belief in their infallibility. Nor is there any recognition of the personality cult that has been employed by charismatic dictators to intensify or renew the charismatic emotions. It will be the task of our subsequent chapters to ascertain the forms, examine the extent, and assess the significance of these two deliberate stabilizers of charisma. But there can be no doubt about the central point: Weber's theory of religious equivalents, backed up by his extensive comparative studies, disproves the contention of the critic that charismatic leadership is necessarily limited by its divine origin and doctrinal content to the sphere of religion.[28]

### CHARISMA AND DEMOCRACY

In analyzing political history, Max Weber came to the conclusion that certain forms of political charisma develop outside and independent of religion. In presenting systematically this second part of his theory, we have to take into account another critical charge that denies the compatibility between democracy and charisma. We shall thus examine the relationship between charisma and democracy as well as dictatorship.

The study of totalitarian movements has given rise to the thesis that every kind of charismatic leadership is inherently and necessarily dictatorial. An outward expression of this dictatorial element is the oath of allegiance to the leader. "These oaths show that supreme leadership is not an institution regulated by rules and precedents, but the investiture is in one person, Adolf Hitler. The justification of this principle is charismatic: it rests on the assertion that the leader is endowed with qualities lacking in ordinary mortals. Superhuman qualities emanate from him; pervade the state, party and people."[29] The leader orders his power according to superiority and inferiority which makes charismatic leadership unavoidably dictatorial in its application.

While this earlier thesis merely uses Weber's theory to interpret Nazi leadership, a more recent exposition seeks to attribute a personal responsibility to Weber for the rise of charismatic leadership in Germany. "I cannot help thinking there is something rather Teutonic, suggesting the *Führerprinzip,* about [Weber's] description." It is "described as a romanticized kind of personal authority inspiring blind obedience in devoted followers."[30] The hypothesis that Weber somehow anticipated Hitler was augmented by a similar inference by a German historian. While examining Weber's proposal that the German president of the Weimar Republic should be chosen by a popular vote, Wolfgang Mommsen concludes "that Weber's theory of charismatic leadership has contributed its part to making the Germans willing to accept Hitler's position by acclamation,"[31] even though Weber had no intention of doing so.

The subsequent debate[32] clearly revealed that the undoubted charismatic disposition for such a leader by certain rightist German groups in the 1920s was not attributable to Weber's proposed plebiscitarian presidency. Hitler derived his sense of calling directly from his own experience. He proclaimed this mission to the court trying him for the coup of November 1923: "The man who is born to be a dictator is not compelled; he wills it. He is not driven forward, but drives himself. There is nothing immodest about this. . . . The man who feels called upon to govern a people has no right to say: If you want me or summon me, I will cooperate. No, it is his duty to step forward."[33]

It is quite obvious that Hitler could not possibly have derived his "duty" from Weber's theory or from the few plebiscites in the 1920s. Weber's ideas on charisma, published in 1921, had hardly been mastered by sociologists and remained unknown to politicians before Hitler's trial. Indirectly, a detailed study of the role of the leader in rightist German political literature of this period reveals three historical sources for the belief in the leader: "the German youth movement, the visionary interpretation of World War I, and the history of Germandom."[34] While Weber's plebiscitarian president was to be complemented and limited by an effective parliament, the rightists saw the leader as the destroyer of parliament. The presidential dictatorship of von Hindenburg from 1930 to 1932 was possible only because the constitutional limitations upon presidential power were ignored. The whole attempt to cite Weber's theory or Weber himself as the godfather of Nazi dictatorship must be viewed as an exercise in political ideology, of little significance for political sociology.[35]

In concentrating attention upon Weber's theory of leadership democracy, the debate established that, for Weber, charismatic leaders have operated within democracy and dictatorship. This presupposes a distinction between democratically and dictatorially inclined types of charismatic leaders. The participants in the debate raised but did not settle the central issue: How and why can charismatic leadership be simultaneously compatible with democracy and dictatorship? For reasons of exposition Weber divided his analysis of the relationship between charisma and democracy into two parts. One is a theory of leadership that contrasts charismatic and noncharismatic politicians. The other is a theory of democracy that compares it with bureaucracy and charisma. We shall follow Weber's procedure, present here his theory of leadership, and consider his theory of democracy in chapter 7.

The theory of leadership in democracy begins logically with a discussion of the place of representatives in parliament. There is a considerable difference between the "free" and the "instructed" representatives. The former "is obligated only to express his own genuine convictions, and not to promote the interests of those who have elected him" (p.293). The latter are nominated by and have to act as "the agents of interest groups" (p.297). For both kinds of representatives Weber was primarily concerned with the dependency of political leaders upon private interest groups. Once elected the individual representative has to make a living in either a nonpolitical occupation or in a job created by his political party. As a result many of the representatives are either politically or economically dependent. They tend to become mere delegates, who deal in "things," are not committed to any particular values, and tend either to vote the party line or to follow the instructions of interest groups. The result is that "the representative bodies of this kind tend to lead to a democracy of delegates, not of leaders" (p.298).

Quite different is the situation for genuine politicians who are guided by the public interests, propose corresponding policies, and are ready to assume publicly the responsibility for their actions. The opportunity for such leaders to arise and to obtain the support of the electorate and the parliament is greatest in a presidential democracy. Consequently, Weber proposed in 1919 that the president of the Weimar Republic should be directly elected by the voters,[36] and be given significant executive powers. Deriving his authority from the consent of the people, the elected leader could concentrate upon national issues, promote national unity, and permit the people to keep him responsible for his policies.

Universal suffrage and personalist competition permit leading politicians to influence public opinion and to promote rival ideologies. Political parties are formed in support of ideologically oriented programs and to win adherents for their ideological beliefs. The men heading such parties are often ideological leaders. If elected to parliament, they utilize the parliament foremost for promoting their ideals, are committed to "the ethics of politics as a cause,"[37] and often argue against the political system as such, thereby reducing the opportunities for compromises in parliament.

Mass participation in elections provides the opportunity for the outburst of mass emotions in the political field. There develops an "emotional accessibility of the masses for gaining personal power" (p.1319). These opportunities are utilized by two quite different kinds of leaders. One is the demagogue who is "compelled to count upon 'effect.' He is constantly in danger of becoming an actor as well as taking lightly the responsibility for the outcomes of his actions. . . . His lack of objectivity tempts him to strive for the clamorous semblance of power rather than the actual power."[38] He remains a mere mass agitator who cannot translate the confidence of the voters into a purposeful policy, and thus fails to become a genuine charismatic leader.

Instead of following a demagogue, masses may respond to a man endowed with a sense of an "inner calling." Those who recognize his special gifts will become his followers. In the case of pure charisma, the leader "rules by virtue of the devotion and trust which his political followers have in him personally" (p.268). As soon as his authority extends beyond his immediate following, his legitimacy is derived from two quite different sources. Deep emotional attachment to the leader provides and remains the basis for his charismatic legitimacy. Election by a majority of voters to the highest position of the state creates a democratic legitimacy. The combination of both principles of charismatic worship and of electoral consent brings forth the leader of a charismatic democracy (p.268).

There are three kinds of such charismatic leaders in democracy, depending on how and why they were elected by the voters. One is the democratic party leader who has transformed his charismatic community into a political party. As head of the party he has to acquire political expertise and "prove himself through conventionally prescribed participation in parliamentary committee work," while retaining the trust of the masses in his extraordinary personality. "The position of the present

British Prime Minister (Lloyd George) is based not at all on the confidence of the parliament and its parties but on that of the masses in the country and of the army in the field" (p.1452).

The civilian Caesar, as the second type, obtains the democratic consent by means of the plebiscite. His chances for gaining power do not depend upon the party's success in taking over the government. Decisive is the emotional attachment of the voters to the leader who at the same time combines ethical principles with mass appeal. Gladstone won the elections of 1886 because "of the firm belief of the masses in the ethical substance of his policy, and, above all, their belief in the ethical character of his personality. It soon became obvious that a Caesarist plebiscitarian element—the dictator of the battlefield of the elections—had appeared on the plain."[39] Instead of being an independently granted consent, voting changes into a compulsively given acclamation of the charismatic qualities personified in the leader.

The military Caesarist usually arises during a war or a warlike crisis. His heroic military deeds establish his charismatic qualification. As soon as not only the soldiers, but also civilian voters develop an "empathy for the leader's will," he takes over the highest political office. "A military dictator like Napoleon had his position affirmed through a plebiscite." The democratic principle of consent functioned as a disguise for a military dictatorship which emerged from a revolution (p.268), and is thus also linked with Weber's type of charismatic revolution.

This typology of leaders in democracy suggests several important hypotheses, each of which will be carefully examined in later chapters. There is a recognition of the coexistence of charismatic and noncharismatic leaders. Instead of being elected, Weber telescoped the two groups into two single kinds of personality that unavoidably struggled with each other for superiority. It was his thesis that "there is only the choice between leadership democracy with a (political) 'machine' and leaderless democracy, namely, the rule of professional politicians without a calling, without the inner charismatic qualities that make a leader."[40] We will have to see whether this thesis of a single alternative between only two kinds of personalities has been confirmed through the actions of the charismatic giants.

There also is a thesis on the superiority of the charismatic personality in competitive elections. There is "in general a highly emotional type of devotion to and trust in the leader. This accounts for the tendency to favor the type of individual who is most spectacular, who promises the most or employs the most effective propaganda measures in the competition for leadership" (p.269). Implicitly, the charismatic leader not only has oratorial gifts, but also is a kind of organizer of mass actions. Confirmation of this superiority thesis occurs in elections when the leader turns his natural charisma into a majority of the votes and thereby shows that only he has the capacity to turn mass emotions in his favor.

A single leader and "charismatic excitement" with its glorification brings a personalistic tendency into democracy. To be sure, the democratic institutions of competitive elections, of voluntary political parties, of a respected parliament which together exert some degree of supervision over the leader (p.1452), and independent courts remain in effective operation, but the great popularity of the charismatic leader has the effect of creating an "intellectual proletarianization" by no longer tolerating free discussion within the leader's party and of imposing the leader's will upon the majority in parliament. There emerges an implicit thesis that charismatic leadership creates two different kinds of democracy, one personalistic, the other pluralistic in nature.[41] While Weber lays all his emphasis upon the former, and very little upon the latter, such a thesis, if correct, would provide an adequate place for charismatic leadership, while modifying democracy in turn.

There is an attempt to draw a line between the civilian and the military Caesars. Their common feature is that both "shift toward the Caesarist mode of selection," of relying upon "the specifically Caesarist technique of the plebiscite" (p.1452). Simultaneously, the plebiscite is "antagonistic to the parliamentary principle." But both charismatic Caesars differ in the method of coming to power. The one Caesarist leader "rises . . . in military fashion" and acts as a military hero who "has his position affirmed through a plebiscite." Or "he rises in the bourgeois fashion, through plebiscitary affirmation, acquiesced in by the army" (p.1415). In the military case, however, the plebiscite is a mere acclamation of the military hero and is thus hardly an instance of democratic charisma. The "military fashion" implies the thesis that military dictatorships are not uniform. The worshipped hero imposes a personalistic dictatorship upon people and army, whereas in an organizational dictatorship the top military heads divide political power among themselves, often without any plebiscite. There will be ample opportunity to test this thesis of two kinds of military dictatorships in our discussion of the leaders of modern war in chapter 9.

In addition to these explicit or implicit hypotheses, there are two ambiguities that concern the relationship between charisma and democratic organizations. In the process of growing from a charismatic community to a mass movement, charismatic leaders acquire various kinds of administrative assistants who in turn appropriate powers and economic advantages for themselves (p.249). For Weber, these paladins—as we shall call them—are an indication of routinized charisma, whereas most of the charismatic giants established their administrative staff during their period of growth of charismatic qualifications and power. We shall have to ascertain how these paladins succeeded in adjusting themselves to the leader's charisma as well as to the bureaucrats in the state headed by the leader.

In principle there is tension between charisma and party organization. When a political boss is in full command of his organization and assured of getting his candidates elected, he will reject any charismatic aspirants as well as ideologists. On the basis of this rivalry Weber ventured a hypothesis. "As a rule, the party organization easily succeeds in this castration of charisma. This will also remain true of the United States, even in the face of the plebiscitary primaries, since in the long run the continuity of professional operations is tactically superior to emotional worship" (p.1132). But the validity of this thesis depends upon the two conditions of emotional mass tranquility and a charismatic pretender without any followers. In the absence of these conditions there is likely to be an eruption of charisma. "However, in times of great public excitement, charismatic leaders may emerge even in solidly bureaucratized parties, as was demonstrated by Roosevelt's campaign of 1912" (p.1132). In place of Weber's organizational superiority, available evidence suggests an alternative thesis. In a situation of an emotionally saturated plebiscite a rejected charismatic aspirant will act as a spoiler and deprive the majority party of victory (Senator Eugene McCarthy in 1968), whereas accepting a charismatic as its leader will enable even the minority party to capture the highest office in the state.

There is also some ambiguity about the specific political mission of the charismatic leader. In a situation of natural charisma a strictly personal attachment to the personality of the leader may suffice for the followers, and the "demagogic effect of the leader's personality"[42] may arouse the passive voters in campaigns as well. In religious charisma the various kinds of prophets attain for themselves "a unified view of the world derived from a consciously integrated and meaningful attitude toward life."[43] In contrast to his theory of religious missions, there is no explicitly stated value charisma for democracy. There are only some hints that point very guardedly to some values. In referring to Gladstone, Weber speaks of a "belief in the ethical substance of his policy," and attributes to his followers "a belief in the ethical character of his personality."[44] There is thus a significant gap in Weber's theory of democratic charisma, since the meaning and content of this ethic remains unspecified. It is our thesis that democratic charisma does not exhaust itself in voters granting their consent to the leader, but he also has to proclaim and personify specifically democratic values that guide his beliefs, order his priorities, and enter into his policies for his movement, party, and state. We shall have to discover which values Weber specifies in his theory of democracy before we can study the more recent democratic giants.

One thesis, however, surpasses all others in significance for our study. Instead of only recognizing the coexistence of charismatic and noncharismatic features, Weber emphasized the interaction of both components in charismatic leadership. In democracy, "the personally legitimated charismatic leader becomes leader by the grace of those who follow him since the latter are formally free to elect and to dispose of him" (p.267). This situation of two authorities and legitimacies, one charismatic and the other democratic, is typical for charismatic leadership in democracy. The mutual fusion of both principles and their largely equal significance presents the core of synergistic charisma, which is thus located in Weber's work itself. It is only in regard to the particular meaning he attributes to this fusion that we cannot follow him. Weber saw in synergistic charisma only a transitional phenomenon from genuine to routinized leadership because the free consent of the voters created a "freely elected leader" who had lost his charisma. It is our thesis that the fusion of charismatic and democratic components leads to a persistent and durable kind of leadership because the interaction gives rise to dual authorities and legitimacies that strengthen charisma as well as democratic government, headed by charismatic giants.

There is a strong emphasis upon the role of emotions, or natural charisma, in Weber's incomplete theory of revolutions. Revolutionary charisma is seen as an emotional and antirational force. The charismatic quality "revolutionizes men 'from within' and shapes material and social conditions according to its revolutionary will" (p.1116). This psychological transformation is at the heart of natural charisma. "In its most potent form charisma disrupts rational rule as well as traditions altogether and overturns all notions of sanctity." In this general form, "charisma is indeed the specifically creative revolutionary form of history" (p.1117), possessing the capacity to undermine bureaucratic and traditional orders.

In addition to their general dynamism, there existed a list of charismatic revolutionaries in the political sphere. Apart from certain leaders in antiquity, "in modern states the best examples are the dictatorships of Cromwell, and the leaders of the French revolution and of the First and Second Empire" (p.268). In their thought and action, "both traditional legitimacy and formal legality tend to be equally ignored by the revolutionary dictator" (p.268). Toward the end of World War I, Weber expected "the rise of charismatic leaders against the legal authorities" of the monarchies (p.265). He easily identified Kurt Eisner as the charismatic leader of some soldiers' councils, establishing with their help a revolutionary government in Bavaria in 1919. He also expected that the victorious countries would be governed by charismatic heroes and some of the defeated countries by charismatic revolutionaries.

Systematically, there are in Weber's abbreviated statements at least four different kinds of charismatic revolutionaries and the respective situations. Religiously inspired uprisings, led by prophets, often start as acts of self-defense because the lower classes are provoked by acts of landlords taking away their traditional rights, if not their livelihood. A few religions only and their prophets provided the ideals for resistance against such deprivations. Calvinism "made it a religious obligation to defend the faith against tyranny by the use of force" (p.595). But this defense could be "undertaken only at the initiative of the proper authorities" (p.596). In many of the peasant revolutions against feudal lords, who had violated traditional laws, excited masses reclaimed their rights with religious arguments provided by religious charismatics.[45]

In some revolutionary situations, charismatic ideologists seek to link mass excitement with beliefs in revolutionary ideals. But contact with the implicit values was often not enough. It was only when the selected ideals had been internalized that a "cause" was generally accepted which entered into the charismatic message of revolutionary leaders and followers. The result, among others, was "the glorification of

'Reason' which found a charismatic expression in the apotheosis of Robespierre." It "was the last form that charisma has adopted in its fateful historical course" (p.1209).[46] When successful, the dictatorship of the charismatic ideologist will lead to "an administration of justice emancipated from formal procedures . . . or a social dictatorship" claiming to use its power for the benefit of the poor (p.270).

There were also religious prophets of a social revolution who lived and preached among Pariah people. "The Jew anticipated his own personal salvation through a revolution of the existing social stratification to the advantage of the Pariah people" (p.494). Such revolutions were generated by the tension between the social claims based on God's promise of a Messiah and "the actual conditions of dishonor under which the Pariah people lived" (p.497). It was expected that such a revolution, if successful, would bring religious salvation and terminate forever the dishonorable position of the believers. Charismatic and religious values simultaneously would authorize and legitimize the expected revolution which in turn would bring the new society.

Finally, there was the revolution of the charismatic military hero who saw himself as the implementor of a revolution. Cromwell accepted the values of the English Independents, while Napoleon claimed to realize the political ideals of the French revolution. The heroic deeds were said to justify a charismatic dictatorship, which was subsequently legitimized "by the sovereign people through a plebiscite" (p.268). At first the leader's aim "was the destruction of the traditional, feudal, patrimonial, and other types of authoritarian power and privileges" (p.269). But then the charismatic leader dispensed with these revolutionary goals when the voluntary army of the faithful became a professional army or the administrative assistants turned into the governors of a bureaucratic administration. For Weber, these shifts signified the routinization of revolutionary charisma.

For each of these leaders there evolved a twofold authorization and legitimation of the expected or actual revolutions. The leader not only felt his inner calling but also believed in the revolutionary ideals. The followers were not only emotionally attached to the leader but also shared his revolutionary ideals. Whether the revolutions were originally defensive or revengeful, destructive or constructive, the respective actions and the authority of the leaders were legitimized by revolutionary ideals. The same was true for the charismatic claim of the leader whose power was legitimized by the worship of the followers. As in democratic so in revolutionary leadership: The fusion of two kinds of authorities and legitimacies signified the existence of synergistic charisma, whether for the movement or for the respective government.

For Weber, however, dual legitimacies were not a mutual reenforcement of a gigantic leader, but a transitional process from a genuine to a routinized charisma. This interpretation of fusion was not merely a logical inference from the inherent instability of charisma. Two specific arguments were offered for explaining the revolutionary misfortunes. One was that revolutionary ideals contained an inherent "utopian component" (p.269) that rendered them unrealizable in concrete historical situations. The other fatal handicap resided in the use of violence in establishing a new regime. In reflecting on these defects, Weber formulated his thesis that revolutionary movements unavoidably suffer from an unintended self-destruction. If successful, unworkable policies engendered the disintegration of the state and a breakdown of the economy. If unsuccessful, revolutionary violence creates counterviolence of the still intact armed forces which destroy the revolutionary movement and then establish a military dictatorship without any trace of charisma.

The sole exception to this self-destruction, emphasized by Weber, was the rise of the charismatic military hero whose victories gained him the devotion of the soldiers and the plebiscitary consent of the masses. Of the four kinds of revolutionary leaders and movements, just the charismatic hero could establish and maintain a new regime. It was a hybrid regime of "democratic dictatorship" because the essentially military rule was supplemented by plebiscitary acclamation of the charismatic qualities.

In all, Weber presented an outline of a theory of political charisma that can be condensed as in table 2.2.

TABLE 2.2. Types of political charismatic leadership.

| Democratic Charisma | Revolutionary Charisma |
| --- | --- |
| Charismatic Party Leader | Revolutionary Ideologist |
| Charismatic Demagogue | Glorification of Reason |
| Caesarist Charisma | Prophet of Social Revolution |
| Aristocratic Charisma | Charismatic Hero |

As soon as any of these leaders became a political force, his power was unavoidably authorized by the dual charismatic and ideological legitimacies. Even when the revolutionary ideals were accepted only by a minority, the charismatic appeal confirmed the leader's rule by popular consent. But there enters here an inherent contradiction in Weber's theory because of his ambivalent attitude towards plebiscites. Instead of distinguishing between democratic plebiscites with their free choice between two or more candidates, and the dictatorial plebiscites with a single candidate excluding any choice, Weber regarded each and every plebiscite as a product of mass democracy. As a result, all Caesars became hybrids, and the charismatic dictatorships of revolutionaries appeared as democratic dictatorships.[47]

These various types of charismatic leadership in revolutions have created considerable analytical difficulties for sociological theorists. The crucial question is of whether and how charismatic qualities and beliefs can be reconciled or united with an extensive concept of revolutionary ideology. According to one specialist in the sociology of revolution, (1) a revolutionary leader must neither possess nor claim any God-like qualities, (2) he has to be the most important articulator of his own ideology, (3) the conviction of his ideals must be shared by his followers, (4) these ideals must be promoted by a mass movement that aims at the breakdown of the old order, (5) an effective and rational organization is required to administer the final pushover of the obsolete order. The result of these features is an ideological leadership and mass movement.

In comparing the features of revolutionary charisma with these requirements of ideological leadership, critics advanced the thesis that such a leadership is inherently incompatible with "the psychological factor that produced charismatic commitment of the followers." If Weber would have isolated the psychological factor, "he would have recognized that charisma is not the primary cause of change."[48] Additionally, if Weber would have inquired into the psychology of the charismatic leader, he would not have fallen in the trap of attributing special qualities to a transcendental source, and he would have avoided the unscientific "glorification of the charismatic leader." On account of the missing psychology of followers and leader and the adoption of the "hero myth," Weber "had no theory of charisma."[49]

What is the missing psychological factor, and how do the ideals find their proper place in revolutionary charisma? A survey of the psychoanalytic theories reveals three motives for voters to become followers of a leader. First, social strain leads to fear, intensifies anxieties that cannot be handled by many persons. They revert to infantile patterns of behavior and demand a leader "who conforms to infantile ideas of adult behavior."[50] Second, intrapsychic distance leads to a conflict between the ego and the ego-ideal, which conflict is projected to the outside and hated world. The threat of the external scapegoat is minimized by the affectionate feelings of the child for the father. For adults, the feelings for the father are transferred to the leader, who is expected to grant protection.[51] Finally, there is the identification of the follower with the leader, thereby ending the identity crisis of the follower. "The leader increases the follower's confidence and self-esteem" which in turn "increase the ego's feeling of trust." These psychic needs of persons are regarded as the psychological "causes of charisma" for the followers.[52]

Unfortunately, these three motives do not produce the same results. Anxiety leads to conformity and submissiveness of the followers to the leader; the transferred father image improves an underdeveloped ego-ideal; the terminated identity crisis generates confidence in the leader and raises the self-esteem of the follower. The motives can thus not be condensed into one psychological factor that would uniformly determine when and why psychic suffering would transform the inflicted person into a charismatic follower of the leader. Nor can any of these motives exert a directional influence upon the leader's choice of the charismatically relevant ideas.

Weber's explanation of the charismatic disposition is quite different. Evoked by the external crisis and attracted by the leader's appeal, addressed persons become followers because of their experienced internal reorientation and subsequent shift in attitudes toward the leader and his movement. Instead of merely releasing anxiety, the masses in huge meetings do lose their inhibitions and exhibit openly their emphatic euphoria, expressing their own passions as well as the admiration for the leader. Instead of psychic suffering, there are overflowing emotions which find their climax in an emotional union that creates a psychic bond between followers and leader. An "acutely emotional faith" becomes the personal foundation of the natural charisma which in turn grants legitimacy to the authority of the leader. The psychoanalytic theories neither come to grips with this mass emotionality nor can explain how mass euphoria generates the legitimacy for charismatic authority.

A laudable attempt is made by the critic to ascertain the role played by ideals in the revolutionary movements of the Bolsheviks and the Nazis. Great emphasis is placed upon the origin but none on the content of the respective ideals. A person becomes a revolutionary not because he becomes an adherent to specific ideals, but he acquires a belief by a kind of osmosis in a revolutionary situation. The same is said to be true of the leaders. Prison terms made them more, not less, determined to invest resources in the revolutionary life. Prison "assures them positions of leadership with the active masses."[53] Lenin and Hitler are presented as highly qualified organizers who were both "obsessed with the bureaucratic responsibility and efficiency" of their party organizations. This one-sided view leads to the critique of the Weberian theory for not having given "sufficient attention to the rational and traditional aspects of the commitment process" of revolutionaries.[54]

It is reluctantly admitted that Trotsky and Hitler acted as charismatic heroes in the few months of taking over power. But this is of little consequence for their leadership. A comparison of the two extremist movements leads to the conclusion that "bureaucratic regime could be overthrown by bureaucratically revolution organizations in the name of the new ideals."[55] Since these ideals were presupposed, the critic did not discover that the leaders of both movements justified their takeover of power with pretended ideals, as we shall see in chapter 6.

There is a strong aversion to the "God-like qualities" of charismatic leaders. Weber is accused of having engaged in "a glorification of the charismatic leader."[56] He had not shown the origin of the "qualities" in the transcendental realm. The superhuman type of charisma is to be rejected because "Weber failed to explain the follower's tendency to identify a transcendental source of power from which the leader is thought to derive his special qualities."[57] Such a claim is to be regarded either as a rationalization or as a noncharismatic inspiration. It is thus proposed that the inspirational leadership should replace the superhuman charisma, and only the natural charisma shall be retained, because it emanates from the need to complete the ego-goal of the followers. In helping us to "enlarge our understanding of the emotionally fanatical followers"[58] charismatical leadership becomes a therapeutic device of psychiatry of little political significance.

Instead of accepting these strictures, it seems more relevant for our study of synergistic charisma to draw some inferences from the analysis of the critic. It is hardly the task of the analyst to deduce from certain theories the nonexistence of certain kinds of charisma and to support others. Nobody can know, or insist that others present information on, the nature of the supernatural will and its bestowal on certain charismatic leaders. If and when charismatic actors claim a supernatural calling and such a claim is accepted by certain followers, the existence of such a charismatic group has to be accepted as a fact that belongs in the typological description of charismatic leadership. Our inference is that whenever theory and description seem to conflict, priority has to be given to the description. An adequate description provides the basis for a theory of charismatic leadership.

Rather than search only for the possible incompatibility of the various subtypes of charisma, it behooves us to discover also the possible cumulation of the various kinds of charisma, personified by one specific leader. Neither Weber nor the critics have given us a comprehensive typology of the various kinds of charisma. Rather than limiting ourselves to different reactions of followers, our presupposition is that charismatic giants will have the tendency to combine, at least, the superhuman and the natural charisma in their person and that such cumulation will strengthen their authority and enlarge the size of their movements.

Charismatic dispositions and emotional attachment of followers to a leader cannot be satisfactorily analysed by an individualizing psychology. Charismatic euphoria and admiration present forms of mass emotionality that engender modes of passions not readily attainable by single individuals. For admiration and adulation of the leader to be dominant in mass meetings leading to emotional union, psychic suffering or substitution must be surpassed by a differently motivated mass longing for union with the leader. Our inference is that an adequate explanation of the "psychological factor" calls for the psychology of groups acting in situations of extreme passions that turn into love of one leader.[59]

The most important insight of the critic is the recognition of the presence of noncharismatic components in a charismatic movement. But it cannot be assumed that the ideals and organizations act always rationally in all situations. The specific role of ideals and organizations, at the command of such a leader, may very well be different from those acting in noncharismatic situations. Our expectation is that the giants will be able to charismatize ideals and organizations in such a way as to strengthen their charismatic authority.

Finally, we cannot exclude or neglect the particular political setting in which giants establish their rulerships. As a minimum, we have to distinguish between charismatic leadership in democracies and in dictatorships. Acting in the political sphere, we can predict, charismatic leaders cannot assume a position of political neutrality but act as rivals to other political parties, and their success will necessarily modify or fundamentally change the political system.

## DICTATORIAL CHARISMA

What then is the relationship between charisma and dictatorship? Weber correctly anticipated the suppression of the Bavarian and Hungarian revolutions in

1919 and the return of reactionary governments by military counterviolence. But what was Weber's interpretation of the Bolshevik revolution in Russia?

In February 1918, Weber characterized the budding Bolshevik regime as a military dictatorship that was hardly to last longer than a few months. The new government is "necessarily a purely military dictatorship; not of the generals but only of the corporals. . . . It is nonsense to say that behind the dictatorship stands the conscious proletariat comparable to the one in West Europe. Nothing but a proletariat of soldiers is supporting this regime. This has its consequences. Whatever may be the ideals of the intellectuals in Petersburg, their political machine is based upon the soldiers who expect and demand special pay and booty. . . . It is the purest militarism that presently exists anywhere. . . . As long as it exists the Bolshevist soldier's imperialism threatens the security and self-determination of all the adjacent nations, and it is entirely unlikely that a government depending so much on the militarist mass instincts could negotiate a sincere peace even if it intended to do so."[60] This militarist interpretation clearly supports the statement of Reinhard Bendix that "Weber did not at all foresee the development of totalitarian government."[61]

This inability to understand the nature of the Communist revolution and of Lenin's charismatic leadership is not merely a mistake in assessing the empirical conditions of the historical situation; it also reveals some serious defects in his theory of ideological dictatorships. There prevail, I submit, three misinterpretations of the relevant facts and several theoretical shortcomings that need to be identified and removed by a revision of his analysis.

In speaking of military dictatorships of the corporals, Weber's interpretation fitted the subsequent military uprisings in many less developed countries, originated and typified by the first Battista revolt in Cuba. The corporals followed their leader because a successful revolt brought them additional income and political power, and stabilized their military, bureaucratic position. Such a military revolt could not happen in the Russia of 1917–18 because the soldiers were peasants at heart and had no military interest of their own. Lenin shrewdly realized that the soldiers wanted to go home and grab a piece of the feudal landholdings. In legalizing the disorderly redistribution of land, Lenin accepted the main goal of the bourgeois agrarian revolution, and thus extended his base of power from the soldiers and workers to the peasants. Instead of following up his previous observation of "a sense of solidarity felt by the workers for the Russian peasants"[62] and of investigating the interaction of the simultaneous worker and peasant revolutions, Weber merely recognized that Russia was an exception to his general rule that revolutionary uprisings had a chance of success only if they were initiated or at least supported by a significant segment of the bourgeosie and bureaucracy (p.266).

Equally surprising and fully unexpected was the transformation of some of the revolting soldiers and militant workers into a revolutionary army, willing and able to fight successfully a civil war for a Bolshevik dictatorship. In his study of the Russian revolution of 1905, there arose in Weber the conviction that improvised military units had no chance of victory in a battle against a bureaucratized army. But this generalization depended for its validity on two not fully appreciated conditions. It was necessary that the soldiers placed full confidence in their officers,[63] and that the regular army had not been defeated by a foreign enemy. The revolutions in Russia and later in Germany undermined the internal cohesiveness and striking power of the armies. In other words, Weber failed to realize that his theory of the superior position of the army and its effective counterviolence was inapplicable in an intensive revolutionary situation. Absence of these conditions was later acknowledged for the German revolution of 1918 (p.266).

Finally, there was Weber's support of the German generals and their dictated peace: "We can give an assurance in all sincerity that on the German side the discussions in Brest-Litovsk were carried on in the most loyal manner in the hope of achieving real peace with those people." The responsibility for the interruption of the negotiations and the subsequently dictated peace was placed by Weber publicly upon the shoulders of the Bolsheviks in the following words: "There is no making peace with fanatics, one can only make them harmless, and that was the import of the ultimatum and the imposed peace at Brest."[64] Of course, Lenin overruled Trotsky and signed this dictated treaty in the correct expectation that external peace was an indispensable condition for the success of the Bolshevik revolution at home. Weber's inference that their ideology will prevent revolutionaries to make peace was unwarranted in the prevailing situation.

These empirical misjudgments were aggravated by an inadequate theory of revolutions. Instead of extending his four condensed types of revolutionary charisma, Weber had formulated two theoretic versions of revolution. The first was a negative inference from his theory of the objective indispensability of the bureaucracy. Relying upon the French experience, Weber inferred that the bureaucratic "apparatus makes 'revolution,' in the sense of the forceful creation of entirely new political orders, more and more impossible—technically, because of its control of the modern means of communication . . . and also because of its increasingly rationalized internal structure. The place of 'revolution' is under this process taken by *coups d'etat* as again France demonstrates in the classical manner since all successful uprisings there have been of this nature" (p.989). *Coups* could be successful only if initiated, or at least supported, by a significant segment of the military and civilian bureaucracy. If this displacement theory had been correct, the two Russian revolutions could not have occurred.

Under the impact of the German revolution of 1918 Weber formulated his theory of revolutions undertaken by councils. The extreme exhaustion and privation of the people on account of the war led to illegal behavior, and undermined the discipline both in the army and industry, thus preparing the way for the overthrow of the old regime. Military defeat generated a tremendous loss of prestige for the government followed by a declining will to resist the rebellion of sailors. In the German revolution "a new administrative staff came into being in the councils of workers and soldiers. In the first place it was necessary to develop a technique of organizing these new staffs. Furthermore, their development was closely dependent on the war, notably the possession of arms by the revolutionary element. Without this factor the revolution would not have been possible at all" (p.265). But revolutionary situation, councils, and weapons were only the first steps. Success was possible "only by the rise of charismatic leaders against the legal authorities and by the development around them of groups of charismatic followers," and "furthermore through the maintenance by the bureaucratic organizations that power once achieved could be retained" (p.266). Such a revolution could only bring the political constitution "desired by democracy,"[65] but neither create a new type of economy, nor extend beyond the limits of a bourgeois revolution.

While this theory of revolutions by councils turned out to be a fairly adequate interpretation of the German revolution, including its charismatic component in Bavaria, it did not help in understanding the Bolshevik revolution. In treating it as an exception, Weber presented arguments for his belief that the uprising in Russia was not a revolution led by either ideological or charismatic leaders. On the one hand, the Bolshevik ideology did not fit the revolutionary situation and could not function as an adequate guide for establishing a new order. Arguing along Menshevist lines, the evolutionary branch of Russian Marxism, Weber insisted that the feudal Russia was not ripe for a Communist revolution, that socialism could be achieved only by evolutionary means, that continued revolutionary violence could only lead to civil war, and end only in a widespread destruction. The ultimate victors would be "the peasantry and the petit bourgeoisie . . . the most radical opponents to *any* socialism."[66] Since their ideals misguided the Bolshevik leaders, one cannot properly characterize their uprising as a genuine ideological revolution.

In principle, a "dictatorship of the proletariat for the purpose of carrying out the nationalization of industry required an individual 'dictator' enjoying the confidence of the masses" (p.278). But Weber could not convince himself that either Lenin or Trotsky possessed any charismatic qualities. In a private letter he spoke of Trotsky as a "militarist . . . who is a Caesar of the soldiers, not a Napoleon of the generals, but a praetorian leader of the corporals and simple soldiers, and his sole aim has to be to satisfy the wishes of the mutinizing rabble so as to keep them together as an instrument of revolution even if the people have to suffer for it."[67] For Weber, the Bolshevik revolution was and remained merely a militarized uprising bare of any charismatic beliefs, devotions, charismatic leaders, or attached followers (p.278).

There emerge several reasons for Weber's inability to identify the charismatic component in the Bolshevik revolution. Being ideologically opposed to communism, he experienced a sense of aversion, to the revolution, and of political opposition to communism. In examining the nature of this revolution Weber's thesis on the need of a bourgeois participation in a successful revolution created a hurdle for his understanding of the Bolshevik revolution. In assessing the future chances of this revolution, Weber accepted temporarily Marxen's theory of historical materialism in order to show that communism could not possibly succeed in a semifeudal country. Focusing his attention on the insurrection as the most conspicuous aspect, Weber saw in the Bolshevik revolution nothing but a "military dictatorship."[68]

Aside from this misinterpretation, there is the interesting methodological fact that Weber had not worked out the various ways of how the noncharismatic features interacted with the charismatic ones in a revolution.[69] His difficulties indirectly suggest a list of the most important noncharismatic components in a dictatorial charisma. First, insurrection or usurpation of power requires a semimilitary force that obeys the commands of the charismatic leader. Second, once in power there arises a need for a secret police and labor or concentration camps for punishing and mistreating the most articulate of the political enemies as well as the opponents to the leader within the charismatic movement. Third, within the center of the charismatic movement there is a single political party that suppresses all other parties and secures for itself a monopoly for all political activities. Fourth, next to the party there operates either a revolutionary or a paramilitary army that is politically controlled by the paladins and is fighting for the leader his open or disguised civil wars. Finally, there is a tendency for dictatorial charisma to become associated with two kinds of ideologies, one for the period of gaining and consolidating power and the other for seeking to implement the ultimate goals of the leader and paladins.

Given these noncharismatic components that interact with the charismatic ones, we can infer a major hypothesis. Leaders in synergistic charisma face two quite different sets of noncharismatic components to which they must adjust and which they will employ for gaining and holding authority. One set of these components is clearly democratic in nature and will thus give rise to democratic charisma. The other set is clearly dictatorial in meaning and effect and thus generates dictatorial charisma. Our study will thus be primarily concerned with these two basic types of political charisma. In the immediately following part we shall investigate dictatorial charisma, using Hitler's leadership as our leading prototype. In the subsequent part we shall analyze democratic charisma, giving major emphasis to the leadership of Franklin D. Roosevelt.

The linkage between charismatic and noncharismatic features combines personalistic with pluralistic materials and calls for an individual and group analysis. Instead of separating institutional structures from unstructured collective behavior,[70] we shall show in detail the interaction between mass and group phenomena. This mode of interaction, via the leader and his devoted followers, creates a distinct semi-institutional sphere in which the charismatic giant and his followers operate. The personalist features of leaders and followers will be carefully identified but not subjected to a detailed analysis of subconscious drives or strictly personal motivation. Major emphasis will be placed upon the ideologies and organizations that such leaders and paladins will adopt or develop for their particular purposes. The reason for limiting the scope lies in the sociopolitical nature of this study. The need for giants to incorporate ideologies permits us to identify the objective meaning of personal drives and desires. The ideologies give a fairly definite direction to the charismatic beliefs and feelings, lead often to distinct goals, broaden the leader's appeal to additional masses, and put leader and followers into a distinguishable place in the constellations of politics and government. The interacting network of charismatic circles, political associations, and semibureaucratic organizations enables leader and followers to capture political power for the purpose of establishing a charismatic rulership.

Given this semi-institutional setting of the giants, we shall concentrate upon three topics for dictatorial and democratic movements. Beginning with the specific nature of the leader and followers, we will investigate the adopted or originated ideologies, then identify and analyse the new organizations and show their impact upon the old organizations. Parts II and III will thus receive the same treatment, but still permit us to emphasize their respective differences in spite of the same type of gigantic leadership.

# PART TWO

# DICTATORIAL CHARISMA

# CHAPTER THREE

# HITLER'S DICTATORIAL CHARISMA

STUDY OF DICTATORIAL CHARISMA faces two quite different hurdles. One lies in the fact that Weber did not develop a theory of dictatorship that was imposed and exercised by the single party and secret police. Nor has contemporary political theory supplied us with a unified theory of modern dictatorship.[1] It is thus impossible to follow the procedure of the previous chapter of examining the reasons of, and occasions for, charismatic leadership in dictatorship *per se*.

Nor is it possible to synthesize the various dictators of so-called totalitarianism into one prototype of charismatic leadership. In the Soviet Union, Stalin was not a charismatic leader, and Lenin's personal qualities have been overlaid by the fabricated legendary charisma. Mao was undoubtedly a charismatic leader but the relevant information is not accessible to outside observers. The new processes of first legendizing and then deglorifying him will further complicate separating facts from fictions. Since the neo-Fascist government of Italy turned against the Nazis at the end of World War II, the Allied command refrained from capturing the secret files of Mussolini and his minions. It is only in Hitler's case that the formerly secret documents and extensive literature on the nature and policies of the regime permit a detailed analysis of his charismatic leadership.

The credit for having first identified Hitler's leadership as charismatic belongs to Hans Gerth.[2] He tried to show how Hitler combined his charismatic qualities with the actions of party and state bureaucracy. While the basic thesis of charismatic leadership seems beyond dispute, there was an incomplete description of the leader and movement because of fragmentary information available at the time. The huge quantities of formerly secret documents permit us to fill this gap. Gerth stated the fusion of two types of domination (*Herrschaft*) very clearly, but the subsequent development to a synergistic charisma is missing.

In our case study of Hitler's charisma, we are concerned with Weber's "basically authoritarian principle of charismatic legitimation" (p.266). Our interpretation of Hitler's record will proceed in terms of Weber's theory. We shall seek to identify the dictatorial components in the charismatic qualities, and analyze the specific subtypes of alternative and cumulative charismata, personified by Hitler. The last section will compare the unconditional authority of dictatorial charisma with the arbitrary authority and illegitimacy of despotic power.

## PERSONAL MAGNETISM

Hitler's exceptionally great impact upon his listeners is attributable to the compulsive self-inflation of his personality that differed in two respects from ordinary self-image. First, Hitler displayed an extraordinary self-confidence. One of its expressions was that he alone could be the leader of the movement. While serving in prison for having led the *coup* of November 1923, the Nazi party had split into two groups. When he was asked which one of the factions he would recognize, Hitler answered: "Neither, when I come out I shall expect everyone to rally to me who realizes there can be only one leader. If this is necessary in the party, it will be double so later in the state."[3] This expectation materialized. One faction submitted to Hitler and dissolved itself; the other splintered and six out of its twenty-four representatives in the Bavarian parliament accepted Hitler as their leader. Hitler's self-confidence was effective because the subleaders themselves believed in the need for *one* leader and thus accepted Hitler's claim to the top position in the movement.

Another aspect of Hitler's self-confidence was his practice of incorporating desirable objects, such as the fatherland or the deeds of others, into his own personality. In many of his speeches he claimed to be the founder as well as *the* promoter of the party, who had built up this organization by his own hands. His self-esteem could grow to such an extent that he lost his sense of reality and proclaimed: "Nothing is impossible; one can do everything if one has the necessary will."[4]

Self-inflation was often followed by Hitler's second psychological ability, his self-intoxication in front of audiences. To be sure, Hitler prepared himself carefully for his speeches; he studied his own gestures in front of a full-length mirror; he acted the culminating points of his speeches during dictation; he reread and endlessly corrected the typescript in order to remember each argument and find the most expressive word for each thought.[5] As a result, Hitler did not merely act in front of an audience but intoxicated himself by his own emotions until he reached the point of near hysteria. In spite of these extensive preparations, it was Hitler's passion and fanaticism which enabled him to unleash "the great masses."[6] The quality of his voice changed as his passion succeeded in reaching the inner springs of his listeners. They not only lost their own distinctiveness in the mass, but came into the ban of the speaker's will who pulled them towards himself as if he possessed an irresistible magnetic power. The magnet was his ability to turn the feeling of masses into an ecstasy.

In the moment of overexcitement, Hitler was able to lead his listeners into two, logically speaking, opposite directions. He singled out *the* enemy, defamed and insulted him in the extreme and aroused his audience into unlimited hatred. As he said himself: "If a people is to become free, it needs pride and will power, defiance, and hate, hate, and once again hate."[7] His own hatred of the enemy was followed by exaltation of the party and movement, by expressions of fraternal love or at least concern for his followers. The other line was his self-glorification when Hitler presented himself as the savior of the nation and movement, who would free both by his own personal will power. The result was usually a tremendous enthusiasm for the leader who promised to lead the masses into a glorious future.

The final act of his emotional intoxication and the ecstasy of the masses arose when Hitler found the appropriate words to express the emotional bond that united leaders and followers. At a meeting of 30,000 SA-men (Storm Troopers) in January 1936, Hitler said: "I have founded this SA. . . . I have led you for the last fourteen years. I have learned to know you. Everything what you are, you have become through me; everything what I am, I have been able to do only because of you."[8] This emotional union, which Weber regarded as the culmination of natural charisma, was here achieved through the psychological process of mutual identification of the leader and the led. It was this union that placed Hitler above all other Nazi leaders and that provided the emotional basis for the willingness to obey his commands, for the mutual loyalty as well as for the effectiveness of the personality cult by the party.

The readiness to be attracted by Hitler's magnetism was so great in the German middle class that millions of them participated, in the words of Max Weber, in this "epileptical ecstasy." Even intellectuals, such as Albert Speer, became the victims of Hitler's gripping appeal.[9] There existed only two general conditions that created a limit to Hitler's magnetism. One resided in the ideological or religious beliefs of voting groups that were committed to the Catholic, Social Democratic, or Communist parties. This immunity of ideological groups points to the fact that it was primarily a clash between ideologies, not foremost emotional resistance, that reduced the impact of Hitler's appeal. The other could be found in the status consciousness of many members of the upper class. Their critical attitude was expressed early by General von Lossow, commanding officer of the *Reichswehr* in Munich during the time of Hitler's coup in November 1923. He subsequently testified in the court: "The well-known eloquence of Hitler at first made a strong impression upon me. But the more I heard him, the fainter this impression became. I realized that his long speeches were almost always about the same thing, that his views were partly a matter of course for any German nationalist, and partly showed that Hitler lacked a sense of reality and the ability to see what was practicable."[10] Believers in oppositional ideologies and bearers of a status honor were thus immune to Hitler's charismatic appeal.

These two external limits were more than compensated for by favorable conditions that greatly enhanced Hitler's magnetism. Related to his ecstatic ability was the technological invention of the microphone that permitted Hitler to communicate his emotions to his listeners and dominate huge mass meetings. Eventual exclusive control over the radio brought millions of others into his spell, that listened to him in their homes. Charismatic dispositions as a mass phenomenon came into being only in periods of extreme stress, such as the hyperinflation and the Great Depression, in which misery and frustration created the psychological readiness for accepting unconditionally one man as the savior of the nation. If any of these favorable conditions had been missing, the impact of Hitler's magnetism would have been substantially reduced.

## SUPERNATURAL CHARISMA

As soon as Hitler tried to explain the psychological excitement created by him in his meetings, he leaned towards his well-known theory of the masses as an object of manipulation. In a speech to businessmen of Hamburg in February 1926, Hitler summarized in one sentence his attitude towards the masses: "What the great mass has to feel is the triumph of one's own power, the contempt of the enemy, and especially the conviction of their own right" as a group.[11] But this manipulative interpretation failed him when he tried to explain his own capacity to excite the masses in his meetings. He then turned to transcendental terms of a supernatural calling, to his infallibility, and to the right of the leader to command obedience from others.

For Hitler, his calling as a political leader had a supernatural origin. His decision to become a politician, he said, was made during his sickness shortly after World War I. "As I lay in the veterans hospital, I said to the Almighty—if I do regain my eyesight, I shall take that as a sign that I should become a politician. When I could later see again I was so deeply stirred that I regarded my recovery as a heavenly act of calling me to a higher task."[12] The Almighty thus not only made Hitler healthy again but also indicated what kind of vocation he shall choose.

Shortly after the takeover of Austria in March 1938, the date of Hitler's selection for a leading political role was shifted back to the time before 1910. When Hitler spoke to the people of Linz, the first larger town he had lived in, he presented his military occupation of Austria as an act predestined by the Almighty. "I believe that it was the will of God to send the boy from here to Germany, give him the commission to lead the nation so that he could return his homeland into the *Reich*. There is a higher power and we all are nothing but its tools." The German march into Austria was celebrated as a "miracle" which was an expression of "the wish and will of providence."[13]

The semidivine calling came at the right time after the defeat of Germany. A military victory in World War I would have been, Hitler asserted, a misfortune for Germany. A state based exclusively upon military power would not have found the way to a rejuvenation of the German blood. "By having to go through a catastrophe but being saved from the abyss, Germany escaped the danger of internal disintegration. . . . A wise proverb applies fully to us: The love of providence for his people expresses itself in the form of punishment."[14] Hitler thus said in 1937 that the postwar misery was a sign of God's wrath which had the effect of generating the psychological conditions for the origin of national socialism.

This punishment was beneficial because the Germans are God's chosen people. In the middle of 1937 Hitler proclaimed: "Not men but God has created the German people who watches over all of us. He has formed this folk; we have grown according to His will, and because of our will Germany shall live eternally. . . . One folk has been resurrected, our *Reich* has been created new. The German has found himself and, in doing so, he has lived up to the will of his maker. . . . One strong state, one proud people, so great and noble that every German can happily confess: I am a German and I am proud to be and remain a German."[15] The belief in a chosen people thus was turned by Hitler into an extreme form of national self-glorification.

Religious saturation of nationalism served a twofold political purpose. The Third *Reich* was to be identified with the glorious past. "Reverence for the great men has to become the holy legacy for our youth." Historical continuity was pronounced so as to win the support of the conservatives for his regime. His "national revolution," too, had to be fitted into the heroic past of the nation. "Every state has to disintegrate whenever there prevail irreconcilable ideological conflicts." Suppression of other parties and free associations was presented as indispensable means for gaining national unity. Faith in the nation thus aimed at a "national and ethical rejuvenation of our people."[16]

Linking religious with nationalistic beliefs prepared the ground for the claim of charismatic leadership. Every successful attack upon his enemies was subsequently claimed as a great achievement that could be successful only because it was blessed by providence. "Could we have achieved so much if we had not been assisted by providence? I know that all the work of men is difficult and transient if it does not receive the blessing of the Almighty. Once providence has approved of such work, as it has of ours, then no man will be able to destroy our achievements."[17] As usual it was more the work of himself and of his movement than of the people that Hitler had in mind. "When I look upon the last five years, then I must say: This was more than the work of men. If I had not been directed by providence, then I could not have found my giddy way"[18] in politics. Hitler thus believed that his work was blessed by God.

He was convinced that he deserved the grace of God because he saw in the success of his policies a providential response to his public prayers. Hitler said on May 1, 1933: "Lord, you see we have changed. The German people are no longer the folk without honor, of shame, internal fights, small courage and little faith. No, O Lord, the German people are united again in one will, strong in their steadfastness and ardent in their readiness to bear sacrifices. O Lord, bless the fight for our freedom and protect our German people and fatherland."[19] Providential blessing was thus also linked to national freedom.

National unity and internal renewal, however, could come only through faith in the leader. "Great tasks have been accomplished only by strong leaders but even the strongest leader will labor in vain if behind him there is not a truly united and faithful people. . . ." To whose faith did Hitler appeal? His answer was definite: "My will—that must be our creed—is your faith. My faith is for me—as it is for you—

everything in the world. The highest gift that God has given me is my folk. My faith rests in the German people whom I shall serve with all my will and for whom I shall give my life."[20]

In Hitler's view, his leadership was the apogee of faith charisma. Faith was here the synthesis of his will, his belief in himself, his belief in a supernatural assignment by a God as well as the people's faith in a God, and the personal endowment granted to one leader by the Almighty. It was because of this synthesized faith that Hitler felt a calling to be the savior of the German nation. He saw in himself the incarnation of God's will in the political sphere. His calling as a kind of political apostle by a super-human being generated a feeling of commitment to his task and aroused a sense of responsibility in him to devote all his energies to his fight. "When I view this miracle [of a fighting union between the leader and the led], then I bow my head before the grace of God who has blessed this fight. I thank all of you my comrades who have made my fight possible and effective."[21] His co-workers translated his claimed incarnation into a peculiar form of intuition. Goebbels said, Hitler "acts intuitively in his great decisions. He begins to hibernate for days whenever he has to arrive at a great decision. It is as if he tried to listen to an inner voice. He suffers even physical pain during this period of gestation. He has often confessed to me his physical pain—and how wonderful he feels when a decision has been reached and action can begin. He places his ear to the ground to listen to his fate."[22] It was claimed that charismatic leadership created its own process of political decision making.

In his own mind Hitler went beyond intuition and instead claimed infallibility for his decisions. Interestingly enough, he got this idea by comparing himself with the pope. When, in 1931, Hitler looked out of the window of his Brown House to the residence of the pope's representative in Munich, he said: "I do not question the infallibility of the Holy Father in Rome in all religious matters. But nobody can dispute that I do understand more about politics than anyone else in the World. I thus proclaim for myself and my successor the right to political infallibility."[23] It was because of this belief in having an unerring judgment that he claimed the right to make all the major decisions in party and state. Repeatedly he rejected the notion that he could or did ever make a mistake. Even his abortive *coup* of 1923 was presented by him as a wise decision because otherwise Bavaria would have become a separate state and that would have destroyed the territorial unity of the *Reich*.

Occasionally, he could admit in small circles, as by speaking confidentially to the German editors in November 1938, that his decisions could stand some improvements. "It could be of course that I cannot agree with other Gentlemen . . . on a certain problem . . . but it is immaterial whether a certain decision was correct. Decisive is that the whole nation stands behind me in such a decision. . . . There has to be a united front so that the wrong part in a decision will be corrected by the resolution with which the nation does stand behind me."[24] This distinction between personal mistakes, admitted only in confidential circles, and unconditional obedience of the masses to the leader's decisions, solved one important dilemma for the subleaders.

They did not have to regard Hitler's decision as infallible but they did have to obey without question because unity of will was in the interest of party and nation. Infallibility is a new feature that was not present in Weber's typology and theory of charisma.

In deadly seriousness Hitler tried to establish a causal nexus between faith in his person and his ultimate infallibility. A mistaken decision would be corrected by the unswerving loyalty of the whole nation to him personally. Full confidence would increase German power to such an extent that even the wrong decisions would be rectified and adequately implemented. It was in this way that he asserted the correctness of his decision to spring a verbal attack upon Czechoslovakia which led to the Munich agreement of September 1938, and the "peaceful" incorporation of the Sudetenland into Greater Germany. The German editors were subsequently told by him that the people have to be "educated to the absolute, stubborn and confident faith in the leader. . . . Consequently, it is necessary that the press blindly follows the principle: The Leader is always right."[25]

In all there was a relationship of reciprocal reenforcement between Hitler's magnetism, the absolute faith in his personality, and the faith of the leader and led in a supernatural selection. Confidence in him received much of its credibility through the emotional experience of his magnetic power. The feeling of interacting ecstasy of the leader and the led was lifted from the psychological to the moral level through the absolute faith in each other and in the Almighty. The recurrently reenforced psychological and moral forces, blessed from above, achieved one great result. Both created Hitler's faith charisma and generated the legitimacy for his charismatic authority up to the beginning of 1938.

There were three major differences between a charismatic prophet and this political apostle of the Nazis. Hitler did not preach a religious ethic; he did not dispense any grace of salvation to individuals or groups; he had great difficulties in formulating the ethics of value charisma. He did, however, claim on many occasions that his will was the incarnation of God's will. Just one example may stand for many: "The single individual is . . . extremely weak when facing the will of the Almighty, but the individual becomes immensely strong in the moment when he acts according to the will of God. In that moment he feels coming to him from above a stream of energy which has distinguished all great phenomena in the world."[26] This hardly disguised claim of being the incarnation of God's will sounded like blasphemy to many devout Christians. This religious charge, coinciding with the power conflict between party and churches, created a churchly opposition to Hitler's religious justification of his charismatic authority. What were the effects upon, and the significance of, this opposition to charismatic leadership?

## RELIGIOUS LIMITS TO CHARISMA

It was Hitler's practice to justify his belief in his personality by claiming the moral support of the Almighty. Most of the key terms in his charisma—calling, chosen people, faith, blessing, salvation—came from or were strikingly similar to the expressions of the Christian prophets.[27] It seemed to many of his followers that Hitler regarded belief in the Christian God as indispensable for authenticating his charisma. Such an expectation had assisted the Nazis in gaining the confidence of many church people during the years of hunger in the depression.

In interpreting belief in God as demanding personal confidence in him, Hitler had adopted the policy to assist the German Christians and to use the power of the state for unifying all the Protestant churches. The original spirit of cooperation between Catholic church and Hitler's government, following the signing of the concordat in July 1933, was replaced by a wave of persecution of priests who allegedly had violated the laws of exchange control. These state interventions were aggravated by those of the Nazi party which dissolved church related trade unions, youth organizations, and social clubs, and drastically reduced the activities of the religious charity organizations.[28] The result of these measures was a rising distrust of Nazi intentions by church leaders and laity who wondered whether Hitler still believed in any Christian teachings.

The many protests by church leaders against Nazi violence in church affairs and the religious dispute within the party induced Hitler to change his policy. Looking backwards Hitler publicly admitted his earlier mistake in January 1939: "This state has only once taken a hand in church affairs when I myself tried in 1933 to unite the impotent protestant churches into one great and powerful evangelical *Reichskirche*. This attempt faltered on the resistance of leading bishops of the various churches. Thus we dropped our unification policy because it could not be our task to protect and strengthen by force the evangelical churches against the will of its leaders."[29] Why did this shift in Nazi church policy arise and how did the new intentions affect Hitler's attempt to widen his faith charisma into a religiously oriented value charisma?

The Nazi effort to unify the Protestant churches clearly failed because a compromise between the Confessing church and the German Christians could not be achieved. Angered by the resistance, Church Minister Kerrl threatened to take over the administrative functions of the churches, forbade all internal elections, and expelled all Christianized Jews from the churches. This policy of repression was disowned by Hitler, who announced on February 15, 1937, a free election of a General Synod which should produce a new constitution for the Evangelical churches.[30] Not the state but the church members themselves should decide what kind of internal order shall prevail within the Protestant churches.

The formal request of Kerrl to be given the power to determine church policy for the party was rejected by Hitler. In an interview with a group of noblemen (*Deutsche Adelsgenossenschaft*), Hitler declared that Rosenberg's book on the *Myth of the Twentieth Century* was strictly a private work. Rosenberg's attempt to discover religious elements in Nazi ideology, Hitler emphasized, did not express the religious position of the party.[31] Nazi officials were ordered to refrain from meddling in church affairs. A confidential message of Hess contained the following warning: "Whoever in the future is undertaking or preparing actions in church matters without being expressly authorized has to expect that he will be publicly disowned by the *Führer* if such actions may be harmful for party and state."[32]

In a confidential speech of November 1937, Hitler described the new division of functions between party and churches. "We will give you (the churches) unconditional freedom in your teachings and in your conception of God. . . . The churches may dispose of the German men in the other world, but the nation shall decide through its leaders over the worldly views of the Germans." This separation of functions involved a constraint for the party. "The organization of national socialism is the movement of the people, but under no circumstances will we engage in any kind of religious cult or rituals."[33]

Consistently, the office of Hess tried to enforce a neutral attitude of the party in church affairs. The Nazi flag could not be hoisted together with any church flag. Insignia of the party could not be engraved upon any tombstones. Names of Nazi heroes could not be given to any church or its buildings. All pastors and priests had to resign from their offices in the party and all its affiliated organizations. Nazi teachers had to stop giving religious instruction in churches, and party officials had to relinquish their church offices. At any funerals or church celebrations, party members could participate only in civilian clothes. The attempt of some bishops to have pastors swear allegiance to Hitler personally was rejected by the deputy leader of the party. Official representation of the party at church ceremonials required a special permission of the *Gauleiter*. From 1937 to the middle of 1939, great ingenuity was employed to sever all connections between party and churches.[34]

Similarly, various Nazi ministers tried to deprive churches of most of the privileges granted to them by the state. Churches were no longer allowed to use public buildings or to have priests and sisters teach in public schools. Religious instruction was curtailed by allowing pupils to excuse themselves from such classes. Teachers could no longer act as organists or choirmasters in their churches. School classes could not be obligated to participate in church affairs outside of school.[35] Governmental employees were specifically authorized to give up their church membership.

Most detailed were the instructions of Himmler to the police whose members had to refrain from assisting churches while on duty. At the same time all help was to be granted to those *Schutzstaffel* (SS) men who resigned their church membership provided they confessed a belief in a church free deity. Atheists had to be instructed to give up such a belief or their personnel dossiers had to be sent in immediately. Hitler's assured freedom of religion thus turned into pressure to become a believer in a non-Christian deity. The internal statistics of religious affiliations (table 3.1) record the extent of such pressures.

While the total members and the percentage of Catholics had increased because of

TABLE 3.1. RELIGIOUS ATTITUDES OF SS-MEN.[36]

| Affiliation | 1937 | | 1938 | |
|---|---|---|---|---|
| | Total | Percent | Total | Percent |
| Evangelical | 110,581 | 60.0 | 122,668 | 51.3 |
| Catholics | 38,810 | 21.1 | 53,937 | 22.8 |
| Deity-Believers | 34,369 | 18.7 | 61,030 | 25.7 |
| Others | 407 | 0.2 | 524 | 0.2 |
| | 184,167 | 100.0 | 238,159 | 100.0 |

the incorporation of Austria in 1938, the number of believers in a deity rose from 18 to 25 percent. The shift toward a neutral religious policy did not constrain Himmler's push for a non-Christian religion.

In fact, party neutrality towards the churches turned into a religious dispute among Nazis who were either adherents of the old churches, of the German Christians, of a German National church, or of the non-Christian deity. The central issue among the last three groups was the precise relationship between Nazi ideology and religion. Church Minister Kerrl gradually became the spokesman of the German Christians. He concentrated upon Luther's distinction between reason and faith, saw in the party ideology a product of reason and science, and claimed that Lutheran religion was free of all Jewish influences and thus compatible with Nazi ideology. Rosenberg was the most articulate speaker for the "religious experience" embodied in Nazi ideology which assertedly contained new values that over a longer period would provide the foundation for a new religion.[37] While Hitler had no use for a Lutheran religion and personally believed in the potentially religious power of Nazi ideology, he studiously refrained from siding with either group in his speeches, but continued to claim divine origin for his leadership.

In turning against any perversion of the Christian creed, leaders of both churches felt quite disturbed by his claim of incarnation. A group of Evangelical leaders, in the Barmer Confession of May 1934, declared their opposition to any non-Christian kind of belief: "We do reject the false doctrine which suggests that the church could and should recognize, in addition to the word of God, also other events and forces, personages and truth, as a part of providential revelation."[38] In a subsequent memorandum of May 1936, the leaders of the Confessing church came close to accusing Hitler of blasphemy when they spoke of "monstrous human presumptiveness" by political leaders.

In an Encyclical of March 1937, distributed in all Catholic churches in Germany, the pope argued strongly against the perversion of Christian doctrines and condemned the "idolatrous cult of Race or People."[39] While these accusations in no way endangered Hitler's power, they did contain a challenge to his asserted ability to incarnate the will of God. Either religious values had to underpin his charisma, and he had to accept Christian teachings, recognize the established churches, and drop his infallibility; or he had to reject Christian teachings, play the role of the anti-Christ, and also risk excommunication by the Catholic church.[40] Did Hitler find a way out of this dilemma of a religiously oriented value charisma?

In a confidential speech to the county leaders of his party in November 1937, Hitler examined the first alternative: "We National Socialists are convinced believers in God. But there is no universal agreement as to the specific nature of God. Nevertheless, belief in God is one of the most ingenious and noblest presentiments of man which lifts us above animals. Such an apprehension induces us to search for the reasons of why and for what man does live. The whole world, so clear in its external form, is not translucent for us in its purpose. Faced by the unknowable, men have humbly bent low before the power of the Almighty, convinced that they stand before a higher Being so inscrutable and deep that we cannot comprehend Him."[41] In these words Hitler rejected any kind of anthropomorphic conception of God. Consistently, Hitler expressed his disbelief in the Catholic faith or teachings. For instance, he said in January 1940, in a private conversation to Rosenberg, "I have never allowed any church representative to address a party meeting or to bury a party comrade. The Christian-Jewish pestilence is coming close to the end of its influence. It is a degrading situation that there once was an influential religion which demanded of its believers to eat their God in the act of Holy Communion. Good deeds of Christians were believed to be religiously significant only if one enjoyed the grace of God. And it was the privilege of the church leaders to decide who deserved his grace."[42]

In place of a Christian God and doctrine, Hitler expounded the notion of a creative God who had the power to create life, to give some individuals extraordinary abilities, and who endowed each nation with certain racial qualities. The greatest values are those that give us the knowledge to recognize our racial endowment and to educate the young in the art of maintaining and purifying the racial strains. This belief in a creative God was accompanied by a racial concept of a religious prophet. Hitler informed his followers that "Jesus was an Aryan. But Paul distorted his teachings so as to mobilize the underworld and to prepare the ground for the rise of a pre-Bolshevism."[43] Hitler thus felt himself as an especially endowed individual selected by a creative God. Because of this endowment, Hitler felt a mission to be a political prophet who had a right to claim charismatic authority in party, state and nation.

Unlike the religious prophets, however, Hitler did not expound any religious doctrine or lead an exemplary life to be imitated by others. Explicitly he emphasized his disinterest in specifying new religious beliefs or accepting the concept of another world for the faithful. He saw before him only the rise of an Olympus "in which I will enter, and in which I will find the most enlightened minds of all times."[44] Hitler accepted the thought of an eternity only in the racial sense that the special endowments would enter into some fundus and then regenerate themselves in future generations. "I am very sorry that I can see the Promised Land—like Moses—only from a remote distance."[45]

Could the new vision of a pagan deity supply the desired values? In 1937, Hitler indicated some doubt and uncertainty. Some of the second string leaders not only believed in a new kind of religion but suggested definite legal actions supporting such a religion. Church Minister Kerrl presented one proposal which not only was designed to renew his mandate but also to assist one of the Nazi groups attacking the Protestant churches. The underlying intent of this proposal was revealed in a confidential letter by Hess: "Kerrl has said that the German Christians should be granted a wider range of action within the protestant churches. . . . This desire to build up a counterweight to the Confessing church by means of state law can only lead to an involvement of party and state in the theological disputes of the quarreling church groups."[46] Kerrl's efforts came to naught. Hitler deliberately refused to see him and granted Hess veto power over all decrees to be issued by the church minister. Apart from various tactical considerations, Hitler refused to support the German Christian movement because he was not willing to accept its version of Luther as the true founder of a German Christianity.[47]

While stalling Kerrl, Hitler considered a second bill that was to authorize Alfred Rosenberg to be responsible for "the unity of National Socialist ideology" and also to direct all measures for the "concentrated resistance to Bolshevism." All ministers and party officials would have had to act according to the directives of the new party ideologist. This power to give binding orders was weakened into guidelines in a reformulated bill by Lammers. His modification removed the objections of the other ministers. The bill was to be signed and published together with Hitler's decree of February 4, 1938, which dissolved the Ministry of War and made Hitler the head of the armed forces. Interestingly enough, Hitler did not sign either the original or weakened bill because he regarded the appointment of an official ideologist as too "risky."[48] Hitler hesitated primarily because of his intended march into Austria. The Austrian Catholic population might have been less enthusiastic about Hitler's Great Germany if an open enemy of the churches would have been appointed as the official ideologist of party and state.

In principle, however, Hitler fully agreed with Rosenberg's intention of not only codifying the ideology but also of preparing the ground for a new pagan religion. This became quite obvious in the religious dispute within the party during 1939, when both Kerrl and Rosenberg wrote and circulated long memoranda, each one seeking to win Hitler to his side. When it became known that Kerrl had almost completed a book on "National Socialism and Religion," the Gestapo confiscated the manuscript and Rosenberg's bill was again presented to Hitler. Not only Bormann and seven *Reichsleiter*, but also Goering supported the bill. The latter even proposed that Rosenberg should become a member of the Council of Ministers. Hitler personally promised Rosenberg to sign a reformulated copy of the bill.[49] As a countermeasure, Kerrl proposed a new decree on "Safeguarding Religious Freedom" which would have nullified the ideological assignment of Rosenberg. In- formed of these disputes within the party, Mussolini asked Hitler three times not to undertake any negative actions against the German churches.[50] The requirements of the alliance with Italy and the need to retain the churches' moral support of the war induced Hitler to reject both bills in January 1940.

This merely tactical decision in no way reduced Hitler's opposition to Christianity nor diluted his belief in a pagan deity. Within the fences of his military compound he expressed his determination to break the power of the churches. "When the war is over, then it will be our last great task to solve the church problems. . . . The state has to become the absolute master. It is only then that the German nation will be secure" for national socialism.[51] While not excluding a terroristic takeover of the church properties, his desire to avoid any religious war induced him to favor a slow but systematic strangulation of the churches.

There developed a twofold religious limit for Hitler's supernatural charisma. One resulted from the charge of blasphemy by the church leaders. The accusation af- fected Hitler because his racial ideology prevented him from sincerely believing in Christ and in most of his teachings. In the absence of a Christian belief, Hitler was prone to derive his calling directly from God and to present himself as the incarna- tion of God's will, thereby preempting the traditional place of Christ. Since he could not assume the role of the anti-Christ, he had no choice but to accept the blasphemy limit to his charisma prior to war.

The victorious *Blitzkriegs* inflated his self-esteem to such an extent that he saw himself as a charismatic hero. Any restrictions upon his power became increasingly unbearable for him, while his successes emboldened him to formulate his "last great task." In allowing the first steps toward a religious counterrevolution by Bormann and others, Hitler saw the elimination of the churches as an ideological crusade, similar to his fight against liberalism and Marxism. But while their preparatory at- tack upon the churches affected only their power, not yet their existence, many Christians regarded these actions as an assault upon religion. The danger of a reli- gious war, constituting the second limit, thus forced Hitler to refrain from openly linking his belief in a pagan deity with his charisma.

### Providential Charisma

What kind of changes did the two religious limits and the internal disputes engen- der in Hitler's charisma? Was he forced to give up his claim for a supernatural origin of his charisma?

There is no evidence that Hitler ever considered giving up his claim to the super- natural origin of his calling. In public proclamations, Hitler continued to express a neutral position to the churches. He declared in his speech of January 30, 1939: "The new state has neither interferred with the individual beliefs nor with the teach- ings of any denomination. Everyone can worship according to his own wishes in the new Germany."[52] In part, this was designed to create the impression that Hitler was not only against any religious quarrels but also was remote to Christianity itself. A careful reading of his speeches reveals that Hitler ceased to claim any religious values as a moral support of his charismatic authority. It was in this way that Hitler accepted incarnation as a limit to his charisma.

Surprisingly enough, Hitler made a distinction between incarnation and divine origin of his calling. His desire—in Weber's words—for "a purely personal reliance upon God's providence" was as strong as ever.[53] But he now appealed to his creative, not to the Christian, God. Continuously he searched for indices that he still enjoyed the grace of his God. For instance, the attempt upon his life in November 1939 failed because he had left the beer hall earlier than intended. This accidental escape was interpreted by him as a sign of providential protection.

Hitler's experience thus demonstrates that the charismatic calling can even be successfully derived from a pagan deity. From his point of view, he avoided the danger of believing in a false God. The leader and the led do not have to believe in the same God, since Hitler failed to reveal explicitly his shift from a genuine religious to a mystic but creative God. Any deeply Christian people are prone to assume that the leader's prayer to an unspecified Almighty can only refer to their own Christian God. The second religious limit was thus clearly sidestepped by Hitler: his own commitment to a pagan God was kept an effective secret. Strangely but truly, deliberate deceit in the real source of grace did not hinder or diminish the strength of Hitler's charismatic appeal nor limit the accepted duty of his followers to obey his commands.

Faith charisma changed into providential charisma. The quasi-religious faith in a Christian God was reduced into mere subsequent blessings of the leader's completed deeds. The shift entailed a negative consequence. A merely providential leader cannot receive a charismatic message from an unspecified God. Hitler's war policies were not derived from any providential force. These policies generated from a secular source, namely, from his ideology. Hitler could thus readily accept the first religious limit because he had found an alternative source of inspiration.

But Hitler could not remove the second religious limit to his previous faith charisma, namely, the danger of a religious war. For some of his violent action he relied upon his belief in a pagan deity. "If I believe in any law of God at all, then it can only be the commandment to protect and maintain the [Aryan] race."[54] Following this self-selected "obligation," Hitler ordered the burning of the synagogues and other Jewish buildings. In hiding behind Goebbels, who took the responsibility in top party circles, Hitler got away with his atrocities. Since there was only shock but no public protest, Hitler initiated the policy of euthanasia. Incurably sick and mentally deranged people had to be killed on Hitler's secret instructions to his personal secretary, Phillip Bouhler. Giving the order on the day of the invasion of Poland, Hitler expected that "such a problem could be solved and executed quite smoothly in time of war without any resistance of the churches."[55] Without knowledge of the regular bureaucracy, the secretary formed an agency of party and SS personnel who brought the victims into special hospitals and killed them secretly. Relatives were informed of the sudden "natural" death of their beloved and received the ashes in an urn. In all, 80,654 victims were murdered in this fashion.[56] Death was inflicted upon these people not to relieve them from unnecessary pain but to serve the purity of the Aryan race.

There was a clear violation of the Christian commandment "Thou shalt not kill." Many Christian believers were shocked and horrified. Catholic bishops issued a pastoral letter, to be read in all churches, in which the mercy killings were openly condemned. Best known became the sermon of Bishop von Galen: "Woe unto the German nation when not only innocent people can be killed, but their slayers remain unpunished."[57] This was not only a risky challenge to the power of the SS, but it also signaled a legitimacy crisis. The leaders of the SS requested permission to arrest the courageous bishop and throw him and other protesters into a concentration camp. Hitler, however, refused to take action against the bishop and forbade any polemic in newspapers against the pastoral letter. Faced with a court case for murder against unknown assailants, Hitler terminated the euthanasia campaign.

By this retreat Hitler did not acknowledge any legitimacy crisis. Advancing a new interpretation, providential charisma did not entail any moral obligation or code of ethics for the leader. He felt free to select any of his dictatorial goals, tried to turn might into right, and employed cunning and deception to achieve his ends. If a certain policy failed, some tactical maneuver was called for to defuse the anxiety of protesters. Instead of meeting the challenge to his pagan beliefs, Hitler pretended to adhere to faith charisma and its Christian ethics. "The Ten Commandments are a code of living to which there is no refutation. . . . They are inspired by the best religious spirit, and the churches supporting them are on a solid foundation."[58] These deceptive phrases created the desired impression that Hitler was against these mercy killings and terminated the campaign as soon as it came to his attention. But in his confidential circle he swore "to pay back Bishop von Galen penny for penny after the war."[59] Then the great "revenge" would come, the concordat with the Vatican would be cancelled, state subsidies withdrawn from the churches, and each bishop would have to beg for money from his *Reichsstatthalter.*

There occurred in this instance a clash between charisma and the racism in Nazi ideology. Providential blessing could not be claimed for the dastardly deeds. While providential charisma covered Hitler's urge for deception and permitted violence, the lack of ethical principles provided no justification for mercy killings. Hitler could thus overcome the legitimacy crisis only by pretending a continued belief in faith charisma.

## PERSONALITY CULT

In religious charisma, apostles and disciples of a prophet engaged in a cult of their god as soon as they formed organized congregations. As these religious communities became permanent, the religious doctrines turned into dogma, supported and strengthened by cults and rituals. If he was still alive, the prophet himself became a priest, or his apostles became officials of a church. Cult was thus opposed to true prophecy; cult arose only in situations in which personal charisma had perished.

In the Nazi setting, however, there developed a coexistence of personal charisma and a semireligious cult. There was an extensive worship of party, ideology, and top leader. In limiting ourselves to the latter, we shall have to distinguish three different components of the personality cult. At the center was the deliberate glorification of the top leader that usually went beyond admiration of his charismatic qualities. This was accompanied by a mere propagandistic image-building in which Hitler was presented as the humane man living up to all traditional virtues. But there was also a systematic attempt to transform Hitler into a superman that was built mainly on the notion of his infallibility.

The manifold attempts to present Hitler as a humane and considerate man were usually guided by the existing moral code. The image was created that Hitler was a devoted friend and comrade of simple party members and felt great sympathy for all ordinary citizens. An endless stream of pictures showed him as a lover of children, as the admirer of women and mothers, and the strong supporter of family life. Hitler was praised as the man of truth, of true modesty and honesty, and of simplicity and generosity. He was portrayed as the man of simple tastes, avoiding any luxury, pomp, and formality. Great stress was laid upon his fight against any corruption in public life.[60] His personal dislike of smoking, and drinking, and his aversion to eating meat were turned into indicators of his strong will. His few grants to young men of promise were advertised as a steady and generous support of every talent and ability. Finally, Hitler was presented as the father of his people who watches carefully over the affairs of the state, assumes all the great responsibilities of his high offices, and asks in return only for the confidence of the people.

While not directly connected with his charisma, this skillfully repeated propaganda produced the effect that Hitler became much more popular than his party.[61]

Not churches or sects but the Nazi party and its affiliates transformed themselves into cultic organizations. This happened especially at the party created holidays, such as the Oath Day of party leaders, Hitler's Birthday, Labor Day, Peasant Day, Martyrs' Day, and, of course, the annual congresses. Instead of cultic congregations becoming attached to political associations, the party organized its own cultic celebrations that were skillfully linked with its political propaganda and ideological indoctrination. The propaganda and educational apparatus of party and affiliates employed artistic specialists, who not only staged the celebrations but also assured widespread participation by non-Nazis. The latter was achieved by dictatorial means. Workers in factories and offices were forced to listen to the main speeches over the radio. The celebrations were filmed and the products were imposed upon movie theaters.[62] It was because of this element of compulsion that Nazi cult included an important element of involuntary participation of many who were not Nazi adherents.

The main thrust of the cultic efforts, however, was directed to the actual and potential Nazis, and especially the youth of the nation. Albert Speer, Hitler's architect,
reports about his reaction to Hitler in a Nazi meeting of 1931: "His persuasiveness,
the particular magic of his by no means pleasant voice, the oddity of his rather banal
manners, the seductive simplicity with which he attacked the complexity of our
problems—all that bewildered and fascinated me. . . . I was not choosing the
NSDAP [National Socialist German Labor Party] but became a follower of Hitler
whose magnetic force had reached out to me the first time I saw him and had not,
thereafter, released me."[63] Hitler's natural charisma was thus especially effective
with young people who possessed the greatest capacity for enthusiasm.

Awakening was accompanied by a renewal of ecstatic feelings. Another listener
described the repeated impact of Hitler's voice upon himself: "Always when I hear
his voice I go home deeply stirred. I feel that I was permitted to see how he could be,
how he should be and how he really is. His voice awakens my conscience and lets me
appreciate the good. He shows everyone the general goal but reveals to everyone . . .
his particular goal. The most gratifying feeling is, however, that his voice creates the
courage to realize this goal; the voice strengthens one's will and confidence in one's
own energies. . . . This voice is a helper, acts like a shield, is a true magnet, an illuminating star in the dark."[64] Unfortunately, this was not a single or exceptional experience, since whole groups could be stirred to tears simultaneously. At a demonstration in Breslau in 1938, the following happened: "When the folk comrades of the
Sudetenland passed Hitler, a wall suddenly built itself in front of Hitler. . . . The
people who had come . . . to look into the beloved face of this man could not be
prodded to march on. Weeping women came up to the *Führer* to touch his hand.
One could hardly understand what they said to him, for their voices were choked by
their tears."[65] While inconceivable for enemies of the Nazi regime, Hitler did not
only generate temporary ecstasy in his followers but was able to incite their lasting
love of, and veneration for, their leader.

Cultic actions were transformed into rituals. In special prayers children had to
thank God for giving the country a leader, the savior of Germany. All subleaders of
the party had to swear loyalty to the leader each February, which ceremony was
broadcasted to every corner of the nation. Each affiliated organization had formulated its own oath to the leader. Most extensive was the worship of the various Nazi
flags. The sixteen victims of the Nazi revolt of 1923 were declared as martyrs of the
movement. The flag carried at that occasion was called the "blood flag." Each year
Hitler touched the blood flag as he dedicated the flags of regional party or of affiliated organizations. The consecrated flag was to be kept as a relic at the respective
headquarters. Hitler and his consorts marched every year through the streets of Munich, reenacting the abortive revolt of 1923. A whole host of Nazi songs praised the
political struggle and worshipped the movement. Indeed, it was in these songs that
Nazi beliefs and worship found their most vivid expression.[66]

At the center of the Nazi cult stood Hitler, who was the main performer as well as the glorified object of the subleaders. Best known were the annual party congresses, in which Hitler's appearance generated into the emotional culmination of the ceremony. One report of the congress of 1936 hints at the emotional seizure of speaker and listeners: "Each time as Adolf Hitler begins to speak, an uproar of Heils rages over the arena lasting many minutes. . . . As he comes to an end, a storm of excitement and enthusiasm embraces the *Führer* . . . one fire has taken a hold of all."[67] The subleaders glorified Hitler as the semireligious apostle, sent by God. After Hitler's speech to 140,000 political leaders in 1936 at Nuremberg, Ley concluded the meeting with the following words: "We believe in an Almighty who directs and protects us and who has sent you to us, my *Führer*." Other subleaders did the same at other occasions. At the party congress of 1935, Goering celebrated Hitler as "the leader and savior of the nation." Shortly before World War II Hess exclaimed: "We believe that a Higher Being has sent us the leader to save our nation in the hour of our deepest misery. In standing behind the *Führer* we fulfill the will of the Higher Power who has given us this savior."[68]

A critical comparison of these glorifying speeches of the subleaders reveals an evolution of thinking similar to the one of Hitler. Ley clearly expressed the belief in a providential mission and in Hitler's ability to incarnate God's will. Hess does not speak of God but of a Higher Being who has placed his will into Hitler. This suggests that Hess knew of Hitler's belief in a creative God but this did not deter Hess to express the incarnation thesis. The personality cult thus not only created the conditions for glorifying Hitler but also compensated for the two religious limits upon Hitler's charisma. From his point of view, emotional renewal and glorification were indispensable because they freed the leader from the transitory limits of natural charisma and also from any religious limits of supernatural charisma.

Nazi cult and glorification enabled Hitler to claim the power of the superman, thereby going beyond the charismatic ability. For charismatic capacity stressed the exceptional quality of the leader as an attribute of his personality. The superhuman man is a form of idolatry that constitutes the worship of a false God. Hitler as a superman lost his human limitations, knew the future, could do no wrong, never made any mistake, and was the true incarnation of a higher will. It was the claim of infallibility that provided the basis for grafting the superman upon the charismatic leader.

The claim of the superman became especially relevant in three concrete situations. One was the assertion that Hitler had become a superior statesman who could manipulate the heads of other governments according to his will. Goebbels translated this into the slogan that "Hitler took up Bismarck's work and is about to complete it."[69] In situations requiring expert knowledge, Hitler frequently claimed to be or to become an expert in any discipline. This was true not only in the political and diplomatic, but also in the military and technical fields. For instance, he saw himself as the creator of the network of superhighways and stood fully behind the building program of *Volkswagen*, even before he meddled in the construction of tanks and super artillery guns. Finally, Hitler was possessed by an architectural megalomania, which flowered into the colorful grandstands of the various celebrations. Executing faithfully his master's wishes, Speer confesses: "It was always scenic drama I was after. I arranged for veritable orgies of flags in the narrow streets of Goslar and Nuremberg, with banners stretching from house to house, so that the sky was almost blotted out."[70] Then came the craze of building party forums at Berlin, Nuremberg and most other *Gau* cities. Berlin was to become the most bombastic metropolis of the world. Sure of his victory, Hitler first stopped but then had his construction program continued so as to have the triumphal arch ready for the greatest of all celebrations: to inaugurate the new German empire after victory.[71]

How and why could the contrived cult intermingle with the genuine feelings in the natural charisma and offset the limits implicit in supernatural charisma? Most puzzling of all, how could genuine charisma legitimize unlimited dictatorship of the top leader?

The Nazis succeeded in establishing a positive relationship between the leader's ecstatic abilities and cultic mass celebrations. Instead of contributing decisively to the forming of churchly institutions, the cult of the personality by a dictatorial political party enhanced the leader's natural charisma. The contrived component of the cult was either not recognized or discounted because manipulation was primarily directed towards the aim of magnifying the size and power of Hitler himself. Cult and manipulation intensified mass emotionalism because they were applied indirectly through the leader. His infallibility was thus a necessary feature of personality cult.

The obvious difference between charisma and idolatry presented no difficulty for the more robust glorifiers. For Goering, for instance, there was an easy transition from glorification to the superman. Of charismatic qualities he said: "There is something mystical, unsayable, almost incomprehensible about this man. . . . We love Adolf Hitler because we believe, with deep and unshakable conviction, that he was sent to us by God to save Germany." A few lines further he shifted to the superman: "There is no single quality . . . which he does not possess to the highest perfection. For us the *Führer* is infallible on all matters political as well as all others which affect the national and social interests of the nation."[72] In this interpretation, glorification becomes the link between natural charisma and infallibility.

Significantly, this particular link was not acceptable to Hitler. He personally connected his asserted infallibility with both natural and heroic charismata. The faith in providence became more and more faith in his own personality, in his own will. Instead of accepting the notion of something "mystical" in his nature, Hitler emphasized his will, his courage, and his honor which were linked with the honor of the nation, and the heroism of the great leader. In many of his speeches he claimed to fight for "*one* folk, *one* Reich, *one* will." In defense of the "national honor," he would "never capitulate." The nation's honor was not for sale. "It is better to be honorably isolated than to be tolerated without honor."[73] In gradually personifying the national honor, Hitler not only struck a heroic pose but increasingly justified his right to top leadership with his daring in politics and his exceptional heroic qualities. As every additional sneak attack of Hitler led only to protest on paper by the foreign powers, there arose "to a rising degree the belief in Hitler's infallibility. His prophesies were nearly always correct."[74] The simultaneous belief in providential and heroic charisma, coupled with cult and infallibility, produced the effect that Hitler became for his most ardent followers the only person to be worshipped.

Heroic charisma manifested itself early in 1938 when Hitler dismissed the top leaders of the army, demoted or pensioned off many of the leading generals, promoted younger careerists, assumed the role (but not the title) of the minister of war, and claimed the right to determine military strategy for the *Reich*.[75] At the same time, Hitler reorganized the top agencies of the state in such a way that his four secretaries for administrative, military, party, and presidential affairs, as well as his delegate in economic matters, reported exclusively to him. They all had to be ready to formulate and execute his commands.[76]

It is our thesis that this purge and reorganization of 1938 cannot be adequately explained by either providential charisma or personality cult. The former existed priorly, the latter was greatly magnified by the purge and its consequences. After Hitler had overcome his self-doubt about providential charisma, there occurred a significant rise in his own self-esteem. His notions of indispensability and infallibility were linked by him with the problem of military expansion. The new living space "had to be gained during his life. Coming generations could not provide a solution. He alone could settle the question."[77] When Hitler presented his new military strategy to the top military leaders on November 5, 1937, he requested that his decision to start a war by 1943–44 be regarded as his "testament to be bequeathed" upon his successor. When he decided upon the invasion of Austria, Hitler took the army under his direct command. General Keitel proposed to Hitler that he should give his orders to the head of the army personally. "Since Brauchitsch was on an inspection tour, I drove with [General] Beck to the Chancellery. Beck's objection [against the invasion] was rejected by Hitler out of hand. Beck could do nothing else but to obey and to report within a few hours which troops were ready to march at midnight."[78] Shortly after the invasion there was an attempt to impose the *Führerprinzip* upon the army. A memorandum of March 22, 1938, tried to establish a new principle: "The Highest Commander of the Armed Forces [Hitler] directs the war and carries the full responsibilities."[79] While this rule was not formally accepted, it is an established fact that all the subsequent invasions, with the partial exception of Norway, were initiated and decided upon by Hitler himself.

How could the corporal of World War I believe that he would possess the military competence to direct a series of wars effectively? There are two answers to this question. Politically, he did convince himself that his success in Germany could be readily repeated in Europe.[80] Charismatically, he increasingly believed that his exceptional ability extended also to the art of leading large-scale wars. There set in a shift to the charismatic hero. It began shortly after the incorporation of Austria when Hitler wallowed in a huge wave of enthusiasm. The leading newspaper of the party greeted him at his arrival in Munich with the words: "Return of the Victorious War Lord."[81] His many victories in the first years of the war, especially the defeat of France, induced an increasing number of his followers to share his belief and worship his heroic charisma. Personality cult thus culminated into hero worship.

## PLEBISCITARY CHARISMA

Parallel to faith and providential charismata, to personality cult and infallibility, runs the development of a plebiscitary charisma. This additional kind of charisma resulted from two contradictory motives. Plebiscites were used as a deliberate tactic of disguising the dictatorial nature of Hitler's charisma and policies; but they also sprang from the desire to provide for the people a form of affectual participation in Hitler's great deeds.

The failure of the putsch in 1923 had convinced Hitler that he could come to power only if he would pretend to seek power by a vote of confidence by the majority of voters. The purpose of his strategem was to gain sympathizers and steal the voters of other parties and undermine them prior to taking over power. There also was the tactical aim of preventing the democratic government from suppressing the Nazis because of their obvious intent of tearing apart the constitution. Questioned on this point by the Supreme Court in 1930, Hitler gave the following answer: "The constitution prescribes only the method of the political struggle, not its goal. We enter parliaments by the votes of the people, and form governments by peaceful majorities. Once we possess the power by constitutional means, we shall transform the state in accordance with our ideology."[82] The duplicitous distinction between method and goal worked very well. Not only did many voters of the middle and conservative parties accept Hitler's promise of peaceful change, but even the Supreme Court was impressed by Hitler's "charismatic sincerity" and accepted his misinterpretation of the constitution.

There was only one occasion when Hitler exploited for his purpose the plebiscite provided for in the Weimar Constitution. In the presidential election of 1932, Hitler was able to run against the incumbent president von Hindenburg. It was not a contest between parties but between personalities. In comparison with 1930, the Nazis doubled their votes when von Hindenburg received 53 and Hitler 47 percent of the votes. In a democratic country, the loser would have accepted his defeat gracefully, while Hitler took this charismatic contest as a vital step in his push for power. Nevertheless, it was not by majority vote but by an alliance with the reactionary forces that Hitler was appointed as a presidential chancellor of Germany in 1933.

After his ascent to power Hitler granted himself the right to call at will for a "plebiscite of the people." Deviously he said: "In every year I shall give the German people the opportunity to determine the extent of my power."[83] Actually, what happened was a shift from a democratic plebiscite with two or more candidates to a dictatorial plebiscite offering the voters only the right to vote for or against the single leader.

In his many speeches prior to these plebiscites, Hitler emphasized three different themes. One was the identity of will of the leader and the people. "The people have the right to affirm or reject my policies." Then there was the notion that the source of strength lay in the people. "The energy of the people is my energy, its strength is my strength . . . the folk is the fountain of my power." The idea of the strong nation was then contrasted with the humble son. "I have no bank account, no shares, no partnership in any enterprise. I do not receive any dividends. . . . My people alone are the judges of my actions." Being just a simple German, it was the duty of every citizen to give his vote to the leader. Indeed, Hitler claimed to be fully devoted to the people. "I am nothing but your speaker; I will only be your agent who defends your life and interests." As the genuine man of the people, Hitler claimed the right to the vote of everyone. "I appeal to the German people in this hour to show our unity of steel in which every man stands behind his leader who is the personification of the people." But none of them had a right to criticize the leader. "In my view, critique does not fulfill an important function. . . . I protest against a vocation [of journalists] who bear no responsibility, but claim the right to know everything better than those who do the work."[84]

Each of the major surprise attacks against foreign states prior to war was followed by Hitler calling a plebiscite. After the march into the Rhineland he said: "I cannot conclude this historical period of restoring our honor and freedom without asking the German people to give me and all my co-workers the subsequent approval for all the seemingly arbitrary decisions and all the great sacrifices I had to ask of you during these years."[85] Often popular affirmation was accompanied by a reelection of the German parliament. But there was only one list of candidates, so that voting amounted to a mere affirmation of the leader's actions. The occasions and results can be summarized in table 3.2.

These acclamations were first of all the combined effect of massive propaganda and coercion. But they also induced millions to admire Hitler's deeds and to adopt a

TABLE 3.2. Hitler's plebiscites.

| Occasion | Date | Percent of Affirmation |
|---|---|---|
| 1. Withdrawal from League of Nations | Dec. 12. 1933 | 95.1 |
| 2. Combining Chancellor and President | Aug. 19, 1934 | 89.9 |
| 3. Return of the Saar | Jan. 13, 1935 | 90.6 |
| 4. March into the Rhineland | Mar. 29, 1936 | 98.8 |
| 5. Annexation of Austria | Apr. 10, 1938 | 99.2 |
| 6. Annexation of Sudetenland | Dec. 4, 1938 | 98.9 |

new attitude to Hitler personally. Conservatives and nationalists felt that Hitler was a true national leader who possessed the capacity to restore German greatness without having to pay a price for his exploits.[86] Many non-Nazis of a liberal or democratic persuasion gradually adopted a favorable attitude to Hitler. Millions saw in him the incarnation of the political genius. Whatever daring policy he initiated and executed was bound to be successful. The dictatorship of the single party turned for many into a government of the political genius, an apparent dictatorship from and by the masses.

Actually, there was a clear distinction between a democratic and a dictatorial Caesarism. The former could be criticized and terminated by the voters; the latter could not. Each plebiscite was at the center of a deliberately contrived and manipulated personality campaign that made it a national obligation for everyone to acclaim the leader by his vote. The space for "no" on the ballot was extremely small, whereas the one for "yes" was greatly magnified so that no voter could have any doubt what was expected of him. Anyone who did not vote or who rejected the claim of a superman was identified and punished. Secrecy was eliminated from the ballot box and voting became coercive. These contrived excitements and threats became so clearly identified with the plebiscites that this kind of Caesarism fell into the dictatorial category.

There was no doubt in Hitler's mind that he would not permit any plebiscite to limit the extent of his power. He said in a confidential speech to his county leaders on April 29, 1937: "I have acted first and then wanted to show the world that the German people stood behind me. . . . If I had been of the conviction that the people would not back me up, I would have acted anyway, but I would not have issued the call for a plebiscite."[87] This admission reveals that Hitler did not see his power dependent upon any popular will. Staged plebiscites performed for him quite different functions. One was confirming and finalizing of his unilateral decisions. Neither internal opponents or disbelievers nor foreign statesmen should have any doubt in their minds that Hitler policies could not be modified by negotiations or pressures. Another reason was the opportunity for all people to identify themselves with the leader. At no moment should anyone get the impression that Hitler had become a bureaucrat who was ruling only by formal law. Finally, there was the element of deception involved in this plebiscitary charisma. Using the demonstrative votes as an indicator for his almost hundred percent mass following was one of the effective devices of imposing dictatorial rule upon the disbelievers among the people.

## GIGANTIC CHARISMA IN DICTATORSHIP

What does this case study reveal for the theory of dictatorial charisma? Hitler was undoubtedly an outstanding example of a charismatic giant. Magnification sprang from deriving his extraordinary qualities from natural as well as supernatural sources, from developing different subtypes of unconditional authority, and from combining various forms of exceptional actions into an unusual kind of cumulative charisma. On top of these were grafted his personality cult and belief in his infallibility.

Magnification expressed itself most visibly in the larger number of charismatic features of the dictatorial giant. In bringing together the various characteristics discussed in the previous sections, we arrive at table 3.3 that shows schematically presented features.

TABLE 3.3. CHARACTERISTICS OF DICTATORIAL GIGANTISM.

| Sources of Charisma | Cumulative Charisma | Types of Authority | Sources of Obedience | Personality Cult | Idolatry |
|---|---|---|---|---|---|
| Supernatural | Faith | Duty | Duty | Rituals | Megalo-mania* |
| Semireligious | Providence | Oath | Loyalty | Cults | Superman |
| Calling | Plebiscite | Plebiscite | Affirmation | Glorification | Infallibility |
| Pagan Calling | Heroism | Discipline | Submission | Worship | |
| Natural | | | | | |
| Love | | | | | |
| Hatred | | | | | |
| Seizure | | | | | |
| Emotional Union | | | | | |

*Megalomania expressed itself mainly in Hitler's architectural and construction plans for party and cities. See Albert Speer, *Inside the Third Reich* (New York: Macmillan, 1970), chap. 5.

Most obvious was the addition of the personality cult and of idolatry that were usually missing in the democratic kind of charismatic giants. This raises the question of how these semicharismatic features were combined with the genuine charismatic qualities.

Another case of magnification was the diverted alternative charisma. In regard to the supernatural sources, Hitler was compelled to give up a religiously oriented faith charisma and to adopt in its place providential charisma. But the shift had either very little significance for the attached followers or could be compensated for by greater emphasis upon loyalty and discipline. Hitler's doubt and uncertainty in the year 1936–37 were removed by his belief in a creative God. His extreme self-confidence was not diminished in the slightest, and his course of action became decidedly more aggressive. The alternative to a pagan calling was thus considered and accepted secretly by Hitler but did not hinder or change his plans and policies.

Closely associated with magnification was cumulative charisma. There emerged a distinction between the roles and the personality of charisma. Various roles were performed by the same leader. From 1933 to 1938, Hitler desired to demonstrate his popularity and called for dictatorial plebiscites. Charisma of the plebiscite was coupled with providential charisma. Heroic charisma began with the march into

Austria and continued until the severe defeat at Stalingrad. Providential and heroic charisma coexisted during his political and military victories and reenforced each other without becoming identical. In cumulative charisma the leader's power was not only derived from his original qualities, but his prestige and political position were greatly increased by his exceptional deeds. No other mortal could legitimately challenge his authority and get away with it. Cumulative charisma thus lent itself readily to dictatorial rule by a supreme commander.

Most original was the symbiotic relationship between natural charisma and personality cult on the one hand, and between supernatural charisma and idolatry on the other. The two sets of components remained inherently dissimilar, but they became so intimately associated in specific situations that the leader could readily shift from one to the other, and most of the believers did or could not readily identify the line of distinction. How was this twofold symbiotic relationship possible?

In interpreting his supernatural calling, Hitler emphasized his own will and strength, his right and ability to make the most important decisions, and his phenomenal capacity to mold the course of history. When heroic deeds were added to this overweening self-assurance, the resulting awe induced many followers to see in Hitler the personalized superman. He was expected to be able to do anything he was determined to do. This notion of unlimited possibilities became linked with Hitler's belief in his own infallibility. His emphasis was not on the external opportunities, but on the internal gift to turn every situation into his favor. His claim that the "leader is always right" thus sprang as much from his supernatural gifts as from his personal belief in infallibility. Even defeat did not compel him to admit that he was fallible.[88] He attributed defeats either to disloyalty of followers, opposition by generals, or inadequate belief of the German people in his ideology.

A similar link was established between natural charisma and personality cult. Love and hatred became equally important components in Hitler's interpretation of natural charisma. The hatred was directed towards one specific enemy: international Jewry. This enemy must be destroyed at any price. The leader was the only man who could lead in this fight to reveal and terminate the conspiracy of the enemy. Hatred of the enemy and his destruction provided one source for the indispensability of the leader. The other source was the emotional attraction of the followers that turned into love of the leader. It was quite natural for many followers to turn in their fraternal or erotic love to glorifying and worshipping the leader in the form of various cults and rituals. Love turned into glorification and natural charisma was linked with personality cult, in spite of the obvious contrivances used in the latter. Paladins, engaged in building up the contrivances, such as Goebbels or Albert Speer, did not fall for the cult, but they retained their fraternal love almost to the final defeat.

The twofold symbiotic relationship goes far in explaining the paradoxical fact that the followers loved their dictator. For the true believers as well as worshippers, the leader was not a dictator but a genuine savior of the nation. Hatred of the enemy and the desire for his destruction were for them only the other side of the coin of loving the leader, of accepting voluntarily his rule, and of regarding the punishment of disbelievers and deserters as morally justified and politically indispensable. Personality cult and glorification of a superman extended the spell and power of the leader even to those who did not feel deep love or were not consumed by hatred of the enemy.

These three sociopsychic processes effectively explain the success of gigantic charisma in a dictatorship. Magnification by means of the two charismatic sources presents the reason for the continued inner consistency and the absence of fickleness of the charismatic quality. Cumulation of several kinds of charismata in the same leader constitutes the cause for the rising strength of the leader and the charismatic movement. The two kinds of symbiosis explain the persistence of the affectual participation of the masses in most of the leader's appeals and policies. Each of the processes contained an element of reciprocity of the followers to the actions of the leader and vice versa. It is the fatal defect of the alternative theories of either a demoniac or mob leadership[89] that they do not identify these processes and miss their respective reciprocity.[90]

What were the major "dictatorial" components in Hitler's charismatic leadership?[91] There was first and foremost an emotional exploitation of the followers by the leader. In natural charisma, emotional union contains a mutual taking and giving that brought satisfaction and permitted affectual participation of the masses in the leader's appeal and action. In the personality cult, however, the emotional union was transformed by the leader into an unquestioned and one-sided glorification or worship of his person *per se*. Admiration in natural charisma was contingent upon exceptional deeds, performed or expected. The intensified feeling in worship served the leader only, who derived from the concentrated emotions an enlargement of his power and privileges. These advantages were obtained without the intention and explicit consent of the worshippers. When the expected and demanded worship was not forthcoming, then the attempted emotional exploitation was followed by compulsion. Refusal of worship was punished whether the withholding sprang from distaste, disinterest, disbelief, disloyalty, or emotional desertion. The leader must be glorified or the nongiving follower was punished.[92]

The second dictatorial element was contained in the new meaning given to legitimacy as a justifier of charismatic authority. In democracy, legitimacy contained the voluntary approval of the leader's right to lead as well as the followers' readiness to comply with his decisions. In the single party dictatorship, however, charismatic authority was no longer dependent upon the approval of the followers. The right to lead was said to be automatically justified by the two interacting sources of his exceptional qualities. Approval was replaced by the sanctification of the already enjoyed and justified power. The inner willingness of the followers to comply with the leader's wishes was superseded by unlimited obedience. The voluntary elements in legitimacy were replaced by compulsion. Instead of authority resulting from legitimacy, sanctified authority was the cause of obedience.

The third dictatorial element consisted in the widening of the unconditional authority of the leader. In the first phase of the Nazi regime, not all contingent authority had been removed. There coexisted a normative and prerogative state.[93] But the rights of the courts to review the laws and administrative rulings diminished rapidly from 1938 onwards, and the orders of the leader were increasingly held above the law. The prerogative state was enlarged when parliament was deprived of its legislative function, when the presidency was combined with the office of the chancellor, when the cabinet was reduced to a mere administrative agency, when the leader became the *de facto* head and actual commander of the armed forces. Combining of offices and centralizing of power for the charismatic leader became the indicators for eliminating the previously existing authorities of co-responsibility and the rise of his authority. The leader became all-powerful in the political sphere.

The fourth dictatorial element resided in the increased claims of the leader for justifying obedience to his unconditional authority and applying it to particular situations and groups. Similar to the religious prophet who "preaches, creates, or demands new obligations by virtue . . . of his own inspiration or of his own will" (p.243), Hitler insisted that it was the moral duty of paladins and followers to accept and implement his orders. This dutiful authority was demanded in general appeals. For specific groups or actions, however, Hitler created three other kinds of authority. Instead of being satisfied with admiration and enthusiasm, he institutionalized oath-taking authority. All officials in the Nazi movement had to swear annually unlimited loyalty to the leader. The oath translated emotional attachment into a norm that morally committed all members of the movement to be eternally loyal to him personally. A plebiscitary authority was fashioned for the voters. Phenomenal deeds of the leader were to be affirmed by all eligible voters. Whoever refused to partake in the plebiscite was punished by the secret police. Finally, there was the invention of disciplinary authority. Each state official and soldier had to swear unlimited fealty to the leader personally. "A charismatic hero may make use of discipline . . . if he wishes to expand his sphere of domination" (p.1149). What was said of Napoleon fitted Hitler perfectly. Of these four kinds of charismatic authority[94]—dutiful, oath taking, plebiscitary, and disciplinary—the last one increased in relative significance and became predominant during the years of defensive wars.

As a desired side effect of the dictatorial elements, personality cult linked charisma with idolatry. Personality cult under conditions of a monopoly of all means of mass manipulation transformed the leader into a superman. His supremacy became so great that even disbelievers acquiesced in his rule and opponents felt the futility of their intended resistance. Acquiescence of the nonfollowers became an effective substitute for charismatic authority. The leader himself became a victim of self-aggrandizement when he mistook his claimed infallibility as an extension of his superhuman qualities. Personality cult linked genuine beliefs with idolatry when superman and infallibility became adjuncts to dictatorial charisma.

This leads to the question of arbitrary authority and illegitimacy. What was the place of violence in dictatorial charisma? How far did the compulsory elements in dictatorial charisma justify violence or was there a normative political limit to violence even for the charismatic dictator?

As we have seen in chapter 2, Weber tried to establish a twofold relationship between revolutionary charisma and violence. One is the thesis of a distortion of charisma. Minimal violence is compatible with charisma if it is limited to the mere act of overthrowing the old regime and of protecting the leader against assassination. Any violence going beyond these limits leads to a distortion of the values implicit in revolutionary charisma. The other thesis culminated in the prediction of an unintended self-destruction of revolutionary charisma. Adopting wholesale violence, whether by the masses or by a revolutionary dictator, breeds the military dictatorship that suppresses the revolution by force. Did these two theses also apply to Hitler's dictatorial charisma?

It so happens that Hitler's earlier violence was neither minimal nor distortive of his charismatic qualities and appeals. His concealed civil war shortly after his appointment as chancellor was minimal in the sense of neutralizing the regular police and armed forces, but maximal in destroying all democratic and leftist groups and wantonly killing many of their leaders. The same was true of the murder of SA leaders, although they merely disagreed with him politically, and did not threaten him or his leadership. Instead of being limited to the period of violent upheaval, secret police and concentration camps became permanent instruments of violence, serving the goals and policies of the leader. Rather than diluting his charismatic quality, the two occasions of concerted violence in 1933 and 1934, and the new agents of violence greatly increased Hitler's appeal as well as popular fear. There was a shift from compliance to obedience for the believers, and an increasing acquiescence of the nonbelievers, undercutting any effective opposition within the movement and rendering hopeless any nonviolent resistance of his opponents to him and his regime. In fact, the two occasions and instruments of violence were sanctified by the loyal and disciplinary authority of dictatorial charisma and supported by affirmative and submissive obedience.

Other wholesale kinds of violence were either justified as acts of self-defense or as retaliations for insults to the leader or the German people. Deception took the place of charismatic legitimacy. Claiming the right to call German soldiers to war and death was justified as an act of self-defense against foreign aggression. Killing hostages in occupied lands, killing allied paratroopers landing in Germany, closing universities and decimating intellectuals in dominated countries, were all falsely defended as retaliations for criminal acts against the German people or armed forces.

The three greatest atrocities, however—the systematic mercy killings of hapless victims, the deliberate starvation of Russian prisoners of war, and the expropriation, deportation, and extermination of the Jewish people—were kept secret from the majority of the German people. The reaction of those who heard of it did not indicate a limit of authority: "The *Führer* does not know these things, otherwise he would put a stop to it." Hitler himself drew a private line against violence incompatible with his charismatic authority. He refused to invite Himmler to his social parties by saying: "I need such policemen . . . but I don't like them."[95] But this personal dislike was not enough. When the mercy killings threatened to become a public scandal, Hitler was forced to stop this particular violence. Reluctantly, he had to admit that even dictatorial charisma did not legitimize deliberate killings of hapless victims for reasons of populational-racist policies.

Racist genocide continued as charismatically illegitimate campaigns. To be sure, the agents of extermination excused themselves with blind obedience and disciplinary authority. Commander Hoess of the Auschwitz extermination camp confessed subsequently: "It did not occur to me at all that I would be kept responsible. You see, in Germany it was understood that if something went wrong, then the man who gave the order was responsible."[96] While the political and military leaders were given detailed reports by Himmler on extermination, he declared emphatically "that the *Führer*'s name must never be linked with these deeds." Himmler assumed personal responsibility for the massacre by the SS. But at the same time he boasted that the extermination policy was "carried out . . . without our men and our leaders suffering the slightest damage to spirit and soul."[97] His reference was not to charismatic legitimacy but to Nazi ideology.

Instead of self-destruction of charisma, racial and imperialist violence coexisted with dictatorial charisma. There were three reasons for this coexistence. One was the veil of secrecy covering the despicable atrocities. The second was Hitler's belief in his creative God that called upon him to purify the German blood from any form of racial pollution. The third and most important reason was Hitler's particular ideology that replaced his charismatic message and that demanded of him the extermination of the racial enemy. In living up to this ideological obligation, but going far beyond dictatorial charisma, Hitler established a form of racist and eventually also of political despotism that is truly unique in modern history.

Since the arbitrary authority of this despotism was based upon his ideology, we will have to investigate the nature of his ideology. How could the same set of ideals provide the "message" for dictatorial charisma and simultaneously supply the guidelines for the most brutal kind of despotism, both operating in the same kind of political system?

# CHAPTER FOUR

# CHARISMA AND IDEOLOGY

COMMITMENT TO AN IDEOLOGY means believing in or worshipping of a certain set of values. Such a belief provides a guide for the actions of individuals. The same values turn from personal beliefs into guides of groups when many people share the same ideals. When personal beliefs become the points of orientation for others, the ideology becomes a social phenomenon. Max Weber expressed the social nature of values in the following words: "The orientation of value-rational action is distinguished . . . by its clearly self-conscious formulation of the ultimate values governing the action and the consistently planned orientation of its detailed course to these values. . . . Examples of such value-rational orientation would be the actions of persons who, regardless of possible cost to themselves, act to put into practice their convictions of what seems to them to be required by duty, honor, pursuit of beauty, or religious call, personal loyalty or the importance of some "cause" no matter in what it consists" (p.25).

Ideologies as "causes" become activated politically and socially in five different forms. First of all, certain ideals will be selected from the larger cause for realization in the immediate future. These are the so-called action programs promoted by the ideological believers. Then there are the fundamental principles, explicit or implicit in the ideology, that become major points of orientation and crystalize themselves in a distinct view of the world. The relevant values of these views will be turned into long-range goals and even plans to be implemented in the future. Moreover, ideals do find their bearers who hold the values, accept the goals, and engage in the corresponding actions. Interaction of the bearers often gives rise to an ideological group that constitutes "a voluntary association motivated by an adherence to a set of commonly held ultimate values" (p.41). Further, the internal structure and leadership of the group engenders an ideological authority that is legitimized by the belief in, and adherence to, the ultimate values. Finally, leaders and adherents feel a moral commitment to the immediate and ultimate goals that engender sentiments for worshipping the values and of devoting the personal life to their implementation, of turning the "cause" into a reality.

The resultant ideological movements differ in regard to leadership, content of ideals, and legitimizing authorities as well as attitudes to other ideologies and to the prevailing political regime. An ideological group may be headed primarily by an organizer or by an ideologist. The latter usually possesses the gift of personifying the values of the group, of enunciating most vividly the immediate and ultimate ideals, of formulating the goals and mobilizing voters for their acceptance, of articulating specific action programs, of pushing for their realization, and of inspiring actual and potential adherents to intensified efforts on behalf of the ideology. Organizers usually do not perform these functions themselves but distribute them among various kinds of leaders and thereby promote various forms of collective leadership.

Ideological movements enjoy a certain degree of choice in selecting their particular theories and ideals. The chosen set of ideals and corresponding principles may either be revolutionary or counterrevolutionary, progressive or restorative, evolutionary or resurrectional, liberal or conservative, pacifist or militarist, national or international in nature. Content of the chosen ideology is closely associated with certain attitudes toward other ideologies and toward the prevailing political regime. Revolutionary and counterrevolutionary ideals are intolerant and mutually exclusive of each other. Each of the other pairs of ideals is competitive to the other. Liberals try to persuade conservatives and vice versa, and seek to capture each other's voters. But revolutionaries may accept certain progressive and evolutionary ideals, while counterrevolutionaries may ally themselves with restorative or resurrectional ideals for certain phases of their development. The result of this interrelationship is an ideological structure that coexists with economic, political, social, military, and cultural structures in the same kind of society.[1]

In regard to ideological authority, the right to lead must be supported by those who are expected to obey. There occurs a special ground for ideological legitimacy. Decisive is the mutual belief in the validity of the ideology by the leader and led. It is the ideologist who is sought and confirmed as the leader of the group. Intensity of commitment, ability to articulate the goals, effectiveness of appeal, and capacity to implement the goals, constitute the criteria for selecting the ideological leader. Once chosen as the leader, he can enjoy conditional, unconditional, or arbitrary authority, as it has happened in charisma. Conditional authority depends upon the voluntary accord of the believers that the old or new leader fully meets the three qualifications for ideological leadership. Unconditional authority shifts the right to formulate the specific qualities to the leader himself who demands obedience of the believers to his command. In arbitrary authority the leader also obtains the power to determine the content of the ideology, decides freely upon the immediate and long term goals, and uses force to obtain obedience when it is not forthcoming voluntarily. In arbitrary authority, the leader enjoys the privilege of determining the acceptable beliefs and claims the right to engage in ideological imposition of his own ideals and oppression of any alternative or deviating ideals. Arbitrary authority is not supported by ideological legitimacy, but the ideology may serve as a self-justifier of the leader and his policies.

Finally, a distinction develops between status quo and advocate ideologies. Some ideologies take a positive or a negative position to the prevailing regime.[2] Positive ideologies express the rationale, expectations and hope of the existing regime or contain the arguments for defending the system against its attackers. Oppositional groups present the ideals that seek either to replace the prevailing regime, reform it in a progressive or evolutionary way, or restore it to a previous status.[3] In either supporting or challenging the prevailing regime, ideologies of mass movements act as agents for or against change in political systems. Change may be hindered by an effective positive ideology. The change may be forward looking to a new regime, whether revolutionary, counterrevolutionary or reformist, or moving backwards by either restoring a deteriorating system or achieving its resurrection.

Ideological diversity or a conflict-laden ideological structure creates serious problems for the interaction of charisma with ideology. As a rule, most democratic ideals are incompatible with dictatorial charisma. Conversely, dictatorial ideals are not convergent with democratic charisma. A theory of synergistic charisma has thus to distinguish between the two basic forms of democratic and dictatorial fusions. The process of fusing democratic charisma and corresponding ideals, as exemplified by Franklin D. Roosevelt, will be investigated in chapter 8. The interaction of dictatorial ideals with charisma, as personified by Hitler, will be the central topic of this chapter.

Even within these two kinds of fusions, the ideological and charismatic components were often not of the same relative significance. One ideology may be more relevant as a guide to action than the other. Indeed, we have to distinguish between two kinds of linkages within the democratic as well as dictatorial fusions. If the emphasis is placed primarily upon charisma, we shall speak of ideological charisma. Vice versa, when the ideology is predominant, then we are faced with charismatic ideology. While charismatic aspirants do often have a choice of acting mainly as an ideologist or a charismatic, charismatic giants can increase their power and create a stable authority only if they find an appropriate combination of ideology and charisma.

It is our conviction that Hitler exerted the greatest catastrophic impact upon public affairs of any one man in the twentieth century. It behooves us to know precisely how much of his power was attributable to his charisma, ideology, or organization.

## CHARISMATIC IDEOLOGY

The Nazi range of programs was so broad, including legitimate and illegitimate actions, that they could not all be guided and justified by one single and uniform ideology. It is our thesis that the Nazis promoted and believed in two distinct ideologies. Resurrection of the nation was one set of ideals; the other comprised a theory and ideals of a comprehensive counterrevolution. We shall first examine the relationship between charisma and national resurrection, and then turn to the interaction of charisma and counterrevolution.

National resurrection contained two sets of ideals, one generally accepted and the other heatedly disputed within the Nazi movement. Widely shared were the ideals of regaining full national sovereignty, rebuilding an independent armed force, replacing democracy by dictatorship, and creating a Greater Germany. The specific relationship between these goals and charisma will be discussed in the next section. The controversial set of ideals included a desired national bolshevism, a demand for economic socialism, getting back South Tyrol, and a practice of antiparliamentarism.[4] Each of these four ideals was strongly opposed by Hitler but vehemently proclaimed by some subleaders. How did this factional dispute about goals turn into a conflict between these ideals and charismatic authority?

National resurrection required an "awakening" of the national spirit and a regaining of national freedom from the shackles of the Treaty of Versailles. There was full agreement between Hitler and the dissidents in the party that the French hegemony over the Continent had to be broken. But there was disagreement on who would be the best ally in this fight. Dissident groups, led by Gregor and Otto Strasser, fought for an alliance with the Soviet Union, while Hitler insisted upon an alliance with Fascist Italy and an arrangement with Britain.

In response to the Treaty of Locarno of 1925, Gregor Strasser wrote an article on "Russia and We" in the official newspaper of the party. He rejected the treaty as an attempt to incorporate Germany into the front of the Western Allies whom he accused of seeking to invade the Soviet Union. In international affairs the national interests of Germany and Russia run parallel, he asserted, providing the basis for an alliance. The conflict between the respective ideologies could be minimized if the Soviet Union would drop its support of the German Communists, and Germany would not interfere in the internal affairs of the Soviet Union. Strasser formulated the slogan: Together with Russia against the West.[5] This Nazi version of "national bolshevism" was incorporated into a draft for the revising of the program of the NSDAP and accepted by a meeting of the dissidents in Hannover.

In response Hitler called a leadership conference in February 1926. In his speech of two hours, he rejected any form of collaboration with Russia. Greatest emphasis should be placed upon rebuilding German military power. Any German ally would have to be useful in the eventual defeat of France. Russia could not provide effective help because there were no common borders, nor was there an effective army or a reliable ruling class in the Soviet Union. Hitler's most telling argument was stated later: "If today Germany would conclude an alliance with Russia against the West, tomorrow Germany would become the great historical battlefield."[6] The official report of the conference emphasized the Jewish influence in the Soviet government and predicted that any alliance with the Communists would lead to the immediate political Bolshevization of Germany."[7] Instead of defending their position, the dissidents meekly withdrew their draft, and Hitler declared the program of the party of 1920 as eternally valid.

A similar dispute arose on the issue of South Tyrol. While point one of the party program called for a Greater Germany, Hitler proposed in a separate pamphlet that South Tyrol should permanently belong to Italy in order to provide a basis for an alliance with Fascist Italy. Germany and Italy could realize their imperialist ambitions only if they could jointly defeat France. Hitler implicitly proposed a twofold trade-off. Italy should retain South Tyrol in return for supporting Austria's incorporation into Germany; Italy should receive the right to control the Mediterranean Sea while Germany would be able to get its living space in Eastern Europe. While Hitler disguised these intentions after 1930 and did not publish his second book, he took strong actions against his opponents and removed all critics of his foreign policy from influential positions in party and state.[8]

The party officially demanded national socialism and sought to sever the links between socialism and internationalism. But there was no agreement on the economics of national socialism. On April 13, 1928, Hitler single-handedly revised point 17 of the party program by declaring that "the NSDAP fully accepts the principle of private property." Confiscation of land for public purposes without compensation was limited by Hitler to "Jewish real estate speculators."[9] This view was rejected by the dissidents in the party. In 1929, Otto Strasser published his "14 theses of the German revolution." In addition to supernationalism and racism, Strasser took a definite position on national socialism: "The German revolution rejects the individualistic economic system of capitalism, the elimination of which is an indispensable condition for the success of our revolution. We believe most devoutly in the corporative economic system of socialism, the purpose of which is to satisfy the needs of the nation, not to accumulate wealth and profits."[10] Strasser aimed at a significant reform of capitalist property. Of the available capital of private enterprises, 49 percent should be retained by private owners, 41 percent should be taken over by the state, and 10 percent be given to workers. Of the realized profits, 51 percent should be kept by the owners, while 49 percent should be distributed among the workers of corporations.[11] There was thus an open conflict on the economics of socialism within the party.

The dispute culminated in a two-day private debate between Hitler and Otto Strasser in May 1930. Hitler accused Strasser of deviation from the party line: "The tone of your papers is a public disgrace. Your articles infringe upon the elementary laws of discipline. They are an insult to the Party program." Strasser countered, "If you wish to preserve the capitalist regime, Herr Hitler, you have no right to talk of socialism. For our supporters are socialists, and our program demands the socialization of private enterprise." Hitler objected, "That word socialism is the trouble. . . . I have never said that all enterprises should be socialized. On the contrary, I have maintained that we might socialize enterprises prejudicial to the interest of the nation. Unless they are so guilty, I would consider it a crime to destroy essential elements in our economic life." When Strasser referred to the unresolved conflict between capital and labor, Hitler retorted, "Profit sharing and the right of workers to be consulted are Marxist principles. I consider that the right to exercise influence on private enterprise should be conceded only to the state, directed by the superior class."[12]

The record of Hitler's action reveals a clear and unflinching stand on the issue of capitalism versus socialism. In 1925, Hitler successfully prevented his party from voting for a referendum that called for the expropriation of properties held by the royal princes. In 1928, he turned against the "eternal" program of its party by dropping expropriation of land without compensation for Aryans and committed himself and the party to the principle of private property. In 1930, he emphatically declared that if he would come to power he would leave the Krupp Works alone. "Do you think me crazy enough to want to ruin Germany's great industry?"[13] In 1931, Hitler compelled the representatives of his party in parliament to withdraw their own bill that had demanded the nationalization of private banks. In 1936, Hitler decreed a law that threatened the death sentence for any businessman who kept foreign currency abroad, but the law was never implemented. In 1937, the steel industrialists opposed the large-scale exploitation of domestic iron ore, but Hitler merely imposed a forced sale of the ore deposits against compensation. In 1939, when Thyssen left Germany and denounced the war Hitler did not nationalize these properties but had them administered as a private trust. In 1942, Director Reusch refused to obey certain war orders; he was deprived of his managerial rights but his own and the company's properties remained in private hands.[14]

Of course, politically and ideologically sensitive property was not respected. Properties of the forbidden political parties, of the trade unions, and of the consumer cooperatives were confiscated by the party without any compensation. Property of Jews was partly taken away and then expropriated outright in 1938. Most of the private newspaper concerns were put under such pressure that most of them became property of the party or *Gauleiters*.[15] Since expropriation of capitalist property did not occur in Germany proper, one must conclude that Hitler acted as an ideologist in regard to the institutions of private capitalism. Private property and profits, private enterprise and entrepreneurial initiative, and even "German" capitalism as a whole, constituted for him intrinsic values that had to be respected and cherished for their own sake.

Sanctity of property established a causal relationship between Hitler's capitalistic beliefs and the support of the Nazis by big business. Hitler's belief in the sanctity of private property lent credence to his promises that he would assist particular private investment projects as soon as he would come to power. As soon as Hitler coupled his belief in private property with the promise to destroy the independent trade unions, which he did in July 1932, leaders of the heavy industries used all their influence with von Hindenburg to get Hitler appointed as chancellor of the *Reich*.[16] After

Hitler's ascent to power, Gustav Krupp von Hallbach created the so-called Hitler Donation which collected contributions from trade associations on a regular basis, that were made available to Hitler personally, throughout the Nazi regime. Hitler's belief in the capitalist institutions supplied the reason, the political and financial support of big business constituted the means for the de facto alliance between many leading industrialists and the Nazi party.

This similarity of beliefs was most clearly expressed by Hitler in his confidential meeting with business leaders in February 1933. He carefully linked private property with the unrestricted right to inheritance, with private initiative and achievement of private enterprise, with an ethical legitimation of private power.[17] This was also the theme of another speech to the industrialists in 1932: "An ethical justification of private property is possible if I have reason to believe that men differ in their capacities. It is then sensible to leave wealth in the hands of their originators. . . . Lower income indicates that the less able men are not qualified to manage the property created by the exceptional man."[18] Hitler thus justified private property in terms fully compatible with a capitalist ethic and with the charismatic belief in the exceptional personality. Capitalism and charisma were not incompatible, but a chasm separated economic socialism from Fascist charisma.

In acting as an ideologist, Hitler scored a threefold success. In rejecting national bolshevism, antifascism, and prosocialism, Hitler committed the party to antibolshevism, to a pro-Italian foreign policy, and to support of private property and enterprise.[19] In winning this ideological struggle, Hitler became the selector of goals and the determinator of the rightist direction of his movement. In dissipating leftist sentiments and defending private property, Hitler prepared the conditions for the subsequent alliance with reactionary political parties and industrialists. But the belief in the capitalist institutions was stated only in confidential meetings of businessmen because in his propaganda he rooted for anticapitalism and garnered much middle class support.[20] Nor did Hitler openly reject socialism. He opposed ideas of economic socialism within the party, but at the same time he tolerated the ideals of social peace in industrial relations, social honor, and status equality of workers, sponsored and promoted by the Labor Front. The propaganda of these ideals by the social Nazis also helped to obtain mass support among workers during the depression.[21]

What was the role of charismatic authority in these ideological disputes? Why did Hitler not use his persuasive powers to lure the dissidents to his views? The answer is that he tried but failed. In his long discussions with Otto Strasser in 1930, Hitler sought to placate his opponent: " 'You have been an officer, and you see that your brother accepts my discipline, even if he doesn't always see eye-to-eye with me. Take a lesson from him; he is a fine man.' Hitler seized my hand, as he had done two years before. His voice was choked with sobs, and tears flowed down his cheeks."[22] There was thus a clear charismatic appeal designed to emotionally mesmerize the will of the doubter. But Strasser's insistence upon an ideological agreement revealed an astonishing fact: Hitler's charisma did not work with convinced ideological opponents.

Faced with this refusal to obey his disciplinary authority, Hitler reacted in a charismatic fashion. He refused to discuss the issues further and terminated the debate within the party. No ideological reconciliation took place. Rejected ideals could only be retained as strictly private beliefs. Hitler acted decisively as soon as this restriction was forgotten. Most difficult to take was the giving up of South Tyrol. In May 1937, the Labor Front disobeyed the order by publishing a map which included South Tyrol as a part of Greater Germany. On Hitler's orders, the whole issue of the magazine had to be recalled and destroyed, followed by an apology to Mussolini. Hess instructed all party officials to cease interfering in any way with Hitler's foreign policy. The imposed party line thus was clearly extended to crucial ideological beliefs. Subsequently, the two dictators swore eternal friendship and mutual solidarity.[23]

In the absence of ideological reconciliation, Hitler achieved ideological conformity by using his natural and supernatural charisma. Doubters were subjected to charismatic appeals; their wills were mesmerized and their private beliefs undermined. Ideological disagreements were effectively minimized and the wisdom of the leader so glorified that most doubters dropped their own beliefs and gladly accepted the one of the leader. Emotional union of natural charisma effectively legitimized Hitler's ideological authority.

In terms of his supernatural calling, Hitler interpreted his charismatic authority as including the privilege to decide unilaterally which ideals and action programs had to be rejected, postponed, or activated in particular situations. He arrogated to himself a veto power of designating certain ideals as fundamental, as expandable, or as openly condemnable. He even exercised the right to reverse himself as in the 1939 contract with Stalin, but still demanded ideological obedience because of his superior wisdom and genius. Supernatural charisma embodied in the leader thus gave rise to a unilateral process of decision making: he alone could know what was best for party, state, and people and everyone was bound by his will and decisions.

If there would have been recourse to ideological legitimacy, then the leader would have been bound by the content of the ideals, and the beliefs of the leader and led would have been substantively identical. But in determining unilaterally the meaning of the ideals Hitler substituted discipline for identical beliefs. At every possible occasion, Hitler emphasized the role of discipline and linked it with punishment. He told his county leaders in 1937 that if "anyone tries to undermine the principles of discipline, such as putting up democratic claims, then one has to tell him: 'Stop! Cease immediately, otherwise you will be thrown out [of the party].' If this is not enough, then you will be thrown somewhere else [concentration camp].''[24] Privilege of policy selection, veto power, and disciplinary punishment were the selectively employed devices that enforced ideological conformity and insured ideological indoctrination. It was in negatively delimiting the ideological mission and of employing natural charisma as the justifier, and disciplinary charisma as the enforcer, that there developed in the Nazi regime the new phenomenon of a charismatically sanctioned ideology.

## IDEOLOGICAL CHARISMA

At the center of the resurrectional ideology stood three goals. A German mass army had to be reestablished; all restrictions on German sovereignty had to be removed; Austria and Sudetenland had to be incorporated into a Greater Germany.[25] These and similar goals were infused by love of the fatherland and by chauvinism. "We National Socialists do love our Fatherland above everything else and will not tolerate any other idol. We know of just *one* interest and that is the one of our people."[26] Internally, this love led to the claim of a classless society in the form of a people's community. The military purpose was to reestablish a German army by imposing compulsory recruitment of all young men unilaterally in 1935. A year later Hitler sent German troops into the demilitarized zone of Rhineland as a surprise attack. This march induced Hitler to proclaim: "In this hour we bend our knees and beg the Almighty that he will give us the strength to fight and win the struggle for the freedom, honor, peace, and future of our people."[27] In undertaking these civilian and military actions, Hitler effectively fused his resurrectional ideology with his providential charisma. The chauvinist belief specified the ideological mission, from which he deduced his actionable programs. His success in outsmarting the governments of the Allied powers was approved by providential blessing. Changing the military power constellation was thus the first proof of the effectiveness of ideological charisma which was also presented as a struggle for freedom, honor, and peace. There is little doubt that this ideological charisma was widely approved by the German people who thus lent a voluntary legitimacy to these actions.[28]

The same was true for the goal of incorporating Austria and Sudetenland into the *Reich*. The first point of the Nazi program of February 1920 bluntly claimed: "We demand the union of all Germans into one Greater Germany on the basis of national self-determination of all people."[29] When the days for action came, Hitler delivered a speech to the submissive parliament that gave a charismatic justification for his coming forceful action, but it was put into dictatorial terms. The man who dutifully "takes over the leadership of the people is not responsible for parliamentary procedures . . . is not bound by laws or democratic institutions, but has to follow exclusively his assigned mission. Whoever disturbs this mission, is the enemy of the people. . . ."[30]

The march into Austria took on the form of a national liberation and aroused great ideological enthusiasm in Germany and Austria. The Nazis regarded it as the realization of their resurrectional ideology. Conservatives and nationalists interpreted the Austrian absorption as completing Bismarck's work, of transforming little Germany into Greater Germany.[31] Both official churches celebrated the incorporation of Austria by ringing their bells—in the words of the Catholic bishop of Regensburg—"as an expression of joy over the return of our Austrian brothers to the Greater German Reich."[32] There was thus widespread joy on both sides of the border over the act of unification—although it was accomplished by ultimatum and military invasion. Conservatives, nationalists, and churchly groups thus surrendered joyously their restorative ideal of regaining the Germany of 1914 to Hitler's national resurrection.

In addition to justifying his cunning surprise ideologically, Hitler also employed two other legitimizers. One was in the style of a charismatic Caesar. Speaking in Munich three weeks after the incorporation, Hitler exclaimed in a mass meeting: "This miracle [of unification] was accomplished by the German people themselves because they followed me with a devout heart year for year. I trust you so fully, you German folk, that I can say to the world: Not I did complete this act of unification but 75 millions dearly wanted it."[33] Accordingly, he called for a plebiscite both in Germany and Austria. The question on the ballot reveals the charismatic intent: "Do you pledge yourself to your *Führer* Adolf Hitler and thus to the reunification of Austria with the German Reich?"[34] Officially, not less than 99.5 percent said yes. Just one Catholic bishop refused to participate in this "holy acclamation." The Nazis regarded this as an "act of disloyalty," and the bishop was banished from his diocese by the Gestapo. Significantly, his refusal was not directed against the ideology or practice of Greater Germany, but he was punished for his protest against the idolatry of the leader. Although by law voting was a voluntary act, disbelief in Hitler's charismatic quality was thus punishable by violence.

The final legitimizer was Hitler's particular providential charisma. In his proclamation to the party congress of September 1938, Hitler celebrated the Greater Germany in the following words: "The highest gratitude we owe to the Almighty who has blessed the return of Austria to the new Reich. It was through his grace that the new Reich could achieve such a success which was possible without shedding the blood of our German comrades. May the German people never forget that this deed was attained only because the German nation was united through National Socialism."[35] Providential blessing thus was linked in the same breath with praise for the unifying influence of Nazi ideology. His providential charisma did not stand alone nor did it function as the single short range cause for the incorporation of Austria. For Hitler, Greater Germany was primarily the result of his ideological mission, his own masterful foreign policy, the increased power of the German armed forces, and of his military alliance with Mussolini.[36] Indoctrination of the German-speaking people in Nazi ideology and the providential blessing of all the deeds of the leader and the Caesarian acclamation by his people were seen as supplementary approvals for the rise of a Greater Germany.

There was thus an intermingling of two kinds of charismata and one definite ideological goal. The ideology of Greater Germany set the specific goal to be attained by party, state, and army. From this goal were inferred the two policies of incorporating Austria and Sudetenland. Providential blessing gave Hitler the inner certainty and assurance that his indoctrination with Nazi ideology, his ultimatum to the Austrian anti-Nazi government, and the final military invasion of Austria would be successful. The "holy acclamation" in the style of a Caesar articulated the charismatic disposition of the people, who were given the opportunity to affirm the leader's foreign policy and to rejoice with him in the fulfillment of their charismatic longing as well as in the realization of their ideological dream. The result of these interactions was Hitler's ideological charisma.

Incorporation of one ideological goal into the charisma required two important reinterpretations of the ideology. Hitler was willing to associate his goal with the national-liberal demand for a Greater Germany by the revolutionists of 1848. Speaking in Frankfurt on March 31, 1938, Hitler said: "I have come to this grand city at a great historical moment, ninety years after the attempt was made here to give to the German people its own Reich."[37] Quickly he added that this dream has now been fulfilled by his own actions so that nobody could draw the conclusion that current Nazi policies were linked with the liberal ideology of the past. The second interpretation was politically more relevant. Up to the takeover of the Sudetenland, Hitler had justified his policy of Greater Germany with the principle of national self-determination so as to minimize resistance to his policy in foreign countries. After the incorporation of the Sudetenland, however, this liberal principle was replaced by a folkish one. Hitler's speeches for a "holy acclamation" by the Sudeten-Germans culminated in his enunciation of the Third Reich: "The birthday document of the Second Reich was signed by the German princes. The birthday document of the Third Reich will be affirmed by the German people."[38] This symbolic act of establishing the Third *Reich* presented simultaneously an ideological and charismatic achievement. Incorporation of the Sudetenland also constituted the end of Hitler's practice to employ successfully and peacefully his resurrectional ideals as a reliable guide for Nazi foreign policy.[39]

Hitler already combined passion and ideology in his first book. Emotions were "the great magnetic force which alone attracts the great masses who always respond to the compelling strength that emanates from the absolute faith in the ideology put forward, combined with an indomitable zest to fight for and defend these ideals."[40] Faith in the ideology was linked with natural charisma in the first years of his regime, when the unity of ideological belief was reenforced by an emotional bond between the leader and followers. Hitler expressed this sense of belonging together at the party congress of 1936 in the following words: "Not everyone of you can see me, nor can I see each of you. But I feel you and you can feel me. We are now melted into one. It is very wonderful for me to be your leader. Who can be more proud of his followers than he who knows that his comrades are motivated by nothing but pure idealism. What has brought you in my spell . . . what could I possibly give you? One thing has united us: the fight for a great common ideal."[41] Such a feeling of an emotional bond and shared idealism gave a new direction to the life of the believers in the ideology. This new meaning for the participants in an ideological movement was expressed by Hitler at the party congress of 1937: "What would my life be without you? That you have found me, that you have believed in me, has given your life a new meaning, has placed before you a new task. That I have found you has given me a new life and has really made possible my fight."[42] These utterances of Hitler constituted the emotional climax of his annual speeches to the "guard of the national socialist revolution" and to the Hitler Youth. They reveal his innermost feelings for, and his assessment of, the Nazi movement for his *Reich*. Without specifically saying so, Hitler was combining natural charisma with his providential charisma.

What was the role of the ideology in this relationship? If Hitler would have regarded the ideology as the common cause for the realization of which leader and followers devoted their lives, then he would in effect have claimed ideological legitimacy for his authority. In such a case, the leader would have been the enunciator of the new ideals; he would have personified the ideals but would always have been the servant of the ideology. The followers, in turn, would have felt an emotional bond between themselves and the leader because he most eloquently could express the longing for the new society. The leader and the followers would mold their lives according to the mission contained in their ideology. Did Hitler grant the ideology such an exalted position?

The answer is clearly in the negative. In 1930, the issue of whether the ideology was superior to the leader became a point of dispute between Hitler and the Nazi dissidents. On April 27, 1930, Herbert Blank published an article in which he inferred a law from German history: "It is an essential part of German greatness that the loyalty to the idea was always placed above the loyalty to the personality." Blank regarded it as "a great conceit to believe that Germans would even then follow the leader if he should betray the idea." In such a case "the betrayed gray army would . . . march over the leader so as to rescue the idea."[43] Hitler was furious. Rosenberg published an article on "Leader and Idea," printed in all Nazi newspapers, in which he asserted that Hitler personified the idea to such an extent that both had become inseparable. In a heated discussion with Otto Strasser who had published the article of Blank, Hitler declared the superiority of the idea as "bombastic nonsense." Such an interpretation "would lead to the dissolution of our organization which is based upon discipline. I have no intention of allowing our organization to be disrupted by a crazy scribbler."[44]

For Hitler, discipline within the party meant loyalty and obedience to himself personally. He saw in himself not only the sole enunciator but also the creator of Nazi ideology. Intellectually and emotionally, he incorporated the ideological mission into his charisma. Nazi ideology and movement were included into his requests for providential blessing. "It was not the meaning of providential approval, which has accompanied the wonderful growth of our movement, that all our struggle should in the last act count for nothing. The Almighty has shown us the wonderful way of success and he will bless our actions in the future."[45] There thus arose a genuine fusion between charisma and ideology which created an ideological charisma.

Being able to shift between ideological and charismatic legitimizers brought Hitler some great advantages. Emphasis upon the ideology of national rejuvenation enabled him to overcome barriers to his dictatorial rule. Restorative and traditional beliefs could be linked with his resurrectional ideal so that a part of his ideological mission was also accepted by nationalists and conservatives. Churchmen miffed by the claim of incarnation could still accept Hitler as the great leader because they could readily adopt some version of the ideology of national rejuvenation. Emphasis upon providential blessing or ecstatic feeling also drew those into his spell who were indifferent or allergic to any intellectual form of legitimacy. The mixture of ideology with intuition increased the certainty of his own expectations while making others more uncertain as to what line of action could be expected of him next. Deliberate cunning was occasionally combined with intuition. Staged irregularity in his behavior was to confuse not only potential assassins but also foreign statesmen.[46] Actions of a strict ideologist would have been more effectively predictable and more readily anticipated by counteraction. Hitler was so greatly convinced of the advantage of surprise that he tried to keep secret certain lines of his own ideals.

Beyond those immediate advantages, fusion of the two subtypes of appeal permitted Hitler to avoid Max Weber's law of a return to everyday rule. Including the ideological mission into his charisma[47] sustained Hitler's claim that power did not corrupt or deter him from building up his Third *Reich*. Renewal of ecstasy and enthusiasm maintained, if not strengthened, the devotion of the followers. Hitler Donation and subsidies by the state made the Nazi party independent from most pressures of economic interest groups. Charismatic and ideological fusion thus additionally explain why mass fervor did not subside as the movement turned into a successful political regime or why the Nazis could not be "tamed" as they took over state offices and carried the burden of responsibility for the affairs of the state.

In linking ideology with charisma, Hitler overcame the greatest handicap of charismatic authority, its instability. As Weber emphasized, "by its very nature, the existence of charismatic authority is specifically unstable." The longer the rule of the personal leader lasts, the weaker it tends to become. Eventually, charisma "becomes efficacious only in short-lived mass emotions of incalculable effects, as on elections and similar occasions" (p. 1146). Clearly, Hitler was able to overcome this tendency towards instability. He achieved charismatic stability through the renewal of the emotions of natural charisma, through his personality cult, through his linking of the resurrectional ideology with his providential charisma. Rather than diluting the genuine charisma, the ideological mission not only provided a source of actionable programs, but also strengthened the charismatic authority which was legitimized simultaneously by the duty to obey and by the sharing of the indoctrinated ideology. Both legitimizers reenforced each other thereby increasing enormously Hitler's power as leader.

What were the dictatorial components in this cumulative charisma and its link with ideology? Linkage is inevitable in a dictatorial situation in which: (1) ideological competition is impossible because all other ideologies have been suppressed; (2) indoctrination of the official ideology moulds public opinion; (3) the leader is simultaneously the highest ideologist and *the* bearer of charisma; (4) personal indifference to the official ideology is not permissible and thus punishable; and (5) personality cult relies both on charisma and ideology. After the first phase of development, all of these features existed both in German and Italian fascism.

## INTERNAL COUNTERREVOLUTION AND CHARISMA

Why did the Nazis develop two different ideologies? The original version of the resurrectional ideals was stated in the party program in 1920 and then enlarged by an intensified anti-Semitism. The idea of a counterrevolution in the form of trying to overthrow the Weimar Republic developed during the French invasion of the Ruhr and the hyperinflation of the stormy year of 1923. For their illegal putsch the Nazis possessed a limited but definite action program. The constitution of Weimar was to be annulled; an embargo was to be imposed upon all bank deposits; all major enemies were to be herded into concentration camps. But there was as yet no counterrevolutionary ideology.[48]

It so happened that Hitler's claim of possessing charismatic qualities and of formulating his counterrevolutionary ideology came shortly after the abortive putsch. One was conceived as being in the presence of the other. Hitler told his court: "The man who feels called upon to govern a people has no right to say: If you want me or summon me, I will cooperate. No, it is his duty to step forward."[49] This sense of a calling became linked with his desire to formulate a theory as a guide for himself and his party. "Without my imprisonment, 'My Battle' would never have been written. This available time offered the opportunity to arrive at certain theories about which I had only some instinctive inkling."[50] It was thus more a theory than an ideal that was to provide his political mission. Those who knew him before and after his prison term noticed a distinct change in the man. Hans Frank, his lawyer, designated "the year of 1924 as the decisive turning point in the world-shaking life of Hitler." While he never regarded himself as an intellectual, he was very proud of his book. In 1938 Hitler said: "I would not like to change any of its ideas. . . . One thing is clear. If I had known in 1924 that I would be chancellor of the Reich, I would never have written the book."[51] There was thus a note of regret as if he had revealed too much of his mission.

Hitler was in search of a theory that would provide the core for his ideology and give a definite direction to his charisma. Hitler's counterrevolutionary view of the world included his "laws of nature" and two sets of ideals and actions. Laws and ideals were used to set goals of actions and to justify an internal as well as an external counterrevolution. All three can be presented schematically as in table 4.1.

While there was no clear dividing line between theory, ideals, and actions, Hitler saw in his laws of nature definite causal relationships that were imposed upon men.

TABLE 4.1. THEORIES, IDEALS, AND ACTIONS OF COUNTERREVOLUTION.

| Theories | Ideals and Actions | |
| --- | --- | --- |
| | Internal | External |
| Social Darwinism | Inherent Inequality | Racial Purity |
| Law of Population | Creative Personality | Purification by War |
| Living Space | *Führerprinzip* | Series of *Blitzkriegs* |
| Racial Purity | Party Monopoly | Charismatic War Lord |
| | Destruction of Democracy | Rule of the Superior Race |
| | Extermination of Marxism | Exploitation of Occupied Countries |
| | Imposed Ideology | Racial Expropriation |
| | Perpetual Coercion | Extermination of Inferiors |
| | | Racial World Empire |

Ideals were normative values that had to be in accord with the laws but designated a commitment for believers.[52] Goals and actions had to implement both the laws and the ideals. Rather than separating theories from ideals, we shall discuss both under the headings of internal and external counterrevolutions and examine the link of each with charisma.

Theoretically, both kinds of counterrevolutions were necessary and unavoidable because of the Darwinian law of the eternal struggle. Available opportunities are too scarce to satisfy all the needs of men so that the division of goods and services generates conflict inevitably. "Man must realize that a fundamental law of necessity reigns throughout the whole realm of nature and that his existence is subject to the law of eternal struggle and strife."[53] In the multitude of the people, "the two most powerful drives of men, those of hunger and love, presuppose for their satisfaction an unending struggle." His very biological and psychological nature forces man to conform to the fundamental law. Thus ruthless competition prevails among men who are not guided by any principles of humanity. Force, not ideals, rules the world. "Through all the centuries force and power were the determining factors. . . . Only force rules." The strong find it necessary to impose their will upon the weak. Powerful states and strong individuals are morally better than weaklings. "There is only power that creates justice."[54] Strength and force together create rights. Always before God and the world, "the stronger has the right to carry through what he wills."[55] Behind natural law there stood God's will. Implicitly, the charismatic leader is the executor of this will of the Almighty who has created nature.

The theory of the eternal struggle was linked with the ideology of the great personality, the rule of the party, indoctrination, and the extermination of Marxism. "Whatever goal man has reached is due to his originality and brutality. The basis of all development is the creative urge of the individual, not the votes of the majorities. The genius of the individual is decisive, not the spirit of the masses."[56] Charismatic quality is thus also claimed for superior human abilities. "Every deed of a nation, in each and every field, is the result of the creative act of a personality. . . . The great man alone has been the generator of human progress." Belief in the creative personality, the genius, became a second reason for Hitler to proclaim his leadership. "Nations have to arrive at a decision. They must either elect representatives or choose great personalities. Both are incompatible with each other. Great things have always been created on this earth by great men, but their accomplishments have frequently been destroyed by majorities."[57] Democracy exerts a leveling effect upon the quality of leadership which leads to political inefficiency. "The greatness of a nation is not counted as the sum of all actions but as the sum of the extraordinary achievements."[58]

Condemned democracy was linked with racial inferiority and Marxism. Democracy "is the belief of all inferior or racially mixed bastards as well as of the Jews. Such a belief leads necessarily to a racial chaos. . . . to a bastardization and mongrelization of all races. The general decline of all racial values enables the nonassimilated Hebrew slowly to rise to a position of the master over the world."[59] As an ideal of the racially inferior, democracy as a political system leads thus to the domination by the racially intact Jewry. Additionally, democracy is also responsible for the rise of Marxism. "The democracy of the Western states is the forerunner of Marxism which could not have developed without democratic institutions. Democracy provides the fertile soil for this [Marxist-Jewish] pestilence that spreads like a disease over the world. Parliamentarism, as the external form of democracy, is the most monstrous institution"[60] that greatly facilitates the growth of Marxism and Judaism. Democracy had thus to be destroyed first *before* the two arch enemies of Hitler could be eliminated.

The rule of making decisions by majority must be replaced by the leadership principle. Hitler's formulation of this idea of the *Führerprinzip* is well known: "Authority of every leader over those below and responsibility of everyone below to the leader above." This rule was to be applied to all governmental bodies, from the village to the *Reich*. "There shall be no body of representatives but only councils of advisors who assist the elected leader. He alone assigns them their specific tasks. The leader assumes full responsibility for all actions just as does the top executive in the corporation."[61] All others have no right to participate in major decisions but must follow the leader obediently.

The same rule of unquestioned personal authority must be applied to the Nazi party. In the party, "the ruling principle is: Never must a resolution be passed by majority decision. Never! The leader in charge of special sessions listens to the various expressions of opinion and then decides by himself. There will be no decision for which one man does not assume full responsibility. That is the ruling principle of our movement."[62]

Strangely, but typically, Hitler did not see this leadership rule as the most extreme form of dictatorship. Neither his theory nor his ideology contains a specific rationale for dictatorship. The rule of an oligarchic group headed by the leader was called either the aristocratic principle or true Germanic democracy. In his main book he defined the latter "as the free choice of the leader [among alternative policies] who assumes full responsibility for what he does or does not do."[63] In later speeches, however, Hitler placed himself above the party. "The party stands as the living organism of the people behind the leadership. The party is the people. . . . The party as an organization of picked men thus fulfills all the conditions necessary for a government closely bound up with the people because the whole leadership, which determines the actions of the state . . . runs from base to summit through the movement."[64] It was in this disguised form that Hitler described the dictatorship of the single party.

The party arrogated to itself the task of educating and indoctrinating the people. The ideological aim of the party was to "stamp upon Germany the new *Weltanschauung* so durably that it does become the element of cohesion among the German people." Acceptance of Nazi ideals was not voluntary. "National socialism as an ideology is bound . . . to be intolerant, that means to . . . insist upon the rightness of its views and of its policies in all circumstances. . . . When a nation is already bewildered . . . it is only the harshest principles and iron resolution which can unite the people into a single body capable of resistance—and thereby able to be successful in politics."[65] Dictatorship by a single party was thus expected to lead to ideological indoctrination and domination over the people.

Hitler wanted to derive programs of action for his internal counterrevolution. The ideological features were thus regarded as articles of belief that were self-evident for him. Creative personality, superior leadership, unquestioned authority in the party, its political monopoly, and universally valid ideals of the inequality of men were all seen as binding values. These could not be tested, but had to be believed. One purpose of formulating the ideology was to identify the acceptable values to be believed in and to establish their relative priority. The other was to identify the negative and positive programs of action to be implemented by party and troopers.

Negative actions—from the point of view of Nazi ideology—were to be taken against Marxism, Democracy, and the related ideologies. The internal counterrevolution began on February 28, 1933, one month after Hitler's appointment as chancellor. The burning of the *Reichstag* was used as an excuse for suspending all civil liberties. Without possessing any reliable evidence, the Nazis blamed the Communists for burning the parliamentary building. In Goering's words, "This is the beginning of the Communist revolt."[66] About four thousand Communists were arrested and thrown into concentration camps or torture chambers. Justification of this violence was that the ever watchful Nazis had restored law and order. In Hitler's words: "The Communists before us dominated the streets and public places, and imposed a criminal terror upon the people. Now we have restored security, peace, and order. This was the deed of my storm troopers."[67]

On May 3, 1933, came the unprovoked but violent occupation of all the buildings of independent trade unions and consumer cooperatives, the confiscating of their properties, arrest of their officers, and installing of Nazis in the compulsory Labor Front. The justification for this takeover was the asserted corruption and misdirection of the workers by union leaders. Consequently, Hitler gave an ideological justification: "Marxism could not be allowed to present itself as an economic movement for the benefits of laborers."[68]

The multiparty system was destroyed in July 1933. Political parties were forbidden or they dissolved themselves under threat of violence by Nazi troopers. Already in January 1932 Hitler said: "The middle groups will be hacked to pieces and destroyed. The age of compromise will find its end. International bolshevism will be checked in Germany by the powerful movement of National Socialism. The Almighty Himself by His gracious will creates the necessary condition for the salvation of our people. By destroying the lukewarm in the middle, He wants us to gain victory."[69] In claiming providential blessing for his ultimate victory, destruction of the multiple party system was indirectly justified by providential charisma.

There was finally the elimination of the various forms of democratically elected officials in states, provinces, cities, and villages. This action was based upon the dictatorial decree of February 28, 1933. The central government was authorized to take over the powers of any state government temporarily "if it does not take the necessary measures for reestablishing law and order."[70] The authority for this purge was deduced from a pretended "Law and Order" legitimacy.

There thus follows an important inference on the justification of this internal counterrevolution.[71] Three different grounds of legitimacy were given to justify this counterrevolutionary violence. One was a fictitious, legal legitimacy. The Nazis claimed to have protected the state against a nonexisting Communist revolt or falsely removed state governments for not upholding "law and order." The counterrevolutionaries passed a "law for the protection of the national state" and destroyed democracy under this "legal" cover.

For the Nazis themselves, there was an ideological legitimacy that justified violence. It was in the name of the counterrevolutionary ideals that the Nazis destroyed the trade unions, eliminated all political parties, and imposed their ideology also on non-Nazis. For Hitler himself, however, his actions "against the national decay" were charismatically legitimized. "The parties of class hatred may be convinced that my determination to eliminate them will be unlimited so long as the Almighty gives me life and energy."[72] Ideological and charismatic legitimacies thus supported and reenforced each other in the internal counterrevolution, but both were also disguised by a legal legitimacy, by the defense of "law and order." Leader and paladins justified their internal counterrevolution by the charismatic, ideological, and legal legitimacies.

Adding legal legitimacy brought the Nazis two great advantages. In defending law and order, a significant number of the SA divisions acted as an auxiliary police, enjoying the benevolent neutrality of the regular army. Counterrevolutionary violence did not breed the counterviolence of the armed forces, avoiding Weber's law of the unintended destruction of the original agents of violence. Also, disguising the counterrevolution as a defense of "law and order" and political violence as police power enabled the members of the upper middle classes to be either indifferent to or approve of Nazi violence. Neither group found it necessary to protest against Nazi tortures and murders because the victims deserved their punishment for "attacking" the prevailing law and order. In tolerating the counterrevolution, these groups could continue their alliance without as yet approving of Hitler's charismatic authority.

## IDEOLOGICAL SCHISM AND CHARISMA

In emphasizing his ideological mission, instead of a divine one, Hitler regarded his ideology as a binding commitment for himself and his followers. He insisted that "ideologies proclaim their infallibility."[73] Any deviation from or schism of his ideology could thus easily be interpreted as a disbelief in the charismatic quality of the leader. Nevertheless, there occurred two ideological conflicts in the first phase of the Nazi regime. The one culminated in the purge of the SA leaders in June 1934, and the other in the dismissal of the leading generals in February 1938. What was the relationship between these ideological conflicts and the charismatic leadership?

While there was full agreement on the political counterrevolution, there was a serious disagreement on the military counterrevolution among Nazi leaders. The most conspicuous proponent of a military upheaval was Röhm, the chief of the SA. He confidentially said to another Nazi late in 1933: "Adolf knows exactly what I want, I have told him many times. [There should be]no recasting of the monarchic army. Are we revolutionaries or not? . . . If we are, then something new has to develop similar to the mass army of the French revolution."[74] A Nazi army, ousting the generals, was to be the core of the then widely expected "second revolution" by the Nazi storm troopers.

It so happened that Hitler was opposed to a military counterrevolution. Already in 1928 Hitler expressed his conviction that the coming war could be executed and won only by a modern mass army, highly trained and equipped for modern warfare. "The present *Reichswehr* has to provide the framework for the coming [compulsory] mass army."[75] This view was repeated before the German Supreme Court in 1930 under oath: "Out of the present *Reichswehr* will grow the army of the German people."[76] In getting the generals and SA leaders together at a joint meeting in August 1933, Hitler formulated a principle for the future cooperation and division of tasks between these organizations. The regular army "is the sole bearer of the arms of the nation; the SA is responsible for the political education of the nation."[77] By subsequently appointing Röhm as a minister and member of the secret defense council, Hitler aimed at a coordination of the respective tasks of the military and semimilitary organizations, limiting the SA to the political education of the recruits prior to their military training.

But Röhm proposed a quite different program which he submitted to General von Blomberg on February 1, 1934. Aiming at a "revolutionary army," Röhm recommended a fundamental reorganization along three lines. All matters of military security should be brought under the jurisdiction of the SA; the *Reichswehr* should be limited to training of officers and soldiers in modern warfare; the trained units should be transferred to the SA whose commanding officers should be advised by the technically competent general staff officers. It was implied that Röhm should be appointed as the new minister of war.[78]

On June 3, 1934, Hitler talked for two hours to Röhm who only agreed to send the SA on a furlough for one month. Coming under pressure of the military and von Hindenburg, Hitler decided to remove Röhm from his position. On June 22, Hitler called SA leader Lutze of Hannover to his chancellery, claimed a secret plot of the SA against himself, and revealed his decision to appoint a new leader of the SA.[79] A fabricated news item that Röhm was after the life of Hitler, and another one that the army was preparing for a showdown, led to his decision of a wholesale slaughter of the SA leaders.

How did Hitler justify his bloodbath for which he bears the main responsibility? There was not one word about the ideological conflict. None of the accused and murdered SA men was blamed for having deserted the Nazi ideology. In his speech on July 13, 1934, he gave a charismatic reason for his violence: "It became finally clear that I alone was the man who had to confront the Chief of the SA. He had broken his oath of allegiance to me, and I alone had to keep him responsible for his violation."[80] Hitler thus had integrated the ideological mission into his charismatic authority to such an extent that he shifted the ideological dispute to the charismatic level. He called himself "the highest judge" of the land and turned the illegal bloodbath into a charismatic purge.[81]

The outcome of this particular ideological schism suggests some important inferences. Once a specific set of ideals and subsequent policies has been internalized in the charismatic mission of the leader in a dictatorial setting, all paladins are morally bound to accept these ideals as their own and live accordingly. If they do not do so, then such disbelief will be considered as charismatic disloyalty deserving severe punishment. In interpreting his authority extensively, Hitler claimed the right of acting as a charismatic law creator, issuing the orders of execution on the spot, disregarding all legal or procedural requirements. What was (and is) regarded as unmitigated and unjustified violence in a legal order became a severe but fully justified execution in a charismatic order. It was because of the acceptance of this right of the leader to decide over the life and death of his paladins that the SS performed the executions, and none of the divisions of the SA protested in any way against the beheading of their leaders. The deliberate bloodbath reenforced Hitler's position in the dictatorship, created an "intellectual proletarianization" in the Nazi party and movement, and cemented the alliance between Hitler and the upper class.

The second ideological conflict between Hitler and one group of army leaders was concerned with the differences between military and Fascist imperialism. Both participants in this dispute were engaged in an extensive military and economic rearmament and believed in the necessity of war for the future development of Germany. But they adhered to different versions of imperialism and anticipated different kinds of war and warfare.[82] Why did Hitler at first support the right of the generals to lead the regular army, but then deprived them of this right at the end of the rearmament period? There are charismatic and ideological reasons for this dispute which have to be depicted briefly as causes leading up to the ideological schism.[83]

In his main book Hitler had formulated a law of population and living space that reversed the sequence in Malthus' law of population. Instead of beginning with land, Hitler started with population. Any healthy people will have a natural fertility and a rising population. Such an increase is a necessary law of nature. "Germany has an annual increase in population of almost 900,000 souls. The difficulty of feeding this army of new citizens will become greater with every year, and is bound some day to end in catastrophe if no means are found to avert this impending danger of hunger and pauperization in time."[84]

Instead of regarding the land as a fixed quality, history of agriculture "is full of significant progress, of steady improvements, of rising yields. There has been either an improvement in the methods of cultivation or an increasing use of fertilizers." While agricultural output has exceeded significantly the inputs of factors per acre, this method does not provide a solution of the food problem. "There can be no doubt that there is a limit to these improvements."[85] Either the rates of increase in yields will decline or the demand for products and for a higher standard of living will exceed the rising productivity of land. The result will be a Malthusian discrepancy between land and population. "Finally, the time comes when it will be no longer possible to satisfy the daily needs and famine will have become the eternal companion of such a people."[86] This danger faces especially the German people. "The German nation has found itself in a situation of insufficient living space ever since its entry into world history. The scarcity of land has determined German political actions in world politics. Ever since the great migrations in ancient times did Germany remove its land scarcity only by employing its sword or by permitting a decline of the size of its population."[87]

Under no condition was Hitler willing to adjust the population to the food supply. In truth, "the whole life struggle consists in getting more land so as to adjust its size to the rising number of people" But scarcity of land is not universal. "The excess of land of some nations coexists with the extreme poverty of others who cannot secure the necessary food supply in spite of all their efforts."[88] Unequal distribution of land is completely unjustified." It cannot be the intention of heaven to give fifty times as much land . . . to one nation as compared to others. . . . If this earth has room enough for all to live in, then one should give us the space we need for living."[89]

Hitler thus invoked "the right to self-preservation . . . what has been denied by kindness will have to be taken with the fist." Germany is in great need of land suitable for settlement. "The only possibility of carrying out a sound land policy is to be found in the acquisition of new soil in Europe proper." It has to be clear that "this goal can be achieved only through fighting. . . ." The desired land can be obtained only "at the expense of Russia," secured "with the help of the German sword."[90] Already in his first book Hitler set himself the goal of a war with Russia for the purpose of acquiring the necessary land for German settlement. The theory of an insufficient food supply provided the basis for Hitler's ideology of Fascist imperialism and conquest. His value goal called for the expansion towards the East so as to obtain the land for the rising population, for settling German peasants, and for obtaining a large but reserved market for German industry.

Convinced of the "necessity" of a war, Hitler actively promoted the secret military rearmament by supporting the two secret defense laws. In 1936 he produced a memorandum for a Four-Year Plan, devoted to an extensive economic rearmament, which ended with the following directives: "The German armed forces have to be ready for war in four years; the German economy has to mobilize for war in four years."[91] These military preparations did not yet foretell the new strategy to be adopted. It was in the secret meeting of November 5, 1937, that Hitler revealed his own ideas about the need for a *Blitzkrieg* strategy. In case of a conflict between Britain and Italy over the control of the Mediterranean Sea in 1938, the German armed forces should occupy Austria and Czechoslovakia. He calculated that "the incorporation . . . would bring an increased food supply for five to six million Germans. This would be possible under the assumption that about two million Czech-Slovaks and one million Austrians would be driven from their land by compulsory emigration." Hitler believed "that in all probability England and perhaps also France have already silently written off Czechoslovakia. . . . Military participation by Russia must be countered by the speed of our operations."[92] It was in this form that Hitler presented his strategy of lightning warfare with its separate attacks against one single enemy at a time, and a speedy as well as conclusive operation by mobile and coordinated forces on the ground and in the air.

In the subsequent discussion, however, the leaders of the army opposed Hitler's strategy as well as the early date of invasion. The heavy Czech fortifications would prevent a quick victory in the east, and the incomplete German fortifications could not contain the attacking French forces in the west. Instead of a series of *Blitzkriegs* there would occur an international war involving Germany on its frontiers in the east and in the west. Neither militarily nor economically was Germany strong enough to win such a two-front war, whether in 1938 or in 1943, Hitler's two likely dates for invasion. There was thus an ideological clash between the two military strategies of lightning warfare and of preparing for a total war.

Instead of arriving at a compromise, Hitler remained convinced of the superiority of his strategy, and adopted the attitude of a charismatic genius whose extraordinary gift was not appreciated by the highest military officers. He had craved for the role of a charismatic hero for years. Already in 1934 Hitler told Rauschning and others in confidence: "I do not allow the 'generals' to give me orders. The war is [to be] conducted by *me*. There will only be one time that will be truly auspicious, and I will wait for it with inflexible determination. And I will not pass it by. I shall bend all my energies bringing it about. That is my mission."[93] It was the ideological military mission of a charismatic hero.

While there was the will to punish those who did not recognize his gift and refused to accept his strategy, Hitler could not stage a violent charismatic purge because another bloodbath would have demoted the army, undermined its internal cohesion, and destroyed the will of the officers to fight in Hitler's war. Instead of one lightning stroke, there occurred a series of three deceitful manipulations. The first was a despicable intrigue. When it became known that General von Blomberg had married "a lady with a past," Himmler and Goering dug out an old charge of homosexuality against General von Fritsch and linked both together as the most serious violation of the military code of honor. In the same night of January 24, 1938, when Hitler discussed these matters with Goering, it was decided that the honor of the army required the removal of the two highest military officers.

Dismissal was followed by usurpation. In fending off all proposals for the appointment of other officers to these positions, Hitler formally abolished the Ministry of War, made himself the head of the armed forces, and thereby destroyed the organizational autonomy of the army. Military planning and general supervision came under the direct command of Hitler. His orders were formulated by two military paladins, Generals Keitel and Jodl, who worshipped his exceptional genius and assisted him in usurping the military leadership of the armed forces. One of the first actions was a peaceful purge of many of the other generals who were either politically too conservative or imbued with the wrong military strategy.[94] Dismissal, usurpation, and purge resolved the second ideological schism in favor of Hitler who thereby reduced the generals to minor holders of power in the dictatorial regime, and who abolished their major institution, the Ministry of War.

As in the previous purge, Hitler did not justify his usurping of military leadership with ideological legitimacy. Temporarily, he used the honor code of the aristocratic officer corps and the general antipathy against homosexuality as surrogate legitimizers for his usurpation. But his sudden invasion of Austria changed the situation. While this was a military campaign, Hitler had ordered the invasion, gave binding commands to the generals, and then minimized their actions to the one of a military police. The "liberation" became first and foremost an extraordinary charismatic deed, not only for Hitler and his followers, but for the great majority of the Austrian and German people. The occupation itself became the charismatic legitimation of Hitler's usurpation of military leadership. In order to demonstrate this popular legitimacy, Hitler arranged for an affectual participation of the masses by calling for dictatorial plebiscites after incorporating Austria as well as Sudetenland into his Greater Germany. In the overflow of emotion and general jubilation, the masses truly and sincerely loved their charismatic dictator, and approved of his annexations.

If Hitler and his paladins would have been guided only by the ideology of national resurrection, and if he would have been satisfied with plebiscitary charisma, then the two incorporations would have been the sole military actions, leaving the Danzig question to peaceful negotiations. Greater Germany would have become the largest power of the European continent, the leader and the party would have enjoyed the obedience of the masses, and a world war would have been avoided. If Hitler would have recognized and respected his own limits, fascism and its charismatic leader would have enjoyed the prospects of a fairly secure future.

## EXTERNAL COUNTERREVOLUTION AND CHARISMA

Nazi ideology of external counterrevolution comprised two related but still distinct sets of ideals. One was the aim of a Fascist imperialism and the creation of a charismatically led empire. The other was the belief in a racial purity and the subsequent deportation and extermination of the inferior races. In this and the following section we shall examine how these two ideologies were related to charisma and implemented by the gifted leader.

Hitler's two theories of an excess population and limited living space, already outlined, provided the rationale for the ideology of Fascist imperialism. To overcome this scarcity required a policy of large-scale settlement of German farmers in the east of Germany. The land itself could be obtained only by means of a decisive military victory. The purpose of the war was thus "to gain the greatest profit at the lowest cost" for Germany.[95] In proposing his strategy of lightning warfare, Hitler not only tried to economize the number of military divisions and the equipment for fighting the war, but also tried to overwhelm the enemy forces by concentrated and powerful strokes so as to obtain the greatest possible booty for his own war machine. The confiscation of the land, compulsory deportation, the strategy of lightning warfare and subsequent booty, and sequestration turned the prospective war into a policy of an external counterrevolution.

Internal and external counterrevolutions required for their success effective command over military forces. The former was executed by the SA troopers acting as an auxiliary police of the state, being imbued with the Nazi ideology. The latter was a much more formidable task that depended first on effective command over the regular armed forces by the charismatic leader and second on a belief in the ideology of Fascist imperialism. The promoted younger officers to the leading military positions were either charismatic worshippers of the military genius or military technicians of modern warfare, able and willing to execute Hitler's military orders.

Fighting a counterrevolutionary war with the help of officers of conservative or politically indifferent persuasions entailed two significant hurdles for charismatic, ideological leadership in leading and winning counterrevolutionary wars. Inevitably, there were clashes between decisions based upon charismatic vision and military expertise. While the two sets of criteria were effectively reconciled in the earlier *Blitzkriegs,* charismatic rulership prevailed in the second half of the war, leading to some costly mistakes and catastrophic losses (e.g., Stalingrad).[96] The string of earlier victories led to Hitler's underestimating the military power of Russia and the likelihood of American involvement, and to his belief that the *Blitzkrieg* strategy was applicable to all theaters of war.

It so happened that Hitler developed a peculiar process of charismatic decision making that can be readily observed in his attempt to implement his imperialistic ideology and policy. What were the conditions, components, and consequences of this process?

Indispensable were the two charismatic conditions. One resided in Hitler's ideological mission which engendered the belief in the necessity of imperialism and war. In the attempt to prepare for the invasion of Austria, Hitler told Chancellor Kurt von Schuschnigg, "I have a historic mission, and this mission I will fulfill because Providence has destined me to do so. I thoroughly believe in this mission, it is my life."[97] In preparing and executing the series of invasions, Hitler was obsessed by this mission. Second, the rapid and bloodless incorporation of Austria and Sudetenland into Greater Germany had aroused such a mass euphoria that not only the majority of the people, but also important segments of the bureaucracy, turned into his devoted followers.

In addition, there were two military conditions. Hitler benefited from the more advanced military technology and more extensive rearmament of Germany. The other European powers were also handicapped by the genuine and widespread desire for peace. Both these limitations of the prospective enemies minimized the will and capacity to resist Hitler's invasions by military means.

Given these favorable conditions, there evolved a pattern of charismatic decision making. The first component was the fixing of a target for aggression. On May 30, 1938, Hitler ordered the preparation for a military attack: "It is my irrevocable decision to destroy Czechoslovakia by military action." October 1 was set as the day of invasion. Again on April 11, 1939, Hitler issued the military directive: "I have decided upon a solution by force" in settling the Polish question.[98] In all the subsequent preparations and military attacks, it was Hitler alone who exercised the exclusive privilege of deciding unilaterally and finally over war and destruction. This privilege was institutionalized in the well-known commands of the leader (*Führerbefehle*), in military as well as in civilian affairs.

The next component was a combination of secrecy and deliberate deceptions. Not only were the military directives kept secret, but all the preparations had to be accomplished without ordering explicitly mobilization of the military forces. "Secrecy is the decisive condition for success." It required a small military staff at the direct disposal of Hitler. Secrecy was accompanied by deliberate deception and dishonest promises. In a speech to the generals, shortly after picking Poland as his next target, Hitler declared: "I would have to be an idiot if I would on account of Poland slide into a [world] war."[99] In his public speeches Hitler promised, during negotiations of the Sudetenland, that this demand would be his last one in Europe. Shortly afterwards Hitler assured France that he would never ask for a return of Alsace-Lorraine to Germany. In combining strict secrecy with false promises, Hitler deliberately sought to dispel any apprehension about his counterrevolutionary intentions and at the same time to prepare the ground for a surprise attack.

Another component of decision making employed by the charismatic leader was the use of ultimatums in seeking to disintegrate the will of selected victims. Hitler invited the representatives of Austria, Slovakia, and the truncated Czechoslovakia and threatened them with invasion and destruction of their states and armies. He offered them the alternative of avoiding this disaster by signing an agreement that would allow the German army to enter their states without meeting any military resistance. While Austria was given a few days of respite for legalizing such an agreement, President Hacha had to sign on the spot, and President Tiso arranged for the "consent" by telephone. Charismatic quality was here linked with brutality towards the victim. The cunning insight that the previous protectors of these small countries would not come to their rescue, and that ultimatums would turn invasions into peaceful occupations reenforced Hitler's demand.

Somewhat similar was the decision making of negotiation under duress, of exercising coercion under the label of bargaining. The outstanding example of such coercion was the well-known appeasement in Munich. In order to prevent Hitler's unilateral invasion of the still intact Czechoslovakia, England and France signed an "agreement" that provided for the four-staged evacuation of the Sudetenland by the Czech army, beginning on October 1, 1938. To disguise this occupation by the German army, Hitler signed Chamberlain's statement that the two countries would never go to war with one another again. This "peace with honor," misconceived by Chamberlain as a great achievement, was actually a great defeat for the West because Hitler obtained his consent without war.[100]

This process of decision making produced two important consequences. The internalizing of the counterrevolutionary ideology into the charismatic mission enabled the leader to link the dictatorial components of planned aggression, ultimatums, disguised coercion as well as strict secrecy, deception, and dishonesty with his charismatic leadership. It was because of the internalized, but violence-prone, ideology that these dictatorial components became compatible with charisma. The resulting synergistic charisma in the party dictatorship registered a great achievement: It accomplished the incorporation of two countries into Greater Germany which under strictly military leadership would have required the coordinated force of ninety divisions of the German army.

The situation changed, however, when there was potential military resistance so that actual war became the means for realizing the leader's imperialist goals. In order to isolate Poland for an effective conquest by lightning warfare, there occurred a hurried bargaining between two dictators. The Hitler–Stalin pact arranged for the division of Poland and granted Russia control over Finland and the Baltic states. In order to avoid a possible war with Russia, Hitler felt obliged to share the booty of conquest with the Communist dictator. But dishonesty was also linked with the agreement because Hitler was determined to take all this back at a more auspicious occasion. This determination to break the agreement created a spurious ideological legitimacy. When Hitler was asked how his followers would react to his deal with communism, Hitler answered: "My party members know and trust me; they know I will never depart from my basic principles, and they will recognize that the ultimate aim of this gamble is to remove the Eastern danger and thus to facilitate under my leadership . . . a swifter unification of Europe."[101] A pragmatic deal in the style of old-time power politics could thus be concluded and executed without besmirching the ideology or undermining the belief in the charismatic qualities of the leader.

But how could the deliberately chosen wars be justified to the soldiers and their mothers? Hitler did not use his ideology for legitimizing outright aggression. He pushed the responsibility upon the enemy. One week before the invasion of Poland, Hitler told the generals: "I shall find a propagandistic excuse for the start of the war, whether believable or not. The victor will not be asked whether he told the truth."[102] He instructed the SS to put common criminals into Polish uniforms, forced them to stage a surprise attack upon the transmitter at Gleiwitz, and thereby sought to place the responsibility for the war upon the Polish government. For Hitler any kind of lie and deception was justified by his counterrevolutionary ideals as long as they were propagandistically effective.

In seeking to motivate the soldiers to fight his war, Hitler invented a charismatic legitimacy in the form of mutual sacrifices. "When I call upon the armed forces and demand sacrifices of the German people . . . I have a right to do that because I was once ready, as I am now, to make every personal sacrifice. I do not demand anything else of the German man as I was willing to do over four years. There shall be no deprivation for any German that I am not willing to endure immediately. My whole life shall now fully belong to the people. I shall be nothing but the first soldier of the German Reich."[103] This minimal kind of natural charisma, of being united in mutual sacrifices, was a temporary phenomenon which was only loosely linked to the "honor of the nation," but not at all to the counterrevolutionary ideology.

Victory in Poland enabled Hitler to find a way for claiming heroic charisma. In his speech at Danzig he asserted: "The Almighty has blessed our weapons. . . . Providence has called upon me to be . . . the liberator" of the city of Danzig.[104] When leading generals argued against an attack of the West, Hitler presented himself as the military genius who knew best how wars should be fought. He celebrated victory in the West with the following proclamation: "German People: This most glorious victory in history has been achieved through the daring of your soldiers who have won this battle by their extraordinary deeds and fearless actions in the face of dangers to their health and lives. I herewith order that for eight days the Nazi flags shall be flown everywhere in honor of our soldiers. I also order the ringing of the bells by all churches for three days. Bells and prayers shall unite us and shall accompany our soldiers who will continue their fight for the freedom and future of our nation."[105] In a subsequent speech, however, the extraordinary deeds became the ones of the leader who had devised military strategy and directed the whole war, and who in turn was guided by providence. The extraordinary enthusiasm and worship of the leader grafted heroic upon natural and providential charismata and all three legitimized Hitler's wars and victories.

Instead of also claiming ideological legitimacy, Hitler found it advisable to fabricate a sham ideology. In his proclamation to the soldiers ordered to attack in the West, Hitler said: "It has been the intention of the British and French rulers for 300 years to prevent every consolidation in Europe, and to keep Germany in weakness and impotence. . . . England and France have tried . . . over Holland and Belgium to invade our Ruhr district. Soldiers of the West, your hour has come. . . . Do your duty."[106] This bogus claim of a war of defense was followed by Goebbels' instruction to the editors that they must put the full blame of the war on Western powers. "On no account must we allow ourselves to be maneuvered once more in the role of the aggressor."[107] After the defeat of France, Hitler turned from the defender to the generous victor when he appealed to "the reason of the Englishmen" to stop fighting because there was no conflict of interest between the two countries. The bogus ideology had a role to play because he could place the responsibility for the war upon his enemies and then demand that they recognize his increased victories and power.

The theories of external counterrevolution experienced a significant specification. The theorems of overpopulation and scarce living space were turned into goals for an imposed annexation of French territory. A new principle guided the respective proposals and policies. The peace of Westphalia of 1648 was seen as a historical crime by means of which the French had prevented the development of a greater Germany. Consequently, the borders prior to 1648 had to be restored. Burgundy, all of northern France, and of the Atlantic coast had to be united into a satellite state, controlled by German soldiers and open to German settlers. Hitler instructed the Nazi Stuckart to work out a plan for annexation along these lines. While it could not be immediately implemented, Hitler ordered various measures in preparation of eventual annexation. A northeastern line was drawn specifying a territory into which evacuated Frenchmen could not return. Two northern provinces of France came under the jurisdiction of the German military commander of Belgium, thereby preparing for a coming Flemish state. The provinces of Alsace and Lorraine were incorporated into Germany proper, expelling all those French families who had come into these provinces after 1918. Hitler specified that "Alsace and Lorraine should become completely German within ten years."[108]

Next to specification there was a deliberate and comprehensive secrecy about the goals and policies of annexation. None of the various measures were published in Germany. French complaints were either not answered or rejected as groundless. None of the German newspapers were permitted to report about the wholesale expelling of Frenchmen or of German settlers living on expropriated French farms. Germanization was implemented with great dispatch and utter ruthlessness. There was no fundamental difference between the French and the preceding Polish dismemberments, except that the former was stretched over a longer period and required a higher degree of secrecy.

There thus emerged two different relationships between charisma and the imperialist beliefs and policies. There was an effective interaction between charismatic beliefs and military victories. In accepting Hitler's interpretation of God having blessed German weapons, the *Blitzkriegs* were regarded as charismatic deeds that justified the worshipping of the leader. Annexation, expropriation, and the building up of a Fascist empire, however, did not find open and outright charismatic legitimacy. Hitler refrained from asking publicly for the approval of these policies by the masses who either had no occasion or no emotional urge to legitimize these policies. For Hitler, his paladins, and many in his movement, the ideal of a Fascist imperialism had become a part of the charismatic mission so that there was an interaction between the charismatic belief and the policies of annexation. But this part of ideological charisma was not a mass phenomenon, nor did it excite mass enthusiasm or elicit great admiration of the leader. Ideological charisma was limited to the ideological believers, bound the leader and his paladins, justified their actions to themselves, but was not infused by emotional charisma.

## RACIAL COUNTERREVOLUTION AND CHARISMA

So much has been said about Hitler's racism and its awful consequences that we can limit ourselves to the relationship between this ideology and charisma.[109] Could Hitler obtain charismatic legitimacy for his racial policies?

In his theory Hitler claimed that racial purity was the basic reason for human quality and national greatness. The purer the blood, the greater was the value and the stronger the character of the personality. The Aryan alone "is the founder of the higher mankind, the archtype of what we mean by a superior human being."[110] Pure blood leads to personal superiority and to a racial consciousness, and both together produce the monuments of human history. In the racial hierarchy, the Aryan stands at the top and the Jew at the bottom of the ladder. The former has the right to rule and also the obligation to eliminate the inferior race. Conquest and oppression are essential for the development of mankind because only in racial empires of the Aryans can the genius flower and create the master works of a superior culture.

The law of racial purity provided the basis for a racial ideology. "The realization of the fundamental racial consciousness, reborn by the National Socialists and expressed in the thesis of 'Blood and Soil,' will bring about the deepest revolutionary transformation that the world has ever seen. Our major ideal of a racial rejuvenation of our people . . . will determine all the internal and foreign policies of our party."[111]

Hitler tried to tie his racial law and ideology to charisma. "Eternal nature revenges relentless the violation of its laws. I do believe that I do act in accord with the will of the Almighty. In defending myself against the Jews, I honor the work of God."[112] There was thus an easy transition from a biological law of nature to a supernatural charisma. Only when a supernatural will stood behind the law could Hitler claim to know the superior will and to act as the charismatic apostle of God.

The supernatural will turned into the measures of his counterrevolutionary racism. There was the boycott of the Jewish stores in 1933. As he predicted in his main book, a law of compulsory sterilization was passed that sought to prevent the mentally and physically unhealthy from perpetuating their genes in their children. The marriage laws of Nuremberg in 1935 contained the obnoxious "Aryan Clause" that prevented marriage between gentiles and Jews and deprived the Jews of their citizenship. But this law was not justified publicly with the racial ideology. Hitler pushed the marriage laws through parliament because, he said, it was necessary to forestall violent demonstrations by the German people. Nor did Hitler personally assume the responsibility for burning the synagogues in 1938. Goebbels reported to Hitler that sporadic fires had broken out in two provinces, burning Jewish buildings. Goebbels said to the *Gauleiters:* "I have reported these actions to the Führer. He has decided that the party shall not organize such demonstrations. But if such actions should arise spontaneously, then such demonstrations should not be suppressed."[113] This backhanded directive induced the *Gauleiters* to order party and SA groups to deliberately burn down Jewish property in most cities. Two days later Hitler imposed a special levy of one million marks upon the Jewish community for the murder of a German diplomat by a young Jew in Paris. Revenge was thus added to the pretended defense against Jewish aggression. Hitler claimed to react only to Jewish provocation. But this disguise was dropped when Goering demanded the punishment of those SA men who were involved in the murder of 90 people. Hitler replied: "Murders committed in the service of the ideology have to remain unpunished."[114] Hitler thus placed the anti-Jewish actions into his racial counterrevolution, justified murder in the name of this ideology, while pretending to the public that he knew nothing about arson, levy, and murder of Jews. There was no attempt at charismatic legitimacy of this deliberate violence.

In the field of indoctrination, however, Hitler was able to link emotional charisma and racism. On the one hand, there was for him a linkage between Jewry and bolshevism. "The Russia of today is in principle nothing other than the Russia of two hundred years ago. A brutal dictatorship of an alien race has imposed its rule upon the whole of Russia. . . . In the Soviet Union of the so-called socialist paradise more than 80 percent of the leading positions are occupied by Jews."[115] On the other hand, if there should be war, then the Jews would be the instigators. This conviction led to his well remembered threat: "If the international financial circles of Jewry should again push the nations of Europe into another world war, then the end result will not be a Bolshevization of the world but the destruction of Jewry in Europe."[116] Antibolshevism and anti-Jewish racism were thus melded into one deeply held ideological belief.

This ideology became fused with emotional charisma. In the process of dictating his speeches, Hitler's face got red and his voice became harsh when he spoke the words bolshevism or Jewry.[117] His immense hatred of both enemies produced in him a self-intoxicating effect. Hatred of the enemy became the opposite but equally important feeling to charismatic enthusiasm. His charismatic calling involved for Hitler the irrevocable assignment to smash the two enemies. But his waves of insults were not followed by any specific programs, apart from systematic discrimination and deportation of Jews, calling for mass actions that could have found the approval of the voters. While his threat of destruction was laden with overflowing charismatic emotions of his audiences, there was no publicly presented program for the coming mass slaughter of the Jews and the starvation of Russian prisoners.

In explaining his invasion of the Soviet Union, Hitler declared it as a preventive war against the Jewish-Bolshevist and Anglo-Saxon plot to destroy Germany. His decision for the extermination of the Jews was made at the same time and passed on orally to Goering who gave a written instruction to Hydrich "to bring about a complete solution of the Jewish question in the German sphere of influence in Europe."[118] The subsequent conference on January 20, 1942, officially adopted the code word of "deportation"' and secretly formulated the program of building gas chambers for the extermination of the Jews.

Hitler's slogan was that "faith moves mountains." In his headquarters he emphasized: "The Jews must clear out of Europe. . . . If they refuse to go voluntarily, I see no other solution but extermination."[119] The final solution was presented as a "disinfection" of the polluted race. In public speeches, as the one to young officers in May 1942 or to the *Reichstag* in July 1942, Hitler justified his war by his need for living space to settle German peasants and soldiers in the occupied territories of the East. Extermination was thus for him the destructive and resettlement the constructive part of his racial counterrevolution. Hitler thus claimed an ideological, not a charismatic, legitimacy for his war, extermination, and resettlement.

Instead of trying to arouse sympathy for their "disinfection," the Nazi rulers expected different reactions of the people. Hitler anticipated popular consternation. Prior to gassing, he said: "It's not a bad idea . . . that public rumor attributes to us a plan to exterminate the Jews. Terror is a salutary thing."[120] The fear aroused would prevent any resistance to extermination. The party headquarters tried to give direction to rumors. When soldiers on furlough from the East reported cases of atrocities, Bormann informed his provincial and county officials that Jews from occupied lands were transported to the East and were "employed as laborers in camps or behind the front . . . while the old Jews were resettled in the new camp of Theresienstadt."[121] In trying to get support for his "total war" slogan in 1943, Goebbels tried to strengthen the will of party members to resist. He blamed international Jewry for instigating the war and promised that Germany would retaliate "with the total and radical extermination . . . of Jews." The wild shouts of "Hang them!" revealed that Nazi hatred demanded extermination for reasons of revenge for military defeats.[122] Such a will for destruction was no longer covered by any legitimacy.

As news percolated among civilians, especially among church members, there were a few protests by church leaders against the policy of genocide. In a secret memorandum submitted to the government, the Protestant Bishop Wurm wrote on July 16, 1943: "The killing of members of other nations and races who are not even accorded a civil or military trial has to stop. . . . The day will come when we will have to pay dearly for these deeds." Half a year later came the pastoral letter of the Catholic bishop of Berlin who insisted on "the fundamental human rights of everyone regardless of his ancestry."[123] Such protests led only to the occasional hiding of individual Jews, but never did crystalize into a significant passive resistance. Either lack of information or repulsion against mass murder prevented the holocaust being legitimized either by charismatic or ideological mass beliefs.

There thus developed two opposite notions about the leader's right to decide over life and death of human beings. In the minds of those opposing extermination, the leader had a right to start a war, force soldiers to fight and in the process be maimed or killed. Dying in the name of patriotism, or giving one's life for the fatherland, was morally justified. But it was quite different for any person, however exalted he might be, to order his extermination squads to deliberately kill people, just because they were sick or belonged to an "inferior" race or enemy group. The Christian Commandment "Thou shalt not kill" underlay such an opposition to the policy of genocide. It was certainly a minority of those informed who lived up to their Christian belief in a dangerous situation, since they were likely to be punished for defamation of the leader. Hence, opposition to wanton killing of hapless victims was expressed only in private memoranda or in euphemistically phrased human rights.

In all, our investigation reveals four different relationships between dictatorial charisma and ideologies. There was an effective fusion between charisma and the resurrectional ideology, leading to ideological charisma. This was followed by a selective affinity between charisma and internal counterrevolution which was also disguised by legal legitimacy. There was a conflict between military counterrevolution and charisma, and also between two alternative military strategies. Both conflicts were resolved by charismatic purges of those opposing the ideologies of the leader. The imperialist ideology and military victories were legitimized by several modes of charisma, but the subsequent annexations and exploitations were justified only secretly by the counterrevolutionary ideology. Racism as a form of indoctrination was approved of by a form of natural charisma, while racism as a policy of extermination was either kept secret or disguised as deportation publicly, but secretly justified as an unavoidable obligation placed upon the leader and SS execution squads by a fateful ideology.

The identifiable product of these four kinds of interactions was synergistic charisma in a single party dictatorship. Its achievement can be condensed into three theses. Adoption of two separate but compatible ideologies strengthened charismatic leadership because the specific ideals provided the goals appropriate for the two quite different situations of peace and war. The four kinds of interaction greatly enhanced the power of the charismatic leader because he could and did utilize charismatic as well as ideological authority and legitimacy in his personal rulership. Charismatic nonbelievers and the millions of politically indifferent people carried no political weight because of the widespread fear of the secret police and the brutal punishment by the agents of terror. Those who carried such weight were either worshippers or noncharismatic supporters of Hitler, at least prior to either the military purge or major military defeats.

Our analysis of the four interactions of charismata and ideologies suggests four specific inferences on Hitler's major initiatives. First, the overthrow of the Weimar Republic by means of Nazi arson and terror was dually "justified" by the interaction of supernatural charisma and the ideology of an internal counterrevolution. Second, the synergistic linkage between providential charisma and resurrectional ideology gave rise to the Munich "agreement" and the subsequent invasion of Austria, Czechoslovakia, and Poland. Third, the interlacing of heroic charisma and Fascist imperialism prompted the invasions of Western and Eastern Europe by a series of *Blitzkriegs*. Fourth, the interpenetration of natural charisma with the belief in racial pollution induced Hitler to feel a sense of obligation to "purify" the Germanic race that culminated in the wholesale extermination of Jews and Slavs.

Since Hitler not only personified these four modes of synergistic charisma, but also translated them into policy initiatives and subsequent campaigns, it is he who foremost bears the personal responsibility for the course of events in the Third Reich and in the Nazi empire, and for imposing the Second World War as well as the holocaust upon mankind.

# CHAPTER FIVE

# CHARISMA AND ORGANIZATION

CHARISMATIC AND IDEOLOGICAL BELIEFS require an effective organization for their implementation. This raises the question as to the fundamental relationship between charisma and organizations. In Weber's theory there are two kinds of organizations, one of which is alien to charisma, while the other is effectively assisting charisma. How can charisma be linked with and opposed to organization at the same time?

An alien relationship is said to exist between bureaucracy and charisma. "In radical contrast to bureaucratic organization, charisma knows no formal and regulated appointment or dismissal, no career advancement or salary, no supervisory and appeals body, no local or purely technical jurisdiction, and no permanent institutions in the manner of democratic agencies, which are independent of incumbents and their personal charisma" (p. 1112). As soon as a charismatic leader becomes the head of the state, he invariably runs into a conflict with the official bureaucracy. On the one hand, bureaucracy is indispensable for the daily operation of the government; on the other hand, the charismatic leader has a personal relationship to his paladins, is accustomed to informal assignments, irregularities of tenure or promotion, and despises formalized spheres of jurisdiction. Since some of the charismatic giants did experience various kinds of conflicts with the regular bureaucracy, they should confirm Weber's rule of an inimical relationship between bureaucracy and charisma.

Yet the charismatic leader cannot realize his mission if he does not find manifold assistance. As Weber has emphasized "charismatic authority does not imply an amorphous condition; it indicates rather a definite social structure with assistants and an *apparatus* of services and material means that is adapted to the mission of the leader. The personal assistants constitute a charismatic aristocracy composed of a select group of adherents who are united by discipleship and loyalty and chosen according to personal charismatic qualification" (p. 119).[1] There thus developed a nonbureaucratic organization, personally attached to the leader, ready to implement his wishes, in whatever form they may be expressed. Instead of a uniformly alien relationship between charisma and organization *per se*, there developed one conflict

129

between organizational and charismatic leaders, and another between bureaucracy and charismatic apparatus. But there was also a supportive relationship between a leader and his apparatus.

In synergistic charisma, the problem is not that of avoiding bureaucracy or perishing. It is the task of the leader to build up an effective charismatic apparatus for accomplishing two different purposes. One is to turn this apparatus into the leadership corps of a political party. The other is to superimpose the apparatus upon the regular bureaucracy as soon as the leader comes to power. While the tension between the two types of organization remains alive, a separation of functions or a division of labor develops that enables the leader to control both party and state for the sake of implementing his policies and realizing his mission.

Control depends upon certain conditions. "A party's general character is significant for the chances that charisma has in its struggle with the party bureaucracy" (p. 1133). Status parties led by notables or parties directed by ideologists have frequently avoided charismatic leadership. Parties devoted to promotions of private interests frequently resisted charismatic leadership when they were given a choice. Charismatic parties originated in two different ways. Either a charismatic community entered the political sphere and struggled for power. If successful, the leader became head of a party and his paladins turned into party officials. Or, "in times of great public excitement, charismatic leaders may emerge even in solidly bureaucratized parties as was demonstrated by [Theodore] Roosevelt's campaign in 1912 . . . only extraordinary conditions can bring about the triumph of charisma over the organization. As a rule, the party organization easily succeeds in this castration of charisma" (p. 1132).

It is at this point that there emerges the central difference between pure and synergistic charisma. Weber was inclined to expect that in the struggle over administration, bureaucracy will win over charisma. The information available at his time largely supported his alternative. But he did not close the door to synergistic developments, although he did not investigate this possibility. He merely admits that "it is probably not possible to generalize on this score. The internal dynamics of party organization, and the social and economic conditions of each concrete case are all too intimately interwoven in any given situation" (p. 1133). A party machine may thus collaborate or be controlled by a charismatic leader.

In the twentieth century wars, depressions, and national independence movements have greatly increased the opportunities of charisma. Not only has the number of political parties increased, but a new type of dictatorial party has arisen that seeks to suppress all other parties and destroy democracy. Weber defined political parties as democratic organizations. "The criterion of formally voluntary solicitation and adherence in terms of rules of the group within which the party exists is treated here as a crucial point" (p. 287). Free admission and voluntary membership are seen as indispensable for political parties. "But when a party becomes a closed group which is incorporated by law into the administrative staff . . . it ceases to be a party and becomes a part of the polity" (p. 287). In pointing to closure, Weber took the first step to an explanation of a dictatorial party, but he did not anticipate the subsequent development to a political monopoly.

Instead of becoming a part of the administrative staff of the state, the dictatorial party ushered in two important political changes. One was the shift from the multiple to the single party system; the other was the replacement of democracy by dictatorship. These changes led to the coexistence of democratic and dictatorial parties in two opposed political systems. This corresponds to the distinction between democratic and dictatorial charismata as well as democratic and dictatorial ideologies.

This parallelism has produced great consequences for the relationship between charisma and organization. The cleavage between the two has been significantly reduced because of the affinity between democratic charisma and bureaucracy or between dictatorial charisma and dictatorial bureaucracy. A fundamental antagonism prevails only between democratic charisma and dictatorial bureaucracy or between dictatorial charisma and democratic bureaucracy.[2] At the same time, opportunities for building up a charismatic apparatus have increased both in democratic as well as dictatorial charismata. As the executive branch became stronger relative to the legislative branch of modern states, so the opportunities grew for creating and promoting a charismatic apparatus, in democracy as well as in dictatorship. The result has been, as we shall see in chapter 10, that the relative significance of routinized charisma fell, while a new avenue opened up for the phenomenal growth of synergistic charisma. This new kind of leadership in itself gave rise to a positive interlinkage between charisma, ideology, and organization.

As in charisma and ideology, we have to study separately democratic and dictatorial organizations. The Nazi party is the most appropriate dictatorial object of such an investigation because charisma and organization were closely intertwined through most of its existence. This party was also organizationally separated from the administrative staff of the state. Hitler stated a rule of separation in the following words: "The tasks administrative in nature will be assigned to the state (bureaucracy). Tasks beyond the capacity of the state will be solved by our movement."[3] The strictly political matters in all their forms were the prerogative of the "more dynamic organizations of the party." In Hitler's phrase, "the party gives commands to the state."[4] The separation permits us to concentrate our discussion to the party sphere, the prerogative of which demands an investigation of the political monopoly established by the combined efforts of charismatic leadership, ideology, and party machine.

## DICTATORIAL PARTY

In his sociology of political parties, Weber identified four characteristics that together presented the internal structure of such organizations. A political party consists of "(a) leaders and their staffs . . . (b) active party members [who] . . . under certain circumstances may exercise some form of control. . . .(c) inactive masses of electors or voters . . . (d) contributors to the party funds [who] usually remain behind the scene" (p. 285). These four features are typical for the majority of political parties in modern times.

The difference between democratic and dictatorial parties resides in the particular relationship among the four groups of participants within political organizations. The major share of power in democratic parties lies in the hands of active members whose decisions select the leaders and give the directives for the policies chosen and implemented. In dictatorial parties, power is concentrated in the hands of the leaders who decide who shall be the active members, select the tasks for the members, determine the means of manipulating the voters, and accept and utilize the funds coming from contributors. A dictatorial party operates according to the rules of closure of membership, compulsory assignments of tasks, conditional admission of new members, centralized control over the staff actions, financial independence from the diverse contributors, and policy determination by the top leader.

*Closure.* The NSDAP was at first an open political association that accepted anyone as a member who paid his dues and adhered to its ideology.[5] Entry into the party usually meant joining a particular local group. Right of admission by the locals was taken away by party headquarters in 1927. Applications had to be referred to the central financial office in Munich which alone issued membership cards which were valid only if signed both by Hitler and the party treasurer. A national numbering system was introduced that gave the highest prestige to those members with the lowest number. Officially, on May 1, 1933, the party became a closed association. The overall ban on new members was modified by granting membership only to those who demonstrated their political reliability in other Nazi organizations and could demonstrate their Aryan ancestry. Members of the Hitler Youth, for instance, who had served honorably for four years and came from a pure Nordic race were readily accepted in the party in spite of the general ban. Party leaders thus aimed at an exclusive membership by adopting the rules of closure and racist selection of the admitted few.

*Selection.* Prior to the general ban there was a great rush to become a member of the party. Many wanted to belong to the privileged political class. A special rule was applied to the leaders of the associated Nazi organizations. Anyone in this group who had been appointed to his position prior to January 31, 1933, could become a member of the party. Others appointed to such positions in the next five months were accepted only on probation for two years. The data on membership shown in table 5.1 came from diverse sources because the official membership roles were destroyed prior to the end of the war.

Insofar as closure was ineffective, extensive screening of the once admitted members took its place. The rough figures on membership indicate that about 1.5 million members were expelled by decision of the party leaders.

*Compulsory Assignments.* Party members were given unpaid work assignments by party officials. The system of local branches was subdivided into blocks and cells. By

TABLE 5.1. APPROXIMATE PARTY MEMBERSHIP.

| Dates | Consecutive Numbers | After Resignations and Expulsions |
|---|---|---|
| July 1926 | 49,523 | 35,000 |
| Sept. 1930 | 300,000 | 129,653 |
| Jan. 1932 | 800,000 | 450,000 |
| Jan. 1933 | 1,200,000 | 719,000 |
| Jan. 1935 | 4,000,000 | 2,500,000 |

Source: Dietrich Orlow, *History of the Nazi Party: 1919–1932* (Pittsburgh: University of Pittsburgh Press, 1969), pp. 76, 239.

May 1936, a block comprised forty to sixty households, and a cell four to eight blocks. In each apartment building of a block, there was an informer who had to report any suspicious detail, much of which was passed on to the Gestapo. The wardens of the blocks had to explain the policies of the party and indoctrinate the people in the ideology. The wardens of the cells, who were responsible for the political reliability of their blocks, received their instructions from the chairmen of the branches. There was a steady increase of this interwoven network of party functionaries. The more than 100 percent increase in the local officials attests to the tight network of the party bureaucracy. The position of the local leader became a paid vocation. These leaders established regular offices, hired personnel, introduced managerial rules, and acted according to instructions from above. A bureaucratic hierarchy thus developed from extending the local organization and giving compulsory assignments. Yet the local officials were not hired according to administrative competence nor were the positions protected by tenure. Decisive for appointment was political reliability and compliance with the will of the leaders. The firing and hiring of many local officials during the years 1937–39 indicated that politicians of the districts and provinces controlled the local party bureaucracy. The local turnover coincided with the entry of many professionals, state bureaucrats, and industrialists into the party by special dispensation from Hitler. Anyone unable to fulfill his assignment had to present a valid excuse or was expelled from the party.

*Concentration.* The power for organizational activity was concentrated in the hands of the leaders. The top leader was self-appointed. In appointing himself *Gauleiter* of Munich and having the local organization of Munich acting in the name of the national organization, Hitler assured legally his permanency in office. The four divisional heads of the party were appointed by Hitler. First, came the party treasurer, in 1931, then the party judge, then his deputy as leader in 1933, and the organizational leader of the party, in 1934.[6] Each head was given an imperative mandate to act in the name of the leader. There were neither well defined jurisdictions nor prescribed procedures for coordinating the activities so that organizational disputes were built into the organization. The *Gauleiters* were also appointed by Hitler and their tenure depended upon his pleasure. Outsiders were selected whenever there were squabbles in a particular district. Traveling inspectors were chosen by Hitler for the purpose of checking upon the locals. Up to 1928, local leaders were appointed by the *Gauleiters*. Even as the head of the government, Hitler insisted upon his right to appoint all the leaders down to the county level.[7] While there was no manual prescribing the specific rights and duties of this hierarchically arranged set of leaders, Hitler possessed a veto power against any kind of decision made at any level of the organization.

*Centralization.* The financial administration was the most centralized in the party. Treasurer Schwarz built up an effective system for collection of dues and rigorously enforced delivery of the share to headquarters. A network of financial officers was appointed who were all responsible to Schwarz personally. This was especially true for the financial officer at each *Gau* office. He had to follow the treasurer's specific instruction for controlling the financial outlays of each *Gauleiter*. A network of trained auditors examined the books of all party officials and most of the associated organizations. Many financial deviations were reported and some of them led to a cutoff of funds. Annual budgets had to be submitted by the districts for the approval by the central office. Treasurer Schwarz also possessed the right of an overall checkup of the finances of a number of subordinate Nazi organizations. His struggle over the financial transactions of the Labor Front was successful in 1937 when a financial scandal forced Ley to let the party treasurer impose a new financial administration upon this largest Nazi controlled organization.[8] Of all the offices of the party, technical competence, managerial rules, and office procedures stamped the financial administration as the most bureaucratic organization of the Nazis. Centralized control was here translated into top party power over the subordinate organizations.

*Financial Independence.* The former ad hoc payments by private supporters were replaced by regular payments by business organizations to the party. The idea of making regular payments to the Nazis originated in 1933 in the top employer organization which was presented to Hitler by Gustav Krupp von Bohlen. Hitler contributed only the charismatic title—Hitler Donation. The purpose was to collect funds from business concerns in order—in the words of Hess—"to furnish the party headquarters with the means required for the centralized execution of those tasks that are for the benefit of the SA, SS, party staff, Hitler Youth, and the National Socialist Flying Organization. The donation gives the contributing enterprises the assurance that their work for the rebuilding of the German economy will not be disturbed by unauthorized and unpredictable collections" by Nazi outfits.[9] When at the beginning of the war the payments were reduced, Bormann threatened: "The payments have to be collected compulsorily from industry if they should not be paid voluntarily." Incomplete information suggests that the organizations of business paid from 500 million to 600 million marks to the top Nazis during a period of eleven years.[10] Hitler thus held in his hands the purse for financing the integral organizations attached to the party.

Largely unknown have been the annual payments of the Ministry of Finance to the treasury of the party. According to the records of the ministry, the payments shown in table 5.2 were received by the party.

TABLE 5.2. ANNUAL PAYMENTS OF THE STATE TO THE PARTY IN MILLION REICHSMARKS.

| Year | Payment | Year | Payment |
|------|---------|------|---------|
| 1934 | 66.0 | 1940 | 289 |
| 1935 | 72.0 | 1941 | 385 |
| 1936 | 86.0 | 1942 | 436 |
| 1937 | 100.0 | 1943 | 540 |
| 1938 | 145.0 | 1944 | 524* |
| 1939 | 240.0 | | |
| | | Total | 2,883 |

*Estimated.
Source: *Reichsfinanzministerium* R 2, folder 31096, BA.

All attempts of the minister of finance to either examine the need or the proper allocation of these funds were rejected by the party treasurer who successfully emphasized his "right to a free disposition over these funds." These almost 3 billion marks, which far exceeded the membership fees of the party (16 million marks by 1942), were received by the party not as subsidies but as a tribute to be paid by the subdued state agency to the victorious party. Instead of a routinization of charisma that "adapted itself to the conditions of the economy"—as Weber expected (p. 254)—the Nazis got most of the funds desired, without having to make any significant concessions.[11] After the Röhm purge, the party was financially immune to any pressure from business or state agencies, and could extend its activities far beyond its own financial resources.

*Specialization and Coordination.* The major divisions of areas of activity were not clearly defined within the party prior to 1932. In that year, Gregor Strasser established the new division called "organization." This division took over control over the subordinate organizations and appointed a set of inspectors who tended to control the regional heads of the party. The result of the reform was the creation of six specialized divisions consisting of organization (Strasser), propaganda (Goebbels), finance (Schwarz), business matters (Bouhler), youth organizations (Schirach), and paramilitary organizations (Röhm). All divisional heads were officially responsible to Hitler, which shows that officially definite jurisdictions were established along bureaucratic lines.

Actually, Strasser increasingly took over top coordination of the divisions and moved towards monocratic administration. This became evident when Schleicher offered Strasser the position as vice-chancellor in a new government. The personal clash between Hitler and Strasser involved not only a conflict over future policies but also between charismatic and monocratic-bureaucratic leadership. A discussion between the two rivals did not lead to a compromise; one had to go. Strasser called a meeting of the ten inspectors, who were all *Gauleiters,* and told them that he had resigned from all his positions in the party because he could no longer tolerate Hitler's type of leadership. While the inspectors urged Strasser to reconsider his decision, they all succumbed to Hitler's subsequent charismatic appeal. Hitler then removed this bureaucratic threat to his leadership. He objected especially to a monocratic administrator, to the inspectors, and to the subordinate position of some of the *Gauleiters.* Hitler appointed himself as head of the "political organization" and selected Ley as his deputy. A few days later, Hitler established a "political central commission" and appointed Hess as its head. Control over the subordinate organizations was divided between Hess and Ley. There were thus two deputies, heading the administrative and political divisions, but one leader. The nature of this leadership was revealed in Hitler's accusation of Strasser as a traitor "who tried to stab me in the back five minutes before final victory." In Hitler's mind, Strasser had questioned the charismatic quality, turned against charismatic authority, and had to pay the penalty of demotion for his defiance of the genuine leader. (Hitler sensed correctly that Strasser felt himself free of any "suggestive influence" of the leader. See Wagener, *Hitler aus nächster Nähe,* p. 405.)

The reorganization divided the party into the four divisions of finance, administration, political affairs, and party courts. Hitler officially kept control over political affairs, making Hess only his deputy. In 1934, Ley was appointed head of administration but excluded from political matters. Hitler officially kept for himself the right of coordinating the tasks of the four divisions, but he engaged only in sporadic interventions that mitigated but did not settle the recurrent disputes among the major divisions in the party.

In all, the formal organization of the party engendered two kinds of conflict. Separation of the jurisdictions between state and party bureaucracies tended to break down when some of the *Gauleiters* tried to add regional plans to the official Four Year Plan or when the Labor Front sought to supplement the economic plan with a social plan of its own.[12] While both attempts were rendered abortive by Goering, the closure of the party was temporarily lifted for some bureaucrats and businessmen who were subjected to party control in performing their tasks of preparing for war. Removal of the monocratic by the charismatic leader led to four independent divisions and built-in squabbles among their heads, indicating an inadequate handling of coordination.[13] But sporadic interventions were enough for imposing the will of the leader upon the party. It was the dictatorial nature of the unconditional charismatic authority that explains why the sporadic decision making, full of periods of uncertainty, did not paralyze the activities of the party. Hitler's commands laid down the new party line that had to be followed by all officials and members of the party.[14] Commands and obedience made the formal party organization compatible with dictatorial charisma.

## IDEOCRATIC ORGANIZATIONS

A relatively small and closed political party, of and by itself, would never have succeeded in destroying in 1933 the multiple party system and suppressing the independent labor movement. Agents of violence as well as a network of auxiliary organizations were required for performing these tasks for the party. In addition to these negative actions, there were the positive actions of providing a set of new organizations that permitted control of the masses in new compulsory organizations. How were these tasks accomplished?

*Conjunction.* One of the most important decisions of Hitler as a political organizer was to establish two party armies. In reflecting upon his failure in 1923, Hitler concluded that the party needed the strength of paramilitary organizations, but that these must be under the control of the party. The "Fundamental Instructions for the SA," signed in 1926 by Hitler and von Pfeffer, established the principle of a political army. "The SA is an institution of the NSDAP. Every SA man has to be a member of the party. Anyone excluded from the party will lose his membership in the SA. . . . The SA is a means for securing our main purpose; victory of our ideology. The party as the bearer of the ideology decides how the SA shall be used in the fight for National Socialism. . . . The political leaders of the branches, districts, and provinces determine how and when the SA units shall appear in public."[15] These rules established the political superiority of the party over the SA which was clearly seen as a party army.

Organizationally, however, the SA was kept separate from the party machine. While the political leaders alone set the specific tasks to be performed by the SA, execution of the assignments was placed clearly into the hands of the SA leaders. They alone decided upon the details of each operation and determined the internal organization of the SA. Cross-membership for the SA men could not be extended to the leaders. "It is forbidden that political leaders enter into the SA. . . . Nor is it permissible that SA leaders undertake political tasks . . . even when party membership does grant such a right."[16] Leaders of both organizations were obliged to work closely together in daily operations. Any differences of opinion had to be reported to the respective superior together with suggestions of how such conflicts could be resolved. These rules institutionalized the principle of organizational conjunction between party and paramilitary troopers.

In deciding upon the internal structure of the SA, Pfeffer had to follow Hitler's program for reorganization. "The organizational form of the SA, its uniforms and equipment, shall not be modelled after the old army. . . . The training of the SA shall not be oriented towards military ideals but shall be in accord with the requirements of the party." Not military exercises or training in the use of weapons, but physical training, shall occupy the SA. "Bodily accomplishments shall give each man the feeling of superior physical ability so that he can always rely on his own strength." The SA shall be a mass organization, not a secret club or conspirational cell, so that its huge street demonstrations can win followers for the party. The SA shall turn into "hundred thousands of fanatical fighters for our ideology." In waging this ideological war, it will be "the highest task of the SA to destroy Marxism and all its institutions."[17]

The services of the SA for the party were substantial. Hoping to take over this paramilitary organization in subsequent years, leading generals took a benevolent attitude towards the Fascist party.[18] The SA dominated the streets and executed the internal counterrevolution. There is little doubt that without the well organized mass organization of these paratroopers, the internal counterrevolution would not have been so prompt and so successful. Instead of "the party being the instrument of terrorism,"[19] it was the command of the party leader and his control over the party army that directed and utilized the paratroopers in their counterrevolutionary activities. Charismatic leadership was capable of directing paramilitary organizations.

*Organizational Fusion.* The SS and Hitler Youth were originally subdivisions of the SA. Both became separate organizations whose leaders became directly responsible to Hitler. Receiving their political and organizational instructions from him, both implemented the principle of organizational conjunction. Building up its own bureaucratic administration, with its own leaders and officials, the Hitler Youth cooperated with the *Gauleiters* in the various provinces. These provincial leaders issued the directives for the political programs. The SS organization, however, acted as the police within the party in the beginning of 1930. In June of 1931, the SS established an intelligence division which spied mainly upon other political parties, but on particular occasions also within the party. The membership of the SS rose "from 200 in 1929 to 50,000 in 1933, to 500,000 in 1939, and to a maximum of 950,000 in 1944."[20] In absorbing the tasks of the official police of the state and running the concentration camps, the SS implemented the principle of organizational fusion between party and state. Such fusion was the ideal and ambition of all other Nazi organizations.[21]

Financially, however, all the integrated organizations of SA, SS, Hitler Youth, NS Motor Corps, NS Flying Corps, and others remained dependent upon Hitler and party treasurer Schwarz. The latter received and allotted the funds obtained from the state treasury. The Hitler Donation, through Bormann, distributed its funds to the various integral organizations. The division of the money of the donation in table 5.3 indicates the financial dependence of these integral organizations upon Hitler.

Hitler also gave grants for special projects of these and other Nazi organizations. He also bestowed huge birthday gifts upon his immediate favorites so that loyalty to the leader could be sufficiently remunerative. The party treasurer used various formulas for allotting the funds received from the state. Payments usually entailed an auditing of the books and an indirect control of the special projects proposed by the integral organizations. Charismatic leadership was reinforced through dispensing of funds to subleaders.

TABLE 5.3. PAYMENTS TO NAZI ORGANIZATIONS, 1937–38.

| Recipients | Marks |
|---|---|
| The Führer | 30,000,000 |
| Führer in Obersalzberg | 11,500,000 |
| Reichsfuhrer SS | 200,000 |
| Air Sport Führer | 1,200,000 |
| Hitler Youth Leader | 300,000 |
| Air Defense Leader | 750,000 |
| Reichs Sport Leader | 300,000 |
| Leader of Sailboat Union | 180,000 |
| NS Welfare Organization | 200,000 |
| Costs of Collection | 163,186 |
| | 44,593,186 |

Source: Nurnberg Industrialists document 761, T–303, National Archives.

The integral organizations constituted the specialized units of the party. They all had one common goal: to implement the ideology of the leader and the party in particular lines of actions. Implementation took two forms. One was to indoctrinate its members with the ideals of the movement; the other was to run an organization that would implement these ideals in specific situations. The means employed could be peaceful and thereby related to particular groups seeking to change their outlook on life and live up to the ideals of the movement. Or the means could be violent— searching and fighting the opponents and breaking their resistance by force. The SA and the SS were the two party armies assigned the task of destroying the bearers of oppositional ideologies and punishing those who deviated, disrespected, or rejected the ideals and policies of party and regime.

### INTERLOCKING ORGANIZATIONS

The various auxiliaries comprising Nazis and their sympathizers in various professions and occupations came under increasing control of the party machine. Several secondary organizations were established with their headquarters as departments in either the organizational or political division of the party. Comprised mainly of party members, each could present a claim to a leadership position in the new affiliated organizations. Anyone employed in the various occupations and professions was herded into these new and compulsory organizations, directed by new Nazi leaders. The network of organizations for teachers illustrates the relationship between secondaries and affiliates. The main department of education at headquarters decreed early in 1934 that all party members engaged in teaching at elementary and secondary schools would have to join the Front of National Socialist Teachers; all other teachers not members of the party would be compelled to become members of the League of National Socialist Teachers; and all leaders of this affiliated organization would be selected from the front. These leaders received their directives from the main department of education.[22]

The affiliated organizations controlling nonparty members were given the two tasks of establishing a political class system by undercutting any persistent form of joint interest representation and of imposing ideological indoctrination. An official memorandum in 1936 emphasized especially the means of control. "The affiliated organizations are institutions of the party, which have been formed for implementing our ideas in each social or economic area of activity. Each of the affiliates receives its political directives from a main department at party headquarters. All leaders of the affiliates are political leaders (*Hoheitsträger*) and are appointed by the party."[23] Party control over the affiliates created many staff positions that were usually occupied by ordinary party members, often favorites of the major officeholders. The 16,000 staff offices of the Labor Front alone exceeded the one of the party machine. The affiliated organizations were dominated by a corps of leaders that compelled workers in the mass of occupations to join the organization so that they could be prevented from engaging in their own independent interests.

The network of the party's formal organizations consisted of four divisions that were united by the same kind of leadership, but separated by different tasks and organizations. The kingpin was the party machine that contained a set of departments acting as the heads of the secondary organizations. These were comprised of leaders occupying the major bureaucratic positions in the new affiliated compulsory organizations, the masses of which were compulsory members. There was thus an interlocking network of departments, secondaries, and affiliates that all were dominated by the same group of Nazis. Selection of the top leaders, financial dependence, and coordination of tasks, tied these organizations to the party. An abbreviated schematic presentation (table 5.4) may illustrate the components of this organizational network.

The important discoveries of this analysis are: (1) that the single party alone was not sufficient for establishing and maintaining its exclusive political and ideological control over the masses; (2) that a network of auxiliary organizations was necessary to extend the party's control over the masses; and (3) that there was not merely interaction between the party and the other organizations, but the former effectively

TABLE 5.4. ORGANIZATIONAL NETWORK.

| Personal Dictator: Hitler | Party Organizations |
| --- | --- |
| 1. Permanent Party Chief | 1. Party Machine<br>  a) Financial Administration<br>  b) Organizational Administration<br>  c) Political Organization<br>  d) Party Courts |
| 2. Commander in Chief | 2. Paramilitary Organizations<br>  a) SA<br>  b) SS<br>  c) NS Motor<br>  d) NS Flying Corps |
| 3. Superior Leader | 3. Integral Organizations<br>  a) Hitler Youth<br>  b) Labor Service<br>  c) NS Women League<br>  d) NS Student Club |
| 4. Ultimate Chief | 4. Interlocking Organizations<br>  a) Secondary Organizations<br>    (1) NSBO<br>    (2) NS Hago<br>    (3) NS Teacher Front<br>    (4) NS Journalists<br>  b) Affiliated Organizations<br>    (1) Labor Front<br>    (2) NS Farm Folk<br>    (3) NS Civil Servants<br>    (4) NS Teachers League |

directed and dominated the latter. Far from being the rule of an unstructured elite, the new types of paramilitary, integral, secondary, and affiliated organizations had to be created in order to permit an oligarchical group to dominate the polity and control the governmental administration.

## POLITICAL MONOPOLY

The effect of the party's dominance over the interlocking organizations has been the rise of a political monopoly. Specific internal and external conditions were responsible for party's domination of the political sphere. The counterrevolution was the main agency of political change. Its success depended very largely upon the alliance with the propertied classes, generals, capitalists, and bureaucrats that had dominated the state under Hindenburg's presidential dictatorship. In forming a coalition government, Hitler was able to get ahold of the government peacefully. The internal counterrevolution could then be carried through under the condition of the benevolent neutrality of the armed forces and controlling the state police.[24] Being appointed to the government peacefully permitted the Nazi leaders to stage and win the violent counterrevolution subsequently, and without any conflict with the state's instruments of power. The effect of the political alliance between the Nazis and the power holders behind the president was that the upper and middle classes were not affected adversely by the internal counterrevolution. Its furor was limited to the destruction of democracy and the labor movement. The overthrow of the Weimar Republic thus proceeded under the most favorable external conditions, ensuring victory for the Fascist party.

Once the destruction of the enemy was completed, the Nazis established a legal monopoly for their party. A law of December 1, 1933, declared: "The NSDAP has acquired the status of an agency of public law; its bylaws will be issued by the *Führer*."[25] The party was thus placed above, and organizationally separate from, the state. Accordingly no state law could regulate the activities of the party. This was a prerogative enjoyed only by Hitler. At the same time, the enforcement agencies of the state, including the secret police, were employed to protect the monopolistic position of the party. A law of December 24, 1934, protected the party and its leaders, organizations, uniforms, flags, and insignia against any malicious gossip or inflammatory agitation.[26] People's courts were established to punish anyone who engaged in any kind of political activity against the ruling party or its organizations or ideology. There was established a peculiar sort of political monopoly. The party's leaders and organizations were protected by the enforcement agencies of the state, while being at the same time above the laws of the state. The result was a division of the state, one sector being guided by legal norms and the party creating a prerogative state.[27]

The two most important conditions internal to the party for the political monopoly were the paramilitary organizations and the interlocking organizations. How could these mass organizations be dominated by the relatively small single party? One reason was the shared ideology and the fanatical belief in its values and goals. The other reason was new methods of interorganizational control. Differentiating the methods for the integral and semimilitary from those for the interlocking organizations was one of the secrets of Nazi success.

Domination of the affiliated organizations was accomplished through compulsory membership, imposed leadership, dictated goals, and frustrated or limited realization of collective interests of the herded members. These methods of dictation can only be summarized briefly.

*Compulsion*. The first and basic claim was that the party had the sole right to create new mass organizations. Freedom of association was abolished. New mass organizations were created that either absorbed previously autonomous organizations or replaced them by new ones. These new organizations were based upon occupations and professions or upon social and cultural interests. The underlying rule was that each type of major activity had to be organized by the party. For making a living in a special line everyone was compelled to become a member of the respective organization. The pressure exerted by party and paramilitary troopers was so great that no one could afford to stay out of the organization. This was especially true when employers made membership a condition for employment and accepted the obligation to deduct the dues for the compulsory organizations. Compulsory organizations and membership for those not belonging to the ruling party tend to be a universal feature of one-party regimes.

*Imposed Leadership.* All positions of leadership in compulsory mass organization became a prerogative of the ruling party. Leadership positions were the basic feature of the political monopoly. Non-Nazis had no right or opportunity to aspire to or occupy any leadership position. Nor did compulsory members have any right or chance to elect or otherwise influence the selection of leaders. All leaders were appointed either by the respective department at party headquarters or by the top leader in the compulsory organization. Candidates were taken from the secondary organizations who were committed to Nazi ideology, known as trusted paladins of the leader, and possessing skills and experience in the occupation or profession of the respective mass organization. Leaders were not responsible for their policies to the members, but exclusively to the top party leaders. The *Führerprinzip* was thus adapted to interorganizational control. All leaders in the affiliated organizations were responsible directly or indirectly to the leaders of the ruling party.

*Multiple Goals.* Selection of goals was not a right of the members, but a privilege of the leaders. There was one regime goal for all affiliated organizations. Their overriding task was to maintain and promote the rule of the dominant party and its ideology. This was closely associated with the charismatic goal: leaders and members were morally obliged to glorify and worship the great leader at all suitable occasions. The superior and ultimate chief of the secondary and affiliated organizations was not a mere figurehead but the most exalted personality in the world. The third goal was to derive support for the party within the affiliated organizations, most importantly to marshal support for the most recent political campaigns and to engage in extensive indoctrination in party ideology. Finally, there was the goal oriented towards the respective occupation or profession of the members of the affiliated organization. This specialized goal had to be compatible with the other three goals insisted upon by the party and the leaders of each affiliated organization.

*Curbed Behavior.* The test for the efficiency of the imposed leaders was their degree of success in curbing and redirecting the aspirations and behavior of the compelled members. There was no fundamental respect by the leaders for the vested interests of the simple members. Three rules were usually applied to redirect the interests of the members. Certain kinds of interests were supported but there was then a new justification. It was not the personal benefit in getting a job or securing a contract, but the leader's will or the regime's policy that led to the leader's approval of such actions. Other kinds of actions desired by the party, from improving occupational skills to participating in political demonstrations, were actively promoted by the leaders. Finally, any push of the members for realizing class or sectional interest collectively, such as engaging in collective bargaining or striking for better working conditions, was outlawed by the government, and actively frustrated by the Labor Front.[28] While preventing the rise of all wage rates in situations of full employment was difficult to attain, it was remarkable how effectively the patterns of curbed behavior could be imposed upon a formerly class conscious, but then organizationally destroyed, labor movement.

The resultant political monopoly, established by organizational domination, indoctrination, and terror, was incomplete in the first phase because of an alliance with the generals and big business and ideological conflicts among various segments within the party. The economic and military alliance had the effect that the respective departments at party headquarters were deprived of the right to control separate allied organizations. The economic and military departments were withering on the vine and eventually dissolved. All business firms were compelled to join the respective compulsory organizations, but their leaders were big businessmen, the goals were self-selected, and their collective behavior did not follow the Nazi pattern. Hitler himself recognized this relative independence of business groups when he said publicly in July 1933 that "the minister of economics was responsible for economic policies."[29] While the rules of compulsory organizations and appointed leaders were fully implemented in the economic and military fields, the specialized goals had merely to be compatible with the governmental—not party—goals, and the pattern of behavior permitted the realization of the respective personal and group interests. In the second phase from 1938 to 1942, however, additional qualifications for leadership were imposed. Economic leaders not only had to be acceptable to the large business concerns, but also had to present proof of their political reliability, as attested to by party leaders.

There were considerable differences among Nazi leaders about the goals and scope of the internal counterrevolution. Hitler and his coterie favored a counterrevolution largely limited to the political field, while others favored a "second revolution" also in the military and economic fields. Organizationally, there were three alternative modes of coming to power that presented themselves as different options for a counterrevolution, which can be stated schematically (see table 5.5).

It so happened that Hitler combined different features of these three options. He formed an alliance with the leaders of the old upper class, shared political power with them, used plebiscites to affirm his unilateral actions, and employed terror for carrying through the internal counterrevolution.[30] The ideological and organizational disputes concentrated upon the issue of whether the counterrevolution should be lim-

TABLE 5.5. OPTIONS OF FASCIST DICTATORSHIPS.

| *Main Actors* | Leader + Party | Party + Allies | Troopers + Party |
|---|---|---|---|
| *Main Action* | Plebiscite | Agreed Usurpation | Civil War |
| *Ideology* | Resurrectional Counter- revolutionary | Resurrectional + Restorative | Counter- revolutionary |
| *Kind of Power* | Partial + Bilateral | Partial + Bilateral | Total + Unitary |
| *Political System* | Plebiscitarian Dictatorship | Usurpational Dictatorship | Violent Dictatorship |

ited to the political sphere or also and subsequently be extended to the economic and military fields.

In preventing the extension of the counterrevolution, Hitler limited organizational domination in two ways. The SA was demoted from a full-fledged paramilitary to a mere preparatory organization engaged in physical training of future soldiers or reservists. The SS was promoted into the position of the sole agency of violence. The two secondary organizations of the NSBO for workers and the NS Hago for artisans were reduced to paper organizations of actual or potential office holders in the Labor Front. Their separate budgets were eliminated in 1935 and only the minority of the earlier members of these two organizations were admitted into the party.[31] The secondary organizations were eliminated for laborers and artisans, and their members were incorporated in the leader corps of the other affiliated organizations.

There developed a cleavage between the expectations and the roles performed by the leaders in many of the affiliated organizations. In charisma, the expectations engendered by the leader carry a high degree of creditability. In return for the trust of the followers, the leader's promises become definite expectations that are turned into definite personal goals of devotees. This was especially true for the SA whose members expected to be the nucleus of the future Nazi army. Hitler made a half-hearted promise on October 3, 1930: "The SA has to be conscious of the fact that it will be the reservoir of the future national army. The increase in the manpower of the Reichswehr . . . will come from those men who are imbued with the national socialist ideology."[32] When 300,000 of these men were appointed as the auxiliary police for carrying through political counterrevolution, they regarded this as the first step of a military career. Thus, there developed a conflict between the expectations inspired by the leader and the actual roles assigned by him to the paratroopers. Why did these frustrated expectations, resulting from a dubious promise by the leader and the denials of definitely desired roles, not lead to a credibility crisis for the Nazi regime?

If the socioeconomic interests had guided the action of the paratroopers, then there would have been a serious conflict between the SS and SA. Many of the SA men were unemployed or holding unsatisfactory jobs. They believed in their right to obtain substantially improved jobs in the military or administrative bureaucracy of the state. Moreover, the SA was fairly well equipped and sufficient men were trained for combat. After the purge, the SA possessed 177,000 rifles, 651 heavy machine guns, and 1,250 light machine guns.[33] In terms of the required means, the SA would have been in a position to defend their interests and to avenge their leaders by armed resistance, even after the sneak attack by the SS in 1934. Why did the SA not engage in a counterattack? Hitler had split the leadership and placed the opponents to Röhm into strategic positions. He defamed the beheaded leaders as homosexuals, not deserving loyalty and protection by their subleaders. Most important, Hitler had mesmerized their will to resist his purge or to avenge the killing. While "suspicious characters" were thrown into camps, Hitler's renewed charismatic appeal was effective: in obeying his orders, the SA became incapable of promoting and realizing their personal and organizational group interests. Confidence in the leader was restored as if the bloodbath had not occurred.[34]

In terms of power, the purge increased the charismatic authority of the leader because he was now supported by genuine devotion as well as acquiescence. Eliminating the threat of the SA to the military establishment reinforced the alliance. The military leaders immediately supported Hitler's quest to take over the presidency of the state also. Rendering the SA incapable of realization of interest increased the power of Hitler as well as that of the military and economic allies, which simultaneously broke the backbone of the economic counterrevolution of the artisans.[35] Although some of the short-term interests were recognized, the Nazified artisan organizations were deprived of their opportunity to realize their counterrevolutionary ideals in the economy.

Charismatic leadership thus promoted four quite different organizational policies in the first phase of the regime. First, the leader was able to enlarge and to strengthen the party and most of its integral organizations. Increased power and actions established the organizational nucleus for building up the political monopoly. Second, all police forces of the state were federalized and their leadership taken over by the SS. The secret police and the concentration camps became dual organizations that acted in the name of the state, but were manned and controlled by the SS as a party organization. Actions and power of this dual organization increased so rapidly that the SS and its agencies of violence became as powerful in the area of police work as was the party in the political field. Political and police monopolies were intertwined by the leader and both organizations became his obedient servants after the purge of 1934. Third, by purging the leader and demoting the organization of the SA, Hitler consolidated his personal power in the state, united the chancellorship with the presidency, and increasingly enjoyed the confidence of his allies. Consolidation and confidence prepared the ground for establishing his personal dictatorship over the military, the bureaucracy, and the economy in 1938. Finally, the network of interlocking organizations not only survived the opposition of some recalcitrant elements in the leader corps, but also extended its control over the compelled members of the affiliated organizations to such an extent that a whole range of new policies became possible without leading even to a significant degree of passive resistance from the populace. The four successful organizational policies created together a system of organizational domination.

We thus find that there was not an affinity, merely, between dictatorial charisma and dictatorial organization. The charismatic leader prevented the rise of a monocratic bureaucracy in the party and established a charismatic chain of command that centered around himself. The result of these organizational policies was an organizational domination by or for the benefit of the charismatic leader. How could one charismatic leader build up such a comprehensive but pliable organizational network and subject it to his authority? Why did some of the organizations not turn against the leader and destroy his authority and chain of command?

## CHARISMATIC GROUPS

In seeking an explanation of this organizational domination, we have to search for the elements of charisma in the party organization. Our thesis is that the NSDAP was a hybrid of a charismatic and bureaucratic organization, as originally suggested by Hans Gerth. But his evidence was limited to devotion and loyalty of the followers. The specific charismatic elements of leaders and paladins, and the role they played in the organizational network, still have to be identified and appreciated. Were these charismatic roles accidental and eventually terminated by the victory of organization over charisma?

The search for an explanation becomes possible if we build our interpretation upon modern organizational theory. Important are the three findings that "every organization creates an informal structure," that the goals are modified . . . by processes in [each organization] itself," and that "the process of modification is effected through the informal structure" of the organization.[36] The primary agents modifying the organizational goals are usually small groups. Their specific nature differs considerably in large-scale organizations. In industrial relations it has become customary to distinguish friendship circles from command groups, and interest groups from task groups.[37] The novelty in the Nazi organizations was that their most important small groups were of a charismatic character. While differing from mere command groups, these charismatic groups acquired the right to make the most significant decisions in the organizations while serving simultaneously the charismatic leader. What were the distinguishing features of these small charismatic groups in dictatorial organizations?[38]

*Charismatic Cliques.* Charismatic cliques are small groups dominated by a charismatic leader. It was Hitler's privilege to select members, assign them a particular role in, or expel them from, the group. Selection usually depended upon possession of three traits. Prospective members must have shown at various occasions the sustained feelings of devotion to and worship of the leader. Candidates must have exhibited comradely qualities in various critical turns of the movement, whether in the fight against the enemies or in strictly fraternal situations. Candidates must also have shown some special qualities, whether as political fighters, as useful henchmen, or as links with allies or other supporters. Given these traits for admission, those among the members were most effective who provided the leader with special personal services so that he could entrust them with special assignments for which the chosen members were solely responsible to the leader.

As chancellor, Hitler developed two related charismatic cliques. One was his table community. Whenever he resided in Berlin certain comrades were either expected to join him at his luncheon table or they were invited as special guests. The interaction was more on the comradely than on the worship level, although nobody could for one moment forget Hitler's exalted position. The general rule was that daily business would not be discussed at the table. Questions of history, ideology, and philosophy were the topics preferred by Hitler.[39] These were interspersed with telling humorous stories, intermingled with banter, usually at the expense of persons not present. Goebbels prepared his stories very carefully so as not only to entertain Hitler but also to arouse his animosity against some enemy of the minister of propaganda. Reputations could thus be made or destroyed at the luncheon table, depending upon Hitler's moods or reactions to the informal, if not planted, reports that came to him in a strictly personal fashion. Each table partner sought eagerly to please or to impress Hitler or at least to avoid his displeasure.

The second form of Hitler's cliques appeared in the monologue chambers, taking place at long sessions during the night. Since Hitler suffered from insomnia, he engaged in long monologues until the early hours of the following day. These rhetoric efforts fell into two categories. One was the presenting of stories aimed at entertaining or at creating a laughing fit. The more serious monologues sought to commit facts to memory through repetition, and to find their most suitable interpretation by looking at the same problem from different sides. The overall impression was one of a manifold personality—from the memorizer, repeater, debator, cunning defamer, and imitator, to the ideologist, brutal racist, admirer of war, and self-inflated hero. The monologues thus provided a forum for preparing his speeches, for impressing his favorites, and for retaining their beliefs in his exceptional gifts. The official recorder of his rhetoric talents said: "The puzzle of his fascination is partly explainable through his method of considering the same problem from all angles before a partner in the debate came to grips with the same issues."[40] Hitler's appeal and his exalted position permitted him to create his loyal audience. The obvious intention was of maintaining a kind of charismatic community in small groups of disciples, even after he had reached the pinnacle of his monopolistic power. The psychological need of giving and receiving adulation was thus satisfied in an institutionalized fashion.

Hitler's creation of charismatic cliques was imitated by some of the subleaders, especially by some *Gauleiters* or SA leaders. They employed some of the cruder methods of self-glorification, demanded adulation from their immediate employees as well as from their subordinates in command. Negatively, many of the charismatic imitators hated desk work and clerical procedures. Positively, many of the subleaders revealed an extraordinary urge for action, assumed unusual risks, engaged in questionable enterprises, or got themselves into debt. Following Hitler's example, these imitators formed their own cliques of adulation, parading as great men in front of self-chosen listeners, and thus illustrated that the distance between megalomania and imitated charisma could be very small indeed. Adulating henchmen were usually used to build up regional or affiliated power centers that created much trouble for the managers of the party machine.[41]

*Comrades of the Old Guard.* A typical effort of Hitler was to portray the years prior to the ascent to power as the "period of struggle" *(Kampfzeit)* by and for the party.[42] The struggle not only elevated the party but also provided the opportunity to celebrate the courage and accomplishments of the "old fighters." Without their manifold sacrifices, the *Führer*'s struggle "could not have been successful." The services rendered justified the claim for special privileges in the new political order. Party leaders carried through an extensive campaign to get an office for each old member. It became a publicly recognized duty *(Dankespflicht)* of the people to thank the "co-fighters of the *Führer*." The main office for civil servants at party headquarters pestered the various ministries of the government. The new law for restoring the rights of the professional bureaucrats was reinterpreted as giving preference to party members in the hiring and promoting of civil servants.[43] All previous officials who had been pensioned off because of their membership in the Nazi party had to be reinstated. Excluded from promotions were all members of previous democratic parties, all those who fought against the "national revolution," and all Jews and Germans married to Jews. In the session of the Cabinet on March 23, 1935, Hitler decreed that all National Socialists who had joined the party up to September 14, 1930, had to be appointed to positions of the lower and middle levels of the civil service. Towards the end of 1936 about one thousand Nazis had been installed in the Ministry of Finance.[44]

Granting these privileges did not transform the "old fighters" into bureaucrats. Hardly any of them possessed the necessary education, training, or technical competence for their new positions. The minister of the interior suggested that these requirements should be waived because of the new appointees' loyalty to the *Führer* as well as the political will and their perseverance during the period of the "struggle" which would enable these candidates "to compensate fully for their educational defects," given an adequate period of preparation.[45] A confidential memorandum of May 1934 on "National Socialist Personnel Policies," revealed that it was not only the desire to get these old fighters into staff positions but also to employ them as dispensers of Nazi ideology. It was thus not supernatural but ideological charisma that motivated the leader to place fanatical Nazis in the civil service without their adopting the bureaucratic mentality or a sense of status or honor.

In honor of the old fighters, Hitler invented a symbolic union between himself and his earlier assistants. In 1933 he created the Golden Party Emblem which was to be granted to all party members whose number was below 100,000 in the membership registry. The medal was supposed to express the gratitude of the party for the services rendered and the sacrifices borne during the first years of Hitler's struggle. It was also to be a sign for the emotional union linking the leader with the earliest disciples. Rather than signifying natural charisma, the medal became the source of a bitter dispute. Most apparatchiks, who had joined the party at a later date, could thus not receive the coveted emblem. In response to their protests, Hitler extended the list of recipients and, thereby, demonstrated the difficulty of endowing the Old Guard as a group with the halo of natural charisma.[46]

*Charismatic Oath.* Granting an emblem to the old fighters implied a kind of mutually belonging together and comradely feelings on both sides. Early in 1934, however, Hitler dropped this cloak of humility. He presented himself as the *Führer* who was standing at the summit of party and state. In fact, he was above both organizations, and all its officials owed their positions as well as their allegiance to him personally. The *Führerprinzip* was translated into *Führergewalt*. This new claim of Hitler was eagerly presented as a universal rule by the Nazis. "The will of the leader is the only source [of authority] and he alone is the sole enunciator of German law, whether within the sphere of the party or the state. It is of secondary significance in which form—law, decree, or ordinance—the leader proclaims the new law."[47] Political sovereignty thus became personified in the leader; all his claim and actions were said to emanate from his charismatic authority.

All bearers of political sovereignty in the party owed loyalty to the leader. Such an allegiance was to be attested by a proper oath. There thus took place on February 24, 1934, "the greatest oath taking in history."[48] No less than 795,000 party leaders, 130,477 leaders of the Hitler Youth, 43,063 leaders of the Nazi girls, 1,900 leaders of the NS Student League, and 18,500 leaders of the Labor Service had gathered in their local party buildings. Raising their hands in unison, all of them repeated the words of their oath of loyalty to their leader, spoken to them over the radio by deputy leader Hess. This national ceremony was repeated in subsequent years at the same day. It was by all odds the most symbolic act of dictatorial charisma. For all swore "blind obedience" to their leader without obtaining any promise in return.

Five months later came the testing of this allegiance. The oath given was interpreted by Hitler dictatorially as giving him a blank check for any action he might desire. The ideological and organizational conflicts between party and SA leaders were resolved charismatically. The first indication of this came in a speech of Hess on June 25, 1934: "The command of the leader, to whom we have sworn loyalty, has alone validity. Woe upon him who breaks his oath with the belief to serve the revolution by a revolt of his own. Wretched are those who believe to have been selected to help the leader through revolutionary action. Adolf Hitler is the greatest revolutionary; he remains innerly the revolutionary of the greatest style. He needs no crutches. Woe upon him who clumsily tramples into the fine net of his plans in the delusion of claiming to act faster. He is an enemy of the revolution—even if he is motivated by the most sincere belief. The beneficiaries would be the real enemies of the revolution, whether the reactionaries or the communists."[49] The charismatic ideological authority thus made the leader's commands incontrovertible. He alone was the fountainhead of the "revolution." It was within his unlimited discretion to decide upon the most appropriate policies and he had a right to destroy anyone who in the Nazi movement insisted upon another line of action. As we have seen, Hitler justified his bloody purge with the charge that Röhm had broken his oath of loyalty. "I have suffered the greatest breach of faith and fidelity which I have ever placed in one man whom I have shielded to the last moment and for whom I have made many sacrifices."[50] To be sure, Hitler linked charismatic with legal authority when he accused Röhm also of treason by having negotiated secretly with the French ambassador. But Hitler redefined the law against treason and claimed that not the Supreme Court but he was the "highest judge" to impose the death penalty without trial upon the accused traitors. In thus violating himself the legal norm, Hitler felt his purge justified through his charismatic authority.

*Subsidiary Charisma.* All the leaders of the network of organizations had sworn their oath of loyalty to the leader. It was their duty to fulfill the wishes of the leader in their organizations, even if they had no face-to-face relationship with him. Charismatic devotion and actions had to be guided not only by the emotions but also by the multiple goals of the respective organizations. While the regime and charismatic goals were clear in their intent, the particular meaning of Nazi ideology for the particular controlled groups was often not specific enough for concrete action. The leaders were enjoying a certain discretion of how to apply Nazi ideology in their field of activity. Diverse interpretations led to an emphasis of particular strands of Nazi ideology. The leaders of the Labor Front primarily promoted the honor of work and of industrial peace in industrial relations. The majority of the SA men insisted upon the realization of the Military counterrevolution. The SS tried eagerly to live up to the counterrevolutionary ideal of a pure Aryan race. The result was at least an ideological differentiation or at its worst an ideological conflict within the movement, as discussed in the preceding chapter.

Organizational domination did not readily assure an easy and effective fusion of charisma and ideology. Too great emphasis or push for a particular ideal invariably accorded the charismatic goal a subsidiary place in some organizations. The resulting tension between charisma and ideology gave rise to warnings or vetos from party headquarters or to prohibitions or suspensions from the leader himself. It was because of ideological differentiations and tension between ideological and charismatic goals that charisma had to struggle for maintaining its proper place in the organizational network. In case of an outright conflict—as in the pressure of the SA, the guild control of the economy, or the unification of the Protestant churches—the charismatic will of the leader always won over the ideological intentions and organizational promotions of particular groups of Nazis.

There emerge three significant differences between the small groups in American industrial relations and the charismatic groups in the Nazi organizational network. There was a difference in the nature of the groups. While the small groups of workers were unofficial and often deviated from the rules of the official organization, the charismatic groups were comprised mainly of the officials and were part of the command structure of the organization. There was also a difference in the linkage between group and organization. The groups of workers constituted the center of the informal organization, while the charismatic groups were the kingpins of the formal organizations in the network. There was also a difference in purpose of the respective groups. The unofficial groups tried to protect themselves against impositions of the agents of the formal organizations, while the groups of charismatic leaders aimed at preventing the ordinary members of the affiliated organizations from engaging in collective but independent actions for their own benefits.

### CHARISMATIC AND IDEOCRATIC APPARATUS

For the control of organizations, especially of the bureaucracy and party machine, charismatic groups provided only the indispensable personnel and emotional attachment. There also had to be a chain of command that would enable the leader to obtain the administrative services of bureaucracies, but permit him to employ his charismatic power (*Führergewalt*) to impose his will upon the various organizations. A charismatic or an ideocratic apparatus had to be superimposed upon the various organizations that would assure an efficient and sincere implementation of his policies.

What were the components and the essence of this apparatus? Did Weber's thesis apply that a bureaucracy can be fought only by a counterbureaucracy "that is equally subject to bureaucratization" (p. 224)? If not, how did Hitler immunize the members of his apparatus against the status, honor, and administrative procedures typical for a bureaucracy when he permitted his apparatchiks an office, substantial income, rank, and title of professionals?

*Plenary Authority.* In Hitler's mind, the party was primarily a "dynamic organization," the core of which was the leaders, not the members. In creating new branches of the party, he followed one rule: "First the *Führer*, then the organization, not the other way around."[51] If the new local branch did not grow, his remedy was to change the leader. The main task of such a leader was to imbue the members with a sense of loyalty and to concentrate upon making the right decisions. The trait of a good leader was to relieve himself of administrative tasks, stay away from factional disputes, and be a leader of men. It was only secondarily that a leader was also an office holder. In this capacity he had to supervise the work of the officials, mainly to arouse their enthusiasm for the leader and party and thereby increase the efficiency of his office. The party machine was seen as a mere instrument to serve the political and ideological purposes of the leaders, not possessing any independent significance of its own.

In selecting subleaders, Hitler paid little attention to administrative competence. He had only a small interest in assigning definite tasks, allocating functions, and specifying precise jurisdictions. Selection was mainly guided by two other requirements. Candidates for leading positions had to be able to act as his personal trustees who were fully devoted to him personally. Selectees had to know Hitler's personal preferences and habits, his ideas and ideals, so as to be reliable and to require only a minimum of instructions. Whoever was not fully devoted to him did not deserve a position of confidence. Next to the charismatic qualification was the commitment to the ideology. Subleaders had to be motivated by the right kind of ideals and had to use their own enthusiasm for exciting others and winning followers for the leader and cause.

In party matters, Hitler was not interested in bureaucracy, but in ideocracy. A distinction developed between ideology and ideocracy. Ideology comprised the ideals to be believed in and the goals to be attained. Ideocracy referred to the programs of actions, the will, ability, and enthusiasm, to realize the programs against all kinds of obstacles.[52] The party needed fighters who knew how to overcome all hurdles and to win the confidence of the voters in the shortest possible time. Assignments of tasks to such fighters had to be highly flexible and had to allow for a high degree of initiative and self-responsibility. Hitler thus institutionalized the device of plenary authority. The recipient was granted the right to act in the name of the leader as his trustee, and had the right to improvise all means essential for realizing the programs assigned to him, but had to stay within the ideology.

There were, however, two limits for the transfer of such unspecified authority. One affected the authority of Hitler himself, the other concerned the legislative proposals to the government. Each caused some decline in efficiency in the ideocratic organization.

When Hitler was appointed chancellor he did not appoint a monocratic head who would direct the party for the leader's benefit. Instead of a monocratic head, there was an appointment of three trustees leading the party. Treasurer Schwarz had already been granted unlimited control over the financial affairs of the party in 1931. In April 1933 Hess was appointed deputy leader and had the right "to decide all questions of the party leadership in the name of the leader."[53] A year later came the transformation of the mediation into a party court, and Buch was given the very general authority to act as the party judge and head the court system of the party.

But Hitler hesitated to grant Ley the authority to be the organizational leader of the party. When Ley questioned the superior position of the party by speaking of the "three pillars of the movement"—the SA, SS, and the political organization—Hitler stepped in decisively. While granting the title, but not a plenary authority, Hitler delimited Ley's jurisdiction "to the creation, maintenance, and supervision of the inner organization of the party, including administrative training and personnel, but excluding the integral organizations of the SA, SS, NSKK. . . . The political leadership of the party, including the secondary and affiliated organizations, belongs exclusively to me. The same is true for introducing, naming and renaming of offices in the party organizations, the selecting of new titles as well as the appointing or dismissing of political leaders down to the county level."[54] Ley was thus limited to strictly organizational matters, while political affairs remained in Hitler's hands. Although the separation was by no means strictly enforced, the limits put on Ley enabled Hess to greatly enlarge his own division in the party.

Instead of a monocratic head, as usual for a dictatorial party, there were four divisional trustees all directly responsible to Hitler. Since there was no regularized access and reporting to Hitler, there developed a gap in the decision making process at party headquarters. A whole host of jurisdictional disputes ensued from this broken link in the ideocratic hierarchy, followed by controversial or disputed decisions at the divisional level. Rather than being accidental, the gap was a necessary feature of Hitler's peculiar charismatic apparatus which could be at his direct control only at the price of some bureaucratic inefficiency.

The second limit related to the coordination of all organizational activities under the control of the party. While Schwarz had the legal right to audit the books of all organizations—except the SS—there was divided control over the secondary and thus affiliated organizations between Ley and Hess. After the collective meetings of all the departmental chiefs (*Reichsleitung*) had become inactive in 1935, there continued a fraternal conflict between Hitler's two trustees about the power and rules of coordinating and directing the controlled organizations. Hitler himself was the real bottleneck because he did not enforce the limitations imposed upon Ley in 1934. Circumstantial evidence suggests that his main reason was disappointment with Hess and continued discipleship by Ley. Hess dropped out of the monologuical meetings, while Ley attended and profusely admired his leader and excited him with many new plans, some of which were paid for by the Labor Front.[55] The charismatic clique thus interfered with the effective organizational domination by the party. But this deficiency was largely made up by the ideocratic organization of the SS and its concentration camps.

Behind Hitler's actions, there was the not clearly expressed idea of a fusion of charismatic and ideocratic organizations. The two lapses in decision making caused by himself indicate that this goal was not achieved at the apex of party and organizational network. Nevertheless, the Nazis congratulated themselves for having avoided bureaucracy in the party. The accomplished bureaucrat Schwarz said that the party has replaced the bureaucratic hierarchy by the "new principles of loyalty, responsibility, and voluntary participation in the work" of the leader.[56] Actually, a hybrid party machine was intermingled with charismatic and ideocratic elements of organization.

*Gau Kings*. In the organization of the party, provincial leaders operated as the dependent officials acting on instructions from the divisional heads at party headquarters. Schwarz especially had succeeded in making the financial officers of the *Gaus* directly responsible to himself. It was Schwarz, not the *Gauleiters*, who decided how the available funds should be spent in the provinces. A group of auditors, acting for the party treasurer, examined the books of the provincial and county offices and submitted detailed financial reports to Munich.[57]

Protest against this bureaucratization came not only from the political leaders in the field, but also from Ley himself. In a letter of April 14, 1936, Ley told Hess: "I have as organizational leader protested with hands and feet against the fact that the *Gauleiters* were deprived of their financial autonomy. Today we have the grotesque situation . . . that the financial authority of the *Gaus* lies in the hands of the treasurer in Munich. No financial officer at the *Gau* can dispose of a significant sum without the prior approval of the treasurer. I recall the fact that he stopped the payment of salaries for a certain period in Mecklenburg, and is preventing the *Gauleiter* of Düsseldorf to move into new quarters although the old ones are completely inadequate."[58] There thus occurred a clash between bureaucratic requirements and the charismatic apparatus of the leader.

Most of the *Gauleiters* regarded themselves as independent political leaders, who were responsible for their actions directly and only to the leader. Hitler had taken the same position in his reorganization of the party in December 1932.[59] The regional leaders were said to be fully and solely responsible for political events and moods of the people within their territory and responsible for their decisions directly to Hitler. The paladins were thus given the position of trusted charismatic disciples of the leader. As a result, *Gauleiter* Koch of East Prussia accepted orders only that originated from Hitler directly. *Gauleiter* Florian of Düsseldorf said of himself: "I am alone the Master in this *Gau*."[60] Even in 1942 Hitler was proud that he had elevated his paladins to "*Gau* kings."[61] Thus there developed a regional charismatic apparatus responsible directly to Hitler. The main extralegal, if not illegal, actions of the *Gauleiters* were usually legitimized by the leader's charismatic authority.

Since the leader required his charismatic apparatus, and the dictatorship its machine, the two modes of organization had to be reconciled to each other. Financially, a special fund of about ten percent of the regular dues was placed at the disposal of the *Gauleiters*. Additional sources could be tapped for special projects, such as the fashionable building of the *Gau*, youth or sports centers, most of which were financed by donations from enterprises. *Gauleiter* Terboven of Essen collected 557,000 marks for the construction of youth hostels.[62] Expropriated Jewish property was another source of special income of the *Gauleiters* if they remained within the rules set by Goering.[63] These financial advantages granted to the *Gauleiters* reconciled charismatic tendencies with bureaucratic requirements of the machine.

Hitler himself was very much concerned about the permanent tenure of the *Gauleiters*. No deputy *Gauleiter* was permitted to replace his boss. The attempt of the Hess office to use these deputies for watching over the *Gauleiters* was largely unsuccessful. Over a period of ten years, Hitler removed only three *Gauleiters*—Bruckner, Streicher, and Joseph Wagner. He also resisted all efforts to redistrict the territory of the *Gaus*. At the same time, he favorably received the claim that each *Gauleiter* should be granted some state office. In Bavaria, several *Gauleiters* became heads of governmental districts, and in Rhineland the administrative districts of the state were divided according to the ones of the party. The *Gauleiters* effectively succeeded "in transforming . . . charismatic blessing . . . into a permanent possession of everyday life" (p. 1121), by performing simultaneously the duties of a party bureaucrat and a charismatic apparatchik. In conflicts with the trustees, they could seek a decision from the ultimate leader.

*Charismatic Regents.* In the organization of the state, Hitler fully developed the monocratic headship of the state. He even went to the extreme of merging the chancellorship and the presidency in the new office of the *Führer*. Formally, this looked as if Hitler had shifted from personal to official charisma. Actually, the tasks and power of the *Führer* were never officially defined or delineated so that the office was merely a convenient device for strengthening the personal dictatorship. The major gain of linking personal charisma with the two merged offices was that Hitler gradually extended his power to all the various branches of the official bureaucracy. Up to 1943, the major goal of the Nazis in the state was to reduce the regular bureaucracy to an apolitical administration but utilized its technical competence primarily for Nazi ends.

Hitler desired a direct political control instrument at the middle level of the regular bureaucracy. It was on his initiative that the cabinet passed a law on April 7, 1933, to appoint regents (*Reichsstatthalters*) who officiated at the seat of each state government (*Länder*).[64] Hitler got Hindenburg to appoint only *Gauleiters* to these positions. The two exceptions related to Prussia and Bavaria in which Goering and von Epp received these titles. But Goering had to appoint the other *Gauleiters* to the positions of provincial presidents in Prussia who obtained an authority similar to the regents. The regents received the same salaries, expense accounts, and official residences as did the ministers of the central government.[65] Organizationally, the principle of personal union of state and party offices was thus implemented on the level of the *Gaus*.

In terms of tasks assigned, the new regents acted as state officials, party leaders, and Hitler's confidence men simultaneously. As state officials, the regents operated as the agents of the central government by seeing to it that the state governments followed the policies specified by the chancellor. In Hitler's own words: "The regents do not represent the interests of the state governments, but act as the agents of the *Reich* relative to the *Länder*)."[66] Without being able to govern in the states, the regents became the watchdogs over the regional bureaucrats.

Hitler assigned the regents also two kinds of party functions. On the one hand, the regents had to prevent party leaders from replacing state agencies. "It is the responsibility of the regents"—said Hitler—"to prevent organizations or party leaders from usurping functions of the state, to dismiss or to appoint officials, because these functions belong exclusively to the central government."[67] On the other hand, the regents had to induce regular bureaucrats to respect the party and its policies. The personal union of state and party offices enabled the regents or provincial presidents to intervene in the normal affairs of the administration whenever the prerogatives of the party had been slighted. For instance, *Gauleiter* Bürckel ordered the regional administrators to ignore a law of the *Reich* on subsidies for building small houses. Bürckel claimed that the party was not given enough influence in selecting the candidates for such subsidies for the Saar region. Hitler intervened and asked Hess to mediate between the minister and the *Gauleiter*.[68] A reformulation of the ordinance made the rights of the party more explicit and mollified the *Gauleiter*.

In terms of functions assigned, the regents did perform a few official tasks, but their range of activity was not limited by a restricted sphere of competence. In the summer of 1933 Hitler said: "You are the first regents, and it is up to you what you do make out of this position."[69] In these words, Hitler delegated a portion of his charismatic authority to the regents. As his alter egoes, the subleaders were authorized to act on their administrative level as if they were the *Führer* himself. If in doing so they would get into a conflict with the ministers, then the regents would call for a binding decision by the *Führer*.

Very soon this charismatic position of the regents collided with the policy of the Hitler government to abolish all forms of federalism. Minister Frick prepared a bill on the "reconstruction of the *Reich*" that became law on January 30, 1934. Hitler had given his signature as a symbol for unifying the people in one unitary state. As soon as this became known, the regents protested loudly to their *Führer*. Hitler had these letters forwarded to Minister Frick "for further action."[70] Assuming Hitler's full support for the law, Frick called a special meeting of the regents. His written speech revealed that he tried to expound the limited jurisdiction of the regents as well as the separation between party and state. But Hitler acted promptly. He cancelled the meeting and thereby prevented a confrontation between the minister and the regents.

Here was a clear clash between the bureaucratic principles of hierarchy and specified jurisdiction and the charismatic principles of equality between minister and regent, preferred access of the regents to the leader, and the regents' responsibility only to the leader. In his bureaucratic way of thinking, Frick was convinced that Hitler would opt for bureaucracy. When he was ready, Hitler made two related decisions. In normal administrative matters, the regents could accept instructions from the ministers. But "an exception has to be made . . . in cases of special political significance. Such an exception is fully in accord with the special position of the chancellor as the leader of the nation."[71] Hitler was not willing to give up his alter egoes on the middle administrative level.

From the middle of 1934 to the end of 1937, the right of the regents did not include taking any initiatives in legislative or administrative matters. Various efforts in this direction were usually cancelled by the affected ministries. The original intention of monthly meetings between the *Führer* and his regents was not implemented. The few meetings held were dominated by Hitler's speeches. The irritation of the regents expressed itself at a meeting on August 20, 1936, which was called by Schacht to get the regents' support against Goering's attempt to take over economic leadership.[72] Subsequent efforts of various regents to take over execution of the Four Year Plan in their territory were effectively stopped by Goering. The increased centralization of administration at the expense of the regents found its expression in a long memorandum of Sauckel in 1936 who complained to Hitler about the over-centralization and the loss of influence suffered by the regents.[73] This dissatisfaction led to a special meeting of the regents in December 1937, chaired by Hess, at which it was demanded that the regents be recognized as the executive heads of the regional administration.

This demand was accepted by Hitler after the purge of February 1938. On the one hand, there was a definite ruling by Hitler on the political tasks of the *Gauleiters* that came in 1939. "The *Gauleiters* are in all instances responsible for all measures of political significance, especially those affecting the mood of the population. Agencies of the state do have to assure themselves of the approval of the *Gauleiters* in general. Political measures by state agencies must have the prior consent of all the participating *Gauleiters*. If an agreement between state and party agencies is not possible, then the final decision will be made by the deputy leader of the party."[74] This instruction aimed at dividing the political from the bureaucratic decisions, concentrating the former in the regional heads of the party, and limiting the bureaucrats to nonpolitical decisions. *Gauleiters* were given the discretion to decide what was "political" in an administrative policy. The sole constraint of the *Gauleiters* was to get the approval of the deputy leader on controversial issues. The period of a bureaucratic superiority in administration had come to an end by 1940.

Austria became the first land for experimenting with the rule by regents. At first Hitler had signed a directive authorizing an office in the ministry of interior to supervise the legal incorporation of Austria in the *Reich*. But he also appointed Bürckel as the campaign manager for the plebiscite. Bürckel immediately overstepped his authority, passed new laws—an exchange rate of three shillings to two marks—and asked for Hitler's consent by telegram.[75] Hitler not only approved but instructed Frick to obtain Bürckel's prior approval to all new laws.

Bürckel tried to institutionalize his newly won power. On March 30, 1938, he submitted a bill which was to authorize the regent of Austria to be the sole legislator for the province and to exercise a veto power over the legislative actions of the district leaders. Hitler refused to sign this bill and rejected the veto power. Instead he approved the new party organization for Austria which was divided into seven new *Reichsgaue*. His intention was to "create in Austria a situation that can be taken as a model for the *Reich*."[76] This denied the regents but offered the *Gauleiters* the power of being the governors of their districts.

There were extensive negotiations between the new governors of Austria and the ministries of the *Reich* as to who should control the specialized agencies—railways, postal service, finance, and economy—which lasted from June 1938 to March 1939. Hitler twice instructed the cabinet to find a compromise. When this failed, Hitler called Frick and Bürckel to Berchtesgaden. In the main, Bürckel's proposal of making the seven *Gauleiters*, the executive governors of their districts responsible only to Hitler, was accepted, but the redistricting of the special agencies was rejected. To console the disturbed ministers, Hitler agreed to leave the watchdog position of the regents unchanged in Germany proper and limit the new satrap organization to Austria and Sudetenland.[77]

The new system of executive governors was liked so much by the Nazis that it was applied to the incorporated and occupied territories. Hitler appointed *Gauleiters* as *Reichs* commissioners of Alsace, Lorraine, Warthegau, and West Prussia, and favorites for Poland, Holland, and Norway. Each commissioner received his instructions from Hitler directly and was responsible only to him. Enjoying the status of a minister and receiving an equal salary, the commissioners refused to discuss the principles of their administration with the ministers. Frick presented a bill to Hitler which was to require the commissioners to report regularly to the various ministries. Hitler furiously rejected the bill. Frick was told that "it is the expressed wish of the *Führer* that the *Reichs* commissioners of Holland and Norway, as well as the protectors of reduced Czechoslovakia and Poland, were directly subordinate to him and not bound by any directives of the ministers."[78]

In regard to the power structure, regents remained watchdogs of the civil and military administrators in Germany proper because the Nazis needed economic, military and administrative expertise. As providers of such services, these three groups became minor power holders that could effectively oppose direct party domination of their own activities. Party power could be brought to bear only indirectly through the charismatic agents, and these had to be careful not to reduce expert efficiency. Regents who became governors in the incorporated and in some of the occupied countries merged personal with office charisma. In these territories, even the officials of the lower ranks came from party officials who were transplanted into the occupied lands.[79] Governing mainly by means of the police was effective for resettlement, deportation, exploitation, and extermination but not for inducing the subdued populations to work "voluntarily" for the German war machine.

## CONTROL OF STATE BUREAUCRACY

The party machine functioned as a counterbureaucracy in the state. Hitler centralized all top positions of the state in his hands. He acted in his capacity as party head as well as charismatic leader. Hitler took over first the office of the president, then he dominated and overruled the cabinet, and finally he merged the office of the chancellor with the one of the *Führer*. After the purge in 1938, Hitler became his own minister of war, forced the commanders of the armed forces to take orders directly from him, and in 1941 took over the strategic direction of the war. In the economic field, Goering lorded over the economic state agencies and enterprises, acting according to Hitler's instructions. As a result, a party counterbureaucracy was superimposed upon the state bureaucracy, military forces, and economic agencies. Party control became simultaneously a personal and charismatic rulership.

How could one man take on so many offices, determine their major policies, and control their implementation? The answer lies in a system of devoted secretaryships, linked with superministries. General Keitel became head of the military administration and functioned as Hitler's personal secretary, assisted by the military strategist General Jodl. Goering took over the ministry of economics for six weeks, during which eighteen top officials were dismissed, and the agencies of the Four-Year Plan incorporated into the ministry.[80] The decline of the cabinet was followed by the promotion of its secretary to the minister of the chancellory. All other ministers could get access to Hitler only through an arrangement with the new minister, Lammers, who became in effect Hitler's secretary for administrative affairs. Although Himmler was officially not a minister in the second phase, he had united the regular with the secret police, possessed his own budget, controlled almost all quasi-police function—border and foreign exchange control—administered the concentration camp, directed the militarized SS, and thereby established a superministry in police affairs. As head of an ideocratic organization of party and state, Himmler acted on instruction from Hitler and was responsible for the police and extermination policies solely to his leader.

To be sure, these four secretaries did not have the same charismatic relationship to Hitler. Goering and Himmler were Hitler's paladins and acted as his trustees. For instance, Goering appointed over twenty plenipotentiaries, each in charge of an industry or program, reporting only to Goering. A semicharismatic apparatus was thus superimposed upon the economy, assuring its mobilization for war. Goering and Himmler received delegated charismatic authority that enabled them to give commands in their own rights, acting within the policy lines of Hitler. Keitel and Lammers were bureaucrats, able to handle the administrative matters of their superministries, but neither one was given the power of issuing commands. It was their task to prepare the bills or ordinances that were then accepted, rejected, or modified by Hitler. Although the particular linkage to the charismatic leader differed, the effect of these secretaryships was the same. All spheres of the state came under direct command of the *Führer*. Charisma turned into a personal dictatorship directing a super-Fascist regime.

In legislative and related matters, deputy leader Hess established a "party ministry."[81] His specialists examined all bills and major ordinances of the ministries. Hess possessed a veto power over all legislation, since Hitler signed bills only when they were countersigned by his party deputy. The office of Hess also had to give its consent to the appointment of bureaucrats at the upper levels.[82] The *Gauleiters* had this right of participation at the regional levels. Party officials usually imposed two political conditions: candidates had to be members of the party in good standing who in the past had acted favorably to the Nazi party. Eventually, most state bureaucrats—except for the military—became members of the party and were subjected to its discipline. The regents, additionally, were the watchdogs of the provincial governments and in wartime also did check upon the actions of the military commanders insofar as they had political significance.

In political and personnel matters, the party machine was a counterbureaucracy. Its leaders at the regional and local levels acted as watchdogs of the state bureaucrats, while all top political positions tended to be occupied and effectively controlled by the superior party leaders. In a party dictatorship, Weber's thesis on the superiority of bureaucratic experts does not hold. It is only in democracy that "the political 'master' always finds himself, vis-a-vis the trained official, in the position of the dilettante facing the expert" (p. 991). Politicians of the single party develop a sense and practice of superiority. This is based upon the political monopoly of the party and the devotional-trustee relationship to the charismatic leader. The counterbureaucracy would have been much less effective if its rulers would not have possessed the prerogative of monopolized political power.

There thus emerge four different kinds of Nazi organizations operating within and for the dictatorship. There was first the bureaucracy of the party and all its secondary as well as affiliated organizations. Then there were the paramilitary organizations acting as the agents of secret police and terror as well as implementors of the internal and external counterrevolutions, responding to the specific commands of the leader. Moreover, there were the ideocratic organizations of which the educational and propaganda divisions of the party were directly engaged full-time in systematic indoctrination, whereas the party pushed the party line, and the paramilitary organizations forced Nazi tenets and slogans upon those who did not voluntarily accept Nazi ideals and policies.[83] Finally, there were the charismatic organizations that consisted not only of the leader's direct assistants or delegates but also comprised all office holders in all Nazi organizations. In demanding an oath of loyalty from all of them, Hitler institutionalized his charismatic paladins into a distinct corps of subleaders. Each one held office only so long as he enjoyed the leader's confidence.

Beyond the four Nazi organizations, the civilian and military bureaucracy of the state also had to swear a charismatic oath to the leader. Civil servants not only had to profess to believe in Nazi ideology, but also had to implement any law bearing Hitler's signature regardless of its legality. Officers and soldiers committed themselves to the following oath of allegiance: "In the name of God I swear this sacred oath that I shall serve in unconditional obedience to the *Führer* of the German people, Adolf Hitler, as the commander-in-chief of the armed forces, and as a gallant soldier I am ready to give my life in fulfilling this oath.''[84] Millions continued fighting even when they knew that wholesale disobedience would have terminated a hopeless war and could have possibly prevented a dismemberment of Germany.[85]

The result of superimposing charismatic loyalty upon party and state organizations was the rise of a synergistic charisma in organizational matters. The effect of the charismatic infusion can be condensed into four inferences. First, Hitler's exalted position was maintained even in a period of relative tranquility, because he united his strategically placed paladins into one charismatic corps of leaders who regarded his commands simultaneously as administrative instructions and as charismatic orders. Second, charismatic domination over the civilian and military bureaucracy of the state increased the leader's power as he, step by step, centralized all top positions in his hands and got his commands enforced either because of the counterbureaucracy or because of the bureaucrats becoming his devotees. Third, a charismatic apparatus was also built into the organizational network in which trusted party members and worshippers were occupying all important offices in these mass organizations. The leader was thus simultaneously assured of effective political supervision of the masses and of charismatic obedience of his agents in these organizations. As a result of their devotion, these agents usually did not feel themselves as oppressors, but regarded themselves as trusted paladins of the leader, eager to live up to his expectations and ready to fulfill all of his commands. Fourth, while there were underground groups of opponents, most of them were discovered and punished by the secret police. Of the many attempts on Hitler's life, only the Stauffenberg coup had any political significance. At no point did the agents of terror show any significant weakness that could be exploited by underground groups. It was because of this synergistic fusion of charismatic obedience and systematic terror that the counterrevolutionary regime of the Third Reich could not be overthrown by an internal revolution. External defeat in a two-front war alone could terminate the rule of charismatic dictatorship.

# CHAPTER SIX

# CHARISMA AND DESPOTISM

THE ESSENCE OF DICTATORSHIP is a tyrannical rule by one person or by a small group of persons who impose their will upon the population at large. Depending upon the instruments of oppression utilized, it is customary to distinguish between military, police, and single party dictatorships. Violation of their own constitutions and suppression of freedom and liberty for the oppressed, prerogatives and privileges for the dictators and their agents, are the well-recognized hallmarks of all three kinds of dictatorships. Max Weber added a fourth kind of dictatorship, despotism, which rules by means of a centralized bureaucracy in which there is a "complete dependence of the administrative staff upon the chief so that every limit to his power is missing."[1] Political history is replete with these four types of dictatorship and their modifications, none of which inherently requires a charismatic leader. Our problem is how and why charisma becomes a part of dictatorship.

Loss of individual and political freedoms and oppression by a violence galore has created resentment and hatred for dictators and their political systems. Democrats feel a deep-seated animosity towards dictatorial regimes. It is thus taken for granted that no group in oppressed nations can and ever will love its dictator. Yet it is precisely this new phenomenon of millions loving their particular dictator that points to charismatic leadership. The waves of emotional upsurge in mass meetings, elicited, directed, and exploited by the leader, prove effectively that some dictators do possess the exceptional quality of the charismatic personality.

There also is extensive evidence for the development of charismatic communities surrounding a dictatorial leader. This is true even when the leader and the disciples live in different places, and when the political party acts as the nucleus for a charismatic community. Subleaders turn into charismatic paladins. For instance, the cynical and sophisticated Goebbels wrote in his diary in 1926: "Adolf Hitler I love you because you are strong and sincere. He is what one has to call a genius."[2] The slightest disfavor by Hitler engendered deep depressions in Goebbels. The "old fighters" acted as if they were Hitler's aristocratic community. The vanguard nature of the

Bolshevik party often performed the same function for Lenin's paladins. Young Stalin loved his leader, saw in him the hero with whom he identified himself. The careful selection of party members by Lenin, chosen for their courage and revolutionary spirit to engage in secret political activity, was turned by Stalin into a source of status distinction. He proudly regarded the party as an "organization of leaders" and exclaimed that "only the party committees can worthily lead us; they alone light up for us the path to the 'promised land' called the world of socialism."[3]

The charismatic community and the superiority feeling of belonging to the select can thus also nest in a dictatorial party. The leader's wishes are gladly fulfilled, though they take the form of commands. It is because of this willing submission to the will of the leader, acting as a dictator in the political sphere, that there developed the "basically authoritarian principle of charismatic legitimation" (p. 267). Given this reciprocal relationship between the leader and his paladins, two questions call for specific answers: Which particular beliefs and actions permitted the leader and his inner circle to act as a genuine charismatic community within party and state? Was charismatic leadership a kind of an idiosyncrasy only of the Nazi regime, or can the same kind of leadership also be found in other single party dictatorships?

It is the main task of this chapter to engage in a comparative study of charismatic leadership of fascism and communism. Our aim is twofold. On the one hand, we want to identify the basic similarities between the respective leaders and their paladins in the two dictatorial regimes. On the other hand, it is also necessary to indicate the specific differences between leaders and circles and discover whether the divergencies result only from the different situations or derive also from the contrary ideologies, organizations, and respective policies.

Given this specific purpose, we shall select the same criteria for our comparison of the leadership in both regimes. Our two prototypes will be Hitler for fascism and Lenin for communism.[4] What was the nature of the crisis faced, the superhuman qualities possessed, the modes of mass appeal employed, the ideologies used as guides, and the organizations utilized by each leader in building up his charismatic rulership? How were the charismatic and legal authorities combined, the particular forms of discipline imposed, the personality cult developed and practiced by each one of these charismatic dictators?

In tracing the similarities and differences of leadership we expect to find an increasing consolidation of the leader's power in party and state. As in Weber's theory, there occurred a gradual and occasionally violent change in the nature of the charismatic qualities. But the nature of the change was of a quite different character. Instead of a depersonalization of the qualities, and of a routinization of the relationships between the leader and the noncharismatic forces, there developed the tendency towards the infallible superman who tried to break all barriers to his personal power and thereby moved into the direction of despotism. Potentially or actually, each leader tries to rule supremely over the party and paramilitary as well as civilian and military bureaucracies. Our provisional hypothesis for this chapter is that despotism became the alternative to depersonalization and routinization in the last phase of Hitler's rule, and in a modified form, Stalinism in the Soviet Union.

## DIFFERENT CRISES

Two specific conditions permitted the rise of charismatic leaders in communism and fascism. One was a severe crisis undermining the authority of the state and other ruling organizations. The other was the rise of a collective excitement that destroyed the belief in the validity of power enjoyed by the prevailing rulers. These two conditions were fully recognized by Weber when he emphasized that the gifted leaders became known in "the moment of distress [be they] psychic, physical, economic, ethical, or political" in nature (p. 1112). While several of these crises coexisted and interacted, the major crisis was different for each one of the charismatic leaders. In the Communist situations, Lenin and Mao faced primarily a military crisis in their respective states. The regular armies had been defeated by foreign powers, the regular bureaucracy was disintegrating, the formerly docile peasants were in a state of revolt, and the provisional or traditional governments were paralysed. In these catastrophic situations it became possible for a small revolutionary party with a charismatic leader to engage in an insurrection and establish a new regime by means of victorious civil wars.

The main crisis facing the Fascist leader was a severe economic depression, aggravated by prior military defeat and grievances following the hyper-inflation and Ruhr invasion. While the suffering of most previous downswings fell mainly upon the labor classes, the Great Depression also imposed severe deprivations upon the lower middle class in city and countryside. Combined with the resentment of inadequate punitive peace terms, two quite different kinds of emotional excitements developed. Emotions of deprivation felt by workers were politically stultified by the inner split within the labor movement. The increasingly ferocious hatred of the middle groups was exploited by a counterrevolutionary party and leader. Seizing the opportunity created by the depression and the particular antilabor anxiety enabled the Fascist charismatic leaders to build up a major mass movement and—by means of an alliance with conservative forces—placed themselves at the head of a new government.

The different military and economic crises were thus accompanied by a two-pronged psychological crisis. Mass excitement of Russian peasants and workers created a revolutionary situation, while the emotional upheaval of the German middle classes moved in the direction of a counterrevolutionary situation. One emotional wave provided an opportunity for a Communist party and leader, the other for a Fascist party and leader, to move into the leading positions of new political systems. The respective crises provided the opportunity for a fundamental change, but the divergent directions resulted from the intentions and actions of the respective charismatic groups.

In addition to these external crises, there followed a set of other crises that arose because of systematic policies of the two kinds of regimes. The Bolsheviks generated a major internal crisis through their collectivization of the private holdings of the peasants. The Nazis created another kind of crisis when they invaded one Continental country after the other. Dictatorial regimes of major size have the capacity and inclination to initiate new crises that they tend to exploit for their own benefit and impose great sacrifices upon other social classes or other countries.

## SUPERHUMAN QUALITIES

Fascist charismatic leaders possessed an abundant flow of emotions which they magnified to such an extent as to become the magnets for the masses. Hitler and Mussolini were outstanding leaders of the charisma of the rhetoric. Operating within a democratic system in their earlier years, they were given the opportunity to cultivate their natural endowment to the hilt. Quite different were the emotional and external situations for Lenin and Mao. Having to operate under conspirational conditions, requiring secrecy and full reliability of the paladins, Lenin found that love and friendship had to be sacrificed to the demands of his cause. Always on guard against possible spies, and in the wake of the schism within the Social Democratic party of Russia, Lenin "had eliminated the danger of love and had kept his emotions under control, at least as reflected in his political activities."[5] It was only after the February revolution in Russia that Lenin discovered his oratorial capacity and developed a considerable emotional appeal in mass meetings. He was reported as "the most powerful man I ever saw on the platform."[6]

Another kind of difficulty arose with the supernatural calling of the leader in dictatorial movements. As we have seen, Hitler experienced the clash between supernatural charisma and the Christian canon of incarnation. God's will was only once incarnated in His son. This conflict was officially resolved by Hitler's shift to providential charisma, but personally he increasingly believed in a pagan God. Mussolini carefully avoided this predicament by widening the concept of religion. "Fascism is a religious belief . . . in an objective spirit which goes beyond particular individuals and includes everyone as a participant in a religious community."[7] The pope called the Fascist leader a "man of providence" and permitted church members to swear an oath of loyalty to the Duce. Such an oath was not a religious sin, because the oath was accompanied by the mental reservation of not violating any religious commandment. But Hitler's increasing reliance upon heroic charisma involved more of a superhuman than a supernatural source of his charisma. His claimed infallibility was then more an expression of the superman and less a belief in a supernatural incarnation of God's will.

Communist charismatic leaders have no use for religion because they are convinced atheists. The Communist giants became prophets of revolution who claimed omniscience for themselves, and universal validity of their laws of history. At first, the new Marxist science became the Gospel that had to be taught to the ignorant. There was also a veneration for Plekhanov, the first Russian Marxist. In the subsequent disputes, Lenin was "beginning to feel within himself the capacity to lead the movement, if necessary, without the master."[8] Gradually he became the sole authentic interpreter of his laws of history. The subsequent leadership contained the two charismatic elements of omniscience on the side of the leader, and the readiness of the paladins to accept his interpretations and policies and to obey his orders. Obedience was rendered in the dual form of admiring the leader personally and of venerating the science collectively as containing the eternal truth. While the Fascist leaders openly proclaimed their superior qualities, the Marxists believed that the position was thrust upon them because they alone were perceiving the "scientific truth."

There were thus two changes in the specific nature of charismatic qualities of the leaders. While originally attributing their qualification to supernatural sources, Fascist leaders at a certain point shifted to heroic charisma of the superman. Communist leaders derived their superior abilities from a certain theory of history and veneration of a revolution. Because of these beliefs, paladins claimed superior knowledge and foresight, and combined omniscience with worship for their great leaders.

### Charismatic Appeal

The aim of the appeal was to secure the unbounded love of the followers and guard against any potential and actual disloyalty. For Lenin as well as Hitler, effective appeal developed in two distinct phases. During the period of preparation, each aspirant concentrated first upon gaining a group of devoted paladins. While forbidden to speak in mass meetings for almost a year after his release from prison, Hitler engaged in organizational action and built up new local and regional branches of his party.

Working in exile, Lenin demanded full reliability and devotion from his paladins. Speaking of underground work, Lenin wrote: "In order that the center should always be able not only to advise, persuade, and argue . . . but actually conduct the orchestra, it is necessary that it should be known precisely who is playing which fiddle, and where and how he does it; where any person has been trained to wield an instrument; who strikes a false note, and where and why . . . who ought to be shifted, and how and whither, in order to eliminate the discordant tone. . . ."[9] Whoever was not reliable or devoted was either demoted or expelled, whereas the true paladins were advanced to the most coveted positions in the organization. The lad Schirach became the leader of youth as well as student groups. Strength of the belief in the leader was thus accompanied by the dictatorial discretion of the leader to shift or expel anyone from the party not submitting to the leader's wisdom.

The period of consummated appeal began only after the leader was given the chance to meet masses in huge meetings. But there was a striking difference in the modes of appeal. Hitler excited, aroused the emotions, created a hysterical outburst against the enemy, and an overflowing enthusiasm for himself. Lenin presented arguments, sought to convince, tried to gain adherents, and aroused the masses as much for his cause as for himself. Indeed, in the mass meetings of the summer of 1917, Trotsky's rhetoric outshone that of Lenin.[10] When Lenin went into hiding in

Finland, there occurred the exceptional event of two charismatic leaders working hand in glove. While Lenin worked out the strategy of insurrection, Trotsky executed it in his own way. He was the darling of the masses, expressing their hatred and arousing their enthusiasm for himself and the cause. It has been said of Trotsky's most memorable speeches: "He then listened to his own voice as to that of a stranger, trying to keep pace with the tumultuous rush of his own ideas and phrases and afraid lest like a sleepwalker he might suddenly wake and break down. Here his politics ceased to be the distillation of individual reflection or of debates in small circles of professional politicians. He merged emotionally with the warm human mass in front of him, and became its medium."[11] Trotsky personified the revolution. When the soldiers in one garrison of Petrograd hesitated to put themselves under Bolshevik direction, he went there and persuaded them to swear the oath of allegiance to the Soviets. "The revolution worked mainly through its titanic power of persuasion, and it seemed to have vested the greater part of this power in a single person."[12] Instead of fighting against each other, as Weber expected, they collaborated to such an extent that Lenin proposed Trotsky as head of the first Bolshevik government and only after he refused did Lenin accept this position. In a sense, Trotsky personified more natural charisma and Lenin superhuman charisma. In political matters, Lenin was the major, Trotsky the minor or partaking, charismatic leader.

## DICTATORIAL IDEOLOGY AND CHARISMA

Fusing ideology with charisma was typical for democratic and dictatorial charismata. Interpenetration provided two significant advantages. The respective ideology supplied the leader and the led with a set of immediate goals and a vision for the future. Ideology strengthened charisma because the leader could extend the enthusiasm for his person into an admiration of his cause, and a willingness to accept his goals. Ideological charisma increased the opportunities for masses to participate vicariously or actually in the respective movements.

There was, however, a fundamental divergency in the role played by ideology in democratic and dictatorial— and here in Fascist and Communist—leaderships and movements. There was first the basic difference in the particular content of the respective ideologies. This was followed by the different sets of goals, the priorities selected, and the policies chosen by the respective leaders. Democratic ideologies are open to all voluntary believers, are often internally diffused, and contain different strands of ideals that appear in different modes of combined beliefs and political manifestations. Dictatorial ideologies are often internally consistent, claim an intransigent righteousness, deny rival ideologies a right to exist, and eventually turn into an indoctrination of the indifferent groups. Disbelievers were ostracized and punished. The monolithic claim for the dictatorial ideology was even more pronounced in communism because of the fusion of ideology with science, but the intolerance was extreme in each case of dictatorship, since the charismatic leader was the sole enunciator of the respective ideals, goals, and policies. Simultaneously, ideals became fused with the belief in the leader; ideals turned into political weapons of dictatorial charisma.

In spite of the exclusive claim of Fascist and Communist ideologies, there did occur another significant event. In each regime, the leaders developed two valid ideologies. While diametrically different in substance, the belief in two ideologies strengthened the influence of ideological charisma. We have already seen how Hitler utilized his resurrectional ideology for keeping his alliance intact and for "peacefully" establishing his Greater Germany, and how the counterrevolution led to war and Fascist imperialism. Linkage of two ideologies with charisma gave the Nazi movement and its leader an inner dynamic and expansive drive that could be stopped only through a total defeat in a world war.

Surprisingly, the Communists of Russia also developed two ideologies that became fused with charisma. One went under the neo-Marxian label of permanent revolution. This theory contained three components that had different authors and had originated at different times but all were merged in the revolutionary situation of 1917. The first thesis, expounded particularly by Lenin, insisted that Russia would have a similar capitalist development as in West Europe. The second was mainly Trotsky's theory of permanent revolution proper with its emphasis upon the working class as the sole revolutionary force, the underdeveloped capitalist class, the political maturity of the proletariat, and its chance of taking over power by an insurrection. A revolution in Russia would be the signal for the revolutions in other states and their socialist governments would help to overcome the backwardness of the Russian economy and society. Finally, there was the vision of the future, in which the state would wither away, social classes would dissolve themselves, coercion would come to an end, and eternal freedom and equality would prevail in socialist countries.[13]

The second ideology went under the heading of socialism in one country and developed out of the two central defects of the first ideology. Instead of the expected democratic dictatorship of the majority of workers and peasants, there developed the minority dictatorship of a small party that could maintain itself in power by means of civil war and police terror. During and partly because of the civil war, there developed the Red Army, the secret police, the "revolutionary terror," the single party, and domination by the party of the increasingly powerful state. The party-military dictatorship provided the basis of, and the missing international revolutions the justification for, Stalinism with its domination of party and state, the extreme personality cult, the ruthless purges as well as the large-scale expropriation of private property without compensation, collectivization of agriculture, overambitious industrialization and central planning.

Coexistence of two ideologies led to factionalism and schism among the paladins in Communist and Fascist dictatorial parties. Some factions either sponsored or supported one of the leader's ideologies, but rejected the other. Or other factions espoused special ideals or interests that they sought to attach to one or the other of the leader's ideologies.

The result was ideological squabbles among Communists as well as Fascists. Three different methods were developed either to mitigate or to terminate ideological disputes. One was a declaration by the leader to specify certain ideals or issues as so sensitive that discussion among the paladins had to cease, and the leader unilaterally would resolve the dispute at the appropriate moment. The other was to distinguish between periods of open discussion and of ideological unity after the leader or the highest party agency had arrived at a decision. The former method was more common to the Nazis and the latter the preferred procedure among Bolsheviks (democratic centralism). Finally, there was the termination of ideological disputes by the leader himself. In minor issues he would act as an umpire by pronouncing *the* authoritative version of the respective ideals. In major issues he would either expel or physically exterminate the protagonists of certain prohibited ideals.

Enforcement of these ideological decisions again took two different forms. One was the voluntary yielding of paladins to the interpretation of the leader.[14] Recantation became the Stalinist method in the Soviet Union. Whoever continued to promote prohibited ideas was usually arrested by the Cheka or the Gestapo. A fundamental ideological conflict led to outright violence. Röhm's insistence on extending the internal counterrevolution to the military sphere ended with the purge of the SA and Hitler's ordered murder of its leaders. Trotsky's eventual opposition to socialism in one country led to his exile and his eventual murder on Stalin's order.

Linkage of ideology with charisma thus entailed advantages and disadvantages for the leader in Communist and Fascist regimes. Promoting a cause politicized the movement and supplied an indispensable condition for establishing a new political system. Sponsoring two compatible ideologies permitted increasing the size of the movement by obtaining the allegiance of additional groups and by forming alliances with nonparty social, political, and economic as well as military groups during certain phases of the revolution or counterrevolution. Opposed to these advantages were the ideological disputes, factions, and extermination of rival political opponents within the ruling party. Two major and several minor ideologies created uncertainties about the meaning of ideological legitimacy. The result was a distinction between partisan and legitimizing ideologies,[15] the distinguishing line of which was usually defined unilaterally by the leader.

The major advantage of two ideologies, however, was that each leader and movement was given the opportunity to instigate and execute a "complete" revolution and counterrevolution. The internal upheaval could be separated in time and program from the external counterrevolution of the Nazis, while the political and military revolution could be consolidated before the program of the economic revolution was undertaken and a new economic system was established by the Bolsheviks. In Nazi Germany, completion referred to the relationship between internal and external counterrevolution, while in the Soviet Union it referred first to political and military revolution before the economic revolution completed the process of violent change. It was only after World War II, that the Bolsheviks undertook the "revolution by conquest" in the East European countries, and this process was continued in Indochina and in Angola. After American atomic power was neutralized through detente, a new phase of revolution by conquest was begun on other continents that may become as dangerous as was Fascist military and counterrevolutionary expansion of the 1940s.

## LEGAL AND CHARISMATIC AUTHORITY

Each dictatorial party tried to seize power without openly violating the prevailing law of accession. This could be accomplished only by cunning and deception. Hitler was appointed as chancellor by presidential decree, not by a vote of parliament. Just one month later Hitler overstepped the limits of the presidential decree when he used the burning of the *Reichstag* as an excuse to impose a civil siege which became the instrument for dissolving the political parties and civil associations, preparing for the takeover of the various state governments, and establishing the Gestapo without recognizing any constraint. "The history of the illegal *coup d'etat* is characterized by the identification of 'order' with Hitler's person."[16] That is to say, legal authority disguised charismatic authority in whose name the constitution was violated by the Hitler government. This was accomplished not with prior or subsequent explicit approval of the people, but with disguise and deception. In claiming to defend public order against an alleged enemy of the state, Hitler deliberately violated the constitution, without asking his followers to grant him specific legitimacy for this action.

A similar kind of deception was employed to cover up the Bolshevik insurrection in 1917. The overthrow of the czarist regime had replaced the monarchic by a legal authority of a provisional democratic government. Soon after Lenin arrived in Russia, he called for a socialist revolution and a democratic dictatorship of the proletariat and the peasantry. His insistence upon a reelection of the workers' and soldiers' deputies was one demand of his April theses. The implicit aim was to replace the new legal authority of the provisional government by the revolutionary authority of the Soviets, intermingled by the charismatic authority of Lenin as well as Trotsky.

Not the Bolshevik party, but the Soviets should be the bearers of revolutionary authority. Under the slogan of "all power to the Soviets," the Bolsheviks won a majority first of the Petrograd and then of the All-Russian Soviet conference. As the leading Bolshevik speaker in these bodies, Trotsky urged that the Red Guards be armed "so that we may build up a genuine rampart against counterrevolution."[17] Taking over power was thus to be accomplished by means of two deceptions. The professed aim was not to establish a Bolshevik party dictatorship but a "democratic dictatorship" of the Soviets. Revolutionary authority was not to be secured directly and openly claiming revolutionary legitimacy but under the disguise of fighting against the counterrevolution. Insurrection came as a conspiracy that claimed, if at all, legitimacy only after its success. When the insurrection was in process, Trotsky denied the conspirational element before the congress of the Soviets: "The rising of the popular masses needs no justification. What has taken place is an insurrection, not a conspiracy. We have hardened the revolutionary energy of the workers and soldiers of Petrograd. We have openly steeled the will of the masses for a rising, not a conspiracy. Our rising has been victorious."[18] But the soldiers participating in the insurrection were told by the same Trotsky that it was their task to fight off the attacking counterrevolutionaries.[19]

In the process of exciting the masses, Lenin played more the role of the ideologist and Trotsky more the one of the charismatic. In the meetings addressed by Trotsky, the masses were usually in an ecstatic mood. In the days before the insurrection, Trotsky tried to prepare his listeners for action. Thus he let the aroused masses repeat the following oath: "Let this your vote be your oath with all your might and power of sacrifice to support the Soviet, which had taken on itself the great burden of bringing the victory of the revolution to completion and of giving the people land, bread, and peace."[20] The oath was the closest Trotsky ever came to a claim of ideological legitimacy.

As head of the Soviets of Petrograd, Trotsky had set up a military revolutionary committee which took over the power of the state when Trotsky had issued his *Order Nr. I:* "The Petrograd Soviet is in imminent danger. Last night the counterrevolutionary conspirators tried to call the Junkers and the shock battalions into Petrograd. You are hereby ordered to prepare your regiment for action. . . . All procrastination and hesitation will be regarded as treason of the revolution."[21] The October revolution was thus justified by a spurious legitimacy of fighting a conspiracy.

Comparison of the seizures of power reveals that neither Communists nor Fascists openly established their dictatorships in the names of their leaders or their parties. Both employed deceptions, engaged in insurrections, and pretended to defend either the revolution or the new state against a conspiracy of their enemies.[22] The respective insurrections were justified with a pretended legal authority. It was only after victory that the violence was justified by the combined authority of charisma and the respective ideologies.

Thus there occurred an intermingling of three different kinds of authority. One was the spurious claim of an alleged legal authority that was deceptively utilized to carry through the respective insurrections. Once successfully completed, there was an open claim and subsequent recognition of the ideological authority, either as revolutionary or counterrevolutionary legitimacy in the two regimes. There was finally the charismatic authority of the leader who claimed to have a right to establish the new political system of his choice. But neither leader was able or willing to have his authority legitimized in a formal and universal election, specifically asking for a subsequent approval by the voters. Charismatic and ideological authority thus contained a special prerogative of the leader that he could claim legitimacy for his insurrection without having to ask and to get the specific consent of the majority.

Finally, there arose the new phenomenon of arbitrary authority and illegitimacy. In building up paramilitary troops and using them as secret police forces of the regime, the rule of the single party and dictatorial charisma were effectively supplemented by a police dictatorship. The combined secrecy and violence were outside the legal system, and were despotic and oppressive at the same time. The leader and delegate handled the police forces as fully submissive instruments, and these forces used violence freely against their enemies. All these actions were based upon arbitrary authority and illegitimacy and could hardly ever be covered by charismatic authority.

## CHARISMA AND ORGANIZATION

There was a clear interlinkage between charisma and organization in the prototypical regimes of Hitler and Lenin. In each case the leader personified a dictatorial party and headed the government of a dictatorial regime. The bureaucracy of party and state had to accept the orders of the leaders as binding norms. It was because of the command over the Red Army and the respective secret police that the violent takeover could lead to a consolidated regime. Without these two kinds of party and police organizations, charismatic leadership would not have determined major policies in the new states. Equally, each dictatorial party controlled a network of auxiliary organizations which were headed and dominated by paladins of the leader. Interlocking organizations were thus an important part of the instruments available to the respective leader.

Nevertheless, Lenin did not possess a charismatic apparatus in a way created by Hitler. The reasons for the difference resided in the particular nature of the charismatic personality; in the peculiar process of decision making in the top leadership. These distinct divergencies produced special modes of an apparatus as the agents of the leader, different methods of translating the emotions into normative duties and discipline of the followers, and diverse ways of glorifying the leader.

In Nazi Germany, Hitler was the sole charismatic leader. His supremacy was carefully institutionalized. He was president of the party, head of the SA, chancellor of the government, and *Führer* of the *Reich*. All the other subleaders took second place, and most were his paladins. Gregor Strasser, who had a mass following of his own, undercut himself, while Goering's aspirations as deputy leader were kept in bounds. Goering lost his control over the secret police and over most of the ministries of Prussia in 1934. Not even Röhm ever sought to rival Hitler as the supreme leader.

In capitalizing upon his charismatic quality and fourfold offices, Hitler centralized all major decisions in his own hands. Most of the major decisions were made by him unilaterally. While granting Goering full power in economic affairs, it was Hitler who decided upon the Four Year Plan and imposed the construction of the Westwall upon a fully employed economy. Although Goering paraded as the minister and commander of the air force, Hitler alone decided upon the size of the air force and the production programs of airplanes. The process of unilateral decision making expressed itself also in the fact that Hitler's commands could overrule any ordinance of the party or law of the state.

Supreme leadership and unilateral decision making were used by Hitler to build up a decentralized charismatic apparatus. Instead of appointing one general secretary, control over the Nazi party was divided among three subleaders in charge of politics, organization, and finances. In the districts, *Gauleiters* were Hitler's confidence men who were solely responsible to Hitler personally for political affairs in their region. All members of the personal apparatus enjoyed definite tenure in their offices, received salaries equal to those of ministers, and occupied the status of Hitler's comrades in power. In consequence the so-called *Gau* kings did not regard themselves merely as the staff of a unified party bureaucracy, but acted as the trusted friends of Hitler, his agents as well as his admirers. Personal allegiance and decentralization at the top prevented the party bureaucracy from ever infringing upon or diluting Hitler's charisma.

During Lenin's time, the situation in the Soviet Union was very different. He was only head of the government, but not the formally installed president of the party nor the official chairman of the central committee or politburo. Instead of enjoying the power of command, Lenin had to find a majority for his proposals because of the party's rule of collegial decision making. While he could usually convince others, he was outvoted on some important issues. As Lenin himself said at the time: "The old Central Committee [1919–20] defeated me on one gigantically important question. . . . On organizational and personal questions I have been in the minority countless times."[23] Lenin's superior qualities expressed themselves in his ability to persuade and his greater insight and experience. On each major issue his charismatic quality was tested in extensive debates that often turned into heated disputes. Lenin had thus to develop his talents as persuader and teacher to make his charismatic abilities effective.

In other words, Hitler operated under conditions of organizational charisma, while Lenin acted in situations of charismatic organization. Instead of being equally effective in their mutual interpenetration, the decision making process was determined more by charisma in one case and by organization in the other. As a result, Hitler possessed his own decentralized charismatic apparatus that managed and controlled the party machine for him, at a minimum of time and energy for himself. Lenin was himself engulfed in organizational matters and could control the party machine only if he devoted an inordinate amount of work and time to its operation. To relieve himself of this burden, he first formed an organizational office as his implementing agency. But he committed a major mistake as a charismatic leader when he agreed that Stalin should be appointed as General Secretary of the party machine. Not the charismatic leader, but the machine politician was institutionalized as the head of the single party.

In the Soviet Union, the party machine won over charismatic leadership in the last months of Lenin's life. Formally, this seems to verify Weber's major organizational thesis of the incompatibility of charisma with organization. Actually, the party machine succeeded only because of Lenin's sickness and untimely death. Had he recovered, he could have removed Stalin and found for himself a genuine technician—such as Hess and Schwarz were for Hitler—who would have managed the party for the benefit of Lenin. This interpretation is reenforced by the fact that Lenin tried to correct his mistake shortly before his death. In a postscript to his political testament he wrote: "I suggest that the comrades think about a way to remove Stalin from that post and appoint in his place another man who in all respects differs from Comrade Stalin in his superiority, that is, more tolerant, more loyal, more courteous, and more considerate of the comrades, less capricious, etc."[24] Instead of a universal law of incompatibility, our comparison reveals that organization wins only if the leader permits a monocratic head of the single party next to himself, and is not able to determine the main lines of party policy. The incompatibility does not hold if and when the leader builds up a decentralized charismatic apparatus composed of devoted paladins who obey his orders and implement his personal policies.

There was another important organizational difference between Lenin and Hitler. The secret police and its concentration camps were not actually a part of the party machine, but were handled for Hitler by his delegate Himmler. At Lenin's time, the head of the secret police was not responsible to him personally but to the politburo. The secretary general of the party assumed control over the secret police so that he could, and did, use this despotic instrument against his political enemies in the party after Lenin's death. Control over the secret police exerted a significant influence in the subsequent succession crisis for a new leader.[25]

## CHARISMA AND DISCIPLINE

Establishing a new political system by means of a single party gaining a political monopoly calls for extensive discipline as well as for paramilitary or military forces. While the need for discipline was the same in fascism and communism, the modes and justifications for such discipline differed considerably. Hitler demanded obedience in the name of charismatic authority, whereas Lenin and Trotsky insisted upon discipline on the grounds of revolutionary authority.

It was one of Hitler's most surprising accomplishments that he obtained discipline without destroying the emotional bond between leader and followers. The emotions of natural charisma were translated into a duty to obey the leader. Enthusiasm and love were subjected to a process of normatization by means of oath taking by the paladins as well as all office holders in party and state. As we have seen, party officials had to renew their oath of loyalty each year. Soldiers had to swear allegiance not to the state but to Hitler personally. Hitler based his demand for unquestioned discipline upon an ethical commitment of loyalty to the leader. Emotional surrender, normative duty, and unlimited loyalty to the leader were followed by the complete destruction of individual wills of the police forces. In speaking to uniformed Nazi troops on Martyr's Day in 1933, Hitler rejected any limit to his commands: "I demand of you that you give your life as did the 16 men who perished on this place in 1923. There can be nothing else in your life than this loyalty [to the leader]. These martyrs must be the standard for your life which shall furnish an unattainable goal for all others."[26] Hitler thus knew two kinds of discipline. In one the leader's will was substituted for that of the oath taker. In the other he claimed the right to require such extreme actions from his followers that they most likely would perish. Absolute obedience thus gave the leader the right to decide unilaterally over life and death of the members of his oppressive instruments. Unquestioned obedience to the leader's will, but without any demand upon their lives, was the fate of compliant paladins of the charismatic apparatus and later also of the party army, called Waffen S.S.

The oath of the soldiers and officers was enlarged to include not only military but also ideological obedience to the leader. Military criteria alone were not enough for promotion in military ranks. Simple soldiers could be moved up into positions of officers if they had taken great risks in combat or assumed great responsibility in performing assigned tasks. Evidence of a strong belief in Nazi ideology often became a substitute for training of an officer, because his "oath to the leader binds him especially to his military duties."[27]

Charismatic leadership of the armed forces expressed itself in a creation of a second type of officers whose special tie to the leader was said to strengthen the will to fight and to fulfill most accurately his commands. Full ideological obedience came only in 1944 after the abortive assassination when Hitler got himself a chief of staff, General Guderian, who demanded that all his associates had to become members of the Nazi party.

In the Soviet Union, insurrection called for Red Guards; civil war and external intervention could be won only through a Red Army. The danger of the revolution being destroyed induced the leaders to demand discipline within the party by prohibiting any kind of faction opposed to the leaders. For a short period there occurred a militarization of workers who were conscripted and pressed into a semimilitary service. Millions of non-Communist and even former Czarist officers were compelled to join the fight in the newly organized Red Army. The Red Guards of Petrograd comprised four thousand men in October 1917, while at the end of the civil war not less than 5 million men had at some time served in the Red Army.

Fighting spirit and obedience were obtained through ideological appeals and discipline. Both were clearly expressed in the oath to be sworn by the soldiers of the Red Army, written by Trotsky: "I, a son of the toiling people and a citizen of the Soviet Republic assume the title of a soldier of the Workers' and Peasants' army. I undertake to observe revolutionary discipline and unflaggingly do my duty. . . . I undertake to come forward on the first call of the Workers' and Peasants' government to defend the Soviet Republic and for the cause of socialism. For the brotherhood of the peoples I shall spare neither my own strength nor my own life. If by evil design I should depart from this my solemn promise, let general contempt be my lot and let the severe hand of the revolutionary law punish me."[28] There were two elements in this Bolshevik oath. One was the ideological inspiration from which was derived the duty to fight for the cause of communism. The other was the demand that each soldier had to obey the orders of his superiors whatever the content of the commands. Disobedience entailed extreme penalties. Terror was used in regard to the professional officers. If they did not serve the Red Army unflaggingly, or deserted to the White armies, then their families were to be executed in their place. Bolshevik discipline thus became intermingled with terror. While both assisted in winning the civil war, terror has become a hallmark of communism, whether in suppression of opponents in the Soviet Union or insurgency in other lands.

In Weber's theory we find a twofold relationship between charisma and discipline. On the one hand, discipline is neutral towards different kinds of leadership and political systems. "It places itself at the disposal of every power that claims its service and knows how to promote it." On the other hand, discipline is "intrinsically alien to charisma" because "heroic ecstasy, loyalty, spirited enthusiasm for the leader" is incompatible with "drill for the sake of habitually routinized skill." (p. 1149). Surprisingly, we find both attitudes towards discipline developing in the Soviet Union during the civil war. Inside the Bolshevik party, the Workers' opposition argued furiously against, while Trotsky pushed for, a militarization of workers and trade unions. In the Red Army, Trotsky was simultaneously a strict disciplinarian and also a partaking charismatic leader.

Eruptive charismatic leadership often occurred at critical moments of the civil war. One well-known case happened on the western bank of the Volga, opposite to Kazan. When Trotsky arrived in his armored train he was faced by mass desertion of the soldiers. "He descended into the panic-stricken crowds of soldiers, poured out on them torrents of passionate eloquence, rallied them and, on occasion, personally led them back to the fighting line. At an especially critical moment, his own escort joined in the battle."[29] Of course, Trotsky could inspire the soldiers because his own troops were few and the enemy weak so that his personal courage and entreaty established his fame as a charismatic hero.

There was a short period in the civil war when discipline and victory did provide the opportunity for Trotsky to establish himself as a charismatic leader in his own right. Trotsky let this chance pass by because his Marxist theory did not permit him to see and translate victory into personal power. But his opponents in the politburo saw this danger, dismissed his chief of staff in Moscow, appointed another one over Trotsky's protest, and adopted a new military strategy opposed by Trotsky. Although this strategy turned out to be a mistake, Trotsky never had a chance to link discipline effectively with his personal charisma. The partaking charismatic leader had to be demoted so as to make him accept the discipline of a compliant paladin.[30]

Lenin also tried his hand in seeking military victory through authority and discipline. He personally approved the shift from defense against the Polish attack to military expansion into the territory of another state. When the Red Army was defeated in its attempt to capture Warsaw, Lenin changed the policy and admitted his mistake in the next party congress. As a result, military victory did not become a source of charismatic heroism, nor could it provide an opportunity for the leader to claim infallibility, if this had been his intention.

There occurred a significant difference between the two regimes in regard to discipline and its effect upon charisma and party. Hitler effectively utilized discipline and victory for shifting to heroic charisma. He linked one kind of discipline with the terroristic instruments and also the armed forces, and their victory could be, and was, claimed as an accomplishment of the personal courage and wisdom of the leader. In linking the other discipline with the charismatic apparatus whose members controlled the bureaucracy of party and state for him, neither one did come in a position to derive exclusive glory for itself from victory. The charismatic leader was the sole beneficiary from each discipline.

Nothing similar happened in the Soviet Union because the specific discipline of the charismatic apparatus was missing and neither military nor the terroristic discipline could be linked with charisma. Since the successful civil war ended with a Soviet defeat by Poland, the main charismatic leader admitted his mistake publicly, and the partaking leader solidaristically shared in this responsibility. While Trotsky was widely regarded as the victor of the civil war, his second position in the leadership did not permit him to go beyond enjoying passively the glory granted to him.[31]

The party became the victor of the civil war mainly because of the extensive use of arbitrary authority. Such arbitrariness expressed itself in various forms, including Trotsky's militarization of trade unions, Lenin's prohibition of factions within the Bolshevik party and attempted occupation of Warsaw, Stalin's inspection commission and occupation of Georgia, Dzerzhinsky's secret police and spy system, and the various acts of terror during and after the civil war. None of these actions was in accord with the Bolshevik ideology as it prevailed prior to the insurrection. Instead of ideological legitimacy, there was revolution by conquest at home. Each of these actions involved some form of violence that was committed in the name of the dictatorial party. While practiced first by the various members of the politburo, arbitrary authority became gradually the personal prerogative of Stalin and turned into the essence of Stalinism.

The two kinds of discipline, distinguished in Weber's theory, find their practice in Communist and Fascist dictatorship. One was the discipline in military organizations. "The content of discipline is nothing but the consistently rationalized, methodically prepared and exact execution of the received orders . . . and the actor is unswervingly set for carrying out the commands" (p. 1149). This kind of discipline prevailed in the Red Army and in the German Army, except for their respective periods of defeat in World War II. As in Weber's theory, appeal to inspirational emotions of the superiority of the Fatherland did not diminish the uniform conduct achieved through systematic discipline.

The two regimes acted differently in the interaction between charismatic heroism and discipline. For Weber, there is a positive relationship: "A charismatic hero may make use of discipline . . . indeed he must do so if he wishes to expand the sphere of domination" (p. 1149). While introducing strict discipline in the Red Army, the Communist leaders rejected personal heroism, accepted it only for the party. Hitler deliberately linked personal heroism with strict discipline, for paladins and officers as well as for armed units, beginning with his strategic plans for war in 1938. The combination of heroism and discipline led to the formation of a new status group in the *Waffen SS*, which became Hitler's pride and joy, and turned into the most ferocious fighters on the German side during the war. Synergistic charisma claims to increase the will and ability to fight because the soldiers are conscious of enjoying the trust of the leader.

## CHARISMATIC SUCCESSION

In his theory of bureaucracy, Weber distinguishes between formal and substantive justice. The former requires equal treatment before the law, whereas the latter includes "irrational sentiments" that may lead to unequal treatment of certain clients and grants a degree of discretional power to judges (p. 980). Similarly, in comparing ideological parties with charisma, Weber suggests that a charismatic leader has a greater chance of rising to the top in a spoils party than in a party with a well-developed ideology (p. 1133). The ideology contains elements of rationality and thus presents a hurdle for the rise of a charismatic leader. Can this thesis of a rational influence also be applied to the problem of succession?

To a certain extent there were differences in assignments of tasks and granting of favors between Hitler and Lenin. The great emphasis of the Bolsheviks upon the vanguard position of the party led to certain rational rules for political actions. The principle of democratic centralism involved two directives. There had to be an open discussion within the politburo inducing the leader to consider opinions of others. Decisions had to be made by majority vote after which the minority was bound to defend the majority decision as if there had been unanimous agreement. The politburo met in regular sessions in which Lenin was occasionally defeated. Assignments of the tasks were made by appointment but could be refused by individual members. Democratic centralism and appointment minimized the influence of favors granted by the leader. At a later date the formation of definite factions was disallowed, on insistance of Lenin. It was not only the ideology, but also the principle of collective leadership, that were responsible for the collaboration at the top of the party.

As we have seen, there was only the *Führerprinzip* in the Nazi party. The meetings of the *Reichsleiters* were discontinued, whereas the *Gauleiters* were only occasionally called together and then were not given a chance to decide issues by votes. Assignments to tasks were made by Hitler and granted as a gift by the leader. Charismatic favoritism was thus built into the party organization. The exception was limited to the salaries and to the tenure of the *Gauleiters*, so that economic considerations did not negatively influence the loyalty of the *Gauleiters* to the leader.

Nevertheless, it was Hitler and not Lenin who arrived at a designation of his successor. It was at the beginning of the war that Hitler designated Goering as his first successor, asserting that he would go to the front and subject himself to the same dangers as his soldiers: "Should I perish in this fight, then party comrade Goering will be my first successor."[32] The decision to start a war and the desire to distinguish himself as a hero provided the immediate reasons for the designation of a successor.

But why did he designate Goering? Why did he not designate Himmler or some one else of the party? Although Hitler did not reveal his personal motives, the past assignments and delivered services could provide the answer. Goering was at the time the most power hungry paladin, the most involved in military preparation, and the one enjoying greatly the ruthless use of violence. Goering played a decisive role in the burning of the *Reichstag* and the internal counterrevolution. As minister of interior of Prussia he neutralized the regular police, elevated 300,000 SA men into the auxiliary police, who then murdered their political enemies or tortured them in concentration camps. Goering also played a significant role in the Röhm purge, directing also the killing of men who had been in the past his personal rivals. For his violent services, Goering built up a secret police for Prussia, independent of the SS. But Hitler undercut this attempt, forced Goering to give up the regular and secret police forces which were united with the SS and placed under the command of Himmler. Hitler did not appoint Goering to any office in the party and allowed him only to control the wire-tapping of telephone conversations with foreign countries. There was no interference, however, with Goering's pompous way of living and fantastic uniforms. When asked about this bombastic behavior and imitated royalist performance, Hitler gave a prompt answer: "This is a unique case. I let him have his pleasures. Goering is a baroque personality. His occasional weaknesses have been more than compensated by his accomplishments."[33]

Recognized as special plenipotentiary, Goering was appointed as head of the Four Year Plan office and given plenary powers. It was Goering who approved the detailed economic plan, confiscated the iron ore deposits, established the Hermann Goering Works, reorganized the ministry of economics, appointed about twenty of his own plenipotentiaries who had to report to him. While Hitler was fully informed, he intervened only for military reasons, such as the building of the Westwall.[34] Shortly before the invasion of Poland, Goering was appointed chairman of the Council of Ministers, which new agency issued the immediately relevant economic war legislation. The Goering Works grabbed a whole range of industrial properties and the planning office obtained jurisdiction for exploiting the economies of the occupied countries. In putting Goering in charge of economic affairs, Hitler could concentrate upon political and military affairs and transform himself into the charismatic warlord.

Hitler's confidence in the "baroque personality" was destroyed by British saturation bombing. Goering could not keep his promises that the air force would defeat Britain and protect German airspace and cities from any foreign bombers. Early in 1942 Hitler dissolved the holding company of the Goering Works, reduced the jurisdiction of the planning office, and undercut all exhibitions and propaganda stunts of Goering, who ceased to be the confidant of Hitler. It was only in the last days of the war that Goering claimed the right to succeed the isolated Hitler, who in turn issued an order for the arrest of this pretender. At the trials of Nuremburg, Goering adroitly played the role of the star defender and committed suicide rather than being executed on order of the International Military Tribunal.

It follows that not the charismatic quality itself determines the selection of a successor in a dictatorial regime. It was charisma in its heroic form, linked with the finality of death, and assuring his fame in history, that induced Hitler to designate a successor. When war turned into defeat, when the armies of the charismatic warlord crumbled and his power was destroyed, then the once designated pretender had to be condemned and punished. Forced into a bunker, surrounded by ruins, suicide was the only and appropriate way of terminating a charismatic rulership in Fascist dictatorship. Defeat eliminated the problem of succession.

Lenin's attitude to his potential successors confirms the thesis that a dictatorial giant is unwilling or unable to designate his own successor. In his testament Lenin examined the pretenders to his position, but did not name one as his successor. Trotsky was favored only indirectly by being given one instruction to reveal to the congress Lenin's break with Stalin. It was more anger about Stalin's arrogance than dispassionate selection of the charismatically most qualified man that moved Lenin before his death to turn against Stalin.

As long as Lenin lived, Stalin was neither deputy to, nor pretender for, but the understudy of the charismatic leader, effective since his illness. The general secretary was only the office manager of the Central Committee. It was in his capacity as commissar of nationalities that Stalin got in conflict with Lenin. Stalin not only pushed for the annexation of Georgia by the Soviet Union, but also replaced the new Communist government with his own agents in the occupied land. Lenin fumed about the use of terrorist methods against party members. The terror, he said, was borrowed "from tzarism and was barely touched by the Soviet world."[35] Lenin wrote a memorandum against Stalin that was to be presented to the next party congress. Stalin retained his position only because Lenin was too sick to have his "bombshell" exploded at the party congress.[36] The difference between the two power hungry paladins, Goering and Stalin, was that Hitler could keep a lid on Goering's power, whereas the sick Lenin could only indicate who should not be his successor. The result was a crisis of succession in the Soviet Union.

There is an abundance of evidence for the charismatic qualification of Trotsky, whether in his own mind and behavior or in the widespread recognition of this quality by party members and other followers. At the first party congress without Lenin, there was a thunderous applause when Trotsky's name was mentioned. He was widely regarded as the victor of the civil war. Lenin himself had offered the position of vice-chairman of the government three times, but Trotsky always rejected it. At first, Lenin was trying to use Trotsky for offsetting the influence of Stalin. But in the postscript to his testament, Lenin had given Trotsky the instrument for eliminating

Stalin as general secretary. If Trotsky would have accepted the position and read the postscript to the congress, as Lenin had asked him to do, his road to becoming the second charismatic leader of the Soviet Union would have been clear. Instead, he made a rotten agreement with Stalin and passed up this unique opportunity.[37]

Why did Trotsky turn into a charismatic failure? It was only many years later that Trotsky revealed his reason for not fulfilling Lenin's wish. "What retained me was the fear that any sharp conflict in the ruling group at the time, when Lenin was struggling with death, might be understood by the party as a casting of lots for Lenin's mantle."[38] Nevertheless, when he was not recognized as the primary leader, he resigned all his positions in protest and asked to be sent abroad "as soldier of the revolution" which he predictably expected to occur in the Germany of 1923.[39] This request was denied, presumably out of fear that allowing Trotsky to be the leader of another revolution would make him the new charismatic leader in Russia. The charismatic quality could not be hidden effectively, "Trotsky . . . had a terrible personal visibility about him. . . . Trotsky always overwhelmed others with Trotsky."[40]

But there was another barrier that prevented Trotsky as well as Stalin from proclaiming their right to charismatic leadership. It consisted in the Marxian theory of Bonapartism. In analyzing the role of the two Napoleons in the French revolutions, Marx had condemned them as grave diggers of the revolution. Imbued by this theory no Bolshevik leader of the Left, Center, or Right could claim to be a supreme leader for fear of being accused as the liquidator of the Russian revolution. But this is precisely what happened in the spring of 1927 when Stalin presented his "theses" against the opposition in the party. Trotsky as the leader of the opposition shouted, " 'The First Secretary proposes his candidature to the post of the grave digger of the revolution.' Stalin turned pale, rose, contained himself with difficulty, and then rushed out of the hall, slamming the door."[41] This charge was the greatest insult and led to the final break between Trotsky and Stalin. The succession crisis was then resolved by terrorist means. Trotsky was carried into a train, deported, and exiled, while the secret police rounded up about six thousand of his followers. It was only after many years that Stalin was regarded as a quasi-charismatic leader by some specialists of Bolshevism.[42]

## LEGENDARY CHARISMA

There was a distinctly different attitude between Lenin and Hitler in regard to charismatic glorification. Lenin had a decided aversion to ceremonies and worship of his person. But his magnetic appeal as well as his inner certitude, insight in the ability and wishes of others, and his clear-cut policy decisions turned him into the personification of party and state. While he tolerated the thunderous applause to his speeches, he turned against any deliberate glorification of himself. This precisely happened in September 1918 when he was shot at and wounded in an attempt on his life.

Even Trotsky participated in this chorus of glory by lesser lights: "Never has the

individual life of one or the other among us seemed to be of such secondary importance as it does now at a moment when the life of the greatest man of our time is in
mortal peril."[43] But when Lenin recovered and returned to work, he was appalled
and exclaimed: "Look what they say in the papers. Makes one ashamed to read it
. . . calls me a genius, a special kind of man. . . . Next they will be holding public
prayers for my health. Why, this is horrible. . . . All our lives we have carried on an
ideological struggle against the glorification of personality. We long ago solved the
question of heroes, and now we are again witnessing the glorification of personality."[44] Lenin ordered his assistants to visit the editors and have the whole campaign
stopped. There was thus a mass desire for glorification that was not shared by the
central personality.

The Lenin cult set in one month before his death and flowered into a long lasting
legendary charisma. Widespread grief for the loss of the leader culminated into an
unrestrained worship by the paladins, the party members, and a significant portion
of the people. The Marxist rejection of personal worship as a form of Bonapartism,
spoiling the revolution, was forgotten. The love for the charismatic leader was expressed openly. Bukharin, the Marxist theorist, lamented: "Comrade Lenin was first
of all a supreme leader, a *Führer*, such as history presents to humanity once in hundreds of years, those whose names have become associated with epochs. . . . It
would be hardly possible in all of history to find another leader so loved by his
comrades-in-arms. All of them felt a special feeling to Lenin. Their feeling for him
was precisely one of love."[45] This love, worship and grief constituted the combined
emotions felt for one leader who personified a legendary charisma that was renewed
under Khrushchev and only disintegrated in our time.

Most of the secondary leaders participated in this building up of the Lenin cult.
Trotsky said: "In each of us lives a small part of Lenin, which is the best part of each
of us." The proclamation of the central committee distinguished between the body
and the spirit of Lenin. "His physical death is not the death of his cause. Lenin lives.
In the soul of every member of our party there is a particle of Lenin."[46]

Stalin was overly eager to retain body and spirit of Lenin. Contrary to Lenin's
explicit wishes, Stalin decided that Lenin's body was to be mummified, put up for
display in a mausoleum, ready to be worshipped by the masses. Pilgrimages were
organized and the body of the dead leader idolized all over the country. An elaborate
ceremonial was introduced and everyone was expected to participate in the glorification of the leader. Lenin's portraits, statues, busts, and posters were placed in all
public buildings and in many private homes. All this constituted the emotionalism of
Lenin's legacy as a dead but beloved leader. At the funeral Stalin delivered the following eulogy:

> In leaving us, Comrade Lenin commanded us to hold high and to keep pure the great
> name of Member of the Party, We swear to thee, Comrade Lenin, to honor thy com-
> mand.

In leaving us, Comrade Lenin ordered us to conserve the unity of our Party as the apple of our eye. We swear to thee, Comrade Lenin, to honor thy command.

In leaving us, Comrade Lenin ordered us to maintain and strengthen the dictatorship of the proletariat. We swear to thee, Comrade Lenin, to exert our full strength to honor thy command.

In leaving us, Comrade Lenin ordered us to strengthen with all our might the union of workers and peasants. We swear to thee, Comrade Lenin, to honor thy command.

In leaving us, Comrade Lenin ordered us to strengthen and enlarge the Union of the Republics. We swear to thee, Comrade Lenin, to honor thy command.

In leaving us, Comrade Lenin enjoined us fidelity to the Communist International. We swear to thee, Comrade Lenin, to devote our lives to the enlargement and strengthening of the union of the workers of the whole world, the Communist International.[47]

In formulating these six commandments, Stalin most definitely expunged forever Lenin's stricture that political power should not be personalized and that there should be no worship of any leader. Instead of proclaiming the forces of history, Stalin proclaimed the genius of the dead leader. His teachings and writings had to be made available in authoritative editions. His ideals and ideas had to be dogmatized, sloganized for the masses, and utilized as a standard for judging all other books and beliefs. All members of the party and the factions had to believe in the six commandments. The Communist movements and governments from then on derived the authority for their power from the charisma of the dead leader. Instead of a cult emanating from the charisma of the living leader, authority of the secondary leaders was now derived from the charismatic legacy of the dead leader.

The legacy could either consist of Stalin's six commandments or of accepting Lenin's theory, his concept of leadership, his notion of vanguard party, and the subsidiary role of the secret police. The genuine successor was to be not merely a replacement but the best Leninist in the country. It so happened that Stalin tried to show that he alone was fully capable of inheriting Lenin's legacy; that he had a series of heroic deeds to his credit; and that he alone was the best friend, advisor, and trustee of Lenin. This process of imitation went on for over three years.

Imitation involved maligning the reputation of his rivals, especially Trotsky's. Since Stalin did not possess any charismatic quality of his own, he had to invent a series of legends designed to show that he truly was the best Leninist. As a result, a legendary charisma was added to the derived charisma from Lenin and both were personified by Stalin.

Eager to show that he was a theorist in his own right, Stalin tried to systematize Lenin's diverse ideas into one theory. In his *Foundation of Leninism*, Stalin gave his own definition: "Leninism is Marxism of the era of imperialism and the proletarian revolution."[48] While Lenin had emphasized in 1918 that "a complete Socialist revolution is unthinkable in our country," in 1923 he believed it possible that the missing economic revolution in Russia could be achieved through a building up of agrarian cooperatives that would be peacefully accepted by the middle class peasants. Stalin for the years of factional strife adhered to this notion of cooperatives, emphasized especially by Bukharin, but he later adopted the policy of forced industrialization and got the policy of collectivization of the peasant land adopted by the party congress only by means of an amendment. Stalin's theory was thus a significant extension, if not a revision, of Leninism.

In regard to the nature of leadership, Stalin emphasized that the success of revolution depended on the "science of leadership in the revolutionary struggle of the proletariat." In the vanguard there could be positive and negative leadership. The former was exemplified by Lenin who in the second revolution of 1917 developed a characteristic "hardness" against all deviations.[49] In the years of dispute, Stalin gave the impression that the unity of the party, one of his commandments, could be adhered to only by collective leadership. He said at the congress of 1926: "Collective leadership, unity of the party . . . with the minority submitting to the majority—that is what we need now."[50] But when the other factions had been defeated, Stalin recalled the revolutionary situation of 1917, saw the development of a new revolutionary situation in 1928, which he regarded as a challenge to himself and the party. In initiating the forcible grain requisitions Stalin acted without any pretense of consulting the politburo[51] and saw himself justified by the Leninist hardness of his own leadership.

In his high regard for the party, Lenin had opened up the gate for new members, insisted upon majority decisions, emphasized commitment and honesty among comrades, and demanded that the organizational office be subordinated to the politburo. He also required that all factions must be dissolved for the sake of party unity. The secretariat of the Central Committee was to be nothing but an administrative office. Stalin, however, built up a political faction of his own, established a personal chancery whose agents kept him informed of the activities of the governmental departments. From top to bottom, Stalin organized a personal apparatus within the party machine that increased in number and cohesiveness until his faction made up the majority of the party congress of 1927. Thus organizational manipulation won over strict ideological adherence of charismatic followership. One major consequence of this apparatus was that Stalin had wielded himself as an effective instrument that enabled him to identify his faction with the party, and for seeing himself as the personifier of the party. Whatever was good for Stalin and his faction was also good for the purity and strength of the party.

Finally, there was the legacy of the secret police under the control of the party. The Checka was founded in 1917 for the purpose of combating "counterrevolution, speculation, and sabotage." Mass executions began in 1918 following the attempt on Lenin's life. In the reorganization of the police in 1922, then called OSPU, Stalin was the representative of the politburo on the board of the police. When its first head died in 1926, it was Stalin who replaced him with one of his minions and thereby took over control of the police. In extending the jurisdiction of the police to all anti-Soviet actions, Stalin drove the political actions of the rival factions underground. "The friends, colleagues, or supporters of Trotsky . . . were especially aimed at and gradually eliminated from universities, political institutions and army establishments."[52] Controlled organizations, such as the Young Communists, had to teach the "deviations of Trotskyism." Instead of serving the party as a whole, the secret police gradually became Stalin's instrument who used it to strengthen his own faction.

There was no vote either by the Central Committee or the party congress in positively choosing the new leader. Stalin was picked negatively by exclusion of the other pretenders. Trotsky and Zinoviev were excluded from the politburo in 1926, expelled from the party a year later, and either forced to emigrate or to go to prison. Many of their associates were arrested and punished by the secret police. Exclusion was proposed by Stalin—under threat of his resignation. In 1929, the members of the rightist faction were subjected to the same process of exclusion and dismissal from their jobs. The result of these coercive actions was the preponderance of power in the hands of Stalin. Instead of the party organs participating positively, there was only Stalin's praise for the secret police. "The OSPU is necessary for the revolution" which "will continue to exist for the confounding of the enemies of the proletariat."[53] Not the party or its members but the secret police was elevated to the guarantor of the revolution.

For Stalin, rise to Lenin's position was not so much a result of organizational manipulation, but emanated from a transfer of the charismatic qualities to himself. On the superhuman level, he acted as if he had acquired the same theoretical, inspirational, and courageous qualities possessed by Lenin. As evidence for this transfer he referred to his success over the left and right factions in the party, over his building up of the police forces, and of enlarging the armed forces. By a process of maturation, facilitated by legendary charisma, Stalin regarded himself as Lenin II.

On the level of natural charisma, Stalin possessed only two of the emotional qualities: extreme anger and intense hatred of others. On the basis of these feelings, Stalin divided others into the two categories of friends and enemies.[54] At the same time, Stalin lacked outstanding oratorial ability and possessed no gift of persuasiveness or any ability that could arouse enthusiasm. In their place were the brutality and rudeness which had been severely criticized by Lenin. When Lenin's testament was finally published, Stalin turned the critique into a praise of himself: "Yes, I am rude, comrades, toward those who rudely and treacherously smash and split the party. I have not concealed this and do not now." He thus demanded in 1927: "The opposition must disarm, utterly and completely, both in the ideological and in the organizational sphere."[55]

Stalin thus believed and exemplified that rudeness, not love or enthusiasm, was exactly what the party and revolution required. His concept of Lenin's charismatic qualities was thus one-sided, and legendary charisma did contain only those emotions that were directed towards enemies inside and outside the party. It is in this sense that charismatic beliefs and terrorist practices coexisted and, from Stalin's point of view, supported and reenforced each other.

The test of Stalin's charismatic, terrorist qualities came during the crisis of 1928. A shortage of grain had developed, partly because produce was withheld by peasants, partly because demand had risen due to the increased number of industrial workers. In seeking to overcome this crisis, Stalin formulated his principle of the economic revolution from above. "What is at issue is the change from small individual peasant enterprises to large-scale cultivation, on the basis of collective cultivation of the soil. . . . Using a new and improved technique. . . . The Kulak must be dealt with by economic measures on the basis of revolutionary legality" which "does not exclude the use of certain administrative measures against the Kulak."[56] The task of the new leader was thus parallel to the one faced by Lenin in 1917: a new revolutionary situation that had to be exploited by decisive actions.

Yet the differences between 1917 and 1928 were not mentioned by Stalin at that time. A genuine revolutionary fervor had arisen in Russia in 1917, favoring a revolution from below. Lenin could hope that by organizing the masses, he could reduce violence to a minimum. It was only the Red Army in the civil war that was responsible for the revolution from above. The attack upon the peasants in 1928 was a terrorist and military venture from the beginning. In 1923, Lenin had hoped for an agrarian reform by means of voluntary cooperatives of the peasants, directed but not dominated by the party. Stalin's notion of an agrarian revolution from above was his own choice which could be accomplished only by violence, euphemistically called "administrative measures." Legendary charisma entered into the process of decision making only in the limited sense of providing Stalin with the belief that he as the best Leninist was the only man qualified to undertake such an adventure. The revolution from above itself could be, and was, authorized only by the revolutionary legitimacy.

## MANUFACTURED CHARISMA

Elements of despotism existed in and were indispensable for Communist and Fascist regimes. The "regular" terror aimed and usually succeeded in preventing nonbelievers or nonallies from participating in any kind of political activity. Concentration or labor camps were the means by which active opponents were detained and potential opponents were kept silent. The "disciplinary" terror aimed at the members of the ruling party and army, and demanded full performance and obedience to the commands of the ruler. As we have seen, the oath of the Red Army threatened soldiers with the "severe hand of the revolutionary law" if they shirked their military duties. Hitler imposed strict discipline upon his paramilitary organizations and authorized one of them to be his secret police, acting arbitrarily. Accompanying these built-in agents of terror were the special guards that protected the life and fame of the charismatic leader and thereby foiled any attempt at individual counterterror. Blind devotion by the agents transformed terror into dutiful services for the leaders of dictatorial charisma.

Despotism differs from terrorism in two important respects. First, the leader orders the annihilation of whole groups of the ultimate enemies that stand in the way of either revolution or counterrevolution. Said Stalin prior to the agrarian revolution: "Either we shall pin them down, the capitalists, or they pin our shoulder to the ground."[57] Similarly, Hitler threatened that if the international Jewry would again plunge the world into a war, then the result would be "annihilation of the Jews in Europe."[58] In each case, organized violence or war was interpreted ideologically and regarded as an instrument to destroy the class or racial enemies.

Second, the ultimate enemy was allied with smaller enemies whose destruction was the first task of despotic government. Hitler ordered the mercy killings of incurable patients, demanded the elimination of the Polish intelligentsia, insisted upon the slaughter of Communist commissars, and dictated the killing of hostages and enemy paratroopers. Stalin imposed an agrarian confiscation of peasant lands and deported millions of middle-class peasants. Millions of captured Russian soldiers were threatened with punishment after the war because they were said to have deserted to the enemy. Communist revolutions and Fascist counterrevolutions could thus be implemented only by means of various forms of organized violence that together constituted the components of despotism.

It so happened that such wholesale extermination called for a change in the nature of the dictatorial party. Neither charisma nor ideology sufficed to instigate and execute such mass violence. Many of the party members did not measure up to the bloody tasks demanded of them. Stalin visited disciplinary terror upon his own party. It began with the expulsion of 130,000 members in 1930, increased to more than 800,000 in 1933, and was followed by another 340,000 in 1934.[59] Expulsions fell especially upon peasants and intellectuals. Open entry was replaced by a closure for new members for a period of two years in 1936. Subsequent newcomers entered the party primarily for personal gains and privileges, carefully abstaining from an ideological commitment, but following literally the instructions and discipline required by the top leaders.

Operating in anticipation of their external counterrevolution, Nazi leaders imposed two rectifications upon their party. "A sort of minor purge took place in mid-1938."[60] Party members were not allowed to hold offices in churches. Ministers and priests were forbidden to hold membership in the party. Lay church officials could not hold offices in the party. These measures tried to make the party immune to any influences of churches. The pogrom of the Crystal Night, executed by the party and the SA, led to widespread enrichment of party officials. While Hitler rejected Goering's request to punish the private stealing of Jewish property, the leader declared such property as belonging to the state. Party officials should not be engaged in business activities built on Jewish capital. While increasing the party's submissiveness to the ultimate leader, the two rectifications prepared the party for its new tasks in the occupied territories. Instead of being controlled by the members, Fascist and Communist parties became pliable instruments of the respective leaders.

A kind of internal despotism consisted in the purging of the leaders and subleaders of the Communist party and the streamlining of the Nazi party. Revolutionary victory in agriculture should have made Stalin proud of his collaborators and paladins and praise them for their accomplishments. On the contrary, he staged the purges and showy trials that eliminated about 70 percent of the Central Committee and the majority of the politburo. Stalin himself was investigator, prosecutor, and judge all in one, who on his own convicted the accused prior to the trials. "In those days when a case was closed—and if Stalin thought it necessary—he would sign the sentencing order at the politburo sessions and then pass it around for the rest of us to sign. We would put our signature on it without even looking at it. That's what we meant by 'collective sentencing.' "[61] In staging these purges, Stalin transformed the party into his personal instrument, fully obedient to his will, and staffed with his henchmen. He also warned any potential activists inside or outside of the party that any resisters would be killed without mercy. As a result, Stalin became the personal despot whose power was absolute. It became customary to identify "the general secretary with the Central Committee, then with the party, and then with the State."[62] It was in this form of identity that Stalin's despotic domination of party and state was recognized prior to World War II.

Hitler employed two related but not identical methods of internal despotic actions. One method was the beheading of the SA leaders and the demotion of this paramilitary organization. The other method was directed against former allies, whose members were repressed or punished in various ways because they either did not fully accept Nazi ideology or promoted policies and interests deviating from the Nazi pattern of behavior. As instruments for punishment Hitler employed either his party or the secret police to bring the allied groups in line. The various actions, objected to by the Nazis, were committed by either the bureaucracy of the state, the army, the churches, or economic organizations. The repression imposed upon the judiciary may stand as an example for Hitler's shift to despotism.

The attack upon the judges began with a despotic act of Hitler. A court had given a husband a lenient sentence because he was said to have been insane when he killed his wife. Hitler was furious, set the court's judgment aside, and had the man shot by his order. On Hitler's demand, the *Reichstag* passed a law in spring of 1942 which granted Hitler the right to dismiss any judge, reform the judiciary system for civilian crimes without any regard to existing laws or customs.[63] This was followed by appointing a Nazi as minister of justice who then collaborated extensively with the chancery of the Nazi party for inducing judges to impose draconic sentences upon civilian criminals. Punishment for disbelief in Nazi ideals, doubt about the victory, or violation of rationing rules became increasingly severe so that the judges became agents of despotism.

A short time later, the same kind of arbitrary authority was granted to Hitler in regard to military courts. He was given the right to have soldiers and officers punished regardless of "so called privileged right" or "without any special procedures," if they were not imbued with the proper fighting spirit.[64] Military law and prosecution turned increasingly into despotic punishment exemplified by the rapidly increasing death penalties. In all, not less than 423,000 verdicts were imposed by military courts upon members of the armed forces from the beginning of the war to November 1943.[65] Instead of having their status and honor respected, officers could now become political outcasts by verdict of submissive military courts implementing the despotic rules of the leader. Stalin's arbitrary rule was even more severe when he had generals shot whenever they lost a battle in the first year of Nazi invasion of the Soviet Union.

There was one significant difference between Stalin and Hitler in the handling of their party comrades. Except for the Röhm purge, Hitler did not stage showy trials for eliminating old fighters, nor did he eliminate the heads of the secret police. Hitler used demotion, dismissal, and disfavor to reduce or withdraw the power from some of his paladins, leading to favored and disfavored subleaders or dismantled organizations. The SS and the party chancery were the two most favored organizations in the last phase of the war. The expansion of the SS was accompanied by the demotion of the SA which was given little opportunity to partake in the booties of war. Party chancery and treasury streamlined the party organization, thereby demoted the network of Ley and the party courts of Buch. Many of the integral and affiliated organizations were dissolved and the Labor Front was utilized in exploiting foreign workers. A similar distinction developed between favored and disfavored *Gauleiters*. The former were given new assignments in occupied lands or on the home front, whereas the latter withered on the vine. This streamlining produced a similar effect as did Stalin's purges. The formerly monolithic party and secret police deteriorated into the pliable instrument of a personal despot.

What, then, is the relation between the charismatic and despotic leadership? In each case the leader ruled primarily by means of a dominated single party and a pliable secret police. Despotism was possible only because of this potentially unlimited personal control over these instruments developing out of previous charismatic leadership, whether heroic or legendary in nature. But neither ruler was willing to be regarded as a ruthless despot. Both insisted upon the devotion and loyalty due to a charismatic leader in spite of widespread disenchantment by the masses. Neither could continue to deliver the gifts and achievements of genuine charismatic leadership. The result was a discrepancy between charismatic self-belief and the actual performance of the respective leaders. What kind of charisma was compatible with despotism?

In the very few speeches Hitler delivered during the period of military defeat, Hitler remained able to arouse the admiration of his paladins. Sauckel said at one of these occasions: "We all appeared extremely small. In hours like these one really realizes how immensely great the *Führer* is.''[66] But such enthusiasm did not extend to the masses of followers. Hitler invented a kind of legendary charisma for them. The past pattern of achievement was projected into the future. Speaking of the struggle during the Weimar Republic he claimed that he again would snatch victory out of the clutches of generally expected defeats. Increasingly, he emphasized his ideological mission of defeating Bolshevism and Jewry and the convinced Nazis hung on to their ideals. Rosenberg and others even prepared for a world conference of anti-Semitism to be held in Cracow, Poland, but this was foiled by the advance of the Red Army. Nazi anti-Semitic convictions thus stood up to the very end of capitulation. The same was not true for either the qualities possessed by the leader or the belief in them by the followers of charisma. The defeat at Stalingrad has to be regarded as the turning point from acquired charisma to disenchantment. Hitler still felt his quality, but found less and less believers. A symbolic event of disbelief came in January 1944 when Hitler told his generals: "If it should be the will of the Almighty that this [war] should end into a catastrophe for the German people, then you my generals and admirals must gather around me with upraised swords to fight to the last drop of blood for the honor of Germany."[67] The charismatic circle should defend the leader to the bitter end.

Charisma was reduced by Hitler to a suicidal idea that elicited only deathly silence from the generals. Aware of the rejection, Hitler left the room without finishing his speech. The less enthusiasm he could arouse, the more distrustful he became, and the more did he resort to despotic power uttering vows of vengeance for the destruction of German cities by Allied bombers. But it was the abortive assassination of July 1944 that witnessed the height of Hitler's despotic ferocity when he ordered Himmler: "Shoot everyone who resists, no matter who he is." Despotism was garbed in a charismatic mantle when Hitler claimed over the radio that his escape was a "sign from Providence that I must, and therefore shall, continue my work."[68] While still believing in his mission, he sought to stem the wave of disenchantment by wallowing in despotic actions.

Stalin, too, tried to use charismatic qualities for covering his despotic actions, but the legendary charisma of Lenin stood in his way. So he began to denigrate Lenin. "Nothing was sacred to Stalin, not even Lenin's good name. . . . He wanted to influence us psychologically to undermine our limitless love of Lenin, and to increase his own stature as uncontested leader and great thinker of our era."[69] Stalin regarded himself as the revolutionary superman because his economic revolution seemed to him superior to Lenin's political and military revolution. Sensing his desire for admiration, one of his henchmen suggested: "The time has come to replace the slogan 'Long live Leninism' with the slogan of 'Long live Stalinism.' " Stalinism became an ideology in its own right containing its own set of ideals expressed and implemented by Stalin as the superior leader.

In the context of charisma, Leninism and Stalinism differed in two ways from each other. One related to the ideology; the other to the nature of the respective cult.

Instead of the ideology being shared by and voluntarily believed in, the Stalinist ideology was authoritatively stated and the related policy line dictated by the leader. All members were morally bound to the Stalinism as a distinct ideology. At the same time, the party stood below the leader, was reshaped in his image, and had no longer a will of its own, while the members were nothing more than pawns. Any deviation from the leader's dogma or from his policy line was punished by the leader. After the economic revolution, despotic power became fully compatible with imposed ideology and dictated party line.

There also was a difference between Lenin's charisma and Stalin's personality cult. The core of the former was the emotional union and the sharing of the mission between the leader and his followers. Stalin's personality cult was a form of manufactured charisma. The leader craved glorification of his person and admiration of his revolutionary achievements, but he did not possess genuine charismatic qualities. He then used his power over party and police to command full obedience from the paladins and followers as if he were endowed with genuine superhuman qualities.

At the center of manufactured personality cult stood the self-glorification of the leader. Khrushchev said in his secret speech: "The cult of the individual acquired such monstrous size chiefly because Stalin himself, using all conceivable methods, supported the glorification of his own person."[70] In his *Short Course of the History of the All-Union Communist Party*, Stalin characterized himself in the following words: "Stalin's military mastership was displayed both in defense and offense. Stalin's genius enabled him to divine the enemy's plans and defeat them. The battles in which Comrade Stalin directed the Soviet armies are brilliant examples of operational military skills."[71]

Self-praise turned into the claim of being omniscient. As Khrushchev said: "Everyone can err, but Stalin considered that he never erred, that he was always right. He never acknowledged to anyone that he made any mistakes in the matter of theory and in his practical activity."[72] The result was a claim to infallibility that in his view gave him the right to punish or to kill anyone who did not willingly acclaim his greatness. The charismatically claimed superiority thus provided him with the justification for his systematic purges and relieved him of any sense of guilt for his awful slaughters. One example may stand for the linkage between charismatic infallibility and despotic punishment. Stalin had written a pamphlet on the "Economy of Socialism." In his mind, he alone could have had the ideas expressed there. Suddenly, Stalin accused an unknown economist of having stolen his ideas. It so happened that the economist had written considerably before Stalin started writing and publishing his own work. "So the disgraced economist was arrested and jailed. . . . After Stalin's death we released him." Being infallible in his own mind induced Stalin to dogmatize his ideas and demand their full acceptance as indisputable truth. "When Stalin proposed something, there were no questions, no comments. A 'proposal' from Stalin was a God-given command, and you do not haggle about what God tells you to do—you just offer thanks and obey."[73] Stalin's theoretical "accomplishments" included among others, a new biology, a new linguistics, and also a Stalinist form of anti-Semitism, culminating in the "doctor's plot."

Last but not least, there was Stalin's belief in his own heroic deeds. He saw himself as the greatest hero in both the destructive and constructive aspects of the second revolution. It was he who decided and directed the attack upon the Kulaks, their extensive deportation, and the huge enlargement of the labor camps. Collectivization of the peasant land holdings was seen by him as his outstanding and constructive achievement.[74] Building up the state, its police and armed forces, and using them to break all peasant resistance, was believed to be another heroic deed. Each and everyone of these violent actions was expected to arouse the admiration of the paladins and of the followers. Hence party propaganda was greatly enhanced and became increasingly a worship of Stalin. Posters, statues and busts, films, novels, and photographs presented Stalin as a charismatic superman whom everyone had to obey.

Correspondingly, heroism became the central characteristic of the manufactured charisma for the masses. Every bureaucrat and manager, worshipping the leader in his own right, was urged to look for and report extraordinary deeds in his line of work. Given the overall goal of high growth rates, special accomplishments had to come from lowly workers who were inspired by the leader. Workers with high work quotas in the north were said to be inspired by Stalin because he had spent some years in the arctic circle of the old regime. Pilots and other technicians received prizes for outstanding professional services. Greatest attention was paid to the Stakhanovite campaign, beginning in 1935, in which workers were induced to surpass significantly their assigned quota of work and received in return substantial gifts and prizes. In the official press, the winners were celebrated "as the heroic people who have proven that there are no limits to the heroism of the Soviet people. . . . It was the thought of Stalin which inspired us."[75] Heroism in the work place was thus used as an economic incentive for workers to increase their speed and output by emulating the winners. The new Soviet man was pictured as a charismatic hero.

How were these heroic deeds at high and low places related to despotism. The extreme violence of the economic revolution, followed by the severe famine, created a mood of rebellion in the country. "Not only the immense mass of the peasants but the majority of the army, including its best generals, a majority of the commissars, 90 percent of the directors of factories, and 90 percent of the party machine, were in more or less extreme degree opposed to Stalin's dictatorship."[76] The crisis was so deep that Stalin's fall from power seemed unavoidable. Rather than changing his revolutionary course, or resigning on his own accord, Stalin adopted two new policies, of which the first was despotic in nature, and the second charismatic, both designed to destroy the prevailing mood of rebellion.

Although the internal left and right oppositions had been disintegrated and deprived of power, some of its leaders might have provided leaders for an anti-Stalinist rebellion. After dropping Lenin's rule that no party member could be put to death for political offences, Stalin charged all his opponents with antiparty activities, and treason to the Soviet state. While not agreeing among themselves, each one of the enemies—"Trotskyists, Bukharists, Zinovicvists, saboteurs, wreckers, diversionists, German agents, Japanese agents, British agents"—was guilty of a treason plot and had to be destroyed. Punishment took the despotic form of either sham trials or of mass execution, including not less than 35,000 officers of the Red Army, and eventually also the heads of the secret police. Despotism successfully destroyed all potential leaders of the opposition and translated opposition into an all-consuming fear, flattery and confession of guilt for crimes never committed.

This manufactured charisma, as Stalin's second policy, addressed itself to the masses, especially those outside of the party. Self-glorification, omniscience, and infallibility revealed a charismalike self-esteem that sustained Stalin in the years of famine and unorganized but widespread resistance. It was not so much "vanity and lust for power"[77] as a genuine feeling of his own heroism that motivated him in his destruction of all possible modes of opposition. There was no sense of guilt or fear of revenge for the purges that might have haunted any other mortal being. There was, instead, systematic attempt at building up a personality cult, presented as a belief in the heroic qualities of the leader, whom all the masses and the national groups could look up to in veneration. Despotism alone would not have done the job; successful personality cult as a deliberate contrivance was an essential complement that, together with despotism, sustained Stalin and his regime.

The superman's feeling of superiority, reenforced by the personality cult, pushed the leader into monumental plans calling for an exceptionally large volume of human and material resources. Their allocation to the huge projects could be accomplished only by the use of despotic power. Stalin's agrarian revolution involved wholesale resettlement of peasants and a multitude of labor camps for deported kulaks, causing also immense suffering from the ruthless brutality of the agents of violence. The same feeling of superiority and unrestrained will power induced Hitler to impose his plans of a grandiose empire, requiring a greatly enlarged German army, and the deportation and exploitation of millions of slave laborers.[78] Even if despotism as a distinct political system was not explicitly desired, the very scale and frequency of the grandiose projects forced each leader to employ despotic means for their implementation. As it was, aim and means of despotism complemented each other. Both together destroyed (private) farms in Soviet agriculture, establishing the new institutions of state and collective farms in the countryside. While Hitler expressed his readiness to exploit occupied countries already in 1937, he congratulated himself that the Blitzkriegs would bring him monumental victories by using minimal resources for warfare. While not expecting the buildup of a huge war machine, deportation and exploitation were not less cruel because the respective policies had to be improvised by his minions.

The longer the war lasted, the less Hitler's chances of victory, the greater the exploitation, the larger was the spread of the disbelief in his exceptional qualities. The greater the famine following the agrarian revolution, the stronger became the opposition to Stalin's rule. Both dictators fought ruthlessly any kind of disenchantment as well as infractions of the imposed discipline. For instance, the honor court of the SS sentenced to death more than one thousand SS men during the war[79] because of their disbelief in Hitler's infallibility and chance of victory and because of their physical nausea at having to kill millions of hopeless people.

As his claimed heroism was diluted by military defeat, each despot felt the need to refurbish his manufactured charisma. Stalin incorporated love of the fatherland and patriotism, as supplementary ideologies, into his pseudocharisma. Hitler's response to military defeat was more drastic. While increasing his exploitation of the occupied lands, he shifted his emphasis from the fraternal love of the followers to—in Weber's words—"the negative force of resentment" toward the enemy. Presenting himself as the man of strongest will and greatest ruthlessness, he demanded the trust of the mass of followers in his struggle against his most dangerous enemies. Attacking them as "subhuman beings" who would weaken the race, Hitler and his firing squads developed the brutal will to physically exterminate vast numbers of Jews and Bolsheviks. The result was a revengeful charismatic determination and a justification for the holocaust. The racial theory presented an ideological obligation, whereas hatred and desire for revenge supplied the will for destruction. It was the shift from fraternal love to unlimited hatred that culminated in the worst deeds of despotism.

While despotic means can be found in each phase of dictatorial charisma, despotism as a deliberate policy and practice became the last phase of such a regime. Despotism took the place of a routinization of charisma. Total military defeat terminated Nazi despotism, while Soviet despotism came to an end only with the death of Stalin and the removal of Stalinism.

# PART THREE

# DEMOCRATIC CHARISMA

# CHAPTER SEVEN

# CONSCIENCE
# AND CHARISMA

THE THEORY OF CHARISMA deals not only with the leader, but also with his paladins, his followers, and his supporters. The particular relationship of these three groups to their leader constitutes the internal structure of political charisma. The nature of the relationship changes over time depending upon the four phases in the evolution of successful charisma. In the dormant phase, the leader hears his "inner voice" for the first time, and prepares himself for living up to his calling (p. 400). In the disciple phase, the leader attracts paladins who do his bidding; both together form a communal group that lives on the gifts supplied by the supporters (p. 243). In the third phase the leader succeeds in building up a mass following, establishes an "expansive political movement" (p. 252) and thereby enters in and eventually dominates the political arena. Finally, the original leader dies, a successor takes his place, but he frequently deviates from the ideals of the original leader and may change his close disciples (p. 247). Most important for our purpose is the third phase, in which the internal structure is fully developed, and in which paladins, followers, and supporters have gained a definite position relative to the leader. It is the purpose of this chapter to discover how and why charismatic leadership has also flourished in a well-established democracy.

While Weber has formulated a theory of democratic charisma, as discussed in chapter 2, his distinction between democratic and dictatorial charismata suffers from two ambiguities. One relates to the specific definitions of democratic and dictatorial charismata. The other pertains to the peculiar time perspective he has attached to these two basic kinds of political charismata.

Instead of placing charismatic leadership directly into the respective political systems, we are given two kinds of "interpretations" of charisma. "The basic authoritarian principle of charismatic legitimation may be subject to an antiauthoritarian interpretation" (p. 266). Each interpretation gives rise to a different kind of legitimacy. In democratic legitimacy the gifted person "becomes leader by the grace of those who follow him since the latter are formally free to elect or even to dispose of him . . . now he is the freely elected leader" (p. 267). In revolutionary dictatorship, however, the "voluntary army of the faithful" achieves victory which secures dictatorial power for the leader. "The winning glory and honor in war" permits the leader to give his leadership an authoritarian interpretation. Coexistence of two kinds of directly opposite types of charismatic leaderships gives rise to "several charismatic structures" (p. 267). In terms of legitimacies the "interpretation" amounts to two internally different structures of democratic and dictatorial charismas.

Correspondingly, there are two significantly different sources of charisma. In the dictatorial case, the leader possesses a "self-created qualification"[1] that prompts him to seize power by dictatorial means. The strength of the inner will is the typical source of dictatorial charisma from which he derives the right to command obedience from others. In the democratic case, the extraordinary quality surprises the leader himself. It is a calling that is independent and beyond the self-creation of the leader. The claim to leadership is recognized by followers on their own initiative. Recognition of the clearly visible calling induces voters to give their electoral consent to the charismatic leader in democracy.

Surprisingly, these differences in legitimacy and sources should be, but are not, accompanied by appropriate differences in charismatic authority and in limits of power. Instead of the two kinds of authorities, there are the "interpretations" which a leader gives to his power. Actually, the term interpretation is a misnomer that has to be banned from our analysis. A careful reading of the subsequent text reveals a distinction between democratic and dictatorial authorities. The elected leader faces "a shift in the belief that a group has a right to enact, recognize, or repeal laws . . . both in general and in the individual case" (p. 267). The leader's right to issue orders is dependent upon the consent of the followers, thereby giving rise to a conditional authority.

In the dictatorial case, the leader is largely independent of the popular will, translates his own will into binding orders, choosing his own timing and the forms of his own dictates, leading to an unconditional authority to be complied with by the followers. Dependence upon the election by voters establishes a potential limit to charismatic leadership in democracy, whereas independence prevents any specific and readily enforceable limit to the leader's tenure in dictatorship. It is to be emphasized that these differences in authority and limits are not imposed upon the leader by the respective democratic or dictatorial institutions, but are self-chosen preferences of the leaders that are insisted upon or voluntarily adhered to on their own accord.

The differences in legitimacy and authority and in sources and limits provide us with the salient characteristics of democratic and dictatorial charismatic leadership. These typical features can be easily illustrated by a schematic presentation. To bring out the contrast vividly, we shall add the main characteristics of illegitimate and thus despotic rule in table 7.1.

While the first ambiguity can thus be readily removed by an appropriate definition of the respective terms, the same cannot be done for the time sequence in the

TABLE 7.1. Charismatic *Herrschaftverband*.[a]

| Political System | Leadership | Legitimacy | Authority | Sanctions[b] |
|---|---|---|---|---|
| Democratic Charisma | Elected Leader | Voluntary Consensus | Conditional Directives | Voluntary Obedience |
| Dictatorial Charisma | Self-Appointed Leader | Recognition Out of Duty | Unconditional Authority | Unquestioned Compliance |
| Illegitimate Rule: Despotism | Violent Usurpation | Fear Acquiescence | Arbitrary Commands | Spying Intrigue Violence |

[a]The three different translations of the term *Herrschaft* are either "imperative control" (Timasheff), "authority" (Parsons) or "domination" (Bendix) and the subsequent debate in the *American Sociological Review*, 1975, pp. 666–74, suggests that there is not one English term that includes all four components of the concept *Herrschaft* which are all needed as soon as one analyzes specific political systems. When we are forced to use one term, we shall translate *Herrschaftsverband* as rulership, following the original suggestion of Benjamin Nelson (CIT).
[b]Including sanctions into these four categories presupposes at least a charismatic group. "An organized group subject to charismatic authority will be called a charismatic community" (p. 243).

evolution of charisma. For, Weber presented the thesis that dictatorial and democratic charismata follow each other in time. Dictatorial charisma not only comes first in time, but it is also more pure because its authority and legitimacy are less interfered with by noncharismatic factors. Democratic charisma grows out of dictatorial charisma, and is also contaminated by various alien matters. These penetrators create the "progressive rationalization of the organization" assisting the leader, or indicating a development toward a routinization of charisma. There was only a cursory attempt at verifying this sequence thesis with plebiscitary charisma, (p. 267) but a detailed investigation of a leader with an actual mass following is missing. Presumably, this defect is attributable to the fact that Weber could not observe firsthand in his time a charismatic giant and his followers who started and remained in democracy.

In our time, however, gigantic charismatic leaders in democracy developed independently of the ones in dictatorship. A sequential development of one out of the other is not a part of our experience. This also means that we can study the two basic kinds of charismata independently of each other. It was only in militant charisma, to be discussed in chapter 9, that democratic and dictatorial features could intermingle because the democratic leaders had to adjust themselves to requirements of major wars. Nothing is lost, but much is gained, by discarding this asserted sequence of the two kinds of charismata.

Unfortunately, a study of the relationship between democracy and charisma is hindered by a more recent controversy. Three distinct issues are in dispute. The first one deals with the power state and its impact upon democracy. Weber is accused of seeing in the state nothing but an instrument of power that has a perversive influence upon democracy. In seeking to use the state for an imperialist policy, it is said, he is forced to adopt an elitist position and to overemphasize the role of the bureaucracy. The second issue concerns Weber's attitude to democracy. He is accused of being unable to appreciate genuine democratic values, of overemphasizing the role of the party machine and is, therefore, presenting only a leaderless democracy with a party machine. Finally, there is the contention that if there should be a charismatic leader, he will undermine the values of democracy, reduce parliament to an institution subservient to him, and mistreat the voters as a dishonest demagogue. The conclusion suggested by these critics is that charismatic leadership is either inherently dictatorial or, if tried in a democracy, will inevitably turn into a dictatorial Caesarism.[2]

Subsequent studies have significantly deflated the contentions of the critics. It is wrong to attribute to Weber a constant goal of the power state, since he also supported liberal rights of citizens. Especially his insistence upon a plebiscitary kind of leadership for the Weimar Republic came only after German military defeat, when "Weber recognized that a world-political role was no longer possible for his country."[3] Instead of concentrated power of the state regardless of the popular will, Weber proposed direct election of the president as well as his removal from office if ten percent of the electors demanded a referendum and a majority voted him out of office. The intention was thus not a dictatorial but a democratic plebiscite in Weber's constitutional proposals.

The preference for presidential democracy should not reduce parliament to a rubber stamp. Weber strongly supported a parliament that had the right to approve or reject the respective budgets as well as the general policies of the government. Parliament, also, should guarantee the civil rights of the citizens and be the proving ground for new leaders in whom voters could have confidence. None of these functions could be adequately performed if private interests could win a dominant influence in parliament. Finally, the central problem for democratization of Germany "was to eliminate the abuses of the bureaucratic regime which had developed after the departure of Bismarck."[4] Indeed, Weber presented an incisive comparison between democracy and bureaucracy that will be examined in chapter 9.

In order to obtain the proper framework for our comparison between democracies and leaders, we shall first identify the common denominator of all democracies, then discover the differences between the subtypes of democracy, and add to each of them the appropriate kind of leadership.

All genuine democracies derive their ultimate power from the votes of the electorate which enjoys the rights of citizenship. Elected leaders derive their authority from the two sources of the popular consensus and from the specific rights granted to them by the democratic constitution. These two authorities are conditional because they can be withdrawn by the voters in a subsequent election. As indicated in table 7.1, the difference between unconditional and conditional authority and legitimacy constitutes the specific divergency between dictatorial and democratic political systems.

The differences among the different kinds of democracy can be obtained from the particular roles played by the participants. The four participants of voters, officials, public opinion, and leaders do not possess the same capacities in the process of decision making. We thus will distinguish the subtypes of democracy according to the principle of prioritization. Leaders and officials usually enjoy more influence. Whoever has the greatest influence in ordering the priorities determines the particular type of democracy.

Similarly, each democratic subtype finds a kind of leader who is most congenial to the preferred mode of priorities and/or the policies selected. The leaders among themselves either belong to the group of personalist or of collegiate teams of leaders. In bringing out the affinity between leader and related democracy, we shall speak of one group as belonging to personalist democracies and the other to pluralist democracies, as can be seen from table 7.2.

Our thesis is that there is no single or uniform relationship between democracy and charismatic leadership. Pluralistic democracy normally does not generate tendencies toward charismatic leadership. The reason is that mass emotions are either passively or rationally responding to the slogans of different candidates. The situation is different in personalistic democracies, in which mass emotions become active

TABLE 7.2. TYPOLOGY OF DEMOCRACIES AND LEADERSHIPS.

| Democracies | Personalistic Democracies | | | | Pluralistic Democracies | | | | |
|---|---|---|---|---|---|---|---|---|---|
| | Presidential Democracy | Ideal Democracy | General Democracy | Mass Democracy | Representative Democracy | Interest-Group Democracy | Aristocratic Democracy | Party Machine Democracy | Bureaucratic Democracy |
| Selectors of Priorities | Charismatic | Ideologists | Caesar | Manipulator | Delegates | Agents | Notables | Bosses | Bureaucrats |
| Roles of Leadership | Inspirational | Aspirational | Innovational | Innovational | Pragmatic | Pragmatic | Pragmatic | Paternal | Paternal |

and candidates are selected according to personal and social sympathies. These candidates include the ideologist, who finds adherents to his cause; the manipulator, who arouses mass passion against an enemy without getting any popular admiration for himself; and the leader of armed forces, who gets mass support but is not himself endowed with charismatic qualities. Finally, there is the charismatic aspirant, who finds mass support on the strength of his charismatic qualities.

The contrast between personalistic and pluralistic democracies presents a view that differs in several respects from Weber's concept of democracy. (We are using an extended definition of leadership.) His tendency was to limit the title of *Führer* to charismatically endowed personalities. Regular politicians, including representatives, notables, agents, bosses, and bureaucrats, tend to act as leaderless functionaries. We shall speak of democratic leaders whenever they are engaged in selecting the major priorities leading to specific policies. Weber uses two concepts of mass democracy but does not always keep their meanings apart. One refers to the large number of voters, quantitatively, which are present in all modern democracies, personalistic and pluralistic. The other concept of mass democracy relates to activated mass emotions, which are capable of recognizing charismatic personalities and develop the readiness to follow them.

In consequence, the particular linkage between leader and subtype of democracy is limited to the charismatic movement in an overly restricted sense. The relationship between ideologists, manipulators, and military heros and the corresponding democracies is missing in Weber's analysis. At the same time, there is a careful distinction between ideal democracy, bureaucratic democracy, and political democracy, each of which has some capacity to influence the fate of charismatic leadership. It is our task to examine in detail the impact of these three democracies upon charismatic leadership. We shall consider ideal democracy and leadership in this chapter, turn to political democracy and charisma in chapter 8, and then consider bureaucratic democracy and militant charisma in chapter 9.

## IDEAL DEMOCRACY AND LEADERSHIP

Ideal democracy includes the promotion of pacifist, liberal, social, and equalitarian principles, each of which can provide an ethical basis for political conduct. Pacifism was promoted either by Christian sects in North America or by Jainism and Buddhism in Asia. In these religions, "every relationship to the world and action within the world is broken off, and in which the personal exercise of violence as well as resistance to violence is absolutely prohibited" (p. 594). Indeed, "the unconquered army of Cromwell petitioned Parliament for the abolition of forcible conscription on the ground that a Christian should participate only in those wars the justice of which could be affirmed by his own conscience" (p. 596). Sincere believers should have a right to conscientious objection or even civil disobedience in regard to all other wars.

In formulating the concept of pacifist democracy, the sects had established freedom of conscience as the first and, in their view, the most basic kind of personal freedom. But Weber's historical studies revealed only a few cases of sincere attempts at translating this belief into political organizations. "The most important of these was the Quaker community in Pennsylvania, which for two generations actually succeeded, in contrast to all the neighboring colonies, in existing side by side with the Indians, and indeed prospering, without recourse to violence. . . . The American War of Independence, which was waged in the name of the basic principles of Quakerism, though the Quakers did not participate because of their principle of nonresistance, led to the discrediting of this principle, even inwardly" (p. 596).

In assessing this American experience, Weber placed a high value on the freedom of conscience. In "ethics the pacifists are our betters."[5] Politically, however, the small and neutral states alone can seek to implement political pacifism because their military weakness does not constitute a threat to any other state or nation. A great state with manifold economic interests unavoidably stands "in the way of power plans of other larger states." A possible "drive for expansion" by military powers creates the threat of invasion. This "historical fate," in Weber's view, has "to be borne by all great states" even when they have full respect for the national feelings and desire independence for other states.[6] A policy of national self-determination thus called for trustworthy allies. In 1915, when these ideas were published, Weber furnished unintentionally the central argument for NATO after World War II. By the same token, his respect for freedom of conscience provided a rationale for conscientious objection on ethical grounds against active participation in the Vietnam war.

Radical democracy centers on the ideal of full individual freedoms for every citizen. Radicalism stems here from the period of enlightenment and contains the belief in the superiority of reason which guarantees a "cosmos of abstract norms" that guide men in their daily behavior. The main function of the state was to guarantee these rights against any encroachment by political power. The bills of rights were thus incorporated into the American and French constitutions. The Fourteenth Amendment also included freedom of individual interests by declaring that no state shall "deprive any person of life, liberty, or property without due process of law." Weber especially emphasized the inclusion of private interests into the constitutionally guaranteed rights (p. 1209).

As a national and democratic liberal, Weber personally appreciated the civil rights and called them "our self-evident possessions" that have become inviolable for any West European.[7] But he also noted some unintended consequences of the belief in civil rights. Already before the French and Russian revolutions (1905) liberals became united because of their beliefs in personal freedoms. The same beliefs contributed significantly to the development of modern capitalism. The ideal of an "undisturbed competition in markets" justified the "ultimate appropriation of the means of production" by employers (p. 871). Although not accepted everywhere, "throughout the whole puritanically influenced Anglo-Saxon world this principle [of free competition] has had a great influence up to the very present" (p. 873). Even the fact that the American Constitution did not recognize corporations was turned to the advantage of business. While many of the states granted various privileges to corporations, the Supreme Court for many decades refused to protect laborers against industrial exploitation because this would have been a violation of the freedom of contracts for employers. What started as radical guarantee of freedom for all turned into preferential treatment of the propertied classes[8]—up to the midst of the New Deal.

The ideal of social democracy could be realized only by means of an effective social democratization. Not only individuals but also social groups should receive appropriate rights. Economic and social interests of labor should be fully respected and their unions recognized as bona fide representatives of workers. As a result, laboring groups could develop "a feeling of honor and comradeship" which is essential for the whole epoch of capitalism.[9] At the same time, much of the upper-class arrogance and conceit, as well as privileges, would have to disappear. The worship of titles and degrees and the manifold aristocratic manners and customs of the nobility would have to cease. Nor could the plutocratic conventions, contrivances, and snobbishness be tolerated.[10] Such social democratization would develop the basis for the necessary self-respect and dignity of each person and the appropriate constraint or tolerance toward others. Social democratization was thus regarded as a necessary condition for the effective participation of voters in political democracy and for a willingness of minorities to abide by the decisions of majorities.

As a proponent of a "fully radical form of social democratization" in Germany,[11] Weber held little hope for the chances of peasants to gain opportunities similar to the one of the noble landlords in East Germany.[12] But he was insistent upon the right of small nations to receive full autonomy of their internal affairs in a peace treaty between Germany and old Russia.[13] He also strongly underlined the need for minority rights in a future German parliament. The parliament would have to convene at the request of one hundred members; minorities should be adequately represented in committees and should be able to question publicly members of the cabinet and publish minority reports of commissions.[14] Since radical and social democracies were not politically unrelated, Weber's theory of ideal democracy could have told us that granting voting rights to the blacks in the South could only be a prelude for a great demand for social democratization of all citizens—including women and all minorities—in society.

Minimizing social stratification would have to be followed by a similar style of life in and between social groups. Some similarity would arise unavoidably from a similar fate in political and social affairs or from effective social democratization. But status distinctions, especially of the aristocracy, tended to be self-perpetuating. The self-importance and romanticism of journalists and the *Junkers* aroused Weber's sarcasm and contempt.[15] An appropriate style of the middle class, called bourgeoisie, and a sense of reality constituted an essential precondition for an adequate public opinion that had to provide a guide for those called upon to govern.[16] Appropriate information and popular participation could bring an effective parliament that should provide an indispensable supervision over the administrative actions of the executive.

What then is and should be the role of leadership in these various forms of ideal democracy? The government, selected from and responsible to a representative parliament, should be headed by a leader who combines three major qualifications. He should feel political passion for a "cause"; he should weigh his actions and assume full responsibility for their causes and intended as well as unintended consequences; and he should possess a sense of proportion which would enable him to let "realities work upon him with inner concentration and calmness."[17] There was a very broad definition of the "cause." "The politician may serve national, humanitarian, social, ethical, cultural, worldly, or religious ends. . . . Some kind of faith must always exist. Otherwise, it is absolutely true that the curse of the creature's worthlessness overshadows even the externally strongest political successes."[18] The ethics of responsibility implicit in these causes requires that a leader should voluntarily resign from his position if he is hit by unintended consequences of his decisions.[19]

The leader required in an ideal democracy was clearly and definitely an ideologist. Only he who was absorbed by his "cause" and had the inner motivation to persuade others sought to convince a majority of the voters, and—if elected—let his policies be guided by his own ideology. At the same time, power to implement his cause was limited by universal suffrage, popular elections, public opinion, extensive publicity of public affairs, and a sustained confidence of parliament. On account of these constraints, the "cause" of the leader could reform, but it could not destroy democracy. Most decidedly, an ideal democracy had no inherent need nor objective causes for a charismatic leader who relied foremost on mobilizing emotions and on demanding dutiful obedience because of his supernatural powers.

What was the political relevance of the Weberian theory of ideal democracy? Its principles belonged mainly to the sphere of ideals, the relevance of which depended upon specific situations. Some of the ideals—as in natural rights—operated "besides the positive laws partly as an ideal postulate and partly as a doctrine with varying degrees of actual influences upon legislation or legal practice" (p. 810). Pacifist beliefs were political postulates that could lead to special legislation for small groups or states, not for larger nations. The beliefs of radical (or equalitarian) democracy, in Weber's view, went beyond the commonly accepted interpretations of liberty and equality because he also included competition and private property as sanctified individual rights. This extended list of civil rights has been or should be included in written constitutions.

In two respects did Weber go beyond the accepted bill of rights as believed in democracies of his time. One was his insistence of universal suffrage as an indispensable part of democracy.[20] The other was the right of workers to organize themselves in trade unions and engage in collective bargaining. Indeed, Weber formulated a law of social democracy—not of socialism—that runs as follows: "In everyday life and in the economic struggles of the workers, the sentiments of honor and solidarity are the only decisive moral forces for the education of the masses, and for this reason these sentiments must be given free rein. This and nothing else is the political meaning of 'social democracy' in an age which, inevitably, will still remain capitalist for a long time" (p. 1391). In 1906 Weber predicted in a lecture at St. Louis that this social law would also become important for the United States as soon as free soil had vanished, or when a substantial number of young farmers would move into the cities, or when these centers had been flooded by "the enormous immigration of the untutored elements from Eastern Europe." The displaced farmers would tend to lose confidence in the democratic ideals and the immigrants would never acquire the beliefs of "the Anglo-Saxon spirit."[21] While the rights of organizing trade unions and of engaging in collective bargaining were not granted before the New Deal, the belief in the fundamental civil rights did not diminish among the majority of the white workers. Social democracy became an addition, not an alternative, to the ideals of democracy.

The original and added postulates of ideal democracy provided the justification of civil rights, and granted an equalitarian position to those whose freedom was not based upon ownership of private property. For Weber, these postulates and ideological leadership could co-exist with a great variety of economic systems, including capitalist or socialist in nature.

There developed certain situations in which the ideals were not sufficiently respected as ultimate goals for actions. Deviations occurred in this country (1) when legal rights and protection were denied to an articulate minority of the adult population; (2) when politically privileged groups shunned the principle of universal suffrage and disfranchised certain minorities; and (3) when aggressive wars were fought, as in Vietnam, which were regarded as illegitimate by a significant number of voters. If a permanent distortion of democracy had to be avoided, then a choice had to be made between "material and ethical goals."[22] The subsequent conflict between goals would lead either to a sham constitutionalism, as Weber expected for Russia after the revolution of 1905, or to an eventual granting of citizenship rights to everyone. He implicitly predicted that ideals of democracy would again and again inspire movements aiming at either reform or revolution.

Even when full rights are granted to citizens, ideological leadership may generate its own difficulties. The leaders can promote those ideals that are most feasible, or they may adopt an attitude of an ethics of conviction. The latter will shun all consideration of material interests and reject all kinds of compromises with nonbelievers. The ethics of conviction will be adopted especially when leader and members operate in and with an ideological party. Refusing all compromises has the effect of paralyzing parliament and coalition government whenever the votes of the ideological party are required for effective cooperation. These unintended negative consequences were observed by Weber as resulting from the intransigence of the Social Democratic party in the German parliament prior to the revolution of 1918. The

powerlessness of parliament played into the hands of the bureaucracy, which dominated not only the administration but also politics and the legislature.

In seeking to overcome this unsatisfactory situation, Weber proposed to the constitutional commission a presidential democracy for the Weimar Republic. A president who should either be a gifted politician or a charismatic leader should be elected
by plebiscite. The politician would not only accept parliamentary control of the government, but also be guided by the ethic of responsibility. Given the slim chances of
finding such a man, Weber placed more emphasis upon electing a charismatic leader
whose control of the administration as well as of parliament would assure an efficient
government and a stable democracy.

If given a choice Weber would have preferred the gifted politician who would
have aimed at a synthesis between ideals and the ethic of responsibility. He did regard as detrimental to democracy the combination of a dogmatic ideological party
with an intransigent ideological leader. There were, however, two other dangers
that he did not consider in his extensive writings. One was the danger that a charismatic leader would adopt an ideology and act according to the ethic of conviction,
thereby inflicting upon democracy the negative consequences of the combined ideological party and dogmatic leader. The other was a crisis of conscience that would
arise out of a feeling of guilt, followed by an ethic of conviction, so that the distortion of democracy must be speedily terminated by granting the full voting and participation rights to all citizens, including the black and the young.

It so happened that this crisis of conscience developed in the 1960s in the United
States. It was because of this crisis among the liberals in the North that the new
movement of the blacks could adopt the tenets of ideal democracy as their goal for
terminating their disfranchisement. And it was resistance against implementing these
ideals growing out of the crisis that moved the segregationists to a confrontation
with the Constitution and the federal government. Most surprising of all was that
the struggle for and against the civil rights movement was led by two charismatic
leaders, who both incorporated their respective ideals into their charismatic missions. What were the meaning and consequences of these two modes of synergistic
charismata which combined ideology with charisma in a well-established democracy?

## CHARISMA, CASTE, AND CLASS

Max Weber was fully aware of racism as a special problem of democracy in the
United States. In his theory of races he traced the causes and consequences of racial
segregation for the political community. One cause resided in the belief of racial
purity. "In the United States, the smallest mixture of Negro blood disqualifies a person unconditionally" (p. 386). The other cause consisted of a "tendency toward
monopolization of social power and honor" (p. 386). Monopolization arises out of
the segregated intermarriages, and the closure of social and political activity reserved
for members of the superior race. "Strikingly different racial types, bred in isolation,
may live in sharply segregated proximity to one another either because of monopo-

listic closure or because of migration" (p. 388). The result is a clash between the privileges of the superior and a denial of citizenship rights to the inferior races. Weber anticipated a conflict about "the Negroes' demand for equal civil rights" (p. 386), but he did not foresee the rise of charismatic leadership on both sides of the color line. Why and how did this happen?

For many decades there existed a fundamental cleavage in society and polity. In society, there prevailed a caste system between the white and the black, and a class system between the rich and the poor. Most of the Negro population belonged to the lower caste as well as to the economically and socially poor class. Neither organized movements nor unorganized riots enabled the blacks to grow out of the pit of poverty or to break down the walls of segregation. Something new and effective had to be done if the "inferior" race was to enjoy some sort of social democracy similar to the one of the recent immigrant groups.

In the state, the two-party system and political pluralism prevailed only in the North. Political positions in legislatures and executives could be obtained only through victory in competitive elections. In the South, however, there had grown up a monolithic political system, in which the whites alone enjoyed full rights of citizenship and dominated all forms of government. The blacks were disfranchised, whether by social convention or by law. Caste and class were not coextensive, since most of the poor whites regarded themselves as members of the superior caste, in spite of their poverty.

Corresponding to the divisions of caste and class there had also developed an ideological conflict. Most of the politically active citizens in the North professed a commitment to the ideals of democracy. Ever since the abolitionists, however, the believers in equal political and civil rights suffered from a troubled conscience because suffrage was not universal and not all adults enjoyed equal rights. While conservatives separated equality and discrimination as belonging to two different worlds, liberals hoped that all adults would eventually enjoy the rights of full citizenship. In the South, the ideal of equality had been replaced by the ideal of racial supremacy of the whites because of their racial purity. The blacks were regarded as mentally and socially inferior and were not expected to develop the capacity of exercising full citizenship rights.

The decision of the Supreme Court in 1954 granting every child similar educational opportunities constituted a challenge to the segregationists as well as to the disfranchised groups. Instead of an open and violent rebellion of the Negroes, seeking to enforce the decision of the court, and of an open resistance of the segregationists, there developed two kinds of charismatic leaders with their respective followings. The ultimate goal of the black leader was full racial integration, whereas the white leader and his followers sought to uphold racial supremacy and segregation. Each leader and group sought to realize their respective goals without open rebellion or counterrebellion by building up a respective charismatic movement within the institutions of political democracy. We shall first examine the nature and consequences of the black leader and movement, and then turn to the opposite movement of the whites.

## BLACK CHARISMA

One can readily distinguish the qualities of natural and supernatural charisma in Martin Luther King, Jr. His dormant phase came to an end with his decision to become a Baptist pastor. His oratorial ability was his outstanding achievement as a minister. "He used few gestures. . . . He relied almost totally on his voice, a deep and throaty baritone . . . alternating quiet passages with expansive rhythmic sections, building to a climax in a crescendo of staccato phrases. . . . King attacked his enemies in key phrases . . . his voice rising in anger, in indignation, in wrath."[23] This voice conveyed an inner strength, a troubled calmness, that pulled people to him like a magnet. This personified natural charisma was most pronounced when speaking to huge masses. Best remembered are his two speeches in Washington in 1957 and 1963. On the latter occasion, the nine preceding speakers received little applause. King was given a tumultuous welcome; his voice and words created an emotional bond between him and his 250,000 listeners; the climax of his speech ended in an explosive uproar. For the millions seeing him on the television screen, King had become the leader of the blacks in most parts of the country.

We also can pinpoint the visible rise of his supernatural charisma. Far from being the originator of the first boycott of the buses in Montgomery, King was taken by surprise. As chairman of the Montgomery Improvement Association he aroused the Negroes to united action. But the task of organizing the boycott taxed his abilities severely. In a private prayer he confessed that he was at the end of his powers. But then he heard "the quiet assurance of an inner voice saying, 'Stand up for righteousness, stand up for truth, and God will be on your side forever.' My uncertainty disappeared, I was ready to face anything."[24] It was his vision of being in touch with God that transformed King from a simple pastor into a selected man enjoying the supernatural gift of grace, incarnating a religious charisma. Whenever he found himself in critical situations, King renewed his vision by prayer. The decision of the Supreme Court declaring the Alabama segregation of buses unconstitutional was for him a "revelation of the eternal validity of this [religious] faith."[25]

This sense of a calling was conditioned and reenforced by his philosophy of personalism. King had adopted the belief that personality is the key to the meaning of the universe and that not man but God is the Supreme Personality. Personalism became linked with a personalized view of religion: "If one is truly of the religion of Jesus he will seek to rid the world of social evils. The Gospel is social as well as personal. . . . I still believe that standing up for the truth of God is the greatest thing in the world."[26] But missing is any feeling of his personal superiority, because any believer can partake in the divine and be guided by the truth of God.

Religious charisma became associated and received its specific mission from two ideologies. One was the belief in liberty, equality, and freedom, included in the Bill of Rights in the American Constitution. The other ideology was the belief in nonviolence that was first practiced politically by Gandhi in India and then advocated in the United States by A. Philip Randolph, the black union leader, and finally transplanted by Martin Luther King, Jr., into the black movement.

Far from opposing democracy, King pointed to the discrepancy between the constitutional rights and their disregard in practice. The federal government did not enforce the civil rights of the Negroes; state and local governments openly and deliberately violated the rights of the blacks. In appealing to the conscience of the whites, King demanded that they live up to their own beliefs by granting legal equality to all minorities. The situation required, he suggested, an active federal leadership by issuing a second Proclamation of Emancipation, subscribed to and implemented by the whites in the North and South. The so-called Birmingham Manifesto of April 3, 1963, contained the sentence: "We believe in the American dream of democracy, in the Jeffersonian doctrine that all men are created equal and are endowed by their Creator with certain inalienable rights; among these being life, liberty, and happiness."[27] The emancipation of the blacks thus did not call for a revolution, but for a practical reform that would implement the ideals of democracy in all parts of the nation.

It was King who succeeded at the mass meeting in Washington by saturating the principles of civil rights with strong emotions. "I have a dream that one day the son of the former slaves and the son of the former slave owners will be able to sit together at the table of brotherhood. . . . I have a dream that one day even the state of Mississippi, a desert state sweltering with the heat of injustice and oppression, will be transformed into an oasis of freedom and justice. . . . When we let freedom ring . . . we will be able to speed up that day when all of God's children . . . will be able to join hands and sing . . . 'Thank God Almighty, we are free at last.' "[28] The great enthusiasm aroused by this and many other of King's speeches signified that the ideals of democracy had been effectively fused with the natural charisma of the leader and his followers.

The ideology of nonviolence contained a political and a religious component. It was the task of the leader to integrate both so that they reenforced each other. Politically, the Negroes are a small minority in a huge white majority. The blacks can obtain equality and justice only if they find the sympathy of a nonresistant majority. This support cannot be obtained through violent actions of the black. "In a violent racial situation the power structure has the local police, the state troopers, the national guard and finally the army to call upon, all of which are predominantly white." In seeking their justice by violence, the Negroes will be inevitably defeated. Many whites fear that if the Negroes gain power, they will without restraint and pity revenge the accumulated injustices and brutalities of the past. "Only through our adherence to nonviolence . . . will the fear of the white community be mitigated." Nonviolence is thus a "tactical program of action" that will bring the Negro into the "mainstream of American life."[29] This method has the side effect of disarming the white opponents and exposes the immorality of using weapons against the black.

The religious component of nonviolence advanced a solid theological justification for rejecting violence. It begins with the thesis that God is love and he who loves participates in the being of God just as he who does hate does not know God. Love is the opposite of hatred. The love of Jesus must be our guide for action. "Love must be our regulating ideal. Once we must hear the words of Jesus echoing across the centuries: 'Love your enemies, bless them that curse you and pray for them that despitefully use you.' If we fail to do this our protest will end up as a meaningless drama on the stage of history."[30] These words spoken in the early days of the boycott of buses in Montgomery and repeated in many churches, carried a deep meaning for his listeners who felt that, in suffering the violence of the police and white terrorists, they themselves gained in moral strength over their attackers. "Only with a living faith in God can the technique of nonviolence be employed with complete confidence and to greatest advantage. Without God, nonviolence is without substance and potency."[31] In making nonviolence a religious dogma, King had found a way of letting his followers participate in his supernatural charisma as well as in his manifold nonviolent but organized actions. In his mind he had not only solved the technical problem of how a powerless minority could stand up and obtain concessions from a powerful majority when seeking the rights of equal citizenship but he had also found a moral religious principle for winning the struggle without becoming the victim of hatred and brutality.

There emerges a peculiar and most intricate form of cumulative charisma for a minority in democracy. For the leader the emphasis upon his religion tied the overflowing emotions to faith charisma, and the paramount role of love incorporated the brotherly ethics into value charisma. Instead of acting as alternatives or substitutes for each other at appropriate occasions, both kinds of charisma were of equal importance fusing and reenforcing each other, and were simultaneously emotionally gripping and morally binding. Religious charisma and democratic ideologies interacted and reenforced each other.

In dictatorship as well as in democracy there occurred an effective linkage between the two modes of charisma and two ideologies, binding leaders as well as followers. Yet there were striking differences in specific content, secrecy, and commitment between the two systems. The dictatorial leader enjoyed significant discretion in selecting the acceptable ideals; declared one ideology as knowable and binding, and the other as deeply secret, or temporarily deniable, and as revealable only at the point of action. The democratic leader was fully and equally committed to his ideologies, regarded both as equally significant and binding, and sought honestly to convince all followers and allies of the truth of his ideals.

Moreover, each charismatic movement strove to translate the emotional bond and the reciprocal loyalties into appropriate organizations. The dictatorial organization was simultaneously interlocking and strongly disciplinary, subject to the leader's commands. The democratic leader formed only an umbrella organization of church ministers, known as the Southern Christian Leadership Conference (SCLC). While the Student Nonviolent Coordinating Committee was initiated and partly financed by the SCLC, the offspring then became independent and subsequently a rival of the parent organization. Cooperation with other civil rights organizations, such as the National Association for the Advancement of Colored People (NAACP) and the Congress of Racial Equality (CORE), had to be negotiated for each new program of action. Instead of the leader dominating the organizations, King received only a payment of his expenses from the SCLC, distributed the income from the Nobel Prize among the civil rights organizations, and handed over the larger part of his book royalties to the SCLC.[32] Charismatic leadership thus generated a minimal form of a supportive organization in democracy. Each major demonstration had thus to be preceded by agreements for joint actions.

Finally, in linking the two ideologies with the leader's extraordinary qualities, the synergistic interaction created a value as well as a faith charisma. The major features included (1) the presence of God in the life of every paladin and follower; (2) an intense feeling of love created a sense of universal brotherhood; (3) as equal believers, all men had a right to full citizenship; (4) leader and followers were obliged to oppose injustice whenever and wherever it was practiced; (5) leader and followers had to overcome their inner fear of being subjected to violence and were morally obligated to endure injury without resorting to counterviolence.

## ACHIEVEMENTS OF BLACK CHARISMA

Given these characteristics and peculiarities, what were the achievements, partial successes, or limits of this charismatic movement and its leader? Could the reform of full-fledged citizenship rights be attained? Or would the unorganized rebellion turn into an organized revolutionary movement, closing available opportunities and building up decisive hurdles for the charismatic movement in the 1960s?

The first and most obvious achievement of charismatic leadership was the emotional and political mobilization of the previously inarticulate black community. The charismatic appeal significantly changed the self-perception of many blacks. The imposed image of nonperson was widely replaced by self-esteem. Black consciousness took the place of eternal subservience. Following a nationally and internationally recognized charismatic leader, the usually disunited Negroes began to regard themselves as brothers and formed a sense of group solidarity. In spite of their meager resources, collective actions were undertaken and often carried through successfully. Mobilization turned into a new kind of militant but nonviolent resistance, first against single segregated institutions,[33] and then against segregation as a racial caste system.

The second achievement of the charismatically led black movement was the successful appeal to the moral conscience of white liberals. The oppressive response of the Southern police forces and the killing of some individual but passive resisters by infuriated segregationists was found intolerable by millions of whites in the North.

Leaders of white Protestant churches and of some trade unions supported the black movement. The resulting informal alliance widened the protest against segregation and became a national civil rights movement when President Kennedy declared segregation morally wrong, turned against second-class citizenship, and proposed the first Civil Rights Bill to the Congress.[34] The bill became law in 1964 when it became clear to leaders of both political parties in the North that the black movement and its white allies could not be dispersed and defeated by police oppression and called for a political solution.[35].

The third achievement consisted of the superiority of federal law and the armed forces over the segregation laws and the police forces of the southern states. Federal action was ignited by the biracial demonstrators in Selma, Alabama, in 1965. Segregationist killings of a Unitarian minister and others and the large-scale arrests and beatings by the police were revolting to millions of viewers. President Johnson addressed the nation: "What happened in Selma is part of a larger movement which reached into every section and state of America. It is the effort of the American Negroes. . . . Their cause is our cause, because it is not just the Negroes, but really it's all of us, who must overcome the crippling legacy of bigotry and injustice."[36] The president federalized the National Guard, let federal marshals protect the marchers from Selma to Montgomery, Alabama, and broke the barriers to Negro registration by the subsequent Voting Rights Act of 1966. It was the biracial alliance that, after some other skirmishes, not only granted the Negroes the right to vote, but step by step tore down most of the laws and institutions of segregation in the South.

These three accomplishments of the charismatically led civil rights movement produced two crucial effects. The biracial movement, effectively supported by the federal government, terminated the legally tolerated two-class citizenship by means of a significant political reform. In the segregated South, however, the three accomplishments together amounted to an antisegregationist revolution against the racial caste system. A simultaneous reform and revolution achieved at a minimum degree of upheaval and violence is unique in the history of democracy. If any one man can be singled out as the initiator, driving force, and guiding spirit of these two major political changes, it was the preacher and charismatic leader Martin Luther King, Jr.[37]

The legal reform of citizenship was only the first, but not the ultimate aim of the black movement. King himself in 1967 outlined four additional reform programs that had to be undertaken by the federal and state governments. Most urgent was the improvement of the public welfare system. Instead of being regarded as beggars, the beneficiaries should be recognized as citizens who have a right of "maximum feasible participation" in community planning and assistance, to be advocated and directed by welfare unions. Second was the demand for an end of segregated housing. Segregation had worsened due to the concentration of Negroes in northern cities because of the migration from the South. "Urban renewal has been Negro removal and has benefited big merchants and real estate interests."[38] Rehabilitation and new housing in ghetto areas should be temporary, highly subsidized, and accompanied by tenant unions. Required should also be a long-range plan for integrated housing; meeting standards of adequacy, using features of model cities, and built by an integrated work force.

Very important was the third proposal of eliminating the racial underclass by reforming the whole educational system. The considerable task would be not only to bring Negroes up to a higher educational level, but "to close the gap between their educational levels and those of whites."[39] In addition to substantially improving the schools in the ghetto areas it should be the mission of all educators to rapidly improve the school performance of the Negroes and other poor children. Educational parks in which students would be brought together in one place "will guarantee school integration even before housing is desegregated."[40] Most important of all, the huge unemployment of the Negro youths who suffer from crisis underemployment in a booming economy should be terminated. The necessary steps should include jobs first and training second, on-the-job training, merit awards to employers for hiring untrained workers, and pushing for a rapid expansion of the human services industries, so as to increase significantly the demand for quickly trained laborers. Youth employment should be followed by a program for fair employment practice that would steadily reduce discrimination for reason of color and educational disadvantages.

## CRISIS OF VALUE CHARISMA

It is well known that few of the above mentioned programs were initiated during King's term of activity. Of the manifold reasons for this delay, three are most important for our discussion. There was first the shift from peace to war which diminished the funds available for reform programs. The war created a split between white and black liberals that substantially reduced their political power during the second half of the 1960s. Second, bringing down the caste system was greatly resented by the segregationists. There was a fear for jobs and incomes and other consequences of Negro rehabilitation. A white backlash created a political counterpressure to the attempt of eliminating the Negro underclass. Finally, there eventuated three limits to the charismatic qualities which sprang from a crisis in the belief of charisma. We shall discuss these limits of charismatic values before turning to the white backlash and its own charismatic leader.

The crisis of value charisma arose within the black movement itself. The growing militancy of the black radicals led to a challenge to the doctrine of nonviolence and to King's leadership. The killing of Medgar Evers and the wounding of James Meredith in 1966 provided the occasion for questioning the role of nonviolence. A more tactical argument demanded self-defense against violence by white terrorists or police brutality. The lengthy discussions gave rise to a compromise that the march through Mississippi should be continued peacefully. The other argument was raised by black revolutionists who insisted upon the exclusion of "white phonies" and proclaimed "Black Power" as the new slogan for the black movement, implying that weapons of all sorts would be used to break down any resistance to the black movement.

King's answer to this challenge was clear and foresighted. He rejected the distinction between violence for defense and aggression because the former would become the latter in any real encounter. Emphatically he underlined that counterviolence would bring no gains for the blacks but only suppression by superior military force. He recognized that pride in blackness was valuable in itself but linked it with the dignity and honor due all black people. There was no compromising on the basic issue: "I refuse to be driven to a Machiavellian cynicism with respect to power. . . . Violence is the antithesis of creativity and wholeness. It destroys community and makes brotherhood impossible."[41] But the radicals who did not accept his arguments intensified their call for black power, which was adopted by the Black Panther party and went under with their suppression. The suppression was correctly predicted by King and anticipated generally by Weber long ago, and nonviolence has been accepted by the few surviving members of the Black Panther party (e.g., Cleaver).

The second crisis arose when King extended his nonviolence from civil rights to the Vietnam war. There were two specific reasons for him to speak out against the war. One was his religious belief in nonviolence which induced him in his Nobel prize lecture to deplore America's "failure to deal positively and forthrightly with the triple evils of racism, extreme materialism, and militarism." This was followed by a statement to the Fellowship of Reconciliation. "It is worthless to talk about integrating if there is no world to integrate in. . . . The war in Vietnam must be stopped. There must be a negotiated settlement even with the Viet Cong!" The second reason moving him was the concern for the poor. "I speak for the poor of America who are paying the double price of smashed hopes at home and death and corruption in Vietnam." The soft pedalling of the war on poverty was rejected. "Do we love the war on poverty or do we love the war in Vietnam?"[42]

Calling for a negotiated peace engendered two opposed responses. The "peacenicks" welcomed his shift in policy and sought to incorporate his followers into their movement, while some proposed the forming of a new political party, with King and Spock as their candidates for the presidential election. Those who continued to support the war accused King either of having deserted Americanism and gone over to the Communists or of having downgraded the civil rights movement. King himself rejected either interpretation. In joining the peace movement, "I thought I could serve as a bridge between the old liberals and New Left."[43] Instead of bridging this cleavage, the Vietnam war split the civil rights movement. Not only the black leaders were divided as were the liberals, but the government withdrew its support from King and his followers. While withdrawal from Vietnam was eventually accepted by the majority, the immediate impact of the opposition to the war created a limit for the leader's charismatic power.

Finally, there arose opposition to the values of the movement and indifference to King's charismatic leadership in the northern ghettos. In seeking to mobilize these

Negroes for major demonstrations, King and his assistants discovered the weakness of the Negro churches, the selfish outlook of middle-class Negroes, and the organized gangs of younger Negroes. None of these groups developed a charismatic disposition and thus was not inclined to accept King's leadership. The race riots in Harlem and Watts took him as much by surprise as they were unexpected by the Johnson administration. The racial disorders in the first nine months of 1967 attested to the fact that none of the black organizations was in effective control nor could advance a feasible program for mitigating the miserable conditions in the northern ghettos. In becoming acquainted with the isolation and deprivation of the core of the ghettos, King presented a Bill of Rights for the Disadvantaged that would require more statesmanship and more sacrifices by white Americans. But he found no takers. The Congress had just passed overwhelmingly the antiriot bill, indicating that this violence and the dispute over the Vietnam war had broken the alliance between white and black and that this cooperation was no longer available for regenerating the life in ghettos.

In the last year of his life King was thus faced by a stymied charisma resulting from the threefold value crisis. His most cherished value of nonviolent but organized action had been rejected by the supporters of Black Power, by many of the former white allies, and by the Negroes in the northern ghettos. This utterly unexpected situation induced King to search for the causes of the crisis. He found no definite answers but three untested possibilities. "We have developed an underclass in this nation, and unless this underclass is made a working class, we are going to have problems." The civil rights movement had thus run up against the wall of this hardly modified class structure. He also considered the quite different response of the northern whites to the squalor or riots of the blacks in the ghettos. While police brutality in the South created an outrage of the whites nationally, "police misconduct in the North was rationalized, tolerated, and usually denied." This negative response severely tested King's belief in the honesty of whites, and he began to believe that "most of the white Americans are 'unconscious racists.' "[44] While still committed to the ideal of equal educational opportunities for white and black children, King was able to mobilize twenty thousand demonstrators before City Hall in Chicago. Next day, however, the number of participants fell to the usual two hundred,[45] and the "busing of children for racial reasons" remained an unresolved conflict in many cities a full decade after his death. In whichever direction he turned, the black charismatic leader ran against the walls of a two-race society that perpetuated the inferior position of the blacks and white poor.

Facing his charismatic limits squarely, King arrived at the following reflection: "For years I have labored with the idea of reforming the existing institutions of society, a little change here, a little there. Now I feel quite differently. I think you have got to have a reconstruction of the entire society, a revolution of values." But when he sought to spell out the values of a religious brotherhood, these values also called for reconstructed institutions. Such a change meant "the possible nationalization of certain industries, a guaranteed annual income, a vast review of foreign investments, an attempt to bring new life into the cities."[46] The Negro labor leader Philip Randolph had proposed the outline for such a plan that called for a domestic Marshall Plan of $100 billion to rehabilitate the poor over a period of ten years. King saw in this plan the economic expenditures for winning the war on poverty. These funds, wrote King in introducing the book, shall provide for the needs "of America's poor, for there is no way merely to find work, or adequate housing, or quality integrated schools for Negroes alone. We shall eliminate slums for Negroes when we destroy ghettos and build new cities for all.[47] The political clout for implementing the plan was to be provided for by a Poor People's March to be held in Washington, D.C., on April 22, 1968. "I am going for broke" was King's way of expressing the intended revolutionary nature of this program.

Within the black movement the crisis of values expressed itself as a cleavage between the charismatic quality and the two ideologies. Opposition was directed primarily against the two sets of ideals. Nonviolence was attacked by the adherents of black power who demanded guns to fight the police in the forthcoming demonstration in Memphis. Taking the side of the advocates of black power, Congressman Adam Clayton Powell declared that "the days of Martin Luther King have come to an end." At the same time, King's pacifism in the Vietnam war was attacked by "hawks" who called him "Commie" and "traitor." The crisis of values thus could not be settled by dropping one ideology and by placing full emphasis upon the other.[48]

In seeking to remove these limits to his charisma, King did formulate a third ideology—a social democracy in the sense of Weber. What he called a revolution of values was actually an attempt to raise the standard of living of the black and poor to the level of the organized laborers in the North. The blacks should "stand up against an unjust system without destroying life or property."[49] This new demand was illustrated by linking the economic strike of the Memphis sanitation workers with the boycott of white newspapers and some department stores. It was not a revolution directed against the political system or the establishment of big business, but a set of integrated policies designed to lift the underclass upward to the level of the organized working class. The black and poor should enjoy the same advantages of working conditions, employment, wage scales, housing, and schools, as were available to organized workers of the white race. Under the prevailing conditions of the Vietnam war and the rising backlash, such a program could not be implemented in the foreseeable future. The scepticism among white liberals revealed the declining appeal of black charisma for the allies and especially for the Johnson administration.

In terms of possible actions, black charisma was suffering from an impasse that tended towards depersonalization when King was killed in Memphis.[50] The subsequent Fair Housing Act, which Johnson got through a reluctant Congress, was largely an empty gesture in response to the many riots protesting King's murder.

The act was only a tribute to Dr. King's memory that left undone the reconstruction program for the black and poor.

## WHITE RESISTANCE AND CHARISMA

When the majority of the Supreme Court ordered the integration of the schools in 1954, hardly anyone of the justices anticipated the political explosion emanating from the attempted social desegregation.[51] Yet the court opened the road for the rise of a black civil rights movement. The school decision was followed by the civil rights legislation of 1957, 1960, and 1964 pushed for by white liberals. These efforts of the black and white integrationists were strongly resisted by the open racists in the South and many unconscious racists in the North. The repeated confrontations were accompanied or followed by a series of riots in major cities in which blacks revolted by burning down major parts of the ghettos.

While the riots expressed spontaneous protests, unguided by any national leadership, three other movements were gradually or partially led by charismatic leaders. Martin Luther King, Jr., first gained national prominence. He was soon followed by Governor George Wallace as the leader of the prosegregationalist movement, whereas Robert F. Kennedy, as the young attorney general, turned gradually from an institutionalized federal official into the charismatic leader of the white liberals running for the presidency in 1968.

There is general agreement that the segregationists did not initiate the racial struggle. Resistance grew out of the so-called white backlash, a "shorthand phrase for growing resentment against the pace and tone of the Negro demands."[52] Actually, resistance as the core of the backlash operated on two levels. The unofficial groups consisted of conspirational activists engaged in lynching, burning, beating, bombing, and killing black demonstrators or freedom fighters. Official resistance came from southern governors, courts, police, and national guards who used their institutionalized power to resist the federal pressure for integration. These resisters were amalgamated into one charismatic movement by Governor Wallace. How could racism form the basis for charismatic leadership?

Hardly anyone seemed less likely to become the defender of segregation than George C. Wallace. Having grown up in relative poverty and worked his way through college, Wallace was known as an economic liberal while a member of the Alabama legislature. He was much more interested in social than racial issues when he ran for the governorship in 1958. His defeat by a racist induced a political shift in his ideological outlook. Wallace concluded that "they out-niggered me one time but they will never do it again." He made it his business to become an "expert about niggers."[53]

Actually, there was some charismatic presentiment at an early age. When standing in front of the Alabama capitol to be selected as a page for the state senate, the boy confessed: "I felt chill bumps all over my body. I stood there with my feet on the stair and looked down Dexter Avenue. In my mind I could see my future. I knew I would return to this spot. I knew I would be governor of the people of this state."[54] He soon learned that continual campaigning was the indispensable means for success. Even during the war years, as a mechanic in the Air Force, he wrote Christmas cards to all the families of his county.

In his inaugural address as the new governor in 1963, Wallace presented himself as the new charismatic leader: "Let us, as Alabamians, grasp the hand of destiny and walk out of the shadow of fear, and fill our divine destination. Let us not simply defend, but let us assume the leadership of the fight and carry our leadership across the nation. God has placed us here in this crisis. Let us not fail in this, our most historical moment."[55] Instead of the gift of grace, there was the hand of destiny. The unexpected crisis had brought forth a new leader to fight tyranny. Segregation should not only be protected, but Alabama will provide the new "courageous leadership for millions of people throughout this nation who look to the South for their hope in this fight to win and preserve our freedom and liberties."[56] While not mentioning himself personally, there was little doubt that Wallace saw himself as a genuine charismatic leader, for Alabama as well as for the nation.

While he referred only occasionally to the source of his superhuman quality, his mass meetings revealed his ability to arouse enthusiasm for himself. Young and old, men and women succumbed to his appeal. One blue-collar worker after a mass meeting in Michigan in 1964 proclaimed: "I am sixty. I never voted before, but I shall vote for this man." Wallace also became the magnet for many young people. The polls of October 1968 reported that 25 percent of the younger voters favored him compared with 21 percent of the total sample in this age range.[57] Even critical listeners were swept off their feet by his emotionalism. One female reporter said: "You saw these people in that auditorium while he was speaking—you saw their eyes. He made these people feel something real for once in their lives. You could not help respond to him. Me—my heart was pounding. I could not take my eyes off him, there were all these people screaming. You almost loved him, though you know what a little gremlin he actually is."[58] In January 1972, Wallace spoke at the statewide convention of the Jaycees of Florida, arousing the enthusiasm of the young businessmen. "The crowd loved it. After forty-five minutes of cheers interrupted by fifteen minutes of speaking, Mr. Wallace sat down. But the standing ovation did not sit. 'More, more, more,' went the chant, and, 'Wallace, Wallace, Wallace, Wallace.' "[59] A similar response was forthcoming from other states. For a period of twelve years, from 1960 to 1972, Wallace was riding on one wave of mass emotionality after another.

This rhetoric charisma was followed by emotional union between the leader and his paladins. One committed businessman said: "I don't believe I have ever known anybody who has that total belief in himself that George Wallace had. He is the most remarkable individual I've ever had the pleasure of being around."[60] The feeling of unlimited self-importance, combined with his personal magnetism, aroused three strands of emotions. There was the feeling of fraternal love of his paladins and devoted followers, the deeply felt hostility toward his enemies, and the hope for a new future of his many listeners. The impact of these emotions was such that Wallace was able to unite most of the rightist groups behind his banner.

There was also the negative proof for the effectiveness of his charismatic appeal. Shortly after he was incapacitated, over six thousand people had paid two dollars each for the barbecue at a political rally in Alabama. But most of them left as soon as they learned that Wallace would not be present. One of the organizers said privately: "There really is no substitute for the fiery governor to turn out the crowds. No one can speak with such certainty, with such gusto."[61] Neither King nor Wallace had around him even one paladin who could act as the first disciple of the leader. Nevertheless, the black and white movements as fundamental opponents were guided by and believed in the same primarily emotional type of charismatic leadership.

### IDEOLOGIES OF SEGREGATED DEMOCRACY

There was a quaint coexistence between an ideology centered in racial supremacy and a set of folksy ideas and ideals in the antiblack backlash. It was the special achievement of Wallace to link the notion of a racial mode of aristocracy with the earthiness and irreverence of the plebeian and personify both for over a decade. How could this combination of disparate ideas be made believable?

Ideologically, "Wallace was an unabashed racist. . . . He believed that black people are biologically and genetically an inferior species of the human race. He believed that segregation best preserves the values of both white and black races." The institution of segregation was indispensable and eternal. Indeed, Wallace said, "A segregationist is a man who likes people and knows that when God made some men black and some white He separated us Himself from the beginning." The divine origin of the races is reenforced by the purity of the blood of the whites. Divinity and purity call for a glorification of the white race and its supremacy. In his inaugural address in 1963 Wallace said: "Let us rise to the call of freedom—loving blood that is in us and send our answer to the tyranny that clinks its chains upon the South . . . and I say: Segregation now, segregation tomorrow, segregation forever."[62] This vow expressed his belief in the sacredness of the traditional order of effective segregation of the white and black races.

The decision of the Supreme Court, declaring separate but equal schools as unconstitutional, infuriated segregationists, many of whom refused to obey the law of the land. Candidate Wallace called for resistance in his 1962 campaign and made the following promise: "As your governor I shall refuse to abide to any federal court order even to the point of standing at the schoolhouse door in person if necessary!" He did expect that the "federal government will likely back down because the people of this country will not stand for the jailing of the highest official within a state." That promise led to the confrontation between the newly elected governor and the federal marshals when Wallace personally blocked the entry of Negro students ready to register at the University of Alabama. In the 1968 presidential campaign, Wallace emphasized his opposition: "Separation of schools exerts no negative influence upon students and parents. We have more togetherness in Alabama than you have in Washington." His promise for 1968 was that "when I am president, not a dime will be paid of federal money for busing one single student."[63] Schools belong to local government and are supervised by state government, and the sovereignty of states has to be respected by the federal government under all conditions.

In overthrowing the separate but equal doctrine, the Supreme Court became a major target of rightist defamation. Wallace charged that the Court had "wantonly destroyed the Constitution. The object of the Court was purely political." The Civil Rights Act was for him "the involuntary servitude act of 1964." There had to be a fundamental revision of the Court's decisions. A new tribunal composed of the fifty Supreme Court justices of the states should be convened and charged with the task to review the past and future decisions of the U.S. Supreme Court.[64] Wallace's American Independence party participated in the campaign to impeach Chief Justice Warren. In refusing to submit to an order of federal courts, Wallace complained that the judges favored "mob rule while hypocritically wearing the robes and clothes of. . . great and honest men."[65] "If I did what I'd like to do I'd pick up something and smash one of these federal judges in the head and burn down the courthouse."[66]

Hatred of the courts was even surpassed by the wild contempt for "federal tyranny." The executive was accused of initiating a "trend towards military dictatorship." In a speech against the registration of Negroes in 1963, Wallace charged that the federal action was "a frightful example of oppressing the rights, privileges, and sovereignty of the states." The Civil Rights Act of 1964 was for Wallace "the most monstrous piece of legislation ever enacted by the United States Congress. It is a fraud, a sham, and a hoax." The Housing Act of 1968 he denounced as the greatest attack upon private property in our country. "We must destroy the power to dictate, to forbid, to require, to demand, to distribute, to edict, and to judge what is best and to enforce that will of judgment upon free citizens. We must revitalize a government founded in this nation on faith of God."[67] The individual states must be given the autonomy to protect the rights of citizens against the power of "federal tyranny."

This ideology of racial purity, separate schools, hypocritical judges, and fully respected state rights envisioned an unequal democracy. Instead of uniform citizenship with equal rights for all citizens, there were the two status groups of white and black, privileged and disfranchised voters, of victims and criminals. The racist view of the world separated equality from democracy and translated citizenship rights into privileges of white voters, long effective in a southern single-party democracy.

If Wallace would have limited himself to this ideology of racism and inequality his influence would have been restricted to the area of legalized segregation. A supplementary ideology was necessary for running in the presidential primaries outside of the South and new conflicts had to arise in the North before Wallace could become a viable candidate in most parts of the nation. The riots of Harlem in 1964 and Watts in 1965, burnings in over sixty cities in 1967, and protest riots to the murder of Dr. King in 1968 intensified the fears of the whites, which in turn created a receptiveness for the ethnic ideology articulated by Governor Wallace.

Ethnic groups are not characterized by the color of the skin, but are distinguished by their origins, languages, historical experiences, cultures, habits, and styles of living. Many of the Italians, Irish, Jews, Slavs, and Spaniards live in residential neighborhoods in big cities, constitute ethnic voting blocs, and often place their ethnic beliefs above their economic interests. Their steady process of assimilation into mainstream America languished after World War II under the pressure of the northward migration of the blacks. One ethnic neighborhood after another was taken over by the blacks. In protecting their houses and schools against the penetration of the blacks, the ethnics built up the institution of de facto segregation. While not glorifying race per se, southern racists and northern ethnics held one belief in common: the blacks are inferior beings and deserve no help but contempt. This new affinity provided the opportunity for the ethnic ideology of Wallace.

Starting with the assumption that everyone was obliged to obey the law, Wallace presented the Negroes as habitual lawbreakers. Extraordinary punishment alone could provide law and order. Riots by the black should be suppressed by military means. "My orders are to shoot to kill. That's the way to keep law and order. If you'd have killed three that way in Watts, the other forty would not be dead today."[68] Federal judges were accused by him of coddling the criminals and indicting the police. In 1968 Wallace claimed that if he were president nobody would get stabbed or raped in the shadow of the White House, even "if I had to call out 30,000 troops with two-foot bayonets and put them every thirty feet apart. . . . The police in this country ought to be backed up to the fullest. . . . If the police ran things for two years, we would get law and order restored in this country."[69] There was thus a veiled proposal for a police dictatorship, to be directed and supervised by the governors of the states, that would beat the Negroes into submission and resist "federal tyranny" at the same time.

While he formally accepted integrated schools as the law of the land after 1967, Wallace presented himself nationally as the saver of quality education and as the attacker of the intellectuals. "I think there is a backlash against the theoreticians and bureaucrats in the national government who are trying to solve problems that ought to be solved at the local level."[70] Wallace presented integrated schools as necessarily inferior schools. "To ask us to equate our children, classroom for classroom, with a race that is two years behind in the sixth grade and three years behind in the twelfth grade is to ask us to deprive our children of the education to which they are entitled."[71] Busing of school children was condemned as the instrument for lowering the quality of education. In 1972 Wallace declared that "busing is the most asinine and cruel method I have ever heard of."[72] As an alternative Wallace proposed that ethnically controlled schools of the neighborhoods, free of federal interference, alone were able to provide quality education.

There was also a new interpretation of superpatriotism. His love of country took the form of glorifying the armed force. While he did not favor going into Vietnam, Wallace demanded a prosecution of the war until gaining undisputed victory. The Joint Chiefs of Staff should be given a free hand in directing the war. All our allies should be required to participate fully in the war. Returning from a visit of Vietnam in 1969, Wallace declared that "this war is winnable. . . . There is no way to withdraw combat troops until the enemy is crushed. . . . It would take less casualties to win this war than to withdraw."[73] Monolithic communism was the single and despicable enemy that had to be destroyed by all means possible.

Implementing the ethnic ideologies of law and order, neighborhood schools, and superpatriotism was expected to be a task of the police and armed forces. Riots would be stopped by police brutality, neighborhood schools would be protected by state courts, deserters would be thrown into prisons, and demonstrations would be controlled by the National Guard. The "mobilization" brought Wallace and his followers close to the frontiers of violence and involved clearly unconstitutional actions. But Wallace claimed the right to change the Constitution. "What is the Constitution anyway? It is the product of the people, the people are the first source of power, and the people can abolish a constitution if they want to."[74] Democratic processes and equality would have had to be rejected and a transitional dictatorship accepted for implementing the two ideologies.

Corresponding to the "blackening of the cities"[75] was an effort of Wallace to address himself also to the economic interests of the ethnic groups of workers. His American Independence party published a peculiar social program that was to supplement the ethnic ideology. The party promised to increase the minimum payment of the Social Security program, abolish the deductions of Medicare for those unable to pay. A public works program should reduce unemployment. The rights of workers should be respected and collective bargaining guaranteed. The party favored an equitable minimum wage, reasonable working hours, protection against accidents, and an adequate pay for work performed. This social program, adopted by Wallace, was to show the ethnic groups as well as the "white trash" that they did not have to give up their economic interests in voting for him. A leaflet of American Federation of Labor and Congress of Industrial Organizations (AFL-CIO), harped at this point by saying, "George Wallace could cost you a thousand dollars a year." There was a charismatic reply by Wallace: "It falls flat on its face. Nearly all of the rank-and-file support me."[76] Not only the behavioral segregationism but also the emotional attachment and belief in the ethnic ideology were expected to attach workers permanently to Wallace.

In 1972 Wallace added a special program for the "average man," centering around the lower middle class, which was simultaneously directed against government and intellectuals. In a righteous tone he declared that the government in Washington was run by "bureaucrats, hypocrites, uninterested politicians. . . . Washington is the hypocritic capital of the world." But the voters would stop this. "The American people are fed up with the interference of the government. They want to be left alone." Most unfair was the tax structure. While pointing to the increase in governmental revenues, Wallace told the politicians that "you had better give tax relief to the average man in this country and put it [the tax] on the filthy rich in Wall Street . . . or you might wind up short in the next election."[77] A tax reduction would not cripple essential government services because 82 percent of the supporters of Wallace believed in May 1972 that it was only necessary to cut the funds for the "unreasonable demands" of the Negroes.[78]

The little governor of Alabama used the "average man" as a code word for lower middle and working classes which together rose in protest against the federal government. The average man had, in one respect, a populist connotation in that he stood for the people's uprising against the national government. But the average man was also seen by Wallace as a part of his charismatic following and his ideological adherents. It was because of this combination of protest and attachment, that the "average man" as a voting bloc was expected to rise against the "federal tyranny" and support Wallace in his presidential campaign in 1972.

### CHARISMATIC ACHIEVEMENTS AND FAILURES

The most important accomplishment of Wallace, from his point of view, was his success in getting elected in his state four times. The majority of the active voters supported him because of his charismatic quality and his explicit belief in racial supremacy. This was most clearly visible when he ran his wife as a stand-in for himself. "She's going to carry the banner. I'll serve as her dollar-a-year assistant. And we will continue to sell the South's story to the nation." Such a charismatic surrogate is an exceptional event in the tumultuous history of charismatic leadership. Even when he was paralyzed Wallace received more than seventy percent of the votes in the state primary. His response was that "they love me. All of them love me"[79] in the home state.

His second accomplishment was the build up of a charismatic movement on a national scale, active in four presidential campaigns. In 1968 Wallace ran as the candidate of a third party, thereby transforming a two into a three party system. In a short time he got himself on the ballot in fifty states. His ten million votes almost prevented Nixon from getting a plurality of the votes. The two unintended consequences of the Wallace vote were that the Republicans captured the presidency, but that Nixon became only a minority president. This handicap created the psychological determination for Nixon to work for a landslide in the election of 1972.

The stated intention of Wallace was to prevent the other candidates from getting a plurality so that the House of Representatives would have to select a new president. In order to get his support, the winning candidate would have to negotiate "a kind of a coalition government" over which Wallace would have a continuous influence. But instead of the 177, he got only 45 electoral votes, so that his main purpose was defeated. The third party under his leadership failed. He himself formed a kind of a coalition when he selected a retired general as his running mate. Said one of his assistants retrospectively: "Everything went downhill from that point on." The provision of winner-take-all of the electoral votes in a state defeated the charismatic challenger.

In running in the Democratic primaries in 1972, rather than as a candidate of a third party, Wallace sought to capture one of the two traditional parties. 'I am gambling on trying to change the Democratic party.'[80] He won one-third of the votes in the ten primaries he contested. A comparison (table 7.3) of the most successful primary results shows the persistence of the Wallace vote.

TABLE 7.3. WALLACE VOTE IN THE DEMOCRATIC PRIMARIES[81]
(PERCENT OF TOTAL VOTES).

| State | 1964 | 1972 |
|---|---|---|
| Wisconsin | 34 | 22 |
| Indiana | 30 | 41 |
| Maryland | 42 | 39 |
| Michigan | 0 | 51 |

The impressive showing was foiled by McGovern's manipulation of the mode of electing candidates, and by the shots in Maryland on May 15, 1972. Since the Democratic convention selected a leftist candidate, the sole question was how the Wallace vote would be divided between the official candidates. Already in August 1971, Nixon did adopt the central component of the ethnic ideology: "I have consistently opposed the busing of our nation's children to achieve a racial balance."[82] Nixon got the majority of the passionate but leaderless Wallace voters in the South and a division of six to five in favor of Nixon in the other regions of the country. Nixon got his longed for landslide largely by grace of the gunman, minimally by his own efforts.

Apart from the electoral campaigns, Wallace suffered his major failure in the fight for the racial privileges of the whites in the South. Whenever the blacks demonstrated, the governors sent their police and state troopers to beat down the marchers and freedom riders. When he was asked to grant a permission for a walk from Selma to Montgomery in 1965, Wallace snorted: "I am not going to have a bunch of niggers walking along a highway in this state as long as I'm governor."[83] But the police brutality at Salem created a wave of indignation all over the nation which induced Wallace to request an interview with President Johnson. Wallace was told by the president: "I had seven hundred troops on alert. If the state and local authorities were unwilling or unable to function, I would not hesitate one minute to send in federal troops." To save face, Wallace asked for federal assistance for protecting the marchers. In response Johnson federalized the Alabama National Guard. "So the troops went in after all. . . . But they were not intruders forcing their way in; they were citizens of Alabama. That made all the difference in the world!"[84] The legalized system of segregation of the races was definitely lost to the South for ever.

The winners were the civil rights movement and the federal government. Their somewhat tenuous alliance gradually evolved a sequence of complementary actions. Black leaders organized a nonviolent demonstration; police and state troopers either arrested or dispersed the marchers; private white groups engaged in burning, bombing, and lynching; a wave of indignation aroused public opinion in the North; white and black liberals demonstrated at the White House; and the president responded to these pressures by either sending in federal troops or neutralizing state power by federalizing the National Guard. Finally, the Congress would pass civil rights acts that would outlaw open segregation, assure the right to vote, and gradually dismantle the related institutions of open racial repression. By 1968 even Wallace admitted publicly that integrated schools and accommodations were the "law of the land" and that legal segregation was dead.

Extralegal segregation, however, continued in various forms. Several reasons explain this incomplete reform of the civil rights movement. Neither white not black charismatic leaders found similarly qualified successors. The internal factions split the respective movements, dispersing their accumulated power. Neither leader did nor could have overcome the constitutional hurdle for winning a presidential election. As inherent minorities, neither leader could secure the required majority so that neither one could become a charismatic giant, nor establish charismatic rulerships in their own right. Seeking to win by means of a third party was bound to fail, as Wallace discovered in 1968.

An alliance with one of the major parties offered a promise either for completing the reform of the civil rights movement or reversing the prevailing trend of desegregation. But the long war in Vietnam destroyed such an opportunity. The pro-peace sentiments increased to such an extent as to replace the crisis of conscience and divert attention from implementing the civil right laws. Racial riots and propeace demonstrations culminated in a revolt that split asunder the liberal-black alliance and terminated Democratic control of the presidency. Republicans regarded the Wallace movement as a political rival who could be defeated only by stealing some of his slogans and ideologies. Busing of children and support of ethnic groups and state rights became the new issues of the Republicans. Assisted by the paralysis of Wallace and by the leftists campaign of McGovern, the Republicans did return to the White House by a landslide in 1972.

In the meantime, a kind of token desegregation developed during the 1970s. Officially, the ideology of social integration was accepted which demanded the same opportunities for all regardless of color, sex, age, and nationality. Laws and courts required affirmative action in employment, open housing, and busing of children for reasons of racial equality. While the goal of "color blindness" is not openly questioned, there is a determined opposition to the implementation of the laws of social equality. Many public schools are in an uproar and public housing projects often suffer from vandalism and destruction. Three defects of the reform for a socioeconomic democracy have become common knowledge. Some of the new institutions, such as busing, have been poorly chosen or wrongly implemented. Many blacks either lack the skills or have not yet developed the cultural habits required for making the most of their new opportunities. Finally, there is the resistance of many ethnic or rich groups who fight for retaining their heritage and cultural advantages. Reemphasized ethnic separation has intensified the discrepancy between equal voting rights and unequal cultural rights. There is some hope that better programs and cultural improvements will help to overcome the present stage of social experimentation.[85] But the backlash and the adoption of some of its principles by the radical right, linked recently with the Republican party, will—at least for a period—keep alive the conflict between legal and social democracy.

The conflict might have been  mitigated if the crisis of conscience and of black charismatic leadership would have been able to complete their reform. Apart from the change in the overall situation on account of the Vietnam war, there occurred two modifications effecting the termination of the leadership of the two charismatics. The gifted leader is not only the most important asset of such a movement; his strategic position contains also the greatest vulnerability for his continued leadership. Both movements were permanently derailed by the bullets of assassins. The result was an interrupted charisma: the leader vanished, his movement disintegrated, and his program of reform remained incomplete. This exit extinction or interruption replaced the alternative of Weber's better known gradual decline by the routinization of charisma.

Interrupted charisma is, historically speaking, not a counterpart of "irruption of charisma" which generates "a threat to regular organization" (p.1132). Neither one of the opposed charismatic leaders got into a dog fight with a major political party. The Democratic party benefited greatly from its earlier alliance with the civil rights movement. The break came because of an ideological conflict, not an organizational dispute, over war and peace, between segregation and racial integration. This ideological crisis was intensified by the crisis of charismatic leadership, and these conflicts interrupted the process of democratization.

### DUAL CHARISMATIC LEADERSHIP

In the implementing of the democratic ideals, universal suffrage was expected to grant the rights of citizenship to every adult. Placing citizens on an equal footing would amount to a process of political democratization because it would minimize privileges of certain social groups. The impact of this leveling would tend to engender also a process of social democratization leading to a similar style of life. Not only would the aristocrats lose their special distinction but workers would demand the right to organize themselves and engage in collective bargaining with their employers. The rights to assemble and to organize should be granted if democracy was to "free the road for the development of value forms suitable to our civic, social, and economic structure . . . ."[86] As we have seen, Weber appreciated the special tensions that arise from the task of granting citizenship rights to the black, living under a caste system being superimposed upon the class system. While he believed that the process of democratization—political and social—would be facilitated through a charismatic leadership in democratic Germany, he made no similar proposals for the leadership of the United States. His overall theory of social democracy implied that ideologically committed leaders would face especially great difficulties to overcome the tension between equalitarian and social democracy, because they are usually guided by the ethic of commitment. Leaders guided by the ethic of responsibility could more readily complete the process of democratization because they could adjust the timing and arrive at compromises necessary to reconcile the requirements of the two kinds of democracy. How and why has this process of democratization been suspended in this country?

The first steps toward equalizing citizenship rights were undertaken by leaders guided by the ethic of responsibility. President Truman ordered a gradual removal of the racial restrictions in the armed forces after World War II. The Supreme Court specified a slow implementation of equal rights in schools by the states. The first instances of Negro resistance sought to extend the law to equal educational opportunities to transportation and accommodations. The shift from small pressures to a principled position, infusing ethical absolutes into the racial struggle, occurred in the long boycott of the segregated buses of Montgomery, Alabama. Both sides refused to agree on a compromise because they adopted an unbending ideological stance. There were two charismatic aspirants who most effectively articulated the ideological righteousness and at the same time infused the resoluteness with group emotions. Personal charismatic appeal combined ideology and emotions and led to a cumulative faith and value charisma on both sides of the segregation conflict. Cumulation provided a leadership much stronger than could have been supplied by ideological absolutism alone.

The strength was magnified also by the allignment of two ideologies by each leader. Accepting the belief in nonviolent resistance, black marchers in the South showed great courage when they demonstrated for their rights in spite of being beaten by the police, bitten by dogs, and arrested in great numbers. Similarly, the belief among segregationists in a "federal tyranny" induced three governors to resist the decisions of the Supreme Court by facing the federal marshals in the name of states rights. Both supplementary ideologies created additional support on both sides of the struggle and increased the effect of the respective propaganda.

Equally important was the increased intensity of the emotions that emanated from the charismatic belief in the exceptional qualities of the respective leaders. Huge mass meetings could arouse the listeners, overcome political apathy, and mobilize the required resources for the struggle—out of love for the admired leaders. In addition to enthusiasm, there was also its opposite, hatred. The black marchers hated the institution of segregation and the white protesters hated the new civil rights legislation. Anger and indignation intermingled with admiration and enthusiasm, and both passions were united in fighting for one institution but condemning another one, usually with equal intensity.

While the majority of the voters were not a part of either charismatic following, many of them took a position on the respective claims involved in the confrontation. A number of conservatively inclined citizens looked with sympathy on those fighting for the rights of the states, and the "New Federalism" became a plank of the Republican party in 1980. Many of the liberally inclined experienced a feeling of compassion for those who had been denied their civil rights. As a result of this compassion, white liberals suffered from troubled conscience that was, by some, translated into a feeling of guilt and became the motive for actively supporting the civil rights movement.[87] A similar crisis of conscience led to the political alliance between the national leaders of the Democratic party and administration on the one hand and the leaders of the civil rights movement on the other.

Although each partner in this alliance experienced a symbiosis between feeling and will, the respective group emotions of compassion and charismatic love and of loyalty remained distinct. To be sure, Reverend King called the assisting whites his brothers and sought to fuse compassion with charismatic longing and loyalty, but such a mixture was limited only to those fully committed emotionally on each side. For most others the political cooperation was built upon the mutual belief in the validity of civil rights for all citizens, as embodied in the interpreted Constitution. The cooperation growing out of this intellectual commitment led to the civil rights legislation and the joint attempt at its implementation. "Without the aid of law, man's conscience works in vain."[88]

It has to be noted that Weber did not explicitly include compassion in his theory of interpersonal relationships. This gap was filled by an early work of Alfred Schütz, although the link between compassion and cooperation was somewhat weak.[89] Nor did Weber trace specifically the synergistic link between the charismatic and symbiotic beliefs and the democratic ideals in specific situations. Consequently, in Weber's theory ideal democracy remained unrelated to the mission of charismatic leaders and their movements. For him, mass passions were the necessary condition of the charismatic disposition, followed by submission to the leader. Rising only in mass democracy, the charismatic leader was then introduced either as a military hero or as a civilian Caesar. He commanded the trust of the masses by employing the plebiscite as a "demagogic means" of appeal. All plebiscites were seen as charismatic acclamations and "every democracy tends in this direction" (p. 1451). In stamping passions in mass democracy as the only emotional link between leader and followers, Weber was compelled to overly emphasize plebiscites—as an institutional element—and indirectly designate electoral charisma as the prototype for all other charismata in the political sphere, as we shall see in chapter 10.

Nor did Weber anticipate dual charismatic leadership and movements at the same time and place. There are two reasons for this oversight. One was related to the institutional and the other with the situational element in this dual charisma. Both charismatic forces centered their attention on the interpreted constitution. Blacks and liberals aimed at extending the Constitution by granting effective civil rights and removing the disenfranchisement of the past. Segregationists and conservatives sought to continue discrimination in the constitutions of the Southern states, and to reenforce inequality by separation in the federal Constitution. Taking the opposite side in this constitutional and ideological struggle incorporated conflict into dual charisma. By acting against those with military forces, the federal government put its weight on the side of the civil rights movement.

Equally overlooked by Weber was the racial component of the two movements in the situation. Many participants on both sides perceived their opponents in inhuman terms. Segregationists saw the blacks as subhuman beings, incapable of using civil rights responsibly and apt to engage in rape and murder. A similar fear haunted many blacks, who expected only bombings, lynchings, and police brutality from the whites in Southern communities. Fear and anxiety were thus built into each charismatic movement. The hatred of both groups was so great that a genuine reconciliation between the opposed movements was impossible to attain. The result of intellectual conflict and emotional fear was that neither side could achieve a clear victory. Neither movement could develop into gigantic charisma.

The final outcome was a partial victory for each. Legally, segregation was abolished, and blacks became an electoral constituency of the Democratic party. On the other hand, the backlash was so strengthened through the assistance of the ethnic groups in the North that many of the rights granted, especially in housing and employment, were not implemented by Republican presidents. As a result, the racial split and its antagonism continues to fester the body politic as well as society, and social reform remains incomplete.

While Weber overlooked the special institutional and racial components of dual charisma, his theories on values and democratization give an additional explanation for the outcome of the struggle. In examining the attempts of groups to implement values in politics, Weber concluded that the particular content and multiplicity of ideologies leads to an unavoidable conflict between values.[90] Promoters of one set of values adopt a partisan position relative to the adherents of other values. The very partisanship prevents an amiable accommodation of the respective values.

But there is an exception to this rule of unavoidably conflicting values that is only implicit in Weber's theory. A reconciliation of values is possible if they are compatible in their content and can be realized simultaneously through accommodating actions. This is what happened in the relationship between blacks and liberals. The belief in the same constitutional principles permitted an alliance avoiding a clash between the respective values. But the conflict between the values of the two charismatic movements contributed significantly to the stifling of the civil rights reform.

A crisis in shared constitutional values arose when Reverend King attacked the Vietnam war. His critique was justified with the following words: "I know that I could never again raise my voice against the violence of the oppressed in the ghettos without having first spoken clearly against the greatest purveyor of violence in the world—my own government."[91] In generalizing the principle of nonviolence and in demanding an end to the war, King demanded that the Johnson administration adopt the pacifist principle in international affairs. Dogmatization of one principle and its generalization to other matters dissolved the alliance. Understanding of constitutional values contributed significantly to the success of universalizing civil rights; conflict on the pacifist values terminated mutual cooperation and contributed an additional cause to the stifling of the reforms.

While Weber saw no link between ideal democracy and charismatic movements, his theory of democratization provides a deeper meaning for the process of reform and its consequences. He pointed to certain conditions that permit a simultaneous development of equalitarian and social democracy, while other conditions generate a conflict between these modes of democracy. One is the condition of class and property as both penetrate into the polity. In general, "the modern state has created the concept of the citizen. The modern right to vote means nothing else but the legal equality between citizens."[92] In society, however, social inequalities are generated by different educational opportunities and especially by differences in the possession of property. On account of the dependencies, legal rights can only "mitigate the advantages of privileged groups whose influence upon the policies of the state is always greater than is justified by their numbers."[93] Social dependencies thus lead to a difference between social and political democratization. "The [legally] unlimited democracy in America, for instance, does not prevent the growth of a raw plutocracy or even an aristocratic prestige group, which is slowly emerging."[94] Cultural improvement in the direction of "cosmopolitan personalities" through education and property can reduce the discrepancy between political and social democratization.

The same is not true for the majority of the workers. Such improvement is unattainable because the respective values "cannot be imitated by the broad masses of the people."[95] The class cleavages can only be minimized by a deliberate policy. We "must not forget that in everyday life and in the economic struggles of the workers the sentiments of honor and solidarity are the only decisive forces for the education of the masses, and that for this reason these sentiments must be given free rein. This and nothing else is the political meaning of 'social democracy' " (p. 1391). In concrete terms, social democratization meant that there should be free trade unions and collective bargaining by means of which workers could practice their own solidarity, self-respect, and honor. "When it acts in solidarity, the industrial proletariat . . . is a force at least capable of order and orderly leadership through its functionaries and hence through rationally thinking politicians."[96] If so, workers seek and often obtain the benefits of social democracy.

Universal and equal voting rights have been at the center of political democracy, while holding jobs and earning a regular income have been at the center of social democracy.[97] Recurrently high figures of unemployment, even in periods of prosperity, are an indicator of insufficient social democratization. This insufficiency has been the fate of the American blacks, both before and after granting of the right to vote. Sociologically, continued mass unemployment of the blacks presents a case of an underclass that lives either outside or at the fringes of labor markets. A stifled reform means that social democratization is held in abeyance for the majority of blacks and other groups of the poor. The goal of Reverend King of lifting the blacks into the white working class, receiving all the advantages of trade unions and of the social services of the state, describes the task of social policy for the future.

Historically speaking, a close association between citizenship rights and rising employment opportunities have been the hallmark of all nations in modern democracy.[98] The linkage between political rights and economic opportunities has emanated from lower-class protests, from the desire to obtain national unity, from periods of compassion for the depressed social groups. (National unity moved Weber to support extension of democratization from the political to the social field.) Whichever motive was strongest at a given time, protests, unity, and self-esteem have fashioned a trend from political to social democratization. This historical experience establishes a presumption that the same trend will eventually bring social democratization to the blacks.

In all, dual charismatic leadership and movements have not been able to grow into a gigantic charisma. Neither leader was able to get control of a major political party or could become president of the nation; neither had any chance of establishing a charismatic rulership. All this was accomplished by Franklin D. Roosevelt and the New Deal. The analysis of his leadership is the topic of our next chapter.

# CHAPTER EIGHT

# CRISIS AND CHARISMA

POLITICAL DEMOCRACY COMPRISES four different features, according to Weber, in the modern state. These include independent political parties, an effective parliament of representatives, a responsive executive and judiciary, and the electorate of citizens whose votes determine who among the political groupings is given the right to exercise political power. All these institutions, separately and jointly, operate within the framework of a written constitution, and their power is delimited by the interpreted constitution.

Basic for a political democracy is the linkage between private and public spheres of action. Political parties originate and partly operate in the private sphere. In seeking to organize citizens for political participation, parties solicit either full members or sympathizers who seek to promote the opportunities of their chosen political party. Parliament, administration, and courts operate in the public sphere for the purpose of formulating public policies and implementing them according to the rule of law.

For a charismatic leader to rise to power in a political democracy, it is necessary for him to become the spokesman for a political party. He and his party must win the majority of the votes in competitive elections. Victory in political campaigns grants the leader and party the power to form a government, to control the legislature, to appoint the heads of civilian and military bureaucracies, and to select the judges in the judiciary system. The central questions to be examined in this chapter are: (1) how does a charismatic personality succeed in becoming simultaneously the leader of his party, of parliament, and of the administration, and (2) how does he impress his personal style and policies upon the political system without destroying or fundamentally transforming political democracy?

By the way of introduction we shall briefly summarize Weber's theory of political parties and ascertain how a charismatic personality can establish an exalted position in his own party. We shall then turn to the ideals and policies sponsored by the charismatic leader that bring him to political power in the country. Since Weber did not formulate a theory of charismatic ideologies and policies, we shall have to exam-

237

ine the achievements and failures of one outstanding charismatic leader in a modern democracy. The most conspicuous example was (and is) President Franklin D. Roosevelt whose situation, charismatic appeal, ideals, and policies prior to World War II would furnish the prototype for democratic charisma in the midst of a severe economic crisis.[1]

## POLITICAL PARTIES AND CHARISMA

In his analysis of political parties, Weber concentrates upon the internal structure of such organizations. Such a structure consists of "(a) party leaders and their staffs . . . (b) active party members [who] under certain circumstances . . . may exercise some form of control . . . (c) inactive masses of electors or voters . . . (d) contributors of party funds [who] usually remain behind the scene" (p.285). Active members join the party by formal voluntary solicitation and adherence . . . to the rules of the group within which the party exists" (p.287). The ordinary business of parties is carried on by leaders and staff who by their actions create a party machine. While active members "exercise some forms of control by participating in discussion, voice complaints, or even initiate resolutions" (p.285), leaders and staff usually acquire more control because the task of implementing policies lies in their hands. Inactive masses are merely an object of party activities. Their votes are sought at election time through campaigning by competing parties. Financial backers provide some of the funds for mobilizing voters and capturing their votes; hence, wealthy contributors obtain a share of the power within the party.

Since the controllers of parties are prompted by different motives and often espouse different goals, an affinity develops between particular parties and certain voting groups. In giving preference to certain interest constellations, whether political or economic, the result is the formation of interest groups. Ideological beliefs of party leaders and corresponding ideals of certain voters have led to the formation of ideological parties. When the party leaders become political enterprisers, controlling a party machine for their own profit, active members join them for the spoils of politics, giving rise to patronage parties. Finally, when aroused masses identify with a leader of exceptional qualities, his paladins form a charismatic party that is elected primarily by devoted followers. Weber's theory thus culminated in the distinction of four different political parties.

In democracies with multiple parties, all four kinds of parties can coexist and compete for the backing by the corresponding voting groups. In a two-party system, however, the necessity of getting the support of the majority leads to coalition parties. Not only the various interest groups, but also diverse ideological groups, become allied with one or the other of the two parties. Appeal to certain interests and ideologies may be undertaken by the patronage party so as to be victorious in the electoral campaigns. The amalgamation of different interests and beliefs has given rise to two transformations of parties in this country. Patronage parties are often paramount in local and state politics in which actual or potential office seekers seize upon critical issues and grievances in order to win the election. Amalgamated interest parties on the national level place most of the widely held ideologies in their platforms, make excessive promises, and sponsor a variety of ideological beliefs so that frequently the two major parties cease to differ significantly from each other. The result of these deformations is widespread apathy and a low rate of political participation on the part of many voters, because they feel deprived of any genuine choice in elections.

Pressure groups have developed that seek to impose their will upon party leaders. First and foremost, their particular interests, ideals, ideas, and issues have to be given highest priority. In Weber's theory, these groups are nonpolitical in nature when they are "politically oriented" and if they aim at influencing "the appropriation, expropriation, redistribution, or allocation of the powers of government" (p.54). While this characterization allows pressure groups a wide range of influence, Weber did not anticipate that the power of some pressure groups becomes so large as to transform themselves into voting blocs and reduce the political party into a mere transmission belt for promoting and protecting their special interests.

In regard to the role of political parties in political democracy, Weber developed an interesting standard for assessing the quality of their political activity. The concept of political democracy "includes not only the 'equal rights' of the governed but two further postulates: (1) prevention of the development of closed status groups of officials in the interest of a universal accessibility of office; and (2) the minimization of the authority of officialdom in the interests of expanding the influence of 'public opinion' as far as practicable. . . . Whenever possible, political democracy strives to shorten the term of office through election and recall, and to be relieved from a limitation to candidates with special expert qualifications" (p.965). These two postulates serve the purpose of avoiding exclusion and of keeping the parties open to any newcomers.

Since political parties exercise their power in and through parliaments, Weber tried to distinguish between positive and negative politics by parties and governments. Positive politics prevails when the executive either works according to the political directives of parliament or when the president must obtain the consent of the legislature for his policies. Such consent is usually given in the form of laws or of explicit approval for major administrative decisions. Laws and approval are supplemented by accountability of the executive for adequately implementing laws and ordinances. Under these conditions "the leaders of the dominant parties have a positive share in government and parliament becomes a factor of positive politics" (p.1408).

A quite different situation prevails when the head of the executives either ignores the will of the parliament or when party leaders regard the executive as a "hostile power." Such an attitude gives rise to negative politics. Politicians in parliament then reject "appropriations and other legislation or introduce unenforceable motions." Conversely, if an executive refuses to provide "the indispensable minimum of information" or otherwise injures the reputation of parliament, then there will arise "an assembly of impotent faultfinders and know-it-alls" (p.1408). The result in either case will be "negative politics."[2]

Exercise of power by political parties, whether practicing positive or negative politics, deals not only with substantive issues, "but is also a struggle for personal power. Wherever parliament is strong . . . the power struggle of the parties will be a contest for the highest administrative offices. The fight is then carried on by men who have great political power instincts and highly developed qualities of political leadership" (p.1409). Beyond parliament, the survival of parties, "and the countless ideals, and partly very material interests bound up with it require that capable leaders get to the top" (p.1409). Translating party into personal power creates the necessity of leadership in party and government.

In Weber's theory, two conditions establish the need for leadership. An external requirement flows from the hierarchic arrangement of parties and government and the shifting of decision making to the heads of such organizations. The internal requirement refers to the personal power instinct or ambition that drives certain persons to fight for the top positions.[3] These indispensable requirements provide the starting point for Weber's theory of political leadership, regardless of the type of party or government. Any kind of leadership involves a tendency for a concentration of power in the hands of the top men who decide for the members or organizations.

Fundamental for Weber's theory of leadership is the distinction between masters, officials, and politicians. Masters are those "who do not derive from grant by others the powers of command claimed and exercised by them" (p.952). Such masters act as military, police, or despotic dictators and are outside of democracy. Officials are bureaucrats who are appointed to an office if they have received a certain education and training and are assigned the task of administering certain laws or rules that are given to them by their superiors. When limited to this task, officials exercise power only by implementing laws and do not enjoy any discretionary or independent power of their own. A politician in a democracy is elected, not appointed, to a political position, enjoys no permanent tenure but must fight for his reelection. The political tasks are not rigidly prescribed, but are influenced by unforeseen events or changing sentiments of voters. While the original grant of power comes from the electorate and has to be renewed periodically, there is an element of discretionary power that can be limited by public opinion but not eliminated by voters. Instead of being kept strictly accountable, the politician is responsible only for those uses of discretionary power that are regarded as "politically sensitive" by his voters. It is only when a certain degree of discretionary power is enjoyed that politicians can adequately face uncertainties and anticipate and mold the future.

The peculiar relationship between discretionary power and the uncertainty of future events exerted a significant influence upon Weber's definition of leadership. The bureaucrat is not a leader because his laws tend to disqualify him for developing the right attitudes for meeting the uncertainties of events and for handling the shifts in public opinion. The demagogue worships only his vanity and misunderstands, if not misleads, the masses politically. The mere power politician suffers from "an inner weakness and impotence" which he "hides behind this boastful but entirely empty gesture." The strict "representative of interest groups" acts as a mere agent, follows instructions or mere hunches, and is thus "inwardly defenseless" against the unexpected events of politics. These inner disqualifications of demagogues, power politicians, and agents are aggravated when they depend for their income upon the steadiness of their political positions. Private interests then surpass public interests in making political decisions. The three types of politicians, suffering from a lack of inner calmness and a sense of responsibility, unavoidably create a situation of what Weber called "leaderless democracy."[4]

In two cases only do politicians possess the inner quality and the outer effectiveness for becoming genuine leaders. One is the ideologist who couples to the "passionate devotion to his cause" an inner sense of proportion of letting realities work upon himself with inner concentration, and is also able to assume the responsibility for the consequences of his ideals and actions. Next to the ideologist is the charismatic leader who by the quality of natural and superhuman gifts possesses the capacity to genuine leadership. It is obvious that Weber's restricted definition includes only extraordinary leadership. Extraordinariness refers here to unusual situations, exceptional abilities of the leaders, and distinguished actions leading to great accomplishments. It is quite clear that charismatic leadership falls into the category of extraordinary abilities and accomplishments.

While giving full emphasis to extraordinariness, Weber leaves little room for ordinary leadership. He tends to include not only the experts but also the professional politicians in his broad category of bureaucrats, whom in turn he perceives as being deprived of leadership qualities. If one follows this suggested usage, then most American presidents, for instance, would have to be regarded as nonleaders. Indeed, the full significance of extraordinary leadership comes to the fore only if we know full well the meaning of ordinary leadership in a modern democracy.

Briefly, established professional politicians become recognized leaders for ordinary affairs if they possess the three abilities of cherishing some widely acceptable political beliefs, maintaining a sense of proportion and inner concentration, and assuming a sense of responsibility for their ideas and actions. Endowed with these qualities to some degree, professionals will have to be able: (1) to define fairly definite goals; (2) to foresee some of the major contingencies in the future; (3) to reconcile both into plans for concerted actions; (4) to translate the goals and plans into laws; (5) to simultaneously obtain majority support by public opinion; and (6) to attain the confidence of the voters. If and when presidents or prime ministers possess these abilities and perform these tasks adequately, they are usually accepted as competent leaders, although they cannot be regarded as either charismatic or ideological leaders.[5] When we add to our list of leaders top professional politicians meeting these standards, then it is apparent that political democracy can be guided either by ordinary or extraordinary leadership, depending upon the specific situations, the degree of emotionality by the electorate, the qualifications of the leaders, and the degree of confidence granted them by the voters. While this distinction between two basic types of leadership in democracy makes full use of Weber's theory of charismatic leaders, our contrast with ordinary leadership[6] permits us to put charisma in its proper place and incorporate it into a more comprehensive and internally consistent typology of all kinds of democratic leadership.

This addition of ordinary leaders, but excluding mere experts, does not render worthless Weber's concept of a "leaderless democracy." Such a situation arises when strict bureaucrats occupy the top positions of parties and government or when the professionals do not measure up to the internal and external requirements and turn out to be merely pseudoleaders. The latter may either not possess the inner abilities or their range of political opportunities may be limited either by certain situations or by positive or negative kinds of politics. There is indeed an interlinkage between types of leaders, parties, and situations as shown in table 8.1.

We can thus say that the translation of party into personal power generates a linkage between the type of party and the corresponding kind of leader. Either the respective qualities are embodied in the personality of the leader selected by the party or the already chosen leader is so flexible that he can adopt new patterns of leadership, corresponding to the changing opportunities of his party.

Weber's theory of political democracy, including parties, politics, and leaders, provides the framework for our study of charismatic giants in democracy. In order to be specific in regard to all relevant components of the theory, we shall select the Great Depression of the 1930s as the extraordinary situation, and examine the qualities, ethical beliefs, political ideals, and policies of Franklin D. Roosevelt as the most expressive prototype of a charismatic giant in democracy. In order to be elected president in 1932, did he build up a new charismatic party? Did he merely reform the national Democratic party by imposing a charismatic leadership upon that party? If that party was an amalgamation of divergent interests, patronage, and bureaucracy, what kind of cooperation could there be between the various kinds of professional politicians and the charismatic leader with his particular circle?

## SUPERIMPOSITION OF CHARISMATIC LEADERSHIP

It so happens that Weber examined the various relationships between regular parties and charismatic leaders. His historical findings can be briefly summarized. In exceptional situations only does a bureaucratic party become receptive to a charismatic leader. "In times of great public excitement, charismatic leaders may emerge even in solidly bureaucratic parties, as it was demonstrated by [Theodore] Roosevelt in 1912" (p.1132). Similarly, a charismatic leader may rise out of particular interest constellations. "Since the time of Crassus, a typical figure has been the great sponsor who at times finances a charismatic leader and who expects from the latter's electoral

TABLE 8.1. DEMOCRATIC PARTIES AND LEADERS.

| Parties* | Respected Leaders | Pseudoleaders |
|---|---|---|
| *I. Ordinary Situations, Regular Parties, Ordinary Leaders* | | |
| Interest party | Mediators | Wheeler-dealers |
|  | Manipulators |  |
| Spoils party | Political entrepreneurs | Bosses |
| Bureaucratic party | Organizers | Disciplinarians |
| *II. Extraordinary Situations, Movements, and Leaders* | | |
| Charismatic party | Genuine charismatics | Demagogues |
| Ideological party | Reformers | Fanatical zealots |

*Weber also included religious and status parties in his typology that are beyond the scope of this study.

victory government contracts, tax advantages, monopolies or other privileges, and especially the repayment with interest of his advances" (p.1132).

Some of the bosses behave similarly to the great sponsors in critical situations. A patronage party can make it possible "for impressive personalities to win the necessary following" in an election who then are reduced to mere figureheads during their terms of office (p.1133). The greatest difficulty is faced by an ideological party when opting or permitting the rise of a charismatic leader. "Any attempt to adapt the ideologies to the momentary opportunities [of a charismatic leader] easily precipitates a catastrophe" for the ideological party (p.1133)[7]. These historical findings suggested to Weber two inferences, "Only extraordinary conditions can bring about the triumph of charisma over organization" (p.1132). In ordinary times, however, "the party organization easily succeeds in this castration of charisma" (p.1132).

In taking these historical findings on the relationship between regular parties and charismatic leadership as our guide, we shall have to examine whether in the depth of the Great Depression the regular parties were able to control or castrate a charismatic aspirant. If this was not possible, how far and in which fashion was the rising leader able to impose himself and his policies upon his regular party?

When Governor Franklin D. Roosevelt was seeking the presidential nomination of the Democratic party in 1932, one condition was in full evidence. The country found itself in a severe economic and social crisis. The number of unemployed had risen from 3 percent in 1929 to 26 percent of the labor force in 1933. About five thousand American banks had failed, and the value of the stocks on the New York Stock Exchange had dropped by over 80 percent in the same period. While not anticipating the crash of 1929, Roosevelt adopted two different attitudes towards the depression. Personally and economically he deplored the many sacrifices imposed upon the people. Politically, as we shall see in the next section, he welcomed the end of prosperity because the debacle would terminate Republican rule and offer an opportunity for a return of the Democratic party to power. The crisis as a condition for charismatic leadership was in full evidence in the early 1930s.

Roosevelt was an "organization man" before he became a charismatic leader. He rose rapidly in the Democratic party from the state senator of New York to the vice-presidential candidate on the national ticket in 1920. While Alfred Smith had strengthened the party in large cities over the country, Roosevelt promoted the organization of the party in rural areas, especially in the upstate counties of New York. In early 1929 as governor he said: "It is the moral duty of us to spread the Democratic gospel."[8] In his reelection in 1930, his margin of 725,000 votes over his Republican opponent was in part a result of also getting a majority in the rural counties of the state. Election and reelection turned Roosevelt into the official leader of the Democratic party of New York, providing him with the opportunity to fight for the presidential nomination of the Democratic party in 1932. What was the reaction of the patronage and interest parties to his charismatic claim of leadership?

One early problem was the corruption by Tammany Hall in New York City. While trying to gain the support of the delegates for the convention, Roosevelt initiated the well-known Seabury investigation which documented the acceptance of bribes by city officials, including the mayor himself. Based upon the evidence supplied by the investigation, Roosevelt as governor conducted an objective and dignified hearing which was so damaging for the mayor that he resigned from his office. While demonstrating that he would not tolerate any corrupt officials, Roosevelt did not engage in a fight against the bosses and their patronage parties. Some of the political bosses, such as Curry of New York, Cermack of Chicago, and Hague of New Jersey, opposed Roosevelt's nomination, whereas Pendergast of Kansas City, Curley of Boston, and Flynn of the Bronx supported him. The latter group, in accord with Weber's theory, expected significant benefits for themselves springing from Roosevelt's charismatic appeal. At the same time, Roosevelt did not attack the bosses and their spoils on principle. After the nomination all of the bosses supported Roosevelt in the campaigns and most of them flourished after his inauguration as president.

There arose a similar conflict between Roosevelt and private interests and party financiers. Mr. John Raskob of General Motors was not only the chairman of the National Democratic Committee but also its most important financial sponsor. Seeking to buy certain policies for his contribution, Raskob supported Smith and fought against the nomination of Roosevelt. Prior to Smith's availability, Raskob tried to induce leading businessmen, such as Owen Young, banker Melvin Traylor, or Newton D. Baker, to throw their hats into the ring. Roosevelt could get the nomination only by fighting successfully the moneyed interests in the party. Equally abortive were the attempts of Raskob to commit the National Democratic Committee to a policy of high tariff and of supporting Hoover's proposals for a business recovery. The influence of the large corporations had to be curbed, and the interests of small businesses and farmers had to be supported, before Roosevelt could be nominated by the convention.

Beyond corruption and influence of big business, Roosevelt supported just one organizational reform. Senator Huey Long had unexpectedly proposed that the requirement of a two-thirds majority for selecting a presidential candidate should be replaced by a simple majority. Roosevelt temporarily supported the proposal, but dropped it when other leaders of the South strongly opposed the idea. Roosevelt gave an ethical interpretation for his revised position: "I am not willing to gain the nomination by the methods of a poker game. My hands are clean, and before God, I intend to keep them so."[9] In the fight for delegates Roosevelt respected the unit rule for state delegations as well as the favored sons of the various states. He ran in primaries only when there was an open competition. As a result of these rules Roosevelt was short by eighty votes for nomination on the first ballot. A horse trading was necessary for avoiding a deadlocked convention. In order to get the votes of Texas and California, Roosevelt found it advisable to offer Speaker Garner the vice-presidency.

The crucial question facing the convention was whether there should be a change only in the person or also in the type of leadership. Alfred Smith offered the leadership of a professional politician. He stood for a simple repeal of the prohibition amendment, for an equal political status of Protestants and Catholics, and for overcoming the depression by granting increasing subsidies to large concerns. The first two proposals had contributed significantly to the defeat of the Democratic ticket in 1928 under Smith. Roosevelt proposed solving the liquor problem by local option, keeping religion out of politics, and granting governmental assistance to the "forgotten men," including both the lower and the middle class. Promising such assistance found "hearty approval" by farmers and workers, but was condemned as a "demagogic appeal" by the defenders of the rich.[10] Calling a charismatic challenger a "demagogue" is the usual reaction of professional politicians to charismatic leadership.

It was precisely the special quality of this appeal that was recognized by the majority of the delegates. "It was part of Roosevelt's conscious reliance upon the power of his voice to influence the convention even though he remained in Albany."[11] There was overflowing enthusiasm when Roosevelt arrived at the airport in Chicago. "The crowd, pressing in around Roosevelt, knocked off his hat and sent his glasses awry, but Roosevelt showed no dismay."[12] There was a "thunderous applause" of the delegates when the new leader concluded his acceptance speech with the following words: "I pledge you, I pledge myself, to a new deal for the American people . . . this is a call to arms. Give me your help, not to win votes alone, but to win in this crusade to restore America to its own people."[13]

As soon as he was nominated, Roosevelt formed a charismatic circle within the Democratic party. Farley, Howe, and Flynn took over the national Democratic party, in charge of directing the campaign. Their main instruments were the regular state and country organizations of the Democratic party. Recognition was denied to the "Roosevelt Clubs," and individual volunteers received only occasionally some campaign material from headquarters. There was thus synergistic interaction on the organizational level. The regular state and county units represented either patronage or interest parties which worked for Roosevelt's election for their own personal and organizational gains. Superimposed upon these organizations were the charismatic circle and Roosevelt's personal brain trust, which both together assisted the candidate in directing the campaign. As in Weber's theory, the charismatic leader refrained from building up his own party,[14] but utilized the existing regular parties by taking over their headship on the national level and granting them a certain degree of autonomy on the county and state levels. Charismatic leadership became the directing force in a political democracy. This was achieved by getting control over one of the regular parties, not by forming a new charismatic party.

In spite of the deep depression, the United States was ahead of other equally stricken countries. Economic deprivations created much misery but not a deep political crisis. The shift to charismatic leadership and acceptance of the New Deal were accomplished without the breakdown of the political system. Since democratic government remained intact, the new leader personified democratic—not dictatorial—charisma. What precisely was the nature of this kind of charisma? How did a well-known politician become such a leader, and how did the masses become charismatic followers?

## CHARISMA AND POLITICAL TALENT

There was a kind of presentiment of an illustrious career in the future. Already in his student years Roosevelt confided "that he would run for the office at the first opportunity, and that he wanted to, and thought he had a real chance to, be president."[15] When he ran for and won a seat in the state senate of New York, his only qualification was an illustrious name and a few financial backers. Although he did not yet possess any oratorical talent and was uninformed in political affairs, he successfully led a fight against Tammany Hall, learned to get in the public limelight, and created a public image of himself as a progressive politician. As vice-presidential candidate on the Democratic ticket in 1920, Roosevelt established himself as an internationalist by fighting for the League of Nations. He learned the art of campaigning, made many personal connections, and started an extensive correspondence with political leaders all over the country. After his defeat in 1920 he predicted confidently that "1932 will be our year."[16] This rapid career pointed to a young man who was learning fast, showing little personal depth, but was on his way to becoming a professional politician. The only possible charismatic trait was the high degree of self-confidence that was interpreted by many as a form of arrogance.

Being suddenly stricken by infantile paralysis seemed to crash all his political hopes. While his mother saw him as a permanent invalid whose political career was behind him, the diagnosis of his doctor left some hope for eventual recovery.

Roosevelt himself wrote to a friend in September 1921: "The doctors assure me that I am recovering very rapidly and there is no reason to fear any permanent effects from my illness."[17] There followed a period of seven years of strenuous exercises, of a strict regimen, but complete physical rehabilitation eluded him. He was able to stand with the help of braces, but could never walk unassisted.

Yet there was a psychological and political recovery. "Years later he confided to Francis Perkins that for the first few days he had been in utter despair, feeling that God had abandoned him. Then his buoyancy and strong religious faith asserted themselves; he felt that he must have been shattered and spared for a purpose beyond his knowledge."[18] This sense of having been chosen by a Higher Being was strengthened by the belief of his family in him and especially by the confidence of his assistant Howe who said: "I expect him to be president. . . . As far as I am concerned you . . . are a man of destiny."[19] The ordeal thus created in Roosevelt the conviction that his life was spared for the higher purpose of becoming president of the country.

Being guided by this goal, Roosevelt became a mature man. He ceased to be pompous, became simple, sincere, honest with himself, friendly and charming to others, cheerful, and humorous at most occasions. Gradually he strengthened his will and gained an inner fortitude. The inability to walk freely imposed a new life style. Being forced to sit "removed him from the hurly-burly, the nervous wear and tear which is one of the most exhausting things of city life . . . nor could he resort to the normal human impulse of running away from difficulties."[20] Most important, he increased his already great power of self-control and learned the lesson that "once you make a decision you must not worry about it."[21] He could pull a curtain down and go to sleep. Continual effort to restore his health engendered in him a supreme self-confidence, whereas his own suffering generated a great sympathy for other people, especially the less fortunate.

Far from attributing his increasing inner strength as exclusively a product of his own will, Roosevelt sought a religious explanation for his personal and political recovery. He "believed in a beneficent God, the Ten Commandments, the Sermon on the Mount, and in the direct teachings of the Bible. . . . He regarded the Scriptures as an incomparable source of wisdom and frequently turned to them in his writing and speaking."[22] Instead of separating political activity from religion, he tied them closely together by means of ethical principles, as we shall see presently. Roosevelt believed that there was a divine purpose, which induced humans to cooperate with God in making a better world. The divine plan left a large measure of individual freedom, especially for the leader, in solving the problems that faced us. There is little doubt that his religious faith gave him immense strength, great optimism about the future, and a remarkable serenity in daily as well as momentous affairs.

How was this religious faith transformed into charismatic qualities? Roosevelt felt "in his own estimation . . . destined to leadership in great affairs." He possessed the gift of seeing "hidden meanings in events obscure to others." He learned "to charm others to the point of uncritical approval."[23] Roosevelt enlarged his circle of admirers, but transformed only a relatively few into his disciples. Nor did he explicitly attribute his calling to the Almighty. Circumstantial evidence suggests that the uncritical acceptance of his institutionalized religion and the tradition of democracy prevented him from expressing such a claim at any time. He spoke publicly of the "divine plan" and implied that he had special knowledge of its details, but his religious piety inhibited him from regarding his exceptional abilities as supernaturally ordained. The democratic tradition that the office seeks the man, that nominees are elected by voters, not selected by God, precluded the notion of a superhumanly chosen leader. Roosevelt thus could only feel but not express his supernatural calling. In spite of this hidden origin of his qualities, "what he said and what he did was entirely congruous with a larger destiny."[24]

There was no similar hesitation on Roosevelt's part to present openly and exhibit effectively the abilities of emotional charisma. But these differed in several respects from the personal magnetism of dictatorial charisma. Personal charm was the outstanding characteristic of his personality. Many have attested to his ability to make himself liked, to put others at ease, to enjoy the admiration of the few and the many, and to obtain personal sympathies and bend others to his will, gently, imperceptibly, as if agreeing with him was the only sensible thing to do. The first recognition of the explosive impact of his mass appeal came in 1924 when Roosevelt nominated Alfred Smith for the presidency at the Democratic National Convention. When he spoke for the third time the delegates were on their feet to greet him. His performance impressed even the city boss Tom Pendergast of Kansas City who made the following statement: "I am seldom carried away or become overly enthusiastic in meeting men in all stations of life, but I want to tell you that had Mr. Roosevelt . . . been physically able to have withstood the campaign, he would have been named by acclamation the first few days of the Convention. He has the most magnetic personality of an individual I have ever met, and I predict he will be the candidate on the Democratic ticket of 1928."[25] The voters of the state of New York came to know Roosevelt by his "radio voice." He was the only top Democratic nominee who was elected in his home state in 1928 and reelected by a landslide in 1930. In the campaign of 1932 he demonstrated his emotional impact upon his listeners. He loved campaigning and never lost his sense of humor as his train puffed from one stop to another. He derived strength from "hands extended in welcome, voices warm with greetings, faces reflecting his smile along the interminable wayside."[26] The so-called barnstorming testified to the great enthusiasm that Roosevelt was able to arouse in all parts of the country.

A most lasting impact emanated from his fireside chats which revealed a new attitude towards his countrymen, and which was described in the following words: "Roosevelt never thought of the people as 'masses.' When he talked on the radio, he saw them gathered in the little parlor, listening with their neighbors. He was conscious of their faces and hands, their clothes and homes. His voice and his facial expressions as he spoke were those of an intimate friend. . . . As he talked his head would nod and his hands would move in simple, natural, comfortable gestures. His face would smile and light up as though he were sitting on the front porch or in the parlor with them. People felt this, and it bound them to him in affection."[27] Roosevelt's affection, his compassion for others, was recognized by his listeners as a kind of personal friendship, creating an unbreakable trust. As one soldier expressed it, "I felt as if I knew him, I felt as if he knew me—and I felt as if he liked me."[28] Thus at the core of the emotional union were mutual trust and sympathies. The destructive crowd effect was often missing, and the euphoria engendered primarily a liberating effect upon him and his followers. In the words of a historian: "Roosevelt's patrician concern for mass suffering, his charm, his calm confidence, his gaiety, even his cavalier approach to grave problems of the day . . . had an immediate and lasting effect upon the American people."[29]

In order to be effective in a crisis, charismatic qualities and mass enthusiasm had to be translated into acceptable actions. A combination was required of the ordinary talents of a professional politician and the special talents of a charismatic leader mastered competently by the same personality. Ordinary talents were essential for dealing with other politicians and with bureaucrats who did not believe in the leader's possession of charismatic qualities. Maneuvers, intrigues, and deceptions were used by Roosevelt to retain the services, if not the loyalty, of party or state officials.[30] To concentrate upon the nomination and election of 1932 for a moment, Roosevelt exhibited ordinary talents when he induced the delegates to vote for his candidates for temporary and permanent chairmanships of the convention; when he offered a deal to trade the vice-presidency for the votes of the Texan delegates; when he disowned the Roosevelt clubs and relied upon the regular party organizations of the states; when he decided to use patronage as a reward for senators who voted for his bills.[31]

The extraordinary talents of Roosevelt were usually linked with deliberate dramatization of the respective actions. They included the flight to Chicago to deliver his acceptance speech; his activist campaign in all parts of the country; his refusal to collaborate with President Hoover during the interregnum; his concentration of the major bills into the first hundred days after his inauguration. Rhetoric and drama aimed not only at eliminating fear, but also aimed at mobilizing the voters to participate vicariously in his actions, and thereby become his charismatic followers.

It is obvious that only synergistic interactions between ordinary and extraordinary talents did bring Roosevelt the nomination of his party and the election by the voters. Insistence upon charismatic actions alone, as in not approving the deal with the Texan delegates, would have created a deadlocked convention and would have led to selecting a "dark horse." Avoiding "jaunts around the country" during the campaign—as some senators suggested—would have minimized the enthusiasm of the masses and reduced the emotional strength of the leader.[32] Not pure, but synergistic charisma, brought Roosevelt into the White House.

This immense staying power suggests that extraordinary qualities were primary, and ordinary qualities supplementary, to his leadership. The test of its effectiveness in each of the four elections was Roosevelt's ability to put together a coalition of forces that gave him a majority of the votes. His authority was sustained by popular approval between elections, activated by his periodic talks over the radio. The charismatic appeal exerted its greatest effect in the presidential campaign of 1936. Roosevelt exclaimed privately: "There is only one issue in this campaign. It is myself, and people must be either for me or against me."[33] His overwhelming landslide indicated that the majority of the voters understood and approved of this charismatic leadership. In voting for him the electorate also brought and kept the Democratic party in power. A charismatic leader was simultaneously the head of the majority party, and of the federal executive with its extended powers. Both organizational instruments were also used to implement charismatic policies. The result was a synergistic interaction between charismatic and noncharismatic forces in the same party and democracy.

## CHARISMATIZATION OF THE CRISIS

In his theory of mass democracy Weber pointed to one condition that is inherent in democracy and frequently acts as one of the causes for charismatic leadership: mass emotionality. If and when a gifted personality appeals to the mass emotions, he will readily find many followers who are willing and eager to vote him into office. If he is elected by a majority, there will arise the rulership of electoral charisma. Such a charismatic leadership can arise, as exemplified by the devoted followers of President John F. Kennedy, without depending upon any other conditions for creating an emotional union between the leader and the followers.

But mass emotions may be prompted and intensified by the existence of a severe crisis, which may be political, psychological, social, military, or economic in nature. Max Weber hinted at such a crisis situation when he said: "Charisma . . . *may* affect a subjective or *internal* reorientation born out of suffering or enthusiasm. It may then result in a radical alteration of the central attitudes and directions of action with a completely new orientation of all attitudes toward the problems of the world" (p.245). The suffering emanating from a severe crisis brings forth a charismatic disposition by millions of voters. The appeal of a leader not only engenders their enthusiasm, but also creates the distinct hope that he will be able to lead the country out of the crisis. The sequence of suffering, enthusiasm, and hope together produce a form of crisis charisma. It is only in situations of an interaction between subjective feelings and objective conditions that there is likely to arise a "completely new orientation of all attitudes," experienced by the leader and the followers.

It so happened that Franklin D. Roosevelt personified such a crisis charisma. In order to make any sensible promise for terminating mass suffering, he had to give a special interpretation of the causes and effects of the crisis that went beyond the generally held opinions of others. Specifically, he was moved to take a radically new attitude towards the crisis that would permit him to claim that he was able to effectively alleviate and eventually overcome the crisis. How far did Roosevelt succeed in charismatizing the crisis?

The Democratic candidate adopted a partisan, an economic, and a charismatic interpretation of the Great Depression. In his campaign speeches he eagerly rejected the Republican claim of being the party of prosperity. He countered the assertion of Hoover that the depression was engendered in foreign countries by pointing to the years of agricultural crisis in the 1920s. For Roosevelt, the Republican prohibitive tariff "has been one of the effective causes of the present depression."[34] He told farmers that no tariff on a surplus crop had the slightest chance of raising the domestic price. But the tariff raised the industrial prices. "The farmer sells on a free trade basis; he buys in protected markets. The higher the industrial tariffs go . . . the greater is the burden of the farmer."[35] Foreign governments had retaliated against American tariffs. "The villainy we taught them, they practiced upon us."[36] A considerable portion of the farm crisis was thus attributed to political causes in the form of mistakes of Republican administrations.

The crash of the stock markets was said to be partly the responsibility of the Hoover administration. "It was the heyday of promoters, sloganeers, mushroom millionaries, adventurers of all kinds." Instead of discouraging the lure of easy gains, the Hoover administration initiated the "crop of foreign bonds which American investors know to their cost today."[37] It also encouraged the speculation boom at home. Power companies and public utilities sold too many securities, which led to an extreme overcapitalization, to paying dividends out of capital, to making profits out of speculation, and to luring and eventually wasting the savings of millions in watered stocks. Not less direct was the attack upon the monopolies resulting from corporate growth. "We find two-thirds of American industry concentrated in a few hundred corporations, and actually managed by not more than five human individuals. We find more than half of the savings of the country invested in corporate stocks and bonds, and made the sport of the American stock market. We find fewer than three dozen private banking houses, and stock selling adjuncts of commercial banks, directing the flow of American capital. We find a great part of our working population with no chance of earning a living except by grace of this concentrated industrial machine."[38] An irresponsible governmental policy and the ruthless manipulations of professional speculators had created a speculation capitalism that was condemned as a politically responsible agent for the Great Depression.

In his economic interpretation of the depression, Roosevelt combined two rival theories of his time. The immediate cause was overinvestment. Idle industrial capacity indicated a "gigantic waste . . . superfluous duplication of productive facilities, the continuous scrapping of still-useful equipment, the tremendous mortality of industrial and commercial undertakings . . . the profligate waste of natural resources." Consequently, the country does not suffer from insufficient capital. The root cause of the crisis was that "the purchasing power of other great groups of our population was permitted to shrink." Diminished purchasing power led to the conclusion that we cannot endure this crisis "for long unless we can bring about a wiser, more equitable distribution of the national income."[39]

Emphasis upon the creation of new purchasing power was accompanied by rejecting two "misinterpretations" of the depression. The very depth of the depression demonstrated to Roosevelt that there were no "immutable economic laws" that contained an "invitation to sit back and do nothing."[40] Self-correction of the depression could not be expected under the prevailing conditions of misery. Rejected also was the opposite view of a crisis of the economic system. As emphasized by Reinhold Niebuhr: "Capitalism is dying and it ought to die. . . . Capitalist rule has been convicted of ineptness and injustices."[41] Roosevelt accepted the charge of an inadequate operation of the economy by private interests, but rejected the catastrophic view of the depression as a breakdown of the capitalist system as a whole.

The charismatic interpretation of the crisis emphasized the human aspects of the depression. One cause was unlimited mass fear that paralyzed appropriate actions. The greater the misery, the greater the psychological crisis. The manifold losses not only created widespread discontent but also increasing fear for economic and social survival by those with little or no income. While benefiting politically from the discontent, Roosevelt diagnosed this fear as a paralyzing force that had to be addressed additionally to the economic crisis. "This fear spreads to the entire country." There was only one remedy. This fear can be met only if "with more or less unity we turn to our government in Washington."[42] Roosevelt faced this psychological crisis as soon as he came to power. His attack is well remembered. "First of all, let me assert my firm belief that the only thing we have to fear is fear itself—nameless, unreasoning, unjustified terror which paralyzes needed efforts to convert retreat into advance."[43] Roosevelt's supreme self-confidence radiated out from the Capitol over the country, striking a responsive cord in the hearts of millions.

Roosevelt discerned a moral crisis, a negative impact of the depression on the homely virtues. "This is one of the tragic consequences of the depression. The things that we were taught have not come true. We were taught to work and have been denied the opportunity to work. We were taught to increase the products of our labor and we found while the products increased the return has decreased. . . . The results of our labor . . . have been lost in the smash of an economic system that was unable to fulfill its purpose." While Weber did not include moral injuries as an effect of crises, Roosevelt saw it as his task to bring back the old virtues. "The measure of the restoration lies in the extent to which we apply social values more noble than mere monetary profit."[44]

The interacting economic, psychological, and moral crises turned into a situation of extraordinariness that was termed by him as an extreme emergency which could be mastered only by exceptional measures.[45] Indeed, the crises were regarded as a personal challenge to his talents and sense of responsibility. "Out of every crisis, every tribulation, every disaster, mankind rises with some new share of greater knowledge, of higher decency, with purer purpose."[46] The enormity of the task called for exceptional leadership. The course of objective forces had to come under the direction of a great leader. It was the right of the people to say who should be at the helm. During the campaign, Roosevelt attacked the Republican leadership. It "misunderstood the forces which were involved in the economic life of the country. . . . It encouraged the vast speculative boom . . . and the administration was not frank, not honest, with the people."[47] When he was elected he placed the greatest demands upon himself and claimed the right to terminate the emergency by utilizing to the limit all the resources and powers available to the federal government. In the first inaugural address he said: "I assume unhesitatingly the leadership of this great army of our people dedicated to the disciplined attack upon our common problem. . . . We do not distrust the future of essential democracy. The people of the United States have not failed. In their need they have registered a mandate that they want direct, vigorous action. They have asked for discipline and direction under my leadership."[48]

In translating the economic and psychological crisis into an emergency, Roosevelt had charismatized the economic downswing and found in the moral crisis the key to crisis charisma. The economic crisis required decisive political actions by the government, not merely a new economic policy by economic groups. Faced with the danger of disaster he was tempted to extend his charismatic authority beyond the constitutional limits set for the executive. He said in his inaugural address: "But in the event that the Congress shall fail to take one of these two courses, and in the event that the national emergency is still critical, I shall not evade the clear course of my duty that shall then confront me. I shall ask the Congress for the one remaining instrument to meet the crisis—broad executive power to wage a war against the emergency, as great as the power that would be given me if we were in fact invaded by a foreign foe."[49] The response of the audience to this last sentence was so great that Eleanor Roosevelt commented: "You felt that they would do anything—if only someone would tell them what to do."[50] Charismatization of the crisis thus provided the mass support for a new economic policy and for a government assuming the responsibility for economic recovery and reform. Given this support, the leader had to select and adopt ideals that guided him in overcoming the reinterpreted crisis. Which ideologies were accepted and applied by the charismatic leader in a democracy?

### ETHICAL MISSION

In the years of his first election in 1932, Roosevelt faced a situation of ideological diversity. The traditional policy of a balanced budget, of governmental retrenchment in accord with declining revenue in a depression, was still supported by the conservatives in the Democratic party. Balancing the budget was a part of the party's platform of 1932, and was believed in and expounded by the candidate in his speech at Pittsburgh on the eve of the election.

A second ideology insisted that economic recovery required public works, federal relief payments, unemployment and old age insurances, and a regulation of financial and farm markets. Each of these policies called for increasing activities by government. Roosevelt had already tried to implement such policies as governor of New York,[51] and adopted these policies and others during his first term as president. But there was a guilty conscience about the rising public debt. The principle of deficit financing was not explicitly recognized as the core of a public policy of recovery. Much of the spending was done haphazardly, creating the two unintended and unexpected recessions of the fall of 1933 and the winter of 1937–38.

Two different ideologies sponsored or defended the policies of the New Deal. One view regarded the respective measures as constituting a revolution. "It was this: government was assuming responsibility for the security and welfare of its working populations and for the stability of the whole economy."[52] Another view saw in the New Deal a kind of reform that had been proposed by the progressive movement of Theodore Roosevelt and Woodrow Wilson, and was thus an application of long familiar principles. Roosevelt himself developed two different attitudes to the progressive ideals of the past. Up to the summer of 1935 he regarded progressivism as "a precedent for the major part of the New Deal legislation."[53] In his speeches he developed a program that also took account of the major requirements for a policy of economic recovery. In the campaign of 1936, however, there was a shift from cooperation among all groups with the government to a strong attack upon big business and an increasing collaboration with labor. Democracy was contrasted with plutocracy, and a vigorous antitrust policy was designed to break up monopolies. In this second phase, Roosevelt saw himself "as the embodiment rather than the servant" of this more pointed progressivism,[54] which he combined in various ways with his program of economic and social reform.

Yet Roosevelt contributed a set of ethical maxims which entered into the charismatic mission. Historically, these maxims had some affinity with his religious beliefs and were in accord with Woodrow Wilson's moral law by which "mankind is ultimately governed." The moral values of this ultimate law guide us in our journey "toward moral perfection."[55] While Wilson applied the moral law primarily to political reform, attacking party bosses, Roosevelt's main contribution was to set ethical standards for his economic recovery and reforms.

Facing a rising unemployment in New York, Governor Roosevelt proposed a temporary relief administration and invoked an ethical principle for its justification: "The duty of the State toward the citizens is the duty of the servant to its master. . . . One of these duties of the State is the caring for those citizens who find themselves the victims of such adverse circumstances as make them unable to obtain even the necessities for mere existence. . . . Aid must be extended by the government, not as a matter of charity, but as a matter of social duty."[56] There would be no dole; work would be created in return for the relief payments. An increase of the income tax would provide the funds and balance the budget. The social duty would thus replace private charity that could no longer care for a million unemployed.

The principle of social duty was generally applied to the whole country in the campaign of 1932. Roosevelt claimed that after his election, "no one would be permitted to starve." When states would become unable to provide relief, the federal government would provide the necessary funds. This social duty provided the justification for the subsequent Civilian Conservation Corps, the federal grants for cities and farmers, and the work relief programs. All these programs grew out of "the consciousness of responsibility for the economic well-being of millions of people."[57] A promise of the new leader was: "We are going to make a country in which no one is left out."[58]

The effort to devise a policy of recovery was guided by the ethical principle of the "cooperation of government, business, and labor." In his second fireside chat Roosevelt emphasized: "It is wholly wrong to call the measures that we have taken, government control of farming, industry, and transportation. It is rather partnership between government and farming and industry and transportation, not partnership in profits, for the profits still go to the citizens, but rather a partnership in planning, and a partnership to see that the plans are carried out."[59] When it was called to his attention that such a partnership meant giving up the philosophy of laissez-faire, Roosevelt answered: "I never felt surer of anything in my life than I do of the soundness of this passage."[60] Such partnership depended upon mutual trust of all participants.

The subsequent National Recovery Act aimed at a reform of industrial markets. Negatively, there was a determined fight against the practice of cutthroat competition. Far from being beneficial, this kind of competition had revealed a new form of Gresham's Law: "It was the sorest and most humiliating principle of the system that bad business tended to drive out good business."[61] The unavoidable resentment re-enforced the rejection of the laws of demand and supply. A new institutional arrangement had to be found for implementing a new goal in markets. The new goal for industrial markets was to establish "fair competition and honorable business practices."[62] Fairness should be implemented by setting up voluntary standards as guides for obtaining adequate cost prices. For each industry a code would specify the ethically acceptable behavior. While most of the codes permitted price fixing by industrialists, the president was given the power to approve or disapprove the codes. He did expect sincere compliance with the spirit of the codes which principle he expressed to the members of the chambers of commerce on May 4, 1934: "I ask that you translate your welfare into the welfare of the whole, that you view recovery in terms of the nation rather than in terms of a particular industry."[63]

The same principle of fairness was also to apply to the transactions in labor markets. In the same speech, Roosevelt presented the reason for his request. "It is a simple fact that the average of the wage scale of the nation has gone down during the past four years more rapidly than the cost of living. It is essential, as a matter of national justice, that the wage scales should be brought back to meet the cost of living and that this process should begin now and not later."[64] His wish was formally adhered to when each of the approved codes contained a provision for higher wages. When disputes arose between employers and workers, leading to strikes and violence, Roosevelt at first turned to governmental mediation of the disputes. Eventually he became convinced that a new institution was required for settling wages and working conditions. In signing the Wagner Act, Roosevelt accepted the new arrangement of collective bargaining for setting wages which became the new major institution for reformed labor markets. In the farm sector Roosevelt accepted two ethical principles of individual equality for single farmers and of equality between the farm and industrial sectors. In regard to the latter Roosevelt aimed at "the restoration of agriculture to economic equality with other industries within the United States."[65] There was thus a need for a separate farm program. Production was limited to the agreed crop quotas to be set by elected country committees. Reduced acreage was expected to raise prices so that farmers could cover their costs of production. Whenever prices did not rise, excess supply was stored and farmers were given the opportunity to receive support prices from the government. The new institution of government purchases for storage relieved the farmers of the necessity to sell their products at moments of excess supply in markets.

The goal of economic security was linked in Roosevelt's mind with "social justice through action." On the one hand, justice aimed at protecting human beings and helping people to fight poverty. On the other hand, social justice required adequate help to those suffering from misery in specific situations. "Among our objectives I place the security of men, women, and children of the nation first. . . . People want some safeguards against misfortunes."[66] Most important for him was the suffering from unemployment, industrial injuries, old age, and unsupported children. The principle of social risk, incurred without the fault of the victim, led him to the moral obligation of society to fight for social insurances and effectively overcome poverty.

In the capital markets, property certificates should be handled according to two other ethical virtues, namely, honesty and openness. Secrecy and fraud should be eliminated. Those who "manage banks, corporations, and other agencies handling other people's money should act as the trustees for others." Every issue of the new securities "shall be accompanied by full publicity and information and no element affecting the values of shares shall be concealed from the buying public." For "there is a definite, positive burden on the seller for the first time to tell the truth."[67] Trusteeship required that commercial banks be separated from investment banks, that the shares owned by directors and officers of corporations issuing new shares be fully disclosed, and that the deposits of small savers be federally insured. The purpose of these measures was to protect investors and depositors as well as to restore the confidence of the public in the security markets. There was also deep concern for the debtors. Their interest rates should be reduced, foreclosures would be stopped, mortgages of farms and homes refinanced with the help of governmental assistance.[68]

The last economic goal of economic planning was only remotely linked with any kind of ethics. "I am not speaking of economic life completely planned and regimented. I am speaking of the necessity, however, in those imperative interferences with the economic life of the nation that there be a real community of interests . . . among its economic units and the various groups in these units. . . . I plead not for a class control but for a true concert of interests."[69] The model for such planning became later the domestic allotment plan in which nearly four thousand local committees of farmers confirmed the voluntary acreage restrictions of their crops. By planning farm output "it will pay farmers for the first time to be social-minded, to do something for all," in the words of Tugwell.[70] Social-mindedness was thus expected to take the place of an ethical maxim. At one point Roosevelt envisioned an overall plan for the whole economy. "Most important to me in the long run is the problem of controlling by adequate planning the creation and distribution of those products which our vast economic machine is capable of yielding."[71] But this vision of an overall plan never materialized, partly because of a missing ethical maxim, and partly because theory and practice of indicative planning was not yet available at that time.[72]

It is our conclusion that Roosevelt possessed an extensive set of ethical maxims for the major parts of economic reform. These ideals constituted his charismatic mission which he personally was ready to propose if given the appropriate opportunity. From the ethical ideals of fairness, reasonableness, equality, openness, honesty, mutual trust and social justice, there ensued a "moral responsibility for making life of individuals more . . . decent."[73] What Roosevelt desired and envisioned was a form of ethically responsible capitalism. The major institutions of private enterprise, individual property and production, profit incentive, honest marketing, and informative advertising would be fully respected and retained by his reform. But capital power would be extensively curbed, working conditions and industrial relations would be greatly improved, wage rates would have to be just, prices fair, and profit rates never maximal but only satisfactory. All market transactions would have to conform to specified ethical standards of conduct.

One has to add that these ethical ideals for reform were clearly opposed to the ethical virtues of thrift, frugality, self-reliance, and complete independence deduced from the philosophy of individualism. There occurred a cleavage among the "old virtues" that gave rise to two different philosophies. Roosevelt's ethical maxims implied a social conscience, involved cooperation and partnership, and was based upon the philosophy of mutual assistance which was widely accepted during the depth of the depression.[74] After the National Recovery Act (NRA), however, economic independence became the belief of the majority of businessmen that was turned against the New Deal, leading to a conflict between two sets of ethical beliefs.

## INTERESTS AND CHARISMATIC ACHIEVEMENTS

In adopting his ethical maxims, Roosevelt derived two great benefits for his personal leadership. He "had an almost Wilsonian need for justifying . . . himself, for assuring himself that there was always a 'good' reason for his acts."[75] Since he could not publicly link his ethical maxims with his superhuman qualities, "doing good" was his way of living up to his charismatic calling. Simultaneously, the ethical maxims provided a set of readily acceptable goals for his policies. These goals furnished the guideposts for his recovery and reform programs. Goals and programs helped him to escape from indecisions and from floundering around without personal and political compass, and provided stability and continuity for his charismatic leadership over time.

The great emphasis upon ethical values entailed also two unintended handicaps for the leader. The inability to publicly link ethics with charisma limited the emotional suffusion of the maxims by the followers. The ethical values had to be deduced either from an unspecified moral law or from the Christian commandment of loving your neighbor. Whoever did not believe in the validity of these ultimate values of ethics did not feel a moral obligation to live up to the charismatic appeal. There remained a significant minority, especially among the well-to-do, who either did not or could not understand the charismatic leader, and who provided the reservoir for an ideological and emotional opposition to charismatic leadership. Equally serious was the second handicap. The ethical maxims had to be reconciled with the economic and political interests of particular groups. Compromises had to be found for either adjusting the interests to the ethical goals or modifying the goals so as to be compatible with the interests of organized groups.

As a personification of synergistic charisma, the leader could not be satisfied with proclaiming his ethical goals. He was forced to arrive simultaneously at ethical and pecuniary decisions, to be open-minded to both kinds of considerations, and to aim at a satisfaction of the ethical ideals and the material interests of the majority of his followers.[76] A charismatic achievement thus exists only if there has been a successful interaction of ethical ideals and practical interests. In choosing selectively some of the major issues, we will have to discover what were the major achievements of Roosevelt's leadership.

*Rejection of Socialism.* Early in 1933 faith in capitalism was at a low ebb. The head of the American Farm Bureau predicted in January 1933: "Unless something is done for the American farmer, we will have revolution in the countryside within less than twelve months."[77] Roosevelt himself had drawn the line between revolution and reform in the spring of 1931. "There is no question in my mind that it is time for the country to become fairly radical for at least a generation. History shows that where this occurs occasionally, nations are saved from revolutions."[78] This view guided him in the days of the banking crisis when a senator urged him to nationalize the banking system. Roosevelt emphatically rejected the proposal. "This is not necessary at all. . . . I've every assurance of cooperation from the bankers."[79] Turned down was also the offer of the coal companies. "The operators will sell the mines to the government at any price fixed by the government."[80] Equally negative was Roosevelt's attitude to the schemes for a redistribution of private incomes whether they were proposed by Senator Huey P. Long or Dr. Francis E. Townsend or the "work for all" of Upton Sinclair. His ethical virtues placed a limit on the extent of economic reform. In order to reject socialism and limit his program to recovery and reform, Roosevelt introduced an additional ideological principle: "I believe in the sacredness of private property, which means that I do not believe that it should be subjected to the ruthless manipulation in the stock market and in the corporate system."[81] Rejection of socialism was thus coupled with full support of the capitalist property structure, except for the one of dishonest or fraudulent speculators.

*The Social Service State.* As a first step to a new type of government there was to be a moral rejuvenation of the private sector of the economy. "We must set up new objectives; we must have new kinds of management. Business must think less of its own profits and more of the national function it performs."[82] The second step was to be an increase in the economic functions performed by the federal government. In pursuing its recovery goal, the federal government: (1) created income for specified disadvantaged groups and unemployed; (2) provided temporary jobs through public projects and contracts; (3) stored surplus farm produce and subsidized soil conservation; (4) granted debt relief through refinancing of mortgages for farms and homes; and (5) engaged in extensive subsidy payments or easy loans to avoid bankruptcy of many private firms. The result of these services was the rise of a public sector of the economy. This expressed itself in a substantial excess of public expenditures over revenue, in a rising public debt compensating for the declining private debt, and a large extension of the capital assets owned by the federal government. Not less than thirty-three new federal agencies were created from 1933 to 1939 which employed an increasing number of employees.[83] The time of a limited government had definitely come to an end.[84] But Roosevelt saw the public sector as beneficial for the private sector because the government created private purchasing power, bought increasing quantities of privately produced goods and services, and thereby "became a means of human betterment." The two ideologies of providing minimum protection for individuals and governmentally created purchasing power initiated policies that acted as energizers and benefactors of the private sector. But one has to add the ethical maxim of the social duty of the state before one can regard the transfer payments as the external expression of a government acting as means of human betterment.[85]

*Fairness for Industry.* The major purpose of the NRA was "to bolster private enterprise through cooperation of government, business, and labor,"[86] The ethics of partnership was to be accomplished through "codes of fair competition for trade or industry" provided that implementing trade associations "impose no inequitable restrictions on admission to membership," and that the codes were not designed to promote monopolies or to eliminate or oppress small enterprises."[87] The mutual agreements should be utilized to establish standards of fairness in industrial markets. The ethical ideal of fairness linked recovery with economic reform.

In implementing codes, ideology and fairness became separated. Either there was disagreement among producers about the acceptable prices and quotas, or the prices set in the codes contained elements of monopolistic profit. The implementing trade associations acted increasingly as semicartels, no longer subject to the constraints of the antitrust laws. Profit, not ethics, was their aim in fixing prices and setting production quotas. In seeking high enough profits to compensate for the losses of the depression, enterprises and trade associations rejected the standard of fair competition, meaning minimum average cost of the industry or any close approximation of that standard. Late in 1934, Roosevelt became aware of this deviation from the standard of fairness. He questioned the wisdom "of these devices to control production or prevent destructive price cutting which many business organizations have insisted were necessary."[88] There arose a conflict between the business interests of restoring the property structure of enterprises and the ethical fairness of the president. This conflict rendered the NRA ineffective already prior to being declared unconstitutional by the Supreme Court.[89]

*Social Justice for Labor.* The principle of social justice was incorporated into the National Recovery Act (NRA). The codes were supposed to set standards for the "maximum hours of labor, minimum rates of pay, and other conditions of employment."[90] The precise content of these standards was to be agreed upon by employers and unions in the process of writing the codes. But either independent unions did not exist or employers refused to recognize them as bargaining agents so that bloody strikes occurred in some industries. As a part of the codes, reform of labor markets faltered at first on the company unions and on the divergent interests of employers and laborers. In response to this conflict, Roosevelt proposed the establishing of a Labor Board designed to mediate the disputes. A bill was adopted by the Congress but it satisfied neither employers nor unions. Hence, social justice could not be implemented as a part of the NRA.

Leadership in regard to labor was shifted from the president to Senator Wagner, whose bill became law in 1935. It legitimized trade unions, established a National Labor Relations Board that held elections, and certified as bargaining agent that union which was chosen by the majority of workers in factories. Company unions were forbidden, and employers were enjoined to bargain in good faith. The ethical principles of fairness and faith were thus built into labor legislation. Interestingly, it was not the charismatic leader but the senator from New York who was mainly responsible for linking fairness with collective bargaining.[91]

*Equality for Farmers.* The ethical goal of equality for agriculture was to be achieved by raising farm prices to the level prevailing in 1909–14. This parity price was believed to raise farmers incomewise to the level of industry. But when it came to paying the subsidy involved in price raising equal to the difference between the current market price and the calculated parity price, the New Dealers shifted from mere price fixing to a substantial reduction of output. The first Agricultural Adjustment Act provided two different instruments for helping the farmers. One was the allotment plan for reducing the acres under cultivation. The other was the marketing agreement for increasing the sale of farm products. When exports increased little,

Wallace placed the emphasis upon limiting the acreage for specific crops. This decision was confirmed by Roosevelt, thereby reducing the tensions among the administrators of the law.[92] Restricting future output was linked with taking surplus products out of the current markets. Farmers were granted support prices that in effect
put a floor under market prices. In establishing a government agency as a buyer of
surplus products, instead of financing parity prices, the administrators of the AAA
regarded the ethical and economic equality of agriculture as a goal for the future,
whereas raising current farm income guided the immediate policies for agriculture.
Rising purchasing power satisfied the economic interests of the farmers, but destroying standing crops and killing pigs created an ethical burden for all participants.

*Confidence in Finance.* The financial crisis of the Great Depression created not only
illiquidity and holidays of banks, but also insolvency of many debtors, and a breakdown of confidence between creditors and debtors. In the words of one banker,
instead of the weak being afraid of the strong, the strong were afraid of the weak.
The Reconstruction Finance Corporation provided capital for many enterprises,
and bought preferred stocks of banks. To minimize the danger of speculation, the
new banking act separated investment from commercial banking. The new control
of the stock exchanges tried to forestall the danger of insiders milking the outsiders.
Disclosure of information was required from companies issuing new securities. The
bankers' control over the Federal Reserve System was terminated. The major ethical
component was to induce the "money changers" to regard other people's money as
a sacred trust, and the banks as "public bodies" were obliged to provide full information to the public. Banks were compelled to insure the savings accounts of their depositors under public auspices. But the attempt to create public lending institutions
was smothered by the banking interests. While extensive legislation laid the foundation for a new trust in financial institutions, the financial scandals revealed in Senate
hearings delayed the return of public confidence for several years.

*Minimum Social Protection.* In Roosevelt's thinking social security included three
programs. "These three objectives—the security of the home, the security of livelihood, and the security of social insurance—constitute a minimum of the promise
that we can offer to the American people."[93] Protection of home owners and
farmers was achieved through the refinancing of mortgages at lower rates of interests. In terminating foreclosures, the federal government put a floor under the real
estate markets. A minimum income for the daily expenses was provided for by the
various relief programs, some of which required working in return for getting assistance. While the original bills for social insurance were formulated by others, it was
Roosevelt who insisted that all insurances be combined into a single package. Unemployment insurance was administered jointly by the states and the federal government, whereas social insurance for the elderly became a federal obligation, and federal subsidies for the welfare programs of states sought to help the needy and
handicapped. Most of these insurances were to be financed by deductions from payrolls. Roosevelt's approval contained a moral component: "We put these payroll

contributions there so as to give the contributors a legal, moral, and political right to collect their pensions and their unemployment benefits. With those taxes in there, no damn politician can ever scrap my social security program."[94] While the resistance of business organizations was overcome, the American Medical Association succeeded in killing all staff proposals in the field of health.

In all, there was a peculiar interaction between Roosevelt's ethical maxims and the private interests of organized groups. Equality together with interests set the long-term goals, while the interests alone determined the short-term goals and policies of agriculture. Fairness was the prevailing attitude for arriving at product prices of manufacturers as well as negotiating wage rates by agreement. Trust and honesty were to return to financial transactions, and social protection was granted for all those needing assistance for getting a minimum of income through the actions of the service state. Whatever was the specific contribution, the ethical maxims defined the recognized "public interests" in economic and social affairs. Ethical norms were defined by Roosevelt as rights of individuals. "Every man has a right to life and this means that he has the right to make a comfortable living. . . . Our government, formal and informal, political and economic, owes to everyone an avenue to possess himself a portion of that plenty (from our industrial society) sufficient for his needs, through his own work."[95] In setting ethical goals and in interlinking them with essential private interests, the charismatic leader made his major contribution by pursuing a policy of economic and social welfare.

In addition to the welfare policy, there was an effort to replace competition by cooperation in many markets. Experience in the depression revealed two major deficiencies in markets. One was the cyclical distortion. A drastic decline of demand created a fall in prices so deep that not even the most efficient enterprises could cover their costs. The usual expectation that minimum costs of these enterprises would automatically put a floor under prices or wages did not materialize. Equally disastrous was the rise and impact of cut-throat competition. Fighting for their very existence, many small firms used every possible means for cutting costs and underbidding each other by lower and lower prices. Deception and dishonesty replaced fairness and truth in an increasing number of market transactions. It was Roosevelt's insight to understand this interaction between competition and unfairness. His ethical maxims thus fitted well the practical experience of marketers. Instead of waiting for unfairness to disappear by a rise in aggregate demand, Roosevelt saw in the codes of the NRA a method of assuring a return to truth and honesty. He said to a group of businessmen in 1934: "You and I are now conducting a great test to find how the business leaders in all groups of industry can develop capacity to operate for the general welfare. Personally I am convinced that with your help the test is succeeding."[96] In trying to overcome distrust and deception by means of the codes, Roosevelt tried to replace competition by cooperation among producers as well as between producers and consumers.

Cooperation required not only ethically acceptable goals and attitudes but also a reconciling of private with public interests. The great majority of organized groups insisted upon a reform of private markets. There was widespread agreement that the excess supplies had to be removed from the markets. Removal could either be done by new collective actions of private organizations or by new governmental agencies. Private organizations were given an incentive for cooperation. "In return for exemption from the antitrust laws, each industry met its obligations to the public welfare."[97] When restructuring of markets became a public task, new governmental agencies had to be built into markets. The list of such agencies became very long and only the most important ones can be recorded here (see table 8.2).

Instead of enduring the unbalanced markets, the various governmental agencies engaged in a deliberate and sustained adjustment of markets. The aim was to eliminate the phenomenon of lopsided markets in which there existed a steady tendency toward excess supplies and depressed prices. Farm output of most staples is discontinuous and supply concentrates in harvesting periods. Forced by inadequate resources to sell the total supply immediately, farmers suffered from depressed prices. Finding in the charismatic leader an understanding supporter, farm organizations pushed for storing of the surplus at government expense. In providing for an alternative opportunity for sale, the leader and his government put a politically created floor under market prices.

A similar excess supply prevailed in labor markets, magnified in depressions but created by the propertylessness of workers.[98] When a worker loses his job, lack of resources prevents him from becoming a businessman. The other members of his household are forced to accept jobs at lower wage rates. The result is a lopsided labor market. The law of supply is reversed by the institution of the family: falling wage rates or unemployment of men increase the labor supply of women and children in many markets.[99] Under pressure of labor, Roosevelt consented to support the Wagner Act which introduced a restructuring of labor markets. Employers had to negotiate with the representative union elected by workers. Collective bargaining set wage rates, hours of work, fringe benefits, and conditions of work. A political element entered the labor markets that minimized the influence of excess supply upon negotiated wage rates so that union wage rates replaced lopsided market wages.

There emerge two quite different concepts of the economic crisis and the associated remedy. In the market view, the lopsided markets had to be removed by the extensive economic reform by means of building up new institutions. The charismatic leader personified these reforms and his name remained associated with the institutions in subsequent decades. Charismatic rulership became the leading agency of the reform that was not subject to any tendency of routinization. In the cyclical view, the crisis emphasized the insufficiency of aggregate demand, and recommended deficit financing as the sole remedy for overcoming the crisis. The various relief payments, work relief, and public works programs constituted the core of Roosevelt's recovery program. In his mind, these programs were necessary to help those who suffered for no fault of their own. His compassion for the "little man"

TABLE 8.2. RESTRUCTURED MARKETS.

| Markets | New Institutions | Market Adjustments |
|---|---|---|
| Farm products | Credit Commodity Corporation | Price support |
| Crop lands | Agricultural Adjustment Administration | Allotment programs |
| Tenant lands | Farm Security Administration | Subsidy payments |
| Loan markets | Farm Credit Administration | Lower interest rates |
| | | |
| Manufactured products | National Recovery Administration | Code prices |
| Capital funds | Reconstruction Finance Corporation | Reduced interest rates |
| Transportation | Interstate Commerce Commission | Approved rates |
| Real estate | Home Owners' Loan Corporation | Renegotiated mortgages |
| Stock exchanges | Securities and Exchange Commission | Approved issues of shares |
| Gold markets | Federal Treasury | Embargo, hoarding |
| Silver markets | Federal Treasury | Purchasing offer |
| Foreign currency | Federal Reserve System | Price manipulations |
| | | |
| Social insurance corporation | Social Security Board | Payroll deductions, benefits |
| Deposit insurance | Federal Deposit Insurance Corporation | Loan guarantees |
| | | |
| Labor services | National Labor Relations Board | Negotiated wage rates |
| | | |
| Industrial peace | Conciliation Service | Mediation |
| Electric power production | Tennessee Valley Authority | Reduced prices |
| Electric power distribution | Rural Electrification Administration | Reduced prices |

linked the recovery program with emotional charisma. But Roosevelt could not incorporate the theory of deficit financing because he remained committed to a work ethic that could not justify any form of a "dole."[100] One part of the relief program was abolished, hurting many poor families. As a result, the theory of deficit spending—but not the recovery programs—remained outside the ethics of democratic charisma.[101]

Most students of the New Deal have concentrated on the interest groups and their reforms. In doing so, they assigned to Roosevelt the role of a representative leader who aimed to satisfy the special interests of his political constituency. It is certainly true that Roosevelt performed two roles of leadership, one representative, the other charismatic in nature. The alliance with the organizations of labor and farmers permitted the exercise of representative leadership. But the most novel feature of his combined leadership was his ability to reconcile the respective interests with his ethical maxims. The conflict with John L. Lewis and with the organizations of big business presented the leading exceptions to his attempted reconciliation of class interests with his charismatized ethical principles. In spite of these exceptions, Roosevelt placed greatest importance upon his charismatic qualities which he utilized in being elected four times to the presidency. Only in accepting this greater emphasis upon his specifically personal qualities can one understand his particular leadership and do justice to his charismatic rulership.

## CHARISMA AND THE SUPREME COURT

Charismatic leaders seek to consolidate their power as soon as they head the government. If successful, the leader establishes a charismatic rulership. Combining charismatic and presidential power transforms a purely transitory into a "permanent relationship" (p.246). After his first term in office the leader seeks to renew popular enthusiasm, to keep alive his own special qualities, and to be reelected by the majority of the voters. The landslide reelection of 1936 effectively renewed Roosevelt's charismatic authority.

Renewal also assured the paladins as well as secondary party leaders that their "ideals and material interests" were served best by a continuation of the charismatic rulership. At the same time there was a disenchantment with the leader and with many of his policies by some of the noncharismatic groups which became an anticharismatic opposition shortly after the reelection. Weber had emphasized the rise of an opposition by "ruling organizations" (p.54), but he did not anticipate the distinction between urban businesses as the old organizations, and the development of labor and farmers as new ruling organizations.

In order to come to grips with this new power constellation, we have to adopt and then modify Weber's theory of ruling organizations. "A ruling organization [*Herrschaftsverband*] will be called 'political' insofar as its existence and order is continuously safeguarded within a given territorial area by the threat and application of physical force on the part of the administrative staff." In contrast a "politically oriented" organization "aims at exerting influence upon the government of a political organization; especially at the appropriation, expropriation, redistribution, or allocation of the powers of government" (p.54). In the setting of 1936, Roosevelt and most of his civilian and military bureaucracy, plus the new institutions of the New Deal, constituted the political organizations. The political and economic interest groups belonged to the politically oriented organizations. Labor and farm organizations supported the charismatic leader, whereas most urban business groups had turned against him.

This division of the politically oriented organizations into supportive and resistant groups played a decisive role in the evolution of charismatic rulership. Instead of "the economy" turning unitedly against the charismatic leader, the greatly enlarged farm and labor organizations became the allies of the leader. In receiving the support of one set and facing the opposition of another set of organizations, charismatic rulership was incorporated into a new power constellation that existed in addition to the charismatic relationship between the leader and the followers. In being a charismatic leader and a noncharismatic holder of power at the same time, the president could act, but could also be supported, or opposed, in both spheres of activity.

In the depth of the crisis, the United States Chamber of Commerce had repeatedly accepted the "philosophy of planned economy." In 1935, however, the chamber "voted its opposition to the proposed two-years extension of the NRA, to the social-security bill, to legislation on public utility holding companies, to the government's banking bill, to pending amendments to AAA and to all labor legislation."[102] Roosevelt at that moment believed that he had saved the position and profits of business in the struggle against the depression and felt betrayed by his own class.[103] Mutual animosity governed the relationship between the president and most businesses.

This situation was aggravated by a unanimous decision of the Supreme Court which declared the NRA as unconstitutional. The delegation of power to the president, used in prescribing codes, was said to be "virtually unfettered." Also, the power to regulate business was said to be excessive; the transactions of the chicken business in question were local in character, not a part of interstate commerce. Beyond these special condemnations, the Court proclaimed broad constitutional doctrine so as to ward off any congressional action in the future. In spite of great misgivings, Roosevelt regarded these decisions as final. The partnership with business had ended, partly for reasons of his own. He said: "I don't want to impose a system on this country that will set aside the antitrust laws on any permanent basis."[104] No new codes were signed and old ones were no longer enforced. In terms of power, ideals, and mass emotions, business groups and their organizations had become the ruling organizations in opposition to the New Deal as well as to the charismatic leader and his following.

During the election of 1936, Roosevelt fought the "economic royalists!" While underlining his support of private enterprise, he attacked the concentration of capital in the following words: "This concentration of economic power in all-embracing corporations does not present private enterprise as we Americans cherish and propose to foster it. On the contrary, it represents private enterprise which has become a kind of private government, a power unto itself—a regimentation of other people's lives."[105] But this verbal attack was not followed by any antibusiness legislation that would have reenforced the previously adopted bills on holding companies and the tax on undistributed profits. Roosevelt merely reactivated the prosecution of collusion among business firms, and initiated an extensive investigation of economic concentration. In keeping open the lines of communication, Roosevelt seems to have been willing to come to some accommodation if the opportunity should arise in the future.

In the meantime, an alliance developed between business groups and the judiciary. In the fight against the New Deal, business groups engaged in large-scale litigation. In 1935–36 federal judges issued about sixteen hundred injunctions that prevented federal officers from carrying out federal laws. A significant number of these injunctions were directed against the Tennessee Valley Authority. The attack upon the New Deal was intensified by the decisions of the Supreme Court which declared unconstitutional the AAA, the Bituminous Coal Conservation Act, and the New York Minimum Wage Law. It was especially the fate of the AAA that "turned thoughts of men in the administration towards the impending necessity of a challenge to the Court."[106] The Democratic party platform asked for a "clarifying amendment" if various problems could not be solved by legislation. It was in this conditional fashion that Roosevelt hinted at his future action against the Court.

It so happened that the attack upon the Court was not inevitable. Roosevelt had the choice of seeking a policy of cooperation with the Court so as to get relief from the threat to his legislation. Such a policy would have prevented the danger of a coalition of other branches of government with the ruling organizations opposed to charismatic leadership. Or he could have adopted a charismatic policy of forcing the Court into submission to the presidency by changing the constitutional provisions without accepting the procedures of a constitutional amendment.

Two opportunities for cooperation were close at hand. One was to let the electoral victory work its way upon the members of the Court. On February 1, 1937, "a majority of five overturned both the Tipaldo decision and *Adkins vs. Childrens Hospital.*" This was four days before Roosevelt's message on the "packing" of the Court. Justice Stone had forewarned the president by saying that he should "be more patient and trust to the passage of time to solve this problem."[107] Without the accident of Stone's sickness in the crucial week, Roosevelt would have known of the new majority of the Supreme Court and would never have submitted his Court message. It would have only required to wait a few days until "the opinions could be written and handed down."

Given the more comprehensive interpretation by Justice Robert of the interstate commerce clause, a simple bill on retirement pay would have obtained the desired approval of the New Deal legislation. Six of the nine men on the high bench were over seventy. "The ironical fact is that both Van Devanter and Sutherland wanted to retire before 1937. . . . They had clung to their posts chiefly because . . . the Supreme Court justices did not have the privilege of retirement."[108] If Roosevelt would have submitted a bill providing a pension equal to the salaries, he could have obtained full support in Congress and could have been able to nominate two new justices of his choice. Legislative and judiciary branches would have been on the side of the president, rather than feeling compelled to join in the opposition of the ruling organizations in an unnecessary struggle over the Supreme Court.

As it happened, Roosevelt pursued his charismatic policy to the hilt. Believing that "the people are with me," he was guided by his feeling of superiority and overconfidence of a charismatic leader to overcome any hurdle that blocked his way. Convinced of his invincibility, he prepared his plan in great secrecy, sought no advice or assistance, and sprang the plan on his cabinet and leaders of the party, anticipating the joy of a sure and great victory. Why then did he fail?

There were two tactical mistakes that could have been avoided by proper consultation with party leaders. One professed aim was to improve the efficiency of the Court by adding coadjudicators. It was easy for the chief justice to prove that the Court was not overburdened. The other professed aim was to rejuvenate the Court. But there was no appropriate proposal for an honorable retirement and pension. Apart from the insult involved in insinuating that all the old men were senile, the pension plan initiated and approved by the Senate was not only directed against Roosevelt but cemented the alliance between the two other branches of government.

Involved in the "packing" bill was an overemphasis upon the ideology implicit in the conflict. Roosevelt held that it was the national duty of the Court to "view the interstate commerce clause in the light of present-day civilization."[109] This "duty" was widely associated with the charge that the members of the Court were guided by their ideology of economic conservatism in nullifying the New Deal laws. Actually, it required only a minor modification from a narrow to a comprehensive interpretation of the commerce clause to render the ideological charge obsolete. Approval of the National Labor Relations Act and of the Social Security Act changed the attitudes of the labor leaders. They no longer felt that their gains were threatened by the Court and gave only lip service to Roosevelt's struggle. The expected mass support was much smaller than expected by the leader.

Roosevelt had also underestimated the widespread belief in the inviolability of the Constitution, and had not anticipated the popular admiration for the Supreme Court. It was Felix Frankfurter who explained these feelings to the president during the struggle: "It is a creditable aspect of human nature that it wants some object of veneration, and veneration to no small degree thrives on mystery and mysticism. . . . People have been taught to believe that when the Supreme Court speaks it is not they [the justices] who speak but the Constitution."[110] This form of veneration was nothing else but a form of institutional charisma, as defined by Weber. For Roosevelt, institutional charisma created an additional limit to his personal charisma.

Finally, Roosevelt did not realize how vulnerable charismatic leadership had become to the charge of personal dictatorship. He and his opponents saw his leadership in a quite different light. In his second inaugural address he defined his task as assisting in the discovery of "dominant public need. Then political leadership can voice common ideals, and aid in their realization."[111] He did not for a moment consider the possibility that even a charismatic leader may be wrong in voicing the "common ideals." His opponents, however, saw in his attempt to enlarge the Supreme Court, a desire to establish a personal dictatorship. The Republicans had raised this issue already in the presidential campaign of 1936. Candidate Landon said: "The American people always have been fearful, in the end, of a great man." His running mate, Frank Knox, raised the question, "Upon what food does this our Caesar feed?" His answer was that Roosevelt was on the road leading to Moscow. Herbert Hoover predicted that if Roosevelt were reelected, America could expect "the succeeding stages of violence and outrage by which European despotisms have crushed all liberalism and all freedom."[112] These efforts to identify charisma with dictatorship could have been taken as warning signals by the leader of democratic charisma.

When the Supreme Court approved several laws of the New Deal but the president refused any compromise, the suspicion of dictatorship became paramount. Raymond Molcy in his testimony before the judiciary committee of the Senate said: "A proposal has been made which imposes upon one man—the present chief executive—the almost sole responsibility of determining the final objectives of liberalism."[113] This charge was adopted and incorporated into the report of the committee. The rejection of Roosevelt's bill was supported by the argument that "it contains the germ of a system of centralized administration of law that would enable an executive so minded to send his judges into every judicial district in the land to sit in judgment on controversies between the government and the citizen . . . [and] it would . . . destroy the independence of the judiciary, the only certain shield of individual rights."[114] Instead of recognizing democratic charisma, the committee and eventually the majority of the Senate saw nothing but an attempted dictatorship. Unintentionally and unfortunately, the president's proposal had abetted this wrong identification of charisma with dictatorship.

### LIMITS OF DEMOCRATIC CHARISMA

There was once a theory of constitutional dictatorship that came close to the concept of charismatic leadership. "In time of crisis a democratic constitutional government must be temporarily altered to whatever degree is necessary to overcome the peril and restore normal conditions."[115] The specific form of this alteration was also indicated. "In a crisis, public opinion compels the abrogation of the separation of powers. There is only one will in effective operation, and that is the will of the president."[116] If this theory were correct, then there could (and would) have been no leadership of democratic charisma. The "packing" of the Supreme Court would have been successful, and an amendment would eventually have made the presidency the predominant power of government. Charisma would have started democratically but ended dictatorially.

Instead of a constitutional dictatorship our analysis suggests a theory of cumulative democratic charisma that permits us to take account of different subtypes of charismatic leadership operating in divergent situations. In the depth of a crisis, the presence of an extraordinary personality leads to political victory of that party which nominates him as its candidate. The election takes the form of a charismatic plebiscite. If the leader retains the confidence of his voters, there will be new modes of renewed enthusiasm, leading to subsequent plebiscites. Repetition of three subsequent reelections was clear evidence that Roosevelt was the bearer and beneficiary of electoral charisma. No other candidate in the history of the United States was elected four times to the presidency or stayed in office for twelve successive years. Death alone terminated this rulership of electoral charisma. The sole constitutional amendment that grew out of this experience was a new provision that limited the tenure of any subsequent president to two terms. Such an amendment could be adopted only subsequently when no charismatic personality was visible anywhere. Nobody can guarantee that such an institutionalized limit will stand up against a future gifted person able to capture the imagination and votes of the majority of the voters.

Quite different from electoral charisma was the appearance of crisis charisma. The fight against the Great Depression led to the two major policies of governmentally directed recovery and of economic reform. Both policies reenforced each other and were quite effective in the midst of the crisis. As long as these policies were regarded as vital and beneficial to the majority of the people, charismatic leadership simultaneously satisfied mass emotions as well as interests and ideals of organized groups. But the crisis, defined as an emergency of extreme proportion, could not last forever. As soon as enterprises were again profitable, businessmen pushed for terminating the New Deal, and increasingly turned against the charismatic leader. An open conflict arose between employers and employees as evidenced in the sit-in strikes of workers in mass production industries. Socioeconomic conflict not only differentiated the concepts of the crisis, but business opposition created a class limit for the effective operation of charismatic rulership.

The perception of the crisis and the nature of its remedies also played a role in the struggle over the composition of the Supreme Court. Business leaders "were aroused to a pitch of wildest excitement by the Court bill, and, being rich, their instant reaction was to spend large sums of money on the fight."[117] All kinds of businesses financed cover organizations that helped to defeat the Court bill. But the members of the Supreme Court developed their own concept of the crisis. In the process of the fight, the two swing votes—Hughes and Roberts—of the Court became convinced by the landslide reelection that the major laws of the New Deal had to be sanctioned by the Court provided they were derived specifically from constitutionally granted powers and did not inhibit directly the profit opportunities of big business. Beyond this compromise the Court did (and would) not go because it benefited from the widespread veneration of the Supreme Court across various voting blocs.[118] A twofold result ensued from the constitutional conflict. While the major laws of the recent past were declared constitutionally legitimate, institutionalized charisma effectively limited the power of personal charisma towards the end of the crisis.

Finally, there was the disintegration of the synergistic charisma. Instead of following Roosevelt's legislative lead, the Democrats split into almost equally strong factions in the Senate, and conservative Democrats formed a coalition with the Republicans that controlled the Rules Committee in the House. Roosevelt was no longer the leader of a united party; party loyalty became severed from the devotion to the leader. Struggles for power over party and legislature took the place of following the leader. In the maneuvering over the Court bill, senators were "pointing out to one another that if the president won in the end, he would be the absolute boss" dominating the Congress as well as the Supreme Court.[119] Belatedly, Roosevelt and his advisers bemoaned the fact that he had decided not to create a charismatic party in the heydays of his power. Now the spoils party administered to him a barely disguised defeat of his Court bill. In order to remove this limit imposed upon him, Roosevelt entered the primaries of some states in 1938 to prevent the relection of some of his party opponents. This attempt largely failed because the state leaders fought for their autonomy from the national leader of the party. The party limit remained effective until the next presidential campaign of 1940.

The limits administered by the ruling organizations, the Court, and the party did not significantly affect electoral charisma, restricted crisis charisma in regard to the interests and ideals of big business, but effectively stymied synergistic charisma. Instead of a Weberian "depersonalization of charisma" (p.1135) there was an overemphasis of personal charisma in the Court fight, indicating that in the last phase of his rulership the leader had to rely more upon his noncharismatic instruments of power to avoid an "antidictatorial" coalition of all his opponents against him. The lesson is that the leader's temptation of a frontal attack upon legislature and judiciary has to be effectively resisted if synergistic charisma shall remain in effective operation.

A distinction developed between limits and routinization of charisma in the sense of the quality becoming attached to "an office or to an institutional structure regardless of the person involved" (p.1135). Actually, a deep crisis induced the legislature to follow the president's lead, and genuine compromises were required only after the extreme emergency had subsided. The judiciary is likely to lag behind, nullify some laws, but will relent under the pressure of landslide reelections. While the power of crisis charisma tends to decline with the success of such leadership, its main achievement was to turn economic reform into permanent institutions. Rather than regarding electoral charisma as transitional, the giant and his followers saw in electoral victories the main weapon of success that was incorporated as an indispensable segment in the process of cumulative charisma.

The reform put a floor under most farm product prices and secured decent wage rates, plus limited working time and improved working conditions for most blue collar workers. Social insurance provided a minimum income for the unemployed and elderly people. The new institutions drastically reduced the economic risks and social uncertainties that had become the worst scourge inflicted upon the whole working population. These new institutions, put in place prior to the stalemate, became equally significant to the granting of equal political rights to all citizens. It was only when this plight of industrial poverty had been removed that social democracy with its self-organization of masses could bear fruit and generate the fullness of the mutually reenforcing civil and economic rights to which free men were entitled.

For many decades, workers had been prevented from organizing trade unions in mass production industries. Employers used all the weapons at their command to maintain sweatshop conditions for the semiskilled and unskilled workers in their factories. The Wagner Act gave workers the opportunity to organize, but this right had to be translated into practice by breaking down the agencies of repression. This was accomplished by the sit-down strikes in the car and rubber industries and by the hearings of the La Follette committee of the Senate.[120] The revolutionary strikes and the public exposure of the methods by which workers were held hostage eventually terminated the period of industrial servitude. Roosevelt neither initiated nor approved this occupation of factories by workers.[121] But he effectively prevented the National Guard from removing the workers by military violence. He thereby assured the institutionalization of trade unions in mass production industries. None of the limits imposed upon synergistic charisma could undermine this bulwark of reform. The new institutions became the main features of the charismatic rulership.

The leadership of democratic charisma (and its allies) had demonstrated its worth as an agency of political and economic progress. The election of 1940 not only broke the tradition against a third term, but also rejuvenated charismatic leadership to be ready for meeting the equally serious military crisis.

# CHAPTER NINE

# WAR AND CHARISMA

IN WEBER'S THEORY OF heroic charisma there was a distinction between peaceful and militant leadership. Heroism could be attained by exploiting the available opportunities at the time of peace. But heroic deeds could also be accomplished by superior methods of warfare that lead to a decisive victory over armed enemies. The charismatic quality enables the leader to perform extraordinary deeds, either in diplomacy or warfare, that induce soldiers or citizens or both to great enthusiasm for the personality of the leader. The worship of one exceptional man gives rise to charismatic rulership which is established by means of a popular plebiscite. "Viewed technically, as an organized form of domination, the efficiency of 'caesarism,' which often grows out of democracy, rests in general upon the position of the 'caesar' as the free trustee of the masses . . . who is unfettered by tradition" (p.961). While there is a distinction between peaceful and militant rulership of the leader, greater emphasis is placed upon the military caesar who alone will be considered in this chapter. "Such a 'caesar' is thus the unrestrained master of a body of highly qualified military officers and officials whom he selects freely and personally without regard to tradition or any other impediment." Such a "rule of the genius," however, stands in conflict with the formally "democratic principle of a generally elected officialdom" (p.961). Our major concern is to discover whether all military caesars are necessarily dictatorial in nature or whether some present a subtype of democratic leadership.

In examining military leadership Weber placed the military caesar into the category of the "Napoleon of the generals," not the "leader of the corporals."[1] In each case the militant leader is a part of the military establishment and has acquired military training and experience. He is not a civilian politician who is on his way up to or has been installed as commander in chief. The general and the corporal, however, act in two quite different situations. Coming to power because of their military deeds, both militants are inherently dictatorial in nature. The general exhibits his courage and daring in wars between nations, whereas the corporal organizes revolutionary troops for the purpose of overthrowing his own military establishment by means of a revolution. A war turning into a revolution occurred only under Mao in China and Tito in Yugoslavia but was not happening in the lands of the main belligerents in and after World War II. Since we are mainly interested in the relationship between major wars and charismatic leadership, especially in World War II, we shall neglect revolutions and concentrate upon charismatic leadership in time of war.

Weber derived his theory of the charismatic warlords from two different sets of experience: first, mainly from the patrimonial period, and secondly, from the wars since the French revolution. We shall have to ascertain whether the main proposition of his theory also explains the experience of World War II. His major contention was that in the earlier periods most wars were led by charismatic personalities, whereas the main features of modern wars had changed so drastically that military leadership was laid in the hands of military bureaucrats, thereby reducing significantly the military opportunities to be exploited by charismatic leaders.

## Military Bureaucrats and Charismatic Rivals

In earlier periods of tribes the peacetime chieftain and the militant warlord existed in the same time and place. "Frequently, each of these kinds of charisma has a special bearer. Next to the peacetime chieftain . . . , whose power originates in the household and who has mainly economic functions, stands the hunting and war leader, who proves his heroism in successful raids undertaken for the sake of victory and booty" (p.1142). While temporary at the beginning, one condition leads to the institutionalizing of the militant leader. "The charisma of the warlord rises and falls with its efficacy and also with the demand for it; the warlord becomes a permanent figure when there is a chronic state of war" (p.1142).

In subsequent periods, the military hero becomes a king in his own right. "Kingship originates in charismatic heroism" (p.1141). The successor can activate the same kind of heroic quality "through a regeneration of the whole personality. . . . The real purpose of charismatic education is regeneration, hence, the development of the charismatic quality" (p.1143). Such education seeks to "awaken the capacity for ecstasy and regeneration . . . through shock, torture, and mutilation." Those who stand up in these continuous tests will graduate by "ceremonious reception into the circle of those who have proven their charisma" (p.1143). The new king will then be chosen from those charismatically trained persons. In the course of generations, one family inherits the highest office in the state provided it can live up to the well-known requirements of the institutionalized lineage charisma. Eventually the democratic element of selection disappears and with it goes the charismatic quality, retaining only the ceremonies of traditional monarchies.

The first step to a military establishment (*Militärverfassung*) occurred in the Near East of antiquity. On the one hand, there developed the military bureaucracy; on the other, the concentration and public ownership of the military equipment and means of provisioning. "The necessity of river regulation and an irrigation policy in the Near East and in Egypt . . . caused the development of royal bureaucracies. Initially these were charged only with the construction tasks, but from this core ensued the bureaucratization of the entire administration which enabled the king, through this apparatus and the revenues supplied by it, to take the army administration under his own bureaucratic management" (p.1261). To this military bureaucracy came the recruited army. Indeed, "the 'officer' and the 'soldier,' an army recruited by compulsory draft and equipped and fed from the [public] storehouses, became the foundation of military power. The result was the separation of the soldier from the ownership of the means of warfare and the military defenselessness of the subjects" (p.1261).

Nothing similar occurred at that time in the Occident. The earlier patrimonial kings followed the principle of the self-equipment of the armies. "The lord is to a large extent dependent upon the good will of the soldiers whose obedience is the sole basis of his political power. . . . The lord lacks the bureaucratic apparatus—an instrument of compulsion which is blindly obedient because of its complete dependence" (p.1261). It was the significant change in the economy, the rise of large landholdings, and the control over the annual produce that enabled patrimonial rulers to equip and feed a standing army and to transform the officers into military bureaucrats dependent upon the lord.

Building upon these two fundamental pillars of a military bureaucracy and public ownership of the means of war, the modern state followed two quite different principles of military service. In some states the soldiers and officers were hired on a contractual basis. Military service became a profession for soldiers and often a status designation for the officers, who often were members of the nobility. This kind of professional army was especially cultivated in Great Britain. On the Continent most of the power states followed the principle of compulsory draft of soldiers and of selecting officers on the basis of professional competence. Military service became a legal obligation which was placed most severely upon the shoulders of the propertyless masses. The most important effect of the increased size of the armed forces and their bureaucratization was the imposition of strict military discipline. Soldiers were put in uniforms and systematically drilled until they performed their required tasks automatically. "The sociologically decisive points . . . are, first that everything is rationally calculated, especially those seemingly imponderable and irrational emotional factors. . . . Secondly, devotion is normally impersonal, oriented towards a purpose, a common cause, a rationally intended goal" (p.1150). The immediate goal was the effective control of the uniformed troops by means of commands by military bureaucrats who directed their wars from the safety of their bureaucratized offices.

Modern wars, especially World War I, sprang from two important tendencies of a military and ideological nature. The armed forces greatly raised their striking power by using a rising number of war machines. Production, supply, storage, and use of the machines created a war sector in the economy. "Economic forces interested in the emergence of military conflagrations *per se*, no matter what may be the outcome of their community, are called into life" (p.918). The military establishment becomes almost the only purchaser of war material which "enhances the capitalist nature of the process" (p.918). Wars were financed by credits that enlarged the profit chances of banks and led to a "mass of private bondholders" interested in maintaining the military establishment. Finally, there were the traders of imported raw materials and exported finished products who were supporting an extensive military expansion. All these economic groups together comprised the sector of "imperialist capitalism" which pushed for as well as contributed to the policy and followed military expansion.

This imperialist policy was opposed by another segment of the economy whose "capitalist interests [were] of a pacifist orientation" (p.918). Producing and selling goods in private markets at home, instead of supplying state agencies, capitalists earned a lower rate of profits. Similarly, private traders buying and selling goods abroad in open markets had to accept greater degrees of risks than those trading with companies in colonies or protectorates. The higher profit chances in the imperialist sector "withdraw capital from alternative uses and make it more difficult to satisfy demands in other [pacific] fields" (p.920). In terms of relative growth for the predictable future, "the prognosis will have to be made in favor of the imperialist tendencies" (p.919).

The trend towards wars with machines was accompanied and reenforced by nationalistic emotions that tended to place their own nation above all others. The high prestige claimed for their own nation became intertwined with the belief in the need of political expansion for the sake of becoming a super power (*Grossmachtgebilde*). To be sure, there have been "pacifist sympathies" based upon the ideals and interests of "the petty bourgeois and proletarian state [but these] very often and easily fail. This is partly because of the easier accessibility of all unorganized "masses" to emotional influences and partly because of the vague notion . . . of obtaining some unexpected advantages arising through the war" (p.921). As a result, the nationalistic feelings reenforced and idealized the military and economic imperialism, and all three together provided the underlying causes for World War I.

National leadership in the wars of machines developed along two quite different principles. There was a kind of duality in the sense that the general staff of the military bureaucracy selected miliary strategy and followed military rules in its implementation. Ordinary political leaders determined the political lines of policy in regard to internal and external affairs, including the decisions over war and peace. Such a division of military and political tasks between two groups of leaders prevailed on the side of the Allies in the early period of World War I. Weber underlined this principle of duality for the Prussian Wars. There was "Bismarck's strict principle that the generals conduct the war according to military rationale but that the head of the government conclude peace according to political considerations" (p.1426), although the political leader in this case possessed significant charismatic qualities.

In the major wars of machines there occurred a preference for the "principle of personality" in leadership.[2] An unpopular war, unsupported by enthusiastic patriotism, may be imposed by an autocratic monarchy. Such a leader will and has relied upon support of the military forces not only against the external enemy, but also against the political opposition at home. When the demands of the war became extreme and more and more machines had to be thrown against the enemy, one general would seize political power and establish a military dictatorship during wartime. General Ludendorff was the outstanding example for such a dictatorship in Germany.[3]

If the war should be won, then the victorious general becomes a popular hero and tends to seize or accept political power for the subsequent period of peace. Whatever the outcome of the war, Weber saw a general tendency towards a military dictatorship. "As in any major war so in the present one. Without exempting any belligerent [of World War I], England, France, Russia, and Germany experienced to the highest degree the rise of a political military dictatorship, regardless of the official form of government in time of peace."[4] Whatever the outcome of the major war, Weber's thesis was that the struggle of millions of soldiers must lead to military dictatorship, not only for the war period but also for the immediate time of peace.

But he recognized one important exception that emanated from the peculiar relationship between war and revolution. Either military defeat weakened the internal discipline and fighting power of the regular armed forces to such an extent that revolutionized soldiers used their arms to overthrow the old government and dismissed most of the officers, for the purpose of establishing a revolutionary government.[5] Or the revolution preceded in time the war itself and became ideological because the new leaders invaded other nations for the sake of installing the revolutionary institutions in the defeated countries. A victorious general built up a military establishment and claimed for himself military and ideological leadership for his own and the occupied countries.

For Weber, revolutionary dictatorship had a chance of success only if the victorious general was a genuine charismatic leader. It was Napoleon I who personified such a charismatic war leader. While rising primarily as a military leader, his "rule of genius" expressed itself in military victories. Military power was extended into political power by means of a popular plebiscite. The claim for popular consent arises "where the chief feels himself to be acting on behalf of the masses and is indeed recognized by them. Both Napoleons are classical examples, in spite of the fact that legitimation by plebiscite took place only after they seized power by force" (p.267). Especially Napoleon I was a military Caesar whose military heroism created the enthusiasm and followership for his successful plebiscite. His charisma was also evident in the field of administration. In creating a new military bureaucracy, Napoleon "elevated people of humble origin to thrones and high military commands" (p.244). Also in building up a civilian administration, selection of officials did not depend upon professional training and belief in the special office honor (*Amtsehre*), but upon the personal ability and adaptability to the needs of the charismatic rule. "The French system of administration by prefects is derived from the charismatic administration of the revolutionary democratic dictatorship" (p.268). Indeed, "revolution and Bonapartism have made the bureaucracy all powerful" in France (p.985). Finally, Napoleon's charismatic leadership was also compatible with legal and economic rationality. The *Code of Napoleon*, as a new legal system, not only survived him in France but also in Rhineland.

In all, Weber's theory of war by machines points to three tendencies of successive development in time of war. The preponderance of war machines creates a military necessity to transform the peace economy into the war economy. This transformation requires not only a military bureaucracy but also an effective civilian bureaucracy. A close cooperation of the two bureaucracies is required for reducing civilian consumption and increasing war production. As soon as the military imposes its will upon the civilian bureaucracy, there arises a situation of absolute bureaucracy.

Military necessities create the tendency to employ coercion. In the armed forces a strict discipline is enforced so that the armed forces become the pliable instrument of the generals. As the demand for war machines increases, the top generals will increase their pressure upon the civilian government and population. Reluctance of granting all of the military demands induces the top general to establish a military dictatorship. He eliminates the civilian government and imposes his will upon the civilian bureaucracy and the people. The effect is an exploitation of the civilians who not only have to work more and eat less, but who also lose their liberties and have to tolerate the privileges granted to the military rulers.

Since the machine war tends to deromanticize modern warfare, there arises a need to manipulate mass emotions. A military dictator will seek to employ a war pathos that is based upon an emotional nationalism. Or a military hero succeeds in attaching mass emotions to himself. Heroism and civilian admiration for exceptional deeds brings forth the charismatic leadership of the war hero.

The question arises whether the two world wars confirm Weber's predictions of an absolute bureaucracy, of military dictatorship, and/or charismatic heroism. It is the purpose of this chapter to examine these three issues and examine especially the relationship between the military dictators and charismatic leaders.[6] Was there a necessary sequence from the one to the other, did they exist simultaneously in different countries, or was charismatic leadership limited to democracies in time of war?

## DEMOCRATIC AND DICTATORIAL BUREAUCRACIES

It is one of the best known propositions of Weber's theory that bureaucracy is indispensable for every modern state. The need for bureaucratic services lies in the fact that laws do not implement themselves but have to be administered by competent officials or officers. Since the size and tasks of the modern state increase unavoidably with the growth of economies, "the need for mass administration makes bureaucracy completely indispensable" (p.223). The capacity to provide administrative services lies, individually, in the professional competence and expertise of its members, and, organizationally, in an integrated system of official bureaus. "The decisive reason for the advance of bureaucratic organization has always been its purely *technical* superiority over any other form of organization" (p.973, italics in the original.)

A bureaucracy is basically politically indifferent, but can adjust itself to any political system, as long as it is limited to the use of its technical abilities. The bureaucratic core is "characterized by formal employment, salary, pension, promotion, specialized training and functional division of labor, well-defined areas of jurisdiction, documentary procedures, hierarchical sub- and super-ordination" (p.1393). But such an apparatus can be linked with certain underlying principles that are taken from specific political philosophies and accepted as guidelines for bureaucratic actions. When a bureaucracy links the principle of equality with administrative efficiency, such a commitment entails a "proto-democratic process of legitimation."[7] When the greatest emphasis is placed upon "law and order," implemented by discipline and hierarchy, then the bureaucracy is fully or primarily dictatorial in nature. Max Weber has stressed the role of equality in the relationship between bureaucracy and democratization, but only hinted at the "authoritarian bureaucracy" (p.1453). In order to ascertain the specific tasks and interactions of civilian and military bureaucracy in time of war, and to identify the appropriate leadership for each, we shall briefly summarize the similarities and differences between the democratically and dictatorially inclined bureaucracies.[8]

In an effectively operating political system of democracy, bureaucratic officials respect the civil and political rights of citizens. One very important aspect of these rights is the equal access of all citizens to administrative services offered by officials and bureaus of the state. On the one hand, this means that the services should be either free or available at minimal costs. On the other hand, obligations imposed upon citizens should be equally distributed to all or be guided by ability to pay. Open access has thus to be accompanied by fairness in providing opportunities or imposing uniform penalties. It is only when openness and fairness are generally respected and practiced that citizens can enjoy a minimal participation in administration.

Closely related is the equal treatment of all citizens by governmental bodies. Legal equality grants equal rights and reject discrimination of all sorts. Equal treatment creates a spirit of formal impersonality because all persons are judged "without hatred or passion, hence without affection or enthusiasm. The dominant norms are concepts of straightforward duty without regard of personal considerations" (p.225). Equal treatment produces two socially enormously important effects. Modern bureaucracy has gained the capacity to handle administrative tasks of considerable size and variety so that administrative decisions affect the life of the majority of the citizens. "The demand of a society accustomed to absolute pacification for order and protection [by police] in all fields" is satisfied by means of an enlarged and growing bureaucracy (p.972). At the same time, "the development of bureaucracy favors the leveling of status" (p.226). Possessing or gaining privileges by bureaucratic decisions is in violation of the principle of equality before the law. Equal treatment of all persons exerts a leveling effect upon all those who are affected by administrative services.

Laws set the standard for bureaucratic behavior and laws do demand an unquestioned respect and adherence by the bureaucrats. They are especially obliged to be-have in accord with enacted and constitutional law. It is a part of the "honor of office" [Amtsehre] to apply the laws and rulings competently and efficiently. Stan-dards and efficiency call for arriving at decisions based on "purely objective consider-ations" (p.975). Uniform standards and objective criteria lead to rational decisions by bureaucratic agencies which are akin to modes of calculation. The subsequent certainty makes bureaucratic decisions predictable and permits definite expectations. Administrative law requires officials to organize their offices, establish procedures according to the due process of law, estimate their future requirements and budgets, and thereby become accountable to higher bureaucratic officials. Private parties, looking at civil and criminal laws and their interpretations, can anticipate future bu-reaucratic rulings and formulate their private plans accordingly. These modes and consequences of bureaucratically performed calculations comprise the essence of the substantive and formal rationality of bureaucracy (p.226).

In considering these and other characteristics of rational bureaucracy, Weber em-phasized two parallel developments, one between bureaucracy and capitalism, and the other between bureaucracy and democracy. An elective affinity tends to prevail that is beneficial for the enforcement of the laws and that minimizes the danger of conflict among these institutions.

Modern bureaucracy provides an unintended benefit for capitalism as an eco-nomic system. "Calculable rules are the most important element of modern bu-reaucracy" (p.975). Calculation is coordinated with, or applied to, "the principle of specializing administrative tasks" (p.975), leading to the employment of experts. Calculation and specification can be found in the bureaucracy of the state as well as in the capitalist enterprise. "Normally, the very large modern capitalist enterprises are themselves unequalled models of strict bureaucratic organization. Business man-agement throughout rests on increasing precision, steadiness, and above all, speed of operation" (p.974). Beyond the similarity of these two features in private enterprises and official bureaus, there are definite benefits obtained by private concerns from the provision of official administrative services. "Today, it is primarily the capitalist market economy which demands that the official business of public administration be discharged precisely, unambiguously, continuously, and with as much speed as possible" (p.974).

There emanated a high degree of mutual assistance by governmental offices for enterprises and vice versa. "On the one hand, capitalism in its modern stages of de-velopment requires the bureaucracy, though both have arisen from different histori-cal sources. Conversely, capitalism is the most rational economic basis for bureau-cratic administration and enables it to develop in its most rational form, especially because, from a fiscal point of view, it supplies the necessary monetary resources" (p.224). While not aiming at the same goals, both kinds of bureaucracies favor the same methods of rational calculations, employ experts, achieve the same degree of bureaucratizing work, and depend upon each other for the mutual provision of administrative services.

In the relationship between democracy and bureaucracy, there is a similarity of goals as well as effects, but a significant difference between the methods employed. The principle of equality is adopted by both, but each contributes differently to the realization of equality. Democracy gives full emphasis to an independent public opinion, supports the consensus on major issues, and stipulates the specific rights of individuals. Bureaucracy, while respecting the independence of public opinion, provides the rules and machinery for obtaining popular consensus, and implements as well as protects the equal rights of the citizens. In being committed to the principle of equality and of each providing service to the public, democracy and bureaucracy produce the same effect of reducing or eliminating status differences among individuals and groups. In exerting a leveling effect, "bureaucracy inevitably accompanies modern mass democracy" (p.983). In turn, active democratization sets limits for the bureaucracy by giving "content and direction to administrative activities by means of 'public opinion' " (p.985).

There is also tension and conflict between democracy and bureaucracy. "Under certain conditions, democracy creates palpable breaks in the bureaucratic pattern and impediments to bureaucratic organization" (p.991). The holders of power in the bureaucracy tend to build their power upon specialized knowledge and official secrets, reenforced by formalism and overemphasis of procedures (p.225). But "political democracy strives to shorten the term of office through election and recall, and to be relieved from a limitation to candidates with special expert qualifications. Thereby democracy inevitably comes into conflict with the bureaucratic tendencies" (p.985) that can hardly be eliminated once and for all. At the same time, "propertyless masses are not served by the formal equality of the law." They neither possess significant properties, nor can shape their lives according to the rules of bureaucratic calculations. "Naturally, in their eyes justice and administration should serve to equalize their economic and social life-opportunities in the face of the propertied classes" (p.980). Equality before the law does not lead to social democracy with equal rights, possessions, and opportunities for all citizens. In its place, bureaucracy creates a passive democracy in the sense of "leveling the governed" (p.985).

These conflicts lead to the question of "who controls the existing bureaucratic machinery" (p.224). There are two bureaucratic tendencies that must be curbed. One is the insistence upon autonomy from parliamentary control. The other is the appointment of a bureaucrat as monocratic head of the bureaucracy, thereby seeking independence from the control of the government. In order to keep the bureaucracy accountable for its actions, there has to be an effective parliamentary and executive or judiciary control of the bureaucracy. If effective, the control assures active democratization of government and of the people. All strategic positions of leadership have to be occupied by politicians in order to prevent malfunctioning of the administration. Since the electorate cannot keep the bureaucracy directly responsible, it is the obligation of politicians to effectively control the bureaucracy so that the voters can keep the politicians responsible for the actions of the bureaucracy.[9]

What is the role of leadership in democratic control over the bureaucratic machinery? Bureaucratic domination is achieved through a concentration of specialized knowledge in the organization. "Bureaucratic organization, or the holders of power who make use of them, have the tendency to increase their power still further by the knowledge growing out of experience in the service" (p.225). Since the knowledge is valuable and indispensable, control means two things. It has to be prevented that knowledge is translated into "official secrets." This secrecy is "a product of the striving for power" (p.225), and it is the curbing of this power that can make the knowledge open and accessible to the public, thereby increasing the quality of public opinion. It is the task of politicians or of counterorganizations to transform the secrets into publicly available information essential for formulating and evaluating the various public policies.

Control also means that bureaucrats should not occupy positions of leadership, whether for large but single organizations or as monocrats of segments or of all state organizations. Top administrative positions must be occupied by politicians. Even when bureaucrats are models of "integrity, education, conscientiousness, and intelligence" (p.1405), they tend only to know how to administer, not how to govern. The difference between politicians and bureaucrats "lies in the kind of responsibility . . . and the different demands addressed to both kinds of position" (p.1404). Being guided by their "ethos of office" (*Amtsehre*), bureaucrats have to accept and implement the policies selected by politicians; not formulate policies of their own. "If a man in a leading position is an 'official' in the spirit of his performance," if he "works dutifully and honorably according to rules and instructions, then he is useless at the helm . . . of government" (p.1404).

As a leader, a politician is guided by his own values which he believes are in the public interest. In seeking to get his particular policies adopted by legislatures or voters, he enters "the realm of the struggle for power." He must tell them: "you either give me now the authorization I want from you, or I will resign" (p.1404).[10] In defining the central issues and formulating policies, the political leader has to win popular support and the approving actions of legislatures or judiciary, and subsequently to receive obedience from the bureaucracy.[11] In democracy, the leader provides the link between the bureaucracy and the voters and determines on which policies they both can agree and cooperate. What is required is not "a political genius, to be expected only once every few centuries, not even a great political talent, but simply . . . a politician" (p.1405).

Democratic leadership by politicians is in a position to draw a line between policy and administration. This is accomplished by the decisive role of legitimacy and the prerogative of law making over administration. A democratic bureaucracy is subordinate to the law in dispensing justice equally. Political leaders have a right and a duty to place themselves at the head of administrative departments, to make the major political decisions, and to exercise effective supervision over the actions of administrators. This arrangement not only breaks off the hierarchic order at the top, but it also calls for, at least intermittently, administrative accountability to the political leadership. When direction and accountability are strictly adhered to, politicians can be responsible for the bureaucratic performance and can themselves be kept accountable by the people for mistakes of the administrators.

As a by-product of this analysis, bureaucracy never brings forth, or prepares the ground for, a charismatic leader. If he does arise at all, then it is as the opponent of bureaucracy. As a rule, however, his antagonism is directed not against the "democratizing" but against the "dictatorializing" bureaucracy. The latter is also more prone to prepare the ground for a military dictatorship.

## NEFARIOUS AND ABSOLUTE BUREAUCRACIES

Under certain conditions bureaucracy can refuse to accept the principle of equality and adopt in its place either the principle of preference or of punitive law and order. The choice "depends upon the distribution of economic and social power, and especially upon the sphere that is occupied by the emerging bureaucratic mechanism" (p.989). The bureaucracy "is easily made to work for anybody who knows how to gain control over it" (p.988). Pressures can come from inside the organization or impinge upon it from the outside. If effective, there occurs a change in the goals accepted by the bureaucracy. Whenever there is a bias for preferential treatment we shall speak of nefarious bureaucracy because it violates the principle of democratic equality. Whenever the bureaucracy adopts the principle of law and order for its own sake and sees itself authorized to accept any available method to defend internal order or external security there has arisen an "authoritarian organization" (p.1453) or an absolutist bureaucracy.

There are two well-known types of nefarious bureaucracy.[12] One springs from the association between bureaucracy and propertied classes. The other emanates from the elective affinity between bureaucracy and certain status groups. In each case the administrative services are no longer distributed equally among all concerned; some benefit either from indulgences or from special claims and recognized rights. Social stratification penetrates into the organization and differentiates the services according to status or class positions of the recipients.

In a world of increasingly strong interest groups, the prevailing bureaucracy is subjected to deliberate pressures for respecting, protecting, and promoting the vested interests of private groups. Various kinds of inequities arise in response to such urgings. The goal of serving the public interest is supplemented or superseded by private interests of particular groups. New special agencies are established, such as the departments of commerce or agriculture, that concern themselves primarily with promoting the respective private interests. Or existing agencies appoint or recognize certain persons as liaison officers who seek to coordinate the programs and actions of public and private agencies. As a result, private and public interests become so often intermingled that private and public spheres no longer remain separate. Bureaucracy loses its independence in the interpretation and enforcement of certain laws and rulings. Regulatory commissions of the federal and state governments are often the leading cases in which the regulators lose their moral integrity and in fact become the assistants of private interest groups.[13] The available or redirected services are unequally distributed, expressing the fact that certain branches of the bureaucracy have become subservient to "the economically and socially most influential strata" (p.997).

A peculiar elective affinity has developed between some bureaucracies and status groups. One kind of status distinction arises within the bureaucracy itself. The modern bureaucrat in public bureaus "attains a distinctly elevated social position relative to the governed" (p.959). Titles and ranks indicate membership in such an esteemed group, while the reputation of the offices claims a high prestige for the public organization. The other status groups exist in the society at large. "There is also the possibility . . . that bureaucratization of the administration is deliberately connected with the formation of status groups or is entangled with it by the force of the existing groupings of social power" (p.990). The ethical beliefs and the mutual self-esteem of both status groups intermingle to such an extent that the external group claims the right of exclusively providing the aspirants for the higher and highest positions in the state bureaucracy. Keeping the doors open only for the aristocracy or for the graduates of leading universities has the effect of a "guild-like closure of officialdom" (p.960). Gradually, but surely, the beliefs and conventions of the aristocracy become the norms for the behavior of state officials. Although the interpenetration of the internal and external status groups originated in the patrimonial state, "the desire to resurrect such policies in changed forms is by no means infrequent among modern bureaucrats" (p.960).

The response to these kinds of inequitable bureaucracies has been either negative or positive, depending upon the political system. In democracy, the reputation of the state bureaucracy suffered more or less severely. Either the bureaucracy was identified with inefficiency, corruption, and dishonesty, or the bureaucrats were identified with arrogance and snobbishness, and seen as climbers or hunters for honor. The set of derogatory terms or other expressions of antagonism depended upon the culture of the various countries[14] and upon whether the nefarious nature of the bureaucracy was attributable to the special privileges enjoyed by private interests or status groups. It is especially to these types of organizations that Weber's dictum applies: "Democracy as such is opposed to the rule of bureaucracy" (p.991).

While private interests motivate the respective administrative actions in nefarious bureaucracy, absolute bureaucracy seeks to obtain political power for itself and aims at becoming the sole bearer of public interests. Instead of leaving law making to the political leaders and implementing laws according to the rule of law, the bureaucracy frowns upon any "outside" influence, whether it comes from private groups, a king, a parliament, or any kind of supervisor. Internally, an absolute bureaucracy tends to keep all its secrets, extends its control over the entry to official positions, strictly enforces the rules of promotion and compensation, and rigidly imposes the bureaucratic code of honor.[15] If allowed to move along this line of independence, there develops a bureaucratic self-control that enables one high official to occupy the position of the monocrat in the state. Externally, the monocrats and the department heads accumulate discretionary power which they use to manipulate public opinion, enlarge the scope of executive power, usurp legislative functions of parliament, pressure the courts, and effectively determine the policies of the state. The end of such a development is bureaucratic absolutism in which one bureaucrat becomes the dictator of the country.

## MILITARY DICTATORSHIP

For Weber the military was the most likely candidate for establishing a dictatorship, because it was the agency in which centered most of the state's monopolized legitimate violence. In ordinary times, "violence acquires legitimacy only in those cases . . . at least initially . . . in which it is directed against members of the fraternity who have acted treasonably or who have harmed it by disobedience or cowardice" (p.906). Use of extensive violence against whole groups usually requires an emergency that justifies a declaration of military siege followed by extralegal action. The bureaucratic monocrat, whether a military or a civilian, becomes a dictator when he deduces a "specific legitimacy of violence" from the need to defend the legal order at home or against a foreign enemy.

Weber formulated an interesting thesis on military dictatorship. Wars between major powers call for military service of millions of men and for extensive production of war materials. The imposed sacrifices create resistance which can be broken only by a military dictatorship. It is this enlargement of the public sector and its redirection of the private economy, plus extensive deprivations, that lead inevitably to a military dictatorship in all the belligerent countries.

Actually, this thesis of an inevitable dictatorship, springing from an uncontrolled bureaucracy and war necessities, happened only in the German, Austrian and Russian monarchies in World War I. Weber's generalization was (and is) unwarranted for the Anglo-American countries in both world wars, nor could it fit the specific kinds of Fascist and Communist dictatorships before and during World War II. The much more diverse situation calls for a modification of his thesis on absolute bureaucracy.

Weber's starting point was "the monopolization of legitimate violence" in the state (p.904). When its external security or its internal legal order are threatened, the military organization is authorized to wage war against a foreign foe or to suppress any revolution. The military forces are thus regarded as the sole bearers of arms in the state. Police, courts, and intelligence forces are seen as agents of law enforcement that do not exercise extralegal violence. But the single party regimes, especially of the

Communist and Fascist variety, introduced the secret police forces and militarized the regular police, the personnel of which were largely recruited from the paramilitary forces of both types of parties. There has occurred a proliferation of the bearers of arms, each of which has on occasion become the agent of violence. The result is an extension of the modes of dictatorship, depending upon who possesses the means of violence in the state: bureaucratic dictatorship, military dictatorship, police dictatorship, intelligence dictatorship, and judiciary dictatorship.

There are thus two quite different tendencies toward dictatorship. Weber correctly saw the first line emanating from the absolute bureaucracy and the military organizations. He did not anticipate the more recent development of revolutionary and counterrevolutionary parties which utilized the police, spy services, and courts as agents of violence, operating in times of peace as well as war. The new agents of violence not only destroyed civil liberties and suppressed or controlled private organizations, but the Fascist parties used these agents to impose the will of the leader and party upon the old bureaucracy and military forces, whereas the Communist parties established new civilian and military bureaucracies. Instead of the old bureaucracies dominating the state, they themselves became pliable instruments of the leader and gradually succumbed to his combined dictatorship of party, police, and courts.[16] Rather than fighting according to military rules in the Second World War, the generals of Communist and Fascist armies were compelled to execute the orders of their respective political dictators. The Fascist dictators were a cause, not an effect, of World War II.

There is also a need to modify Weber's thesis on the inevitability of military dictatorship arising in democratic countries. His argument contains two major parts. There was said to be a mutual complementarity between civilians and military dictatorships. In time of peace the bureaucratic monocrat tends to become the head of the government but he needs the support of the generals for effectively imposing his bureaucratic absolutism. In time of war, however, one of the generals seeks to become the military dictator but the new tasks of the war economy, such as rationing, require the active assistance of the civilian bureaucracy. This mutual interaction is reenforced by the code of honor cherished by both groups, and also by the similar status position of the landholding aristocracy. Technical abilities and the combined honors of office and status generate the belief that the heads of both organizations alone know what is best for state and society. The claim to govern the country was justified by "the strictly 'objective' idea of the *raison d'état*." But this includes also "the sure instinct of the bureaucracy for the conditions of maintaining its own power in the home state. . . . Most of the time only the power interests of the bureaucracy give a concretely exploitable content to this by no means unambiguous idea" (p.979). The argument of the *Staatsräson* was thus employed for explaining the development of bureaucratic absolutism.

How much of this "idea" could be implemented? Weber predicted that "the Prussian administrative organizations . . . will in the future be an advance of the bureaucratic, and especially monocratic, principle" (p.974). But he saw this only as a "normal," not as an inevitable possibility. "For two of the most expansive political formations, the Roman empire and the British world empire, rested upon bureaucratic foundations only to the smallest extent during their most expansive periods. . . . [For] later on the English state did not participate in the Continental development towards bureaucratization, but remained an administration of notables" (p.970). The main reasons for this line of development were seen in the insular geography, the absence of a standing army, and the desire to limit the scope of governmental activities. "The United States still bears the character of a polity which, at least in the technical sense, is not fully bureaucratized" (p.971). But he believed that bureaucratization of the political parties had an effect similar to the one of civilian bureaucracy.

While Weber presented the rules of notables and of bureaucrats as "two autonomous developments" (p.977), each governed by its own *Eigengesetzlichkeit*,[17] there was no doubt in his mind that bureaucratization would win the struggle in all industrialized nations. Greatest emphasis was placed upon the overriding need of business and administrative offices to operate according to calculable rules. To this we have to add the impact of the more recent military technology which has removed the protection granted previously by the oceans and has created the necessity to maintain standing armies. The current race in atomic weapons clinches Weber's argument of a general tendency towards bureaucratization in all industrial countries, whether democratic or dictatorial, capitalist or Communist in nature.

Yet there is implicit in this thesis an untenable inference. The trend toward bureaucratization does not necessarily entail a general trend toward bureaucratic absolutism. The notion of a bureaucratic superiority over nonbureaucrats or the claim that bureaucrats alone are best qualified to govern their countries is emphatically rejected in genuine democracies. Practically all politicians attack the nefarious features of bureaucracy. Rather than claiming a right to political leadership, the majority of governmental employees are motivated by pecuniary interests, insisting mainly upon special material gains. The heads of agencies satisfy their desire for power by fighting for larger budgets and seek to build up personal empires within the federal bureaucracy. In recent periods of deep crises, the American generals and admirals never claimed a right to political leadership. Our modification thus is that there is a danger of nefarious bureaucracy, but no unavoidable tendency toward bureaucratic absolutism or military dictatorship as long as worship of bureaucrats is rejected, entry is not limited to one status group, and military leaders are kept accountable to political leaders.

These restrictions upon bureaucratic developments have opened up two important political opportunities. Our analysis reveals a rationale for an effective political control of the bureaucracy. First, a policy of democratic bureaucracy is possible and meaningful that can transform a nefarious into an equitable bureaucracy. Second, as an alternative, charismatic leaders are given a chance to break bureaucratic resistance to their policies by inducing the welter of personal empires to tolerate and serve the leader during his reign.

President Roosevelt has shown that bureaucracy is not necessarily incompatible with charismatic leadership. He adroitly developed distinct policies for handling the bureaucrats. In time of peace he created a whole slew of new agencies for implementing the policies of the New Deal. He often laid the foundation for rivalry among administrators by permitting overlapping jurisdictions or by vaguely defining administrative tasks. While Congress foiled his plan to incorporate the new agencies into regular departments in 1938,[18] Roosevelt was successful in bringing most of his appointees into the civil service system. In time of war, most of the new tasks of the war economy were again assigned to special agencies, some of which lived in tension with the military departments. Advisory commissions were often attached to the new agencies so that representatives of private groups could lend support or modify the policies of the administrators.[19] Multiplication of the new offices called for coordination of programs and policies. This was accomplished by establishing "superior" offices by means of which Roosevelt was able to obtain the relevant information and to supervise the implementation of his policies. Last but not least, the leader kept for himself the prerogative to initiate programs, to push for their legislative acceptance, to appoint administrators, and to give overall directives for their actions. The prerogative was used judiciously to retain most of the discretionary power in his hands and to undercut any hidden proclivity of generals or admirals to establish a military dictatorship.[20]

## MILITARY CRISIS AND CHARISMATIC LEADERSHIP

There was a widely recognized clash between leaders of dictatorial and democratic charismata in World War II. Aggression emanated from the Fascist leaders of dictatorial charisma, whereas the bearers of democratic charisma became the leaders of the defense against attack. The Nazi assault was a modernized version of war by machines. It was not so much the machine gun and the rapid-fire artillery, but the sudden attack by tanks, airplanes, and armored infantry that permitted the German armed forces to defeat France within six weeks. Trench warfare was replaced by mobile warfare and surprise strategy. It was only in the second half of the war that the *Blitzkrieg* turned into a total war in which victory was won by the anti-Nazi forces because of their larger manpower, greater quantity, and better quality of war machines.

The military crisis, caused by the defeat of France, led to a change of leadership in Western Europe. Churchill and de Gaulle, the one a civilian politician and the other a regular army officer, became the charismatic leaders of their countries. Their charismatic quality was militant in regard to overcoming the military crisis, political in terms of creating national unity, and emotional in turning despair into the will to resist. Is it true that "the democracies enlisted dictators to lead them in war"[21] or was there a genuine militant charisma that was not of a dictatorial nature?

*Superhuman Qualities.* There can be no doubt that both Churchill and de Gaulle were endowed with exceptional qualities. Already in early adulthood each of these men became convinced that he possessed the quality of greatness, of being designated to perform great deeds. Each showed typical charismatic readiness to engage in risky actions, to attach glory to his name, and to dramatize plans or campaigns. Both aspirants exhibited the traits of personal courage, initiative in the face of danger, and the desire for greatness. This applied to de Gaulle's five attempts to escape from German POW camps during World War I and his voluntary service in the subsequent war between Poland and the Soviet Union. The same adventurous spirit was expressed in Churchill's participation in wars in Sudan and India as well as his activities as a journalist-soldier in the Boer War or as a journalist in the Spanish campaign against Cuban rebels. These military exploits were accompanied or followed by extensive study of military literature. Preoccupation with military problems and knowledge of military strategy—technology for de Gaulle—were the personal characteristics of militant charisma, whereas the previous political experience was useful but of secondary importance.

In waiting for their golden opportunity for greatness, and steeling themselves for great exertions, each acted as a charismatic aspirant. In contrast to the dormant quality, these men felt it in their bones and "knew" of their designation as future great leaders. Both were forced into periods of preparation without being able to present openly their claims to charismatic leadership. De Gaulle prepared himself from 1927 to 1940 and then waited again from 1946 to 1958, while Churchill was in the political wilderness from 1929 to 1939.

There is no evidence that the inner voice to a higher calling was derived from or attributed to a supernatural being. Given Churchill's religious skepsis or indifference, there were only some vague presentiments of being protected by some unknown being. When the foxhole in the trenches was blown up during his temporary absence in World War I, he said, "[I] had the strong sensation that a hand had stretched out to move me in the nick of time from the fatal spot."[22] De Gaulle's strong belief in the Catholic religion prevented him from claiming supernatural selection. Both pretenders saw themselves designated for superior tasks by an undefined destiny, which linked them with the destiny of their respective countries and empires. Churchill aimed at heroism for himself and immortality for his country. As for de Gaulle, "Grandeur becomes his motto, for himself, others, and for France."[23] Judging by the results, destiny served as the source for the belief of being called to great tasks in the future. It was not a supernatural being but a superhuman quality of heroism that appeared as the source of charisma.

There was a significant difference between the two aspirants in regard to natural charisma. Whereas de Gaulle possessed great insight in the feelings and intentions of others, he could not play with the emotions of millions. "De Gaulle was not 'popular' in the ordinary sense, he aroused no mass enthusiasm, still less mass hysteria."[24] He also was often awkward in his relations with others and at a disadvantage with his superiors in earlier years. He said of an obscure army officer in 1927, obviously meaning himself: "He is too sure of himself, too conscious of his strength to let himself be influenced by the mere wish to please."[25] But in the extreme military and political crises of France, de Gaulle's patriotic fervor did bring forth great admiration for his personality by millions of his countrymen.

Far from being awkward, Churchill was a polished and arresting conversationalist as well as an outstanding orator, who knew how to adjust himself to his audiences, sense and express their feelings, arouse their emotions, and gain their enthusiasm. He was capable of overflowing emotions himself and could employ them for his political ends. Just as in democratic charisma, Churchill possessed the gift of natural charisma.

*Appeal and Goals.* An interesting connection exists between war and the recognition of charismatic leadership in a democracy. Being in the defense, military charisma becomes effective only after the state of belligerency. Churchill succeeded to the position of prime minister only after the phony war had almost come to an end. De Gaulle could present himself as leader of the Free French only after Nazi victory over France. The emergency thesis thus expresses correctly the beginning of militant charisma in an attacked democracy.

Threat to security and national independence predetermined the nature of the charismatic appeal and pointed to the goals for action. The main task of the leader was to express the desire and to achieve national unity, to strengthen the moral fiber of the people as well as the will to resist. Appeals turned into enunciating goals for the people as well as the government. The immediate goal was to shift from peace to war production and to mobilize the military and economic forces for effective defense. The ultimate goal aimed at victory over the enemy. Specification of this ultimate goal was well done in Churchill's speech as the new premier on May 13, 1940: "Our policy is to wage war against a monstrous tyranny, never surpassed in the dark lamentable catalogue of human crime. . . . Our aim is . . . victory, victory at all cost, victory in spite of terror, victory however long and hard the road may be, for without victory there is no survival. . . . At this time I feel entitled to claim the aid of all and to say: 'Come then, let us go forward together with our united strength.' "[26] This appeal was so successful that even some of the defeats, as the evacuation of British troops from Dunkirk, became victories in the minds of many people because it showed the courage and the will to resist even under the most difficult circumstances.

Quite different was the nature of de Gaulle's appeal. In June 1940, he could only speak to defeated France by means of the British radio: "At the present hour, all Frenchmen understand that the usual forms of government have disappeared. Confronted with the confusion of French souls, confronted with the liquidation of government which has fallen under the yoke of the enemy, confronted with the fact that our institutions cannot function freely, I, General de Gaulle, French soldier and leader, am aware of speaking in the name of France."[27] This appeal was regarded by the Vichy government as an act of treason. A military court condemned de Gaulle to death for desertion from the French forces. This leadership of the Free French was regarded in Vichy as, and actually was, an act of rebellion. However, there was not only an inner reorientation by the leader and followers, but also an adoption of immediate goals required by the specific military-political situation. Churchill employed all his energies to build up state and economy into an effective war machine, whereas de Gaulle had to fight against the Vichy government in the process of seeking a territory and armed forces for his new government of Free France.

*Ideology and Authority.* In their earlier ideologies, both personalities were definitely conservative, not clearly immune to some ideals of Fascism. Churchill was once an admirer of Mussolini and doubted whether "institutions of adult suffrage could possibly overcome unemployment in the midst of the great depression."[28] De Gaulle in his youth was a sympathizer of the *Action Française* led by Charles Maurras. But increasingly each aspirant concentrated upon the power of their respective states and especially their military strength. A distinct imperialist predilection for the respective empire was a dearly cherished belief. For their nations to be, to remain, or to become again, world powers was the main personal and political concern. De Gaulle proposed after the Normandy invasion that the Saar should be incorporated into France, the Rhineland be separated from Germany, and the Ruhr valley be internationalized.[29] Churchill had fought furiously against granting independence to Egypt, and giving India the status of a dominion. He said publicly in 1932 that "Gandhism and all it stands for will, sooner or later, have to be grappled and finally crushed."[30] Nationalist-imperialist ideology thus preceeded militant charisma.

Accordingly, neither leader was sorry that his authority could not be based upon the formal consent of the majority in an election. In Britain, Churchill formed a coalition government of all three parties, which decided jointly to suspend elections during war time. Recognition of the charismatic leader was thus granted by the heads of parties, and approved subsequently by the members of the prewar parliament. The popular will expressed itself in the great applause given to Churchill in response to his great speeches. Eager for decisive actions, Churchill confessed on the day he became premier: "At last I had the authority to give directions over the whole scene. I felt as if I was walking with destiny, and that all my life had been a preparation for this hour and this trial."[31] But it is quite clear that there was no formal democratic consent by the electorate. At the same time, Churchill respected the reduced power of parliament. He said on January 22, 1941: "I think I have said before that to try to carry on a war, a tremendous war, without the aid and guidance of the House of Commons would be a superhuman task. I have never taken the view that the debates and criticisms of the House are a drag and a burden."[32] When the criticisms became too intense, Churchill one year later demanded and received a vote of confidence from the House.

De Gaulle assumed the direction of Free France by a unilateral act all his own. Years later de Gaulle explained his action in the following words: "It was by adopting without compromise the cause of national recovery that I could acquire authority. It was by acting as the inflexible champion of the nation and of the State that I could gain the consent, even the enthusiasm of the French, and win respect and consideration from foreigners."[33] There was thus a claim of legitimacy for the authority of a charismatic hero. The ideological belief of patriotism justified the claim; popular enthusiasm provided the charismatic legitimacy for his authority. Actually, there was at first merely a kind of symbolic legitimacy by means of the "plebiscite of silence." De Gaulle had requested that all Frenchmen in the occupied zone stay in their homes for one hour on January 1, 1941. "France will let the world know that it sees its future only in freedom, its greatness only in independence, its salvation only in victory."[34] The empty streets amounted to symbolic legitimacy.

In contrast with democratic charisma and its legitimizing formal consent, militant charisma brings forth four quite different modes of legitimacy. One was of a charismatic nature. Admiration of the leader's courage, iron will, inner strength, and clearly expressed certitude created a willingness to obey his orders. The other legitimacy was ideological. An all embracing patriotism, including unlimited love of the fatherland as well as an increasing determination of national survival, generated the readiness to accept the leader's war goals and endure any necessary sacrifice. The third ground of legitimacy was the one related to the authority of expertise. Churchill had acquired considerable competence in military strategy. In the words of Eisenhower, "During the war Mr. Churchill maintained such a close contact with all operations as to make him a virtual member of the chiefs of staff; I cannot remember any major discussion with them in which he did not participate."[35] Finally, there was the legal authority because of Churchill's official position as prime minister, minister of defense, and chairman of the war council. Insofar as his will expressed itself in laws and ordinances, citizens were obliged to obey the laws and regard them as valid. Militant charisma thus enjoyed the confluent authority of charismatic, ideological, expertise, and legal legitimacy.

To be precise, it was only Churchill, not de Gaulle, in whom were vested these four kinds of authority. The belief in the heroic quality of de Gaulle was more latent than manifest in the early war years. Symbolic legitimacy in the occupied territory was expressed more by negative than positive actions. Resistance groups were at first either hate groups or ideological groups, disinclined to any form of charismatic worship. It was only when the Nazis were driven in the defensive that more of the resistance groups recognized de Gaulle as their leader and public opinion changed in his favor. Even more difficult was it for de Gaulle to have his legal authority recognized.

A leader in exile, his Free France was only a potential state, a promise of the future, while the usual attributes of the state were missing. This expressed itself in the long struggle of de Gaulle to be truly recognized as the head of the French state by Roosevelt and Churchill who at a few occasions were ready to replace him by another man.[36] But it was precisely because of his behavior as a hero and the rising belief in him that he eventually succeeded in becoming the national savior of France.

The phenomenon of a confluent authority, in its latent and manifest forms, is empirically identifiable for militant charisma, and typical for synergistic charisma. Such a confluent authority goes counter to the theoretical thesis that "one organization cannot be governed by two distinct ultimate principles of social action."[37] The principles involved could not only be effectively combined but their cumulation greatly increased the power of the leader.

*Charismatic Apparatus.* Executing and winning a war could be accomplished only if the respective leaders possessed control over their own apparatus. The men appointed must serve the leader out of charismatic allegiance as well as their tested ability to execute his orders. While Churchill had acquired a small group of trusted assistants, de Gaulle arrived in London with hardly any paladins.

Churchill was in a much better position because he could select his assistants either from his few political friends of long standing or from aroused experts of the bureaucracy. The latter became the official personnel of his three offices. His assistants had to attune themselves to Churchill's working habits, his political intentions, and strategic ideas. Great inputs and full devotion were demanded in support of many of Churchill's enterprises. The result was a more militarily and administratively than charismatically qualified apparatus of the giant leader.

Top civil servants viewed with distaste Churchill's appointment as prime minister. But there soon occurred a "transformation of opinion in Whitehall and of the tempo of business conducted. A sense of urgency was created in the course of a few days and respectable civil servants were actually seen running along the corridors. No delays were condoned; telephone switchboards quadrupled their efficiency; the chiefs of staff and the Joint Planning Board were in almost constant sessions; regular office hours ceased to exist and weekends went with them."[38] The top bureaucrats and most of their staff became so emotionally involved in the new tasks and attached to their charismatic leader that they became an adequate substitute for the charismatic apparatus.

General de Gaulle suffered from tribulations of having to build up an apparatus without either a political party or a reliable group of paladins. The available personnel were very few because of "an almost general abstention of French personalities vis-à-vis my enterprise."[39] Extraordinary means had to be employed to obtain men technically able to perform the assigned tasks who would remain devoted followers of the leader. Politically, members of his various committees prior to the liberation admired him personally, but many of them believed in a different ideology. Internal political squabbles were thus happening among the assistants of the leader. Militarily, the few generals and admirals recognizing de Gaulle as their leader were motivated by nationalist ideals, but hardly ever moved by personal devotion. Best known became the "rebellion" by Admiral Muselier who felt better qualified to be the French leader in exile. He could be readily replaced because the French sailors admired and supported de Gaulle. His military reputation, however, suffered when the Vichy troops resisted the takeover of Dakar, and when the Allied forces occupied north-west Africa without de Gaulle's knowledge. Allied appointment of General Giraud as the commander of the occupied region created a crisis which was overcome only when de Gaulle was given equal rights and eventually succeeded in becoming the only president of the Committee of National Liberation. There was only one division under de Gaulle's command that entered the south as a part of the Allied liberation of France. Indeed, two divisions had to be "borrowed" from General Eisenhower so that de Gaulle could enter Paris as the savior of France.[40] Insofar as there was a charismatic apparatus in the military field, it was barely able to accomplish its task.

In regard to the resistance movement, the de Gaulle apparatus had to recognize the various groups, including the Communist party and its paramilitary troops. The sole task achievable was to establish links among the many groups and obtain their support for de Gaulle. This could be accomplished only by an agreement with the Communists as the best organized group of the resistance. A coalition of political opponents not only assisted significantly the Allied invasion, but was continued after the liberation. After a visit of de Gaulle to Moscow, the leader of the French Communists returned to Paris, became a member of the de Gaulle government in 1945, but the Communist party dissolved its own paramilitary organization. In regard to resistance de Gaulle and his apparatus achieved a notable success.

Militant charisma in a crisis situation did not possess the paladins required for a charismatic apparatus. Two advantages arose that could be utilized for building up such an apparatus. The close affinity between the ideology of patriotism and heroic charisma permitted such ideological adherents to serve de Gaulle without necessarily becoming his followers. Moved by the fear for national survival, a significant number of British bureaucrats could become emotionally attached and thereby developed the belief in the leader, ready to serve in his charismatic apparatus. In an extreme crisis, a division of tasks developed between the military and civilian bureaucracy, which limited the armed forces to performing their strictly military duties. The domination of the military over the civilian bureaucracy was missing in Anglo-Saxon countries.

*Violence and Militant Charisma.* Violence occupied a central place in militant charisma. But it became customary to distinguish between war and warlike actions as well as between aggressive and defensive wars, and permissible and contemptible warlike actions.[41] In each case there was a systematic employment of physical force by armed forces seeking to obtain an otherwise unattainable objective. Defensive wars against the attack of an aggressor as well as permissible warlike actions were usually regarded as morally justified actions. Aggression and contemptible warlike actions were usually not covered by the prevailing moral code of the international community. Militant charisma became involved in the use of wars as well as warlike actions on a small or large scale.

Militant charisma in the English and French cases contributed in two ways to military defense and counterattack. The war goal was victory, and the peace aims were independence and freedom. The other contribution was to fight against any form of defeatism and create the will and enthusiasm for the defeat of the enemy in spite of toil, sweat, and tears. Churchill "made each one feel that the fate of England rested upon him." De Gaulle "became something of an anti-Vichy hero" as well as a symbol of resistance against the Nazis in French public opinion.[42] While its impact cannot be measured, charismatic leadership contributed significantly to the effectiveness of the Allied counterattack. Military, economic, psychological, and political warfare were sanctioned simultaneously by charismatic and ideological legitimacy. Military actions were perceived as just wars.

For France, de Gaulle was primarily concerned with civil war. The forces of Vichy and of the Free French were not only engaged in political and ideological warfare, but also in various military encounters. Several governors of Vichy were dismissed in colonies, while the battle in Syria was partly successful and the attack upon Dakar was unsuccessful for the Free French. Fighting between Frenchmen could not be justified ideologically by patriotism, but was sanctioned mainly by charismatic legitimacy. Outcome of these fights depended less upon the kind of legitimacy and more upon the extent of manpower and military equipment in the field. Civil war was terminated largely by the victory of the Allied forces over the Nazi armies.[43]

While some forms of warlike actions, such as genocide, were not practiced by the defenders against the Nazi attackers, others did clearly violate the moral code prevailing in a democracy. Best known was the British saturation bombing of German cities in which civilian workers and their families were the specifically selected targets. Early in 1944 the provisional government under de Gaulle undertook a systematic purge of the officials of the Vichy government in Algeria. Most dramatic was the handling of Pierre Pucheu, former minister of the interior at Vichy, responsible for executing some hostages. After siding with the Free French, he was arrested in Algiers, and condemned to death by a military tribunal. After pondering the decision for three days, de Gaulle thought the crimes forgivable, but still ordered the execution because he explained: "I must rise above my passions and only reasons of state must dictate my judgment."[44] Other purges and executions of Vichy leaders followed after the liberation. Neither in England nor in France was there an effort of justifying these violent actions by charismatic legitimacy. Implicitly, certain forms of violence could not be vindicated by the legitimacy of militant charisma.

*Charismatic Accomplishments.* Crisis charisma in wartime experienced one accomplishment and suffered one failure. Crisis leadership clearly succeeded in mobilizing the emotional and intellectual resources of Britain, and established a Free French movement and government that became the junior partner in the Allied counterattack and invasion of the Continent. Without such leadership the will to resist Nazi aggression would have been less strong and unified. Charismatic leadership contributed significantly to the political and economic mobilization for building up a war economy and preparing Britain for the counterattack. American participation in the Allied invasion would have been much more difficult if the Battle of Britain had not been won by the successful resistance of the Spitfires, the use of radar, and the endurance of the British people. Charismatic leadership restored the French Republic and avoided a second occupation, this time by Allied forces.

In a sense, victory over the enemy terminated crisis leadership at home. Each leader tried to continue his leadership in time of peace but failed. Victory had significantly diminished the willingness of the people to follow a giant leader. Political parties reclaimed their right to leadership. Defeat of the conservative party meant also the end of Churchill's charismatic leadership. Return of French political parties to power left little room for the preponderant leadership of de Gaulle who resigned in the expectation that his "rally" would become the instrument for his return to power. But this effort failed so that there was no direct transition from crisis to plebiscitarian charisma in France.

## IDEOLOGICAL SPLIT AND CHARISMA

World War II created the same kind of political, ideological, and military dilemma as did World War I for the United States. The striking power and volume of the modern war machines made it increasingly clear that only the large resources of the United States could eventually defeat the Axis powers. Militarily, however, the country was utterly unprepared, whether for defense of the Western Hemisphere or for intervention abroad. Ideologically, the belief in isolation, or the aversion to participating in foreign wars, was even stronger than in 1917. In September 1939, public opinion was divided into three different groups of adherents. Of those with definite opinions, 37 percent favored positive help of the European democracies, 30 percent would sell goods to belligerents only on a cash-and-carry basis, and the remainder favored strict isolation, not supporting either side of the war.[45]

An ideological split created a personal dilemma for Roosevelt. Reelected in time of peace, he could not readily transfer his charismatic mandate to the new war situation. Roosevelt was fully aware of his new condition of personal powerlessness. Shortly after the defeat of Poland in 1939, he wrote: "I am almost literally walking on eggs, and, having delivered my message to the Congress and having good prospects for the bill [repealing the embargo] going through, I am at the moment saying nothing, seeing nothing, hearing nothing."[46] Roosevelt had learned the lesson of the conflict with the Supreme Court. In a situation of deep ideological cleavage, a charismatic leader cannot take the lead but has to wait for the ripening of the events that will open up new opportunities for decisive action.

*Revision of the Charismatic Mission.* Up to 1937 Roosevelt was deeply committed to a policy of peace. It was he who had initiated the Neutrality Act of 1935. In 1939, he expressed his disappointment with this Act. "We have learned that when we deliberately legislate neutrality, our neutrality laws may operate unevenly and unfairly—may actually give aid to the aggressor and deny it to the victims."[47] He was then willing to take the blame for his own earlier mistake. "I regret that the Congress passed the Act. I regret equally that I signed the Act."[48] There was thus a clear shift in Roosevelt's belief. His charismatic mission no longer included any trace of pacifism. The war in Europe called for a quite different ideal. His newly accepted ideal was national unity among all groups of society. "In meeting the troubles of the world we must meet them as one people—with a unity born of the fact that for generations those who came to our shores, representing many kindreds and tongues, have been welded by common opportunities into a united patriotism. If another form of government can present a united front in its attack on a democracy, the attack must and will be met by a united democracy. Such a democracy can and must exist in the United States."[49] National unity and patriotism, in the face of dictatorial aggressors abroad, became the leading ideal of Roosevelt's renewed charismatic mission.

National unity became associated with two complementary goals. The Fascist threat abroad called for a policy of military defense at home. After a long debate, Congress passed the Vinson Naval Expansion Act which aimed at a two-ocean navy. This was followed by building up a huge air force. When Hitler invaded the Western democracies, Roosevelt requested an appropriation of over one billion dollars and set the goal of producing 50,000 airplanes in one year. The concept of defense was gradually widened so as to include all parts of the Western Hemisphere, including the western side of the Atlantic.[50]

Self-defense was accompanied by the other goal of allowing the potential allies to obtain American military equipment. This policy was partly based upon Churchill's private request that the United States should proclaim nonbelligerency and (1) supply several hundreds of the latest type of aircrafts; (2) loan fifty old destroyers; (3) provide antiaircraft equipment and munitions; and (4) permit purchase of American steel.[51] The request for destroyers could be accepted only after the fall of France and the fierce air attack upon Britain. The subsequent executive agreement was even approved by isolationists when the destroyers were exchanged for eight islands, important for the American defense of the Atlantic coast. Of greatest ideological and practical significance, however, was the lend-lease program which was justified by the new ideal of the United States becoming "the arsenal of democracy." The Lend-Lease Act empowered the president when he deemed it "in the national interest . . . to sell, transfer title to, exchange, lease, or otherwise dispose of . . . any defense article" to any government. Roosevelt admitted that this course of action involved risks, but it is "the least risk now and the greatest hope for world peace in the future."[52]

The new ideal of the arsenal of democracy could become a part of Roosevelt's charismatic mission only after a significant change in the war situation. One important event was the extensive effort of the Committee to Defend America by Aiding the Allies, the six hundred chapters of which contributed significantly to the transfer of the destroyers.[53] The merciless bombardment of Great Britain created a wave of sympathy in this country. Yet it required the reelection of Roosevelt as the undisputed war leader before the Lend-Lease Act was adopted in March 1941. A poll of public opinion revealed that 61 percent were for, 23 percent against, this major act of assistance for the Allies.[54] The shift from loans to gifts in international war finance was seen by Roosevelt as a kind of brotherly act, fully in accord with charismatic leadership.

*Renewal of Electoral Charisma.* In contrast to Great Britain, the electoral process was not suspended in the United States. The presidential elections of 1940 and 1944 were held in spite of the war. Instead of generals occupying the highest office in the land, there was universal insistence that only elected politicians could be the leaders in time of war. Why was there a renewal of charismatic leadership?

Prior to the fall of France, Roosevelt spoke of his retirement and first thought of Hopkins and then of Hull as his successor.[55] The sudden victory of the Nazis on the Continent, however, increased tremendously the military threat to this country. The new task of steering the nation through another crisis overcame his desire for retirement and reenforced the clamor of his followers who wanted him to run again. But there were rivals who were eager to be nominated in his place. When Farley suggested that he should withdraw by making a Sherman-like statement, Roosevelt answered: "If nominated and elected, I would not in these times refuse to take the inaugural oath, even if I knew I would die within thirty days."[56] Two closely related motives prompted his decision. One was the charismatic self-confidence that he was the best and only man strong enough to face the military crisis. The other was the strong sense of responsibility that he had to serve the nation regardless of the risk to his health.

Yet reelection of the charismatic leader created a challenge to a long established tradition. There was an injunction that no president should hold the office longer than two terms. In disregarding this rule, Roosevelt referred to the military emergency and to the wide experience of his administration in foreign affairs. Indeed, Roosevelt broke other well-established precedents. It was customary for an administration not to propose new major policies that could be attacked by the opposition. Roosevelt, however, strongly supported the Selective Service Act which was adopted by Congress and authorized the first peacetime draft in American history.

There was another innovation that had been spurned by President Wilson. The goal of achieving national unity suggested bipartisan support of foreign and military policies. Already in 1939 Roosevelt had contacted the Republican presidential nominees of 1936 about entering the cabinet in a national crisis. Governor Alf Landon asked for Roosevelt's promise that he would not seek a third term. This stipulation caused Roosevelt to nominate Henry Stimson as secretary of war and Colonel Frank Knox as secretary of the navy prior to his reelection. The two most important positions for military preparedness came into the hands of interventionists, reducing the isolationist influence in the cabinet.

The Republicans nominated an outsider, Wendell Willkie, whose charismatic drive outflanked the old-timers at the convention. Willkie was an internationalist who supported the swap of the destroyers against military bases. But others saw in the deal an act of war. An advertisement appeared in leading newspapers which charged: "Mr. Roosevelt today committed an act of war. He also became the first American dictator."[57] While Willkie had no objection to the deal, he criticized the method of bypassing the Congress. This executive agreement "was the most dictatorial action taken by any president."[58] Towards the end of the campaign, Willkie compressed the third term with entry in the war into one slogan: "The third term will mean dictatorship and war." In reply, Roosevelt made a definite promise that was also stated in the Democratic platform. He pledged that the United States would not "fight in foreign lands outside of the Americas, except in case of attack."[59] The charismatic authority was emphatically renewed by the majority of the voters, but consent was mortgaged by the promise that the United States would not enter the war by its own voluntary decision.

It so happened that Roosevelt kept his pledge. He did not ask Congress for a declaration of war nor did he commit the country to war by his own decision. Of all his actions, this antiwar pledge was the one least expected; it was widely regarded as a deliberate deception. In retrospect, one can only conclude that he was sincere and tried his best to avoid involvement in a shooting war. Even some of the critics do admit that "the President felt with great sincerity that his policy would not lead to American involvement but to a British victory that alone would keep the nation out of war."[60] This belief was based on Churchill's promise that Britain would not ask for an expeditionary force. "Give us the tools and we shall finish the job."[61]

As the war progressed there occurred Nazi attacks upon a few American ships and the wholesale sinking of British merchant ships. Roosevelt responded in declaring an unlimited national emergency: "From the point of view of strict naval and military necessity, we shall give every possible assistance to Britain and to all who . . . are resisting Hitlerism or its equivalent with force of arms. Our patrols are helping now to assure delivery of the needed supplies to Britain. All additional measures necessary to deliver the goods will be taken."[62] This was followed by the so-called shoot-on-sight speech of September 1941 after a German submarine had torpedoed the American destroyer *Greer*. In a fireside talk Roosevelt declared: "This was piracy. . . . We have sought no shooting war with Hitler. We do not seek it now. But . . . when you see a rattlesnake poised to strike, you do not wait until he has struck before you crush him. . . . From now on, if German . . . vessels enter the waters, the protection of which is necessary for American defense, they do so at their own peril. . . . The sole responsibility rests upon Germany."[63] Military events had led up to the fringe of war which Roosevelt called "active defense," just short of outright war.

While the reelection renewed charismatic leadership, the scope of its authority was restrained in three different ways. A majority of voters was against a shooting war, keeping Roosevelt bound to his pledge: "No leader of democracy dares to carry a divided people into war."[64] Moreover, there was no majority in Congress able and willing to issue a declaration of war. The extension of the Selective Service Act was just barely accepted in the House in August 1941. Finally, Roosevelt personally and definitely preferred peace, hated the carnage and violence of war, and was reluctant to assume personal responsibility for getting the country into war. "His own personal hatred of war was deep and genuine, and it was this conviction that set him apart" from the interventionists.[65] While objectively restricted, Roosevelt could and did keep his pledge in good conscience. He could honestly say that the sole purpose of our policy "is to keep war away from our country and our people"[66] He could not be persuaded to ask Congress for a declaration of war.

The relationship between the antiwar pledge and the situation of unpreparedness is thus apparent. The lack of military readiness created the objective inadvisability, the pledge engendered the subjective reluctance, against entering the war voluntarily. Democratic charisma is thus adaptable to specific adverse conditions and adjustable to different internal convictions of the leader and different groups of public opinion. The infamous attack of the Japanese at Pearl Harbor removed these restrictions and opened up an opportunity for shifting from a constricted to an empowered charismatic leadership. Roosevelt could now face the military crisis directly and act as the fully authorized war leader, for the pledge was now superseded by the enemy's invasion[67] and created the necessity for a large-scale counterattack.

## PEACE GOALS AND EMPOWERED CHARISMA

Churchill and Roosevelt differed in their respective attitude to war and victory. Churchill's supreme goal was victory over the enemy. His was a heroic charisma because the celebrated victory was a heroic act. Roosevelt felt a deep repulsion towards war which to him was a carnage and slaughter of human beings resulting from organized but morally unacceptable violence. Once the country was attacked, then war and victory became unavoidable but necessary means to achieve a better international order that would guarantee a secure peace. Roosevelt thus became the simultaneous bearer of peaceful and militant charisma who sought to win the war so as to establish an international democratic order after victory. Militant charisma guided him in military preparation and the execution of the war, whereas peaceful charisma induced him to search for the principles of the new order before the Japanese attack and before America's entry into the shooting war. The personal friendship between Roosevelt and Churchill was reenforced when the British leader fell in line with Roosevelt's peace goals.[68]

Opposition to fascism and genuine democracy at home were the starting points for his new charismatic mission. He said on May 27, 1941, when he declared an unlimited national emergency in the war: "We will not accept a Hitler-dominated world or one in which the seeds of Hitlerism can again be planted and allowed to grow. We will accept only a world consecrated to freedom of speech and expression—freedom of every person to worship God in his own way—freedom from want—and freedom from terrorism."[69] The subsequent peace goals, based upon these freedoms, were initiated and expressed in four declarations that stated Roosevelt's personal and official beliefs.

In the Atlantic Charter of August 14, 1941, Roosevelt and Churchill laid down "certain common principles on which they based their hope for a better future of the world." The eight principles of international democracy included a rejection of any aggrandizement by the Allied powers. Territorial changes should be in accord with the freely expressed wishes of the people concerned. Self-government shall be restored in all countries that have been deprived of their sovereignty. All states shall have equal access to the trade and materials of the world. There shall be cooperation among all nations in improving labor standards, economic advancement, and social security. After defeat of the Nazis, all nations shall live safely in freedom from fear and wants. In the new peace all nations shall enjoy the freedom of the seas. All nations must eventually come to abandoning the use of force, to a disarmament of aggressor nations, to an agreement aiming at reduced armaments, and to a permanent system of general security.[70]

In desiring a new future, the two leaders aroused great enthusiasm with their peace goals. Among the many letters was one by Justice Frankfurter who said that the charter "appealed to the spiritual forces, the hopes, the purposes, the dreams, and endeavors of the human fraternity."[71] In his vision of the future Roosevelt combined peace with freedom and wanted the charter to apply to all humanity.

The civil rights day provided the opportunity for another declaration in honor of the one-hundred-fiftieth anniversary of the Bill of Rights. In his statement one week after the attack upon Pearl Harbor, Roosevelt renewed his and the nation's allegiance to individual liberties. "We will not, under any threat, or in face of any danger, surrender the guarantees of liberty our forefathers framed for us in the Bill of Rights. We hold with all the passion of our hearts and minds to those commitments of the human spirit."[72] The earlier Bill of Rights and the new charter were personalized and incorporated in the charismatic mission of the leader. His allegiance was widely cherished by his followers. Not less than 84 percent of the respondents in a sample were ready to vote for Roosevelt if there had been an election in January 1942.

The Declaration of the United Nations was signed at the same time by twenty-six nations. They all subscribed explicitly to the principles of the Atlantic Charter and confirmed that "complete victory over their enemies is essential to defend life, liberty, independence, and religious freedom, and to preserve human rights and justice in their own lands as well as in other lands." Guided by these principles, the signers pledged that each government would employ its full resources against the common enemy. Each government would cooperate in the military task and agreed "not to make separate armistice or peace with the enemies."[73] In this document there was a direct linkage between the war and the subsequent peace. Complete victory and effective cooperation in war were seen as the instruments for building up a democratic order for the whole world. The destruction of the war had to be accepted because war was the only available means for a just peace.

The Declaration of the Four Nations, accepted by the foreign ministers at Moscow in the fall of 1943, specified some of the previously accepted principles. The four nations will "act together in all matters relating to the surrender and the disarmament of the enemy." The nations "will establish a general international organization based on the principle of sovereign equality of all peace-loving states, open to membership by all such states . . . for the maintenance of international peace and security." After World War II the signing nations "will not employ their military forces within the territories of other states except for the purposes envisaged in this declaration and after joint consultation."[74] While the original draft was presented by the American representative, it was revised on two points and then also signed by the Soviet Union and China.

Supported by the Connally resolution of the Senate, a conference was called at Dumbarton Oaks for drawing up the charter of an international organization. The three delegations of the United States, Britain and the Soviet Union agreed upon the distinction between assembly and security council. The five leading powers were granted permanent membership while the rotating smaller members should be elected by the assembly. But no agreement could be reached as to when the permanent members could exercise their veto right. A compromise was reached at the Yalta Conference. Roosevelt proposed a majority vote for procedural questions and a unanimity of the permanent members on substantive issues. In cases of disputes, however, a permanent member should refrain from voting if it is a party in the conflict. Stalin opposed the voluntary abstention but gave in when Roosevelt and Churchill agreed accept two additional "Socialist republics" as members of the United Nations.[75]

The American government proposed at Yalta the Declaration on Liberated Europe. The three heads of state affirmed "their mutual agreement to concert during the temporary instability of liberated Europe the policies of these three governments in assisting the peoples liberated from the domination of Nazi Germany and the peoples of the former Axis satellite states of Europe to solve by democratic means their pressing political and economic problems." The freed nations were urged to form representative and democratic governments by holding free elections and be thereby responsive to the will of the peoples. In granting their assistance the three victorious governments would "consult at once on the measures needed to discharge these joint responsibilities."[76]

A comparison of these declarations reveals that they together comprised the principles for the coming democratic world order. The initiative and most of the ideas were contributed either by Roosevelt or his closest assistants. In making his proposals he was guided by two crucial insights. On the one hand, neither he nor the American people were willing to fight a war primarily out of fear or hatred. There had to be a hope that a better world was going to emerge from the terrible slaughter of the world war. It was a charismatically felt need to state a set of moral principles and to let the people know what the peace would look like before they would and could be asked to risk their lives and resources.[77] On the other hand, Roosevelt was not willing to win the war and lose the peace, as had happened to President Wilson. While he rejected another League of Nations, he did agree—after some hesitation— to a "permanent system of general security."[78]

In proposing and insisting upon the democratic nature of such a future peace, Roosevelt elevated himself to the position of a world leader. He took great pride in linking the internal freedoms of individuals with the external independence and voluntary cooperation among nations. Of course, there were millions who looked to Moscow for leadership. But Roosevelt and Churchill found reasons to believe that they would be able to work with the Soviet Union and to trust Stalin's word. They did not demand ideological concessions from Stalin, such as dissolving the Communist International. In spite of various disagreements, Stalin in the end did accept the declarations as if he genuinely believed in a democratic world order after victory.[79] Most important, in formulating these peace goals, Roosevelt came close to believing in fighting a just war.

## WAR GOALS AND PREPONDERANT CHARISMA

Defining war goals depended on the choice of a military strategy. General Eisenhower summed up the decision of the military leaders. "We've got to go to Europe and fight—and we have got to quit wasting resources all over the world—and still worse—wasting time."[80] While "Europe first" was a military decision, it was Roosevelt who made this strategy binding for all: "I am opposed to an American all-out effort in the Pacific against Japan. . . . Defeat of Japan does not defeat Germany. . . . Defeat of Germany means the defeat of Japan, probably without firing a shot or . . . losing a life."[81]

The American strategists had decided upon a cross-channel invasion in 1942, then in 1943, and finally in 1944. The British Joint Chiefs of Staff, however, stipulated three conditions for a successful campaign. There should be an increased air warfare to reduce the strength of the German fighters; there should be secrecy so as to keep the German defenders down to twelve mobile divisions; there should be an assault on the means of transportation so as to keep the German transfer down to fifteen qualified divisions in the first two months of combat. The lack of military preparations, the increasing demands of lend-lease shipments, and the time consuming concentration of forces for the final assault, compelled Roosevelt to agree to the diversions in North Africa and the defeat of Italy. It was primarily the negotiating skill of Roosevelt which overcame the disagreements among the military leaders and minimized the dissatisfaction of the Russians. A full agreement was reached at the conference of Teheran in November 1943 which set the date for the cross-channel invasion and synchronized the schedules for simultaneous offensives in west and east.

While Roosevelt acted mainly as a reconciler in the disputes about combat programs, his contribution was more direct and decisive in formulating the political goals of the war. Following a suggestion of his military chiefs, Roosevelt announced the basic war aim at the conference at Casablanca. "Peace can come to the world only by the total elimination of German and Japanese war power. . . . The elimination . . . means the unconditional surrender by Germany, Italy, and Japan. . . . It does not mean the destruction of the population of Germany, Italy, and Japan, but it does mean the destruction of the philosophies of these countries which are based on conquest and the subjugation of other peoples."[82] Although the principle involved was discussed at the conference, the timing and announcing were the unilateral actions of Roosevelt himself. In committing himself personally, Roosevelt wanted to ensure "that the war was won and that it would stay won."[83] He also wanted to make certain that the forces against the Axis powers would stay together at least until victory.

When it came to the treatment of postwar Germany, Roosevelt approved a proposal of the Departments of State and War that there should be a capitulation by the German forces, occupation of Germany by the victorious forces, elimination of the Nazis from government, release of all political prisoners, demobilization of German armed forces, and delivery of their weapons. In regard to the new government of Germany, there should be a "broadly based democracy, operating under a bill of rights to safeguard individual liberties." Allied controls should aim only at security and allow the German people "a tolerable standard of living."[84] This program was in full accord with the peace plans; retribution was to be limited to "their guilty, barbaric leaders."[85] Roosevelt acted as the bearer of preponderant charisma overestimating the power at his command.

In regard to the occupation of Germany, Roosevelt was faced with two different proposals. General Eisenhower objected to dividing Germany into "national sectors" and insisted upon one joint regime of occupation. Such an experiment would "quickly test the possibilities of a real quadripartite action"[86] (At a later date Eisenhower proposed a joint Anglo-American zone.) Roosevelt was impressed but did not commit himself. The Department of State argued against a punitive peace and a dismemberment of Germany, but supported the idea of zones of occupation. Zoning was originally proposed by the British and then adopted by the foreign ministers meeting in Moscow. Roosevelt accepted the three zones, but placed the western borders of the Russian zone about two hundred miles to the east, beginning with Stetin.[87] The final division into three zones and the establishment of the Allied Control Council, taking the place of a German government, was agreed upon on September 12, 1944, and was finalized at Yalta. France was then granted its own zone of occupation. Berlin was to be governed jointly but no access roads were formally specified. Roosevelt limited the use of American troops to two years and from the beginning saw the occupation of Germany as primarily a responsibility of her neighbors.[88]

There arose a distinction between military and economic policies of occupation. While the Joint Chiefs of Staff aimed primarily at law and order, and at creating the conditions for a new democratic state, Secretary Morgenthau presented a plan for a punitive policy of occupation. He proposed the elimination of the war-making industries in the Ruhr and Saar and the transformation of Germany into a primarily agricultural and pastoral economy. The Allied military government should assume no responsibility for the German economy, but direct the destruction of the war-essential factories and the dismantling of most other industries. "The primary responsibility for the policing of Germany . . . should be assumed by the military forces of Germany's continental neighbors."[89] At the second conference in Quebec, Roosevelt persuaded Churchill to accept this punitive plan as a guide for Allied occupation policy. At the same conference, Roosevelt agreed to ship lend-lease materials to Britain after victory, and consented to American soldiers to occupy the southern zone of Germany, leaving it to the British to destroy the Ruhr industries.

When a leak revealed the Morgenthau plan, there was pointed criticism of Roosevelt's approval of such a punitive peace plan. Facing the Republican opposition in the reelection campaign of 1944, Roosevelt dissolved the cabinet committee on Germany and divided the task of planning among the Treasury and War as well as State departments. The financial section of the subsequent directive 1067, issued by the Joint Chiefs of Staff, contained some of the crucial ideas of Morgenthau. After the successful reelection in 1944 Roosevelt supported Morgenthau's demand that the directive should be rewritten. Since the Departments could not agree on how much centralization of German administration and economy should be permitted, a compromise was reached that "left the initiative with the zone commanders."[90] The revised direction 1067 was officially in effect only for six weeks and then superseded by the Potsdam Agreement, but dismantling of industries was continued until May 1946 when output had fallen to 20 percent of capacity in the American zone.[91]

The agreements on the war aims of coordinated campaigns in east and west, the unconditional surrender, zones of occupation, and government by the victorious commanders were accompanied by conflicts over the fate of the Central European countries. How was this conflict between war and peace aims resolved?

The Declaration of Liberated Countries envisioned democratic governments, self-government, and national independence after liberation. But the Russian claim to regain their borders of 1939, and to insist upon "friendly" governments beyond these borders, created an insurmountable stumbling block. Long negotiations produced two compromises at Yalta. In regard to the borders, Roosevelt and Churchill did recognize the Russian western borders that had been established under the Hitler-Stalin Pact. In regard to democratic governments, Roosevelt and Churchill were unable to dislodge the puppet Communist governments established by Stalin, so they obtained an understanding that these provisional governments should be transformed into coalitions that included non-Communist leaders. The Declaration on Poland emphasized that the reorganized provisional government should be "pledged to the holding of free and unfettered elections as soon as possible on the basis of universal suffrage and secret ballot."[92] American and British ambassadors should meet with Molotov to work out the appropriate procedures. But this pledge and others were not kept by Stalin. With the exception of Finland, Czechoslovakia, and Greece, all other Central European countries were eventually ruled by Communist governments.

Roosevelt sincerely believed that in recognizing Soviet territorial gains, Stalin would permit genuine democratic governments in the smaller countries if they espoused a friendly foreign policy toward the Soviet Union, as it happened in Finland. Stalin broke his promise in this regard. It was only a few days prior to his death that Roosevelt recognized the deception. His response to a cable from Harriman was: "Averell is right; we cannot do business with Stalin. He has broken every one of the promises he made at Yalta."[93] Harriman had concluded his analysis of the Soviet intentions with the words: "We must clearly recognize that the Soviet program is the establishment of totalitarianism, ending personal liberty and democracy as we know and respect it."[94]

## ACHIEVEMENTS AND FAILURES

In his combination of peaceful and militant charisma, to be considered further in the next chapter, Roosevelt obtained several achievements and suffered several failures. His achievements contained elements of charismatism.[95] The enunciated peace goals not only established the superiority of democracy over dictatorship, but placed peace above war. Instituting the United Nations was for him a part of his obligation as a charismatic leader of the world who felt personally responsible for establishing a new democratic order for the whole world. Lend-lease shipments were not only assistance to partners in resisting aggression, but provided voluntarily granted brotherly help for most of which no compensation was asked. Unconditional surrender contained an element of contempt for the enemy who was regarded as barbaric and to whom the honor of a respected warrior had to be denied. Nothing but his complete capitulation in the field and the destruction of his political system at home was acceptable to the charismatic victors of democracy.

Most important has been the impact of Roosevelt's peaceful charismatic mission upon the self-image and attitudes of mind felt by the majority of the Americans. In not asking for reparations or other war booty in strongly suggesting the end of colonies, in pushing for a functioning United Nations, in providing for the needs of hungry people in the American zone and in Japan, and in supplying the funds and goods for the Marshall Plan, the Truman administration followed the Rooseveltian goals of a genuine international democratic order. The rise to world leadership was not accompanied by a popularly accepted imperialist ideology. Nor has the building up

of the greatest superpower in our time been generally justified by a feeling of nationalistic or chauvinistic pride. The occasional feelings of self-congratulation or superiority are regularly submerged by a dutiful sense of responsibility to fight for a sustained peace in the world.

The failures emanated partly from a need of vengeance to be visited upon the
enemy, and from the conflict between democracy and despotism. Not only
Morgenthau but also Roosevelt derived "moralistic legitimation"[96] from the Nazi
mass murder of Jews and Slavs. In keeping all the German people responsible for the
holocaust, Roosevelt temporarily violated his own peace goals which implied that
the Allied forces were waging a just war, just also to the oppressed peoples of the
defeated dictatorship.

The second failure originated from Communist despotism which led to Stalin's
breaching his promises on liberating the Central European countries, and his insistence on recapturing the loot flowing from the Hitler-Stalin Pact, and on transforming his German zone of occupation into a Communist state. It was primarily
Roosevelt's excessive esteem of his own charismatic ability of personal persuasion,
plus his willingness to give to the Soviets as much as possible, that induced Roosevelt
to minimize Stalin's despotism and overlook his policy of hegemony abroad. It took
the Marshall Plan and the building up of NATO to put a stop to Soviet expansionism in Europe.[97] In spite of the concerted efforts of Allied leaders and armies, world
war victory over fascism did not usher in a sustained peace.

In all, World War II did not confirm Weber's thesis that all major wars must
create military dictatorships in all belligerent countries. The leadership in Western
countries lay in the hands of those personifying militant charisma. Instead of democracies enlisting dictators to lead them in war, leaders of militant charisma directed the
war effort in the democracies. In Britain and France, the war crisis brought forth
new militant leaders, but in the United States there occurred a cumulation of electoral and militant charisma. The synergistic interactions of these charismata differed
from the one in the crisis charisma of the 1930s. Instead of charismatic power being
superimposed upon the civilian and military bureaucracy, these organizations become now an ally of the charismatic leader. But this happened only after an attempt
to deprive Roosevelt of control over industrial mobilization had failed.[98] Military
requirements and intensified patriotism induced the military and civilian bureaucrats
to respect Roosevelt's charismatic position and to collaborate with him in the war
effort. Military and charismatic leaders together created a series of new institutions.
Rather than bureaucracy creating a barrier for charismatic leadership, both cooperated effectively in fighting a defensive war.

While Roosevelt left a significant charismatic legacy after his death, nothing similar was accomplished by Churchill and de Gaulle. Churchill lost his sense of mission
even before the war ended. He confided to his physician in September 1944: "I have
the strong feeling that my work is done. I have no message. I had a message. Now I
can only say 'fight the damned Socialists!' I do not believe in their brave new

world."[99] While Roosevelt passed away naturally, Churchill was voted out of office soon after the war, and de Gaulle resigned as president when he was reduced to a figurehead. Dilution of the particular mission and termination of the war and of mass anxieties together brought an end to the leadership of militant charisma. This termination is still a variation of Weber's routinization because of the simultaneous decline of the leader's qualifications and the exhaustion of mass anxieties.[100]

# CHAPTER TEN

# CHARISMATIC RULERSHIP

AT THE END OF our journey, we can now point to the specific differences between the charismatic giants and luminaries. On the side of the leaders, the giants are invariably bearers of cumulative charisma. They combine either superhuman with natural charisma or peaceful with militant charismatic qualities. As a result of this fusion of two sources and qualities, charismatic leadership increases in strength, becomes durable for a certain period of time, enlarges its radius of appeal, and permits persistent goals and policies over a wide range of issues. Charismatic luminaries, however, are frequently limited to one charismatic source and quality. Most of them derive their inspiration and claim to leadership from natural charisma that is perceived as being fickle, highly variable in strength, and very uncertain for the future.

The two types of leaders face different situations in which they present their claim for leadership. Charismatic giants face an external crisis that is beyond their making. Seizing the need for extraordinary actions, they formulate for themselves a charismatic assignment that tells them how they have to meet the crisis and overcome it in the period of emergency. Indeed, the emergency becomes the external justifier for their charismatic rulership. Luminaries in advanced democracies face merely a randomly occurring mass emotionality to which they appeal for support. In most cases, mass emotionality is maneuverable and responds to the charismatic appeal that turns indifferent masses into charismatic followers.

In his summary statement about charismatic leadership, Weber points to the differences in origin and situations of the two kinds of leaders. "Genesis of charismatic rulership in the typical pure sense . . . always results from unusual, specifically political or economic situations or from extraordinary psychic, particular religious states, or from both together" (p.1121). It follows that charismatic movements do not arise randomly. They require either an external crisis or great psychological disturbances or both together. These favorable conditions provide indispensable opportunities for the leader and his paladins to claim his right to leadership because he alone has the capacity to overcome either the political and economic crisis or psychic disturbances.

Based upon our analysis, we can go one step beyond Weber. When the psychic disturbance is the only favorable condition facing a charismatic claimant, the result is a luminary who is often unable to establish and direct a charismatic rulership. This type of leader is typically the bearer of a euphoric charisma. His main accomplishment is the transformation of ordinary listeners into deeply involved charismatic followers. But the euphoric emotions last only for short periods. Such waves usually occur in electoral campaigns that can be effectively utilized by the leader and his paladins. If successful, the leader personifies electoral charisma who is able to capture the presidency, but faces extraordinary difficulties in making his charismatic authority effective relative to the other branches of government and public opinion. In spite of all efforts, such a leadership represents transitional charisma, unable to build up a charismatic rulership.

Charismatic giants are not only faced by exceptional crisis but also by psychological disturbances. The crises intensify the need for an exceptional leader who has to fulfill his charismatic assignment and also release the fears of his followers. Consequently, his is a crisis charisma that has the tendency to be sustained by the emergency, at least until the worst of the crisis has been overcome. None of these tasks can be performed without an effective charismatic rulership. The charismatic leader can rule only if he induces the other branches of government, public opinion, and the majority of the electorate to accept his goals and policies and permit his movement to establish new institutions and remove some of the old ones. If such new institutions are not installed or permitted to operate effectively, the rulership is bound to be emphemeral, in some respects akin to the luminaries, and subject to an earlier routinization of charisma.

Did the four types of crisis charisma, discussed in the three preceding chapters, build up effective rulerships or did they suffer from an early routinization of their qualities and policies? In order to answer this question, we shall summarize our findings schematically so as to facilitate our comparison.

It is obvious that each of the four leaders faced his own particular crisis that generated for each a fairly definite assignment. Each leader operated in his own particular subtype of democracy in which specific tensions developed that were overcome by the charismatic leaders because each one was endowed with a subtype of charisma appropriate for facing the specific crisis. With the exception of Wallace, all others succeeded in achieving their main goal that led to the installing of more or less adequate institutions.

While all four personalities personified crisis charisma, King and Wallace were not full-fledged charismatic giants. The reason lies in the peculiar relationship between the charismatic and noncharismatic features for their movement. Neither one of them was able to obtain control over one of the major political parties. Wallace relied heavily upon the resources and organization of the State of Alabama. King built up a mere coordinating organization that was composed of the assisting Negro churches. Both appealed only to distinct minorities in the electorate and thus had little chance of being elected to the presidency. The black movement could termi-

TABLE 10.1. CRISES, POLITICAL SYSTEMS, AND LEADERSHIP.

| | Constitutional Crisis | Traditional Crisis | Economic Depression | War Crisis |
|---|---|---|---|---|
| *Situations* | | | | |
| *Political Subsystems* | Ideal democracy | Privileged democracy | Political democracy | Bureaucratic democracy |
| *Types of Charisma* | Compassionate charisma | Traditionalized charisma | Reformist charisma | Militant charisma |
| *Personalities* | King | Wallace | Roosevelt | Churchill |
| *Main Results* | Universal voting rights | Defeat of legal segregation | Major economic reforms | Military victory |

311

nate disfranchisement only because of the coalition with Democratic administrations, whereas the Wallace movement failed in protecting the traditional order of segregation. There arises thus a distinction between the cases of crisis charisma. Major synergistic charisma is enjoyed only by those leaders who have control or full cooperation between the charismatic and noncharismatic components of the leadership, while those who do not present instances of minor synergistic charisma.

While Weber provided the name of charismatic rulership and mentioned most charismatic and a few noncharismatic features, the relationship between crisis and euphoric charisma is not clear, and the distinction between major and minor types of synergistic charisma is missing in his treatment. These descriptive defects we have tried to remove in our chapters. More deplorable are the deficiencies of his theory of charisma. He merely compared two phases of pure and routinized charisma. "Indeed, in its pure form charismatic authority . . . cannot remain stable, but becomes either traditionalized or rationalized or a combination of both" (p.246). This unfortunate phasing means that there is no adequate distinction of the crisis and euphoric charismata and that the period of growth of the charismatic rulership is almost completely missing.

The great variety of charismatic structures created a special problem for the theory of charisma. Since no single composite of all charismata was available, it appeared necessary to select one of its subtypes as the core for *the* theory of charisma. For this purpose Weber chose the charismatic community comprising only the leader, his paladins, and a few supporters. This effort amounts to a theory of a small group that turns into a movement; the emotional union is said to be replaced gradually by disenchantment and by the pressure of noncharismatic forces. There emerges Weber's law of routinization which must occur unavoidably as soon as the group is replaced by a developing movement. In our discussion of the euphoric charisma below, we will have to see whether this law adequately explains the experience of electoral charisma.

A prototypical, not an idealtypical, theory is necessary to explain how charismatic rulerships arise and how they are able to establish new institutions and experience cumulative charismata which are all personified by one leader. Such a second theory would have the rulership as its factual counterpart and would have to explain how and why the synergistic interactions of charismatic and noncharismatic components strengthen the power of the leader to such an extent that he is able to modify the political system of democracy. Since the empirical features of crisis charisma have been presented above, we now have to condense our findings by stating definite propositions for a theory of synergistic charisma.

## THEORY OF SYNERGISTIC CHARISMA

A theory of synergistic charisma consists of historically derived propositions on the linkages among different subtypes of charisma and between the charismatic as well as noncharismatic features operative in charismatic rulerships.[1] Most important for our purposes are relations between conditions and exceptional qualities, cumulation of different subtypes of charisma, merger of charismatic and noncharismatic components, and the intended and unintended consequences of charismatic rulership.

A list (table 10.2) of the charismatic and noncharismatic components can readily be distilled from our previous chapters. The two sets include the following:

TABLE 10.2. COMPONENTS OF CHARISMATIC RULERSHIP.

| Charismatic Features | Noncharismatic Features |
| --- | --- |
| 1. Inner Voice | 1. Political Parties |
| 2. Personal Magnetism | 2. Mass Movements |
| 3. Devoted Paladins | 3. Guided Public Opinions |
| 4. Enthusiastic Followers | 4. Missionary Ideologies |
| 5. Committed Supporters | 5. Neutralized Armed Forces |
|  | 6. State Bureaucracies |

While one can separate logically the charismatic from the noncharismatic components, the crucial question is how the coexistence leads to interactions that create synergistic charisma. This kind of interlinkage is indispensable for the rise and strength of charismatic rulership. For instance, if the leader is not elected president, then there can be no fusion of legal with charismatic authority and legitimacy. Without official position, the leader cannot coordinate the actions of the masses with the actions of the state, and their joint impact cannot generate significant political or economic reforms. It is thus the purpose of this section to present propositions that deal with our main findings on synergistic charisma in democracy.

Our first and conditional proposition concerns the locus and rise of the leader's exceptional qualities. We can readily follow Weber's thesis of charismatic dormancy. "Charismatic powers can be developed only in people or objects in which the germ already existed but would have remained dormant unless evoked by some ascetic or other regimen" (p.400). A gestation period is required for the potential qualities to become actual qualities in the prospective leader. The greater his emotional depth, the more genuine is the subsequent ability to act as a magnet. The stronger his belief in his exceptional calling to greatness, the greater his inner sense of obligation to lead the masses. The gestation period will come to an end when he feels an inner certainty of being chosen *the* leader (p.539).

Second is a contingent proposition that is concerned with the self-explanation of the charismatic qualities. Most of the democratic giants attributed their calling to greatness, to an unspecified destiny. The calling required an extraordinary effort to prepare himself for his great tasks. On the one hand, there was a discovery of the ability to understand the emotions of others and to turn these emotions into admiration for himself. On the other hand, the charismatic aspirant enlarged his innate abilities by acquiring many talents of a successful politician. The intertwining of these abilities made themselves felt by attracting to himself a group of paladins. In forming a charismatic group, the members were not only bound by loyalty to the leader, but also turned into political activists who spread the gospel that the leader was the greatest political genius. In democracy, however, the paladins hardly ever formed a "charismatic aristocracy" because they were used by the leader to perform primarily specialist services in promoting the goals and policies of the leader.

The third is a sequential proposition that deals with the reaction of a mass following in response to the leader's charismatic appeal. When the appeal takes on an emotional outburst and/or a missionary zeal, the listeners experience an emotional union and a kind of vicarious participation in the ideals of the leader. Subsequently, union and participation lead to "a subjective or internal reorientation" which entails "a radical alteration of the central attitudes and directions of action with a completely new orientation of all attitudes toward the different problems of the world" (p.245). The consequence of such a radical alteration is the formation of a charismatic mass following, the emotional and spiritual attachment of which enables the leader and paladins to establish a new political force.

The fourth proposition is deterministic in nature because the course of action taken by the leader and his followers is determined by the elective principle. Whenever the mass following provides a potential voting group, the leader enters the political competition and eventually runs for the highest office in the state. Political campaigns subject the leader and his followers to the critique of other parties. In response, the charismatic appeal is enlarged by engaging in political propaganda, the noncharismatic component of which seeks to arouse public opinion in favor of the charismatic group. The struggle between parties is decided by a plebiscite in which each contender seeks to outbid his rivals. "The plebiscite has been the specific means of deriving the legitimation of authority from the confidence of the ruled" (p.267). The consensus of the majority of voters determines who shall be the leader of the country. As a result, presidential democracies provide a readily available electoral structure that can elevate the charismatic leader to the top of the government without any constitutional change, whereas some constitutional revision is usually required in parliamentary democracy (e.g. in the case of de Gaulle). Instead of being transitional, giants regard electoral charisma as one crucial segment of their cumulative charisma.

The fifth proposition deals with the coordination of charismatic and legal authorities in the process of establishing the charismatic rulership. This phase begins with the leader becoming the head of the government. Once in power, the leader will appoint his paladins to political positions in the state, who act as his agents of confidence and seek to supervise the regular bureaucracy of the state. At the same time, the elected leader performs the legal functions of his office which he seeks to combine and reconcile with his tasks as charismatic leader. His authority to lead is thus partly derived from legal and charismatic legitimacies. In exercising both authorities, the leader employs his political power to divide the prevailing institutions into two categories. There is the one group that supports and complements the tasks of his charismatic agents, while the other group is either neutral or opposed to the charismatic "upstarts." As a result of this division, the leader seeks to undercut the deterrent institutions, promotes the supportive institutions and, insofar as possible, incorporates them as noncharismatic components in his charismatic rulership. Weber's thesis that institutions indicate routinization does not hold for the rulership.

The sixth is a substitutable proposition that concerns the shift from collective to personalized leadership and decision making in government. The power of government is redistributed among its branches and a greater share is arrogated by the executive, at the expense of the legislative and judiciary branches. There arises a prerogative of presidential power in democracy. The process of making decisions "takes place under pressure of feeling that there can be only *one* correct decision, and it is a matter of duty to arrive at" it unitedly (p.267). All the branches and departments feel morally obliged to take the leader's will into account and assure themselves of his approval. In case of divergencies, the will of the leader is substituted for the collective decisions of other agencies, whatever may be their constitutional rights. This substitution is a result of the admiration felt by the many who defer to him because he "knows best." As a result, the unity of purpose and the priority of policies are not seen as an expression of dictatorship of the leader, but are accepted in a spirit of loyalty to the leader.[2] Charismatic worship does not tolerate any disagreement with, much less criticism of, the exalted leader. He himself is not motivated by the desire to accumulate power, but he merely uses power to implement the ideologies of his mission or to meet the contingencies of the crisis. Appropriation of power and economic advantages by the paladins is not favored by the leader.

The seventh proposition is developmental since it seeks to discover the reasons for the growth of charismatic rulership. In comparing and evaluating different goals, there emanates a distinct preference for the ideologies favored by the leader. Other ideologies are either rejected or accepted only insofar as they can be made compatible with the ideals of the leader. Selecting and implementing policies become the tasks of supportive institutions. Depending upon the special assignment, suspected institutions will be either outlawed or given new assignments, or a whole range of new institutions will be built, usually outside of the existing bureaucracy. The decisive criterion is whether the new institutions embody the spirit of the new ideologies, and whether they are innovative enough in their methods to implement adequately the new policies.[3] The unavoidable result is that the public sector is significantly enlarged and that the number of governmental employees increases appreciably. The new offices and agencies, often defamed as the "alphabetical chaos," constitute a pseudocharismatic bureaucracy because it is hierarchically organized but depends for its very existence upon the charismatic leader and his policies.

The eighth sequential proposition pertains to the new power structure in the charismatic rulership. Prior to the ascent to political power, the leader and his followers operate as one power bloc in a political democracy, the ideals of which are subjected to an ethical interpretation by the leader. Victory by the leader in the elections by a substantial margin ushers in three significant changes. There is first the widespread euphoria of the charismatic believers who nourish great expectations for the future. The millions suffering from the depression hope and pray for an effective relief from their miseries. The old ruling organizations give up their opposition to the charismatic leader, join his supporters as temporary allies, in the hope of modifying his policies in their favor.

Almost all American business organizations asked for governmental assistance, not for private gain, but assertedly as a means for promoting recovery. Forced by the depression to adopt a recovery policy, the new government adopted the National Recovery Act and allowed the private trade associations to write the codes of behavior for industries. This alliance soon disintegrated when business again became profitable, and when the leader finally decided to modify his goal of social justice for workers into a decisive support of trade unions. A class conflict penetrated into the recovery policy of the government. The conflict culminated into the sit-down strikes in mass production industries which were furiously resisted by the most powerful employers. Once the leader was reelected by a landslide, class harmony was transformed into class conflict, first between employers and trade union and then between the leader and business organizations.[4]

The uniform power structure was replaced by a dual power structure. The charismatic movement and rulership were confronted by infuriated business groups in economics, and the coalition between Republicans and Southern Democrats in politics. There emerged a counterpolity[5] that organized a frontal attack upon the charismatic rulership. Not anticipating this shift in the power structure, Roosevelt unintentionally played in the hands of his opponents when he proposed a reform of the Supreme Court. The slogan of dictatorship enabled his enemies to split public opinion. They organized a well-financed anticharismatic movement that succeeded in tabling his judiciary reform and it stymied almost all of his future charismatic policies.

The ninth proposition refers to the relationship between synergistic charisma and economic reform. Guided by his goal of social justice, the leader promotes decent wage rates and social security for laborers. Wage disputes are to be settled by mediation, not by collective bargaining or by strikes. The leader is not eager to establish industrial unionism, which problem "was substantially resolved by civil war."[6] The labor rebellion leads to a new kind of trade union which is essentially legalized through the provisions of the Wagner Act and related laws. The leader supports the Wagner Bill only after the Senate was ready to pass it even without his support. He merely tolerates the sit-down strikes when he refuses to have the workers thrown out of the factories by the military. It was up to the workers, not to the charismatic leader, to establish their new institutions.[7] Accepted at first pragmatically by the leader, these noncharismatic features in the Wagner Act become a part of synergistic charisma only by the Congress acting first, and then through an alliance between the leader and the more progressive trade union leaders.

In fact, a distinction developed between synergistic interaction and elective affinity in the relationship between the leader and the supportive but private organizations. The principles of equality for agriculture and social justice for labor covered and justified, in Roosevelt's mind, the respective farm and labor policies of the New Deal. In the view of the supportive organizations of laborers and farmers, the charismatic leader and his administration provided only some assistance but could not prescribe the pattern of their institution building.

There thus emerged a most important differentiation between charismatic mass following and the allied mass organizations. The mass following was headed and directed by the leader, included the paladins and the charismatic apparatus, one segment of the political party as well as the charismatic constituency of voters in elections, especially the farm and labor voters. The mass organizations were directed by indigenous leaders, who represented members according to their occupational positions in the economy, and promoted primarily their specialized occupational and class interests.[8] In doing so, they utilized their power to restructure the respective markets, accepting thereby the assistance of the charismatic leader. Both movements belonged to the New Deal, but only the mass following was a part of synergistic charisma.[9] In the conflict with the ruling organizations, however, the supportive organizations usually stood on the side of the leader, thereby underlining the duality of the power structure in the second phase of charismatic rulership.[10]

The tenth proposition considers the relation between charisma and bureaucracy in the rulership. The leader finds most of the departments and regulatory commissions ill equipped in tackling the tasks of recovery and reform. Roosevelt adopted two strategies in meeting the bureaucracy. He deliberately created many agencies outside of the regular bureaucracy. More than four-fifths of the 250,000 employees hired were exempted from the civil service requirements.[11] The emergency agencies served the president as a means of counteracting bureaucratic resistance. In parceling out authority, the overlapping was often deliberate. Coordination among the irregular agencies was seen as the prerogative of the leader who built agencies on top of each other and had the highest agency report to himself exclusively. A strictly bureaucratic hierarchy was suspected by him as an attempt to curtail his power. The proposal of having one board directing industrial mobilization for war was rejected by him with the following words: "I would simply be abdicating the presidency to some other person."[12] In making himself the "general manager," the charismatic leader largely succeeded in directing the activities of the pseudocharismatic bureaucracy.

He failed, however, in getting effective control over the regular bureaucracy. Early in 1937 he presented to the Congress a bill for reorganizing the federal administration. Aiming at rational management by centralizing all responsibility in the hands of the president, the bill proposed six presidential assistants, one director for the civil service, an integrated salary and promotion scheme, a separation of administering from auditing, two new departments for welfare and conservation, and placement of all regulatory commissions into their respective departments. The subsequent debate revealed that the proposed reorganization had no sizable constituency of its own. An avalanche of interest groups, in and outside of the bureaucracy, flooded the Congress with objections, strengthening the opposition in the legislature. The bill was emasculated in the Senate with thirty-two amendments and defeated in the House in 1938. This result amounted to a reversal of political forces. Instead of the bureaucracy pushing for rationalizing the charismatic rulership, no Weberian principle of rationality was held by the opponents to the reform. The opposed votes in the Congress were either motivated by personal interests—gain, power, or prestige—or by hatred of the charismatic leader. It was traditionalism in the form of defending special but past interests that prevented the leader from establishing his control over the regular bureaucracy. Many of the bureaucrats joined the counterpolity against the charismatic leader.

The eleventh consequential proposition traces the impact of charismatic rulership upon the prevailing political and economic systems. While Weber defined the state in terms of its ultimate means of a legitimate use of physical force, Roosevelt's ethical view emphasized the capacity of the government to contribute to human betterment. Roosevelt's rulership exemplified a state that primarily served the people, assisting especially the disadvantaged groups and those suffering from the misery of the depression. The services provided fell into three categories. There were first the relief payments for those who did not have any form of regular income. Then there were the services aimed at removing defects inherent in the economic system. Remedies were granted as specific rights that guaranteed a specified benefit in the future, as in the case of the social insurances.[13] Finally, most significant were the newly established institutions, such as collective bargaining, that provided a framework or at least a procedure for private as well as governmental actions. Continuous availability of such institutions was assured only if the beneficiaries could wield the political power required for their defense. The result of granting these services, usually available without or below cost, was a significant increase in the public sector. The most obvious indicators of such growth were the substantial rise in governmental expenditures and employees. Since many expenditures were transfer payments, the government undertook a redistribution of private incomes. For those payments financed out of budgetary deficits, there was also some growth of the private sector. While not fully accepting the rationale of deficit financing, the charismatic ruler was not only very proud of the assistance granted, but he transformed the federal government into an agency of human betterment.

In the economy, too, reforms divided themselves into different categories, as seen from the point of view of the groups initiating and benefiting from such actions. First place took those measures which were initiated or justified by the leader's charismatic ethic, as described in chapter 8. The other segment of reforms pertained to the field of industrial relations and primarily benefited different groups of laborers. Additionally, there was an extensive body of reforms that were either initiated or favored farmers and their organizations. There was a fourth attempt to assist businesses, but only some programs favoring small businesses—Robinson Patman Act—were successful, while many of the reforms aiming at big business were either rejected or frustrated. In seeking a common denominator of these reforms, we can accept Roosevelt's own term, social and economic security. He included all those reforms that sought "a greater physical and mental and spiritual security for the people of this country."[14] In their intention, if not always in their effect, the reforms together established one distinct sector of the economy that we can call security capitalism, created by or during the New Deal.[15]

In all, synergistic charisma grew into an effective leadership because of the four fusions and the seven combinations between charismatic and noncharismatic components of the interacting leader and followers. These linkages can be condensed, as in table 10.3.

TABLE 10.3. CHARISMATIC LINKAGES.

| Fusions | Combinations |
| --- | --- |
| Inate + Acquired abilities of leader | Leader + Party head |
| Devotion + Activism of paladins | Appeal + Propaganda |
| Emotional union of leader + Followers | Leader + Charismatic apparatus |
| Organizational core + Mass following | Mission + Ideologies |
| | Legal + Charismatic authority |
| | Regular + Countervailing bureaucracy |
| | Charismatic + Oppositional power |

While these linkages were not necessarily fixed, since changes in personnel did take place, the fusions and combinations remained intact through most of the charismatic rulership. The interactions did assure an exceptional resilience and durability of the rulership.[16] Instead of being transitional, the leader and followers did succeed in renewing the authorities and legitimacies and in institutionalizing many of the adopted policies.

Substantively, charismatic leadership accomplished two major reforms. Politically, the anxieties of mass democracy were replaced by the steadiness of leadership and the enthusiasm of the masses for the leader and his policies. Most of the policies found popular support and often vicarious participation by the masses. The limited government was transformed into the service state which promoted primarily the welfare of the people. Charismatic rulership achieved a revitalization of democracy in, and partly because of, the Great Depression.

Economically, charismatic rulership promoted the two policies of recovery and of reform. The former fell short of full employment, mainly because the leader and his advisers hesitated too long in adopting an adequate policy of deficit financing. Economic reform was greater than the one justified by the ethical principles of the leader. It was primarily the linkage of the ethics with the interests of the allies that together achieved a significant reform in agriculture and in industrial relations.

While Weber was greatly impressed by revolutionary charisma, he did not specifically single out the charismatic giants and he largely overlooked charismatic rulership as an agency of political and economic reforms. This raises the fundamental question of how and why such a reform was possible? Was reform an accidental side effect or can we locate specific causes that made reform the major goal of the charismatic giants in democracy?

## TRANSITIONAL CHARISMA

In examining the origin of charismatic movements, Weber pointed to two situations impregnated with emotional opportunities. As we have seen, the growth of giants depends upon some deep but external crisis. It was the great depression that provided the exceptional opportunity for Franklin D. Roosevelt. It was in a severe military crisis only that Churchill became the national leader of Britain. This meeting of the charismatic leader with his external opportunity suggests an important generalization. Charismatic rulerships are most likely to occur in severe crises. Periods of tranquility are not prone to promote the rise of such rulerships. Seen from point of view of the participating conditions, giants appear as bearers of crisis charisma because it is their historical task to overcome the particular crisis imposed upon their people.[17]

There is a second opportunity for charismatic success that arises in the psychological field and consists of mass anxieties of great force. While every major crisis is accompanied by mass excitements, the reverse is not necessarily true. While originating in the psychological sphere, the situation of mass democracy fosters the potential rise of mass emotionality. Charismatic leaders, if successful, become bearers of euphoric charisma. Candidates in political campaigns appeal to the emotions by either treating the masses as malleable crowds or as potential followers. If the charismatic magnetism is successful, then the leader of such a movement tends to become the bearer of electoral charisma.

In order to come to grips with this electoral charisma, we have to go briefly beyond giantism and consider just one of the charismatic luminaries. Luminaries typically seek to personify electoral charisma, but the rivalry among themselves reduces their influence. Various circumstances often prevent them from reaching their goal of a charismatic rulership.[18] President John F. Kennedy became an active luminary who effectively moved towards giantism. We shall thus select his experience for bringing out the pecularities of electoral charisma, not preceded by a crisis.

Given the essential facts of mass democracy, mass emotionality is a potentially charismatic force. When responding to the charismatic appeal, these emotions become focused on and attached to the charismatic aspirant. The most important contribution of the televised debate between Nixon and Kennedy was that the latter was able to display his special qualities to sensitive listeners. Subsequently, "wildly cheering crowds surged around him as he crisscrossed the country. One has an unmistakable feeling when a campaign catches fire. . . . It was plainly happening to Kennedy in the third week of October, 1960."[19] But the candidate himself addressed these emotions only indirectly. "This race is the contest between the comfortable and concerned, between those who believe that we should rest and lie at anchor and drift and . . . those who want to move this country forward into the 1960s."[20] There was thus a strong emphasis upon compassion and action, but not upon love and personal loyalty, for generating an emotional union. The emotional frenzy was not reached in the last weeks so that Kennedy almost lost the election.

Actually, the charismatic appeal of Kennedy in 1960 had been preceded by more conspicuous efforts in his earlier campaigns. To be sure, in none of these elections did the candidate indicate an inner voice or an endowment of divine grace. There was only an oblique reference to a Supreme Being. Kennedy quoted Lincoln: "I see the storm coming and I know that His hand is in it. If He has a place and work for me, I believe I am ready."[21] But already there were all the indications of superhuman energy and charismatic self-assurance in the prior senatorial campaigns of Kennedy.

While the inner urge to greatness was only implied, there was plenty of evidence for the candidate's possession of natural charisma in 1952. His personal charm was especially effective with the ladies who felt his magnetic power most vividly. The special impact of this appeal was well illustrated by the remark of a leading Republican: "What is there about Jack Kennedy that makes every Catholic girl in Boston between eighteen and twenty-eight think it is a holy crusade to get him elected?"[22] John F. Kennedy won by a majority of seventy thousand votes for his first Senate seat in 1952.[23] In the reelection of 1958 Kennedy increased his margin by 847,608 votes which was the greatest landslide scored for any office of either party in his state. While the organization and money of the Kennedy family helped significantly, the overwhelming vote amounted to an electoral charisma with a vengeance.[24]

In the seven primaries of 1960, which Kennedy won, and the subsequent campaign, he was handicapped by opposition to his religion. "What they objected to was the imposition . . . of Catholic standards . . . on education, censorship, marriage and divorce—and other matters. . . . Ultimately, they feared that American freedom would give way to Catholic power." On the central issue of whether he was guided by the Constitution or papal doctrine, Kennedy took a clear stand: "The First Amendment to the constitution is an infinitely wise one. There can be no question of federal funds being used for support of parochial schools. It is unconstitutional under the First Amendment as interpreted by the Supreme Court. I am opposed to the federal government extending support to sustain any church or its schools."[25] While this explicit commitment to the Constitution persuaded some Protestants, there is little doubt that Kennedy barely won the election because of his charismatic magnetism, and he was close to a failure because of his religion.[26]

Kennedy's ambivalent position on political ideology also created much dispute during the campaign of 1960. On the one hand, he wanted to be nominated by the liberals. His brother Robert said on the eve of the convention in Los Angeles: "I want to say a few words about civil rights. We have the best civil rights plank the Democratic party has ever had. I want you fellows to make it clear to your delegations that the Kennedy forces are unequivocally in favor of this plank and that we want it passed by the convention."[27] On the other hand, Kennedy chose Senator Johnson as his running mate. This created an uproar in the convention. Johnson stood at that time for Southern conservatism and racial distinctions. Instead of adhering consistently to the ideology of racial integration, Kennedy pushed for unity within the party, at a time when his organization was taking over the Democratic party. Of the two noncharismatic components in the convention, ideology and party, organization counted for more than did ideology.[28]

In his inaugural address, the new president underlined two themes. One was the request for internal unity, sacrifice, and cooperation. "And so my fellow Americans ask not what your country can do for you—ask what you can do for your country." The other was a promise of a global defense of freedom. "Let every nation know, whether it wishes us well or ill, that we shall pay any price, bear any burden, meet any hardship, support any friend, oppose any foe to assure the survival and success of liberty."[29] But his call of getting the country moving again was not easy to implement. Destiny did not grant him his wish to establish a forceful and decisive charismatic rulership immediately after election.

Soon after his inauguration, there began a power conflict between the new president and the Congress. Neither the tiny majority in his own election, nor the losses of two senators and twenty-two members of the House by the party in 1960, presented a mandate for an effective charismatic rulership. Since the leaders of the House had been returned to office with more impressive majorities, most of them felt free to disregard or overrule the bills proposed by the new president. Although popular consensus was not the consequence, but the cause, of charismatic rulership (p.266), the effective and relative power of the new president was measured in terms of the number of excess votes garnered in the presidential election.

The conflict between the president and the House amounted to a clash between a push for change and a resisting traditionalism. In conference with Speaker Rayburn, Kennedy had formulated five legislative priorities which included a minimum wage rate of $1.25 per hour, federal aid to education, substantial assistance to public housing, funds for revitalizing depressed areas, and medical aid for the aged through the Social Security system. Acceptance of these bills had been blocked by the Rules Committee prior to Kennedy's election. Not in charismatic fashion, but by "patronage, preferment, party loyalty, and power"[30] did Kennedy and Rayburn succeed in removing this roadblock to new legislation.

There arose considerable optimism for legislative innovations which expressed itself in a series of messages and bills presented by the new president to the Congress. This optimism "had been created by Kennedy's excellence as a campaigner and his personal charisma."[31] But the presidential proposals ran counter to the various traditions developed in the Congress over a long period of time. Kennedy's minimum wage bill in the House was opposed by a conservative bill that insisted upon a very restrictive definition of the commerce clause of the Constitution. The president's reformulated education bill ran afoul of two other traditional institutions. The conservatives insisted upon the rights of states to determine educational policies, and others fought for continued separation of state from church. When it was whispered that federal aid would be made contingent upon school desegregation, the modified Rules Committee killed all education bills. These established traditions smothered the charismatic influence in the Congress. "John Kennedy had lost Congress. Nothing could put his education package together again. . . . He could be defied with impunity."[32] Weber's one thesis that charismatic leadership will be frustrated by entrenched traditionalism was here confirmed (p.246). On being soundly defeated in the Congress, Kennedy's electoral charisma lasted just a few months with the legislative bodies. It was a typical example of a transitional charisma which was limited to the short period of the last phase of the campaign and the first months after his inauguration. The charismatic phase was largely terminated by the coalition of Southern Democrats and Republicans who acted as the political contingent of the ruling organizations in the country. But the "internal reorientation" of most of the followers was still alive in spite of the barrier.

While in office Kennedy shifted from an electoral to a heroic kind of charisma. Unintentionally, his military policy began with a defeat. Approved by Eisenhower, the Central Intelligence Agency (CIA) had organized the Cuban Brigade for the purpose of overthrowing the Castro regime. While giving his consent, Kennedy stipulated that there should be only a large-scale infiltration that would usher in an internal revolution. The revised plan was accepted by him "on the categorical understanding that there would be no direct United States military support," especially no air cover of the landing troops. But his decision was also influenced by his belief in a charismatic invincibility, "by his enormous confidence in his own luck . . . he had the Midas touch and could not lose."[33] There was thus an unspoken desire for a heroic deed. When the campaign failed, Kennedy was forced to assume the responsibility for the misadventure. There was a most surprising response of the American people. A gallup poll reported that 82 percent expressed their support of the president.[34] Just as the British people refused to accept their defeat at Dunkirk, so the American people—patriotism intermingled with charismatic euphoria—approved the deeds of their president who could do no wrong. Even in defeat he was seen as a hero, not in need of having to deliver on his promises.

The real heroic deed of the charismatic leader came in the Cuban missile crisis of 1962. The discovery of Soviet missiles and their sites in Cuba raised the question of whether this military penetration into the Western Hemisphere should be tolerated or stopped. From the beginning of the crisis Kennedy took the position that this secret move had to be resisted and the missiles withdrawn from Cuba. It was decided to impose a naval quarantine upon Cuba for intercepting the Russian ships, and to reenforce this action by a concentration of the regular armed forces in Florida, ready to strike if and when absolutely necessary. While the Organization of American States approved of the quarantine, a prospective invasion was not considered. At first Khrushchev proposed a swap of withdrawing American missiles in Turkey against Soviet ones in Cuba. This swap was rejected and a date was set for American military action. It was only then that Khrushchev accepted Kennedy's demand that the sites be destroyed and the missiles taken back to Russia. The overbearing Khrushchev got panicky and did surrender. The effective withdrawal of offensive weapons was Kennedy's heroic deed. He had been victorious in his policy that this nation would "regard any nuclear missiles launched from Cuba against any nation in the Western Hemisphere as an attack by the Soviet Union on the United States, requiring a full retaliatory response upon the Soviet Union."[35] Withdrawal was not only a victory for charismatic leadership but the deed also restored America's confidence in her own power.

The heroic action presents a typical example of Weber's heroic charisma (p.267). The successful quarantine revealed the exceptional qualities of the leader whose qualities justify popular legitimacy of his charismatic authority. In its particular setting, however, Kennedy's feat was unique. In its inception and execution, the plan presented a "climatic period," a segmental charisma in the form of a hero. But the execution was possible only because of the preceding electoral charisma which gave the president the inner assurance and readiness to undertake the great performance, certain of the overwhelming approval of his countrymen.[36] If his life had been spared, there would have been a sequence of two segmental charismata—separated by a time lag—that would have become cumulative in the reelection of 1964. Cumulation of electoral and heroic charisma would have transformed the luminary into a gigantic leader, capable of establishing a genuine charismatic rulership.

While the bullets of the assassin prevented the completion of the charismatic leadership, Kennedy's experience permits us to infer two important principles that greatly enlarge Weber's radius of charisma. One principle enlarges the causes for the rise of giants; the other suggests a possible sequence of subtypes of leaders, climaxing in the phenomenon of cumulative charisma.

In terms of external conditions, a charismatic leader may spring from (1) severe constitutional, economic or military crises, (2) sporadic mass emotionality, or (3) sudden but dangerous threats to the security of the nation or the interdependence of the polity. Each event is external to the charismatic leaders and cannot be created by them but only seized at the right moment of time. If and when that happens, the external events become causes for charismatic leaders and movements.

Each cause may arise independently or separately or the causes may be so inter-linked that they become either single or multiple causes for charismatic rulerships. When causes and movements meet, we have to deal either with crisis charisma, euphoria charisma, or shock charisma. When all these causes and movements merge into each other, we are faced by a developmental charismatic rulership. Once in office, the leader is not free in the choice of his policies. He has to come to grips with the extraordinary events and seek to overcome them. The particular causes impose upon him fairly specific charismatic assignments that tend to climax into the reform of certain institutions. The shock charisma reenforces the euphoria charisma and both together open another road to charismatic rulership.

A similar extension and differentiation affects the exceptional qualities on the personal side of charisma. In various contexts, Weber has distinguished between alternative and cumulative charismatic qualities, the former being borne by different personalities and the latter being combined in and by the same person. Militant and peaceful charismata can call for different leaders, acting in diverse situations. Natural and supernatural charismata may develop together and become different abilities of the same aspirant. As Kennedy's experience suggests, a leader may start with one quality and subsequently develop another, so that electoral and heroic charismata follow each other, but then become cumulative and segmental over time. The result is the principle of combined or cumulative charisma personified in the same leader.

An important lesson may be derived from Kennedy's experience for the theory of charisma. Weber's theory of transitional charisma is plausible only if electoral charisma occurs in complete isolation from any other charismatic development. Such an isolated charisma has just two phases: the rise of the euphoria in the electoral campaign and the subsequent routinization after the inauguration of the new president. His legislative program will be rejected by parliament, and the entrenchment of traditional forces in that institution will frustrate the charismatic feelings and eliminate all opportunities for a development toward gigantic charisma. If and when that happens, the law of routinization applies only to such a transitional charisma, but is not relevant for any other charisma.

The revival of Kennedy's opportunities shows that electoral charisma does not have to appear in isolation and does not have to be suffocated. Another crisis can appear that revives electoral charisma. That is likely to happen if the leader still feels his extraordinary qualities, if the followers still keep their "internal reorientation," and if the leader knows how to master the new crisis. The disaster of the invasion of Cuba shows the inherent uncertainty of such military undertakings. But Roosevelt as well as Kennedy eventually learned how to shift from a peaceful to a militant charismatic leadership. The military shock enabled them to combine electoral with heroic charisma. While elements of rational calculations were essential for military preparations and executions, such rationalities merely enhanced the opportunities for military victory. Instead of routinization, there was only a change in the sequence of events. Weber's Caesar had to achieve military victory before his special qualities could be sanctioned by means of a plebiscite. In the American experience, however, electoral charisma occurred prior to, and was one of the causes for, the subsequent victory and the incorporation of heroism into cumulative charisma of the same leader.

As Churchill and Kennedy experienced it, electoral and militant charisma can occur in isolation for a certain period of time. If nothing else would have occurred, the law of routinization certainly would have become effective. Such transitional charismata may happen again in the future, but we cannot say that they must happen. Weber's grand generalization is not confirmed by our findings. "Every charisma is on the road from a turbulently emotional life that knows no economic rationality to a slow death by suffocation under the weight of material interests; every hour of its existence brings it nearer to its end" (p.1120). We can say only that every transitional charisma is likely to be suffocated by such forces.

When there is a combination of electoral and heroic charisma, the charismatic movement is likely to experience a revival and soon is on the road to gigantice charisma. There emerge two different roads to charismatic rulerships. A peaceful leader overcomes an economic crisis by means of reform, the institutionalization of which modifies the prevailing economic system. A militant leader wins over the enemy by military victory, combines electoral with heroic charisma, and the subsequent peace treaty institutionalizes a new international order of the world. Roosevelt experienced both modes of charismatic rulership successively. While our statement of the factual evidence seeks to cover both roads, the theoretical propositions above deal only with the peaceful rulership and would have to be supplemented for the militant road, if completion had been intended.

## Pure Type of Weberian Theory

As it happened, Weber did not include either kind of rulership into his theory of charisma. Even his theory of transitional charisma was not based upon the findings of isolated electoral charisma. Weber's theory contained an ahistorical element. Factually, he was engaged in a comparative study of charismatic leaders in history, leading to the description of unstable and stable charismatic leadership. Theoretically, he "starts with an ahistorical concept and then discusses the depersonalization of charisma" which "tends to give the impression of a unilinear devolution or deterioration. This impression results from an artifact of exposition." The ahistorical component of his theory involves the "paradoxical assertions that charismatic leadership gives way to routinization and that it represents an ever recurrant phenomenon."[37]

The confusion arises from the fact that one theory was used for explaining two quite different descriptions for two factual counterparts of charismatic leadership.

The ahistorical component is not accidental but inherent in Weber's method of theorizing. The core of the theory is not derived prototypically from history, but is ideal-typically obtained from an ahistorical principle. This principle is rationality in the case of bureaucracy, and purity for the theory of charisma.[38] The purity is obtained by means of an "as if" construction: just the pure essences of the charisma of the small community make up the core of pure charisma. The belief of the leader in his calling, the belief of the followers in his special qualities and their emotional union constitute the "essences of charisma" (p. 1123). These are accompanied by the economic gifts of the supporters, by the alienation to all economic or rational intentions and actions, and by the estrangement to the world as a whole. The shift from pure to impure charisma requires that all five characteristics of the pure phase are contaminated in the impure phase, leading unavoidably to a routinization and disappearance of charismatic leadership.

If one compares this ideal-typical procedure with the two historical descriptions, there appear two fictional elements in this ideal-typical theory. The five features of the original charismatic community undergo a process of idealization, especially if the aspirant is at the same time a budding or already established politician such as Churchill or Roosevelt. The subsequent impure phase entails a distortion of the electoral charisma, since all the five characteristics are subjected to suffocation or deterioration, simultaneously and completely. Instead of a series of different types of charismata, co-existing or following each other, there is just one process with its two phases of purity and impurity. It follows that the ideal-typical method is inadequate for a reliable theory. It has to be replaced by the prototypical method, in which each of the characteristics has to be taken from the historical record and in which the different types of charisma retain a certain autonomy in adopting their noncharismatic features. Most important, the noncharismatic opponents have to be divided in those which effectively harm and those which strengthen the leader and the movement of charisma. Typification by means of purification reveals itself as an inadequate method for arriving at a reliable theory. This can be done only by a prototypical selection of the relevant characteristics that can be identified with the two historical descriptions of the actual historical movements.[39]

In order to bring out the differences between these two kinds of typological theory, we shall present Weber's pure theory of charisma in terms of propositions so as to make them comparable to the propositions of charismatic rulership stated above.

1. The supernatural qualities of the leader and the euphoria of the followers are essentially irrational in character.
2. The leader cannot be sure of the continued efficacy of his inner voice which alone prompts him to do his charismatic duty.

3. Mass emotions of the followers are subject to fluctuations over time so that there arises an instability of leadership and often a diversity of followership.
4. Transition from purity to impurity involves a process of institutionalization that unavoidably leads to a devolution of the charismatic qualities.
5. In facing the requirements of everyday life, the "charismatic blessings [turn] from a unique, transitory gift of extraordinary times and persons into a permanent possession of everyday life."
6. Charismatic assistants tend to "enter into a deliberate agreement in order to obstruct or even consciously oppose their chief so successfully that his leadership becomes impotent" (p.262).
7. There arises an antagonism between charisma and the capitalist economy, especially the "rational management of an ordinary large-scale enterprise. . ." (p.1118).[40] The vitality of charisma "is immediately endangered when everyday economic interests become permanent, as it threatens to happen everywhere" (p.1120).
8. "Charismatic domination is also the opposite of bureaucracy" (p.1113). Its rational rule disrupts charismatic rulership. Either the leader becomes a figurehead and the bureaucracies of party and state rule, or the bureaucrats win over the paladins.
9. The result is a process of routinization of charisma in which "the charismatic message becomes dogma, doctrine, theory, *règlement* or law" (p.1122) and in which the "charismatically dominated masses become taxpaying subjects, dues paying members of a church, sect, party or club, soldiers or law-abiding citizens" (p.1120).
10. "As soon as charismatic domination loses its personal foundation . . . its alliance with tradition is the obvious and often the only alternative . . . In such an alliance the essence of charisma appears to be definitely abandoned" (p.1122).
11. "Every charisma is on the road from a turbulently emotional life that knows no economic rationality to a slow death by suffocation under the weight of material interests: every hour of its existence brings it nearer to its ends" (1120).

Insofar as these propositions envision an empirical counterpart, it is the notion of a disrupted charisma, creating a kind of *Herrschaftslosigkeit*,[41] that has not been identified in Weber's empirical studies. Disruption seems to be the implied turning point between the two phases, and "death by suffocation under the weight of material interests" (p.1120) is the inevitable end of charismatic leadership. It is only when one regards these eleven propositions as an explanation of routinization that a meaningful comparison is possible with either the euphoric or synergistic charismata.

At no time in the electoral charisma of Kennedy was there any indication that the belief in himself was significantly impaired. The emotional attachment of his followers showed some weakness just prior to the election, but it was fully revived in response to the disaster of the Cuban invasion. The traditional opposition in Congress and the military defeat on the beaches of Cuba administered a serious setback to the charismatic leader and movement. But neither of these external obstacles spelled the end of the charismatic leadership. The implicit linkage between internal belief and external hurdles, so that the outside deterioration did necessarily bring an inside dilution, did not hold of this electoral charisma.

In the militant charisma of Churchill, the reverse relationship prevailed between these two forces. In the dark days of Dunkirk, Churchill's self-confidence was the highest and his mass appeal most forceful. It was only when military victory was assured that his mission failed him, and he had no message for the people in the prospective period or peace. A quite different linkage between the internal and external features could be observed that was not a part of Weber's pure theory. Self-confidence of the leader and trust of the followers were linked with the charismatic message: the strong belief in the charismatic mission sustained leader and followers, even in the darkest days when Great Britain seemed to be completely defenseless against the military forces of the Nazis.

While Weber correctly sensed the conflict between charismatic and noncharismatic forces in his pure theory, he misinterpreted the suffocating influence of the latter. The beliefs of the leaders and their followers were strongest at the time when the external threat was the most dangerous. The charismatic mission entered as an intervening variable; its specific content was such as to furnish grounds for an intensification of the beliefs. Being political and ideological, and thus noncharismatic in origin, such an ideological mission should definitely have diluted the respective beliefs. The pure theory did not incorporate such ideals and did not appreciate the fact of a charismatization of political ideals into the charismatic mission, and thus missed the vitalizing effect upon the followers.

Similar defects reveal themselves when the pure theory is compared with cumulative and synergistic charisma. Reestablishing French democracy after World War II restored the rule of the political parties, reducing again the president to a mere figurehead. In protest to being forced into a powerless position, de Gaulle resigned as president. But his self-confidence remained undiminished. He waited for a dozen of years before he was recalled to the headship of the state so as to forestall a civil war or a military dictatorship because of the conflict over the future of Algeria. But he presented a demand for his acceptance, a new constitution had to be adopted that put presidential in place of parliamentary democracy, giving him charismatic authority for most of the remaining years of his life. This experience reveals two defects of pure theory. One was the inner strength and tenacity of de Gaulle's belief in his destiny. Instead of being depressed by his failures after the war, he remained convinced that his time would come when he would liberate France for the second time. The same self-confidence led to two periods of charismatic leadership, personified by the same person. Similarly, there occurred an affinity between two similar crises that brought forth the same leader who was able to establish a charismatic rulership at the second turn.

There appeared an exceptionally strong inner conviction of his calling that was immune to the adverse effects of external obstacles. While pure theory envisioned only emotional fickleness, most charismatic giants felt committed to their charismatic assignment for life. The pure theory implied unrelated crises, each one generating a challenge to another charismatically gifted person. The giants, however, did possess the resilience to face different crises and meet their challenges in succession or after a period of inactivity in between. The element of time, permitting only a positive and negative phase for leaders in the pure theory, shows a greater diversity of patterns, varying from irregular phases with interruptions to the sequential phases of electoral, synergistic, and militant leadership of Roosevelt.

The pure theory stipulates an adversary relationship between the charismatic leader and the bureaucracy. Actually, the giants were able to attract one segment of the bureaucracy that assisted them and developed pseudo-charismatic attitudes toward the leaders and their policies. The few who turned against the leader had been hired more for their specialized talents than for their loyalty towards him. Others represented certain interest groups that were allied to the leader. Finally, Roosevelt had the advantage of building up an extensive federal bureaucracy, and many of his appointees favored his policies and were grateful for being given professional positions in the bureaucracy. These associations and alliances acted as a counterbureaucracy to those who persistently opposed the charismatic leadership. Enjoying the confidence of the masses and having direct access to the radio and thus to public opinion, the leader's authority was so great that opposition of the unfriendly bureaucrats was more latent and became manifest primarily in situations critical for the leader.

The existing conflict between charismatic and capitalist leaders and organizations centered not on the issues of rationality or irrationality but on profits and social honor. In blaming big business for the depression and in condemning the concentration of capital, Roosevelt seriously injured the social honor of business leaders. They answered in kind by accusing him of waste, mismanagement, calling him a demogogue and a dilettant, and resented his desertion from the upper class. This social conflict was aggravated by the conflict over wages and profits that arose in connection with administering the National Recovery Act. The social and economic conflicts culminated in an open struggle when the service state supported the trade unions, and Roosevelt refused to evict strikers who had occupied factories. Weber fully appreciated these conflicts, but he overly emphasized the role of rationality and failed to include in his pure theory the transformation of the ruling organizations into a counterpolity which, in this *Führerkampf*, imposed a significant limit upon synergistic charisma.[42]

An equally serious omission is that charismatic rulership is not mentioned in the pure theory. The growth of rulership is accomplished by an increase in charismatic authority and in the accomplishment of the movement's major goal of overcoming the crisis. For King, this goal was equal voting rights for all citizens, white or black;

for Roosevelt, the carrying through of economic and social reform. Neither goal could be implemented without accepting new laws and institutionalizing new rights. But institutions were said to be an indicator of a deteriorated charisma. "For charisma is by nature not a continuous institution, but in its pure type the very opposite" (p.1113). The most crucial distinction between supportive and deterrent institutions is missing in the theory. Without the former, the leader could not finalize his achievements, could not secure definite benefits for his followers and peoples, and could never leave behind him a definite legacy for future generations.

The missing concrete ideals in the mission, and the absence of institutions supporting the movements, produced the effect of letting the routinization begin too early. In one version, "the reign of genuine charisma comes to an end when it can no longer withhold the unqualified permission to found families and to engage in economic pursuit" (p.1120). Routinization begins here as soon as the paladins form their own families and earn a regular income. In the other version, routinization starts when "the charismatic message becomes dogma, doctrine, theory . . . and law." For "acquired rights" are "alien to the essence of charisma" (p.1123). In case of militant charisma, the issue of war legislation would kill the essence of charisma. But we know that the "acutely emotional faith" which indicates the essence was revived with the Japanese attack at Pearl Harbor. In fact, Churchill's charismatic authority was not recognized prior to the start of World War II, and his rulership lasted through the whole period of the military struggle. The whole period of rulership is thus excluded, and genuine charisma is limited to the incipient phase and ends when the charismatic group tends to become a larger movement, comprising "charismatically dominated masses" (p.1122).

It should be underlined that our criticism of the pure theory does not reject Weber's definition of the central charismatic act. We agree that the core is an "acutely emotional faith," followed by reciprocal mutual actions of leader and followers.[43] But Weber overlooked completely the fusion of such emotions with the appropriate ideals, or the merger of the charismatic and chiliastic emotions and beliefs in one person and following. Thus we disagree that such a faithful essence disintegrates as soon as the leader accepts ideals, formulates a theory, communicates his belief by means of modern media, builds up his own organizations, enters into alliances, and generates new institutions. All these are features of charismatic rulership which are almost all included in Weber's description of crisis charisma, but excluded from his pure theory.

Why did Weber formulate such an untenable theory? In the absence of relevant information, one can express only two conjectures. One concerns the empirical relevance of the pure type of charisma. He explicitly stated that "entirely pure charismatic authority is rare" and is visible only in the incipient phase. So he refrained from writing a separate section on pure theory in his chapters on charisma and was satisfied with placing his theoretical dicta into his empirical description of charismatic movements.[44] The other conjecture is more methodological in nature. He

failed to distinguish between the ideal-typical and the prototypical procedures of typification. Only the later can provide the empirical counterpart of a relevant theory;
the former can provide nothing but working hypotheses formulated prior to empirical research and modified or discarded according to the empirical findings leading to
a relevant and verifiable theory.[45]

A beginning of such a theory has been presented in our eleven propositions stated
at the beginning of this chapter. We now assume with Weber that charismatic leadership has been transformed in a "perennial institution" (p.1123), turn to the ending
of the synergistic charisma, and investigate its distinction between limits and routinization of the charismatic leadership.[46] This empirical survey will permit us to complete the relevant theory by adding additional propositions.[47]

<h2 align="center">STYMIED CHARISMA</h2>

From the struggle over the reform of the judiciary to the presidential campaign of
1940, Roosevelt was faced with a political stalemate. His charismatic appeal in mass
meetings was still effective, as was his own sense of being called by destiny. Yet he
had lost control over Congress, faced an increasingly hostile press, and suffered from
divided public opinion and a split in the Democratic party.[48] Why did this political
stalemate merely handicap the leader rather than subject his leadership to a clear
process of routinization?

The period of standpatship began with the negative reaction to the proposed reform of the Supreme Court. In submitting his bill, Roosevelt was guided by two
beliefs. Being the bearer of legal and charismatic authorities, he liked to use both
simultaneously in making his decisions. When both conflicted, he was inclined to
give preference to charismatic authority. It was from this charismatic viewpoint that
he assessed the refusal of the Supreme Court to sanction important laws of the New
Deal. He believed that his reelection in 1936, with its great majority, gave him a
mandate to stand up to anyone who obstructed the will of the people. Belief in his
charismatic qualities and in the confidence of the people in him led to a charismatic
exuberance that motivated his decision to reform the courts. These beliefs culminated in a sense of charismatic invincibility that was not effectively challenged by
anyone.[49]

The proposed reform bill was premature in timing and mistaken in its intention.
Shortly after the bill was submitted, the Supreme Court sanctioned a series of New
Deal Laws, including the Wagner Act. Roosevelt was given the opportunity to withhold his bill since his major purpose had been accomplished. In failing to do so
Roosevelt unintentionally created a constitutional crisis. Public concern shifted from
the bill to the long-range intentions of the charismatic leader. He was accused of
moving in the direction of a dictatorship. It was this fear that was used in the Senate
to table his bill, and this suspicion was mainly responsible for the fact that many
voters accepted the argument of his enemies and believed that each and every kind of
charisma would necessarily turn into a dictatorship. This mistaken belief lingers on

even today. If a leader disregards this fear, then he will provide his enemies with the opportunity to stymie his charismatic leadership.

The shift to a stymied charisma, resulting from the abortive attempt to reform the judiciary, suggests an important proposition that has to be added to the previous ones. In a democracy, the leader is required to aim at a full coordination of his legal and charismatic authorities. He has to avoid any impression or action that tends to replace the separation of power by a charismatic dictatorship. We can call this coordination the law of a self-respecting democracy in a period of charismatic rulership.[12] It was the constitutional crisis, producing the stymied charisma, that was the first reason for the political stalemate of the charismatic rulership.[50]

The second reason for the political stalemate emanated from the class struggle between employers and employees in industrial relations. The Wagner Act tried to minimize this struggle by legalizing three institutions. It recognized independent trade unions and outlawed company unions; it arranged for the election of a single bargaining agent in plants; it stipulated collective bargaining for agreeing on wage rates, working hours, and working conditions. Seeing employers rejecting these institutions, workers in rubber and automobile industries invented the sit-down strike, taking possession of company property and evicting managers from plants.[51] These turbulent actions were widely regarded as a "labor rebellion." Most of the press and many employers called for an eviction of the workers by military force and for punishment of the leaders.

Faced with these demands Roosevelt refrained from taking a public position. Privately he neither favored the new kind of strike, nor was he willing to use military force. Sit-down strikes, he said, are "illegal but what kind of law are they breaking? The law of trespass and that is about the only law that could be invoked. . . . But shooting it out and killing a lot of people because they violated the law of trespassing somehow offends me. I just don't see that as an answer. The punishment doesn't fit the crime. There must be another way."[52] Roosevelt thus supported those governors who refused to employ the National Guard against strikers by sending in mediators and by functioning as an umpire for getting private negotiations started. He handled the sit-down strikes as he did any other strike, fostering an agreement between the opponents as soon as possible.

A publicly neutral position of the leader also influenced the actions taken in the Senate. The Pittman Resolution which declared sit-down strikes "illegal and contrary to sound public policy," was defeated in the Senate. The rejected resolution was amended by Senator Robinson who condemned "espionage and company unions as illegal."[53] Roosevelt did not sign this enlarged resolution, although it did express his reservations to both violent methods in the class struggle. The wheeling and dealing about the resolution revealed that the supporters of neither labor nor business could get a majority in the Senate. The political stalemate could be overcome temporarily only if the leader did not intervene and if both groups found a way to condemn violent actions on both sides of the class struggle.

A similar publicly neutral but privately opposed position was adopted by Roosevelt in regard to counterrevolutionary actions by one group of employers. The leaders of "Little Steel" condemned the Wagner Act and tried hard to undermine any independent unions. An open conflict arose when the workers of Republican Steel Corporation were pushed in a premature strike. The conflict reached its climax in the so-called Chicago Massacre in May 1937. The workers organized a public meeting and then marched toward the gate of one of the plants. They were met by a firing squad of private and public police. Ten of the marchers were killed and twenty-eight wounded. The strike was broken by violence in order to protect the industrial autocracy with its company towns, company stores, company housing, company unions, and generally submissive attitudes of the workers. While the workers lost their strike, the industrial autocracy was broken by the exposure of the violence employed in industrial conflicts and condemned by the La Follette committee of the Senate.[54]

Behind the revolutionary sit-downs and the counterrevolutionary massacres loomed the critical conflict of industrial property of capitalist enterprises and charismatic rulership. Roosevelt carefully refrained from endorsing the theory of job power which claimed that the worker's right to a job entailed his control of the property at the job in order to get recognition of the trade union by employers.[55] Nor did Roosevelt support in any way the theory of the unlimited powers of employers who as full masters of their property should be able to dictate to workers what they had to do at the job and in the home. The master's right was defended in the name of protection as well as freedom. "If minority groups can seize premises illegally, hold indefinitely, refuse admittance to owners or managers, resist by violence and threaten bloodshed to all attempts to dislodge them, and intimidate properly constituted authority to the point of impotence, then freedom and liberty are at an end, government becomes mockery, superseded by anarchy, mob rule, and ruthless dictatorship."[56] These arguments did not impress Roosevelt. For him, "autocratic power was being properly subordinated to the public's government."[57] This means properties and jobs had to be severed from any kind of violence. No group had a right to use force in furthering its own interests or in protecting its own privileges. In disassociating himself from any kind of revolutionary or counterrevolutionary programs and actions, the charismatic leader facilitated the implementing of the Wagner Act. There appears another important proposition. By drawing a line between permissible and forbidden methods of industrial strife and pushing for the former, the charismatic leader limited the stymieing of charisma, salvaged most of the reforms on the books, but had to endure that the political stalemate[58] undercut his charismatic authority for actions in the present and in the future.[13]

One important reason for the effective protection of the reform was produced by the alliance between the charismatic leader and the movements of labor and farmers. The new institutions were jointly created by two different mass movements. One was the mass following of the leader. The devoted mass following accepted and implemented his policies. The other was the organized mass movement comprised of farmers and laborers. The leaders of these independent organizations promoted primarily the interests and ideals of their members, and the subsequent policies were endorsed by the charismatic leader. Roosevelt was never the head of the trade unions; John L. Lewis was never an official of party or government. The separate political and economic organizations collaborated with each other, and combined their efforts in bringing their bills through the Congress.[59] During the phase of rulership Roosevelt was the more powerful partner who had more to give than he received. In the standpatship, however, the relative contributions were reversed. Roosevelt could get bills such as the revised AAA or the Fair Labor Standards Act through Congress only because of the strong support of his allies. The stalemate was temporarily lifted only if and when the allies fully used their power of persuasion.

There follows an important proposition on the relationship between charismatic leadership and reform: charisma was an agency of durable reform because of the joint efforts of the two mass movements and the collaboration between their leaders.[60] Their mutual support offset temporarily the political stalemate, completed the main reform program, and assured the long term survival of the new institutions.[14]

The last reason for the political stalemate came from the rise of the counterpolity of business. Roosevelt saw early the power of the ruling organizations. Privately he wrote to Col. House in November 1933: "You and I know that the financial element in the large centers has owned the government ever since the days of Andrew Jackson and I am not wholly excepting the administration of Woodrow Wilson. The country is going through a repetition of Jackson's fight with the Bank of the United States—only on a far bigger and broader basis."[61] When, subsequently, his partnership with business had failed, Roosevelt viewed the pressures of business as attempts to restore the unilateral centers within an officially pluralist power structure. From 1936 onwards he saw as his major enemy the right wing of big business. What the "economic royalists really complain of is that we seek to take away their power."[62] There evolved a conflict over the distribution of political and economic power between the charismatic leader and all his supporters on the one hand, and all his opponents on the other. We come here to the situation in which certain noncharismatic factors became fundamentally opposed to the charismatic rulership. How did the conflict of interests and political animosity transform itself into a counterpolity that deliberately sought to undermine the charismatic rulership?

Parallel to the unionization of workers, there arose a network of self-organized business groups. The task of formulating the industrial codes under the NRA was mainly accomplished by new or reactivated trade associations. Many of them acted as quasi-cartels even after the NRA had been declared unconstitutional. The eventual sanctioning of the Wagner Act and the rapid rise of independent trade unions induced many industries to organize employer associations which either engaged in collective bargaining or coordinated anti-union campaigns. Finally, there were the overall business organizations, such as the Chamber of Commerce and the National Association of Manufacturers, which eagerly sought to establish a joint front against the New Deal.

Intensified organization was accompanied by formulating a distinct business ideology. Economically the New Deal was declared, in the words of Hamilton Fish, as a "mad orgy of waste, extravagance, and a squander-mania." Protests against inefficiency were accompanied by fear of a nationalization of the public utilities, railroads, coal mines, and even the press. Relief payments were said to "ruin the country by sending it into bankruptcy." Most of the New Deal laws were misunderstood or misrepresented to be a "grandiose and costly excursion into socialism." The fear for the rights of private property were coupled with the contempt for the service state of the New Deal. "We meddle into farms, into factories, and into finances. We meddle into production, into prices and into payrolls. The result . . . will be disastrous."[63] Clearly, the politicians of the opposition could only condemn; they did not present an alternative to the New Deal.

Politically, there was even less understanding of the charismatic leadership. Roosevelt was called an unscrupulous demagogue whose "public approval bordered on idolatry." His hunger for power had induced him to purchase the votes of the unemployed with relief payments so that some conservatives proposed to disfranchise the recipients of welfare checks. The reorganization bill was said to indicate "an incipient Roosevelt despotism." Passage of this bill, one leading senator said, would mean "plunging a dagger into the very heart of democracy."[64] Obviously, the opposition had not yet grown into a counterpolity because its spokesmen were filled mainly with resentments, guided by nostalgia for the past, governed by indignity, and devoid of any program to be implemented by an alternative government.

In defining the New Deal as some form of socialism, the political and economic opposition envisioned a complete destruction of the new system and aimed at a return to the predepression period. In Weberian terms, the opposition was traditional in nature. Experience with this kind of traditionalism hints at an important proposition.[15] When the crisis has been exceptionally deep and the reform has created some significant institutions, restoration of the old order tends to be unsuccessful because the ruling organization does not have the leader or the program for replacing charismatic rulership.[65] The oppositional forces can only contribute to the stalemate and thus prolong the already existing stymied charisma.

The danger of war in Europe, preceded by the occupation of Austria and Czechoslovakia, created a new situation in this country also. The charismatic leader and the ruling organizations had to reassess their political positions. Roosevelt decided to seek a third term and thereby to become the bearer of militant charisma. In seeking a new popular approval, he galvanized his opponents into action. The resistance to a break in the tradition of two terms brought forth a new leader. Wendell Willkie was nominated by the Republicans and received support of the ruling organizations. He adopted an internationalist position of assisting the allies with everything "short of declaring war." But he offered himself as the new leader and called for a drastic shift in domestic policies. His main proposal was to drop reforms and to concentrate upon recovery. The freedom of private enterprises was to be restored and all restrictions were to stop. The country could then rely upon private initiative to increase production substantially and to produce the weapons necessary for effective defense.[66] Such a shift required a new leadership: a third term was to be rejected because it would lead to dictatorship. In discarding the goal of restoration of the old order and concentrating upon long-range freedom of private enterprise and increased production, the new candidate fitted the requirements of the ruling organizations which strongly opposed any "social experiments." A more generally acceptable goal and a new leader—with some charismatic qualities—transformed the ruling organizations into a counterpolity.

In presenting a more appealing alternative, why was Willkie rejected by the majority of the voters? One reason was the rejuvenation of Roosevelt's charismatic appeal which benefited greatly from the military crisis. The other was the renewed division of the American electorate into internationalist and isolationist camps. While both major parties were split on this issue, isolationism was so strong in the Republican party that Willkie shifted gear and became the peace candidate. Roosevelt, called the warmonger, promised, "Your boys are not going to be sent into foreign wars."[67] When both candidates promised peace, the majority voted for a continuity of the charismatic leadership. Stymied charisma might have been ousted, but militant charisma was beyond the pull of the counterpolity and its new leader.

There follow two propositions on democratic charisma. In the phase of standpatmanship, there was little or no dilution of the charismatic quality of the leader, only some disenchantment by the followers. Nor was there routinization by the bureaucracy or tradition nor a suffocation by material interests. The ruling organizations alone had a chance to oust the charismatic leader when they became politically, ideologically, and economically united into one counterpolity, and jointly appointed one alternative leader.[16] Not routinization, but an integrated counterpolity, is the greater danger for the bearer of stymied charisma.

A new military emergency permits the established leader to meet the challenge of the war crisis and to renew his charismatic authority by popular consent. The alternative leader is able to unite most of the opposition, but he cannot overcome the charismatic appeal and is thus deprived of his chance of success. His abortive attempt produces one important legacy of militant charisma. In spite of the patriotic unity during the war, the peaceful death of the charismatic leader leaves behind a tendency towards ideological and political polarization for and against reform.[17]

The combination of electoral and militant charismata modifies the last phase of charismatic leadership. Standpatmanship with its stymied charisma was superseded by the preponderant charisma of wartime. Death in its own right did act as a terminator of the charismatic regime.[18] Death as the last act of the leader closed alternative opportunities for disenchantment of the followers, for the bureaucratic tendencies of the paladins, or for a successful attack by the counterpolity. The sole problem created by the passing away of the leader was the one of succession. This was handled in a constitutional but noncharismatic fashion. The elected vice-president took over the presidential office and thereby ended the phase of militant charisma.

## REFORMIST CHARISMA

What was the charismatic legacy of the giant in democracy in time of peace? In its long-term effect upon society, charismatic rulership with its New Deal was most profound in the three fields of government, labor, and farming. Acceptance of the task of recovery and public welfare created a service state on the federal level which involved an enlargement of the presidency. Recognition of labor as a power broker in the economy led to a broad reform program that eventually and substantially increased the level of living for the majority of workers in this country. Revival of farm income and production entailed the building up of governmental warehouses for staple products, the gradual release of which regulated the quantities and prices in the farm product markets. These reforms confirm one of the main theses of Weber that a charismatic rulership functions as an agency of major changes in polity and society.[68]

But there was one important gap in Weber's description of charismatic change. Weber did not mention reform as an outcome of charismatic movements. This omission in the description stemmed mainly from the fact that Weber relied on the experience of the nineteenth century in which reformist charisma was the exception to the rule of revolutionary and Caesarian charisma. Nor did his "pure" theory induce him to raise the question of reformist charisma. In filling this gap with the accomplishments of democratic charisma, we have to incorporate reformist charisma with all its features and consequences into the description and theory of charisma. The threefold reform became the legacy of the charismatic movement and its leader. The bequest imposed upon the following generations the task of accepting, preserving, and defending the reforms against the enemies of charismatic leadership.[19]

Weber's omission finds its parallel in the prevailing view of the accomplishments of the New Deal. American historians have given us a detailed description of the reforms of the 1930s. But their studies suffer from another hiatus. In presenting the New Deal as an important part of the American progressive movement, a part of the age of reform, they entirely missed the significant contribution of the charismatic leader.[69] By incorporating his ethics into his charismatic mission, Roosevelt and his specific ideals became the core of the charismatic movement and the personification of the New Deal. His ideals and actions contributed one part, his allies the other part, of the extensive reforms. In coordinating both in their overall perspective and in daily operations, the charismatic leader was able to build up a charismatic movement and rulership and developed both into the outstanding example of democratic charisma, rivaling in significance the accomplishments of Gandhi.[70] We can infer from this experience that charismatic movements are an important subdivision of social movements in general and the former find their core in the emotional union of the leader and followers.[20]

How could the reforms survive after the leader's death? In Weber's view, any charismatic legacy has to be institutionalized. This means that reforms lose their emotional support, shed the charismatic ideals, and survive only because they become bureaucratized. Actually, a distinction developed between the regular bureaucracy and the organizational implementors of reform. The subsequent legacy period is akin to the gestation period of the aspirants. Those put in charge of implementing the reforms not only remain attached emotionally to the dead leader, but also act as the sincere believers in the validity of the reforms. Such a commitment leads to rulings in accord with the intention of, and rejecting any deliberate deviations from, the objectives of the reforms. As long as these believers are in office, the bureaucratic requirements are minimized, preoccupations with trivia are limited, and the building up of personal empires is effectively resisted. There is thus no necessity for an immediate process of bureaucratization. We thus arrive at the proposition that the charismatic as well as the ideological reforms do have a chance of being successfully implemented because of this postponed period of bureaucratization.[21]

A second reason for keeping reforms alive springs from the beliefs and actions of the allies of the leader. Many of the trade unions and farm organizations became imbued with the spirit of the reforms. Both organizations insisted, and Roosevelt agreed, that the principles embodied in the reforms had to be retained during the war years. Farm organizations achieved parity prices for the most important products. Most trade unions increased their members and obtained rising wage rates, but at the price of working longer hours per week. After the war and the passing of the leader, most of the reforms had to be defended against the pressure of employers and political conservatives. This happened through the long but successful strikes in 1946. In spite of the Taft-Hartley Act and the outlawing of secondary boycotts, the reform of industrial relations became a permanent fixture of the American economy.

As a third reason for the defense of reform, millions of voters differentiated between the two major parties because of their attitudes toward the reforms. Building upon the charismatic achievements, the Democrats became the reform party and in doing so succeeded in incorporating the workers and lower income groups into their regular constituency. Most Republican candidates glorified personal freedom, eulogized free enterprise, demanded a shrinkage of the federal government, and rejected many of the reforms as unacceptable social experiments. While most of the leaders in both parties came from propertied classes or professions, the bulk of the supporting voting blocs took opposite class positions. In the minds of many voters, the Democrats became the reform party, while the Republicans turned into the free enterprise party. During campaigns many of the voters identified themselves with these goals, professed by the respective parties, and thereby created and maintained a dual political power structure.[22] The side effect of this two-party system and the corresponding division of political power is that independents are forced to either vote for the "lesser evil" or disfranchize themselves by refraining from voting at all.

Finally, the service state created during the charismatic rulership provided two kinds of opportunities for mass participation in government. The long years of the leader personifying the presidency created emotions of institutional charisma and an attachment of the masses to the service state. The various interest groups received assistance from the government by getting tax dollars for financing their various private or public projects. Once these modes of participation were established, a feeling of mutual support arose between politicians and members of the interest groups that gradually modified the dual power structure. As more and more interest groups were organized and received assistance, a plural power structure developed as the emotional commitment of the original reforms was replaced or supplemented by others. In pluralism "the power of the state is shared with the large number of private groups, interest organizations, and individuals represented by such organizations."[71] Charismatically initiated reforms included as one feature of the legacy an openness to other reforms that became either additions to, or deviations from, the original movements and reforms.[23]

Only after decades of living with the charismatic legacy did routinization set in, gradually regularizing or distorting the reforms. The charismatically supported achievements became modified structures of everyday life. The charismatically created agencies became a part of the greatly enlarged bureaucratic institutions. The members of the allied organizations lost their charismatic feelings and were increasingly guided by their major group interests. The straight interest organizations became holders of power in their own right. Older and younger organizations of reform emphasized their particular interests, kept their ideals for rhetoric occasions, exchanged votes for governmental grants or policies, and thereby became a part of the plural power structure.[24]

Routinization of the charismatic mass movement became effective only in the very long run. The previous followers ceased to be believers, discarded most of their ideals, and often turned into adroit fighters for their group interests. But routinization hardly ever ended up with restoration of the precharismatic situation and order. The reform organizations effectively defended their benefits and sought allies in their struggle. For instance, unions supported minimum wage laws for the unorganized so as to support their claim that they represented all the toilers in the economy. But the priority of group interests did not minimize the danger that some of the leaders furthered their personal ends, granted themselves inflated salaries, perpetuated themselves in office, and even demanded payoffs from employers in return for contracts. New laws enforcing democracy in trade unions became an alternative to the lost commitment to the original ideals. Because of their ability to strike and bargain collectively, labor organizations have been able to maintain intact the system of security capitalism, and routinization has rendered permanent a significant change in modern capitalism, initially implemented by the charismatic rulership.[25]

Long-term routinization also exerted its influence upon the counterpolity. Various attempts of the ruling organizations to restore the unilateral power structure, prevailing in the precharismatic order, largely failed. Especially the efforts to annul or circumvent the Wagner Act came to nought. The old ideals of freedom and liberty had to be refurbished before the counterpolity could unite and claim the right to have its candidate occupy the presidency. But it required a military hero, who regarded it as his "duty" to become president, for the Republicans to have a chance to come back to power. Without claiming any charismatic qualities himself, General Eisenhower was seen by many as the man whom they would like to follow. Once in the presidential office, Eisenhower adopted the two major goals of the counterpolity. In a report to Congress in 1956 he said: "Today we believe as strongly in economic progress through free and competitive enterprise as our fathers did, and we resent as they did any unnecessary intrusion of government into private affairs." These two goals of the counterpolity, free enterprise as the sole agent of progress and intrusive government as the enemy, were fully upheld by the military hero. The same report, however, recommended programs of rural development, vocational rehabilitation, and protection against catastrophic illnesses, because the government "can do a great deal to help people who have been left behind in the onrush of progress."[72] It was in these terms that the leader of the counterpolity shifted from a state of significant reforms to a benefactor state assisting only those who had been hurt by the rush of progress. Unavoidably, even those who abhorred the "welfare state" felt compelled to assist at least some disadvantaged groups of society, thus admitting that a systematic policy of restoration was not consciously intended.[26]

## CONSERVATIVE CHARISMA

It was Weber's expectation that "a political genius . . . [can] be expected only once every few centuries" (p.1405). While discontinuous over time, it is more the occurrence of a severe crisis than anything else that gives rise to new charismatic giants. President Reagan, as the new charismatic leader, has repeatedly praised Franklin D. Roosevelt. Reagan even placed himself in line with former presidents, Washington, Lincoln and Roosevelt. This self-image corresponds to his proclaimed mandate that it is his obligation to terminate the monetary inflation. In terms of his own estimate as leader as well as the main task placed upon him by history, Reagan sees himself as the new giant of crisis charisma.

However, a comparison of the charismatic leaderships of Roosevelt and Reagan is beyond the scope of this book. Much of the relevant information is not yet available, and of course many of his deeds will occur in the future. But we can assist future comparisons between the two leaders by formulating a series of hypotheses that can guide those who like to compare past and current charismatic leaders in this country. Instead of repeating the main characteristics of charismatic giants, our hypotheses will emphasize the likely differences between Roosevelt's and Reagan's leadership.

Reagan's emotional appeal was not in its most potent form, because he mixed emotions with ideology. Both were presented by him over television, which follows its own rules of persuasion, less intense than the direct appeal at mass meetings.

The most obvious difference lies in the partisan aspects of leadership. Reagan was nominated and elected as leader of the Republican party. This suggests that each of the two major parties, as a political coalition of various groups, has the capacity to accept a charismatic leader as head of its party and administration.

There has been a decided difference between the ideologies of the two leaders that were fused with charisma. In accepting conservative and rightist ideals as his guide for policies, Reagan clearly adheres to the ideological commitment of conservative charisma.

The shift in political constituencies and in political allies seems to suggest that mass emotions of natural charisma can and have arisen in all social classes. It is not mass emotionality as such, but the class position of voters and supporters that determines the socioeconomic point of view adopted by a charismatic leader and implemented by his administration.

Goals and allies of the new leader led to an attack upon the federal government as "a monster," and concentrated upon a revitalizing of the private sector of economy and polity. These goals entail either a revision or a dismantling of the institutions created by the New Deal. Conservative charisma seeks to displace reformist charisma.

The new charismatic rulership seems to be of shorter duration and its phases seem to follow each other more closely. The election returns of 1982 strengthened the opposition of the Democrats and diminished the unity of the Republicans, and the reelection of the leader is not fully assured. These handicaps seem to point to another case of stymied charisma.

If there is no attempted or successful reelection, the one-term president is unlikely to be judged as a charismatic failure. More likely, the goals and policies of the first two years are indicative of a charismatic giant, whereas the handicaps in the next two years fit more the features of luminary charisma.

Whether these hypotheses will turn out to be true or false, future analysts do not need to start from scratch. Comparison of the two leaders can immediately begin to contrast reformist with conservative claims and deeds. Such a sequence renders inadequate Weber's grand generalization that "every charisma . . . [will die] a slow death of suffocation under the weight of material interests" (p.1120). Two different expectations take the place of his prediction. In terms of mass emotions, natural charisma will disappear as the charismatic followers themselves pass away. In terms of beliefs, however, the institutionalized reforms become a part of the post-charismatic polity and economy. The ideological cleavages will either perpetuate or renew themselves and new crises will occur providing opportunities for new aspirants to build up their new charismatic rulership. The experiences of Roosevelt and of Reagan have shown that successful charismatic leaders can move in the direction of reform or of restoration in a well-established democracy.

# NOTES

## Preface

1. Arthur Schweitzer, "Vom Idealtypus zum Prototyp," *Zeitschrift für die gesamte Staatswissenschaft*, vol. 120, Jan. 1964, pp. 13–55.
2. What Sidney Hook has said of Lenin, that without his "directional leadership" the revolution "would have been lost," applies to all charismatic giants, whether in democracy or dictatorship. But Hook did not rely on the theory of charisma to prove his case. Sidney Hook, *The Hero in History* (New York: John Day, 1943), p. 184.

## Chapter 1: Varieties of Charisma

1. Max Weber, *Economy and Society: An Outline of Interpretive Sociology*, 3 vols., 4th ed., edited by Guenther Roth and Claus Wittich (New York: Irvington, 1968), p. 1405. All subsequent page references to this work will be given parentheses in the text, regardless of the volume.
2. For the purpose of this outline we shall define charisma loosely as the reciprocal relationship between the leader's magnetism and the enthusiasm of his followers. More specific definitions will follow in this and subsequent chapters.
3. The many books on Churchill see him as a great personality but not as a charismatic leader. This seems a symptom of the fact of how little the theory of charisma has become a tool of historical interpretation.
4. Robert Aron in his *An Explanation of De Gaulle* (New York: Harper and Row, 1966) interprets de Gaulle as "a kind of Caesar." Leon Blum not only agrees with him but also nominates Clemenceau as a man "belonging to that same category." *Naissance de la IVeme Republique* (Paris: Albin Michael, 1958), p. 10.
5. Erik H. Erikson, *Gandhi's Truth: On the Origin of Militant Nonviolence* (New York: Norton, 1969), p. 412.
6. I personally hesitate to include Eisenhower because he was almost exclusively a military hero. His policies as president included so few extraordinary actions that one can hardly speak of a political charisma. The father image moved in the direction but did not establish him as a charismatic giant. The interesting study

of James C. Davies, "Charisma in the 1952 Election," *American Political Science Review*, 1954, pp. 1083–1102 deals more with the disposition of some voters than with Eisenhower's conception of himself.

7. Thomas Mann, *Gesammelte Werke* (Berlin: Aufbau, 1957), vol. 12, p. 778. There is still some echo of Hegel's "world-historical individuals" or Jacob Burckhardt's "historical greatness" in recent biography that blocks the road to a charismatic interpretation. See Joachim Fest, *Hitler: Eine Biographie* (Frankfurt: Propylaen, 1973), pp. 19–25.

8. W. C. Runciman, "Charismatic Legitimacy and One-Party Rule in Ghana," *Archive of European Sociology*, vol. 4, 1963, pp. 148–65; David E. Apter, "Nkrumah, Charisma and the Coup," *Daedalus*, vol. 97, 1968, pp. 757–92; Henry Bretton, *The Rise and Fall of Kwame Nkrumah* (New York: Praeger, 1966).

9. P. J. Vatikiotis, *The Egyptian Army in Politics* (Bloomington: Indiana University Press, 1961); Joachim Joesten, *Nasser: The Rise to Power* (London: Odhams, 1960).

10. Kemal H. Karpat, *Turkey's Politics: The Transition to a Multi-Party System*, Princeton, N.J.: Princeton University Press, 1959; Dankwart A. Rustow presents "Ataturk as the Founder of a State," *Daedalus*, vol. 97, Summer 1968, p. 796, as an example of a very cautious charismatic.

11. A representative sample of attitudes revealed in 1965 a high degree of preference for "personalist leadership" in Argentina. Jeanne Kirkpatrick, *Leader and Vanguard in Mass Society* (Cambridge: MIT Press, 1971), p. 217.

12. For the role of manipulation in Kim's charisma see Reinhard Bendix, "Charismatic Leadership," in R. Bendix and G. Roth, *Scholarship and Partisanship* (Berkeley: University of California Press, 1971), pp. 181–83. On the extensive discussion on Castro's charisma see especially Lloyd A. Free, *Attitudes of the Cuban People Towards the Castro Regime* (Princeton: Institute for International Social Research, 1960); Richard Fagen, "Charismatic Authority and the Leadership of Fidel Castro," *Western Political Quarterly*, vol. 20, June 1965, pp. 275–84.

13. Harold J. Gordon, *Hitler and the Beer Hall Putsch* (Princeton, N.J.: Princeton University Press, 1972), p. 50.

14. R. Skidelsky, "Great Britain," *European Fascism* (London: Weidenfeld and Nicolson, 1968), p. 236.

15. Jean Stengers, "Belgium," in H. Rogger and Eugen Weber, ed., *The European Right* (Berkeley: University of California Press, 1966), p. 158.

16. Eugen Weber, "Romania," ibid., p. 532.

17. Eugen Weber, *Varieties of Fascism* (Princeton, N.J.: Van Nostrand, 1968), p. 102.

18. See Paul Kecskemeti, *The Unexpected Revolution* (Stanford: Stanford University Press, 1961), on the role of Nagy in Hungary.

19. Lewis J. Edinger, *Kurt Schumacher: A Study in Personality and Political Behavior* (Stanford: Stanford University Press, 1965), chap. 9.
20. C. A. R. Crosland, *The Future of Socialism* (New York: Macmillan, 1957), p. 195; John P. Roche and Stephen Sachs, "The Bureaucrat and the Enthusiast," *Western Political Quarterly*, June 1965, pp. 248–61.
21. Michael Paul Rogin, *The Intellectuals and McCarthy: The Radical Specter* (Cambridge: MIT Press, 1967), p. 232.
22. See the subsidized book by Victor Laski, *Robert F. Kennedy: The Myth and the Man* (New York: Trident Press, 1968).
23. Even those students who do not see in King a charismatic leader do give him credit for transplanting nonviolence from India to the United States. Lerone Bennette, Jr., *Confrontation: Black and White* (Baltimore: Penguin, 1966), p. 194.
24. *Christian Science Monitor*, Nov. 20, 1975.
25. William H. Friedland, "For a Sociological Concept of Charisma," *Social Forces*, vol. 43, 1964, p. 26.
26. Joseph Nyomarkay, *Charisma and Factionalism in the Nazi Party* (Minneapolis: University of Minnesota Press, 1967), p. 12.
27. For the various abortive attempts on Hitler's life, see Peter Hoffmann, *Widerstand Staatsstreich, Attentat: Kampf der Opposition gegen Hitler* (Munich: Piper, 1969).
28. It is always possible that an interest group or an ideological movement or regime antagonistic to a charismatic leader can hire an assassin who acts for the wirepullers. But an individual opponent has a sufficient motive to kill a charismatic leader. This unanticipated consequence of charisma is as yet not appreciated by those who crave unveiling the suspected conspiracy behind each and every political murder in this country.
29. Jacques Maritain, *Man and the State* (Chicago: University of Chicago Press, 1951), p. 140.
30. "Mass society theory does not account for the fact that Fascist movements draw their followers disproportionally from the middle classes, and that Communist movements draw their supporters disproportionally from the working classes." William Kornhauser, *The Politics of Mass Society* (Glencoe: Free Press, 1959), p. 179.
31. James Stratchey, *The Menace of Fascism* (London: Gollancz, 1933), p. 53. An analysis of British fascism.
32. Henry Pelling, *Winston Churchill* (London: Macmillan, 1974), p. 459.
33. In limiting the charismatic quality to magic acts, Karl Loewenstein concluded to his satisfaction that "charismatic authority in politics is a phenomenon of the pre-Cartisian world." See his *Max Weber's Political Ideas in the Perspective of Our Time* (Amherst: University of Massachusetts Press, 1966), p. 86.
34. Günther Roth, "Personal Rulership, Patrimonialism and Empire-Building," in

Reinhard Bendix and Günther Roth, *Scholarship and Partisanship* (Berkeley: University of California Press, 1971), pp. 156–69.

35. The theories of totalitarianism and authoritarianism could thus not build upon Weber's *Herrschaftssoziologie*. Cf. Juan J. Linz, "An Authoritarian Regime: Spain," in E. Allardt and Y. Littunen, eds., *Cleavages, Ideologies and Party Systems* (Helsinki: Westermark Society, 1964), p. 319 ff.

36. There are a few recognized exceptions to this generalization that will be fully considered at the appropriate occasions below.

37. Reinhard Bendix, *Max Weber—An Intellectual Portrait* (New York: Doubleday, 1960), p. 306. I still remember the many discussions Bendix and I were engaged in during my two years as research associate of the University of Chicago.

38. Ibid., p. 307.

39. The two lines of development became later a part of the theory of "duality of rule." Reinhard Bendix, "Max Weber's Sociology Today," *International Social Science Journal*, vol. 17, 1965, p. 20.

40. Amitai: Etzoni, *A Comparative Analysis of Complex Organizations* (New York: Free Press, 1961), p. 203.

41. Ibid., pp. 213, 210.

42. Ibid., p. 211.

43. Ibid., p. 213.

44. Ibid., p. 203.

45. Edward Shils, "Charisma, Order and Status," *American Sociological Review*, vol. 30, 1965, p. 201. Professor Shils was the first American sociologist I met while engaged in postdoctoral study at the University of Chicago. I remember reading a handwritten translation of Weber's "Objectivity" article which Shils later published in Weber's *Methodology of the Social Sciences*.

46. Edward Shils, "Concentration and Dispersion of Charisma," *World Politics*, vol. 11, 1958, p. 2. Both articles are reprinted in *Center and Periphery: Selected Papers of Edward Shils* (Chicago: Chicago University Press, 1974), vol. 2, pp. 256–75, 405–21.

47. Ibid., p. 4.

48. Ibid., pp. 9, 12.

49. Ibid., pp. 14, 19.

50. Max Weber, *The Protestant Ethic and the Spirit of Capitalism* (New York: Scribner's, 1958), p. 178. The "charisma of disciples" is exemplified by "Jesus freaks," who receive their inspiration directly from Christ, free of any mediator or earthly leader.

51. Shils, "Charisma, Order and Status," pp. 207, 204.

52. Eisenstadt's introduction to *Max Weber on Charisma and Institution Building* (Chicago: University of Chicago, 1968), pp. xx and xxi.

53. Ibid., pp. xxxi, xxxii, and xxxvii.

54. For an earlier attempt to discover charismatic leaders among businessmen see

Heinz Hartmann, *Authority and Organization in German Management* (Princeton, N.J.: Princeton University Press, 1959).

55. Shils, "Charisma, Order and Status," p. 209.

56. Ibid., both quotes from page 205. There seems to be a response to but not a source of this institutional charisma.

57. Ibid., p. 207.

58. The abstract principles, such as centrality and periphery, power and order, are peculiar to the contact theory and do not present grounds for a revision of the Weberian theory of personal charisma.

59. We thus subscribe to the statement that "any theory of leadership must take account of the interaction between situation and the individual." Bernard Bass, *Leadership, Psychology, and Organizational Behavior* (New York: Harper and Row, 1960), p. 18.

60. Hans Gerth and C. Wright Mills, *Character and Social Structure* (New York: Harcourt, Brace and World, 1953), p. 419.

61. Explanation proceeds in terms of configurational theory that seeks to ascertain the patterns of interacting variables and to explain their mutual combinations or coordination, their compatibility or incompatibility in specific situations. For a critical assessment of configurational theory that seems to us too negative, see George C. Homans, "Contemporary Theory in Sociology," *Handbook of Modern Sociology* (Chicago: Rand-McNally, 1964), p. 961 ff.

## Chapter 2: Weber's Theory of Charisma

1. Hans Gerth, "The Nazi Party: Its Leadership and Composition," *American Journal of Sociology*, vol. 45, Jan. 1940, pp. 517–41.

2. Robert C. Tucker, "The Theory of Charismatic Leadership," *Daedalus*, Summer 1968, pp. 731–56.

3. Wolfgang Mommsen, *Max Weber und die deutsche Politik* (Tübingen: Mohr, 1959).

4. Irving L. Horowitz, "Party Charisma," *Studies in Comparative International Development*, vol. 1, 1965, pp. 83–97; David Apter, *The Politics of Modernization* (Chicago: University of Chicago Press, 1966). David J. Butler, "Charisma, Migration, and Elite Coalescence," *Comparative Politics*, vol. 1, April 1969. pp. 423–39.

5. Edward Shils, "Charisma, Order and Status," *American Sociological Review*, vol. 30, 1965, pp. 199–213.

6. Reinhard Bendix, "Reflections on Charismatic Leadership," *State and Society* (Boston: Little, Brown, 1968), pp. 616–29.

7. Claude Ake, "Charismatic Legitimation and Political Integration," *Comparative Studies in Society and History*, vol. 14, 1966/67, pp. 1–13.

8. K. J. Ratnam, "Charisma and Political Leadership," *Political Studies*, vol. 12, 1964, pp. 141–54.

9. Carl J. Friedrich, "Political Leadership and the Problem of Charismatic Power," *Journal of Politics*, vol. 23, 1961, pp. 2–24.

10. Talcott Parsons' introduction to Max Weber, *The Sociology of Religion* (Boston: Beacon, 1963), pp. lxii-lxv.

11. Max Weber, *Economy and Society*, 3 vols., translated by Günther Roth and Claus Wittich (New York: Bedminster Press, 1968), p. 241. Page references to this work will be given in parentheses in the text.

12. Rudolf Sohm, *Kirchenrecht* (Leipzig: Dunker and Hombolt, 1892), vol. I, p. 26.

13. Friedrich, "Political Leadership," pp. 16–17.

14. Hans H. Gerth and C. Wright Mills, *From Max Weber: Essays in Sociology* (New York: Oxford, 1958), p. 79.

15. Friedrich, "Political Leadership," p. 15.

16. Gerth and Mills, *Essays in Sociology*, p. 125.

17. Lewis A. Froman, *People and Politics: An Analysis of the American Political System* (New York: Prentice-Hall, 1963), p. 75.

18. Parsons, *Sociology of Religion*, p. xxxii.

19. Donald McIntosh, "Weber and Freud: On the Nature and Sources of Authority," *American Sociological Review*, vol. 35, Oct. 1970, p. 903.

20. Ratnam, "Charisma and Political Leadership," p. 345.

21. Weber describes these as *Sonder-Charismata* which term was omitted in the translations of Parsons and Gerth. See *Wirtschaft und Gesellschaft* (Tübingen: Mohr, 1956), p. 684.

22. Friedrich, "Political Leadership," p. 13.

23. Ibid., p. 15. After rejecting any relationship between charisma and totalitarian leadership, Friedrich found it necessary in 1965 to call Hitler a "pseudocharismatic" leader. See Friedrich, *Totalitarian Dictatorship and Autocracy* (Cambridge: Harvard University, 1965), 2d ed., p. 44.

24. Methodologically, this inadequate treatment of time and of the phasing of the different subtypes of charisma is an illustration of what has been called the "telescoping of data" associated with Weber's ideal type. See Fischoff, "The Protestant Ethic and the Spirit of Capitalism: The History of a Controversy," *Social Research*, vol. 11, 1944, p. 75.

25. In his eagerness to prove Weber's personal preference for an aristocratic style of life, Mr. Arthur Mitzman mistranslates Weber's term *Gnadengabe*. The charismatic grace as a supernatural gift is identified with the social graces (*Anmut*) of aristocrats. Cf. *The Iron Cage: An Historical Interpretation of Max Weber* (New York: Knopf, 1970), p. 244.

26. This form of connective charisma is not identical with Edward Shils "contact" charisma, which includes all "vital forces."

27. The term "legendary charisma" is derived from "charismatic legacy." See Bendix, "Reflections on Charismatic Leadership," p. 186.

28. In excluding charisma from modern secular life, some students of Weberian charisma predict freely that charisma in the future will be limited to the tribal chiefs engaged in establishing new national states. See Karl Loewenstein, *Max Webers staatspolitische Auffassungen in der Sicht unserer Zeit* (Frankfurt: Athenäum Fisher, 1966), p. 79.

29. Franz Neumann, *Behemoth* (New York: Oxford, 1942), p. 85.

30. Dorothy Emmet, *Function, Purpose, and Power* (London: Macmillan, 1958), p. 233.

31. Mommsen, *Max Weber*, p. 140.

32. See the comments by Reinhard Bendix, Paul Honigsheim, and Karl Loewenstein in *Kölner Zeitschrift für Soziologie und Sozialpsychologie*, vol. 13, 1961, p. 258 ff.

33. *Der Hitlerprozess* (Munich: Deutscher Volksverlag, 1924), p. 269.

34. Kurt Sontheimer, *Antidemokratisches Denken in der Weimarer Republik* (Munich: Nyphenburger, 1962), p. 170.

35. Günther Roth, "Political Critiques of Max Weber: Some Implications for Political Sociology," *American Sociological Review*, vol. 30, 1965, p. 213.

36. "Der Reichspräsident," *Gesammelte Politische Schriften* (GPS) (Tübingen: Mohr, 1958), pp. 486–89.

37. Gerth and Mills, *Essays in Sociology*, p. 117.

38. Ibid., p. 116.

39. Ibid., p. 106.

40. Ibid., p. 113.

41. "Mass democracy has bought its successes since Pericles' times with major concessions to the Caesarist principle of selecting leaders. In the large American municipalities, for example, corruption has been checked only by plebiscitary municipal dictators, whom the trust of the masses gave the right to establish their own administrative agencies" (p.1453).

42. Gerth and Mills, *Essays in Sociology*, p. 103. Occasionally Weber designates "working with loyal personal devotion for a man" as the "charismatic element of all leadership," thinking mainly of the paladins.

43. Max Weber, *The Sociology of Religion* (Boston: Beacon Press, 1963), p. 59.

44. Gerth and Mills, *Essays in Sociology*, p. 117.

45. Horst Buszello, *Der Deutsche Bauernkrieg von 1525 als Politische Bewegung* (Berlin: Colloquium, 1969), p. 34ff. The emphasis is here more on the theological, less on the charismatic goals.

46. It is interesting that this Weberian phrase of "last form . . . of charisma" provided the justification for Ernst Nolte to exclude Hitler's charisma from the political history of the Nazis. See Nolte, "Max Weber vor dem Faschismus," *Der Staat*, vol. 21, 1963, p. 21.

47. In his caustic critique of Weber's theory, Wolfgang Mommsen also missed the

same distinction, but for him plebiscites were inherently dictatorial. Weber's support of a plebiscite for the president of the Weimar Republic was said to be a preparation for Hitler's dictatorship, implying that only parliamentary rule constitutes a real democracy.

48. James V. Downton, *Rebel Leadership: Commitment and Charisma in the Revolutionary Process* (New York: Free Press, 1973), p. 278.
49. Ibid., p. 272.
50. Ibid., p. 225.
51. Ibid., p. 224.
52. Ibid., p. 228.
53. Ibid., p. 199.
54. Ibid., p. 179.
55. Ibid., p. 280.
56. Ibid., p. 276.
57. Ibid., p. 234.
58. Ibid., p. 236. See also Irvine Schiffer, *Charisma: A Psychoanalytic Look at Mass Society* (Toronto: University of Toronto Press, 1973).
59. Compare Rollo May, *Love and Will* (New York: Norton, 1969).
60. Weber, *Gesammelte Politische Schriften*, pp. 280–81.
61. Reinhard Bendix, *Max Weber—An Intellectual Portrait* (New York: Doubleday, 1960), p. 457.
62. Weber, *Gesammelte Politische Schriften*, p. 205.
63. In his speech in 1919 on "Socialism," Weber explicitly recognized this condition: "The soldiers acknowledged the military expertise of the officer completely without reservation"—although they distrusted their instructions for the private lives of soldiers. See a translation of this speech in J. E. T. Eldridge, *Max Weber: The Interpretation of Social Reality* (New York: Scribner's, 1971), p. 192.
64. Ibid., p. 216.
65. Ibid., p. 218.
66. Ibid., p. 217.
67. Theodor Heuss, *Friedrich Naumann: Der Mann, das Werk, die Zeit* (Munich: Siebenstern, 1968), p. 444.
68. Eldridge, *Max Weber*, pp. 217, 216.
69. Max Rheinstein emphasized that Weber's theory of charismatic law creation could be applied to Lenin and Hitler but did not claim that Weber actually did this. See his introduction to *Max Weber on Law in Economy and Society* (Cambridge: Harvard, 1954), p. lv.
70. "Within and between institutional orders and their spheres is the problem area known loosely to sociologists as 'collective behavior.' " Hans Gerth, and C. Wright Mills, *Character and Social Structure* (New York: Harcourt, Brace, and World, 1953), p. 427.

## Chapter 3: Hitler's Dictatorial Charisma

1. For three significant but divergent attempts see Carl Schmitt, *Die Diktatur*, 3d ed. (Berlin: Duncker and Humblot, 1964); Franz Neumann, *The Democratic and the Authoritarian State* (Glencoe: Free Press, 1957); Carl J. Friedrich, "Diktatur," *Sowjetsystem und Demokratische Gesellschaft* (Freiburg: Herder, 1966), vol. 1, pp. 1239–59.

2. Hans Gerth, "The Nazi Party: Its Leadership and Composition," *American Journal of Sociology*, vol. 14, Jan. 1940, pp. 517–41.

3. Heinrich Hoffmann, *Hitler Was My Friend* (London: Burke, 1955), p. 59.

4. Adolf Hitler, *Mein Kampf* (Munich: Eher, 1939), p. 391. All subsequent quotations are taken from this so-called people's edition.

5. Albert Zoller, ed., *Hitler Privat: Erlebnisbericht seiner Geheimsekretarin* (Dusseldorf: Droste, 1949), pp. 17–19.

6. Hitler, *Mein Kampf*, p. 317.

7. Norman H. Baynes, ed., *The Speeches of Adolf Hitler*, (New York: Oxford University Press, 1942), vol. 1, p. 44.

8. Max Domarus, *Hitler Reden und Proklamationen 1932–1945* (Würzburg: Schmidt, 1963), p. 570.

9. Ernst Deuerlein, *Der Aufstieg der NSDAP* (Düsseldorf: Rauch, 1968), p. 235; Albert Speer, *Inside the Third Reich* (New York: Macmillan, 1970), p. 19.

10. *Der Hitler Prozess* (Munich: Deutscher Volksverlag, 1924), p. 120.

11. Werner Jochmann, *Im Kampf um die Macht* (Frankfurt: Europaische Verlagsanstalt, 1960), p. 53.

12. Hans Frank, *Im Angesicht des Galgens* (Gräfelfing: Beck, 1953), p. 315.

13. Domarus, *Hitler Reden*, p. 849.

14. Ibid., p. 727. Sept. 13, 1937.

15. Ibid., p. 712. July 31, 1937.

16. Ibid., p. 233. March 23, 1933.

17. Ibid., p. 700. June 6, 1937.

18. Ibid., p. 704. June 27, 1937.

19. Ibid., p. 264.

20. Ibid., pp. 502 and 503. May 1, 1935.

21. See Hitler's speech of Sept. 1936, a condensed version of which can be found in *Reichkanzlei* 43 II/1211, Bundesarchiv, Coblenz, West Germany.

22. Prinz zu Schaumburg-Lippe, *Dr. Goebbels* (Wiesbaden: Limes, 1963), p. 131.

23. Baldur von Schirach, *Ich glaubte an Hitler* (Hamburg: Mosaik, 1967), p. 98.

24. Hildegard von Kotze and Helmut Krausnick, *Es spricht der Führer* (Gütersloh: Mohn, 1966), p. 283.

25. Ibid., p. 282.

26. Domarus, *Hitler Reden*, p. 704. June 27, 1937.

27. This similarity has been shown by Friedrich Herr, *Der Glaube des Adolf Hitler*

(Munich: Bechtel Verlag, 1968). But the inference that such a similarity sub-stantiates an alliance between Nazis and the Catholic church is not convincing. The role of charisma in Hitler's leadership is completely neglected.

28. On the history of these conflicts between Nazi state or party and the established churches, see the detailed studies of Günter Lewy, *The Catholic Church and Nazi Germany* (New York: McGraw-Hill, 1964); Friedrich Zipfel, *Kirchenkampf in Deutschland, 1933–1945* (Berlin: de Gruyter, 1965); John S. Conway, *The Nazi Persecution of the Churches 1933–1945* (London: Weidenfeld and Nicolson, 1968).

29. Domarus, *Hitler Reden,* p. 1060.

30. R43 II/172, BA (Bundesarchiv).

31. R43 II/153, BA.

32. Schuhmacher-Sammlung 245 I, BA.

33. Domarus, *Hitler Reden,* pp. 762 and 893. Nov. 23, 1937 and Sept. 6, 1938.

34. R43 II/177 and 150, BA.

35. Schuhmacher-Sammlung 245 I, BA.

36. R43 II/245 II, BA.

37. For the many memoranda of Kerrl and Rosenberg in this dispute, see R43 II/1200 and 1200a as well as Hans G. Seraphim, *Das politische Tagebuch Alfred Rosenbergs* (Göttingen: Musterschmidt, 1956), p. 148 ff.

38. Fritz Klingler, *Dokumente zum Abwehrkampf der deutschen evangelischen Pfarrers-chaft gegen Verfolgung und Bedrückung, 1933–1935* (Nürnberg: Mendelsohn, 1946), p. 67.

39. Cf. Conway, *Nazi Persecution,* pp. 163 and 165. In sending their memorandum as confidential letter only to Hitler, the leaders of the Confessing church obvi-ously tried to appeal to Hitler's personal conscience in the hope of making him see the danger of blasphemy.

40. At the beginning of World War II Liddel Hart proposed that the Allied govern-ments should suggest such an excommunication to the pope. Kerrl informed Hitler of this article on Feb. 13, 1940.

41. Domarus, *Hitler Reden,* p. 762. Nov. 23, 1937.

42. Seraphim, *Das politische Tagebuch,* p. 97.

43. Henry Picker, *Hitlers Tischgespräche* (Stuttgart: Sewald, 1965), rev. ed., pp. 154, 168. It has been established that this racial interpretation of Christ by Hitler goes back to the year 1924. See Ernst Nolte, "Eine frühe Quelle zu Hitlers Antisemitismus," *Historische Zeitschrift,* vol. 192, 1961, pp. 584–606.

44. Picker, *Hitlers Tischgespräche,* p. 186.

45. Ibid., p. 186.

46. R43 II/169, BA.

47. While praising him as a courageous man, Hitler accused Luther of having played the role of an "ominous pioneer" of the Jewish menace because he saw the Jewish danger too late in his life and glorified the Old Testament. Cf. Die-

trich Goldschmidt and Hans Kraus, *Der ungekündigte Bund* (Stuttgart: Kunst-Verlag, 1962), p. 110 ff.

48. R43 II/1200, BA.
49. Seraphim's *Das politische Tagebuch* contains Rosenberg's statements and conversations with Hitler, while the memoranda and bills of Kerrl are available in R43 II/1200a, BA.
50. Seraphim, *Das politische Tagebuch*, p. 103.
51. Picker, *Hitlers Tischgespräche*, p. 154.
52. Domarus, *Hitler Reden*, p. 1059. Two months later the Protestant leaders presented Hitler with a detailed list of the secret persecutions inflicted upon the churches and their leaders. The protest was officially ignored but increased Hitler's irritation with the churches. R43 II/169a, BA.
53. Max Weber, *The Sociology of Religion* (Boston: Beacon Press, 1963), p. 195.
54. Picker, *Hitlers Tischgespräche*, p. 153.
55. Statement of Dr. Brandt, Hitler's physician, in U.S. Army Military Court, "Transcript of Proceedings; Case I (Medical), U.S. vs. Brandt," Nürnberg, Feb. 1947, p. 2401.
56. Bert Honolka, *Die Kreuzelschreiber—Aerzte ohne Gewissen* (Hamburg: Rutten and Loening, 1961), p. 98.
57. Heinrich Hermelink, *Kirche im Kampf* (Tübingen: Wunderlich, 1950), p. 254.
58. Martin Bormann, *Hitler's Secret Conversations 1941–1944* (New York: Signet Books, 1961), p. 106.
59. Picker, *Hitlers Tischgespräche*, p. 439.
60. The Film Department of the Bundesarchiv, Coblenz, owns a large collection of photographs of Hitler "among his people." For a typical example, see Heinrich Hoffmann, *Adolf Hitler: Bilder aus dem Leben des Führers* (Altona: Zigaretten-Verlag, 1935), p. 17 ff.
61. For details of this image building, supplementing the charismatic appeal, see Ernest Bramstedt, *Goebbels and National Socialist Propaganda 1925–1945* (East Lansing: Michigan State University Press, 1965), pp. 197–229.
62. Cf. Fritz Terween, "Der Filmbericht über Hitlers 50. Geburtstag," *Vierteljahrshefte für Zeitgeschichte*, vol. 7, Jan. 1959, pp. 75–84.
63. Speer, *Inside the Third Reich*, p. 20.
64. Wolfgang Brugge in *Nationalsozialistisches Bildungswesen*, 1937, p. 578. Quoted by L. Poliakov and J. Wulf, *Das Dritte Reich und seine Denker* (Berlin: Arani, 1959), p. 48.
65. Joseph Goebbels, *Die Zeit ohne Beispiel* (Munich: Eher, 1941), p. 101.
66. For a collection and analysis of these songs, see Hans Jochen Gamm, *Der braune Kult: Das Dritte Reich und seine Ersatzreligion* (Hamburg: Rutten and Loening, 1962), p. 105 ff.
67. Ibid., p. 116.
68. Ibid., pp. 57, 41, and 38.

69. Joseph Goebbels, *Signale der neuen Zeit* (Munich: Eher, 1934), p. 141.

70. Speer, *Inside the Third Reich*, p. 70.

71. Reality turned out to be quite different. The torndown houses of the "East-West Axis" provided an easy guide for Allied bombers to find their targets in night flights over Berlin. Furiously, Hitler ordered the camouflage of the axis. Over 500,000 marks were squandered because none of the disguises worked. Reichsfinanzministerium R 2, 5431, BA.

72. Hermann Goering, *Aufbau einer Nation* (Berlin: Mittler, 1934), pp. 51–52.

73. Domarus, *Hitler Reden*, pp. 323 and 324. Oct. 22 and 28, 1933. Italics in original.

74. Hans Frank, *Im Angesicht des Galgens* (Gräfelfing: Beck, 1953), p. 109.

75. For an extensive history of these events, but without any reference to charisma, see Klaus-Jurgen Mueller, *Das Heer und Hitler* (Stuttgart: Deutsche Verlagsanstalt, 1969), chap. 6.

76. Arthur Schweitzer, "Parteidiktatur und Überministerielle Führergewalt," *Jahrbuch für Sozialwissenschaft, 21*, April 1970, pp. 49–74.

77. Domarus, *Hitler Reden*, p. 745.

78. Walter Goerlitz, ed., *Generalfeldmarschall Keitel: Verbrecher oder Offizier?* (Goettingen: Musterschmidt, 1961), p. 178.

79. Ibid., p. 146.

80. Domarus, *Hitler Reden*, p. 760, Nov. 8, 1940.

81. *Völkischer Beobachter*, March 16, 1938, Munich Issue No. 75, p. 1.

82. Ernst Deuerlein, *Der Aufstieg der NSDAP 1919–1933* (Düsseldorf: Rauch, 1968), p. 332.

83. Domarus, *Hitler Reden*, p. 432. Aug. 5, 1934.

84. Ibid., pp. 432, 443, 612, 613, 442.

85. Ibid., p. 597. March 7, 1936.

86. Even Schacht was moved to praise Hitler in his speech to the employees of the Austrian National Bank at its incorporation into the *Reichsbank*. Chief Counsel for the Prosecution of Axis Criminality, *Nazi Conspiracy and Aggression* (Washington, D.C.: U.S. Government Printing Office, 1946), vol. 7, pp. 394–402.

87. Hildegard von Kotze and Helmut Krausnick, eds., *Es spricht der Führer* (Gütersloh: Mohn, 1966), p. 134–35.

88. Hitler refused to speak to his private secretary for six months because she expressed doubt in his ability to know the effect of alcohol consumption on human health. Zoller, *Hitler Privat*, p. 198 ff.

89. Cf. Hans Bernd Gisevius, *Adolf Hitler: Versuch einer Deutung* (Munich: Rutten and Loening, 1963); Hannah Arendt, *The Origins of Totalitarianism* (New York: Harcourt, Brace, 1951).

90. On the sociological theory of reciprocity, but without reference to charisma, see Alvin W. Gouldner, *For Sociology: Renewal and Critique in Sociology Today* (New York: Basic Books, 1973), chap. 7 and 8.

91. "Dictatorial" in this context means a capacity and utilized opportunities of a

few to exploit and rule, receiving rights and benefits one-sidedly, without consent of the giving, and by imposing conformity upon the majority in the situation.

92. In Stalin's personality cult and purges, the culprits had to accuse themselves of various crimes, glorify the leader, and then were executed. Hitler's personality cult did not necessarily culminate in *repeated* purges.

93. Ernst Fraenkel, *The Dual State* (New York: Oxford University Press, 1941).

94. For quite different interpretations of Weber's theory of authority, see Robert Bierstedt, "The Problem of Authority," in Monroe Berger, et al., *Freedom and Control of Modern Society* (New York: Norstrand, 1954); Peter Blau, "Critical Remarks on Weber's Theory of Authority," *American Political Science Review*, June 1963, vol. 57, pp. 305–16; Martin Spenser, "Weber on Legitimate Norms and Authority," *British Journal of Sociology*, vol. 21, June 1970, pp. 123–34.

95. John Toland, *Adolf Hitler* (Garden City: Doubleday, 1976), p. 764.

96. M. Gilbert, *Nuremberg Diary* (New York: Signet, 1964), p. 251.

97. International Military Tribunal, *The Trial of Major War Criminals* (Nuremberg, 1949), vol. 29, p. 146.

## Chapter 4: Charisma and Ideology

1. Ideological structures differ also according to the freedom of beliefs or dogmatization into creeds, tolerance or indoctrination, openness or closure. Arthur Schweitzer, "Ideological Strategy," *Western Political Quarterly*, March 1962, pp. 46–66.

2. Albert Hirschman in Alexander Eckstein, ed., *Comparison of Economic Systems* (Berkeley: University of California Press, 1971), p. 290. Some authors distinguish between ideologies and regime values. See David Easton, *A Systems Analysis of Political Life* (New York: Wiley, 1965), pp. 194–211.

3. Edward Shils limits the term ideology to the oppositional groups whose opposition to the prevailing regime is total, whose attitudes to other rivals are always intolerant, and who demand complete surrender by the enemy. Ideals promoting, sustaining, or defending the *status quo* find no place in this theory. See Edward Shils, *The Intellectuals and the Powers and Other Essays* (Chicago: Chicago University Press, 1972), chap. 2.

4. Except for South Tyrol, these ideas were first promoted by some conservative radicals, outside of the party. See the excellent study by Kurt Sontheimer, *Antidemokratisches Denken in der Weimarer Republik* (Munich: Nyphenburger, 1962), p. 127 ff.

5. Otto E. Schueddekopf, *Linke Leute von Rechts* (Stuttgart: Kohlhammer, 1960), pp. 187–90.

6. Gerhard L. Weinberg, ed., *Hitlers Zweites Buch* (Stuttgart: Deutsche Verlagsanstalt, 1961), p. 154.

7. *Völkischer Beobachter*, Feb. 25, 1926.

8. Hans Adolf Jacobsen, *Nationalsozialistische Aussenpolitik 1933–1938* (Frankfurt: Metzner, 1968), pp. 206 and 249.

9. Reprinted by Werner Maser, *Die Frühgeschichte der NSDAP* (Frankfurt: Athenaum, 1965), p. 470.

10. For the text of the fourteen points, see Reinhard Kühnl, *Nationalsozialistische Linke 1925–1930* (Meisenheim: Hain, 1966), pp. 288–90.

11. For different assessments of Strasser's ideas, see Karl O. Paetel, "Otto Strasser und die Schwarze Front des wahren Nationalsozialismus," *Politische Studien*, vol. 8, 1957, pp. 269–82; Max H. Kele, *Nazis and Workers: National Socialist Appeals to German Labor, 1919–1933* (Chapel Hill: University of North Carolina Press, 1972), pp. 156–60.

12. Otto Strasser, *Hitler and I* (Boston: Houghton Mifflin, 1940), pp. 101, 112, 114.

13. Ibid., p. 112.

14. For details see my articles "Der ursprüngliche Vierjahresplan," *Jahrbücher fur Nationalökonomie und Statistik*, Feb. 1957, pp. 348–96; "Business Power in the Nazi Regime," *Zeitschrift fur Nationalökonomie*, Dec. 1960, pp. 412–42.

15. See Oron J. Hale, *The Captive Press in the Third Reich* (Princeton, N.J.: Princeton University Press, 1964), chap. 5.

16. For the context and consequences, see my paper "Business Policy in a Dictatorship," *Business History Review*, Winter, 1964, pp. 413–37.

17. Documents D-203 and 204 reprinted in *Nazi Conspiracy and Aggression*. (Washington, D.C.: U.S. Government Printing Office, N.D.), vol. 6, pp. 1080–85.

18. Max Domarus, *Hitler Reden und Proklamationen 1932–1945* (Wüerzburg: Schmidt, 1963, p. 73.

19. The dispute over antiparliamentarism does not need to concern us because Hitler used the parliamentary method only as a tactical device. He was appointed as chancellor under emergency powers of the president and destroyed the power of parliament soon after he took office.

20. On the components and fate of anticapitalism see Arthur Schweitzer, *Big Business in the Third Reich* (Bloomington: Indiana University Press, 1964), chaps. 3 and 4.

21. The basic idea of social honor for workers, included in *Arbeitertum*, was developed first by August Winning, *Vom Proletariat zum Arbeitertum* (Hamburg: Hanseatische Verlagsanstalt, 1930), pp. 42–44, 99ff.

22. Strasser, *Hitler and I*, pp. 104–8.

23. Domarus, *Hitler Reden*, p. 736.

24. Kotze and Kransnick, *Es spricht der Führer*, p. 154.

25. For other features of national resurrection, see Arthur Schweitzer, "Ideological Crisis and Fascism," *Societas*, March 1972, pp. 1–25.

26. Hitler's speech of July 13, 1934, cited in Domarus, *Hitler Reden*, p. 424.

27. Ibid., p. 616.

28. For his success of sending German troops into the Rhineland, the Catholic bishops congratulated Hitler in a special telegram. See the reports of the Gestapo by Bernhard Vollmer, *Volksopposition im Polizeistaat* (Stuttgart: Deutsche Verlagsanstalt, 1957), p. 371.

29. Reprinted in Werner Maser, *Die Frühgeschichte der NSDAP* (Frankfurt: Athenaeum, 1965), p. 468.

30. Domarus, *Hitler Reden*, p. 793, quoting from the speech of Feb. 20, 1938.

31. The phrase of "completing Bismarck's work" was urged already by Franz von Papen in a memorandum of 1935. See document PS-2248, Staatsbiliothek Nuremberg.

32. Gunter Lewy, *The Catholic Church and Nazi Germany* (New York: McGraw-Hill, 1964), p. 215.

33. Domarus, *Hitler Reden*, p. 843.

34. Ibid., p. 850.

35. Ibid., p. 892.

36. On Hitler's overflowing gratitude for Mussolini's support see ibid., pp. 811–13.

37. Ibid., p. 841.

38. Ibid., p. 981.

39. Two recent studies examine in great detail the resurrectional policy in foreign affairs. See Hans A. Jacobsen, *Nationalsozialistische Aussenpolitik 1933–1939* (Frankfurt: Metzner, 1968), and Gerhardh Weinberg, *Foreign Policy of Hitler's Germany: The Diplomatic Revolution in Europe, 1933–36* (Chicago: University of Chicago Press, 1970).

40. Adolph Hitler, *Mein Kampf*, translated by James Murphy (London: Hurst and Backett, 1939), p. 373.

41. Reichskanzlei R43 II/1211a, BA.

42. Domarus, *Hitler Reden*, p. 722.

43. Quoted in Reinhard Kühnl, *Die Nationalsozialistische Linke 1925–1930* (Meisenheim: Hain, 1966), p. 43.

44. Strasser, *Hitler and I*, p. 104.

45. Domarus, *Hitler Reden*, p. 722.

46. Even providence is brought in as a protector of his life as in the case of the bomb placed in the beer hall November 1939 in Munich. See Albert Zoller, ed., *Hitler Privat: Erlebnisbericht seiner Geheimsekretarin*, (Dusseldorf: Droste, 1949), p. 80.

47. Our findings do not support the general thesis "that charismatic authority and ideology are incompatible," Joseph Nyomarkay, *Charisma and Factionalism in the Nazi Party* (Minneapolis: University of Minnesota Press, 1967), p. 20.

48. The most recent and detailed study of the Hitler revolt in 1923 goes to the extent of denying any intellectual capacity of the Nazis. It was "a movement

that was in many ways anti-intellectual and was led by men who were contemptuous of any but concrete goals." Harold J. Gordon, Jr., *Hitler and the Beer Hall Putsch* (Princeton, N.J.: Princeton University Press, 1972), p. 644.

49. *Der Hitlerprozess* (Munchen: Deutscher Volksverlag, 1924), p. 269.

50. Werner Maser, *Die Frühgeschichte der NSDAP: Hitler's Weg bis 1924* (Frankfurt: Athenaeum, 1965), p. 463.

51. Hans Frank, *Im Angesicht des Galgens* (Gräfelfing: Beck, 1953), pp. 45–46.

52. Revolutionary as well as counterrevolutionary movements usually develop a theory, ideological values, and overpowering emotions. Arthur Schweitzer, "Ideological Groups," *American Sociological Review*, Aug. 1944, pp. 415–26. The view that "Marxism is the only great ideology which has had a substantial scientific content" (Shils, *Intellectuals and Powers*, p. 38) does not take account of counterrevolutions.

53. Hitler, *Mein Kampf*, p. 208.

54. Gordon W. Prage, ed., *Hitler's Words 1923–1943* (Washington: World Affairs, 1944), pp. 4, 8, 9.

55. Norman H. Baynes, ed., *The Speeches of Adolf Hitler* (New York: Oxford, 1942), p. 45.

56. Prage, *Hitler's Words*, p. 9.

57. Weinberg, *Zweites Buch*, pp. 66, 68.

58. Domarus, *Hitler Reden*, p. 71.

59. Weinberg, *Zweites Buch*, p. 129.

60. Hitler, *Mein Kampf*, p. 78.

61. Ibid., pp. 389, 390.

62. Norman H. Baynes, ed., *The Speeches of Adolf Hitler* (New York: Oxford University Press, 1942), vol. 1, p. 447.

63. Hitler, *Mein Kampf*, p. 116.

64. Baynes, *Speeches of Adolf Hitler*, p. 203.

65. Ibid., pp. 485, 445.

66. Rudolf Diels, *Lucifer antiportas* (Stuttgart: Deutsche Verlagsanstalt, 1950), p. 193. In the trial of 1934, the Communist responsibility for the burning could not be proved by the prosecutor. The recent claim that the Communist van der Lubbe was alone responsible for the arson is based upon circumstantial, not documentary evidence.

67. Domarus, *Hitler Reden*, p. 322.

68. Ibid., p. 310.

69. Ibid., p. 61.

70. For details on the Nazi purge of democratic governments in the states, see Karl D. Bracher et al., *Die nationalsozialistische Machtergreifung* (Cologne: Westdeutscher Verlag, 1960), pp. 136–52.

71. The positive actions, creating the Nazi political monopoly, are organizational in nature and thus belong to the next chapter.

72. Domarus, *Hitler Reden*, p. 322.

73. Hitler, *Mein Kampf*, p. 393.

74. Quoted by Hermann Rauschning, *Hitler Speaks* (London: Eyre and Spottis-woode, 1939), pp. 154–55. Authenticity of this source has been questioned by some German historians. But this scepticism has been removed by the careful study by Theodor Schieder, *Herman Rauschnings Gespräche mit Hitler* (Opladen: Westdeutscher Verlag, 1972) who has shown that the "talks" were largely free from Rauschning's previous theory of nihilism.

75. Weinberg, *Zweites Buch*, p. 112.

76. Robert J. O'Neill, *The German Army and the Nazi Party, 1933–1939* (London: Cassel, 1966), p. 5.

77. Hermann Foertsch, *Schuld und Verhängnis* (Stuttgart: Deutsche Verlagsanstalt, 1951), p. 46.

78. O'Neill, *German Army*, p. 37; and Joseph Bloch, *Die SA und die Krise des NS-Regimes 1934* (Frankfurt: Suhrkamp, 1970), p. 70.

79. "Tagebuch Lutzes," *Franfurter Rundschau*, May 14, 1957.

80. There was a brief confrontation between legality and charisma. When Hans Frank, Bavarian minister of justice, asked for the specific legal charges against the 110 SA leaders before he would hand them over to the SS for execution, Hitler was temporarily taken aback and reduced the list to 19. But most of those temporarily saved were murdered a few days later. See Frank, *Angesichts des Galgens*, pp. 150–52.

81. Domarus, *Hitler Reden*, p. 421.

82. For the first acount of this dispute over military ideologies and strategics, see Arthur Schweitzer, "Atomic Stalemate and War Economy," *Social Research*, Fall 1956, pp. 281–310.

83. It has been the custom of historians to treat theory, ideology, and policies of Hitler as being separate, if not divorced, from his charisma. See the competent studies of Allan Bullock, "The Political Ideas of Adolf Hitler," *The Third Reich* (London: Weidenfeld and Nicolson, 1955), pp. 330–78; Fritz Dickmann, "Machtwille und Ideologie in Hitlers aussenpolitischen Zielsetzungen vor 1932" in *Spiegel der Geschichte: Festgabe für Max Braubach* (Münster: Aschendorff, 1963), pp. 915–41; Eberhard Jaeckel, *Hitlers Weltanschauung* (Tübingen: Wunderlich, 1969).

84. Hitler, *Mein Kampf*, p. 168.

85. Weinberg, *Zweites Buch*, p. 57.

86. Hitler, *Mein Kampf*, p. 173.

87. Weinberg, *Zweites Buch*, p. 83.

88. Ibid., pp. 54–55.

89. Hitler, *Mein Kampf*, p. 179.

90. Ibid., pp. 180–83.

91. *Trials of War Criminals before the Nurnberg Military Tribunal* (Washington,

D.C.: U.S. Government Printing Office, 1949), vol. 12, p. 439. (TWC)

92. *Nazi Conspiracy and Aggression* (Washington, D.C.: U.S. Government Printing Office, 1946), vol. 3, p. 302.

93. Rauschning, *Hitler Speaks*, p. 19.

94. For details, see Klaus-Jürgen Müller, *Das Heer und Hitler* (Stuttgart: Deutsche Verlagsanstalt, 1969), chap. 6.

95. Domarus, *Hitler Reden*, p. 75.

96. Some generals attribute the German defeat largely to the charismatic interventions of directing the war. See Franz Halder, *Hitler as Warlord* (London: Putnam, 1950); and Erich von Mannstein, *Verlorene Siege* (Frankfurt, Athenäum, 1963).

97. John Toland, *Adolf Hitler* (Garden City: Doubleday, 1976), p. 433.

98. Walter Görlitz, ed., *Generalfeldmarschall Keitel: Verbrecher oder Offizier?* (Göttingen: Musterschmidt, 1961), p. 206.

99. Domarus, *Hitler Reden*, p. 1196; Görlitz, *Generalfeldmarschall Keitel*, p. 206.

100. This was Churchill's interpretation of the "agreement." See Roger Parkinson, *Peace in Our Time* (New York: McKay, 1971), p. 70.

101. Heinrich Hoffmann, *Hitler Was My Friend* (London: Burke, 1955), p. 102.

102. Document 1014 PS, *Trials of the Major War Criminals before the International Military Tribunal* (Washington, D.C.: U.S. Government Printing Office, 1952), vol. 26, p. 523. (IMT)

103. Domarus, *Hitler Reden*, p. 1316. Establishing a "leader's headquarters" was the institutionalized expression of the shared sacrifices.

104. Ibid., p. 1365.

105. Ibid., p. 1520.

106. Ibid., p. 1502–3.

107. Willi A. Boelcke, ed., *The Secret Conferences of Dr. Goebbels* (New York: Dutton, 1970), p. 40.

108. Hermann Böhme, *Der deutsch–französische Waffenstillstand im Zweiten Weltkrieg* (Stuttgart: Deutsche Verlangsanstalt, 1966), p. 265.

109. Some competent students regard racism as the main feature of Nazi counterrevolution. Cf. George L. Mosse, *The Crisis of the German Ideology* (New York: Grosset and Dunlop, 1964); Wolfgang Scheffler, "Factoren nationalsozialistischen Herrschaftsdenkens," in *Factoren der politischen Entscheidung: Festgabe für Ernst Fraenkel* (Berlin: deGruyter, 1963), p. 56 ff. In terms of actions, however, Hitler and his consorts believed racism and imperialism as being equally important and mutually supportive.

110. Hitler, *Mein Kampf*, p. 243.

111. *Völkischer Beobachter*, Jan. 4, 1933.

112. Hitler, *Mein Kampf*, p. 66.

113. Baldur von Schirach, *Ich glaubte an Hitler* (Hamburg: Mosaik, 1967), p. 244.

114. Fritz Wiedemann, *Der Mann der Feldherrn werden wollte* (Velbert: Kappe, 1964), p. 191.

115. Domarus, *Hitler Reden,* p. 729, Sept. 13, 1937.

116. Ibid., p. 1058. Jan. 30, 1939.

117. Zoller, *Hitler Privat,* p. 80.

118. Document 720-PS, *IMT,* vol. 26, p. 266. According to Mr. Elie Wiesel not less than sixty-five books have been published that deny the existence of this document as well as the holocaust.

119. Martin Bormann, *Hitler's Secret Conversations, 1941–1944* (New York: Signet Books, 1961), pp. 257, 238.

120. Ibid., p. 109.

121. Hans A. Jacobson, ed., *1939–1945: Der Zweite Weltkrieg in Chronik und Dokumenten* (Darmstadt: Wehr und Wissen, 1961), p. 585.

122. Toland, *Adolf Hitler,* p. 735.

123. H. D. Leuner, *Als Mitleid ein Verbrechen war* (Wiesbaden: Limes, 1966), pp. 144, 142.

## Chapter 5: Charisma and Organization

1. I have translated the term of *persönliche Hilfskräfte* not as staff, but as assistants. I have also italicized the word *apparatus* so as to indicate its organizational nature.

2. Democratic bureaucracy may be of the responsible or of the nefarious kind, as discussed in chapter 9.

3. Max Domarus, *Hitler Reden und Proklamationen 1932–1945* (Wuerzburg: Schmidt, 1963), p. 525. Sept. 11, 1935.

4. R43 II, folder 1197, BA.

5. On the development of the party organizations see Anton Lingg, *Die Verwaltung der Nationalsozialistischen Arbeiterpartei* (Munich: Eher, 1940); Dietrich Orlow, *The History of the Nazi Party: 1919–1933* (Pittsburgh: University of Pittsburgh Press, 1969); Peter Diehl-Thiele, *Partei und Staat im Dritten Reich* (Munich: Beck, 1969); Dietrich Orlow, *The History of the Nazi Party: 1933–1943* (Pittsburgh: University of Pittsburgh Press, 1973).

6. The first organizational leader was Gregor Strasser, who tended to establish for himself a monocratic position at party headquarters.

7. Reichsorganisationsleiter der NSDAP, folder 365, Berlin Documents Center.

8. Ulf Lükemann, *Der Reichsschatzmeister der NSDAP,* Berlin Dissertation, privately printed, 1963, p. 116 ff.

9. D-151, "I. G. Farben Case," Document Book II, Exhibit 73. Available at the Law School library, Indiana Univ., Bloomington.

10. For details, see Arthur Schweitzer, "Business Power under the Nazis," *Zeitschrift für Nationalökonomie,* Dec. 1960, pp. 414–42.

11. Neither the amounts in full nor the distribution of these funds have been investigated in the books mentioned on the history of the Nazi party.

12. For the documents on the attempts of the Labor Front to build up its own social administration, see Arthur Schweitzer, *Nazifizierung des Mittelstandes,* (Stuttgart: Enke, 1970), pp. 180–203.

13. Mussolini did not eliminate, but dominated the general secretary of his party, who had to report daily to his leader. See Dante L. Germino, *The Italian Fascist Party in Power* (Minneapolis: University of Minnesota Press, 1959), p. 39.

14. For instance, Hitler's agreement with Stalin was not preceded or followed by any discussions within the party about the wisdom of temporarily dropping the fight against Bolshevism. Even the most ardent anti-Bolshevists, such as Rosenberg, accepted the leader's decision as a command.

15. Reprinted in Werner Jochmann, *Nationalsozialismus and Revolution* (Frankfurt: Europaische Verlagsanstalt, 1963), p. 266.

16. Ibid., p. 267.

17. Ibid., pp. 241–42.

18. On the various negotiations between the army and SA prior to the first Hitler government, see Francis L. Carsten, *Reichswehr und Politik, 1918–1933* (Cologne: Kiepenheuer and Witsch, 1964), p. 370 ff.

19. Maurice Duverger, *Political Parties—Their Organization and Activity in the Modern State* (New York: Wiley, 1963), p. 260.

20. Robert Koehl, "The Character of the Nazi SS," *Journal of Modern History*, vol. 34, Sept. 1962, p. 275.

21. This organizational fusion comes close to what one historian has called "partification." Dietrich Orlow, *The History of the Nazi Party: 1933–1945* (Pittsburgh: University of Pittsburgh Press, 1973), pp. 13 ff and 491.

22. Schuhmacher-Sammlung, folder 249, BA.

23. Denkschrift des Hauptorganisationsamtes, Schuhmacher-Sammlung, folder 375, BA.

24. In one instance the counterrevolutionary activities were directly supported by the armed forces. On Feb. 24, 1933, General von Blomberg went to Stuttgart to get the military commander to remove the democratic government of Wuerttemberg, if called upon. See Waldemar Besson, *Württemberg und die deutsche Staatskrise, 1928–1933* (Stuttgart: Deutsche Verlagsanstalt, 1959), p. 34.

25. Domarus, *Hitler Reden*, p. 336.

26. *Reichsgesetzblatt*, 1934, p. 1269 ff.

27. For the detailed evidence of this, see Ernst Fraenkel, *The Dual State* (New York Oxford University Press, 1941).

28. Frieda Wunderlich, *The German Labor Courts* (Chapel Hill: University of North Carolina Press, 1946), p. 137 ff.

29. Domarus, *Hitler Reden*, p. 287.

30. Typical of the terror involved was Goering's infamous bullet ordinance: "Every bullet which runs through a police pistol is my bullet. If this is murder, then I am the murderer . . . because I gave the order and I carry the responsibility." See his *Aufbau einer Nation* (Berlin: Mittler, 1934), p. 86.

31. National Socialism 22, folder 612, BA; R 43 II, folder 530, BA.

32. Heinrich Bennecke, *Hitler and die SA* (Munich: Olzog, 1962), p. 251.

33. Robert J. O'Neill, *The German Army and the Nazi Party, 1933–1939* (London: Cassel, 1966), p. 50.

34. This mesmerizing effect of charisma has been demonstrated for the leaders of factions by Joseph Nyomarkay in his mentioned book, but the same paralyzing impact applied also to demoted suborganizations of the party.

35. Arthur Schweitzer, *Big Business in the Third Reich* (Bloomington: Indiana University Press, 1964), chap. 4.

36. Philip Selznick, "An Approach to a Theory of Bureaucracy," *American Sociological Review*, vol. 8, Feb. 1943, p. 47.

37. Leonard R. Sayles, *Research in Industrial Human Relations* (New York: Harper, 1951), p. 131 ff.

38. Naturally, there were other small groups in the Nazi organizations, especially those seeking to realize particular interests. Pertinent information on these interest groups on a local and regional level is presented by Edward N. Peterson, *The Limits of Hitler's Power* (Princeton, N.J.: Princeton University Press, 1969). The significance of this evidence lies precisely in the fact that Hitler was so powerful that he could ignore the interest conflicts at lower levels, because they were irrelevant for his charismatic, ideological mission.

39. For a detailed assessment of Hitler in terms of these table conversations, see the introduction by Percy Ernst Schramm to the second edition of Henry Picker, *Hitlers Tischgespräche* (Stuttgart: Seewald, 1963), pp. 13–67.

40. Ibid., p. 220.

41. See the attempt of Hess to eliminate the self-inflation of subordinate leaders in an order of July 22, 1934, MicroRoll 12, folder 169, T–580, NA.

42. Hitler even intended to exhibit all the material of this period in a new "Museum of the Party." Picker, *Tischgespräche*, p. 237. The personal museum of the communist Kim II Sung of North Korea "is so vast it is officially said to take five days [to see] the memorabilia recording the revolutionary exploits . . . of this particular charismatic leader." *Christian Science Monitor*, April 25, 1975.

43. *Reichsgesetzblatt*, 1933, p. 245.

44. R 43 II, folder 421 a, BA.

45. Hans Mommsen, *Beamtentum im Dritten Reich* (Stuttgart: Deutsche Verlagsanstalt, 1966), p. 178.

46. Domarus, *Hitler Reden*, p. 674; Hans Frank, *Im Angesicht des Galgens* (Gräfelfing: Beck, 1953), p. 174.

47. Anton Lingg, *Die Verwaltung der Nationalsozialistischen Arbeiterpartei* (Munich: Eher, 1940), p. 109.

48. Domarus, *Hitler Reden*, p. 367.

49. Ibid., p. 392.

50. Ibid., p. 243. Implicit reference is to Hitler's previous protection of Röhm against the charge of homosexuality.

51. Peter Huettenberger, *Der Gauleiter* (Stuttgart: Deutsche Verlagsanstalt, 1969), p. 11.

52. On many occasions Hitler proclaimed the party as the organization charged with the task of making the Germans believe in the Nazi ideology. But neither the party nor the SS became a completely ideocratic organization because of their simultaneous political or police functions.

53. Schuhmacher-Sammlung, folder 117, BA.

54. Reichsorganisationsleiter, folder 365, Berlin Docments Center.

55. Ley even transferred funds of the Labor Front to the navy. *Nazi Conspiracy and Aggression* (Washington, D.C.: U.S. Government Printing Office, 1946), VI, p. 1017.

56. Quoted by Lükemann, *Der Reichsschatzmeister*, p. 233.

57. Schuhmacher-Sammlung, folders 249, 372, BA.

58. Reichsorganisationsleiter, Main group 101, Box 328, folder 746, BDC.

59. NSDAP, roll 60, T–81, NA.

60. Otto Bräutigam, *So hat es sich zugetragen* (Würzburg: Holzner, 1968), p. 367, and Lükemann, *Der Reichsschatzmeister*, p. 59.

61. Picker, *Tischgespräche*, p. 490.

62. Ni = 483—NI = 488, Microcopy T = 301, NA.

63. On Streicher's financial scandals and his eventual removal as *Gauleiter*, see Peterson, *Limits of Hitler's Powers*, pp. 275–85.

64. *Reichsgesetzblatt*, 1933, p. 173. An appropriate bill was already formulated at party headquarters prior to 1933.

65. R 43 II, folder 138, BA.

66. Domarus, *Hitler Reden*, p. 372.

67. Ibid., p. 287.

68. R 43 II, folder 206, BA.

69. R 43 II, folder 1376, BA.

70. R 43 II, folder 495, BA.

71. Ibid., Lammers to Frick, June 27, 1934.

72. Wi/IF 5.203, folder 35, T–77, NA.

73. R 43 II, folder 495, BA.

74. R 43 II, folder 1353e, BA.

75. R 43 II, folder 1353c, BA.

76. R 43 II, folder 1353e, and folder 177a, BA.

77. This promise was kept only in part. In Sept. 1939, Hitler appointed most of the regents (or provincial governors) as commissioners for defense. *Reichsgesetzblatt*, 1939, p. 1570. It was their task to prevent the military commanders from controlling civil affairs in the military districts, as it was anticipated in the Law on Defense of 1933.

78. R 43 II, folder 641, BA, letter of Lammers to Frick, June 17, 1940.

79. For a case study, see Martin Broszat, *Nationalsozialistische Polenpolitik 1939–1945* (Frankfurt: Fischer, 1965), pp. 52–59.
80. R 43 II, folder 888, BA.
81. NS 22, preliminary folder 683, BA.
82. Arthur Schweitzer, "Parteidiktatur und Überministerielle Führergewalt," *Jahrbuch für Sozialwissenschaft*, v. 21, April 1970, pp. 49–74. The charismatic component was still missing in this paper.
83. Limited space prevented the inclusion of these educational and propagandistic organizations in our section of ideocratic organizations. But they are well covered by Ernest K. Bramstedt, *Goebbels and National Socialist Propaganda, 1925–1945* (East Lansing: Michigan State University Press, 1965), pp. 197–229; Rolf Eilers, *Die nationalsozialistische Schulpolitik* (Cologne, 1963); Manfred Messerschmidt, *Die Wehrmacht im NS–Staat: Zeit der Indoktrination* (Hamburg, 1969).
84. Domarus, *Hitler Reden*, p. 430.
85. Hitler had worked out a special plan to suppress any German revolt, known as *Walküre*, but loyalty indoctrination as well as extreme fear kept the soldiers obedient to the bitter end.

### Chapter 6: Charisma and Despotism

1. Max Weber, *Wirtschaft und Gesellschaft*, (Tübingen: Mohr, 1950), p. 553.
2. Viktor Reimann: *Dr. Joseph Goebbels* (Vienna: Molden, 1971), p. 68.
3. Robert C. Tucker, *Stalin as Revolutionary, 1879–1929* (New York: Norton, 1973), p. 129.
4. There is no need for a detailed examination of Lenin's charismatic qualification because most of his features can be found in the extensive studies by specialists. We relied mostly on the books of Issac Deutscher, Max Eastman, Nathan Leites, Roy N. Melvedev, Boris Souvarine, Barrington Moore, Stefan Possony, and Leonard Schapiro. Specific references will be given in subsequent footnotes.
5. E. Victor Wolfenstein, *The Revolutionary Personality* (Princeton: Princeton University Press, 1967), p. 190.
6. Max Eastman, *Love and Revolution: My Journey Through an Epoch* (New York: Random, 1964), p. 334.
7. Benito Mussolini, *Der Geist des Faschismus* (Munich: C. H. Beck, 1943), p. 25.
8. Bertram D. Wolfe, *Three Who Made a Revolution* (Boston: Beacon, 1948) p. 152.
9. Issac Deutscher, *The Prophet Armed: Trotsky 1879–1921* (New York: Oxford University Press, 1954), p. 59.
10. Ibid., p. 269.
11. Ibid., p. 262.

12. Ibid., p. 306.

13. Interestingly, this vision was also sketched by Lenin during his time in Finland in *State and Revolution* (New York: International Publishers, 1932).

14. The leader as the umpire calling for yielding has been especially emphasized by Joseph Nyomarkay, *Charisma and Factionalism in the Nazi Party* (Minneapolis: University of Minnesota, 1967), p. 146.

15. On the definition of these two kinds of ideologies see David Easton, *A Systems Analysis of Political Life* (New York: Wiley, 1965), p. 291.

16. Ernst Fraenkel, *The Dual State* (New York: Oxford University Press, 1941), p. 13.

17. Deutscher, *Prophet Armed*, p. 286.

18. Ibid., p. 313.

19. Lenin's instructions from Finland spoke of "insurrection as an art" but emphasized that his words only illustrated the actions to be taken and underlined that the enemy must "be taken by surprise." If he would have been on the spot, his surprise would necessarily have meant conspiracy. V. I. Lenin, *Collected Works* (Moscow : Foreign Language Publishing House, 1964), vol. 26, pp. 9, 15, 152.

20. Deutscher, *Prophet Armed*, p. 305. The term *completion* was referring here to the political, not to the subsequent economic revolution.

21. Ibid., p. 310. As one instance of the many falsifications of history, Stalin's but not Trotsky's name was mentioned as a member of the Military Revolutionary Committee. See N. K. Krupskaya, *Reminiscences of Lenin* (Moscow: Foreign Languages Publishing House, 1959), p. 385.

22. Stalin himself recognized the deception when he said that "the revolution strove to take every, or nearly every, step in its attack in the guise of defense." *Pravda*, Nov. 26, 1924.

23. Tucker, *Stalin as a Revolutionary*, p. 51.

24. Moshe Lewin, *Lenin's Last Struggle* (New York: Vintage, 1968), p. 84.

25. Significantly enough, Trotsky did not oppose outright the use of the Cheka against the "unheard of bureaucratization of the party apparatus." Issac Deutscher, *The Prophet Unarmed* (London: Oxford University Press, 1959), p. 110. While the Cheka arrested his followers, deported him, and placed him into exile, Trotsky did not single out the secret police but saw the revolution betrayed by a bureaucracy.

26. Max Domarus, *Hitler Reden und Proklamationen 1932–1945* (Würzberg: Schmidt, 1963), p. 329.

27. Helmut Heiber, ed., *Hitler's Lagebesprechungen: Die Protokollfragmente seiner militarischen Konferenzen 1942–1945* (Stuttgart: Deutsche Verlagsanstalt, 1962), p. 820.

28. Deutscher, *Prophet Armed: Trotsky 1879–1921*, p. 410.

29. Ibid., p. 419.

30. Max Weber fully recognized several charismatic leaders coexisting in the same

situation. He spoke of "several charismatic structures which exist side by side," but he saw them as "qualitatively heterogenous" and as applying to different persons (p.267). The partaking charismatic leader is missing in his theory.

31. "Whereas Trotsky emerged from the war with much glory and little power, Stalin emerged with little glory and much power." Tucker, *Stalin as a Revolutionary*, p. 209.

32. Domarus, *Hitler Reden*, p. 1316. Sept. 1, 1939.

33. Gerhard Engel, *Heeresadjudant bei Hitler, 1938–1943* (Stuttgart: Deutsche Verlagranstalt, 1974), p. 22.

34. Arthur Schweitzer, "Plans and Markets: Nazi Style," *Kyklos*, vol. 30, Jan. 1977, pp. 88–115.

35. Boris Souvarine, *Stalin: A Critical Survey of Bolshevism* (New York: Longmans, 1939), p. 307.

36. Leon Trotsky, *Stalin: An Appraisal of the Man and His Influence* (New York: Harper, 1941), p. 374.

37. While Issac Deutscher presented all the relevant facts in his excellent trilogy of Trotsky's life and used "Prophet" in the title of all three books, he did not see this opportunity, because for him charisma was incompatible with the theory of historical materialism. Deutscher, *The Prophet Outcast, Trotsky 1929–1940* (London: Oxford University Press, 1963), p. 244. In this way he was more orthodox than Trotsky, who recognized the gift of Lenin and spoke of him as "the greatest man of our evolutionary epoch." Leon Trotsky, *Lenin* (New York: G. P. Putnam's Sons, 1971), p. 200.

38. Leon Trotsky, *On the Suppressed Testament of Lenin* (New York: Pioneer, 1935), p. 38.

39. Issac Deutscher, *The Prophet Unarmed: Trotsky 1921–1929* (London: Oxford University Press, 1959), p. 111.

40. Wolfenstein, *Revolutionary Personality*, p. 28.

41. Deutscher, *Prophet Unarmed*, p. 296.

42. Raymond A. Bauer, "The Pseudo-Charismatic Leader in Soviet Society," *Problems of Communism*, 1953, vol. 2, pp. 11–14.

43. Leon Trotsky, *Lenin* (New York: G. P. Putnam's Sons, 1971), p. 203. In 1930, however, Trotsky would admit only that "without Lenin the crisis" in the leadership of the party "would have assumed an extraordinarily sharp and protracted character." Leon Trotsky, *History of the Russian Revolution* (New York: Simon and Schuster, 1936), vol. 1, pp. 329–31.

44. Tucker, *Stalin as a Revolutionary*, p. 57.

45. Ibid., pp. 287–88. The Russian term *vozhd'*, translated as supreme leader, seems to come close to the German word *Führer*.

46. Tucker, *Stalin as a Revolutionary*, p. 207–8.

47. Souvarine, *Survey of Bolshevism*, p. 352.

48. Joseph Stalin, *Works* (Moscow: Foreign Language Publishers, 1954), vol. 6, p. 123.

49. On Stalin's use of this concept of hardness, see Tucker, *Stalin as a Revolutionary*, p. 400.

50. Ibid., p. 310.

51. Alex Nove, *An Economic History of the USSR* (London: Allan Lane, 1969), p. 153.

52. Souvarine, *Survey of Bolshevism*, p. 382.

53. Ibid., p. 464.

54. The theory of natural charisma does not claim to give psychological explanations of these concentrated feelings. In his frequently mentioned book, *Stalin as a Revolutionary*, Mr. Tucker in chapter 12 gives a persuasively argued psychological identity theory of Stalin. If this theory can be stated without the assumed "inferiority complex," then such a theory would supplement the one of natural charisma.

55. Souvarine, *Survey of Bolshevism*, p. 400.

56. Quoted in ibid., pp. 567–68.

57. Joseph Stalin, *Works* (Moscow: Foreign Language Publishers, 1955), vol. 12, p. 17.

58. Domarus, *Hitler Reden*, p. 1663. Jan. 30, 1941.

59. Leonard Schapiro, *The Communist Party of the Soviet Union* (New York: Random House, 1959), p. 435.

60. Dietrich Orlow, *The History of the Nazi Party: 1933–1945* (Pittsburgh: University of Pittsburgh Press, 1973), p. 242.

61. Nikita Khrushchev, *Khrushchev Remembers* (Boston: Little, Brown, 1970), p. 256.

62. Souvarine, *Survey of Bolshevism*, p. 534.

63. Orlow, *History of the Nazi Party*, p. 369.

64. *Reichsgesetzblatt*, I, 1942, p. 247.

65. Otto Hennicke, "Ueber den Justizterror in der deutschen Wehrmacht am Ende des Zweiten Weltkrieges," *Zeitschrift fur Militargeschichte* (Berlin-Ost, 1964), p. 715 ff.

66. Orlow, *History of the Nazi Party*, p. 416.

67. John Toland, *Adolf Hitler* (New York: Doubleday, 1976), p. 778.

68. Ibid., p. 811.

69. Khrushchev, *Khrushchev Remembers*, p. 46.

70. Ibid., p. 605.

71. Ibid., pp. 606–7.

72. Ibid., p. 593.

73. Ibid., pp. 273, 279.

74. On the destructive and constructive elements of the second revolution, see Robert C. Tucker, "Stalinism as Revolution from Above," in *Stalinism: Essays in Historical Interpretation* (New York: Norton, 1977).

75. Quoted by Katerina Clark, Ibid., pp. 191–92.

76. Walter G. Krivitsky, *In Stalin's Secret Service* (New York: Harper, 1939), p. 187.
77. Either vindictiveness or lust for power have been the standard explanations for Stalin's motives. See Max Eastmann, *Stalin's Russia and the Crisis of Socialism* (New York: W. W. Norton, 1941), p. 78, and Roy A. Medvedev, in *Stalinism: Essays in Historical Interpretation*, p. 206. Such strictly personal motives cannot explain the wide acceptance of the personality cult which is such an important feature of Stalinism.
78. Edward L. Homze, *Foreign Labor in Nazi Germany* (Princeton: Princeton University Press, 1967), p. 129 ff.
79. Manfred Wolfson, "Constraint and Choice in the SS-Leadership," *Western Political Science Quarterly*, vol. 18, Sept. 1965, p. 565.

## Chapter 7: Conscience and Charisma

1. The German term that is missing in the translation of Talcott Parsons is *Eigencharisma*. See *Wirtschaft und Gesellschaft* (Tübingen: Mohr, 1950), p. 156.
2. For the major contributors to the various aspects of this criticism, see J. P. Mayer, *Max Weber and German Politics* (London: Faber, 1943); Wolfgang Mommsen, *Max Weber und die deutsche Politikx, 1890–1920* (Tübingen: Mohr, 1959 and 1974) with an epilogue; Raymond Aron, "Max Weber und die Machtpolitik," in *Max Weber und die Soziologie von heute* (Tübingen: Mohr, 1965), pp. 103–20; Wilhelm Hennis, "Zum Problem der deutschen Staatsanchauung," *Vierteljahrshefte zur Zeitgeschichte*, vol. 7, 1959, p. 19 ff; Christian von Farber, *Die Gewalt in der Politik* (Stuttgart: Kohlhammer, 1970); Ilse Dronberger, *The Political Thought of Max Weber* (New York: Meredith, 1971); Arthur Schlesinger, Jr., *The Politics of Hope* (Boston: Houghton Mifflin, 1962), pp. 6–16.
3. David Beetham, *Max Weber and the Theory of Modern Politics* (London: Allen and Unwin, 1974), p. 237.
4. Gustav Schmidt, *Deutscher Historismus und der Übergang zur parlamentarischen Demokratie* (Lübeck: Matthiesen, 1954), p. 228.
5. Max Weber, *Essays in Sociology* (New York: Oxford, 1946), p. 39.
6. Max Weber, *Gesammelte Politische Schriften* (Tübingen: Mohr, 1958), pp. 140, 122, 125.
7. Ibid., p. 59.
8. Cf. John Commons, *The Legal Foundation of Capitalism* (Madison: University of Wisconsin Press, 1957), p. 65 ff.
9. Weber, *Gesammelte Politische Schriften*, p. 306. I have not included the discussion of pure and direct democracy because Weber regarded them as either utopian or impractical.
10. Ibid., p. 272 ff.
11. Ibid., p. 437.

12. Weber, *Essays in Sociology*, p. 384.

13. Weber, *Gesammelte Politische Schriften*, p. 290.

14. Ibid., p. 347.

15. For the special difficulties in preparing the German nobles for democracy in contrast with the English gentry, see Weber, *Essays in Sociology*, pp. 386–95.

16. Weber, *Gesammelte Politische Schriften*, p. 343.

17. Weber, *Essays in Sociology*, p. 115. These qualifications are internal to the leader. But there are external qualifications governing the relationship between the leader and respective group. In regard to these external features, any individual is a leader "whose behavior stimulates patterning of the behavior in some group." Alvin W. Couldner, *Studies in Leadership* (New York: Harper, 1950), p. 17.

18. Weber, *Essays in Sociology*, p. 117.

19. Former Chancellor Willy Brandt is the only living politician who voluntarily resigned because of the demands of his ethics of responsibility.

20. Weber fought furiously for replacing the Russian three-class voting system by universal suffrage in the second part of World War I. Mommsen, *Max Weber*, 1974, pp. 264–74.

21. Weber, *Essays in Sociology*, p. 384.

22. Weber, *Gesammelte Politische Schriften*, p. 92. For a discussion of the ethics of responsibility and conviction, see Dennis H. Wrong, *Max Weber* (New York: Prentice-Hall, 1970), pp. 58–69.

23. Lerone Bennett, Jr., *What Manner of Man: A Biography of Martin Luther King, Jr.* (Chicago: Johnson, 1968), p. 191.

24. Ibid., p. 75.

25. Even severe critics indirectly acknowledge King's charismatic qualities, but they call it "tremendously appealing social myth with the power to effect broad and significant changes." Hanes Walton, Jr., *The Political Philosophy of Martin Luther King, Jr.* (Westport: Greenwood, 1971), p. 88.

26. Martin Luther King, Jr., "The Most Durable Power," *Christian Century*, June 5, 1957, p. 708.

27. Bennett, *Biography of Martin Luther King*, p. 133.

28. Jim Bishop, *The Days of Martin Luther King, Jr.* (New York: Putnam's, 1971), p. 328.

29. Martin Luther King, Jr., *Where Do We Go from Here: Chaos or Community?* (New York: Harper and Row, 1967), pp. 68, 69.

30. Bennett, *Biography of Martin Luther King*, p. 66.

31. Martin Luther King, Jr., "Love, Law, and Civil Disobedience," *New South*, Dec. 1961, p. 7.

32. William Robert Miller, *Martin Luther King, Jr.: His Life, Martyrdom and Meaning for the World* (New York: Weybright, 1968), p. 168.

33. The boycott against the Montgomery segregated buses lasted 383 days, and financing the resistance cost close to $300,000. Bennett, *Biography of Martin Luther King*, p. 77.

34. Robert F. Kennedy as attorney general received special praise. "He has done more for us personally than any other public official," said Charles Evers, brother of Medgar Evers. Arthur M. Schlesinger, Jr., *A Thousand Days: John F. Kennedy in the White House* (Boston: Houghton Mifflin, 1965), p. 976.

35. Samuel Lubell, *White and Black: Test of a Nation* (New York: Harper and Row, 1964), pp. 103–4.

36. Lyndon B. Johnson, *The Vantage Point* (New York: Holt, Rinehart and Winston, 1971), p. 165.

37. In an opinion sample of Negroes, not less than 88 percent gave King a favorable rating, and of the 100 leaders in the group a total of 95 percent responded favorably to his leadership. *Newsweek*, July 29, 1963.

38. King, *Chaos or Community?*, p. 233.

39. Ibid., p. 226.

40. Ibid., p. 227.

41. Ibid., pp. 69, 71.

42. Miller, *Martin Luther King*, pp. 225, 254, 283.

43. David Halberstam, "When 'Civil Rights' and 'Peace' Join Forces," reprinted in C. Erie Lincoln, *Martin Luther King, Jr.: A Profile* (New York: Hill and Wang, 1970), p. 207.

44. Miller, *Martin Luther King*, pp. 263, 230.

45. Ibid., p. 228.

46. Halberstam, "Civil Rights and Peace," p. 202.

47. King's introduction to *A "Freedom Budget" for All Americans* (New York: Randolph Institute, 1967).

48. Faced with this opposition King even contemplated undertaking a Gandhian "fast unto death" in order to compel all other Negro leaders to "act under the banner of nonviolence." Miller, *Martin Luther King*, p. 272.

49. Ibid., p. 270.

50. It is likely that King did not appreciate the depth of that impasse because the Poor People's Campaign was acceptable to Senator Robert F. Kennedy. King was prepared to support Kennedy's presidential candidacy. It was expected that another friendly president would support King's new program.

51. Jack H. Pollack, *Earl Warren: The Judge Who Changed America* (Englewood Cliffs: Prentice Hall, 1979), p. 176.

52. Johnson, *Vantage Point*, p. 159. This definition as a bundle of negative attitudes to integrationist policies, which we shall accept here, differs from another concept that identifies backlash with any right-wing extremism. See Seymour Martin Lipset and Earl Raab, *The Politics of Unreason* (New York: Harper and Row, 1970), p. 4.

53. Wayne Greenshaw, *Watch Out for George Wallace* (Englewood Cliffs: Prentice Hall, 1976), p. 3.

54. Ibid., p. 94.

55. Bill Jones, *The Wallace Story* (Northport, Ala.: American Southern Pub. Co., 1966), p. 77.

56. Ibid., p. 78.

57. James McEvoy, III, *Radicals or Conservatives* (Chicago: Rand-McNally, 1971), p. 116.

58. Marshall Frady, *Wallace* (New York: World Pub. Co., 1968), p. 7.

59. *Christian Science Monitor,* Feb. 2, 1972.

60. Greenshaw, *Watch Out,* p. 90.

61. John Dillon, "Barbecue Minus George," *Christian Science Monitor,* June 29, 1972.

62. Theodore H. White, *The Making of the President: 1968* (New York: Atheneum, 1969), p. 344; and Jones, *Wallace Story,* p. 70.

63. Jones, *Wallace Story,* pp. 79–80. See also Schlesinger, *A Thousand Days,* p. 964.

64. Jones, *Wallace Story,* pp. 114, 116, 123. See also Philip Crass, *The Wallace Factor* (New York: Mason, 1975), p. 107.

65. Greenshaw, *Watch Out,* p. 18.

66. Tom Wicker, "George Wallace: A Gross and Simple Heart," *Harpers,* April 1967, p. 46.

67. Greenshaw, *Watch Out,* pp. 151, 153.

68. Wicker, "Gross and Simple Heart," p. 46.

69. "The Public Record of George C. Wallace," *Congressional Quarterly,* Sept. 1968, p. 2565.

70. John S. Synon, *George Wallace: Profile of a Presidential Candidate* (Kilmarnock, Va.: MS Pub. Co., n.d.), p. 83.

71. Greenshaw, *Watch Out,* p. 22.

72. Ibid., p. 40.

73. *New York Times,* "Wallace Ties War to Nixon's Future," Dec. 1, 1969, p. 11.

74. Synon, *George Wallace,* p. 114.

75. Theodore H. White, *The Making of the President: 1972* (New York: Atheneum, 1973), p. 142.

76. Crass, *Wallace Factor,* p. 112.

77. White, *Making of President,* pp. 93, 94.

78. Crass, *Wallace Factor,* p. 212.

79. Greenshaw, *Watch Out,* pp. 291, 192.

80. Crass, *Wallace Factor,* p. 193.

81. Chester, Lewis, et al., *The American Melodrama: The Presidential Campaign, 1958* (New York: Viking Press, 1969), p. 524; *Congressional Quarterly,* July 8, 1972, p. 1655.

82. *Christian Science Monitor,* Dec. 18, 1971.

83. Greenshaw, *Watch Out*, p. 169.

84. Johnson, *Vantage Point*, p. 163.

85. Walter W. Rostow, *The Diffusion of Power* (New York: Macmillan, 1972), p. 340.

86. Weber, *Essays in Sociology*, p. 393.

87. Eric Erikson, *Identity: Youth and Crisis* (New York: Norton, 1968). "The great governor of initiative is conscience."

88. Ranyard West, *Conscience and Society* (Westport: Greenwood, 1972), p. 249.

89. Alfred Schütz, *Der Sinnhafte Aufbau der sozialen Welt* (Vienna: Springer, 1932; reissue in 1960).

90. "The highest ideals which grip us mightily can for all times become effective only in the struggle with other ideals. . . ." Max Weber, *Gesammelte Aufsätze zur Wissenschaftslehre*, 3d ed. (Tübingen: Mohr, 1968), p. 154.

91. Bishop, *Days of Martin Luther King*, p. 454.

92. Weber, *Gesammelte Politische Schriften*, p. 254.

93. Ibid., p. 254.

94. Weber, *Essays in Sociology*, p. 392.

95. Ibid., p. 391.

96. Ibid., p. 395.

97. According to more recent definitions, the range of social rights has included "a modicum of economic welfare and security to the right to share to the full the social heritage and the life of a civilized being according to the standards prevailing in society." T. H. Marshall, *Class, Citizenship and Social Development* (Garden City: Doubleday, 1964), p. 71.

98. Reinhard Bendix, *Nation-Building and Citizenship* (Berkeley: University of California Press, 1977), p. 19 ff.

## Chapter 8:  Crisis and Charisma

1. Roosevelt's charismatic qualities in wartime will be included in our next chapter.

2. For a further discussion on these modes of politics, see David Beetham, *Max Weber and the Theory of Modern Politics* (London: Allen and Unwin, 1974), chap. 4.

3. Weber heavily underlined an organizational requirement which he called the "law of the small number." "The ruling minority . . . is able at any time quickly to initiate that rationally organized action which is necessary to preserve its position of power" (p.952). While such minority rule often happens, it is not a general law because it can be offset by rivalry among the power holders or it can be limited by the actions of groups, such as elected conventions, primaries, or national elections. Minority rule without or in spite of these limitations belongs to "negative" politics and shall not further concern us here.

4. Max Weber, *Essays in Sociology* (New York: Oxford, 1946), pp. 114–16.
5. We prefer the distinction of ordinary and extraordinary leadership over the recently suggested concepts of "transactional" and "transforming" leadership. James MacGregor Burns, *Leadership* (New York: Harper and Row, 1978), parts 2 and 3. The former interpretation permits us to include situations, abilities, tasks, and accomplishments into one theory, while the latter distinction is largely limited to an unspecified vote of leaders in modes of change.
6. While many readers will have their own preferences for the most important ordinary leaders, our own list includes Truman and Humphrey, Callaghan and Thatcher in Britain, Brandt and Schmidt in West Germany, and Giscard d'Estaing and Mitterand in France.
7. While in Western Europe ideological parties often become a "regular" party, we have included them into the irregular parties because they are extraordinary phenomena in the United States, and Weber treats them as such. When the socialist parties become regular parties, subject to pressure by trade unions, the party pays the price of "ossification" of its leadership. (p.1448).
8. Frank Freidel, *Franklin D. Roosevelt: The Triumph* (Boston: Little, Brown, 1956), p. 29.
9. Ibid., p. 300.
10. Smith resented this implicit attack upon bigness by declaring that he would fight "any demogogic appeal to the masses of the working people . . . to destroy themselves by setting class against class and rich against poor." Ibid., p. 269.
11. Ibid., p. 294.
12. Ibid., p. 313.
13. Ibid., p. 315.
14. There was a tendency by the charismatic circle to overestimate the significance of their actions for the character of the Democratic party, which was expressed by Moley in the following words addressed to Howe: "You and Jim have done more than elect a president. You have created a new party that ought to hold power for twenty-five years." Ibid., p. 370.
15. Rexford G. Tugwell, *The Democratic Roosevelt* (Garden City: Doubleday, 1957), p. 70.
16. Ibid., p. 129.
17. Alfred B. Rollins, Jr., *Roosevelt and Howe* (New York: Knopf, 1962), p. 167.
18. Frank Freidel, *Franklin D. Roosevelt: The Ordeal* (Boston: Little, Brown, 1954), p. 100.
19. Alfred Steinberg, *Eleanor Roosevelt* (New York: Putnam's, 1959), p. 61.
20. Ernest Lindley, *Franklin D. Roosevelt: A Career in Progressive Democracy* (Indianapolis: Bobbs-Merrill, 1931), p. 207.
21. Freidel, *Ordeal*, p. 121.
22. Thomas H. Greer, *What Roosevelt Thought* (East Lansing: Michigan State University Press, 1958), pp. 3–4.

23. Rexford G. Tugwell, *In Search of Roosevelt* (Cambridge: Harvard University Press, 1958), pp. 36, 43.

24. Ibid., p. 57.

25. Freidel, *Ordeal,* p. 180.

26. Raymond Moley, *After Seven Years* (New York: Harper, 1939), p. 52.

27. Frances Perkins, *The Roosevelt I Knew* (New York: Viking Press, 1946), p. 72.

28. Ibid., p. 6.

29. John A. Garraty, "The New Deal, National Socialism and the Great Depression," *American Historical Review,* vol. 78, Oct. 1973, p. 924.

30. In analyzing such deviations from the truth, Moley speaks of a "process of self-deception" which he relates to the party instead of to the charismatic personality. Raymond Moley, *27 Masters of Politics* (New York: Funk and Wagnalls, 1949), p. 44.

31. Moley, *After Seven Years,* p. 128.

32. Needless to say, neither type of talent was "taught" or cultivated in the best universities. "A Franklin D. Roosevelt or a Chief Justice Harlan Stone might slip in through the side door as the son of an alumnus or graduate of a distinguished private school—though on the basis of academic performance neither could get in the front door [of Harvard] today." David C. McClelland, "Encouraging Excellence," in Stephen R. Graubard and Gerald Holton, eds., *Excellence and Leadership in a Democracy* (New York: Columbia University Press, 1961), p. 142.

33. Moley, *After Seven Years,* p. 343. The original brain trust had lost its influence, and Moley ironically condemned the emotional appeal as "a kind of St. George" campaign (p. 348).

34. Samuel Rosenman, *Public Papers and Addresses of Franklin D. Roosevelt* (New York: Random House, 1938), vol. 1, p. 762.

35. Ibid., p. 672.

36. Ibid., p. 674.

37. Ibid., p. 672.

38. Ibid., p. 679.

39. Ibid., p. 645. For a detailed discussion of Roosevelt's economic ideas during the campaign of 1932, see Daniel Fusfeld, *The Economic Thought of Franklin D. Roosevelt and the Origin of the New Deal* (New York: Columbia University Press, 1956).

40. Rosenman, *Public Papers,* vol. 1, p. 643.

41. Quoted by Arthur M. Schlesinger, Jr., *The Politics of Hope* (Boston: Houghton Mifflin, 1963), p. 110.

42. Rosenman, *Public Papers,* vol. 1, p. 631.

43. Ibid., vol. 2, p. 11.

44. Ibid., vol. 1, p. 757; vol. 2, p. 12.

45. One of his opponents counted that Roosevelt had used the term *emergency* thirty-nine times in his speeches and papers prior to World War II. See George

Wolfskill and John A. Hudson, *All But the People: Franklin D. Roosevelt and His Critics, 1933–1939* (New York: Macmillan, 1969), p. 325.

46. Tugwell, *In Search of Roosevelt*, p. 57.

47. Rosenman, *Public Papers*, vol. 1, p. 205.

48. Ibid., vol. 2, pp. 14, 15.

49. Ibid., vol. 2, p. 15.

50. Joseph P. Lash, *Eleanor and Franklin: The Story of Their Relationship* (New York: W. W. Norton, 1971), p. 360.

51. Bernard Bellush, *Franklin D. Roosevelt as Governor of New York* (New York: Columbia University Press, 1955), p. 143 ff.

52. Louis M. Hacker, "The Third American Revolution," in Richard S. Kirkendall, ed., *The New Deal: The Historical Debate* (New York: Wiley, 1973), p. 38.

53. Henry Steele Commager, "Twelve Years of Roosevelt," in Edwin C. Rozwene, *The New Deal: Revolution or Evolution* (Boston: D. C. Heath, 1949), p. 26.

54. For the distinction between "precedent" and "embodiment," see Moley, *After Seven Years*, pp. 14, 63, and 350.

55. Henry Ralph Gabriel, *The Course of American Democratic Thought* (New York: Roland Press, 1940), pp. 333, 337.

56. Quoted by Rollins, *Roosevelt and Howe*, p. 302.

57. Moley, *After Seven Years*, p. 191.

58. Perkins, *Roosevelt I Knew*, p. 113.

59. Kenneth D. Yeilding and Paul H. Carlson, *Ah, That Voice: The Fireside Chats of Franklin Delano Roosevelt* (Washington: National Archives, 1974), p. 10.

60. Moley, *After Seven Years*, p. 189.

61. Tugwell, *Democratic Roosevelt*, p. 284.

62. Rosenman, *Public Papers*, vol. 2, p. 202.

63. Ibid., p. 157.

64. Ibid., p. 156.

65. Ibid., p. 704. The principle of "equality for agriculture" was originated by George Peek and adopted by Roosevelt. See Richard S. Kirkendall, *Social Scientists and Farm Politics in the Age of Roosevelt* (Columbia: University of Missouri Press, 1966), p. 57.

66. Rosenman, *Public Papers*, vol. 1, p. 771, and vol. 4, p. 67.

67. Ibid., vol. 2, pp. 93, 96.

68. The proposed reforms in money markets were not guided by any ethical maxim. Control of the money supply was shifted to the Federal Reserve Board. This institution engaged in deficit financing primarily for economic reasons. See Marriner S. Eccles, *Beckoning Frontiers* (New York: Knopf, 1951), pp. 172–76 and 272–86.

69. Rosenman, *Public Papers*, vol. 1, p. 632.

70. Arthur M. Schlesinger, Jr., *The Coming of the New Deal* (Boston: Houghton Mifflin, 1959), p. 72.

71. Rosenman, *Public Papers*, vol. 1, p. 644.

72. Even Tugwell who was deeply committed to planning only proposed "self-planning for each industry . . . so that planning would be taken out of private hands. . . ." These vague ideas did not permit Roosevelt to arrive at a comprehensive plan. He merely placated Tugwell by saying: "You know we ought to have eight years in Washington . . . someday we will have the planning you want." Tugwell, *In Search of Roosevelt*, pp. 209–11.

73. Quoted by Perkins, *Roosevelt I Knew*, p. 333.

74. After the New Deal mutual assistance was incorporated into the principle of solidarity: "We are all, if in different ways and in different degrees, mutually serviceable to one another and collectively serviceable in the common purpose of our whole society." Ernest Barker, *Principles of Social and Political Theory* (London: Oxford University Press, 1952), p. 131.

75. Moley, *After Seven Years*, p. 376.

76. Weber had arrived at a more general formulation of the same relationship. "Not ideas, but material and ideal interests, directly govern men's conduct." Weber, *Essays in Sociology*, p. 280. In charismatic relationships, however, there is not only a greater emphasis upon ideals, but also an incorporation of emotions that have to find recognition and satisfaction.

77. Schlesinger, *Coming of the New Deal*, p. 27.

78. Fusfeld, *Economic Thought*, p. 226.

79. Schlesinger, *Coming of the New Deal*, p. 5.

80. Perkins, *Roosevelt I Knew*, p. 230.

81. Rosenman, *Public Papers*, vol. 1, p. 680.

82. Fusfeld, *Economic Thought*, p. 244.

83. Salomon Fabricant, *The Trend of Government Activity in the United States since 1900* (New York: National Bureau of Economic Research, 1952), pp. 69–70.

84. Prior to World War I a substantial business promotion was accompanied by a very limited government. Arthur Schweitzer, "American Competitive Capitalism," *Schweizerische Zeitschrift für Volkswirtschaft and Statistik*, April 1956, pp. 31–51.

85. From a strictly individualistic point of view, these payments went to "loafers" who were in danger of becoming moral degenerates because they lived on other people's money.

86. Broadus Mitchell, *The Depression Decade* (New York: Holt, Rinehart and Winston, 1947), p. 228.

87. Charles L. Dearing, et al., *The ABC's of the NRA* (Washington, D.C.: Brookings Institution, 1934), p. 117.

88. Schlesinger, *Coming of the New Deal*, p. 162.

89. After invalidating the NRA, Justice Brandeis sent Roosevelt a message: "I want you to go back and tell the president that we are not going to let this government centralize everything." Arthur M. Schlesinger, Jr., *The Politics of Upheaval* (Boston: Houghton Mifflin, 1960), p. 280. The antitrust branch of

progressivism turned against the partnership branch of Theodore and Franklin Roosevelt.

90. Dearing, *ABC's of NRA*, p. 122.
91. When the Senate had to choose between Roosevelt's mediation bill and Wagner's original version of his bill, Senator Wagner voted against his own bill because "no one is in a better position [than the president] to weigh the program in its entirety." See J. Joseph Huthmacher, *Senator Robert F. Wagner and the Rise of Urban Liberalism* (New York: Atheneum, 1967), p. 170.
92. Schlesinger, *Coming of the New Deal*, p. 48.
93. Carl N. Degler, "The Establishment of the Guarantor State," in Richard S. Kirkendall, *The New Deal* (New York: Wiley, 1973), p. 51.
94. Schlesinger, *Coming of the New Deal*, p. 308.
95. Degler, *New Deal*, p. 62.
96. Schlesinger, *Coming of the New Deal*, p. 132.
97. Ibid., p. 108.
98. Erich Preiser, "Property and Power in the Theory of Distribution," *International Economic Papers*, vol. 2, 1952, pp. 206–20.
99. This is an instance of Frank H. Knight's principle of familism in economics. See his *Freedom and Reform* (New York: Harper, 1947), p. 70. For the context, see Arthur Schweitzer, "Frank Knight's Social Economics," *History of Political Economy*, vol. 7, 1975, pp. 279–92.
100. Roosevelt said on Jan. 4, 1935: "Continued dependence upon relief induces a spiritual and moral disintegration fundamentally destructive to the national fiber. . . . The federal government must and shall quit this business of relief." Schlesinger, *Politics of Upheaval*, p. 268.
101. The banker Marriner S. Eccles was almost the only adviser of the president who advocated deficit spending on principle. See his autobiography, *Beckoning Frontiers*, p. 287 ff.
102. Schlesinger, *Politics of Upheaval*, p. 272.
103. Richard Hofstadter. *The American Political Tradition* (New York: Vintage Press, 1954), p. 334.
104. Schlesinger, *Politics of Upheaval*, p. 209.
105. Ibid., p. 631.
106. James MacGregor Burns, *Roosevelt: The Lion and the Fox* (New York: Harcourt, Brace, 1956), p. 333.
107. Merlo J. Pusey, *Charles Evans Hughes* (New York: Macmillan, 1951), p. 757; Donald Richberg, *My Hero* (New York: Putnam's, 1954), p. 220.
108. Pusey, *Charles Evans Hughes*, p. 760.
109. Tugwell, *Democratic Roosevelt*, p. 391.
110. Max Freedman, ed., *Roosevelt and Frankfurter: Their Correspondence, 1928–1945* (Boston: Little, Brown, 1967), p. 383.
111. Burns, *Lion and Fox*, p. 292.

112. Schlesinger, *Politics of Upheaval,* pp. 602, 529, and 544.
113. Moley, *After Seven Years,* p. 427.
114. Joseph Alsop and Turner Catledge, *The 168 Days* (New York: Doubleday, 1937), pp. 232–33.
115. Clinton Rossiter, *Constitutional Dictatorship* (Princeton, N.J.: Princeton University Press, 1942), p. 5.
116. Harold J. Laski, *The American President: An Interpretation* (New York: Harper, 1940), p. 155.
117. Alsop and Catledge, *168 Days,* p. 179.
118. "The popular reverence for the Constitution, the conception of the Supreme Court as its guardian, the ability of the judges . . . to counterattack in their own ways, the deep-seated legal tradition in Congress of a large number of lawyers—all these were obstacles" for Roosevelt's bill. Burns, *Lion and Fox,* p. 314.
119. Alsop and Catledge, *168 Days,* p. 179.
120. Schweitzer, "Countervailing Power Revisited," *Journal of Economic Issues,* vol. 14, Dec. 1980, pp. 999–1018.
121. Social democratization in Weber's theory supported trade unions in order to allow workers to participate indirectly in policies through organized mass actions. While unions were not a part of his original program, Roosevelt recognized the unions in 1937 as an instrument to terminate industrial servitude prevalent in mass-production industries.

## Chapter 9: War and Charisma

1. On the context of these two kinds of militant Caesars, see chapter 2 on revolutionary charisma.
2. Max Weber, *Gesammelte Politische Schriften* (Tübingen: Mohr, 1958), p. 291.
3. While Weber recognized Ludendorff's military brilliance, he condemned the general's politics as "insane gamblings." In a personal conversation, Weber urged Ludendorff and other generals to follow the enemy's demand for extradition after defeat. "The officer corps can be gloriously resurrected some day only if they voluntarily 'offer their head' to the enemy." Marianne Weber, *Max Weber: A Biography* (New York: Wiley, 1975), p. 652.
4. Weber, *Gesammelte Politische Schriften,* p. 278.
5. See the last section of chapter 2 for Weber's interpretation of such revolutions in Russia and Germany after World War I.
6. The other two developments of the building up of a war economy and/or revolutionary dictatorship are either beyond the scope of this book or have been examined in chapter 6.
7. Alvin W. Gouldner, *Patterns of Industrial Bureaucracy* (Glencoe: Free Press, 1954), p. 221.
8. The relationship between bureaucracy and democracy has been declared as an

underdeveloped theme of political sociology. The editor of a collection of articles searched but could not find any contribution that would place bureaucracy into the context of political democracy. Renate Mayntz, ed., *Bürokratische Organisation* (Cologne: Kiepenheuer & Witsch, 1968), p. 23. Our discussion seeks to distill Weber's ideas on the subject.

9. For instance, in Germany Mr. Leber had to resign as minister of defense in 1978 when his own intelligence officers had misinformed him and he had unintentionally lied to parliament.

10. In a presidential democracy with its fixed terms of office, not resignation but veto power is the instrument by means of which the president imposes his will upon the legislature and assumes the responsibility for his policies to the electorate.

11. The wars in Korea and Vietnam illustrate the significance of authorization. Militarily, both were lost by our armed forces, but it was only President Johnson whose reputation was besmirched because he had failed to get a clear authorization for the Vietnam war.

12. There is a significant difference between nefarious and disfunctional bureaucracy. The latter includes all deviations from rational bureaucracy, including over- and under-conformity. See Robert K. Merton, "Bureaucratic Structure and Personality," in *Reader in Bureaucracy* (New York: Free Press, 1952), p. 361 ff. Nefarious bureaucracy is limited to definitely inequitable goals and actions, leading to privileges for the preferred and to disadvantages for the discriminated against groups.

13. John F. Winslow, *Conglomerates Unlimited: The Failure of Regulation* (Bloomington: Indiana University Press, 1973), part 4, p. 270.

14. The condemnation of "red tape" in this country refers to a host of hostile attitudes toward the bureaucracy. See Alvin W. Gouldner, "Red Tape as a Social Problem," in *Reader in Bureaucracy,* pp. 410–18. For negative attitudes towards French bureaucracy, see Michael Crozier, *The Bureaucratic Phenomenon* (Chicago: University of Chicago Press, 1964), p. 203 ff.

15. In emphasizing these negative aspects of a bureaucracy seeking independence from any control, Weber speaks of *"unkontrollierte Beamtenherrschaft."* (Weber, *Gesammelte Politische Schriften,* p. 342.) His main concern was to obtain a parliament for Germany that could effectively control the bureaucracy.

16. In some less developed countries, such as Iran under the shah, the monarchic dictator built his power upon the military, police, and intelligence forces, while the party played an insignificant role.

17. Weber, *Wirtschaft und Gesellschaft* (Tübingen: Mohr, 1950), p. 572.

18. Richard Polenberg, *Reorganizing Roosevelt's Government* (Cambridge: Harvard University Press, 1966), p. 162 ff.

19. The mobilization of manpower provided the participation of management and trade unions in formulating and implementing administrative policies. See

George Q. Flynn, *The Mess in Washington: Manpower Mobilization in World War II* (Westport: Greenwood Press, 1979), p. 112 ff.

20. It was only in the Korean war that General MacArthur overruled the instructions of the Chiefs of Staff and was dismissed from his position by President Truman for his insubordination. See William Manchester, *American Caesar: Douglas MacArthur, 1880–1964* (Boston: Little, Brown, 1978, p. 629 ff.

21. Raymond Aron, *The Century of Total War* (Garden City: Doubleday, 1954), p. 258.

22. Winston Churchill, *Thoughts and Adventures* (London: Macmillan, 1942), p. 92.

23. Stanley Hoffmann and Inge Hoffmann, "The Will to Grandeur: De Gaulle as Political Artist," *Daedalus*, Summer 1968, p. 837; Dietrich Aigner, *Winston Churchill: Ruhm und Legende* (Göttingen: Musterschmidt, 1975), p. 31.

24. Alexander Werth, *De Gaulle: A Political Biography* (New York: Simon & Schuster, 1966), p. 52.

25. Charles de Gaulle, *The Edge of the Sword* (New York: Criterion, 1960), p. 43.

26. Victor L. Albjerg, *Winston Churchill* (New York: Twayne, 1973), p. 123.

27. Robert Aron, *An Explanation of de Gaulle* (New York: Harper and Row, 1966), p. 42.

28. Winston Churchill, *Amid These Storms* (New York: Scribner's, 1932), p. 238.

29. Werth, *De Gaulle*, p. 199.

30. Henry Pelling, *Winston Churchill* (London: Macmillan, 1974), p. 352.

31. Winston Churchill, *The Gathering Storm* (Boston: Houghton Mifflin, 1948), p. 667.

32. Herman Finer, "The British Cabinet, the House of Commons, and the War," *Political Science Quarterly*, vol. 56, 1941, p. 324.

33. Charles de Gaulle, *War Memoirs* (New York: Viking Press, 1955), vol. 1, p. 82.

34. Aron, *Explanation of de Gaulle*, p. 57.

35. Dwight Eisenhower, *Crusade in Europe* (Garden City: Doubleday, 1948), p. 61.

36. On "De Gaulle Against the Anglo-Saxons," see David Schoenbrun, *The Three Lives of Charles de Gaulle* (New York: Atheneum, 1966), p. 108 ff.

37. Peter W. Blau, "Critical Remarks on Weber's Theory of Authority," *American Political Science Review*, vol. 57, June 1963, p. 315.

38. J. W. Wheeler-Bennett, *Action This Day* (London: Macmillan, 1968), p. 51.

39. De Gaulle, *War Memoirs*, vol. 1, p. 84.

40. Eisenhower, *Crusade in Europe*, p. 326.

41. For a typology of warlike actions, see Arthur Schweitzer, "Warlike Actions in Our Time," *Journal of Politics*, Nov. 1945, pp. 343–77.

42. Albjerg, *Winston Churchill*, p. 124; Werth, *De Gaulle*, p. 152.

43. The recently advanced thesis that "the higher the degree of organization of

both conflict groups, the lower the likelihood of violence" does not apply to civil wars. See Anthony Oberschall, *Social Conflict and Social Movements* (New York: Prentice Hall, 1973), p. 339.

44. Aron, *Explanation of de Gaulle*, p. 64.

45. James MacGregor Burns, *Roosevelt: The Lion and the Fox* (New York: Harcourt, Brace, 1956), p. 399.

46. Elliott Roosevelt, ed., *FDR: His Personal Letters, 1928–1945* (New York: Duell, Sloan and Pierce, 1950), p. 934.

47. Samuel Rosenman, ed., *The Public Papers and Addresses of Franklin D. Roosevelt* (New York: Random House, 1938), vol. 8, p. 4.

48. Burns, *Lion and Fox*, p. 396.

49. Rosenman, *Public Papers*, vol. 7, p. 5.

50. "In 1940 the United States had an annual iron and steel potential of more than 70 million tons, but not a single armored division." Raymond Aron, *The Century of Total War* (Garden City: Doubleday, 1954), p. 90.

51. Winston Churchill, *Their Finest Hour* (Boston, Houghton Mifflin, 1949), p. 24.

52. Rosenman, *Public Papers*, vol. 9, p. 640.

53. Walter Johnson, *The Battle Against Isolation* (Chicago: University of Chicago Press, 1944), p. 147 ff.

54. Warren F. Kimball, *The Most Unsorted Act: Lend-Lease, 1939–1941* (Baltimore: Johns Hopkins Press, 1969), p. 191.

55. Cordell Hull, *The Memoirs of Cordell Hull* (New York: Macmillan, 1948), vol. 1, p. 858.

56. Burns, *Lions and Fox*, p. 425.

57. Ibid., p. 441.

58. Basil Rauch, *Roosevelt: From Munich to Pearl Harbor* (New York: Creative Age, 1950), p. 253.

59. Rosenman, *Public Papers*, vol. 9, 1940, p. 415.

60. Robert A. Divine, *Roosevelt and World War II* (Baltimore: Johns Hopkins Press, 1969), p. 40.

61. Churchill, *Their Finest Hour*, p. 558.

62. Quoted by Rauch, *From Munich to Pearl Harbor*, p. 323.

63. James MacGregor Burns, *Roosevelt: The Soldier of Freedom* (New York: Harcourt Brace Jovanovich, 1970), p. 141.

64. Rauch, *From Munich to Pearl Harbor*, p. 326.

65. Divine, *Roosevelt and World War II*, p. 47.

66. Rosenman, *Public Papers*, vol. 9, 1940, p. 607.

67. Until the breakdown of the negotiations with Japan, Roosevelt believed that the American military contribution could be limited to naval and air support in Europe. Cf. William Langer and Everett Gleason, *The Undeclared War, 1940–1941* (New York: Harper, 1953), p. 735.

68. Hitler took the opposite course when he carefully avoided to state publicly his ultimate peace goals for fear that they would create additional opposition. See Paul Kluke, "Nationalsozialistische Europaideologie," *Vierteljahrshefte für Zeitgeschichte*, vol. 3, 1955, p. 240 ff.

69. Quoted in Rauch, *From Munich to Pearl Harbor*, p. 322.

70. Text of the charter is reprinted in Burns, *Soldier of Freedom*, p. 130.

71. Max Freedman, ed., *Roosevelt and Frankfurter: Their Correspondence, 1928–1945* (Boston: Little, Brown, 1967), p. 612.

72. Burns, *Soldier of Freedom*, p. 214.

73. Ibid., p. 185.

74. Herbert Feis, *Churchill-Roosevelt-Stalin* (Princeton: Princeton University Press, 1957), p. 208.

75. Feis, *Churchill-Roosevelt-Stalin*, pp. 551, 553. It took long negotiations before the conference in San Francisco did accept the voting procedure adopted at Yalta.

76. Feis, *Churchill-Roosevelt-Stalin*, p. 549.

77. The eventual opposition to the Vietnam war belatedly confirms the truth of Roosevelt's insight and underlines the insensibilities of President Johnson.

78. Robert E. Sherwood, *Roosevelt and Hopkins* (New York: Harper, 1950), p. 360.

79. Roosevelt said to Churchill that "our two countries should proceed systematically through carefully selected persons to talk Stalin out of his shell, so to speak, get him away from his aloofness, secretiveness and suspiciousness until he broadens his views, visualizes a more practical international cooperation in the future, and indicates Russia's intentions both in the East and the West." Quoted by Hull, *Memoirs*, vol. 2, p. 1248.

80. Maurice Mathoff and Edwin Snell, *Strategic Planning for Coalition Warfare 1941–42* (Washington, D.C.: Department of the Army, 1953), p. 156.

81. Sherwood, *Roosevelt and Hopkins*, p. 605.

82. Samuel Rosenman, *Public Papers and Addresses of Franklin D. Roosevelt of 1943* (New York: Harper, 1950), p. 39.

83. Sherwood, *Roosevelt and Hopkins*, p. 697.

84. Feis, *Churchill-Roosevelt-Stalin*, p. 221.

85. Hull, *Memoirs*, vol. 2, p. 1571. One month after his statement on "unconditional surrender" Roosevelt linked it to his opposition to the extermination program of the Nazis. No government has a right to "commit wholesale murder or the right to make slaves of its own people or of any other people in the world." Sherwood, *Roosevelt and Hopkins*, p. 702.

86. Eisenhower, *Crusade in Europe*, p. 218.

87. William M. Franklin, "Zonal Boundaries and Access to Berlin," reprinted in Robert A. Divine, *Causes and Consequences of World War II* (Chicago: Quandrangle Books, 1969), p. 260.

88. William D. Leahy, *I Was There* (New York: McGraw-Hill, 1950), p. 301.
89. John Morton Blum, *Roosevelt and Morgenthau* (Boston: Houghton Mifflin, 1970), p. 586. Morgenthau also had his specialists work out a plan for an American loan of $10 billion for Russian reconstruction. An American credit was discussed at the Crimean, but not at the Yalta conference and did not receive Roosevelt's approval. See John H. Backer, *The Decision to Divide Germany* (Durham: Duke University Press, 1978), p. 82 ff.
90. Blum, *Roosevelt and Morgenthau*, p. 626.
91. See Manuel Gottlieb, *The German Peace Settlement and the Berlin Crisis* (New York: Paine-Whitman, 1960), p. 126; John Gimbel, *The American Occupation of Germany* (Stanford: Stanford University Press, 1960), p. 58.
92. Herbert Feis, *Between War and Peace: The Potsdam Conference* (Princeton: Princeton University Press, 1960), p. 31.
93. Arthur M. Schlesinger, Jr., "Origins of the Cold War," reprinted in Divine, *Causes and Consequences of World War II*, p. 351.
94. Feis, *Churchill-Roosevelt-Stalin*, p. 597.
95. Weber described "absolutely voluntary participation" of the followers in the leader's campaigns as "pure charismatism." Max Weber, *Ancient Judaism* (Glencoe: Free Press, 1952), p. 44. In our context charismatism refers to typical charismatic actions regardless of which leader and followers engaged in such actions.
96. Max Weber, *The Sociology of Religion* (Boston: Beacon Press, 1963), p. 111.
97. Ambassador Harriman analyzed correctly the danger to peace in such an expansionism when he said on Sept. 20, 1944: "If the policy is accepted that the Soviet Union has a right to penetrate the immediate neighbors for security, penetration to the next immediate neighbors becomes at a certain time equally logical." Department of State, *Foreign Relations of the United States, 1944* (Washington, D.C.: U.S. Government Printing Office, 1966), vol. 4, p. 998.
98. Richard Polenberg, *War and Society: The United States of America 1940–1945* (Philadelphia: Lippincott, 1972), p. 6.
99. Lord Moran, *Churchill* (Boston: Houghton Mifflin, 1966), p. 197.
100. Weber had based his formulation mainly upon the experience of electoral charisma. "As domination congeals into a permanent structure, charisma recedes as a creative force and erupts only in short-lived mass emotions with unpredictable effect, during elections and similar occasions" (p. 1146).

### Chapter 10: Charismatic Rulership

1. For the five different kinds of propositions in sociology, see Hans L. Zetterberg, *On Theory and Verification in Sociology* (New York: Bedminster Press, 1965), p. 69 ff.
2. Early in 1942 the farm bloc cajoled Congress into setting farm prices at 110 percent of parity. When this action tended to undermine price control, Roosevelt demanded of Congress to change the law or he would act on his own.

This threat recently has become a major piece of evidence for the theory of the imperial presidency. Arthur M. Schlesinger, Jr., *Imperial Presidency* (Boston: Houghton Mifflin, 1973), pp. 115–16. Congress revised the law, and consumer prices advanced by less than 2 percent for the last two years of the war.

3. We are now in a position to state the reasons for our scepticism of the charisma theory of S. N. Eisenstadt (see chapter 7). The charismatic rulership, as the foundation of institutions, is missing in his theory so that one is at a loss to know by whom and for whom the new institutions are created.

4. While it is correct to emphasize conflict and class in Weber's theory of politics, as it was done by H. H. Brunn, *Science, Values and Politics in Max Weber's Methodology* (Copenhagen: Munksgaard, 1972), p. 248 ff, one has to realize that periods of class harmony have and may again interrupt such conflicts.

5. I am borrowing this handy term of "counterpolity" from Michael Walzer, who applied it only to the relationship between church and state. It fits also with the conflict between charismatic rulership and the ruling organizations because in each case the opposition went beyond the prevailing political structure and built up a polity of its own. See Walzer, *The Revolutions of the Saints* (Cambridge: Harvard University Press, 1965), p. 51.

6. Irving Bernstein, *Turbulent Years: A History of the American Worker 1933–1941* (Boston: Houghton Mifflin, 1969), p. 778.

7. Franklin Roosevelt's first response to the labor rebellion was "A plague on both your houses." J. M. Burns, *Roosevelt: The Lion and the Fox,* (New York: Harcourt Brace, 1956), p. 351.

8. This difference is in full accord with Weber's distinction between organized and unorganized masses. The former are guided mainly by their interests and values, whereas the latter act according to their emotions.

9. The charismatic mass following is not yet an inherent part of the theory and description of social movements, but leadership has recently been included in the theory. See Joseph R. Gusfield, "Social Movements," *International Encyclopedia of the Social Sciences* (New York: Macmillan, 1968), vol. 14, p. 445 ff.

10. The theory of countervailing power deals with this dual power structure that developed during the New Deal. J. Kenneth Galbraith, *American Capitalism* (Boston: Houghton Mifflin, 1952). But the derivation of the new power of the supportive organizations from the power of the ruling organizations is historically wrong and theoretically untenable. See Arthur Schweitzer, "A Critique of Countervailing Power," *Social Research,* Fall 1954, pp. 253–85. For a revision of the theory, see Arthur Schweitzer, "Countervailing Power Revisited," *Journal of Economic Issues,* vol. 14, Dec. 1980, pp. 999–1018.

11. Richard Polenberg, *Reorganizing Roosevelt's Government* (Cambridge: Harvard University Press, 1966), p. 22.

12. Richard Polenberg, *War and Society: The United States 1941–1945* (Philadelphia: Lippincott, 1972), p. 6.

13. It is only for services in the form of long term legal obligations by the state for

which one can use Degler's term of "guarantor state." See chap. 8, footnote 93.

14. The minimal component of security was a substantial reduction of social risks. Said Roosevelt "We have had to take our chance about old age in days past. We have had to take our chance with depressions and boom times. We have had to take chances on buying our homes. I have believed for a great many years that the time has come in our civilization when a great many of these chances should be eliminated from our lives." Arthur Schlesinger, Jr., *The Politics of Upheaval*, (Boston: Houghton Mifflin, 1960), p. 652.

15. The particular meaning of "security" differed considerably for different groups of workers. There was no guarantee of a job or a minimum income, since millions were by law excluded from the specified minimum hourly wage. For those at the very bottom of the income ladder, relief payments meant that "starvation was no longer possible." Barton J. Bernstein, *Towards a New Past: Dissenting Essays in American History* (New York: Pantheon Books, 1963), p. 280.

16. Weber did not anticipate such an achievement. In reviewing the charismatic experience in the nineteenth century, he concluded "that a political genius can be expected only once every few centuries" (p.1405).

17. The need to bring relief is usually so great that the crisis fashions charismatic assignments which the leader must accept or he will fail his followers.

18. A preliminary study of American luminaries suggests the following typology of charismatic streaks in leadership:

| Euphoric Charisma | Personalities | Outcomes |
|---|---|---|
| Individual Charisma | Jimmy Carter | Depersonalization |
| Frustrated Charisma | Joe McCarthy | Censure |
| Electoral Charisma | Robert F. Kennedy | Assassination |
| Electoral Charisma | Edward Kennedy | Defeat in primary |

It seems that Weber's terms of eruption and suffocation, and all the various hurdles in between, apply to various luminaries. But the study of these and other luminaries has to be left to other investigators.

19. Arthur M. Schlesinger, Jr. *A Thousand Days: John F. Kennedy in the White House* (Boston: Houghton Mifflin, 1965), p. 74.

20. Ibid., p. 75.

21. Berton Dulce and Edward Richter, *Religion and the Presidency* (New York: Macmillan, 1962), p. 151. This quote was used as an answer to the query of President Truman whether Kennedy was "quite ready for the country."

22. Richard J. Whalen, *The Founding Father: The Story of Joseph P. Kennedy* (New York: New American Library, 1964), p. 431.

23. Ibid., p. 433.

24. Mrs. Eleanor Roosevelt noticed that Kennedy's mass appeal was similar to the one of her husband. Senator Kennedy's "intelligence and courage elicit emo-

tions from his crowd which flow back to him and sustain and strengthen him."
Schlesinger, *Thousand Days*, p. 76.

25. James MacGregor Burns, *John Kennedy: A Political Portrait* (New York: Harcourt, Brace, 1959), pp. 239–40, 244.

26. Dulce and Richter, *Religion and Presidency*, chapters 10, 11, 12.

27. Schlesinger, *Thousand Days*, p. 34.

28. Neither nomination, election, or rulership lead to Weber's predicted "intellectual proletarianization," which can hardly be called a typical feature of democratic charisma. Max Weber, *Essays in Sociology* (New York: Oxford, 1946), p. 113.

29. *Public Papers of the Presidents of the United States: John F. Kennedy* (Washington, D.C.: U.S. Government Printing Office, 1962), pp. 1–3.

30. Tom Wicker, *JFK and LBJ: The Influence of Personality upon Politics* (New York: Morrow, 1968), p. 76.

31. Ibid., p. 84.

32. Ibid., pp. 144, 146.

33. Schlesinger, *Thousand Days*, pp. 256, 259.

34. Herbert J. Muller, *Adlai Stevenson: A Study in Values* (New York: Harper, 1967), p. 284.

35. Henry M. Pachter, *Collision Course: The Cuban Missile Crisis and Co-existence* (New York: Praeger, 1963), p. 104.

36. Leading interpreters assess the deed only in strictly individual terms. His biographer said: "It was this combination of toughness and restraint, of will, nerve and wisdom, so brilliantly controlled, so matchlessly calibrated, that dazzled the world." Schlesinger, *Thousand Days*, p. 841. While this praise is justified, it does not recognize the hero worship of his followers who through their belief completed the shift to heroic charisma.

37. Reinhard Bendix, *Max Weber—An Intellectual Portrait* (New York: Doubleday, 1960), p. 327.

38. "The ideal-typical construction does not claim that the different characteristics of the complex bureaucracy do actually and necessarily appear together, but that they *should* be interlinked if the legal rulership shall be purposive-rational in every respect." Renate Mayntz, "Max Weber's Idealtypus der Bürokratie and Die Organisationssoziologie," in *Bürokratische Organisation* (Cologne: Kiepenheuer & Witsch, 1968), p. 31.

39. Compare Arthur Schweitzer, "Vom Idealtypus zum Prototyp," *Zeitschrift für die gesamte Staatswissenschaft*, vol. 120, Jan. 1964, pp. 12–55.

40. While Weber had underlined the "antagonism between charisma and . . . the capitalist enterprise" (p.1118), he attributed this cleavage exclusively to the rationality of the enterprises, opposed to any form of irrationality. In a real setting, enterprises often shift from rationality to irrationality, making them amenable to a temporary collaboration with a charismatic rulership.

41. This term has been used by Ralf Dahrendorf, *Markt und Plan: Zwei Typen der Rationalitat* (Tübingen: Mohr, 1966), pp. 1–19. He sees the absence of *Herrschaft* as the hidden assumption of the theory of free markets. English translation in R. Dahrendorf, *Essays in the Theory of Society* (Stanford: University Press, 1965), chap. 8.
42. Weber, *Wirtschaft und Gesellschaft*, p. 555.
43. In the contact theory of Edward Shils, there is a shift in the charismatic act from the acutely emotional faith of leader and followers to the attribution of sacredness. While this may be adequate for institutional charisma, how can an aspirant regard his quality as sacred, how can a charismatic appeal be sacred for paladins and followers? Edward Shils, *Center and Periphery: Essays in Macrosociology* (Chicago: University of Chicago Press, 1975), p. 119.
44. More recently the ideal-typical method has been extended into the polar type presenting the two extremes of a logical continuum. See John C. McKinney, *Constructive Typology and Social Theory* (New York: Crofts, 1966), and Walter Eucken, *The Foundation of Economics* (Chicago: University of Chicago Press, 1951). For a critique of Eucken's method, see Arthur Schweitzer, "Economic Systems and Economic History," *Journal of Economic History*, vol. 25, Dec. 1965, pp. 660–79.
45. In terms of procedures Weber formulated two ideal types. One was a construct without any empirical counterpart, serving only as a heuristic principle of understanding, such as the marginal principle in neoclassical economics. See Arthur Schweitzer, "Typological Method in Economics: Max Weber's Contribution," *History of Political Economy*, vol. 2, Spring 1970, pp. 66–96. The other was a construction as an interpretation (*Deutung*) in terms of the interests, values, traditions, or affects of the respective actors. See H. H. Bruun, *Science, Values and Politics, in Max Weber's Methodology* (Copenhagen: Mundegaard, 1972), p. 204.
46. The thesis that "institutionalizing of charisma" is achieved by and during the phase of routinization overlooks the strategic role of rulership. See S. N. Eisenstadt, *Social Differentiation and Stratification* (Glenview: Scott, Foresman, 1971), p. 46.
47. The additional propositions will be given arabic numbers in brackets, e.g., [12] [13] onwards.
48. Prior to each reelection there was the same kind of attack by Roosevelt's enemies in the party. One senator from the South said: "The whole idea is going to be indispensability. . . . He cuts down every possibility that's coming along. As soon as they begin to get prominent, he gets rid of them." Allen Drury, *A Senate Journal—1943–1945* (New York: Capo Press, 1972), p. 104.
49. Partisan resentment was a minor motive for turning against the courts. The majority of judges were Republicans, and corporation lawyers had invented the technique of constitutional prejudgment in which nonjudges render opinions

as to why the New Deal laws violated the Constitution. Schlesinger, *Upheaval*, p. 468.

50. Instead of Weber's dictum that "the charismatic organization undergoes progressive rationalization" (p.266), both followers and opponents of the leader were in the grip of extreme anxiety during the Constitutional crisis. Irrationality won over rationality.

51. Sidney Fine, *Sit-Down: The General Motors Strike of 1936–1937* (Ann Arbor: University of Michigan Press, 1969), chap. 1.

52. Frances Perkins, *The Roosevelt I Knew* (New York: Viking Press, 1946), p. 322.

53. Fine, *Sit-Down*, p. 355.

54. Jerald S. Auerbach, *Labor and Liberty: The La Follette Committee and the New Deal* (Indianapolis: Bobbs-Merrill, 1966), p. 75.

55. For the details on gaining union security from the industrial autocrats, see Arthur Schweitzer, "Countervailing Power Revisited," *Journal of Economic Issues*, vol. 14, Dec. 1980, pp. 999–1018.

56. A telegram from civic leaders of Boston to the Senate, as quoted by Fine, *Sit-Down*, p. 333.

57. Elliott Roosevelt, ed., *F.D.R.: His Personal Letters 1928–1945* (New York: Duell, Sloan and Pearce, 1950), vol. 3, p. 644.

58. "Roosevelt lost three successive battles over relief; he barely retrieved his devaluation powers; he witnessed the final destruction of his undistributed profit tax . . . he was denied so much as a shadow of his spending and housing programs." James T. Paterson, *Congressional Conservatism and the New Deal, 1933–1939* (Lexington: University of Kentucky Press, 1967), p. 328.

59. The occasional tensions gave rise only to a few estrangements. Best known was the breach between Roosevelt and John L. Lewis, who felt betrayed because Roosevelt did not publicly support the sit-down strikes. Saul Alinsky, *John L. Lewis: An Unauthorized Biography* (New York: G. P. Putnam's Sons, 1949), pp. 147, 159–60.

60. Weber's specific thesis that allies dilute the essence of charisma was not applicable to democratic charisma because he tied the alliance with tradition and did not anticipate the allies promoting reforms.

61. E. Roosevelt, *Personal Letters*, p. 373.

62. Schlesinger, *Upheaval*, p. 584.

63. George Wolfskill and John A. Hudson, *All But the People: Franklin D. Roosevelt and His Critics, 1933–39* (New York: Macmillan, 1969), pp. 242, 266, 280, 273.

64. Ibid., pp. 256, 284.

65. The same lack of a program prevailed for those who insisted upon the autocratic operation of the economy. Restoration would have called for dismantling the New Deal and then hoping for the self-correction of the economy.

66. Wendell Willkie, *Free Enterprise* (Washington: Home Library, 1940), p. 37 ff.

67. Burns, *Lion and Fox*, p. 448.
68. This change is still not generally recognized in the sociology of social change. One author gave us seven causes for social change, but none of them included charisma or bureaucracy. Cf. Perry S. Cohen, *Modern Social Theory* (New York: Basic Books, 1968), chap. 7. For a detailed examination of Weber's theory of development, see Wolfgang Schluchter, *Die Entwicklung des Okzidentalen Rationalismus* (Tübingen: Mohr, 1979), p. 39 ff.
69. Richard Hofstadter, *The Age of Reform* (New York: Knopf, 1955), p. 317.
70. Some historians even convinced themselves that charisma is entirely useless for the study of the New Deal and irrelevant for historical investigations in general. Arthur M. Schlesinger, *The Politics of Hope* (Boston: Houghton Mifflin, 1962), pp. 9–16.
71. Robert Presthus, *Men at the Top: A Study of Community Power* (New York: Oxford University Press, 1964), p. 10.
72. Milton Katz, *The Things That Are Caesar's* (New York: Knopf, 1966), pp. 199, 200.

# GLOSSARY

**Aristocratic Charisma:** Believers in sacred knowledge formed aristocratic religious groups that were closed to the masses of believers.

**Ascetic Charisma:** The ascetic belief calls upon the prophet and disciples to abstain from an excess of emotion and forgive the sins of the disbelievers.

**Charismatic Acclamation:** The modern plebiscite in democracy has provided a method of recognizing a charismatically gifted person by means of an acclamation.

**Charismatic Act:** The essence of a charismatic qualification is an acutely emotional faith of the leader in his destiny and of the followers in his calling by a Higher Being.

**Charismatic Apparatus:** An organizational network is created and directed by the leader, managed by his paladins, and designed to guide a charismatic movement.

**Charismatic Appeal:** The prospective or actual leader arouses the masses to such an extent that they become euphoric and turn into his loyal followers.

**Charismatic Approval:** The attracted masses feel an inner obligation to be loyal to the leader and recognize his right to leadership.

**Charismatic Aspirant:** A potentially charismatic leader presents publicly his claim to leadership because of his calling to lead.

**Charismatic Assistants:** Devotees of the leader who are appointed by him to positions of trust, are paid for their services, and live with their own families.

**Charismatic Authority:** Consists of the claim of the leader either to give commands to be obeyed or to express recommendations to be voluntarily accepted by the followers.

**Charismatism:** Includes all typically charismatic actions regardless of which leader and followers perform such actions.

**Charismatization:** The charismatic leader presents his own interpretation of a crisis as an emergency that calls for a specific assignment for himself and induces him to propose certain charismatic policies.

**Charismatic Caesar:** A bearer of heroic charisma performs some extraordinary deeds which excite the masses to acclaim him as their new political leader by plebiscite.

**Charismatic Castration:** A charismatic aspirant is chosen by the boss as the candidate of the spoils party but is, after his election, reduced to a mere figurehead.

**Charismatic Challengership:** A successful aspirant faces the challenge of rival candidates in elections and then has to meet the challenge of a severe crisis.

**Charismatic Circle:** A variety of small groups that enjoy face-to-face relationships with the leader and belong to either his table community or to his evening monologues.

**Charismatic Community:** A small group of paladins that lives with the leader, whose members refrain from marrying, shun economic pursuit, disdain personal or group power, and live in devotion to the leader.

**Charismatic Decision-making:** Claiming a high degree of wisdom and foresight, giants say that their decisions are irrevocable and beyond criticism by anyone under their command.

**Charismatic Defects:** A charismatic aspirant experiences a handicap in his appeal because he has committed an immoral act or a political mistake that makes his potential followers reluctant to follow him.

**Charismatic Demagogue:** A man of charismatic qualities whose appeal to the masses has only a symbolic effect because he seeks power only to satisfy his vanity.

**Charismatic Depersonalization:** The unique gift of charisma becomes attached not to a person but to an office or institution that is regarded as sacred by the charismatic followers.

**Charismatic Devotion:** Mass enthusiasm for the leader tends to his glorification and generates a sense of loyalty and readiness to serve the leader and his cause.

**Charismatic Discipline:** A charismatic hero can obtain continuous and blind obedience to his commands when he formulates a disciplinary code and trains his followers in the habits of submission.

**Charismatic Disenchantment:** Internal disbelief in the continued exceptional qualities of the leader is the first step leading to a transitional charisma in democracy and to draconic punishment in dictatorial charisma.

**Charismatic Disloyalty:** In charismatic dictatorship, disputing the leader's decisions leads to the charge of disloyalty to the leader, who takes disciplinary action against the disbeliever.

**Charismatic Discretion:** Having received a "mandate" from the voters, the leader enjoys the discretion of selecting policies of his choice and expects the followers to give him full support.

**Charismatic Disposition:** In situations of widespread dissatisfaction, masses long for a gifted person and await him patiently, ready to receive his appeal and to become his followers.

**Charismatic Dormancy:** Prior to becoming an aspirant, the charismatic germ lies dormant in a person until it is evoked by some ascetic or other regimen.

**Charisma of the Disciples:** One branch of Pietism glorified workers because they possessed the spark of divinity which expressed itself in working for low wages and rejecting any urge to acquire property.

**Charismatic Education:** Special schools and training courses are established by some giants either to indoctrinate the young or to imbue courage and obedience in the future assistants of the leader.

**Charismatic Failures:** Charismatic aspirants may fail because of external obstacles: they may be shot by assassins, castrated by party leaders, trapped by political opponents, or driven from office by superior holders of power.

**Charismatic Giants:** These outstanding leaders combine natural and supernatural qualities and at the same time obtain control of a political party and bureaucracy in their efforts to direct a charismatic rulership.

**Charismatic Hero:** An exceptional deed, whether by rhetoric gifts or by outstanding actions, elevates a man into the position of a hero, who becomes the charismatic leader through the worship of the masses.

**Charismatic Ideology:** Charismatic giants adopt certain ideals, become their first articulators, and charismatize the ideals when they are used to indoctrinate the followers.

**Charismatic Image:** The various ideals contained in the mission permit several self-images of the leader as well as group images of and by the followers.

**Charismatic Infallibility:** Dictatorial giants claim to be infallible in their decisions and predictions because of their intuition or blessing by a supernatural force.

**Charismatic Instability:** In euphoric charisma leadership is of short duration because the feelings of the followers are inherently fickle and outside resistance often limits the spatial spread of charisma.

**Charismatic Invincibility:** The trust in the leader during campaigns is so great that he and his followers feel that they cannot possibly lose and must be victorious.

**Charismatic Luminaries:** These persons fall short of becoming giants because compassions do not become emotional unions, and other political party leaders retain a share of the power so that all kinds of compromises are unavoidable.

**Charismatic Message:** Religious or ideological beliefs, cherished by the leader, provide him with a charismatic message that guides him in his choice of policies.

**Charismatic Mission:** While the message is directed to the leader, the mission moves him to proclaim his assessment of the emergency and to detail his assignment for overcoming the crisis.

**Charismatic Revolutions:** In its most potent form charisma disrupts rational as well as traditional rules. In its impact upon others, charisma is the specifically creative and revolutionary form of history.

**Charismatic Routinization:** The structure of charismatic leadership is transformed from an extraordinary movement into an everyday routine in which the members become tax-paying subjects or dues-paying members of institutions.

**Charismatic Rulership:** In control of party and government, elected by a great majority of the voters, the giant through his legislation and administration establishes a rulership that comes close to his proclaimed mission.

**Charismatic Stabilizers:** Dictatorial giants have used infallibility and personality cult to renew or intensify the belief in the leader, whereas democratic giants have discovered that ethical beliefs served the same purpose.

**Charismatic Standpatship:** In their third phase, democratic giants suffer from an external resistance of the traditional forces, and abortive attempts at changing the constitution give rise to stymied charisma.

**Charismatic Structure:** Charismatic communities have an internal structure that emanates from the leader's belief in his calling and from the belief of the paladins in his exceptional qualities; the former belief brings authority, and the latter belief obedience and loyalty to the small group.

**Charismatic Warlord:** A war leader proves his heroism in successful warfare undertaken for prestige and booty, but his charismatic rule is limited to military affairs, and power has to be shared with the peacetime chieftains of various tribes.

**Comparative Charisma:** Different strength and depth of the exceptional qualities and different degrees of success permit a comparison among aspirants, failures, luminaries, and giants.

**Connected Charisma:** In experiencing an intermingling of trust in God and confidence in the leader, religious followers can make a spiritual connection with God through the prophet.

**Constricted Charisma:** When experts and charismatics operate in the modern organization, the experts tend to restrict the influence of the charismatics because the expert satisfies the needs of the organization directly.

**Conservative Charisma:** When the leader incorporates a conservative ideology into his mission, he will use his charismatic authority to bring as many traditional institutions into his rulership as possible during his time of office.

**Contact Charisma:** If charisma is redefined as a vital force in every line of endeavor, everyone coming in contact with that force is a bearer of charisma, but is hardly a leader.

**Countercharisma:** In the contact theory, the political charismatic claims a monopoly of virtue, which claim is opposed by the economic innovator who has within him a spark of divinity.

**Countervailing Power:** The power of the ruling organizations in democracy opposes the charismatic leader who together with his allies develops countervailing power, originally for reasons of defense only.

**Crisis Charisma:** A charismatic giant faces a severe crisis of whatever nature, but his calling gives him the self-confidence to adopt a radically new policy in order to overcome the crisis.

**Cumulative Charisma:** A gigantic leader succeeds in becoming a bearer of natural and supernatural charisma, thereby enjoying a magnification of his authority and appeal.

**Delegated Charisma:** In dictatorial charisma, the top leader delegates charismatic authority to a few of his paladins, who exercise power in their own right, but stay within the policy lines of the top leader.

**Democratic Charisma:** Enjoying an emotional accessibility of the masses in campaigns, democratic candidates seek to establish an emotional attachment of the voters to themselves. The one with charismatic qualities is likely to win the voters' confidence.

**Democratic Dictatorship:** Democratic and dictatorial features are combined when a military leader, after his victory, gains the devotion of the soldiers and is elected president in a plebiscite by citizens.

**Dictatorial Charisma:** Based on his calling, the dictatorial leader demands that the voters become his followers and insists that they believe in his ideology and obey his commands.

**Discretional Charisma:** Exemplary prophets claim to know God's will and derive from this belief the discretion to select unilaterally their policies and symbols.

**Derived Charisma:** A powerful but noncharismatic paladin seeks to become the successor of the dead leader by asserting that he is closest to the legacy left by the dead leader from which he claims a derived charisma.

**Electoral Charisma:** Arising during an electoral campaign, euphoria helps a charismatic claimant to get elected, but then subsides without lending sufficient support to his policies.

**Emotional Seizure:** At the climax of a charismatic appeal the conscious and subconscious feelings of the masses unite with those of the leader, who proclaims their emotional unity.

**Ephemeral Charisma:** Religious anarchists strongly oppose the state, but their religious faith is superficial.

**Eruptive Charisma:** A leader is able to excite an overflowing of emotions in a critical situation, but he is able to mobilize the mass outburst in his favor.

**Ethical Charisma:** The mission of the leader comprises ethical principles that take the place of political ideologies, but guide the leader and followers in their campaigns and policies.

**Euphoric Charisma:** Comprises all the subtypes of charismatic emotions that climax in an emotional union between masses and leaders, regardless of the nature of those emotions.

**Faith Charisma:** Religious faith engenders a special quality of inwardness and a trust in God whose will is known to the believers. Such faith charisma emanates from supernatural forces.

**Ideological Charisma:** Worldly ideals are adopted by the leader from other sources, but the ideals become beliefs and as such are a part of the charismatic mission.

**Imitated Charisma:** The leader's qualities are imitated by the paladins who behave as if they were charismatically endowed and demand adulation from their subordinates.

**Individual Charisma:** A charismatic aspirant feels his own calling and enters the electoral competition, but his minimal oratorical abilities prevent him from turning the listeners into followers.

**Institutional Charisma:** Sacredness and awe are felt by the masses for a particular institution which is venerated as if it possessed charismatic qualities.

**Interactive Charisma:** The special qualities of natural and superhuman charisma are effectively intertwined and personified by a leader so that the attachment of the followers obtains an exceptional strength and duration.

**Interrupted Charisma:** A sudden emotional wave felt by voters is seen as a threat by controllers of political parties or financial organizations, who hastily take action seeking to control the emotions.

**Intertwined Charisma:** Ideals selected by the leader and those chosen by allies become so interlinked as to unite various groups behind the charismatic leader and his policies.

**Legendary Charisma:** The legacy of a dead leader is worshipped by the paladins and followers as if he were still among the living, and his successors claim to implement his ideals.

**Manufactured Charisma:** A noncharismatic personality fabricates a belief in himself, claims to possess his own ideology, and forces others to behave as if they accepted his claim, often by despotic methods.

**Militant Charisma:** A democratic leader of charismatic qualification personifies the will of defending his country against dictatorial aggressors and contributes his share to the enemy's defeat.

**Mystic Charisma:** In seeking the proper road to religious salvation, specific rituals are selected for their mystic power to achieve redemption of guilt and to obtain grace by sacrament.

**Natural Charisma:** A particular person possesses exceptional qualities by virtue of a natural endowment which enables him to generate similar emotions in others who turn into his followers.

**Reformist Charisma:** In terms of political and ethical intentions a democratic giant forms an alliance with labor and farm organizations for the purpose of carrying through extensive political and economic reforms.

**Restorative Charisma:** A charismatically endowed president forms an alliance with the counterpolity for the sake of restoring old traditions and destroying the reform of a dead charismatic leader.

**Peace Charisma:** A charismatic leader in time of war will proclaim his conditions for peace to be implemented after victory. These conditions of peace are used to justify entering and winning the war.

**Permanent Charisma:** Professional magicians and warriors seek a situation of permanent charisma, but this can be obtained only if the crisis becomes permanent.

**Personality Cult:** The greater the power of the dictatorial giant, the greater the temptation and opportunities to engage in various forms of personality cult. They can have an effect similar to the one of heroic deeds.

**Plebiscitary Charisma:** Instead of being a regular election, the plebiscites of voting for a charismatic leader combine acclamation with worshipping a charismatic hero.

**Political Charisma:** Emotional endowment of the leader and related mass movements can establish extraordinary leadership in any kind of political system. In recent history such leadership has alternated in irregular fashion with pragmatic leadership, whether in democracy or dictatorship.

**Providential Charisma:** Charismatic giants claiming supernatural gifts either assert to know God's will or thank him subsequently for having blessed his policies and deeds.

**Pure Charisma:** The acutely emotional faith constitutes the essence of the charismatic quality which generates a completely new orientation of all the attitudes held by followers. Any interference with this reorientation leads to impure charisma.

**Shock Charisma:** A sudden threat to the national security arouses mass passion against the enemy, who is then confronted by a leader exhibiting or revitalizing charismatic qualities.

**Specialized Charisma:** Disputes between charismatic contenders will be settled by means of specialization so that each one obtains jurisdiction to operate in different areas of activity.

**Segmental Charisma:** A time lag develops in the evolution of several charismatic subtypes so that each one becomes a segment in a chain of subsequential charismata, experienced by one and the same leader.

**Sporadic Charisma:** A charismatic aspirant is handicapped by some moral or political defect, so that the charismatic disposition of the followers dwindles, and he is defeated in a contested election.

**Subsequential Charisma:** Over a longer period of time, the leader shifts from one subtype of charisma to another, from electoral to heroic charisma, as if one were caused by the other.

**Subsidiary Charisma:** Arises in the relations between the top leader and some of his paladins, who derive limited charismatic qualities from the leader and owe him full loyalty.

**Surrogate Charisma:** A genuine charismatic leader runs into legal difficulties in getting elected, so he has a relative elected to a particular office behind which he acts as a charismatic leader.

**Symbolic Charisma:** Taking an oath swearing loyalty to the leader stands as a symbol for unlimited obedience to all the wishes and commands of the dictatorial leader.

**Synergistic Charisma:** Certain charismatic and noncharismatic components interact in such a way as to strengthen the leader who is building up a charismatic rulership.

**Stymied Charisma:** Legal or political barriers impose a handicap upon the leader, who is prevented from taking further initiatives and must rely upon his allies to get his bills through the legislature.

**Temporary Charisma:** The charismatic aspirant suffers from inadequate but innate abilities so that his appeal is ineffectual and his original followers will desert him.

**Traditional Charisma:** A charismatic leader is committed to the goal of restoring a cherished traditional order which he incorporates into his mission but then pursues this goal by charismatic methods.

**Transitional Charisma:** Mass euphoria is strong enough to carry the leader into office, but then passions subside while resistance of opponents increases, limiting the leader's hold of office to a short period of time.

**Value Charisma:** Ethical values are incorporated in the charismatic mission of the giant, who derives significant guidelines from these values for his policies.

# SELECTED BIBLIOGRAPHY

## I. Weber's Original Publications

*Zur Geschichte der Handelsgesellschaften im Mittelalter.* Stuttgart: Enke, 1889.

*Die Römische Agrargeschichte in ihrer Bedeutung für das Staats-und Privatrecht.* Stuttgart: Enke, 1891.

*Die Verhältnisse der Landarbeiter im oestelbischen Deutschland.* Berlin: Duncker & Humblot, 1892.

*Die Boerse.* Göttingen: Arbeiterbibliothek, 1894.

*Wirtschaft und Gesellschaft,* 2 vols. Tübingen: Mohr, 1921.

*Gesammelte Aufsätze zur Religionssoziologie,* 3 vols. Tübingen: Mohr, 1920–21.

*Gesammelte Politische Schriften.* Munich: Drei Masken Verlag, 1921.

*Die Rationalen und Soziologischen Grundlagen der Musik.* Tübingen. Mohr, 1921.

*Gesammelte Aufsätze zur Wissenschaftslehre.* Tübingen: Mohr, 1922.

*Wirtschaftsgeschichte.* Munich: Duncker & Humblot, 1923.

*Gesammelte Aufsätze zur Sozial—und Wirtschaftsgeschichte.* Tübingen: Mohr, 1924.

*Gesammelte Aufsätze zur Soziologie und Sozialpolitik.* Tübingen: Mohr, 1924.

## II. Translations of Weber's Works

*General Economic History.* Translated by Frank H. Knight. New York: Allen & Unwin, 1927.

*The Protestant Ethic and the Spirit of Capitalism.* Translated by Talcott Parsons. London: Allen & Unwin, 1930.

*From Max Weber: Essays in Sociology.* Translated by Hans Gerth and C. Wright Mills. New York: Oxford University Press, 1946.

*Theory of Social and Economic Organization.* Translated by Talcott Parsons and A. M. Henderson. New York: Oxford University Press, 1947.

*The Methodology of the Social Sciences.* Translated by Edward Shils and Henry A. Finch. Glencoe: The Free Press, 1949.

*The Religion of China.* Translated by Hans Gerth. Glencoe: Free Press, 1951.

*Ancient Judaism.* Translated by Hans Gerth and Don Martindale. Glencoe: Free Press, 1952.

*Max Weber on Law in Economy and Society.* Translated by Max Rheinstein and Edward Shils. Cambridge: Harvard University Press, 1954.

*The Rational and Social Foundations of Music.* Translated by Don Martindale, Johannes Riedel, and Gertrude Neuwirth. Carbondale: Southern Illinois University Press, 1958.

*The Religion of India.* Translated by Hans Gerth and Don Martindale. Glencoe: Free Press, 1958.

*The City.* Translated by Don Martindale and Gertrude Neuwirth. Glencoe: Free Press, 1958.

*The Sociology of Religion.* Translated by Ephraim Fischoff. Boston: Beacon Press, 1963.

*Economy and Society: An Outline of Interpretive Sociology,* 3 vols., 4th ed. Edited by Guenther Roth and Claus Wittich. New York: Irvington, 1968.

*Max Weber on Charisma and Institution Building.* Edited by N. S. Eisenstadt. Chicago: University of Chicago Press, 1968.

*Socialism.* Translated by H. F. Dickie-Clark. Durban (SA): University of Natal Press, 1967.

*Max Weber: The Interpretation of Social Reality.* Edited by J. E. T. Eldridge. New York: Scribner's, 1975.

*Roscher and Knies: Logical Problems of Historical Economics.* Translated by Guy Oates. New York: Free Press, 1975.

*Max Weber: Critique of Stammler.* Translated by Guy Oates. New York: Free Press, 1977.

### III.  Charisma and Leadership

Ake, C. "Charismatic Legitimation and Political Integration." *Comparative Studies in Society and History,* vol. 14, 1966/67, pp. 1–13.

Ake, C. *A Theory of Political Integration.* Homewood: Dorsey Press, 1967. Chaps. 3 and 4.

Apter, D. E. *Ghana in Transition.* New York: Atheneum, 1963. Pp. 303ff.

Apter, D. E. *The Politics of Modernization.* Chicago: University of Chicago Press, 1965.

Apter, D. E. "Nkrumah, Charisma and the Coup." *Daedalus,* vol. 97, 1967/68, pp. 757–92.

Bass, B. M. *Leadership, Psychology and Organizational Behaviour.* New York: Harper & Row, 1960.

Beetham, D. *Max Weber and the Theory of Modern Politics.* London: Allen & Unwin, 1974. Pp. 226ff.

Bendix, R. *Max Weber: An Intellectual Portrait.* Garden City: Doubleday, 1960. Chap. 10.

Bendix, R. "Einige Bemerkungen zu einem Buch von Wolfgang Mommsen." *Kölner Zeitschrift für Soziologie und Sozialpsychologie,* vol. 13, 1961, pp. 258–62.

Bendix, R. "Reflections on Charismatic Leadership." In *State and Society.* Boston: Little, Brown, 1968. Pp. 616–29.

Bensman, J. and M. Givant. "Charisma and Modernity: The Use and Abuse of a Concept." *Social Research,* vol. 42, 1975, pp. 570–614.

Berger, P. L. "Charisma and Religious Innovation." *American Sociological Review,* vol. 28, 1963, pp. 940–50.

Binion, R. *Hitler Among the Germans.* New York: Elsevier, 1976.

Bord, R. J. "Toward a Social-Psychological Theory of Charismatic Social Influence Processes." *Social Forces,* 1975, pp. 485–97.

Bowie, L. "Charisma: Weber and Nasir." *Middle East Journal,* vol. 30, 1976, pp. 141–57.

Bullock, A. *Hitler: A Study in Tyranny.* New York: Bantam, 1958.

Burns, J. Mc. *Roosevelt: The Lion and the Fox.* New York: Harcourt, Brace, 1956.

Burns, J. Mc. *John Kennedy: A Political Portrait.* New York: Harcourt, Brace, 1959.

Burns, J. Mc. *Roosevelt: The Soldier of Freedom.* New York: Harcourt, Brace, 1970.

Burns, J. Mc. *Leadership.* New York: Harper & Row, 1978.

Butler, D. J. "Charisma, Migration and Elite Coalescence." *Comparative Politics,* vol. 1, 1968/69, pp. 423–39.

Clague, M. "Conceptions of Leadership: Charles de Gaulle and Max Weber." *Political Theory,* vol. 3, 1975, pp. 423–40.

Cohen, J. "The Concept of Charisma and the Analysis of Leadership." *Political Studies,* vol. 20, 1972, pp. 299–305.

Davies, J. L. "Charisma in the 1952 Campaign." *American Political Science Review,* vol. 48, 1954/55, pp. 1083–1102.

Decken, K. "Der General Hauptmann Kong La: Eine Studie Charismatischer Führerschaft in Laos." *Dritte Welt,* vol. 1, 1972, pp. 305–14.

Dekmeijian, R. H. and M. J. Wyszomirski. "Charismatic Leadership in Islam, The Mahdi of the Sudan." *Comparative Studies in Society and History,* vol. 14, 1971/72, pp. 193–214.

Dettman, P. R. "Leaders and the Structures in the 'Third World' Politics." *Comparative Politics,* vol. 6, 1973/74, pp. 245–69.

Dogan, M. "Le personnel Politique et la personalité charismatique." *Revue Francais Sociologique,* vol. 6, 1965, pp. 305–24.

Dow, Th. E. "The Role of Charisma in Modern African Development." *Social Forces,* vol. 46, 1968, pp. 328–37.

Dow, Th. E. "The Theory of Charisma." *Sociological Quarterly,* vol. 10, 1969, pp. 306–18.

Downton, J. V. *Rebel Leadership: Commitment and Charisma in the Revolutionary Process.* New York: Free Press, 1973.

Easton, D. *A Systems Analysis of Political Life.* New York: Wiley, 1965. Pp. 302ff.

Edinger, L. J., ed. *Political Leadership in Industrialized Societies.* New York: Wiley, 1967. (With an interdisciplinary bibliography.)

Eisenstadt, S. N. Introduction to *Max Weber on Charisma and Institution Building.* Chicago: University of Chicago Press, 1968.

Emmet, D. *Function, Purpose, and Powers.* New York: Macmillan, 1958. Pp. 233ff.

Erikson, E. *Identity, Youth, and Crisis.* New York: Norton, 1968.

Etzioni, A. *A Comparative Analysis of Complex Organizations.* Glencoe: Free Press, 1961. Pp. 201ff.

Etzioni, A. "Dual Leadership in Complex Organizations." *American Sociological Review,* vol. 30, 1965. Pp. 688–99.

Fabian, J. "Charisma and Cultural Change." *Comparative Studies in Society and History,* vol. 11, 1969. Pp. 155–73.

Fabian, J. *Jamaa: A Charismatic Movement in Katanga.* Evanston: Northwestern University Press, 1971.

Fagan, R. "Charismatic Authority and the Leadership of Fidel Castro." *Western Political Quarterly,* vol. 18, 1965, pp. 275–84.

Fischer, L. *A Life of Lenin.* New York: Harper & Row, 1965.

Friedland, W. H. "For a Sociological Concept of Charisma." *Social Forces,* vol. 43, 1964, pp. 18–26.

Friedrich, C. J. "Political Leadership and the Problem of Charismatic Power." *Journal of Politics,* vol. 23, 1961, pp. 3–24.

Gamm, H. J. *Der Braune Kult: Das Dritte Reich und seine Ersatzreligion.* Hamburg: Rutten and Loening, 1962.

Gerth, H. "The Nazi Party: Its Leadership and Composition." *American Journal of Sociology,* vol. 45, 1940, pp. 517–41.

Gifford, A. "An Application of Weber's Concept of Charisma." *Berkeley Journal of Sociology,* vol. 1. 1955, pp. 40–49.

Glassman, R. "Legitimacy and Manufactured Charisma." *Social Research,* vol. 42, 1975, pp. 615–36.

Goetze, D. "Einige Bemerkungen zu einer sociologischen Theorie charismatischer Politischer Führerschaft." *Dritte Welt,* vol. 1, 1972, pp. 315–34.

Goetze, D. "Charisma, Traditionalismus und Innovation: Der Fall Kuba." *Dritte Welt,* vol. 2, 1973, pp. 297–319.

Goetze, D. *Castro, Nkrumah, Sukarno: Eine Komparative Untersuchung.* Berlin: Duncker & Humblot, 1976.

Goldberg, E. F. *The Tragedy of Lyndon Johnson.* New York: Knopf, 1969.

Gouldner, A. W., ed. *Studies in Leadership.* New York: Harper & Row, 1950.

Gustin, B. H. "Charisma, Recognition, and the Motivation of Scientists." *American Journal of Sociology,* vol. 78, 1971/72, pp. 1119–34.

Heer, F. *Der Glaube des Adolf Hitlers.* München: Bechtel, 1968.

Hoffmann, S. "Heroic Leadership: The Case of Modern France." In Edinger, L. E., ed., *Political Leadership in Industrialized Societies.* New York: Wiley, 1967. Pp. 108ff.

Hook, S. *The Hero in History.* New York: Day, 1943.

Horowitz, I. L. "Party Charisma." *Studies in Comparative International Development,* vol. 1, 1965, pp. 83–97.

Horowitz, I. L. "Political Legitimacy and Crisis in Latin America." *Comparative Politics,* vol. 1, 1968/69, pp. 45–69.

Hungar, K. *Emperie und Praxis: Ertrag und Grenzen der Forschungen Max Webers im Lichte Neuer Konzeptionen.* Meisenheim: Hain, 1971. Pp. 86–91.

Jonas, R. A. and R. M. Anservitz. "Saint Simon and Saint Simonism: A Weberian View." *American Journal of Sociology,* vol. 80, 1975, pp. 1095–1123.

Kavanagh, D. *"Crisis, Charisma and British Politics; Winston Churchill as the Outsider.* London: Sage, 1974.

Knoll, J. H. *Führungsauslese in Liberalismus und Demokratie.* Stuttgart: Schwab, 1957. Pp. 149ff.

Knoll, J. H. "Demokratie und Politisches Führertum." *Zeitschrift für Religions und Geistesgeschichte,* vol. 12, 1960, pp. 81–87.

Langer, W. C. *The Mind of Adolf Hitler.* New York: Basic Books, 1972.

Lewis, J. W., ed. *Party Leadership in Communist China.* Ithaca: Cornell University Press, 1963.

Loewenstein, K. *Max Webers Staatspolitische Auffassungen in der Sicht unserer Zeit.* Frankfurt: Athenäum Fisher, 1966.

Loewenstein, K. "Max Weber als 'Ahnherrn' des Plebiszitären Führerstaats." *Kölner Zeitschrift für Soziologie und Sozialpsychologie,* vol. 13, 1961, pp. 311–28.

Marcus, J. T. "Transcendence and Charisma." *Western Political Quarterly,* vol. 14, 1961, pp. 236–41.

Mazlich, B. *The Revolutionary Ascetic: Evolution of a Political Type.* New York: Basic Books, 1976.

McFarland, A. *Power and Leadership in Pluralist Systems.* Stanford: Stanford University Press, 1969.

Mommsen, W. J. "Zum Begriff der 'Plebiszitaren Führerdemokratie' bei Max Weber." *Kölner Zeitschrift für Soziologie und Sozialpsychologie,* vol. 15, 1963, pp. 295–322.

Mühlmann, W. E. *Mahatma Gandhi: Der Mann, sein Werk, seine Wirkung.* Tübingen: Mohr, 1950.

Mühlmann, W. E. *Chiliasmus und Nativismus.* Berlin: Reimer, 1961.

Mühlmann, W. E. "Charisma." In Ritter, J., ed. *Historisches Wörterbuch der Philosophie.* Basel, 1971. Pp. 997–99.

Neumann, F. *Behemoth: The Structure and Practice of National Socialism.* 2d ed. New York: Oxford University Press, 1944.

Nyomarkay, J. *Charisma and Factionalism in the Nazi Party.* Minneapolis: University of Minnesota Press, 1967.

Oommen, T. K. "Charisma, Social Structure and Social Change." *Comparative Studies in Society and History*, vol. 10, 1967/68, pp. 85–99.

Oommen, T. K. *Charisma, Stability and Change: An Analysis of Bhoodan-Gramdan Movement in India*. New Delhi: Thompson Press, 1972.

Parsons, T. *The Structure of Social Action*. 2d ed. Glencoe: Free Press, 1949. Pp. 658–72.

Parsons, T. Introduction to Max Weber, *The Sociology of Religion*. Boston: Beacon Press, 1963. Pp. xix-ixvii.

Ratnam, K. J. "Charisma and Political Leadership." *Political Studies*, vol. 12, 1964, pp. 341–54.

Roth, G. "Personal Rulership, Patrimonialism, and Empire-building in the New States." *World Politics*, vol. 20, 1967/68, pp. 194–205.

Roth, G. "Socio-historical Model and Developmental Theory: Charismatic Community, Charisma of Reason, and the Counterculture." *American Sociological Review*, vol. 40, 1975, pp. 148–57.

Roth, G. "Religion and Revolutionary Beliefs: Sociological and Historical Dimensions in Max Weber's Work." *Social Forces*, vol. 55, 1976/77.

Roucek, J. S. "The Changing Concepts of Charismatic Leadership." *Internationales Jahrbuch für Religionssoziologie*, vol. 11, 1967, p. 87ff.

Runciman, W. G. "Charismatic Leadership and One Party Rule in Ghana." *Europäisches Archiv für Soziologie*, vol. 4, 1963, pp. 148–65.

Runciman, W. G. *A Critique of Max Weber's Philosophy of Social Science*. London: Cambridge University Press, 1972.

Rustow, D. A. *A World of Nations*. Washington, D.C.: n.p., 1967. Pp. 148ff.

Rustow, D. A. "The Study of Elites: Who's Who, When and How." *World Politics*, vol. 18, 1966, pp. 690–717.

Rustow, D. A., ed. *Philosophers and Kings: Studies in Leadership*. New York: Braziller, 1970.

San Juan, E., Jr. "Orientations of Max Weber's Concept of Charisma." *Centennial Review of Arts and Sciences*, vol. 11, 1967, p. 27ff.

Schiffer, I. *Charisma: A Psychoanalytic Look at Mass Society*. Toronto: University of Toronto Press, 1973.

Schlesinger, A. M., Jr. "Democracy and Heroworship in the 20th Century." *Encounter*, vol. 15, 1960, pp. 3–11.

Schlesinger, A. M., Jr. *A Thousand Days*. Boston: Houghton Mifflin, 1965.

Schlesinger, A. M., Jr. *The Politics of Hope*. Boston: Houghton Mifflin, 1962. Pp. 9–16.

Schoenbrun, D. *The Three Lives of Charles de Gaulle*. New York: Atheneum, 1966.

Schram, St. R. "Mao Tse-tung as a Charismatic Leader." *Asian Survey*, vol. 7, 1967, pp. 382–86.

Schütz, J. H. "Charisma and Social Reality in Primitive Christianity." *Journal of Sociology*, vol. 54, 1974, pp. 51–70.

Schweitzer, A. "Theory of Political Charisma." *Comparative Studies in Society and History*, vol. 16, 1974/75, pp. 50–81.

Selznick, P. "An Approach to a Theory of Bureaucracy." *American Sociological Review*, vol. 8, 1943, pp. 47–54.

Selznick, P. *Leadership in Administration*. New York: Harper, 1957.

Seyfarth, C. "Alltag und Charisma bei Weber." In Grathoff and Sprondel, eds., *Alfred Schütz und die Idee des Alltags in den Sozialwissenschaften*. Stuttgart: Enke, 1979. Pp. 155–77.

Seyfarth, C. and G. Schmidt. *Max Weber Bibliographie: Eine Dokumentation der Sekundärliteratur*. Stuttgart: Enke, 1977.

Shils, E. "Concentration and Dispersion of Charisma." *World Politics*, vol. 11, 1958, pp. 1–19.

Shils, E. "Charisma, Order and Status." *American Sociological Review*, vol. 30, 1965, pp. 199–212.

Shils, E. "Charisma." *International Encyclopedia of the Social Sciences*, vol. 2. New York: Macmillan, 1968. Pp. 386–90.

Shirai, N. "Charisma und Irrationalität in der Religionssoziologie Max Webers." *Journal of Religious Studies* (Tokyo), vol. 46, 1972, pp. 1–23.

Smelser, N. and W. T. Smelser, eds. *Personality and Social Systems*. New York: Wiley, 1963.

Spencer, M. E. "What Is Charisma?" *British Journal of Sociology*, vol. 24, 1973, pp. 341–54.

Stark, St. "Toward a Psychology of Charisma." *Psychological Reports*, vols. 23 and 24, 1968 and 1969, pp. 1163–66 and 88–99.

Stark, W. "The Routinization of Charisma: A Consideration of Catholicism." *Sociological Annals*, vol. 26, 1966, pp. 283–311.

Stewart, G. "Charisma and Integration: An 18th Century North American Case." *Comparative Studies in Society and History*, vol. 16, 1974/75, pp. 138–49.

Stogdill, R. *Handbook of Leadership: Survey of Theory and Research*. New York: Free Press, 1974.

Tiger, L. "Bureaucracy and Charisma in Ghana." *Journal of Asian and African Studies*, vol. 11, 1966, pp. 13–26.

Timmins, W. M. "Max Weber's Charisma and the Phenomenon of the Sacred." *Rocky Mountains Social Science Journal*, vol. 6, 1969, pp. 146–54.

Toth, M. A. "Toward a Theory of the Routinization of Charisma." *Rocky Mountains Social Science Journal*, vol. 9, 1972, pp. 93–98.

Tucker, R. C. "The Theory of Charismatic Leadership." *Daedalus*, vol. 97, 1968, pp. 731–56.

Tucker, R. C. "Personality and Political Leadership." *Political Science Quarterly*, vol. 92, 1977, pp. 383–93.

Tucker, R. C. "The Georges' Wilson Reexamined: An Essay on Psychobiography." *American Political Science Review*, vol. 1977, pp. 606–18.

Waddell, R. G. "Charisma and Reason: Paradoxes and Tactics of Originality." In Hill, M., *Sociological Yearbook of Religion in Britain*, vol. 5, 1972, pp. 1–10.

Wagener, Otto. *Hitler aus nachster Nahe*. Edited by H. A. Turner, Jr. Frankfurt: Ullstein, 1978.

Walzer, M. *The Revolution of the Saints*. Cambridge: Harvard University Press, 1965.

Weiss, J. *Max Webers Grundlegung der Soziologie*. Munich: UTB-Verlag, 1975.

Willner, A. R. *Charismatic Political Leadership: A Theory*. Princeton: Princeton University Press, 1969.

Willner, A. R. and D. Willner. "The Rise and Role of the Charismatic Leaders." *Annals of the American Academy of Political and Social Science*, vol. 358, 1965, pp. 77–88.

Wilson, B. R. *Magic and the Millennium*. London: Heinemann, 1973.

Wilson, B. R. *The Noble Savages: The Primitive Origins of Charisma*. Berkeley: University of California Press, 1975.

Wilson, R. A. and R. S. Perinbanayagam. "The Dialectics of Charisma." *Sociological Quarterly*, vol. 12, 1971, pp. 387–402.

Wolfenstein, E. V. "Some Psychological Aspects of Crisis Leadership." In Edinger, L. E., ed., *Political Leadership in Industrialized Societies*. New York: Wiley, 1967, pp. 155–81.

Wolfenstein, E. V. *The Revolutionary Personality*. Princeton: Princeton University Press, 1967.

Wolpe, H. "A Critical Analysis of Some Aspects of Charisma." *Sociological Review*, vol. 16, 1968/69, pp. 305–18.

Worsley, P. *The Trumpet Shall Sound*, 2d ed. New York: Schocken, 1968.

# INDEX

Acquiescence, 91, 92
Affective neutrality, 36
Ake, Claude, 347
Alinsky, Saul, 389
Alliance of Roosevelt, 234, 316, 334–35, 339
Alsace-Lorraine, 119, 122, 159
Alsop, Joseph, 379
Apter, David E., 334, 347
Arbitrary authority, 96, 178, 187, 190
Arendt, Hannah, 354
Aristocracy, in charisma, 42, 286
Aron, Raymond, 369, 381, 382
Aron, Robert, 343, 381
Ascetic charisma, 40
Assassinations: of Hitler, 78, 92, 162, 176; of
    Lenin, 181, 185; of King, 220; of Wallace,
    229; of Kennedy, 324
Auerbach, Jerald S., 389
Austria, 68; Nazi takeover of, 74, 76, 88, 103,
    117, 120; its new administration, 158
Authenticity, of charisma, 42, 43
Axis powers, 296, 302

Backer, John H., 384
Backlash, white, 217, 220, 221, 230
Barker, Ernest, 377
Bass, Bernard, 347
Bauer, Raymond, 367
Beck, Ludwig, 84
Beetham, David, 369
Bellush, Bernard, 376
Bennecke, Heinrich, 363
Bennet, Lerone J., 345, 370
Berger, Monroe, 355
Bernstein, Barton J., 386
Bernstein, Irving, 385
Bendix, Reinhard, 22, 57, 326, 344, 346, 347,
    348, 349, 350, 373
Besson, Waldemar, 362

Bevan, Aneurin, 10, 13, 17
Bhutto, Z. A., 14
Bierstedt, Robert, 355
Bismarck, Otto von, 82, 103, 203, 276
Black movement, in U.S.: and Weber's theory
    of races, 210; ultimate goal of, 211; reform
    and revolution in, 216; demand for integrated
    housing, 217; three civil rights acts, 216; and
    dispute over black power, 218, and search for
    social democracy, 235
Blau, Peter, 355, 381
Blitzkriegs, 77, 288; as charismatic deeds, 123,
    194; as part of Hitler's strategy, 84, 116, 117,
    118, 119
Bloch, Joseph, 359
Blomberg, Werner von (General), 117
Blum, John M., 384
Bolshevik party: vanguard of leaders, 164; as
    venerators of science, 166; and democratic
    centralism, 170, 179; insurrection by disguise
    of, 171–72; network of auxiliary organization
    in, 173; Stalin as general secretary, 174; Lenin
    loses control over, 175; no factions within,
    176; and discipline, 177; Stalin's despotic
    leadership of, 188–93; role of politburo in,
    179; collective leadership spurned by, 179,
    185
Bolsheviks, 55, 57, 58, 59, 101
Bonapartism, Marxian theory of, 182, 277
Bormann, Martin, 76, 77, 125, 134, 353
Bosses, political, 204, 238
Bouhler, Phillip, 78, 135
Bracher, Karl D., 358
Bramstedt, Ernst, 353
Bräutigam, Otto, 364
Bretton, Henry, 344
Broszat, Martin, 305
Brown, Jerry, 12
Bruun, H. H., 385

Buch, Walter, 153, 190
Bullock, Allan, 359
Bürckel, Joseph, 157, 158
Bureaucracy: Weber's theory of, 58, 129, 278;
    modern theory of organization in, 135–46;
    vs. ideocracy, 153, 179; vs. counter-
    bureaucracy, 152, 159, 317, 330; definition
    of the core of, 279; democratic vs. dictatorial,
    278–83; and pseudocharismatic influence,
    315, 330. See also Bureaucracy, absolute;
    Bureaucracy, nefarious
Bureaucracy, absolute: assumes law-making
    authority, 284; imposes bureaucratic
    self-control, 280; internal affairs held
    secret,385; manipulates public opinion, 285;
    monocratic head of becomes dictator, 285;
    party and police seek to monopolize political
    power, 286
Bureaucracy, nefarious: causes of, 283;
    preferential or punitive motives for, 283;
    monocratic head of, 285–88; guild-like
    closure of officialdom, 284; and pressure from
    vested interest groups, 284
Burns, James MacGregor, 374, 378, 382, 387
Buszello, Horst, 349

Capitalism: as a system, 207, 209, 256, 276;
    Hitler supports, 99–100, 101; Otto Strasser
    attacks, 99; Roosevelt seeks revision of, 252;
    conflicts with charismatic leadership of, 330;
    security, 340
Castration: of charismatic leaders, 10, 21, 49; of
    charismatic parties, 130, 243
Catholic Church: signs concordate with Hitler,
    72; condemns racial cult, 74; opposes
    euthanasia, 79; warns against killing of Jews,
    126; priests expelled from Nazi party, 188;
    Pope blesses Mussolini, 166
Caesarian leader, 36, 48, 49, 202; civilian, 48,
    232; military, 49, 232, 273, 277; Hitler as,
    87; Napoleon as, 277
Chamberlain, Neville, 120
Charisma. See Weber's theory of charisma
Charismatic apparatus, Hitler's: rule of
    separation of party from state, 131; no
    monocratic administrator, 136; comprised of
    four organizations, 141; paladins as personal
    trustees, 153; vs. ideocratic apparatus, 152;
    development of regional, 155; personal union
    of party and state, 157; unilateral process of
    decision making in, 174
Charismatic aspirants: definition of, 3, 391;
    characteristics of, 11–13; typology of, 13–14,
    18; as spoilers, 50; and choice of ideology,
    97; in electoral process, 205; test of, in a
    crisis, 243

Charismatic authority: growth of, 19; based on a
    belief, 26; the "authoritarian principle" in,
    65, 164, 199, 200; different sources of, 87;
    dictatorial sanctification of, 90; acquiescence
    of nonfollowers as a substitute for, 91, 92,
    102; and disloyalty, 114; intermingled with
    legal authority, 172; conditional and
    unconditional, 172; democratic vs. dictatorial,
    131, 203; instability of, 107
Charismatic community: inner structure of, 18,
    36, 49, 199, 201; sources of, 119; Hitler's
    cliques as example of, 148–50; charismatic
    oath of, 150; as core of Weber's theory of
    charisma, 312; small group in pure theory of,
    327; Weber's ideal-typical proposition of, 328
Charismatic disposition, 54, 67, 195; and
    spiritual leanings, 55, 56; and group
    psychology, 56; and mass overexcitment, 66,
    232, 332; absence of, in Northern blacks, 219
Charismatic demagogue, 36, 202, 241, 336
Charismatic euphoria, 312, 316, 324, 328
Charismatic giants: definition of, 3, 393;
    characteristics of, 4–6; typology of, 13–14;
    three phases of, 19, 28; alternative roads for,
    22, 28, 88; combine different charismatic
    roles, 56, 88, 310; create semi-institutional
    spheres, 60; and symbiotic relationships, 89;
    need an apparatus, 129, 310; become bearers
    of cumulative charisma, 309; success depends
    on overcoming crises, 309
Charismatic legitimacy: in democracy, 199–200;
    deception as a substitute for, 92; four
    dictatorial substitutes for, 91; voluntary and
    imposed, 103; interchangable legitimizers,
    107; Hitler's mutual sacrifices as, 121; failure
    of, vis-a-vis the holocaust, 126
Charismatism: lend-lease shipment as, 306;
    Marshall Plan as, 306–7
Churchill, Winston, 4; as party leader, 17; as
    head of government, 288–96, 297, 300, 301,
    381; and militant democracy, 288–99
Civil rights movement: troubled conscience of
    whites, 211; compassion in, 232; and
    domestic Marshall Plan for blacks, 220; civil
    rights acts, 216, 220, 224; and bureaucracy,
    279; anti-riot act, 219, 221, 225
Comparative charisma: differences in charismatic
    stability, 16; similar personality cults, 16;
    diverse ideologies, 17; preference for a system,
    18; charismatic criteria for comparison, 164ff
Concentration camps: Nazi, 92, 102, 104, 108,
    111, 146; Bolshevik, 175, 187, 194
Conservative charisma, 341, 342
Constitutional crisis, 270–72, 332
Crisis, as charismatic condition: economic crisis
    in U.S. and Germany, 165; military crisis in

old Russia and France, 165, 288; 1942 military crisis in U.S., 300, 337

Cumulative charisma: increases capacity of charismatic giants, 55, 66; magnification and, 88; lends itself to dictatorship, 89; Hitler's threefold cumulation, 122; interacting cumulation for King, 214; Roosevelt personifies, 270; electoral and military interact, 307; electoral and heroic interact for Kennedy, 324; cumulation facilitates charismatic revival, 326

Czechoslovakia, 71, 120, 127, 159, 306

Dahrendorf, Ralf, 388

Dearing, Charles L., 377

de Gaulle, Charles: charismatic qualities of, 288ff; sense of destiny as source of his calling, 289; patriotic fervor generates admiration for, 290; leadership begins as an act of rebellion, 291; no paladins and only indirect audience, 293; eventually personifies heroic charisma, 293; and plebiscitary democracy, 5, 296, 381

Degler, Carl N., 378

Degrelle, Leon, 9, 13

Democracy and bureaucracy: ethical principles to guide bureaucrats, 279; democracy sets limits for bureaucracy, 280; equality does not lead to social democracy, 281; neither autonomy nor monocracy permissible, 282; democracy opposed to bureaucratic rule, 284

Democratic charisma: definition of, 47, 199, 395; personalistic tendencies in, 49, 203; Weber's typology of, 53; features of democracy, 203; four distinct phases of democracy, 199; democratic subtypes according to prioritization, 203; personalist vs. pluralist democracies, 203-4; personalist subtypes mistaken for dictatorship in 1938, 270

Democratic dictatorship, 53, 169, 171, 277

Democratic leadership: representative leaders, 46, 205; ideological leaders, 47, 205, 238; demagogic leaders, 47, 241; charismatic leaders, 47, 48, 49, 204; leaderless democracy, 202, 205, 241, 242; leveling effect of democracy, 110, 281; leaders develop parallel to democracy, 205; and ethic of responsibility, 208; move to top requires power instinct, 240, 241; mere power politics generates empty gestures, 241; linkage with party, 242; bureaucrat should never occupy position of leadership, 282; bureaucracy never brings forth a charismatic leader, 283; role of charismatic leadership unrecognized by American historians, 338

Democratic party: alliance with labor movement, 234, 316; alliance with black constituency, 233; becomes party of reform after Roosevelt, 339

Despotism: definition of, 163, 188; leader personifies dictatorial party, 173; secret police controlled by Soviet general secretary, 175; and discipline, 177, 187; secret police become Stalin's instrument of violence, 186; annihilation of the enemies of the dictator, 188; Stalin as absolute despot after purges, 189; Hitler as wholesale killer of disbelievers, 189, 195; disenchantment of the masses, 190, 194, 195; mass execution of 35,000 Soviet officers, 194; Roosevelt underestimates Stalin's despotism, 307

Deuerlein, Ernst, 351

Deutscher, Issac, 365, 366, 367

Dickmann, Fritz, 359

Dictatorial charisma. *See* Hitler's dictatorial charisma; Lenin's dictatorial charisma

Dictatorial leadership, Hitler's: Hitler fails to perceive his leadership as dictatorial, 111; stands above party, 111; forms an alliance with big business, 144-45; claims power of law makers, 114; usurps military leadership, 117; claims credit for victory in West, 121; party vs. personal, 144; bureaucratic vs. personal, 145

Diehl-Thiele, Peter, 361

Disciplinary authority: Nazi, 87, 102, 106, 107; Bolshevik, 175, 177, 187

Disrupted charisma, 328

Divine, Robert, 382, 383

Downton, James, 350

Domarus, Max, 351

Dubcik, Alexander, 13

Duverger, Maurice, 362

Eisenhower, Dwight, 303, 304, 341, 381, 321

Eisenstadt, S. N., 26, 346, 385, 388

Eisner, Kurt, 9, 13, 51

Electoral charisma, 233, 250, 270, 298, 320, 321, 325

Emotional seizure, 26, 37, 38, 71, 106; and suffusion, 41, 43; and emotional exploitation, 90, 107; and feeling of compassion, 232

Emotional union, 36, 41, 55, 67, 70, 102, 105, 320

Empowered charisma, 300-303

Engel, Gerhard, 367

Ephemeral charisma, 19, 44, 310

Epp, Franz von, 156

Erikson, Erik H., 343, 372

Eruption of charisma, 50, 177, 230

Eschatology, 40, 44, 331

Ethics: of conviction, 209; of responsibility of
leaders, 208, 210, 231; linked with interests,
320
Ethnic groups, 210, 233
Etzoni, Amitai, 22, 23, 346
Eucken, Walter, 388
Euthanasia, 78, 79
Evers, Medgar, 217, 371
Extraordinary emotions, 37, 39, 81, 83; as a
magnetic force, 105; as mass emotions in
electoral charisma, 233

Fabricant, Salomon, 377
Fagan, Richard, 344
Failures of charisma: definition of, 3; and
castration, 8–11; typology of, 13–14, 18;
early, may be corrected, 307; caused by
charismatic exuberance,386
Faith charisma: definition of, 39; and religion,
42; as gift of grace, 42; dictatorial element in,
43; abscence of ethics in, 42, 43, 79; as
diverted dedication, 44; Hitler's, 69, 71, 79,
88; and infallibility, 88
Farber, Christian von, 369
Farley, James A., 245, 298
Feis, Herbert, 383, 384
Fest, Joachim, 344
Fine, Sidney, 389
Finer, Herman, 268, 301
Fischoff, Ephrain, 338
Flynn, Edward J., 245
Foertsch, Hermann, 359
Frady, Marshall, 372
Fraenkel, Ernst, 355, 362
France: hegemony over Germany, 98; Hitler
invades, 122; fall of in 1940, 298; Hitler
annexes French territory, 122; French
charismatic administration, 277
Frank, Hans (Hitler's lawyer), 108, 351, 354
Frankfurter, Felix, 268, 301
Freedman, Max, 378
Freidel, Frank, 374
Free, Lloyd A., 344
Freud, Sigmund, 37
Frick, Wilhelm, 47, 48, 157, 158, 159
Friedland, William H., 345
Friedrich, Carl J., 33, 348, 351
Fritsch, Werner von, 117
Froman, Lewis A., 348
Führer (Hitler), 73, 81, 92, 104, 124, 139, 149,
152, 159, 173, 191
Führerprinzip, 45, 84, 150, 179; and
Führergewalt, 152

Gabriel, Henry, R., 376

Galbraith, J. Kenneth, 385
Galen, Clemence von (Bishop), 79
Gandhi, Indira, 5
Gandhi, Mahatma, 5, 13
Garraty, John A., 375
Gauleiters, 73, 100, 124, 134, 155–59, 179
German Christians (Nazis), 72, 74, 76
German Supreme Court, 85, 113
Gerth, Hans, 65, 347, 348, 350, 351
Gimbel, John, 384
Gisevius, Hans Bernd, 354
God-King's prayer, 213, 214, 215
God's providence, role of, in Hitler ideology,
68, 69, 70, 71, 72, 73, 75, 77, 78, 81, 82,
83, 109
Goebbels, Joseph, 70, 78, 89, 122, 124, 125,
135, 148, 163, 353, 354
Goering, Hermann, 82, 83, 117, 124, 125, 136,
155, 156, 158, 160, 173, 354, 362
Goering Works, 180, 186
Gordon, Harold J., 344, 358
Gottlieb, Manuel, 384
Gouldner, Alvin H., 354, 370, 379, 380
Greater Germany, 85, 87, 98, 102, 103, 104,
117, 118, 119, 120
Greer, Thomas, 474
Guderian, Heinz, 176
Gusfield, Joseph R., 385

Hacker, Louis M., 379
Halberstam, David, 371
Halder, Franz, 360
Hale, Oron, 356
Harriman, Averell, 306
Hartmann, Heinz, 347
Heiber, Helmut, 366
Hennicke, Otto, 368
Hennis, Wilhelm, 369
Hermelink, Heinrich, 353
Heroic charisma: typology of, 53; Hitler's shift
to, 77, 83, 84, 88, 116; military mission of,
117; derived from victory, 121, 178; military
discipline and, 177–79; Lenin's military
mistake spoils, 178; Stalin claims title of
revolutionary hero, 193; Stalin incorporates
into his manufactured charisma, 193; close
affinity of patriotism to, 294
Hess, Rudolf, 73,76, 134, 153, 154, 157, 159,
160–61, 175
Hindenburg, Paul von, 46, 85, 156
Hirschman, Albert, 355
Hitler Donation, 100, 107, 135, 139
Hitler's charismatic career: his claim of special
qualities, 46, 71; personal magnetism, 48, 66,
71; self-glorification, 68, 81, 82, 83;

supernatural origin of, 68–71, 82; his claims of infallibility, 70; charge of blasphemy, 71, 74, 77; his disbelief in Catholic faith, 75; claims "Jesus was an Aryan,"75; as father of his people, 86, 180; as incarnation of a higher will, 82; magnified by personality cult, 83; his belief in his indispensability, 84, 89; his military testament, 84; his plebiscitarian campaigns, 84; seen as political genius, 87; intermingles three kinds of authority, 91; and self-aggrandizement, 90–91

Hitler's dictatorial charisma: Hitler as personalistic hero, 49, 53; noncharismatic component in, 60; leader is always right, 71; Hitler as bearer of dictatorial ideologies, 126; unconditional submission to, 136; control over organizational network, 137–41; millions loving their dictator, 163; Hitler designated his successors, 180–82; two most favored organizations, 190; his qualities self-created, 200. *See also* Dictatorial leadership, Hitler's

Hitler's militant charisma: demands unlimited obedience, 90; he overcomes two hurdles for invasions, 118; his unilateral decision to start war, 119; secrecy, deception, and false promises in, 120; planned aggression, ultimatum, and occupation, 120; Hitler-Stalin Pact, 120–21; his hopes for unification of Europe, 121; Hitler praised as greatest revolutionary leader, 151, 157, 166, 173, 179

Hitler Youth, 106, 134, 138
Himmler, Heinrich, 73, 74, 93, 117, 160
Hoess, Rudolf, 93
Houss, Theodor, 350
Holocaust, 127, 307
Homans, George, 347
Homze, Edward L., 369
Honigsheim, Paul, 349
Honolka, Bert, 353
Hook, Sidney, 343
Hoover, Herbert, 249, 251, 269
Horowitz, Irving L., 347
Howe, Louis, 245, 374
Huettenberger, Peter, 364
Hughes, Charles Evans, 270
Hull, Cordell, 298, 382
Hydrich, Reinhard, 125

Ideal democracy: and pacifist rejection of military service, 205; radical, and freedom, 206; and process of social democratization, 206; typical leader is an ideologist, 208; Weber formulates law of social democracy, 209; honor and solidarity for the masses, 209; conflict in goals of leads to social reform, 209

Ideocracy, 153–55, 161
Ideological authority, 95,96, 102, 124
Ideological charisma. *See* Hitler's ideological charisma
Ideological groups, 95–97, 238–39
Ideological leadership, 54, 57, 96, 111
Ideological movements, 96, 97, 114, 151, 210
Ideological parties, 230, 238, 241
Imperialism, Fascist, 115–18
Indoctrination, 80, 105, 108, 111, 124
Institutional charisma, 34, 269, 271
Institutions: in personal charisma, 60; divided into two kinds, supportive or deterrent, 315; emphasis upon supportive, 315, 316, 317, 325, 331, 340; deterrent, 315, 331; different modes of establishing, in democracy and dictatorship, 326, 331; vigor of, assures durability of rulership, 342
Interacting charisma: in dictatorship, 38, 89, 107, 126; in democracy, 214. *See also* Synergistic charisma
Interest parties, 239–40, 262
Isolationism, U.S., 296–97, 299, 337
Italy, fascist, 65, 77, 98, 99, 108

Jacobsen, Hans Adolf, 356, 357, 361
Jaeckel, Eberhard, 359
Jews: and burning of synagogues, 78, 124, 188; as main object of Hitler's hatred, 89, 124, 191; extermination policy kept secret, 92; Jewish real estate confiscated, 99, 100, 188; Hitler personally responsible for holocaust, 127
Jochmann, Werner, 351
Jodl, Alfred, 117, 160
Johnson, Lyndon B., 216, 218, 220, 229, 234, 322, 371, 380
Johnson, Walter, 382
Jones, Bill, 372
Junkers (German landholders), 207

Karpat, Kemal H., 344
Katz, Milton, 390
Kecskemeti, Paul, 344
Keitel, Wilhelm, 84, 117, 160
Kele, Max H., 356
Kennedy, Edward M., 12, 34, 386
Kennedy, John F., 216, 250, 386; and electoral charisma, 321–23; and euphoric charisma, 325
Kennedy, Robert F., 10, 37, 38, 221, 322, 371
Kerrl, Hanns, 72, 74, 76
Khrushchev, N., 192, 386

Kim, Il Sung, 7, 363
Kimball, Warren F., 382
King, Martin Luther, Jr: rise of supernatural qualities, 212, 214; philosophy of personalism, 212; belief in civil rights, 213; Birmingham manifesto, 213; adopts principle of nonviolence, 213, 215, 216, 220, 234; several charismata interact, 214; works through umbrella organizations, 215; preaches universal brotherhood, 215; claims full citizen rights for blacks, 215; proposes a series of economic reforms, 216, 218; turns against war in Vietnam, 218; proposes a revolution of values, 219; seeks domestic Marshall Plan and new principle of social democracy, 220, 234, 235
Kirkendall, Richard S., 376
Kirkpatrick, Jeanne, 344
Klingler, Fritz, 352
Kluke, Paul, 383
Knight, Frank H., 378
Knox, Frank, 269, 298
Koch, Erich, 155
Koehl, Robert, 361
Kornhauser, William, 345
Krivitsky, Walter, 369
Krupp, Gustav von Bohlen and Hallbach, 100, 101, 134
Krupskays, N. K., 366
Kuehnl, Reinhard, 356
Kulaks, 193, 194

Labor Front, 101, 112,134–36, 142–44,190
Lammers, Hans Heinrich, 76, 160, 364
Landon, Alf, 298, 336
Langer, William, 382
Lash, Joseph, 376
Laski, Harold, 379
Leahy, William D., 384
Legendary charisma: as alternative road to routinization, 19; effective after death of leader, 43, 65; Lenin eulogized by Trotsky and Stalin, 183–84; Stalin seeks to be the best Leninist, 184–87; Stalin's definition of Leninism, 185; Hitler believes Nazism will survive his death, 190; no direct charismatic legacy survives Churchill and de Gaulle, 307; the New Deal and Marshall Plan, Roosevelt's legacy, 307, 331
Lend-Lease Act, 297–98, 303, 305, 307
Lenin, Wladimir, 4, 31, 41, 55, 58, 164, 166, 366
Lenin's charismatic leadership: no supernatural bestowal, 166; sole interpretor of laws of history, 167; effective persuader of the masses, 167; his ideologies strengthen his charisma, 168–69; Lenin breaks with Stalin, 181; long crisis of succession of Bolsheviks, 181; Lenin cult begins shortly before his death, 183
Lenin's dictatorial charisma: insurrection vs. conspiracy, 171; intermingled authorities, 172; Lenin's special prerogative as leader, 172; no charismatic apparatus, 173; talents as teacher and persuader, 174; postscript to political testament, 175; orders attack of Poland, 177; collective leadership was a hurdle, 179
Leuner, H. D., 361
Lewis, John L., 265
Lewry, Günter, 352
Ley, Robert, 82, 136, 154, 155, 190
Limits of charisma: hypotheses on, 39, 41, 67; religious, 71–77, 78, 82; springs from conditional authority, 200; ideological limits to civil rights movement, 217, 218
Lingg, Anton, 361
Linz, Juan J., 346
Lipset, Seymour Martin, 37
Lloyd George, David, 4, 48
Long, Huey, 244
Löwenstein, Karl, 345, 349
Lubell, Samuel, 371
Ludendorff, Erich, 277, 379
Lükemann, Ulf, 361
Luminary charisma: definition of, 3; characteristics of, 6–8; typology of, 14–15, 18; instability of, 309; as bearer of euphoric charisma, 310; utilized in electoral campaigns, 310; recent American luminaries, 386
Lummumba, Patrice, 18
Luther, Martin, 74, 76, 352

McCarthy, Eugene, 34, 50
McCarthy, Joseph, 10, 17, 386
McClelland, David C., 37
McEoy, James, III, 372
McKinney, John C., 388
Magic charisma, 32, 34, 38
Malthus, Thomas, 115
Manchester, William, 381
Mann, Thomas, 5, 344
Mannstein, Erich von, 360
Mao Tse-tung, 4, 65
Maritain, Jacques, 345
Markets, competitive, 206, 208, 262–63
Marshall, T. H., 372
Marshall Plan (domestic), 306, 307
Marxism, 41, 59, 110, 111
Maser, Werner, 356
Mass emotions, 47, 48, 231, 250, 320; and

interacting masses, 60; Hitler's manipulation of, 68; and affectual participation of masses, 90, 317; and mass democracy and plebiscite, 323; and charismatic appeal, 32, 250; leads to euphoric charisma, 320

Mathoff, Maurice, 383

Maurras, Charles, 291

May, Rollo, 350

Mayer, J. P., 369

Mayntz, Renate, 380

Messerschmidt, Manfred, 365

Militant charisma: democratic and dictatorial components in, 202; and military caesar, 273; war promotes charismatic personalities, 274; and shift from trench to mobile warfare, 288; Roosevelt combines with peaceful charisma, 300; cumulation of electoral and, in U.S., 307; Marshall Plan main legacy of, for U.S., 307; war legislation did not kill, 331; Cuban missile crisis and, 323-24. *See also* Hitler's militant charisma; Roosevelt's militant charisma

Military dictatorship: a temptation for the Bolsheviks, 57, 60; attempts of the SA, 144, 151; industrialized countries do not build up new, 277; no American general claimed right to, 287

Miller, William Robert, 370

Mills, C. Wright, 347, 348, 349, 350

Mission, of charismatic leader: specific content of, 38; mass receptiveness to, 39; inherent values strengthen appeal of leader, 41; several ideologies incorporated into, 105; two unusual ideologies worshipped by Nazis, 108; war crisis induces democratic voters to accept new, 303ff; return to peaceful ideals inhibits militant mission in democracies, 330

Mitchell, Broadus, 377

Mitzman, Arthur, 348

Moley, Raymond, 269, 375

Molotov, Wjatscheslaw, 306

Mommsen, Hans, 363

Mommsen, Wolfgang, 45, 347, 349

Morgenthau, Henry, 305-7

Mosse, George L., 360

Müller, Hans Jurgen, 354

Muller, Herbert J., 387

Munich agreement, 71, 127

Mussolini, Benito, 4, 41, 65, 77, 104, 166, 291, 357, 362, 365

Mystic charisma, 40

Nagy, Irma, 9

Napoleon, 8, 51, 59, 277

Nasser, Gamal Abdel, 6, 7, 13

National Guards, 216, 229

Natural charisma: exceptional qualities of leader, 34, 368; engenders ecstasy, 35, 67, 368; and uncertainty of followers, 43, 44; as electoral advantage, 48, 50, 88; Weber's psychological transformation theory of, 51, 55; and ego-goal of the leader, 55; linked to personality cult, 83, 89; love for leader becomes glorification, 89; linked with providential charisma, 106; and acceptance of mutual sacrifices, 121; linked with racial ideology, 124

Nazi auxiliaries, 134, 137-41, 154. *See also* SA; SS

Nazi counterrevolution: conflicting ideologies of, 98; internal and external, 108-9; Social Darwinism as basis for Hitler's ideology of, 109; to be led by the "great men," 110; values of, 111; negative actions of, 111-12; positive actions of, 114-16; internal precedes external in time, 118-23; ideological justification for external, 125

Nazi dictatorial party: open membership ends in 1933, 65; admission a special favor, 123; dominates over four networks of organizations, 141; two paramilitary organizations engage in terrorist actions, 132; integral and interlocking organizations employ spy system and manipulate public opinion, 139-46

Nazi empire, 83-84, 99, 115

Nazi oppression, 69, 102, 108, 151, 173

Nazi party machine: Führer is eternal leader, 144; no monocratic bureaucrat as head of, 153; four divisions of are led by trustees of leader, 154; charismatic clique at center of, 154; regional leaders are paladins of leader, 155; veto power over governmental legislation, 160; party confidence men as counterbureaucracy of governmental bureaucracy, 159, 161

Nazi political monopoly: leadership corps dominates political life, 130; abolishes all other parties, 131, 142, 146; four features of, 143-44; party receives heavy subsidies from state, 134, 135

Nazi war planning: Hitler's Four Year Plan, 116, 158, 173, 180; Hitler's plan for building the Westwall, 118, 173, 180; Hitler plans production of tanks and war planes, 173-74; Hitler appoints Todt as minister of munition, 180

Nehru, Jawaharlal, 5, 13

Nelson, Benjamin, 201

Neumann, Franz, 349, 357

Neutrality Act of 1935, 297

New Deal, 207, 209, 235, 254, 257, 265, 319–20, 334–35
Nkrumah, Kwame, 6
Non-Christian deity, Hitler's belief in, 75, 76, 77, 78, 88, 93
Nyerere, Julius K., 6
Nyomarkay, Joseph, 345, 357

Oberschall, Anthony, 382
O'Neill, Robert, 359
Orlow, Dietrich, 361

Pachter, Henry M., 387
Paetel, Karl O., 356
Paladins, of charisma: confidence men of the leader, 49, 60; their help a moral duty, 91; adopt life style of charismatic aristocracy, 129; becomes part of leader's corps, 130; claim part in symbolic union, 150; Hitler's regional officials became Gaukings, 155; cash in on charismatic blessings, 156; Gauleiters appointed as charismatic regents, 156; often act as bearers of charismatic authority, 160
Parkinson, Roger, 360
Parties, charismatic: part of dynamics of party organization, 130; leader and his paladins form core of political party, 163; mass emotionality is condition for, 242; Roosevelt regrets failure to transform Democrats into, 271
Paterson, James T., 389
Patriarchism, 20, 52
Patrimonialism, 20, 275, 284
Peasant revlolutions, 57
Perkins, Francis, 375
Personal charisma: compared to institutional charisma, 27, 34; causes for instability of, 37, 39; nonbureaucratic organizations can tolerate, 189; depersonalization follows King's death, 220; charge of personalistic dictatorship leads to Roosevelt's stalemate, 269; institutional charisma limits Roosevelt's, 271
Personality cult, 45, 80, 88, 90; Hitler's agencies engage in cultic activities, 80; Hitler cult extends power over nonbelievers, 80; Hitler combines charisma with idolatry, 91; glorification turns leader into superman, 80, 192; Stalin's cult part of his manufactured charisma, 192; Stalin's claim of omniscience, 194
Peterson, Edward N., 363
Picker, Henry, 352
Plebiscitary charisma: in plebiscitary primaries, 49; in democratic and dictatorial plebiscites, 53; Hitler's repeated plebiscitary acclamations,

86, 104, 105; presidential democracies lend themselves more readily to plebiscitary acclamations, 203
Plutocracy, 207, 243, 254
Poland, 119, 120, 121, 127, 159, 177–78, 180, 191, 296, 306
Polenberg, Richard, 380, 384, 385
Political democracy, 237–39, 242
Political parties, in democracy, 236–40
Politicians: three requirements for success, 208, 240; should feel responsible to voters, 282; provide link between voters and bureaucracy, 282; should keep executive accountable to public, 283; should oppose nefarious bureaucracy, 287
Pollack, Jack H., 371
Power structure, 316–18, 328–29, 339–40
Prage, Gordon W., 358
Preiser, Erich, 378
Preponderant charisma, in wartime, 304–6
Presthus, Robert, 390
Private counterpolity, 334–37
Private property, 100, 208, 334, 335
Prophets of religion, 35, 39, 40, 71, 80
Protestant churches: Hitler seeks unification of, 72; resistance of bishops foils nazification of, 72; priests and ministers of, expelled from Nazi organizations, 73; new confessing church charges Hitler with blasphemy, 74; Hitler privately criticizes churches and believes in pagan God, 75ff
Providential charisma, 42–43, 69, 78, 397
Public sector, 315, 333, 335
Purges, in dictatorships: Nazi purge in 1923, 66–67; Weber's thesis that purges from above replace revolt from below, 58; Nazi purge of other parties in 1933, 82, 85; Nazis occupy trade union buildings, 111; purge of SA leaders from above, 113; usurpation of military leadersip by Hitler, 117, 158
Pusey, Merle J., 378

Racial policies of Nazis: racial endowment and Aryan superiority, 75, 123; racial inferiority and pollution, 93, 110; biological law linked to supernatural gift, 124; racial rejuvenation as Nazi ideology, 123; attack on Jewish stores in 1933, 124; hurried passage of marriage laws, 124; Wannsee conference in 1942, 125; bishops warn against killing Jews, 126; two pseudolegitimacies for extermination of Jews, Nazi revenge for military defeat, 125; racial superiority entails obligations to kill, 195
Rahman, Mujibur, 6, 13
Randolph, A. Philip, 220

Raskob, John, 244
Ratnam, K. J., 347, 348
Rauch, Basil, 382
Rausching, Hermann, 116, 359
Rayburn, Sam, 323
Reagan, Ronald, 11, 341–42
Red army in Russia, 57, 169, 173, 176, 178, 187, 194
Reformist charisma,338–40
Reich (Third), 68, 70, 83, 84, 105, 156, 159, 173
*Reichskommissare,* as Hitler's delegates in occupied lands, 159
*Reichstatthalters* as Hitler's delegates, 79, 156, 157–59
Rejuvenation, as Nazi ideology, 69, 107
Repression, 37, 72, 195
Republican party, 232, 342
Revolutionary charisma: theory of, 41, 44, 48, 59; four types of, 51; utopian component in, 52; Weber's thesis of unintended self-destruction of, 53, 92, 112; limited to democracy, 59; in Asia, 273
Rheinstein, Max, 350
Richberg, Donald, 378
Roberts, Owen (Justice), 267, 270
Robinson, Joseph, 333
Roehm, Ernst, 113, 114, 135, 151, 173
Rogin, Michael, 345
Rollins, Alfred B., 374
Roosevelt, Franklin D.: originally an organization man, 244; ethical position in nomination process, 245; forms charismatic circle, 245; role derives from "larger destiny," 246; personal quality to his charisma, 249; crisis charisma of, 250; addresses mass fear caused by economic crisis, 252; seeks to restore social values, 252
Roosevelt, Theodore, 50, 130, 242, 254
Roosevelt's militant charisma: war creates personal dilemma, 296; ideological split between isolation and intervention makes him powerless, 296; national unity becomes his charismatic mission, 297; renewal of his electoral charisma, 298; strongly supports Selective Service Act, 298; promises not to fight unless attacked, 299, 300; Atlantic Charter of 1941, 301; declaration for liberated Europe, 302, 305; willing to trust Stalin, 305; misunderstands Stalin, 308
Roosevelt's reform through charisma: his economic interpretation of depression, 251; uses broad executive power to restore economy, 253; features of his reform program, 255–61; his reconstruction of

markets, 264; dual roles as charismatic and representative leader, 265; struggle between old ruling organizations and new, 265; his opposition to cutthroat competition in labor and farm markets, 255, 265
Rosenberg, Alfred, 72, 74, 75, 106, 190
Rosenman, Samuel, 375, 382
Rossiter, Clinton, 379
Rostow, Walter W., 373
Roth, Guenther, 343, 344, 345, 346, 349
Routinization: and bureaucracy, 19, 21, 49; causes and effects of, 20; and economy, 21; and process of dilution, 21; and revolutionary charisma, 52; declining significance of, 131; despotism replaces, 195; electoral charisma is followed by, 325; succession and, 338; emotions disappear as followers die, 342; after long legacy comes, 340
Rulership, charismatic: definition and typology of, 201, 310, 393; Roosevelt's long period of, 265; supportive and resistant institutions face, 266; new institutions arise from, 310; single and multiple causes of, 325
Runciman, W. C., 344
Rustow, Dankwart A., 344

SA (Nazi storm troopers): and natural charisma, 67; suppresses other parties, 112; as auxiliary police, 112; agent of internal counter-revolution, 118, 137; internal military organization of, 137; purpose was to destroy Marxism, 138; leaders of, decapitated by Hitler, 145
Sauckel, Fritz, 158, 190
Schapiro, Leonard, 368
Scheffler, Wolfgang, 390
Schiffer, Irvine, 350
Schlesinger, Arthur M., Jr., 369, 371, 376, 377, 384, 385
Schluchter, Wolfgang, 390
Schmidt, Gustav, 381
Schoenbrun, David, 381
Schumacher, Kurt, 10, 14, 17
Schuschnigg, Kurt von, 119
Schütz, Alfred, 232, 372
Schwarz, Xavier, 134, 138, 153, 154, 155, 175
Schweitzer, Arthur, 343, 354, 355, 356, 358, 359, 361, 363, 367, 377, 378, 379, 381, 385, 388
Selznick, Philip, 363
Seraphim, Hans G., 352
Shils, Edward, 23–24, 25, 27, 346, 347, 348, 355
Sit-down strikes, 316, 330, 333
Slave labor (Nazis), 194

Smith, Alfred, 244, 245, 248
Social democracy: Weber's law of, 208, 209, 231, 232; King moves toward, 220; Wallace interrupts, 230; legal equality and, 234; differences between political and, 234; political meaning of, 234; workers benefit from, 235, 272; trend from political to, 235
Social Democrats, 67, 209
Social dictatorship, 52
Social evolution, 41, 44
Socialism, 44, 59, 100, 208, 336
Social revolution, 40
Social strain, 54
Sontheimer, Kurt, 349, 335
South Tyrol, 99, 102, 355
Souvarine, Boris, 367
Soviet Union, 98, 121, 124–25
Speer, Albert, 81, 83, 88, 89
SS (Gestapo), 73, 76, 93; confiscates Kerrl's book, 76; responsible for massacre, 93; creates excuses for invasions, 121; organizes extermination squads, 126, 195; widespread fear generated by, 127; controls concentration camps, 137, 145, 176; core of the militarized SS, 160, 176
Stalin, Joseph W., 65, 102, 156, 165, 174, 178, 181, 189, 190–95, 303–6, 355, 367
Stalinism: definition of, 164, 165, 169; ideological disputes in, 170; purges under, 170; exercises arbitrary authority, 178; uses terror in Georgia, 181; conflict over Bonapartism, 182; succession in by means of terror, 182; organizes personal apparatus, 185; Stalin's control of secret police, 185; deviations from Trotskyism, 186; as form of manufactured charisma, 192, 195; as distinctive ideology, 192; and personal worship of Stalin, 193; Stalin's brutality and personality cult, 186
Stimson, Henry, 298
Stone, Harlan (Justice), 267, 375
Strasser, Gregor, 98, 135–36
Strasser, Otto, 99, 101, 106, 355
Sudetenland, 81, 86, 102, 117, 120
Superman, 82–83, 88–89, 190, 192
Supernatural calling, in charisma: as belief and claim, 33, 55, 56; Hitler's exceptional quality, 68, 77; King's special quality, 212, 214; Wallace's quality, 222; Roosevelt, Churchill, and Kennedy hint at, 322
Syndicalism, 40
Synergistic charisma: definition and hypotheses of, 28, 397–98; fusion of two principles of, 50, 52; two basic kinds of, 60, 130; interaction of charisma and ideology, 97, 126–27; Hitler's fusion of charisma and

imperialism, 120, 123; cumulative charisma is often a part of, 126; intensified discipline in, 179; major and minor modes of, 312; ten propositions on interlinkages of, 313–20; euphoric charisma as alternative to, 328; Führerkampf as limit of, 330
Stymied charisma, 332–34, 337

Terror, political: of the Nazis, 125, 144, 162; Red terror, 169, 193; Roosevelt's goal of freedom from, 301
Third Reich, 69, 105, 107
Tiso, Josef, 120
Tito, Josiph, 7, 273
Toland, John, 355
Totalitarian governments, 57, 65, 306
Trade unions: Hitler promises to destroy, 100; occupation by Labor Front terminated free, 111; Weber's respect for, 200, 207; some American unions support black movement, 216; sit-in strikes a short revolutionary phase of, 270; new laws enforcing internal democracy in, 340
Traditional regimes: Weber distinguishes three phases of, 20; charisma not well received in, 39, 41; private trading interests supported in, 311, 318; oppose Kennedy in congress, 323
Trotsky, Leon: as charismatic figure,167; as politician, 55, 58, 59, 167, 194; personifies revolution, 168; performs role of minor charismatic leader, 168; formulates theory of permanent revolution, 169; uses legal authority to disguise revolution, 172; in Lenin's absence, becomes partaking leader, 177; tries and fails to militarize workers, 178; widely regarded as victor of civil war, 181; makes poor agreement with Stalin, 182; Bonapartism spoils his succession, 182; participates in cult of Lenin, 183; Stalin drives him from politburo and country, 186
Truman, Harry, 231, 306, 374
Tucker, Robert C., 347, 375, 377
Tugwell, Rexford G., 374, 375, 377

U.S. Supreme Court, 207, 211, 221, 223, 224, 231

Value charisma: definition of, 39, 398; religious values in, 40, 41; ideological values in, 41; hypotheses and doctrines of, 41, 43; and Hitler's trouble legalizing SA purge, 71, 72; black power creates value crisis for King, 217; conflicts between value and faith charismata, 233
Value-rational action, 95, 208
Vietnam war, 218, 220, 230, 234, 380

Violence, in politics: and revolutions in Russia, 53; and counterrevolution of Fascists, 53, 58; systematically used by Hitler, 78, 114; typically used in dictatorial regimes, 91, 93; disguised as police power, 113; despotic and oppressive use of, 173; systematically organized for holocaust, 188

Wagner, Robert F., 56, 272, 260, 263, 331–32
Wallace, George C., 222–29, 231
Walton, Hanes, 370
Walzer, Michael, 385
War, and charisma, 275–77
Warlord, in charisma: in history, 38, 85, 180, 274; Hitler as highest commander, 84, 91; a permanent fixture of earlier wars, 85, 117, 180
War power of Germany: defeat of 1918, 58; restricted army, 67, 113, 114; transformed into War Ministry, 76, 84, 117; granted benevolent neutrality to Nazis, 142; opposition of to Hitler's invasion plans, 116; in last year military officers joined Nazi Party, 176; soldiers penalized by military courts, 190

Warren, Earl (Chief Justice), 224
Weber, Eugen, 344
Weber's theory of charisma: definition of charisma, 32, 33; religious charisma, 34, 39; religious equivalents, 41, 45; theory of revolutionary charisma, 47–59; organization and charisma, 129, 161, 173; depersonalization vs. superman, 164; discipline alien to charisma, 177; rational components of ideologies, 179; democratic grows out of dictatorial charisma, 202; misinterpretation of Bolshevik revolution, 57–60; did not anticipate dual charisma, 233; no recognition of reformist or conservative charisma, 230; proposed modification and extension of his theory, 331ff
Weimar Republic, 45, 46, 47, 127, 142
Weinberg, Gerhard, 355, 357
Willkie, Wendel, 299, 336, 389
Willner, Ann Ruth, 14
Wilson, Woodrow, 254, 298, 335
Wolfenstein, E. Victor, 365
Wrong, Dennis H., 370